MOODY GOSPEL
LUKE
COMMENTARY

MOODY GOSPEL
LUKE
COMMENTARY

C. MARVIN PATE

MOODY PRESS

CHICAGO

ISBN: 0-8024-5622-7

1 3 5 7 9 10 8 6 4 2

Printed in the United States of America

In the spirit of Luke's gospel,
this book is dedicated
to the poor and needy of this world.
Therefore, a portion of the profit
of this work will be used accordingly.

CONTENTS

ACKNOWLEDGMENTS

A book is a collaborative effort. This work is no different in that respect. Whereas the bulk of the labor was my own, without the help of other people this commentary would have been impossible. Thus I wish to express my sincere appreciation to the following people: Joseph O'Day, associate managing editor at Moody Press; Linda Holland, managing editor at Moody Press; Cathy Norman Peterson, freelance editor; Bill Search and Ryan Hannah, my research assistants and good friends; Cathy Wegner, my excellent typist; and, above all, my loving wife, Sherry, and our dear daughter, Heather Lee.

Finally, may this work bring glory to God and good to others.

INTRODUCTION
LUKE AND THE SALVATION OF MANKIND

We begin our analysis of the gospel of Luke at a surprising place—Romans 9–11, written by Luke's intimate associate, Paul. In Johannes Munck's famous investigation of the apostleship of Paul, *Paul and the Salvation of Mankind,* he wrote of this passage:

> In Rom. 9–11 Paul describes the destiny of Israel after the flesh in relation to God's plan of salvation as a whole. In ch. 9 he shows that the Jew cannot claim salvation, for it is God who has the sovereignty over salvation and perdition; and God has in fact chosen for himself the Gentiles and a remnant of Israel. In 9.30–10.21 he shows how the Gentiles, but not the Jews, received salvation, because the Jews would not take God's way to it, but sought out their own. And in ch. 11 . . . he asks whether Israel's refusal of salvation by faith involves the rejection of Israel. The answer is No. There remains a chosen remnant of Israel, and it was not God's will that the Jews should fall. Their fall led to the salvation of the Gentiles, and God's plan is that the fullness of the Gentiles shall in the future lead the way to the salvation of all Israel. For the way of God's salvation is: disobedience, and afterwards compassion; and in that way God will save everyone.[1]

The thesis of this commentary on Luke is an adaptation of Munck's title, Luke and the Salvation of Mankind. Succinctly stated, the

---

1. Munck, *Paul and the Salvation of Mankind,* 42.

11

purpose of the third gospel, along with the Acts of the Apostles, is to demonstrate that the twofold promise of salvation of the Jews and the Gentiles predicted in the Old Testament is in the process of being fulfilled in Jesus Christ. As we will repeatedly see in the exposition that follows, these two themes—the salvation of Jew and Gentile—dominate Luke's portrait of Jesus. The point being made is that Christ came to save the whole of humanity.

Clarity in a commentary on any given book of the Bible is achieved in two stages: synthesis and analysis. The first step, synthesis, provides the overview of the writing and includes such necessary considerations as the identification of the author, of his audience, and of the central purpose for which he wrote. Plunging into the second step, the analysis of each verse, without having the big picture or central purpose, runs the risk of losing sight of the forest for the trees. Failure to grasp the author's overriding concern inevitably results in misinterpretation of his material. We seek to avoid that pitfall here by devoting this introductory chapter to a survey of the following essential items: Luke's identity, ministry, reliability, and theology, as well as a summary of the content of his gospel.

THE IDENTITY OF LUKE

The New Testament refers directly to Luke three times (Col. 4:14; 2 Tim. 4:11; Philem. 24; cf. Rom. 16:21?). From these passages, as well as the internal evidence of Luke-Acts itself, two points of identification concerning the evangelist can be established with some certainty: his ethnic background and his medical profession.

LUKE'S ETHNIC BACKGROUND

Opinions regarding Luke's ethnic background fall into two categories. The first, and the predominant view until recently, maintains that Luke was a Gentile, thus distinguishing him as the only Greek writer of the New Testament. Four pieces of evidence are appealed to in support of this perspective: (a) Luke's name is Greek (*Loukas*); (b) the language and style of Luke-Acts is Greek. Centuries ago, the great Bible translator Jerome set the tone for this approach: "Among all the evangelists" Luke "was the most skilled writer of Greek."[2] Elements of Greek language and style in Luke-Acts include an opening prologue

---

2. *Ep ad Damasum* 20.4.4. (Quoted in Fitzmyer, *The Gospel According to Luke I–IX,* 107.)

(1:1-4) that is similar to other ancient introductions to Greek historical works, the avoidance of Semitic expressions such as *hosanna,*
abba, the propensity to use the Septuagint (the Greek translation of
the Old Testament), similar vocabulary to classical Greek authors;
(c) Luke's unique stress on the place of the Gentiles and nonobservant Jews in the divine plan of salvation reveals his concern for his
own race, the classic illustration of which is Luke 15 (cf. 2:14, 32; 4:23-
29; 10:30-37; 17:11-21; etc.); (d) Colossians 4:10-14 seems to distinguish Luke (v. 14) from converts from Judaism (v. 11).

The second broad opinion relative to Luke's racial orientation is
that he was Jewish. Two primary pieces of data are enlisted to support
this view: (a) The author of Luke-Acts relies heavily on the Old Testament. E. C. Selwyn championed this position, stating that no Gentile
could ever have obtained Luke's intimate knowledge of Old Testament phraseology.[3] This is especially thought to be the case with the
infancy narratives of Luke 1–2. Two responses, however, neutralize
this overall argument. First, it underestimates the first-century Gentile
Christian's familiarity with the Old Testament. Second, it overlooks
the fact that Luke utilizes other sources in his document, material that
appears to be Jewish in perspective (for example, a Mary/*anawim* [the
godly poor] tradition for Luke 1–2). Furthermore, the alleged Semitic
hue in Luke-Acts, as Fitzmyer has cogently demonstrated, is due more
to the Septuagint than Jewish ethnicity;[4] (b) Romans 16:21 is supposed
to equate Luke with Paul's relative, Lucius, thereby positing Jewish
background for him. But this view comes to grief in trying to explain
why Paul refers there to Luke as *Loukios,* whereas elsewhere the apostle calls him *Loukas* (Col. 4:14).[5] On balance, then, the third evangelist
is more readily identified as a Greek Christian, who nevertheless possessed a firm grasp of the Old Testament, together with a compelling
love for the Jewish people.

LUKE'S MEDICAL PROFESSION
Regarding Luke's professional career, two conflicting decisions
have been reached. An earlier day witnessed the popularity of the thesis that the author was a medical doctor. The *Collect for St. Luke's Day*
attests to the prevalence of this idea.

3. Selwyn, "The Carefulness of Luke the Prophet," 547-58, 51.
4. Fitzmyer, *The Gospel According to Luke I–IX,* 109-25.
5. See Fitzmyer's discussion in ibid., 42-43.

Almighty God who callest Luke the physician, whose praise is in the Gospel, to be an Evangelist, and Physician of the soul; May it please Thee, that, by the wholesome Medicines of the doctrine delivered by him all the diseases of our souls may be healed; through the merits of Thy Son Jesus Christ our Lord. Amen.

Such a testimony is ultimately based on Colossians 4:14, where Luke is called "the beloved physician." Late last century, W. K. Hobart attempted to corroborate the belief that Luke was a medical doctor by establishing similarities between Lucan language and that of the Greek medical schools, especially writers such as Hippocrates, Galen, and Arataeus. In addition, Hobart claimed that medical jargon occurs more often in this third gospel than in its Marcan counterpart: "suffering from a very high fever" (Luke 4:38), "a man covered with leprosy" (Luke 5:12), "paralyzed" (Luke 5:18, 24/Mark 2:3-10), "her hemorrhage stopped" (Luke 8:44/Mark 5:29), etc. Moreover, the pejorative statement about the woman with hemorrhages not being helped by "many physicians" (Mark 5:26) is omitted from Luke 8:43, thus giving the impression that the author was a part of the medical community.

Early in this century, however, H. J. Cadbury provided a rebuttal to the claim that Luke was a physician. After reexamining Hobart's purported comparisons between Luke and other doctors who were his near contemporaries, Cadbury concluded that Lucan language was no more technical than the language of those who were not physicians.[6] Yet, missing in this critique of the traditional interpretation of Luke's livelihood is the intimate relationship that exists between the author of the third gospel and his understanding of salvation, particularly the concept of deliverance from sickness and malady. For the evangelist, salvation is a holistic concept, transforming both soul and body (Luke 6:9; 8:36, 48; 18:42; Acts 3:1; etc.). Luke's emphasis on the restoration of health as salvific, therefore, would appear to disclose his medical background. Furthermore, the Colossians 4:14 passage labeling Luke as a physician is a stubborn fact to dismiss.

THE MINISTRY OF LUKE

What was said of Jesus in Acts 1:1 concerning that which he did and taught could also be predicated of Luke. His ministry was also two

6. Cadbury, *The Style and Literary Method of Luke*, 50-51.

pronged: doing and teaching. We will summarize these two aspects in terms of Luke's companionship with Paul and his composition of the gospel.

LUKE'S COMPANIONSHIP WITH PAUL

In tracking Luke's association with Paul, three points need to be addressed: the biblical data, the liberal challenge, and the evangelical response. The biblical picture of the relationship between Luke and Paul, though brief, is straightforward: Luke was a fellow worker and companion of Paul (Philem. 24) who was dear to the apostle's heart (Col. 4:14). Moreover, if the "we" sections of Acts (16:10-17; 20:5-15; 21:1-18; 27:1–28:16) include Luke as a member of Paul's missionary team (as many think it does), then an intimate working relationship between the two is thereby confirmed.

However, the traditional perspective has not gone uncriticized. During this century, liberal scholars have attempted to drive a wedge between Luke (especially regarding the book of Acts) and Paul, arguing that the former is at odds with the latter. The classic expression of this approach is the work by Paul Vielhauer.[7] That author popularized four apparent differences, or contradictions, between Luke and Paul: First, comparing Acts 17:22-30 (Luke's presentation of Paul's speech at the Areopagus before the philosophers of Athens) with Romans 1:18-21 (Paul's discussion of natural revelation), Vielhauer claimed that Luke's positive portrayal of Paul's attitude toward natural theology is opposed to Paul's own negative portrayal of the same. Second, Luke provides a positive statement on Paul's view of the Law, whereas the apostle himself reaches the opposite conclusion in his letters. Third, Vielhauer maintained that Acts understands Paul's Christology to be adoptionist in nature (Jesus became deity only at his resurrection) and void of a theology of the cross, teachings at variance with the true message of Paul. Fourth, the Lucan picture of Paul detracts from the centrality of eschatology which is characteristic of Paul's thought. That is to say, the doctrine of the end-times, which is such a constituent part of Paul's epistles, finds no place in Acts.

In response to this challenge, evangelicals have demonstrated that the preceding inconsistencies are more imaginary than real. E. Earle Ellis's critique is a good example of this line of argumentation.

7. Vielhauer, "On the 'Paulinism' of Acts," 33-50.

His reply counters Vielhauer point by point.[8] Concerning the first alleged difference, Ellis observes that Acts 17 does not teach that humankind possesses redemptive life by nature, apart from the gospel, something with which Paul would agree. Second, Luke and Paul are in substantial agreement that salvation does not come from keeping the Law (cf. Acts 15 and Gal. 1–2). Third, Acts 13:33, 37 (cf. 2:31, 36) does not teach that Jesus became the Son of God at the resurrection but, rather, that the resurrection proved that he already was. This is fully in line with Romans 1:3-4. Moreover, Luke does indeed have a theology of the cross, as is evident in the mutual fate of Jesus and his followers (Luke 9:23; 22:35; Acts 7:60), including Paul (Acts 21:11; 23:34). Fourth, Ellis joins a chorus of scholars who cogently demonstrate that in the teachings of both Luke and Paul the kingdom of God is present spiritually now, and in the future will be a physical reality. Both writers are informed, therefore, by the same eschatological tension that exists between the first and second comings of Christ.

LUKE'S COMPOSITION OF THE GOSPEL

Regarding the composition of the third gospel, five matters of importance require some attention here: the authorship question, the sources used, the style of language employed, the date of the work, the audience intended.

The Author of Luke

Although the title, "The Gospel According to Luke," is not a part of the original Greek text,[9] there is strong evidence that it correctly identifies the author of the third gospel as Luke. The evidence is both external and internal. The external support for Lucan authorship of the third gospel consists of longstanding church tradition. Cadbury conveniently presents the sources, beginning with the second century A.D.[10] The first reference to the tradition of Lucan authorship is found in the Muratorian canon (ca. A.D. 170).

> The third book of the Gospel: According to Luke. This Luke was a physician. After the ascension of Christ, when Paul had taken him along with

8. Ellis, *The Gospel of Luke,* 46-47.
9. The oldest extant manuscript containing the title, "The Gospel According to Luke," is found in the Martin Bodmer papyrus, p75, which dates to the end of the second century A.D.
10. Cadbury, "The Tradition," in *The Beginnings of Christianity, Part I: The Acts of the Apostles,* 2:209-64.

him as one devoted to letters, he wrote it under his own name from hearsay. For he himself has not seen the Lord in person, but, insofar as he was able to follow [it all], he thus began his account with the birth of John.

The next piece of tradition verifying Lucan authorship comes at the end of the second century from the pen of Irenaeus, in his work *Adversus haereses* 3.1.1, "Luke, too, the companion of Paul, set forth in a book the gospel as preached by him." Later in that work Irenaeus writes, "Luke was inseparable from Paul and was his collaborator in the gospel" (3.14.1).

A touching testimony about the gospel of Luke occurs in an anonymous extracanonical prologue to the gospel dating to the end of the second century A.D.: "Luke was a Syrian of Antioch, by profession a physician, the disciple of the apostles, and later a follower of Paul until his martyrdom. He served the Lord without distraction, without a wife, and without children. He died at the age of eighty-four in Boeotia, full of the Holy Spirit."

Space does not permit further quotation of the traditional material attesting to Lucan authorship of Luke-Acts. Suffice it to say that the witness continues on into the third century A.D. with the testimonies of Origen (*Comm. in Matth.*), Eusebius (*Ecclesiastical History* 3.4, 6-7), Jerome (*De viris illustribus* 7), and others. In concluding this brief survey of the external evidence, a remark by J. M. Creed is enlightening. Writing of Luke, he says, "If the Gospel and Acts did not already pass under his name, there is no obvious reason why tradition should have associated them with him."[11] To jettison such a continuous line of witnesses to Lucan authorship would seem highly gratuitous.

The internal evidence is twofold: first, the prologue to the third gospel (1:1-4) establishes the fact that the author was not an eyewitness of the historical Jesus. That fact eliminates any of the twelve apostles as viable candidates to be the composer of the gospel. Second, there is a scholarly consensus today that Luke-Acts was written by one author. That being the case, then, the author of the "we" sections of Acts surfaces as the most logical candidate to also be the author of the third gospel. Guthrie, after weeding out other companions of Paul who are mentioned by name in the "we" sections of Acts (Silas, Timothy,

---

11. Creed, *The Gospel According to St. Luke*, xiii-xiv.

Sopater, Aristarchus, Secundus, Gaius, Tychicus, Trophimus), thus eliminating them as options, reduces the choice to one—Luke.[12]

The Sources of Luke

Although this commentary will deal primarily with the text as is, nevertheless it is important to briefly consider the sources Luke used for composing his gospel. This is especially the case since he himself relates to the reader his meticulous attempt to gather information about the life of Christ from reliable witnesses (1:1-4). It is commonplace today for interpreters of Luke to posit three written sources as underlying his gospel: the gospel of Mark, the sayings of Jesus (Q), and Luke's special material. Because the studies devoted to the Synoptic Problem in general and Lucan sources in particular are voluminous, only the most cursory treatment of the subject can be offered here.[13] First, the gospel of Luke contains 55 percent of Mark's material; that is, Luke contains 350 verses found in Mark's 661 verses. The agreement between the two extends beyond topical and geographical items to the very words themselves. Second, Luke shares with Matthew approximately 235 verses, thus indicating some sort of relationship between those two gospels. Whether that relationship is explained by the theory that Luke used Matthew's writing[14] or, more likely, Luke and Matthew, unaware of each other's works, relied on the same source—the sayings of Jesus,[15] is a matter of debate. However, it is clear that the third gospel is dependent on another source for its material on the teachings or sayings of Jesus. The third source utilized by Luke in his gospel is material that is unique to him (L), which constitutes as much as one-third of his work. Because this information provides the reader with insight into the heart of Luke's message, it is listed here:[16] 1:5–2:52; 3:10-14, 23-38; 4:17-21, 23, 25-30; 5:4-9a, 39; 7:12-17; 8:1-3; 9:52-55, 61-62; 10:17-20, 25-28; 12:13-15, 16-21, 35-38, 47-48, 49, 54-56; 13:1-9, 16-17, 30, 31-33; 14:1-6, 7-14, 28-32;

---

12. Guthrie, *New Testament Introduction*, 101-2.

13. For an excellent treatment of this consideration from an evangelical perspective, see Stein, *The Synoptic Problem: An Introduction.*

14. A view thought to be compatible with a statement by the second-century church father, Papias, to the effect that Matthew wrote down the *logia* (sayings?) of Jesus. However, when Papias used the term *logia,* it most likely referred to the entire gospel of Matthew, not just the sayings of Christ; see Stein, *The Synoptic Problem,* 129-30.

15. Q is the first letter in the German word for "source," *Quelle,* and symbolizes the 235 sayings of Jesus shared by Luke and Matthew.

16. Fitzmyer conveniently summarizes this material in *The Gospel According to Luke I–IX,* 83-85.

15:8-10, 11-32; 16:1-8a, 8b-12, 14-15, 19-31; 17:7-10, 12-18, 20-21, 28-32; 18:2-8a, 10-14; 19:1-10, 39-40, 41-44; 20:18; 21:8, 21b, 22, 24, 28, 34-36, 37-38, 39; 22:15-18, 19c-20, 27, 31-33, 35-38, 63-71; 23:1-12, 27-32, 35a, 36-37, 39b-43; 24:44-49. At least two themes emerge from these texts: (1) salvation has come to the Jews; (2) Christ's love and salvation are offered to the outcasts of Judaism: Gentiles, women, sinners, the poor, Samaritans, etc.

The Style of Luke

Luke is generally recognized as a polished writer whose command of the Greek language is rivaled in the New Testament only by the writer of Hebrews. A careful reading of Luke-Acts reveals that the author used three kinds of Greek style: (a) the elegant, literary style of the prologue; (b) the Semitic-flavored Greek (Septuagintal) of the infancy narratives; (c) the customary episodic style in which he wrote the bulk of the Gospel and Acts.[17] As Luke T. Johnson has shown, these three different styles are more a testimony to Luke's theological purpose than to his dependency on various source material.[18] Johnson compares such a diverse style with the ancient rhetorical idea of writing in character (*prosopopoeia*), a manner of writing which fits style to character and occasion. The prologues, with their elegant, historical flair, set Luke-Acts within the broad context of world history. The infancy narratives, with their Semitic underpinnings, are designed to take the reader back into the world of ancient Israel. Finally, as the author develops his narrative plot throughout Luke-Acts, the Greek becomes less Semitic and takes on more of a Hellenistic flavor in an effort to show how the Gospel impacted non-Jews. In other words, Luke's literary style matches his theological interests; after the prologue—like the gospel of Christ—it moves from a Jewish to a Gentile audience.

The Date of Luke

The date of Luke's gospel has been variously set in: (a) the second century A.D., (b) A.D. 70–90, (c) A.D. 60–70. A brief summary of each theory is included here, beginning with the most improbable, (a), the second-century A.D. date.

---

17. See, again, Cadbury's analysis of Lucan vocabulary on this point in *Style and Literary Method*, 4-39.

18. Johnson, *The Writings of the New Testament: An Interpretation*, 201, 237.

(a) A century ago, F. C. Baur and his colleagues at the Tübingen University in Germany, proposed the radical theory that Luke-Acts was a second-century document designed to give the impression that Pauline and Petrine Christianity harmoniously existed together from the very beginning—despite the fact that the two were, in actuality, diametrically opposed.[19]

This perspective has rightly been abandoned by modern scholars, for a number of reasons. First, it is now widely recognized that Baur and company foisted Hegelian philosophy onto the New Testament. G. W. Friedrich Hegel, the nineteenth-century philosopher, argued that history and philosophy followed a definite pattern: thesis, antithesis, synthesis. Baur applied such a presupposition to the New Testament. Pauline Christianity (thesis—salvation by faith alone) versus Petrine Christianity (antithesis—salvation by faith plus the works of the Law) = Lucan Christianity (a second-century synthesis—Paul and Peter were in harmony, their positions representing two sides of the same coin). A careful reading of the New Testament renders this polarization of Paul and Peter artificial. That, coupled with the detection of the Hegelian influence upon Baur, has deemed the Tübingen reconstruction highly improbable. Second, the usage of Luke by early second-century writers like Justin Martyr and Marcion rules out a second-century date, for the third gospel had to have had time both to be accepted as inspired and to circulate in order for it to be used in subsequent works, thus eliminating a late date. Luke's supposed dependence on Josephus's *Antiquities of the Jews* (published A.D. 94) is now almost universally rejected by scholars.[20]

(b) Many Lucan scholars in this century date the third gospel to a time period between A.D. 70 and 90. Their reasoning is basically threefold. First, Luke's dependence on Mark (frequently dated in the late 60s) implies a time period for the former in the 70s. Second, and this is the strongest argument, Jesus' prophecy of the fall of Jerusalem (A.D. 70) as recorded in Mark 13:14 has been adapted in Luke 21:20 to reflect the fact that that event had already occurred. Third, because Luke wrote his material subsequent to others' attempts to compile accounts of the life of Christ, and since there is slim evidence that those attempts were produced before A.D. 70, then neither would Luke's work have preceded A.D. 70.

---

19. The principle writings of Baur in which he sets forth his ideas about early Christiantiy are *Paul, the Apostle of Jesus Christ: His Life and Work, His Epistles and His Doctrine*, and *The Church History of the First Three Centuries*, 3d ed.
20. See Guthrie's treatment of this issue in *New Testament Introduction*, 112.

The following criticisms can be garnered against the preceding arguments for a post-70 date of the gospel of Luke. Guthrie counters the first point by observing that no great interval need have separated Luke from Mark, assuming the former was dependent on the latter. Both Luke and Mark were companions of Paul and, therefore, undoubtedly enjoyed access to each other's materials. Furthermore, an A.D. 68 date for Mark is inconclusive. Concerning the third argument, Guthrie rightly notes that the Lucan prologue (1:1-4) in no way excludes a pre-70 date for gospel literary activity.

It is the second argument, however, that carries the most weight for a post-70 date of Luke. Does the change in language from a more generalized prophecy of the fall of Jerusalem in Mark's gospel (13:14) to a specific account of that event in Luke (particularly reflected in the comment about the armies surrounding and besieging Jerusalem, Luke 21:20) necessitate a prediction after the event? Advocates of a pre-70 date think not, for a number of reasons:[21] (1) If Luke's writing occurs after the event of the fall of Jerusalem, then why, other than verse 20, is Luke 21 still rather vague in its description of such a climactic and far-reaching occurrence? (2) Why could not Jesus have uttered both the saying in Mark 13:14 concerning the abomination of desolation and the saying in Luke 21:20 concerning the surrounding of Jerusalem by the Roman armies? (3) The Lucan statement is no more specific than the predictive oracle of a Christian prophet warning Christian inhabitants of Jerusalem to flee to the Transjordan city of Pella lest they become trapped in the upcoming siege of Jerusalem. The date of that prophecy was the late 60s, before the fall of the city.[22] (4) C. H. Dodd has provocatively argued that the language of Luke 21:20-24 is drawn from Old Testament passages forecasting the fall of Jerusalem to Nebuchadnezzar (586 B.C.), rather than that of the siege of Titus (A.D. 70).[23]

(c) The third proposed date for the writing of Luke is A.D. 60–70. Proponents of this period appeal to the following pieces of evidence: (1) The two-volume work of Luke-Acts mentions no events after A.D. 63, not even the well-known occurrences of the deaths of Paul (ca. A.D. 64) and James, the half brother of Jesus (ca. A.D. 64). (2) The abrupt ending of Acts gives the impression that the apostle Paul was still alive

---

21. Guthrie, *New Testament Introduction,* 113.
22. The Prophetic oracle is cited in Eusebius's *Ecclesiastical History,* 3.4.
23. Dodd, "The Fall of Jerusalem and the 'Abomination of Desolation,'" 47-54. We will have more to say about Dodd in our exegesis of Luke 19:41-44 and 21:20-24.

at the time of Luke's writing. (3) Could Luke's rather positive remarks about the Roman Empire have been given after Emperor Nero's persecution of Christians in A.D. 64, especially after the martyrdoms of Paul and Peter?

Although the dating of Luke-Acts does not ultimately affect its interpretation, nor the exposition that comprises this particular commentary, we concur with the more general conclusion espoused by a number of Lucan commentators today: the Gospel of Luke was written during or shortly after the Jewish rebellion against Rome, that is, in or around A.D. 70. The reasons for this hypothesis are: (1) The climate of Luke-Acts indicates a time of crisis, both political and theological, which is commensurate with the Jewish revolt of A.D. 66–70. (2) The fact that Luke does not record the deaths of Paul, Peter, and James may be explained by the reasonable assumption that their martyrdoms were already well known, hence there was no need to mention them. (3) A part of Luke's theological purpose for his two-volume set may well have been to gather the data indicating, contrary to the aberrant activity of Nero, that the Roman Empire was, on the whole, tolerant of Christianity (at least until the time of the later emperor, Domitian, A.D. 84). Furthermore, because Luke-Acts is a selective, not exhaustive, history of the life of Christ, as well as the progress of the early church, the exclusion of certain material is entirely understandable. (4) The predictive nature of Jesus' prophecy of the fall of Jerusalem (ca. A.D. 30) should be accepted. After all, one of the most significant features of Luke-Acts is its emphasis at key points in the narrative on the present fulfillment of divine Old Testament prophecies (Luke 1:20, 57; 2:6, 21-22; 4:21; 9:31; 21:22, 24; 24:44; Acts 1:16; 3:18; 13:27). Only a prejudice against the supernatural would perceive these passages otherwise. Yet Luke 21:20-24, as a faithful representation of the words of Jesus, need not be restricted to pre–A.D. 70. In actuality, Luke's reporting of them shortly after the fact could serve to reinforce the accuracy of the original prediction. Taking into consideration all sides of the debate, then, it looks to this commentator as if the date of Luke-Acts is in or closely around A.D. 70.[24]

24. The statement is T. W. Manson's in *Studies in the Gospels and Epistles* (Philadelphia: Westminster, 1962), 67.

The Audience of Luke

There is widespread agreement that Luke-Acts was written primarily for a Gentile Christian audience. Numerous factors suggest this to be the case:[25] (a) In 1:1-4 Luke relates his account of Christ to a Greco-Roman literary milieu. (b) He dedicates his two-volume work to Theophilus, a person bearing a Greek name (Luke 1:3; Acts 1:1). (c) Luke eliminates from his narrative matters from Judaism less familiar to Gentiles (for example, Jewish ritual purity regulations; he substitutes Greek equivalents for Semitic names like rabbi [teacher], skull [cranium], scribe [lawyer]; he prefers Judea as the generic name of Israel, rather than its specific provinces). (d) Luke's genealogy traces Jesus' ancestry back to Adam (Luke 3:23-38) in order to set the stage for the universal scope of the gospel, rather than restrict it to Abraham and, therefore, a Hebrew audience (see Matt. 1:17). (e) Most of Luke's quotations are from the Greek Old Testament, the Septuagint. (f) Of major import is the fact that Luke's emphasis of salvation falls on the Gentiles and nonobservant Jews. Fitzmyer expresses this point well, "Luke's discussion serves to explain, precisely to Gentile Christians, what their status is vis-à-vis Israel. They are not the new people of God, but belong to the reconstituted people of God."[26] One need not conclude, however, from Luke's stress on Gentile salvation that God has finished with Israel. Indeed, if, as this Introduction will attempt to show later (along with the exposition of the pertinent gospel texts in the commentary proper), the pattern of partial belief leading to full understanding which characterizes key personages in Luke-Acts is true to Luke's perspective, then one finds therein a "sign" of Israel's future restoration.

The Reliability of Luke

Luke-Acts has been labeled the storm center of modern New Testament study, not least because of the questions raised about the historical reliability of its author.[27] Although the issues are too complex to enter into a full-scale treatment here, the general contours of the debate need to be delineated.[28] Perhaps one way to grasp the subject

---

25. The following discussion draws heavily on Fitzmyer, *The Gospel According to Luke I–IX*, 57-59.

26. Fitzmyer, *The Gospel According to Luke I–IX*, 59.

27. The phrase is van Unnik's, "Luke-Acts, A Storm Center in Contemporary Scholarship," in *Studies in Luke-Acts*, ed. Leander E. Keck and J. Louis Martyn (Nashville: Abingdon, 1966), 15-32.

28. A thorough discussion and bibliography of the related issues is provided by Marshall, *Luke: Historian and Theologian*.

would be to highlight two stages of the debate, or better yet, two sets of opponents intimately involved in the discussion: (a) Sir William Ramsay versus the Tübingen School, and (b) I. Howard Marshall versus Hans Conzelmann.

Sir William Ramsay Versus the Tübingen School

Earlier in this Introduction we had occasion to mention the rather radical viewpoint espoused by the Tübingen School. In their reconstruction of early Christianity through the lens of Hegelian philosophy, Baur and company assigned Luke-Acts to the late second century A.D. One of the fallouts from this approach was the denigration of the historical reliability of Luke. Enter William Ramsay. A century ago, Ramsay was trained at Oxford University and graduated from there enamored with the prevailing Tübingen theory that Luke-Acts was dominated by theological teaching rather than historical reality. He determined to go to ancient Asia Minor (modern-day Turkey) and the Aegean area and once for all put the rumors of Luke's reliability to rest. However, after careful investigation, Ramsay found that the "legendary" historical and geographical data in Luke-Acts proved again and again to accord with the facts.

Two of the more famous *cruces* (interpretive difficulties) in Luke-Acts investigated by Ramsay can be mentioned here as illustrative of the discussion as a whole: Luke 2:1 and Acts 18:12. The reference in Luke 2:1 to the first worldwide enrollment for taxes when Quirinius was governor of Syria has raised the eyebrows of historians because, while the birth of Jesus took place during the reign of Herod the Great (who died in 4 B.C.; see Matt. 1–2 and Luke 1:5), Quirinius was governor of Syria A.D. 6–9. Thus it was assumed that Luke had misinterpreted the chronology of the two. However, Ramsay offered a very plausible explanation—Quirinius may well have been the military leader in Syria from ca. 9 to 4 B.C., in conjunction with the civil governor, Saturninus. Indeed, Ramsay pointed to the famous inscription, *titulus tiburtinus,* which contains the significant line, "as pro-praetorial legate of Divus Augustus, he received again the province of Syria and Phoenicia." This remark suggests that someone was Caesar Augustus's legate (governor) in Syria twice. Although the name of the person is lost from the manuscript, Ramsay suggested that, in light of

Luke 2:1, Quirinius well fits the description.[29] His first activity in Syria took place, along with the census, from 9 to 4 B.C., while his second contact with the area, this time as chief magistrate, stretched from A.D. 6 to 9.

Concerning the second text famous for its hermeneutical difficulty, the reference in Acts 18:12 to Gallio as proconsul of Achaia was thought by skeptics to be historically inaccurate. W. L. Knox, for example, argued that Luke confused Gallio (A.D. 51) with an earlier governor, the latter of whom was the one before whom Paul appeared. Apparently Knox had overlooked the fact that Achaia was a senatorial province from 27 B.C. to A.D. 15, and was ruled by a proconsul. From A.D. 15 to A.D. 44, however, Achaia was made an imperial province and ruled by a procurator, only to be changed back to a senatorial province from A.D. 44 on. Knox, thinking that Luke's use of the term *proconsul,* as applied to Gallio, referred to the 27 B.C.–A.D. 15 period, assumed that the author confused an earlier governor of that period with the later Gallio.[30] However, Ramsay applied the recently discovered *Inscription of Gallio* to the situation. That text was written by Emperor Claudius to Proconsul Gallio: "Tiberius [Claudius] Caesar Augustus Germanicus . . . [in his tribunician] power [year 12, acclaimed emperor] the 26th time, father of the country . . . [Lucius] Junius Gallio my friend and [pro]consul of [Achaia wrote] . . ."[31] The text clearly indicates that Gallio was indeed the proconsul of Achaia, undoubtedly in A.D. 51 or 52. This fact, together with the statements by the Roman historians Tacitus (*Annals* 1.76; 1.80) and Suetonius (*Claudius* 25.3) reporting that Achaia was changed from a senatorial province (27 B.C.–A.D. 15) to an imperial province (A.D. 14–44) and then back again to a senatorial province (A.D. 44 on) shows that Luke, in calling Gallio a proconsul, was precisely accurate.

From these findings, and numerous others, Ramsay reached the following conclusion regarding Luke's historical reliability, "His statements of fact [are] trustworthy; he is possessed of the true historic sense; he fixes his mind on the idea and plan that rules in the evolution of history, and proportions the scale of his treatment to the im-

---

29. Ramsay, *The Bearing of Recent Discoveries on the Trustworthiness of the New Testament*, 238-300; though even such a stalwart evangelical as Marshall (*Commentary on Luke*, 103-4) is not fully convinced by Ramsay's theory.
30. Knox, *The Acts of the Apostles*, 81-82.
31. Ramsay, "Luke's Authorities in the Acts, Chapter I–XII," 450-69.

portance of each incident. He seizes the important and critical events and shows their true nature at greater length, while he touches lightly or omits entirely much that was valueless for his purpose."[32]

I. Howard Marshall Versus Hans Conzelmann

Convincing as Ramsay's appraisal was of Luke's reliability, it did not settle the issue. In the second half of the twentieth century, theologians such as Hans Conzelmann have revived an older attempt to discredit Lucan historiography by arguing that the writer of Luke-Acts was more interested in a theological agenda than sound reporting. In his book, *The Theology of St. Luke,*[33] Hans Conzelmann proceeded on the assumption that the first Christians lived in hope of the imminent return of Christ. However, when Christ did not return during the first generation of Christians, the delay of the Parousia [coming] brought disillusionment. To combat such despair, so Conzelmann postulated, faith needed to be grounded in everyday life, to compensate for the nonarrival of the kingdom of God. To do that, Luke replaced the expectation of the imminent Parousia with the theory of the progress of Christian history through the church. Consequently, Conzelmann hypothesized that Luke divided up world history into three periods: (1) Israel up to and including John the Baptist, (2) the ministry of Jesus, the middle of time, and (3) the period of the church. Obviously, the gospel of Luke emphasizes the middle time frame, while the church occupies the last segment.

Conzelmann has much to offer in his analysis of Luke, but at least two protests have been voiced against his assumptions, especially by I. Howard Marshall. In his judicious work, *Luke: Historian and Theologian,* that author demonstrates, first, that the delay of the Parousia did not cause nearly the commotion Conzelmann and others claimed. In actuality, because Jesus himself stressed that the kingdom of God had already dawned through his life and ministry, but awaited the Parousia for its consummation, the church was prepared for an extended period of history.[34]

Marshall's second criticism of Conzelmann flows from his first point—if the theory of the delay of the Parousia is wrong, then it fol-

---

32. Ramsay, *Trustworthiness of the New Testament,* 222.
33. Conzelmann, *The Theology of Luke.*
34. Marshall, *Luke: Historian and Theologian,* 85-86.

lows that Lucan theology is not a reply to it. Stated another way, Luke's historical perspective is not subordinate to his theological concerns. Rather, the two go hand in hand: Luke is both historian and theologian, and in that order. This means that Luke is fully trustworthy as a historian of the life of Christ. Therefore, to read the third gospel is to encounter the authentic, historical Jesus.[35]

The Theology of Luke

A commentary on Luke must also reckon with Acts when ascertaining the purpose for the gospel. Furthermore, the aim of Luke-Acts is inextricably related to the theology of the Gospel of Luke. Various proposals have been championed concerning the latter: Conzelmann's de-eschatologizing model (toning down the message of the end-times),[36] A. R. C. Leaney's theory of the centrality of the kingdom of God,[37] Ellis's emphasis on the messiahship of Jesus,[38] Fitzmyer's focus on early Christianity as the true continuation of the Old Testament,[39] and Marshall's development of the theme of salvation.[40] The last two mentioned proposals have much to commend them and the approach taken in this particular commentary will utilize their perspective as a working hypothesis, adding qualifications along the way.

The proposal advocated here, therefore, concerning the purpose of Luke-Acts, and the theology upon which it is based, is as follows: the twofold promise of the salvation of *both* Jew and Gentile predicted in the Old Testament is in the process of being fulfilled in Jesus Christ. This two-pronged theory stems from two pervasive pieces of data in Luke-Acts: its penchant for seeing the fulfillment of Old Testament prophecy in Christ and in the early church, and its frequent usage of derivatives of the word group "salvation" and related concepts. The former of these is the veritable substructure of the entire two-volume set while the latter occurs some forty-seven times, along with Luke's distinct understanding of salvation as being both spiritual and physical (in the sense of being made bodily whole).

35. Ibid., 53-77.
36. Conzelmann, *The Theology of Luke.*
37. Leaney, *A Commentary on the Gospel According to St. Luke*, 34-37.
38. Ellis, *The Gospel of Luke,* 10-15.
39. Fitzmyer, *The Gospel According to Luke I–IX,* 9-11.
40. Marshall, *Luke: Historian and Theologian,* 53-215.

Yet, the preceding is not all there is to Lucan theology. The most recent discussions of the matter call attention to the difficulty that pertained to Luke's day: what was the consequence of the apparent failure of the twofold promise to have materialized. That is to say, if Israel disqualified itself from divine salvation (demonstrated in its rejection of the Messiah), then what is the destiny of the nation and, for that matter, the fate of Gentile Christians? To put it bluntly, if God lost his people, Israel, then how secure is the church?[41] The usual answer supplied by current interpreters of Luke-Acts is that the early Jewish Christian population constituted and continued the true Israel and that Gentile Christians were made members of the one people of God. In the opinion of this writer, that answer is true as far as it goes. But what it does not seem to take into account is that in Luke-Acts there is a pattern of partial, leading to full, belief at work in key Jewish Christian persons, which served as a divine sign that Israel, indeed, would yet be restored—more on this suggestion in a moment.

The reader will recognize that the aforementioned twofold problem of the destinies of both Israel and the church is not unique to Luke-Acts; it was also a major concern which the apostle Paul addressed in Romans 9–11. But when one recalls the fact that Luke was a companion of Paul on some of the apostle's travels, then suddenly Romans 9–11, as mentioned at the beginning of this Introduction, becomes a key factor in interpreting Luke-Acts. One might express it this way: as a result of accompanying Paul in his ministry of evangelizing first the Jew and then the Gentile, Luke was led by the Spirit to trace the origin of such a message back to its roots—the Old Testament.

Actually, without doing violence in any way to the intended meaning of Luke-Acts, one gains an insight into the author's perspective by viewing it through the lens of Romans 9–11. If so, Luke-Acts, like Romans 9–11, especially chapter 11, can be seen to provide an answer to the question: Has God finished with His people Israel? For Luke, like Paul in Romans 11, the answer is no, for three reasons: (1) Israel's rejection of the Messiah is partial; some, in fact many, Jews did respond positively to Jesus the Christ. These Jewish Christians constituted the remnant, the ones who were faithful to God (in Luke see: the persons of Zechariah and Elizabeth, Mary, John the Baptist, the twelve apostles and the larger band of disciples; in Acts, see the

---

41. Jervell, *Luke and the People of God: A New Look at Luke-Acts*; Tiede, *Prophecy and History in Luke-Acts*; Joseph B. Tyson, ed., *Luke-Acts and the Jewish People*; Robert L. Brawley, *Luke-Acts and the Jews: Conflict, Apology, and Conciliation*.

portrayal of Paul; cf. Rom. 11:1-10). (2) Israel's rejection of Messiah serves a merciful purpose; it is the means for including Samaritans and Gentiles in the plan of salvation (in Luke, see 2:32; 4:18-19, 24-30; 7:1-10; 10:30-37; 15:1-32; 17:11-19; in Acts, see 1:8; 8:4-40; 9:15; 10:1-4; 11:18; 13:1-12; 13:44–28:28; cf. Rom. 11:11-24). (3) Israel's rejection of Messiah is temporal; it will not last forever (in Luke-Acts, see the characterization of the following individuals who move from partial to full belief, thus serving as divine signs of the promise of Israel's future restoration: Zechariah, Mary, John the Baptist, the twelve apostles, Peter, Paul;[42] cf. Rom. 11:25-36). We defer further discussion of Lucan theology to the commentary proper, especially this last point.

THE SUMMARY OF LUKE

We conclude this introductory chapter by providing a summary of the Gospel of Luke. Two items call for attention: the geography of Luke-Acts and an outline of the contents of the third gospel.

THE GEOGRAPHY OF LUKE-ACTS

It is a commonplace in Luke-Acts studies to follow the movement of the narrative to and from Jerusalem. In the gospel, Jesus resolutely sets his face toward Jerusalem, because there he will be crucified and resurrected (9:51). In Acts, Jesus sends his disciples, empowered by the Holy Spirit, from Jerusalem to Judea, Samaria, and the uttermost parts of the earth (1:8). The progression of the narrative perhaps is best illustrated in chart form, with Jerusalem serving as the center point in the story:

LUKE:
    A The Roman World (Luke 2:1; 14)
    B Judea and Samaria (Luke 9:52–19:27)
    C Jerusalem (Luke 19:28–24:12)

ACTS:
    C′ Jerusalem (Acts 1:1–6:7)
    B′ Judea and Samaria (Acts 6:8–9:21)
    A′ The Roman World (Acts 9:32–28:31)

---

42. The commentary proper will seek to substantiate this theory as we have occasion to comment on the relevant passages.

THE OUTLINE OF LUKE

I. **Salvation in History, chap. 1**
  A. The Prologue, 1:1-4
    1. The Story of Jesus from the Eyewitnesses to Luke, 1:1-2
      a. The Historical Perspective, 1:1a
      b. The Theological Message, 1:1b
      c. The Catechetical Tradition, 1:2
    2. The Story of Jesus from Luke to Theophilus, 1:3-4
      a. The Historical Perspective, 1:3
      b. The Theological Message, 1:4a
      c. The Catechetical Tradition, 1:4b
  B. The Infancy Narratives, 1:5-80
    1. The Prophecy of the Birth of John the Baptist, 1:5-25
      a. The Historical Setting, 1:5-7
      b. The Prophetic Announcement, 1:8-20
      c. The Fulfillment of the Promise, 1:21-25
    2. The Prophecy of the Birth of Jesus, 1:26-38
      a. The Historical Setting, 1:26-27
      b. The Announcement Proper, 1:28-37
      c. The Fulfillment of the Promise, 1:38
    3. Mary Visits Elizabeth, 1:39-56
      a. Elizabeth's Praise of Mary, 1:39-45
      b. Mary's Praise of God, 1:46-56
    4. The Birth, Circumcision, and Manifestation of John, 1:57-80

II. **The Birth of Jesus Christ Our Lord, chap. 2**
  A. The Birth of Jesus, 2:1-20
    1. The Setting of the Birth, 2:1-5
    2. The Birth of Jesus, 2:6-7
    3. The Manifestation of the Birth of Jesus to the Shepherds, 2:8-20
  B. The Circumcision and Manifestation of Jesus, 2:21-40
    1. The Circumcision of Jesus, 2:21-24
    2. The *Nunc Dimittis,* 2:25-35
    3. The Testimony of Anna, 2:36-38
    4. Conclusion, 2:39-40
  C. Jesus in the Temple, 2:41-52

III. **Preparation for the Public Ministry of Jesus, chap. 3**
   A. The Preaching of John the Baptist, 3:1-20
   B. The Baptism of Jesus, 3:21-22
   C. The Genealogy of Jesus, 3:23-38

IV. **The Temptation of the Son of God and the Inauguration of the Servant of the Lord, chap. 4**
   A. The Temptation of the Son of God, 4:1-13
   B. The Inauguration of the Public Ministry of the Servant of the Lord, 4:14-44
      1. The Summary Report of the Galilean Ministry, 4:14-15
      2. Jesus' Programmatic Sermon in the Synagogue at Nazareth, 4:16-30
      3. Jesus' Visit to Capernaum, 4:31-44

V. **Jesus: Friend of Sinners, chap. 5**
   A. The Call of Simon Peter, 5:1-11
   B. The Cleansing of a Leper, 5:12-16
   C. The Healing of a Paralytic, 5:17-26
   D. The Call of Levi and the Banquet, 5:27-32
   E. Jesus and Fasting, 5:33-39

VI. **Jesus and the Disciples, chap. 6**
   A. More Conflict Stories, 6:1-11
   B. The Choosing of the Twelve, 6:12-19
   C. The Sermon on the Plain, 6:20-49
      1. The Eschatological Reversal of the Fortunes of the Poor and Rich, 6:20-26
      2. Love Your Enemies, 6:27-38
      3. Inward Obedience to the Word of Christ, 6:39-49

VII. **The Miracles of the Messiah, chap. 7**
   A. The Healing of the Centurion's Servant and the Raising of the Widow's Son, 7:1-17
   B. Jesus and John the Baptist, 7:18-35
      1. John the Baptist's Question about Jesus' Messiahship, 7:18-23
      2. Jesus' Praise of John the Baptist, 7:24-30
      3. Jesus' Judgment on His Generation's Evaluation of John the Baptist and Himself, 7:31-35

XXII. **The Passion Narrative, chap. 22**
  A. The Plot of the Jewish Leaders, 22:1-2
  B. The Betrayal of Jesus by Judas, 22:3-6
  C. Preparation for the Passover Meal, 22:7-14
  D. The Last Supper, 22:15-20
  E. Jesus' Discourse to the Disciples, 22:21-38
    1. The Prediction of the Betrayal of Jesus, 22:21-23
    2. Jesus' Correction of the Disciples Misunderstanding of Their Role in the Kingdom, 22:24-30
    3. Peter's Denial Foretold, 22:31-34
    4. The "Two Swords," 22:35-38
  F. Jesus' Prayer on the Mount of Olives, 22:39-46
  G. The Arrest of Jesus, 22:47-53
  H. Peter's Denial of Jesus, 22:54-62
  I. The Mocking and Beating of Jesus, 22:63-65
  J. Jesus Before the Sanhedrin, 22:66-71

XXIII. **The Trial and Crucifixion of Jesus Christ, chap. 23**
  A. Jesus' Trial Before the Roman Government, 23:1-25
    1. Jesus and Pilate, 23:1-5
    2. Jesus and Herod, 23:6-12
    3. Pilate's Judgment of Jesus, 23:13-17
    4. Jesus Handed Over to Be Crucified, 23:18-25
  B. Jesus' Crucifixion, 23:26-43
  C. The Death and Burial of Jesus, 23:44-56

XXIV. **The Resurrection and Ascension of Jesus Christ, chap. 24**
  A. The Empty Tomb, 24:1-12
  B. The Road to Emmaus, 24:13-35
  C. Jesus' Appearance to the Disciples in Jerusalem, 24:36-43
  D. Jesus' Final Commission, 24:44-49
  E. The Ascension of Jesus, 24:50-53

STUDY GUIDE

The following questions are designed to help students master the major issues of Luke's gospel. Suggested answers may be found in the commentary. A bibliography at the end of this volume provides further resources for study and research.

1. What is the twofold theme of Luke?

2. Who are the individuals in Luke whose partial, leading to full, faith constitute a sign of the future restoration of Israel?

3. What is the Old Testament pattern of birth announcements informing the Lucan infancy narratives in chapters 1–2?

4. How do the births and ministries of John the Baptist and the Lord Jesus compare and contrast in Luke 2–3?

5. How do Adam and Israel help interpret Jesus' temptation in the desert, according to Luke 3:21–4:13?

6. How is Luke 4:14-37 programmatic for the ministry of Jesus?

7. Describe the three elements involved in the pronouncement or conflict stories regarding Jesus and his opponents.

8. Discuss the problem of interpretation of the Sermon on the Plain, Luke 6:20-49.

9. Discuss the meaning behind Jesus' parables relative to the kingdom of God.

10. How are we to interpret the Transfiguration of Jesus, Luke 9:28-45?

11. Discuss Jesus' three passion predictions in Luke.

12. Discuss the background of the Triumphant Entry, Luke 19:28-44.

13. What are the parallel events referred to in Jesus' predictions about the end-times in Luke 21:10-38?

14. What was the order of events in the Jewish Passover at the time of Christ and how does that shed light on Luke 22:1-23?

15. What was the general course of events of the trials of Jesus, Luke 22:47-23:25?

16. What happened at the crucifixion, Luke 23:26-56?

17. What are the proofs of the resurrection of Jesus as delineated in Luke 24?

ABBREVIATIONS

1 Qap. Gen.	*Genesis Apocryphon* of Qumran Cave 1
1QH	*Thanksgiving Hymns* from Qumran Cave 1
1QM	*War Scroll*
1QpHab	*Pesher (Commentary) on Habakkuk* from Qumran Cave 1
1QS	*Rule of the Community, Manual of Discipline* of the Qumran sect
1QSa	Appendix A (*Rule of the Congregation*) to 1QS
4QFlor	*Florilegium* from Qumran Cave 4
4QpNah	*Pesher (Commentary) on Nahum* from Qumran Cave 4
AB	Anchor Bible
ACNT	Augsburg Commentary on the New Testament
Aem.	*Aemilus Paulus*, by Plutarch
Ag. Ap.	*Against Apion*, by Josephus
Ant.	*Antiquities*, by Josephus
Apel. Met.	*Apelius Metamsephoses*
App. *Wars*	*Wars,* Appian
ASNU	Acta seminarii neotestamentici upsaliensis
Ass. Mos.	*Assumption of Moses*
b.	Babylonian Talmud tractate
b. B. Qam.	Babylonian Talmud tractate *Baba Qamma*
b. Ber.	Babylonian Talmud tractate *Berakoth*
b. Erub.	Babylonian Talmud tractate *Erubin*

b. Hag.	Babylonian Talmud tractate *Hagiga*
b. Sanh.	Babylonian Talmud tractate *Sanhedrin*
b. Shab.	Babylonian Talmud tractate *Shabbath*
b. Yebam.	Babylonian Talmud tractate *Yebamot*
Bar.	*Baruch*
BHT	Beiträge zur historischen Theologie
Bib	*Biblica*
CBQ	*Catholic Biblical Quarterly*
CD	Cairo (Genizah text of the) *Damascus* (*Document*)
Corp. Herm.	*Corpus Hermeticum*
De spec. leg.	*De specialibus legibus*
Dial.	*Dialogues*, by Jerome
Eccles.	*Ecclesiasticus*
EQ	*Evangelical Quarterly*
ExpTim	*Expository Times*
FBBS	Facet Books, Biblical Series
HTS	Harvard Theological Studies
ICC	International Critical Commentary
JBL	*Journal of Biblical Literature*
JRS	*Journal of Roman Studies*
Jub.	*Jubilees*
J. W.	*Jewish Wars*, by Josephus
m.	Mishna tractate
m. Mek. Ex.	Mishna tractate *Mekilta Exodus*
m. B. Bat.	Mishna tractate *Baba Batra*
m. Sanh.	Mishna tractate *Sanhedrin*
Macc.	*Maccabees*
NCB	New Century Bible
Nov T	*Novum Testamentum*
NovT Supp	Supplements to *Novum Testamentum*
NTS	*New Testament Studies*
Prot. James	*Protevangelium of James*
Ps. Sol.	*Psalms of Solomon*
R. Gen.	*Midrash Rabbah Genesis*
R. Lev.	*Midrash Rabbah Leviticus*
R. Num.	*Midrash Rabbah Numbers*
R. Pss.	*Midrash Rabbah Psalms*
RB	*Revue biblique*
Rep.	Plato's *Republic*
SBL	Society of Biblical Literature

SBLDS	Society of Biblical Literature Disseration Series
SBLMS	Society of Biblical Literature Monograph Series
SBLSP	Society of Biblical Literature Seminar Papers
SBT	Studies in Biblical Theology
Sib. Or.	*Sibylline Oracles*
Sir.	*Sirach*
SNTSMS	Society for New Testament Studies Monograph Series
SPCK	Society for the Promotion of Christian Knowledge
Strack-B	H. Strack and P. Billerbeck, *Kommentar zum Neuen Testament*
t.	Tosepta tractate
T. Ben.	*Testament of Benjamin*
T. Dan	*Testament of Dan*
T. Iss.	*Testament of Issachar*
T. Jos.	*Testament of Joseph*
T. Levi	*Testament of Levi*
TDNT	*Theological Dictionary of the New Testament*
Tg.	*Targum*
Tg. Ct.	*Targum Canticles*
TNIGTC	The New International Greek Testament Commentary
TNTC	Tyndale New Testament Commentary
Tob.	*Tobit*
Virt.	Philo's *Virtues*
WBC	Word Biblical Commentary
Wis.	*Wisdom of Solomon*
ZNW	*Zeitschrift für die neutestamentliche Wissenschaft*

SALVATION IN HISTORY

The Old Testament and early Judaism divided up time into two periods: this age and the age to come. Accordingly, this age is characterized by sin and suffering, but when the Messiah comes, he will usher in the age to come or the kingdom of God. That era will be a time of unprecedented righteousness and peace, and it will spell the end of human history, especially Israel's enslavement to the nations. Luke agrees with this basic structure of reality, except that he recognizes that the arrival of Jesus as Messiah, rather than terminating history, actually marked the display of God's salvation *in* history. In other words, the life, death, and resurrection of Jesus Christ caused an overlapping of the two ages, so that the age to come has been introduced into this present age. The intersection of those two eras began with the birth of Jesus of Nazareth, the main subject of Luke 1 and 2. After his prologue (1:1-4), Luke turns to the story of Christ, beginning with the infancy narratives of John the Baptist and Jesus.

THE PROLOGUE, 1:1-4

The introduction to the third gospel consists of one long, elegant sentence in the Greek that, in effect, places the story of Jesus Christ onto the stage of world history. Luke was not the first ancient writer to begin his history with a prologue; others such as Herodotus, Thucydides, Polybius, and Josephus did the same. The last person mentioned serves as a convenient point of comparison with the Lucan prologue, both in his style of writing as well as in his attempt to defend the antiquity of his people, the Jewish race. Josephus, like Luke, includes introductions to his two-volume work, *Against Apion*:

> In my history of our *Antiquities,* most excellent Epaphroditus, I have, I think, made sufficiently clear to any who may peruse that work the extreme antiquity of our Jewish race, the purity of the original stock, and the manner in which it established itself in the country that we occupy to-day. That history embraces a period of five thousand years, and was written by me in Greek on the basis of our sacred books. Since, however, a number of persons, influenced by the malicious calumnies of certain individuals, discredit the statements in my history concerning our antiquity and adduce as proof of the comparative modernity of our race the fact that it has not been thought worthy of mention by the best known Greek historians, I consider it my duty to devote a brief treatise to all these points; in order at once to convict our detractors of malignity and deliberate falsehood, to correct the ignorance of others, and to instruct all who desire to know the truth concerning the antiquity of our race. (1.1-3; cf. Luke 1:1-4)
>
> In the first volume of this work, my most esteemed Epaphroditus, I demonstrated the antiquity of our race, corroborating my statements by the writings of Phoenicians, Chaldeans, and Egyptians, besides citing as witnesses numerous Greek historians. . . . (2.1; cf. Acts 1:1-2)

A careful analysis of Luke 1:1-4 reveals that the sentence is divided into two broad, matching statements: the story of Jesus from the eyewitnesses to Luke (vv. 1-2) and the story of Jesus from Luke to Theophilus (vv. 3-4). Furthermore, the two general statements share three specific parallels, which uncover the key themes of the prologue, the: historical perspective, theological message, catechetical tradition. It is helpful to visualize these intimate connections in advance, in chart form:

The Story of Jesus from the Eyewitnesses to Luke	**The Story of Jesus from Luke to Theophilus**
1. Many compiled accounts (1a)	1. Luke writes an account (3)
2. Concerning things fulfilled (1b)	2. Concerning assurance for Theophilus (3b, 4a)
3. Eyewitnesses passed on the message to Luke (2)	3. Theophilus receives the instruction from Luke (4b)

THE STORY OF JESUS FROM THE EYEWITNESSES TO LUKE, 1:1-2

In the first part of his opening statement, Luke makes three important points about the story of Jesus Christ—it is rooted in historical fact (v. 1a); it conveys the theological message that God has begun to fulfill his promises to Israel (v. 1b); and it has been faithfully preserved for succeeding generations (v. 2).

THE HISTORICAL PERSPECTIVE, 1:1a

1:1a   Luke initiates his own work by acknowledging his debt to others in their attempts to record the events surrounding the words and deeds of Christ. The causal conjunction "since" or "inasmuch" (*epeidēper*) in no way disparages Luke's predecessors. If he had wanted to question their validity, the author would have chosen the concessive ("although"), not the causal conjunction. Who the "many" were is not specified, but probably included at the very least Mark's gospel, a collection of the sayings of Jesus (Q), and Luke's own special material. The purpose of these "biographers" was clearly descriptive in nature —they "set their hand to compiling an orderly account" of the historical Jesus. The word *anataxasthai* means "to repeat or compile in order," while the word *diēgēsin* means "digest or narrative account" (cf. *The Letter of Aristeas* 1.8.322; *Ant.* 11.68; etc.; the last two sources are from Josephus's works).

THE THEOLOGICAL MESSAGE, 1:1b

1:1b   Yet, there was more in the writings of Luke's literary ancestors than just history; there was a theological message as well. Verse 1b identifies that interest—they wrote about "the things fulfilled among us." The word *pēplerophorēmenōn* is a highly significant term that indicates, as the third gospel will thoroughly document, that the coming of Jesus Christ was God's means of fulfilling his promises made to Israel of old—par excellence. The birth, life, death, and resurrection of Jesus, together with His subsequent work through the apostles, was nothing less than divine intervention in the affairs of humanity; it was salvation in history.

THE CATECHETICAL TRADITION, 1:2

1:2   The statement in v. 2 ensures both the authenticity of the story about Jesus Christ as well as its preservation through transmission by the "original eyewitnesses and ministers of the word," who "passed" the message along until it eventually reached Luke himself. That the eyewitnesses are to be equated with the ministers of the word is clear because, among other things, the two expressions have the same definite article (*oi*) that governs the whole construction.[1] Undoubtedly, it is the followers of the earthly Jesus, and especially the twelve apostles, that are intended by the phrase "eyewitnesses," who wrote from first-hand experience.

A couple of terms are employed in v. 2 that attest to the fact that the things (*pragmatōn*) that Jesus said and did were faithfully preserved and transmitted to future generations. The first is *paredosan,* a technical word in the New Testament for the passing on in the early church of the tradition about Jesus (see Mark 7:13; 1 Cor. 11:2, 23; 15:3; Jude 13; etc.). Moreover, B. Gerhardsson has argued that *paredosan,* in conjunction with the phrase "ministers of the word," casts Jesus and the apostles in a similar role to that of the first-century A.D. rabbis who transmitted their teachings through their pupils.[2] With the absolute usage of "the word" (*tou logou*), Luke may also be hinting that God providentially superintended the whole transmission. "The word" takes on special significance in Acts as a designation for the gospel the apostles preached (6:4; 8:4; 10:36; 11:19; 14:25; cf. also Luke 8:12-15). It is almost as if God's word, incarnated in Jesus Christ, possessed a life of its own, refusing to be restricted to the past. It is that message that the apostles encountered from the "beginning" (*archēs*) and to which they bore faithful witness. That "instruction" (*katēchēthēs,* v. 4) reached Luke, a member of the second, or perhaps third, generation of early Christianity—they passed it "on to us" (v. 2).

THE STORY OF JESUS FROM LUKE TO THEOPHILUS, 1:3-4

Like the exchange of the baton between runners in a race, Luke hands off the baton of faith to Theophilus. In vv. 3 and 4 the author of the third gospel reiterates the same threefold concern expressed by his predecessors with regard to the story of Jesus Christ—its historical perspective, theological message, and catechetical tradition.

---

1. See Fitzmyer's comments in *The Gospel According to Luke I–IX,* 294.
2. Gerhardsson, *Memory and Manuscript,* 243-45.

THE HISTORICAL PERSPECTIVE, 1:3

1:3   Luke felt constrained to collect the data in organized fashion relative to Jesus Christ. That the author was committed to accurately and systematically presenting the story of Christ is evident in the words, "investigated carefully from the beginning."[3] Although H. J. Cadbury maintained that the word "investigate" (*parēkolouthēkoti*) meant "to observe," thereby inferring that Luke was an eyewitness of Jesus, recent commentators rightly translate the term as "investigate for oneself"[4] (cf. Josephus, *Ag. Ap.* 1.10). "Accurately" (*akribōs*) reflects Luke's careful consideration of the available material. The author further defines his task as one of writing "in order" (*kathechēs*) the events surrounding the earthly Jesus. The term seems to imply chronological sequence.[5] In light of the overall claim by the third gospel to be historically reliable, one should look askance, therefore, on any attempt to categorize the writer Luke first and foremost as a theologian whose zeal for his message led him to distort the historical facts.

The recipient of Luke's digest is Theophilus. Some have speculated that, because the name means "lover of God," it suggests that Theophilus is a symbolic representation for all Christians. Yet, the data concerning this person is too specific for him not to be a historical individual. The title, "excellent" (*kratiste*) has been variously explained. An older generation of scholars interpreted the title to be the Greek equivalent of the Latin *egregius,* the designation for a member of the equestrian, or knightly, order of Roman society in the period of the empire. They reasoned from this that, because such a label was used for the procurator (the governor assigned by Caesar to an imperial province), then Theophilus must have been an official in the Roman military. According to this view, Theophilus's high-ranking position accounts for Luke's efforts to show that Romans were converted to Christ (for example, the Roman centurion Cornelius, Acts 10) as well as to help secure legal status for early Christianity. Most

---

3. Probably Luke intends by this phrase the beginning of the public ministry of Jesus; cf. Acts 1:21-22.

4. Cadbury, *Beginnings of Christianity,* 2:5-4; *contra,* for example, Marshall, *Commentary on Luke,* 43, and Ellis, *The Gospel of Luke,* 63.

5. For a balanced treatment of the relationship between the four gospels' chronological and topical concerns, see the "Chicago Statement on Inerrancy," a credal document produced by the Evangelical Theological Society, in *Inerrancy,* ed. Norman Geisler, 493-500; 496 (Article XIII).

scholars today, however, believe the title refers to Theophilus's social prominence and thereby argue that he was Luke's patron.[6]

THE THEOLOGICAL MESSAGE, 1:4a

1:4a   Analogous to the first general statement of the prologue that emphasized the theological message of divine fulfillment, so Luke in v. 4 remarks that the assurance (*asphaleian*) that God has entered the world through Jesus Christ, can be more intimately experienced (*epignōs*) by Theophilus. The placement of the word "assurance" at the end of v. 4 stresses its importance to Luke. In doing so, the author guarantees the accuracy of the tradition about Christ. Also, the repetition of the term "word" in v. 4 ties into v. 2 with its implication that God has guided the transmission of the gospel. The same confident conviction that characterized the apostles and Luke can belong to Theophilus.

THE CATECHETICAL TRADITION, 1:4b

1:4b   The "instruction" (*katēchēthēs*) being passed on to Theophilus is a part of the overall transmission process of the narrative of Christ. The fact that Theophilus had previously been informed of such matters suggests that he was a Christian, perhaps a recent convert. Possibly, like Cornelius, he was at one time a God-fearer—one who, as a Gentile, embraced Israel's God but not necessarily its attendant ethnic requirements (for example, circumcision). In any event, Luke intends that his presentation will encourage the faith of Theophilus, who, in turn, will pass it on to others. This is all the more so if Theophilus was indeed Luke's patron, whose financial subsistence would ensure that Luke-Acts be published and therefore read extensively.

THE INFANCY NARRATIVES, 1:5-80

We begin the unit on the infancy narratives by offering four introductory remarks concerning their definition, theme, sources, and structure.

First, by way of definition, Luke 1 and 2 are commonly called the infancy narratives because they relate the origins of John the Baptist and Jesus. This material was probably added last to the gospel genre.

---

6. See Nolland's discussion of the topic in general in *Luke 1–9:20*, though he himself does not reach a settled conclusion on the identity of Theophilus, other than the possibility that he was a God-fearer.

Undoubtedly, the development of the formation of the gospel tradition proceeded as follows: First, the passion and resurrection narratives were preached, the earliest testimony of which occurs in Acts 2:23-24, 32, 36; 3:14-15; 4:10; 10:39-40; Romans 1:3-4; 1 Corinthians 15:3-4; and 1 Thessalonians 1:9-10. The next stage encompassed the composition of the words and works of Jesus (Mark). Finally, in answer to the calumny associated with the birth of Jesus, not to mention the concern to establish his genealogical credentials, the need arose to set the facts straight about the miraculous nature of the birth of Christ (cf. Matt. 1–2 and Luke 1–2).

Second, the infancy narratives function like an overture to a musical piece in that key themes played in the beginning resonate throughout the gospel. The dominant chord struck in Luke 1–2 is that the messianic era has dawned in the personal ministry of Jesus. Various proofs of that reality first appear in Luke 1–2 and then are repeated in the gospel: (a) According to Jewish thinking, prophecy ceased at the close of the Old Testament and its return was expected to occur only with the coming of the Messiah (see *1 Macc.* 14:41; Josephus, *Ag. Ap.* 1.41). Luke's emphasis on this aspect signals the presence of the messianic kingdom (1:67-79; 2:29-38; 3:3-6; 4:17-24; Acts 2:14-36; 3:11-26; etc.). (b) The forerunner predicted in Malachi 3:1; 4:5-6, whose job it would be to prepare the way for the Messiah by effecting repentance within Israel, is fulfilled in John the Baptist (1:16-17, 76-77; 3:1-20; 7:18-35). (c) The activity of the Spirit is replete in Luke-Acts, beginning with the infancy narratives (1:35, 41, 67; 2:25-27) and continuing on (3:16, 22; 4:1, 14, 18; 10:21; 11:13; 12:10, 12; Acts 2:1-21; 8:4-24; 10:34-48; 19:1-10; etc.), and is proof positive of the dawning of the age of the Messiah (cf. Joel 2:28-32). (d) One of the attendant blessings anticipated at the coming of the Messiah was joy and good news (Isa. 40:9; 41:27; 52:7; 60:6; 61:1), notes that resound in Luke-Acts (1:14, 44, 47, 58; 2:10; 6:23; 10:20; 15:7, 32; 24:52-53; Acts 3:19; etc.). (e) Another occurrence connected with the coming of the Messiah was the concept that God's faithful would undergo suffering, but that such affliction would be replaced with eschatological glory in the reign of the Messiah (see Isa. 52–53; Dan. 12:1-2; *4 Ezra* 7:88, 95-98; *2 Bar.* 48:49-50; etc.). This is in keeping with Luke's understanding that the glory of the age to come is a present possession of Christians, despite the continuing reality of trials (1:46-55; 2:35; 24:44-46; Acts 14:23; 20:23; etc.). These ideas, and more, are convincing proofs that Jesus is the Christ, who presented the kingdom of God.

Third, the question of the source material for the infancy narratives calls for a few comments at this juncture. Three traditions, in particular, probably inform Luke 1–2. The first is the Old Testament itself, especially with regard to the pattern of the announcements of the births of John the Baptist and Jesus (see Gen. 16:7-13; 17:1-21; 18:9-15; Judg. 17:20).

The second source in Luke 1–2 may well have stemmed from a John the Baptist circle. Marshall writes of this, "It is . . . probable that some, possibly the most prominent, members of John's circle became followers of Jesus and amalgamated their traditions with those of the Christian group which they entered."[7] This distinct possibility would account for the preservation of the reminiscences about the role of John the Baptist (1:5-25, 57-80; 3:1-20; 7:18-35), as well as that of his followers (Acts 19:1-6).

A final source that Luke almost certainly depends on in the infancy narratives is the Jewish-Christian group of the "poor ones" or *anawim,* which originally denoted the physically poor, who had no one to defend them but God (see Ps. 149:4; Isa. 49:13; 66:2; etc.). These people were equated with the remnant of Israel and they developed a deep piety toward God. There is no reason why Mary, the mother of Jesus, could not have belonged to that group, and it may even be that Luke consulted with her. Indeed, Luke's concern for the poor and the needy fits this milieu well as he meditates on his Lord Jesus (1:53-54; 6:20-26; 12:13-21, 22-34; Acts 2:43-47; 4:32-37; 9:36; 10:2, 4, 31; etc.). It should be noted, however, that positing the preceding three sources (the Old Testament, a John the Baptist circle, the *anawim*) in no way suggests Luke fabricated his story based on those traditions. Rather he, like those writers before him, perceived that the prophetic patterns of the Old Testament had reached their culmination in Jesus Christ.

Fourth, the structure of the infancy narratives centers on the parallelism that exists between John the Baptist and Jesus, with the latter receiving the greater importance. We can do no better than to reproduce Fitzmyer's arrangement of the relationship between the two, along with the other supplemental accounts found in Luke 1–2:

7. Marshall, *Commentary on Luke,* 50.

The Structure of the Luke Infancy Narrative

I. The Angelic Announcements of the Births (1:5-56)

1. About John (1:5-25)	2. About Jesus (1:26-38)
The parents introduced, expecting no child (because barren) (5-10).	The parents introduced, expecting no child (because unmarried) (26-27).
Appearance of the angel (11).	Entrance of the angel (28).
Zechariah is troubled (*etarachtē*) (12).	Mary is troubled (*dietarachtē*) (29).
"Do not fear" (*mē phobou*) (13).	"Do not fear" (*mē phobou*) (30).
Your wife will bear a son (13).	You will bear a son (31).
You shall call him John (13).	You shall call him Jesus (31).
He shall be great before the Lord (15).	He shall be Great (32).
Zechariah's question: "How shall I know?" (18).	Mary's question: "How shall this be?" (34).
Sign given: You shall become mute (20).	Sign given: Your aged cousin Elizabeth has conceived (36).
Zechariah's forced silence (22).	Mary's spontaneous answer (38).
Refrain A: Zechariah "went back" (*apēlthen*) (23).	Refrain A: The angel "went away" (*apēlthen*) (38).

3. Complementary Episode: The Visitation (1:39-45)
Canticle: *Magnificat* (46-55)
Refrain A: Mary "returned" to her home (56)

II. The Birth, Circumcision,
and Manifestation of the Children (1:57–2:52)

4. The Birth of John (1:57-58)	5. The Birth of Jesus (2:1-20)
The birth of John (57).	The birth of Jesus (1-12).
	Canticle of the Angels (13-14).
Joy over the birth (58).	Joy over the birth (15-18).
	Refrain B: Mary treasured all this (19).
	Refrain A: The shepherds returned (20).

6. The Circumcision and Manifestation of John (1:59-80) John circumcised and named (59-64). Reaction of the neighbors (65-66). Canticle: *Benedictus* (68-79).	7. The Circumcision and Manifestation of Jesus (2:21-40) Jesus circumcised and named (21). Reaction of Simeon and Anna (25-38). Canticle: *Nunc dimittis* (29-32). Refrain A: They returned (39).
Refrain C: "The child grew" (80).	Refrain C: "The child grew" (40).

8. Complementary Episode: The Finding in the Temple (2:41-52)
Refrain A: "Went" to Nazareth (51).
Refrain B: His mother kept all this in her heart (51).
Refrain C: Jesus grew in wisdom, age, and grace (52).[8]

THE PROPHECY OF THE BIRTH OF JOHN THE BAPTIST, 1:5-25

The episodes of the prophecies of the births of John the Baptist (1:5-25) and Jesus (1:26-38) are parallel, comprising three parts, the historical setting, prophetic announcement (which contains a fivefold pattern drawn from Old Testament birth announcement narratives), fulfillment of the promise. We begin with John the Baptist.

THE HISTORICAL SETTING, 1:5-7
1:5 The historical setting for the prophecy of the birth of John the Baptist is specified as occurring during the reign of Herod the Great, the infamous ruler of Judea (40–4 B.C.),[9] a client kingdom under the control of the Roman Empire (cf. Luke 9:7). Though under the Roman thumb, Israel nevertheless enjoyed a relative degree of religious freedom. Zechariah, a priest, was involved in conducting the worship. The Jewish priesthood was divided into twenty-four courses, each consisting of four to nine families (1 Chron. 24:1-9; 2 Chron. 8:14). In addition to the three great annual festivals that utilized the entire priesthood (Passover, Pentecost, Tabernacles), each course performed its priestly duties in the temple at Jerusalem for two weeks per year. Zechariah

---

8. Fitzmyer, *The Gospel According to Luke I–IX*, 313-14.

9. In addition to referring to the province, the term *Judea* was also used of Israel as a whole; see Marshall, *Luke: Historian and Theologian*, 70-71.

was a member of Abia, the eighth division (1 Chron. 24:10). Elizabeth, Zechariah's wife, was a daughter of Aaron, meaning her father was also a priest. Karl Georg Kuhn shows that the words, "daughter of Aaron" were synonymous with the rabbinic phrase, "daughter of a priest."[10]

1:6 Zechariah's and Elizabeth's character was impeccable, removing any hint that their childless state (v. 7) was due to sin on their part. They are described as righteous (*dikaioi*), a term expressing a person's conformity to the will of God as expressed in His Law (cf. Deut. 6:25). The aged couple is further characterized as "walking blamelessly in all the commandments." In thus calling attention to the piety of John the Baptist's parents, Luke begins to establish a connection between early Christianity and the Old Testament tradition of the righteous. It is also important to note that in his usage of the word "Lord" (*kyrios*), Luke broaches the subject of the relationship between the God of Israel and Jesus, for that nomenclature is applied to both personages (to God, for example, in 4:8, 12; 10:27; to Jesus, for example, in 1:38, 43; 2:11; 7:13, 19; 10:1, 39, 41; 11:39; 12:42; 13:15; 24:3, 34; Acts 2:36). When it is realized that the Septuagint uses the name *kyrios* for Yahweh more than 6,000 times, it is difficult to escape the conclusion that the same word applied to Jesus signifies his equality with God.

1:7 The elderly couple's plight of barrenness was both ironic and prophetic. It was ironic because the name Zechariah means "Yahweh remembers," while the name Elizabeth can be understood to mean either "My God has sworn" or "God is my fortune." Their childless state appeared to belie God's remembrance of and provision for them. Yet, shortly the narrative will show that God will fulfill their names in a prophetic way by granting to them a son. At that time Elizabeth will join the good company of such Old Testament women as Sarah (Gen. 16:1), Rebekah (Gen. 25:21), Rachel (Gen. 30:1), the mother of Samson (Judg. 13:2), and Hannah (1 Sam. 1–2).

THE PROPHETIC ANNOUNCEMENT, 1:8-20

The announcement proper of the birth of John the Baptist follows a five-element pattern also found in the Old Testament birth announcements: (a) the appearance of an angel (or the Lord) to someone (the mother or father); (b) the expression of fear on the part of the person confronted by the heavenly figure; (c) communication of the

10. Kuhn, "Aaron," 1:3-4.

heavenly message; (d) an objection or a request for a sign by the person encountering the prophecy; (e) the granting of a sign or some word of encouragement. This pattern occurs in the announcements of the births of Ishmael (Gen. 16:7-13), Isaac (Gen. 17:1-21; 18:1-15), and Samson (Judg. 13:3-20). This pattern is the sort of thing one would expect when the supernatural intersects with the natural at the point of human need, and one should not, therefore, attribute its occurrence in Luke 1–2 to the author's manufacturing of it from those Old Testament texts cited.

1:8 The scene for the heavenly revelation is set; Zechariah was taking his turn performing his priestly services before God.

1:9 Luke uses two words in his gospel for the temple at Jerusalem: *naon* (here in 1:9, 21-22; 23:45) and *hieron* (2:27, 37, 46; 4:9; 18:10; 19:45, 47; 20:1; 21:5, 37-38; 22:52-53; 24:53). The latter is the designation for the temple in general, or its precincts. The former refers to either the holy place or the holy of holies, depending on the context of the passage. The reference here in v. 9 is to the holy place, for only the high priest would enter the holy of holies once a year on the day of atonement (see Heb. 9:6-7). It is obvious that the service performed by Zechariah was a daily ritual, not the special observance just mentioned. That daily service included the morning and evening sacrifices, which involved a burnt offering. Before the morning sacrifice, and after the evening sacrifice, incense was offered on the altar of incense in the holy place (Ex. 30:7; cf. Dan. 9:2), one of the three sacred objects therein (see Appendix A). Because the priests were so numerous (20,000), some never received the opportunity to perform this service, and no one was appointed for the task more than once. Therefore, the seemingly casual remark that Zechariah was chosen by lot to discharge the responsibility is, in fact, an indication of providential timing and choice (cf. the divine choice of the twelfth apostle to replace Judas revealed by lot in Acts 1:26). The day Zechariah served in the temple was by divine design—that was the very day the angel of the Lord appeared to him (v. 11).

1:10 It was customary for a crowd of worshipers to gather outside the temple in the courts of the men and the women to pray during the morning and evening sacrifices; not only for themselves but also for the safety of the priest who approached the presence of God. According to *Tg. Ct.* 4:16, the people prayed during the offering, "May the merciful God enter the holy place and accept with favor the offering of His people." This is the first of many occurrences of prayer in Luke-

Acts (Luke, nineteen times; Acts, sixteen times), an activity often accompanied by divine revelation (3:21; 9:28; 22:43; Acts 9:40; 10:9, 30; 13:2; 22:17).[11]

1:11 The first of the five elements found in the birth announcement of a divinely chosen biblical person is the appearance of an angel to a human being (see also Gen. 16:7; 17:1; 18:1; Judg. 13:3). The word used for the appearance of the angel is *ōphthē*, a term in Luke denoting a divine epiphany (24:34; Acts 2:3; 7:2, 26, 30, 35; 9:17; 13:31; 16:9; 26:16). The designation for the heavenly being is "the angel of the Lord," a personage in the Old Testament associated with theophanies (Gen. 16:7-13; 21:17; 22:10-18; 31:11-13; Ex. 3:2-6; 14:19-24; Judg. 2:1-5). The angel appeared to the right side (the favored side) of the altar of incense, probably signifying that "he" came in peace and with good news. This divine visitation in the temple to a human is reminiscent of the appearance of an angel to Manoah's wife (Judg. 13) and Isaiah's vision of God (Isa. 6). Perhaps the closest parallel is the story of John Hyrcanus who, while alone in the temple burning incense as high priest, heard a heavenly voice (Josephus, *Ant.* 13.282).

1:12 The second common feature occurring in heavenly birth announcements is the element of fear on the part of the visionary in the presence of the divine guest (see Gen. 13:22; 16:13; 17:3; 18:2). Zechariah was understandably startled and frightened by the sudden manifestation of the angel.

1:13 The third commonality included in divine birth announcements is the angelic prophecy of the birth itself (cf. Luke 1:13-17 with Gen. 16:8-12; 17:15-19; 18:10-15; Judg. 13:3-23). The angel addressed Zechariah by name, telling him not to be afraid, and then announced the purpose of his appearance—to deliver the message that Zechariah's prayer had been heard: Zechariah would indeed have a son. The typical prayer offered by a priest at the daily sacrifice was somewhat set in form, "Appoint peace, goodness, and blessing, grace, mercy, and compassion for us and for all Israel, thy people. . . . Blessed be thou, Jehovah, who blesseth thy people Israel with peace."[12] Apparently, Zechariah's petition went beyond the generic request for God's blessing for Israel to the specific prayer for a son. Perhaps the two were related in his mind—he asked for a son who would be involved in the blessing and redemption of Israel (cf. 2:38). Using a formulaic

---

11. Cf. Marshall, *Commentary on Luke,* 54-55.
12. For further discussion, see Ellis, *The Gospel of Luke,* 66.

expression, the angel announced to Zechariah that he should name his son John (see 1:31; Matt. 1:21; Isa. 9:6; etc.), whose name (Yahweh has shown favor) matched the prayer request (that Yahweh would show favor on Israel).

1:14   The birth of John, according to the angel, will bring a twofold joy, individually and nationally. He will bring joy to Zechariah (and Elizabeth), especially so since they were childless, and beyond the age of childbearing. John will also produce joy in the people of Israel inasmuch as his ministry will prepare the nation for its Messiah (vv. 15-17).

1:15   In vv. 15-17, four characteristics are predicted of John, based on the Hebrew paratactic structure of the angelic statement;[13] he will be great, drink no wine, be filled with the Spirit from his mother's womb (v. 15), and prepare the way for the coming Messiah (vv. 16-17). In asserting John's greatness, the angel indicated that the child was to be a special instrument for God's purposes, second to none in ancient Israel (cf. 7:28a). However, a comparison of this statement with 1:32 reveals that John will be less significant than the Messiah whose arrival he will proclaim, for Jesus will not only be great, but also will be called the Son of the Most High.

Next, it is emphatically said that John will in no way (*ou mē*) drink alcoholic beverages. Abstinence from such was one of the marks of the Nazirites (Num. 6:2-8; Judg. 3:4-7), whose ascetic lifestyle symbolized that they were set apart for God (cf. Luke 7:33). The point being made here by the angel is that John's life, like the Old Testament Nazirite's, will be consecrated to the Lord. Thus, John will be filled with the Holy Spirit even while in his mother's womb. The combination of the two characteristics, ascetic lifestyle and filled with the Spirit, indicates that John the Baptist represented a transitional period; he lived in the overlap of the Old Testament era and the messianic kingdom. Therefore, Conzelmann is not accurate to assert that John the Baptist belonged exclusively to the period of Israel.[14] We are probably to understand the word "fill" (*plēsthēsetai*) to convey a double meaning: to control (see 1:41, 67; Acts 2:4; 4:8, 31; 9:17; 13:4) and to fulfill (1:23, 57; 2:6, 21-22; 21:22). The conclusion to be drawn, then, from

13. Paratactic style refers to the Hebrew penchant for combining sentences together with conjunctions as differentiated from the Greek language, which is hypotactic, that is, uses subordinate clauses in its sentence structure.
14. For a thorough critique of Conzelmann on this particular point, see Marshall, *Luke: Historian and Theologian,* 145-47.

the phrase, "filled with the Spirit," is that the Spirit's presence and control over John was a sign that the promise of the coming of the messianic era was beginning to be fulfilled. For John, that experience began in his mother's womb when she visited with Mary, the mother of Jesus (see 1:41-42), and it signified the fact that God had set John apart for divine service before he was even born.

1:16 The fourth characteristic of John the Baptist emerges from the aforementioned three qualities—he will be a catalyst in restoring Israel to God. As such, he will play the role of the prophet Elijah. A number of comparisons between the two are pinpointed by Luke. Like Elijah, John will turn or convert the children of Israel from idolatry back to the worship of the one true God (see Mal. 2:6).

1:17 Like Elijah, John the Baptist will precede the coming of the Lord (Mal. 3:1). Although no messianic function seems to be in view in Malachi 3:1 (Elijah goes before "Him" = God), it would be natural for Luke and early Christians to identify "Him" with the Messiah, thus ascribing to Elijah, and John, a preparatory ministry for the Messiah.[15] The angel did not equate John with Elijah, but cast him in the role of that prophet, who will display God's Spirit and power, two terms occurring often in Luke-Acts (1:35; 4:14; 24:49; Acts 1:8; 10:38).

The result of John's ministry will be to turn the hearts of the fathers toward their children as well as the disobedient toward a righteous mindset (*phronēsei dikaiōn*). The meaning of this sentence is best sought by understanding Malachi 4:6, the verse upon which it is partly based. Thus, a two-directional relationship is envisioned: the horizontal, between fathers and their children; and the vertical, between sinners and righteousness. Being restored to God should always proceed in both directions, being restored to God and being reconciled to one's fellow human being. These are the people who will be prepared for the coming of the Lord.

1:18 Zechariah's query, "How shall I know?" mingled confusion and objection, a fourth element found in biblical birth announcements (see Gen. 17:17; 18:12; Judg. 13:8, 17). In effect, Zechariah asked for a sign showing that the angelic annunciation would come to pass and, thereby, joined the company of Abraham (Gen. 15:8), Gideon (Judg. 6:36-40), and Hezekiah (2 Kings 20:8-11).

---

15. Jesus' sayings do not necessarily equate John the Baptist with the prophet Elijah but, rather, with the spirit of Elijah; that is, John the Baptist is a type of Elijah (Matt. 11:14; Mark 9:13; John 1:21).

1:19   Verses 19-20 constitute the fifth element occurring in birth announcements in Scripture—the giving of a sign to reassure the visionary (see Gen. 17:20-21; Judg. 13:9, 18-21). Luke identifies the angel as Gabriel (which means "man of God"), one of the seven angels thought in Judaism to stand in the presence of God to do His bidding (see Dan. 9:21; 10:13; 12:1; Rev. 8:2; cf. also *Tob.* 3:17; *1 Enoch* 20). Gabriel informed Zechariah that he was sent from God to divulge good news to him, namely, that Zechariah would have a son.

1:20   The sign the angel gave to Zechariah was a punitive miracle (cf. Acts 5:1-10; 13:6-11)—muteness. Two reasons appear to account for this drastic action: First, Zechariah did not believe the words of the angel, hence the partial judgment pronounced on him—he would be silent until the day when his son was born, an event which would be fulfilled at its proper time. A second reason flows out of the first, one that the commentators do not seem to recognize—Zechariah's partial judgment was a *prophetic sign to Israel,* a picture of both Israel's present rejection of, and future restoration to, God. As mentioned in the Introduction to this commentary, Luke was an intimate companion of Paul, whose concern for both Jew and Gentile permeates the third gospel and Acts. Furthermore, the reader will recall the connection between Luke and Romans 9–11 suggested in the section of this work entitled, "The Theology of Luke." It is time now to draw out the significance of that proposed association. There are undeniable verbal links between Luke 1:19-20 and Romans 10–11, suggesting that the former (Zechariah's partial unbelief) is a foreshadowing of the latter (Israel's partial unbelief); both texts share the following key words: a messenger (*angelos*) occurs in both texts (Luke 1:19; Rom. 10:15); the messenger is sent (*apostellō*) to both parties (Luke 1:19; Rom. 10:15); the message delivered is good news (*euangellios*) for Israel (Luke 1:19; Rom. 10:15); in neither case was the report believed (*pisteuō*) by the recipient (Luke 1:20; Rom. 10:16). Although there is no verbal connection between the two texts concerning the form of judgment (Zechariah's muteness and Israel's obstinacy), the motif of divine judgment because of unbelief is conspicuous in both incidents (Luke 1:20; Rom. 10:16-21/11:25); both judgments are temporary, they will be in effect until the time is fulfilled (*plēroma*). Compare also the specific words, "the times of the Gentiles . . . fulfilled" in Luke 21:24 and Romans 11:25. These verbal links cannot be coincidental. In the divine scheme of things, Zechariah's temporary unbelief, subsequent judgment, and future restoration (Luke 1:19-25/1:64-66) serve as a picture of Israel's present and future conditions.

THE FULFILLMENT OF THE PROMISE, 1:21-25

1:21 Meanwhile, outside the temple, the crowd of waiting worshipers became alarmed at Zechariah's delay. Their consternation may be explained by the Talmudic text *Yoma* 5:1. Referring to the usual short time the priest stayed in the holy place, that passage says, "He prayed a short prayer. But he did not prolong his prayer lest he put Israel in terror." Presumably, Zechariah's lengthy stay in the temple implied to the audience that he had been physically harmed by the awesome presence of God.

1:22 Typically, whenever the priest exited the temple into the waiting crowds, he would utter the Aaronic blessing upon them, "The Lord bless thee, and keep thee. The Lord make His face to shine upon thee, and be gracious unto thee; and give thee peace" (Num. 6:24-26; cf. *m. Tamid* 7:2). His inability to do so caused the people to realize that Zechariah had seen a vision in the temple. However, Zechariah's condition of muteness persisted, leaving him to communicate with the crowd only by signs. In light of v. 62, apparently Zechariah was also deaf. If so, then another parallel between Zechariah and Israel would be established (cf. Luke 1:62 with Rom. 11:8 "ears to hear not").

1:23 The priestly duty lasted one week (performed twice a year), so that only after completing his term could Zechariah go home. According to v. 39, the elderly couple resided outside Jerusalem in an unnamed town in the hill country.

1:24 After an interval of days, Gabriel's prophecy began to be fulfilled with the pregnancy of Elizabeth (cf. the conception of Hannah after her return from the tabernacle, 1 Sam. 1:19-20). In response, she sequestered herself in her home for five months. Fitzmyer observes that Elizabeth's seclusion, like Zechariah's muteness, functioned to keep the divine secret until the time for its completion.[16]

1:25 Elizabeth's comments remind one of Rachel (Gen. 30:23); both women rejoiced that God, in granting them children, was removing their embarrassment of being barren, something looked upon with chagrin by Jews.

---

16. Fitzmyer, *The Gospel According to Luke I–IX*, 329.

THE PROPHECY OF THE BIRTH OF JESUS, 1:26-38

The same fivefold pattern of the Old Testament birth announcement characterizing the prophecy of John the Baptist's birth pertains to the annunciation of the birth of Jesus (see the chart by Fitzmyer earlier referred to). However, the birth of Jesus will be unique in that His conception will take place supernaturally by means of the Holy Spirit coming upon the Virgin Mary. In other words, Jesus' father will be no human, but God Himself (v. 35). As in the episode of John the Baptist, so in the narrative of Jesus, three points are developed: the historical setting (1:26-27), the announcement proper (1:28-37), the fulfillment of the promise (1:38).

THE HISTORICAL SETTING, 1:26-27

1:26 The former episode and this one are linked together by the six-month time span that elapsed between Gabriel's appearance to Elizabeth and to Mary, indicating that things were moving along according to the divine schedule. Gabriel was sent by God to Galilee, one of the three provinces in Israel (the other two were Samaria and Judea; see Appendix B). The early existence of Nazareth has recently been confirmed with the discovery in 1962 at Caesarea Maritime of an inscription listing, interestingly enough, the twenty-four priestly courses (see Luke 1:5), the eighteenth of which was located in Nazareth.[17]

1:27 Gabriel appeared to Mary, who is called a virgin (*parthenon*; cf. 1:34), which, along with Matthew 1:23, calls forth the imagery of the Septuagint of Isaiah 7:14 ("a virgin shall conceive"). Luke probably interprets the angelic message to be the fulfillment of that great Old Testament text. Mary was betrothed to Joseph. In ancient Judaism, the marriage rite took place in two stages. First, the woman was betrothed to a man, a relationship similar to modern-day engagements, except that the betrothal was legally binding and only dissolved by divorce. The couple was basically married, except their union was not sexually consummated until after the second step, the wedding. This step occurred about a year after the betrothal. At that time, the husband took his bride to live with him (cf. Mal. 2:14; Matt. 1:18; 25:1-13; *m. Ketubot* 4:4-5). The couple is identified as Mary and Joseph. The name "Mary" is the Greek form of the Hebrew name *Miriam*, the sister of Moses; it meant "exalted one," a fitting description of the soon-to-be mother of

---

17. Avi-Yonah, "The Caesarea Inscription of the Twenty-Four Priestly Courses," 46-57.

the Messiah. Joseph ("May Yahweh add") was a descendant of David. Although the text will go on to delineate the true father of Jesus to be God, Joseph will be his legal "father" whose Davidic heritage helped further the legitimacy of Jesus' role as Messiah (cf. 1:32, 34; 3:23-31).

THE ANNOUNCEMENT PROPER, 1:28-37

1:28   The first element of the fivefold pattern of biblical birth announcements occurs when Gabriel entered into Mary's house to appear to her. A three-part greeting from the angel ensued, the first of which was grace (*chaire*). This typical salutation is the Greek counterpart of the Hebrew word, peace (*shalom*). It may be that the word *chaire* should be pressed into its more literal sense than just "grace" and include the idea "to rejoice." For example, S. Lyonnet argues that Luke 1:28, 30-31 is based on Zephaniah 3:14-17 and that the angelic pronouncement intends to compare Mary with the daughter of Zion, thereby forecasting Jesus' birth as the fulfillment of Zephaniah's prophecy of the restoration of Israel.[18] If so, our suggestion that Luke-Acts contains key personages who represent the future salvation of Israel would be further supported.

The second part of the angelic greeting was that Mary is the "favored woman" (*kecharitōmenē*; cf. 1:30). The word is a passive participle and indicates that Mary was chosen to be the recipient of divine favor in that she would give birth to the son of the Most High, the descendant of David (1:32). However, to translate the word as "full of grace" as the Latin Vulgate does (*gratia plena*), thereby assigning to Mary the role of bestower of grace, goes beyond the meaning of the word. Even the erudite Roman Catholic scholar Fitzmyer agrees that such a translation "certainly goes beyond" the Lucan intent.[19]

The third part of the angelic greeting, "the Lord with you," lacks a verb but, in light of the same phrase in the Septuagint of Ruth 2:4 and Judges 6:12, it is undoubtedly to be understood as declarative of the fact that the Lord will be with Mary for the purpose of special service.

1:29   The second element of the fivefold pattern of biblical birth announcements is perplexity at the appearance of the heavenly guest. Mary, unaware as of yet of the full content of the angel's message, was

---

18. Lyonnet, "*Chaire, kecharitōmenē*," 131-41; *contra* Fitzmyer, *The Gospel According to Luke I–IX*, 345.

19. Fitzmyer, *The Gospel According to Luke I–IX*, 346.

understandably confused, even to the point of alarm. She pondered what it meant that God was with her.

1:30 Gabriel attempted to allay Mary's fear, the third element of the birth annunciation, by repeating the greeting that she had found favor with God (cf. Gen. 6:18; 18:3; 1 Sam. 1:18).

1:31 Luke 1:31-33 fills out the contents of Gabriel's message to Mary: she will conceive a son, will name Him Jesus, and He will be greatly used by God. Using a clause reminiscent of other prophecies of the births of extraordinary individuals in the Old Testament (Gen. 16:11; Judg. 13:35; and probably Isa. 7:14 too), the angel predicted that Mary would conceive and give birth to a son. The child's name will be Jesus (Greek = *Iēsous*; Hebrew = *Yeshua*), a popularized form of the honorific Hebrew name Joshua (*Yehoshua*). Jesus' name, therefore, anticipated His role—He will be Israel's savior (cf. Matt. 1:21).

1:32 Jesus' role was spelled out by the angel: He will be great, referring to the essence of Jesus' being. More specifically, Jesus will be regarded as the Son of the Most High. The words "Most High" (*hypsistou*) are employed in the Septuagint as the equivalent for the Hebrew name for God, *el elyon* (God Most High; for example, Gen. 14:18 and Dan. 4:14; cf. also *1QS* 4:11; *Sir.* 4:10). It is that background, rather than the alleged Hellenistic practice of calling the Greek deities such, that informs the term.[20] Furthermore, this uniquely divine Son is destined to receive the throne of David, an obvious allusion to the prophetic oracle of 2 Samuel 7:9-16. In fact, as some commentators point out, the dynastic oracle of Nathan in 2 Samuel 7 undergirds Luke 1:32-33, thereby combining in Jesus both Davidic and messianic roles:

2 Sam. 7:9 "a great name"	Luke 1:32 "He will be great"
2 Sam. 7:13 "the throne of his kingdom"	Luke 1:32 "throne of His father David"
2 Sam. 7:14 "he will be my son"	Luke 1:32 "Son of the Most High"
2 Sam. 7:16 "your house and your kingdom"	Luke 1:33 "King over the house of Jacob forever"

Isolated from its context, and especially v. 35, it could be hypothesized that Luke's Christology in v. 32 is adoptionist; that is, that Jesus will be merely a human Messiah who, like the ancient kings of Israel, acquired an adoptive relationship with God upon his accession to the

20. See Marshall's discussion in *Commentary on Luke,* 67.

throne (cf. again 2 Sam. 7:14, which can be read this way, and Pss. 2:7;
88:26; *4QFlor* 10-13). However, v. 35 makes it clear that Jesus will possess an ontological relationship with God even at His conception, thus
ensuring His deity, long before His death and resurrection.[21]

1:33   Gabriel further attributed to Jesus an eternal kingdom, which
will be nothing less than the actualization of God's promise to David
of an everlasting dynasty, according to 2 Samuel 7 (cf. also Isa. 9:6/
Dan. 7:14). Three ideas in this angelic prophecy are operative. First,
Jesus, as king, will reign over a kingdom (*basileusei*). The scholarly
consensus today is that the main message of Jesus pertained to the
kingdom of God, in at least two ways. In the words and works of Jesus
Christ the kingdom of God was spiritually present. Yet the physical
realization of the kingdom awaits the return of Christ. Second, Jesus'
kingly rule will be over "the house of Jacob," a synonym for Israel
(Ex. 19:3; Isa. 2:5; etc.). Third, such a reign will be eternal. In light of
this last statement, it is difficult to avoid the conclusion that in Lucan
theology national Israel, despite its rejection of Jesus as Messiah, will
nevertheless be restored to God in the future with Christ as its king.

1:34   The fourth element of the birth announcement consists of
Mary's objection, v. 34. Mary's question, "How can this be since I know
no man?" has been variously interpreted. Some hold that the verb "to
know" (*ginōskō*) is a present tense used futuristically, "since I shall
not know a man." The resulting meaning assigned to the verse is,
therefore, that Mary was making a vow of perpetual virginity. However, the present tense should be sustained and, in any case, most
Roman Catholic scholars have jettisoned the "perpetual virginity" view.
Others think Mary's confusion stemmed from her knowledge that Isaiah 7:14 predicts a virgin-born Messiah and that she, a woman soon to
consummate her marriage, did not apparently fit the description.[22]
This view, though plausible, suffers from the paucity of data supporting the idea that pre-Christian Judaism associated Isaiah 7:14 with the
prophecy of a virgin-born Messiah. More recent commentators think the
question is a Lucan literary device designed to advance the dialogue
to the point where the angel can explain the means for accomplishing
the conception. But, as Marshall observes, if that were the case, why

---

21. For an excellent critique of Luke's supposed adoptionist Christology, see Marshall, *Luke:
   Historian and Theologian*, 166-69.
22. For example, see Audet, "L'Annonce à Marie," 346-74.

did Luke not just omit v. 34, for v. 35 would have flowed logically from v. 33?[23] Perhaps the most accurate answer is that Mary assumed that the conception was imminent, which contradicted the fact that she had not yet (*ou*) known (had sexual relations with) a man.

1:35 The angel responded with a reassuring sign, the fifth element typical of the birth announcements in the Bible. The sign was twofold: the prediction of Mary's virginal conception (v. 35) and the revelation of Elizabeth's pregnancy (vv. 36-37). The first aspect of the sign, the prediction of Mary's virginal conception, along with Matthew 1:21-23, is the *locus classicus* for the doctrine of the virgin birth. Technically speaking, however, the angel predicted a virginal *conception,* rather than a virginal birth. As far as anyone can tell, the actual birth of Jesus was normal; not so his conception. Verse 35 somewhat specifies how the process would transpire by using two parallel statements: the Holy Spirit will come upon Mary/the power of the Most High will cast a shadow over Mary. The parallelism indicates that the Holy Spirit will be God's creative power for impregnating Mary and is reminiscent of the creation of the world (Gen. 1:1); God's presence overshadowing the tabernacle via the cloud (Ex. 40:35); the Transfiguration scene (Luke 9:34); etc. In and of itself, the phraseology need not be a euphemism for sexual intercourse, but v. 35a, taken with v. 35b, does seem to imply divine begetting. However, the exact nature of the virginal conception, historical as it was, is ultimately a miraculous mystery incomprehensible to mere mortals and to be believed by faith.

The child to be born of Mary will be holy, called the Son of God.[24] Herein lies the foundation for the relationship of the two natures of Christ later formulated at the Council of Nicea (ca. A.D. 325)— Jesus was the God-man, fully God, fully human, yet without sin (cf. Gal. 4:4-6; Rom. 1:3-4; 8:3-4; 2 Tim. 2:8). The concept of the Son of God is at home in the Old Testament, especially with regard to Israel (Ex. 4:22; Deut. 14:1; Isa. 1:2; Hos. 11:1) and the kings of Israel (2 Sam. 7:14; Pss. 2:7; 89:27), and thus adumbrates the application of the title to Jesus. There is no need here for recourse to supposed Greco-Roman parallels of the births of gods by women.[25] Concerning the documen-

---

23. Marshall, *Commentary on Luke,* 70.

24. The phrase *gennōmenon hagion klēthēthēsetai huios theou* can be translated either of two ways: (1) "that which is born will be holy, He will be called the Son of God"; or (2) "that which is born will be called holy Son of God." Probably the first of these is to be preferred.

25. The classic refutation of the supposed influence of the Greco-Roman myths of the supernatural births of the gods on the account of the virgin birth of Jesus is the work by J. G. Machen, *The Virgin Birth of Christ* (New York: Harper, 1930).

tation of Luke's information on the important point of Jesus' virginal conception, Mary seems to be the most likely source.

1:36   The second part of Gabriel's reassuring sign to Mary was the revelation of Elizabeth's pregnancy, Mary's relative (though the nuance of that kinship is not stated). The design of the remark by the angel was to encourage Mary that, if God could cause Elizabeth, a woman barren all her life and now beyond the child-bearing age, to conceive a son, then so could the same God fulfill his promise to Mary.

1:37   The words, "for nothing" (literally, "no word") "will be impossible for God," recall the divine promise of a son addressed to Sarah (Gen. 18:14 [Septuagint]) and, in so doing, provide another confirming example of God's ability to carry out His promise to Mary.

1:38   The third major movement in 1:26-38 is the assurance that the prophecy of the birth of Jesus will be performed. Though the actual fulfillment does not as yet occur in v. 38, Mary's submission to the will of God leaves the reader with the distinct impression that it will indeed come to pass. Two words highlight Mary's willingness to do the will of God. First, Mary identified herself as God's servant or slave (*doulē*), ready to do His bidding (cf. 1 Sam. 1:11). Second, Mary's expression, "let it be to me" (*genoito moi*) "according to your word" is an optative, conveying an attainable wish.

MARY VISITS ELIZABETH, 1:39-56

The third episode in Luke's infancy narratives is Mary's visit to Elizabeth. It consists of two parts: Elizabeth's praise of Mary (vv. 39-45) and Mary's praise of God (vv. 46-55). The latter is the *Magnificat,* the first of four hymns scattered throughout the birth accounts (the others being: Zechariah's *Benedictus* [1:68-79], the angels's song [2:13-14], and Simeon's *Nunc Dimittis* [2:28-32]).

ELIZABETH'S PRAISE OF MARY, 1:39-45
1:39   Shortly after Gabriel's appearance to Mary, she quickly journeyed to a Judean town, the home of Zechariah and Elizabeth (cf. 1:23). Mary's haste was indicative of her obedient attitude. The trip from Nazareth of Galilee to Judea encompassed eighty to one hundred miles, and probably entailed three to four days, depending on

the location of the town. Since the sixth century A.D., tradition has identified the village as *Ain Karim,* five miles from Jerusalem.

1:40   Upon entering Elizabeth's home, Mary greeted her. The content of that greeting is not recorded.

1:41   Mary's greeting stimulated the child in Elizabeth's womb to leap (*eskirtēsen*; cf. Gen. 25:22), thereby signifying that the unborn baby recognized that he was in the presence of the mother of the Lord. The catalyst for such movement as well as the source of the interpretation of the event to Elizabeth was the Holy Spirit, thus fulfilling the promise to Zechariah (1:15). Already John the Baptist had become the precursor of, and witness to, Jesus.

1:42   Under the influence of the Holy Spirit, Elizabeth pronounced a blessing (*eulogēmenos*) on Mary, the explanation for which comes in the following clause—Mary has been blessed of God with a unique child. The idea behind the statement is the Jewish notion that a woman's greatness was determined by the children she bore. Hence Mary is blessed above all women because she will give birth to a child without parallel, the Son of God. Elizabeth's words anticipated a similar blessing from a woman in the crowd surrounding Jesus, in 11:27.

1:43   Elizabeth's positive attitude attaches new meaning to the question, "Why did this have to happen to me?" The remark expressed her humility and deep appreciation at the privilege of being in the presence of the Lord, not to mention her personal acceptance of Jesus' Messiahship—"my Lord" (cf. Ps. 110:1).

1:44   Elizabeth attributed the baby's leap for joy within her to the greeting of Mary the mother of the Lord, thereby indicating that the messianic era with all its long-awaited joy had now arrived (cf. 1:14, 47).

1:45   Elizabeth pronounced a beatitude (*makaria*) upon Mary (cf. 6:20): Blessed is Mary who believed the Lord's promise[26] because He will fulfill it. One cannot miss here the contrast between Mary's faith and Zechariah's unbelief (1:20), thus accounting for the difference in the divine response to each of them.

MARY'S PRAISE OF GOD, 1:46-56

1:46   In answer to Elizabeth's praise of Mary, Mary uttered her own canticle of praise to God, called the *Magnificat,* after the Latin translation of the Greek word for "praise" or to "make great" (*megalynei*).

---

26. The conjunction *hoti* can either be explicative or causal; probably the latter in this case.

"My soul" is a Hebrew circumlocution for "I" (see Gen. 27:4, 25; Ps. 34:3). In praising the greatness of the Lord, Mary displayed her humility and sense of thankfulness to God, the source of her blessing. In this, she reminds one of Samuel's mother, Hannah (1 Sam. 2:1-10).

1:47 Verse 47 repeats the thought of v. 46, using synonymous parallelism, a poetic device featured in the Hebrew language. Thus "my spirit" is a periphrastic for "my soul." The Hebrew influence may also account for the combination of the present tense verb in v. 46 ("praise") and the past tense (aorist) verb in v. 47 ("delighted"). In Hebrew, the construction called "vaw consecutive" cojoins opposite tense verbs (for example, present and past, or the reverse), but the translation takes on the tense of the first verb. Thus, the translation of both verbs in vv. 46-47 is present tense: I praise, I delight. The delight referred to by Mary was centered in God the Savior, a thought rooted in the Old Testament, especially Psalm 25:5 (Septuagint); Isaiah 12:2; Micah 7:7; etc. This is the first occurrence of the title "Savior" in the Lucan writings, and it refers, as Bultmann puts it, to the "delight of the eschaton";[27] the joy accompanying the arrival of the messianic era.

In the Introductory chapter, we had occasion to note the frequency and importance of the concept of salvation in Lucan theology. Four points need to be made relative to *sōtērios* in Luke: First, the title "Savior" as applied to Jesus in Luke is distinctive among the synoptic gospels (2:11; cf. Acts 5:31; 13:23; etc.). Therefore, in Luke, Jesus' primary role is to "seek and save that which is lost" (Luke 19:10). Second, the background of the title "Savior" is rich, drawing on both Jewish and Greco-Roman traditions. In the Old Testament, the term was applied to individuals raised up by God for the deliverance of Israel (for example, Judg. 3:9, 15), as well as to God Himself (1 Sam. 10:19; Isa. 45:15, 21). In Greco-Roman circles, the nomenclature was used for Pharaoh and Caesar. Probably both nuances inform the Lucan usage of the term. The Jewish backdrop can be seen here in Luke 1:47 (Ps. 25:5). Conversely, passages like Luke 2:11 and Acts 4:12 undoubtedly challenge the imperial claim that Caesar is Savior. Third, as Marshall so ably demonstrates, for Luke, salvation is a comprehensive idea, including spiritual and physical deliverance and wholeness (see, for example, 7:50; 8:48, 50; 17:19).[28] Fourth, Luke is concerned with the

---

27. Rudolph Bultmann, *"Agalliaomai,"* 1:19-21; 20.
28. Marshall, *Luke: Historian and Theologian,* 94-102.

universal scope of salvation, the salvation of humankind, involving both Jew and Gentile.

1:48 Verses 46-47 serve as the introduction to the *Magnificat,* while the hymn proper is developed in three strophes or stanzas: vv. 48-50; 51-53; 54-55.[29] The first strophe, vv. 48-50, praises three attributes of God, His power, holiness, and mercy. Verse 48 sets the stage for accentuating these attributes by calling attention to the great reversal that has occurred in Mary's life—God has removed her from obscurity and a lowly status (*tapeinōsin*) to the pinnacle of being exalted by all future generations. The reason for such blessing on Mary is not due to her own worthiness but rather because of the greatness of her Son (cf. 1 Sam. 2:1-10).

1:49 The two attributes of God praised here by Mary pertained to her particular circumstances. God's power refers to 1:35 and the assertion that God would overshadow Mary and produce through her a Son. It echoes Deuteronomy 10:21 and the salvific intervention of God on Israel's behalf. God's holiness refers to the promise that His Son through Mary would be holy (1:35). Luke 1:49 also draws on Psalm 111:19 and its declaration that God's name is holy. All of this speaks of Jesus as the fulfillment of that salvation Israel had long awaited.

1:50 Verse 50 recalls Psalm 103:17, "The Lord's mercy is from generation to generation on those who fear Him" and prescribes the basis for divine salvation—the mercy of God. This is applicable to Israel, Mary, and all who would be saved (Luke 12:5; 18:2, 4; 12:40; Acts 10:2, 22, 35; 13:16, 26).

1:51 Verses 51-53 constitute the second strophe of the *Magnificat,* containing six verbs in the aorist (past) tense. Probably the aorist tense is used because, from the standpoint of Mary, God's salvific acts on behalf of Israel in the Old Testament are perceived as recurring in the birth and life of Jesus. The theme of the divine reversal of the fortunes of the righteous undergirds the entire strophe. Verse 51 asserts that "God has displayed the might of His arm," undoubtedly on behalf of His oppressed people, Israel. The curious words, "the might of His arm," are an anthropomorphism for God's show of power, and are based on Psalm 89:13 which, along with other old Testament passages, refers to the divine deliverance of Israel at the Exodus (Ex. 6:6;

---

29. *Contra* Fitzmyer's proposed structure in *The Gospel According to Luke I–IX,* 360: two strophes (vv. 48-50 and vv. 51-53) and conclusion (vv. 54-55).

Deut. 4:34; Isa. 40:10; etc.). God's scattering of the "proud in heart" (Luke 1:51b) refers to His routing of Israel's enemies of old, beginning with Egypt, and describes God's intervention on behalf of His people by reversing their fate. Thus, v. 51 already clues the reader in on the nature of Jesus' life and ministry—it will be nothing less than a new Exodus (see Luke 9:31), the sign that God's saving acts are revisiting Israel. Perhaps we are to understand Luke as seeing the event of v. 51 partially actualized in the life of Christ, as He ministers with power to the people of Israel at large, all the while dispersing their arrogant religious leaders (see 6:1-11; 11:14-54; 14:1-6; 20:1-18; etc.).

1:52 God's reversal of the fortune of His people continues in v. 52, where Mary declared that God brought down the mighty rulers but exalted the humble. Three biblical instances readily come to mind, vividly illustrating this truth. The first is Job 12:19, the Old Testament context of Mary's statement in 1:52. There Job boldly announces that God will overthrow the mighty, probably with reference to the reversal of his own status as contrasted with that of his so-called friends (Job 42:7-10) and even Satan (cf. also Hannah's song in 2:4, 7). Second, closer to home, it would be difficult to miss the connection between Luke 1:52 and 10:1-24, especially since the latter passage relates the victorious ministry of the disciples, humble and childlike though they were (vv. 21-24), to the subsequent dethronement and fall of Satan, the ruler of evil (vv. 17-20). Third, the two poignant words in Luke 1:52b used of the fate of the righteous, from humiliation (*tapeinous*) to exaltation (*hypsōsen*) are the same words used to depict the destiny of Jesus in Philippians 2:5-11. Though He experienced humiliation (*etapeinōsen*, v. 8) as a servant among human beings, God highly exalted Him (*hyperhypsōsen*, v. 9) at the resurrection. The coincidence is hardly accidental; it bespeaks the reversal of the status of Jesus and of all His disciples.

1:53 The divine switch of the roles of the righteous also applies to socio-economic status. God fills the hungry but sends away the rich (cf. 1 Sam. 2:5, 7; Job 15:29; 22:9). The divine aid to the poor and subsequent warning to the rich is a prominent theme in Luke-Acts (3:11; 4:18; 5:11; 6:20-21; 9:58; 12:22-23; 16:19-26; Acts 2:44-45; 9:36; 10:2, 3, 31; 20:35; etc.), epitomized in Luke's version of the contrast between the fates of the rich young ruler and the poor followers of Jesus (18:18-30). Luke T. Johnson has rightly seen in this overall motif a blending of literal and figurative language, respectively comparing the rich and the poor with the rejection and acceptance of Jesus the Messiah who announced the message of God's salvation.[30]

1:54   Verses 54-55 form the third strophe of the *Magnificat* and, in summary fashion, point to the birth of Jesus as the continuation of God's covenant with Abraham and Israel. In Jesus, the Messiah, the restoration of Israel will indeed begin to take place. Verse 54 draws on Isaiah 41:8-9 in its reference to God's servant (*paidos* [son]) is used of Israel, the servant in Isa. 42:1; 44:1; 45:4; 52:13; etc.). The connotation of the Isaianic background, together with Luke's choice of the word "mercy"[31] (which is based on the Hebrew idea of chesed; cf. Ps. 98:3; etc.) indicates that Mary had in mind God's faithfulness to His covenant with Israel, despite Israel's repeated failure to live up to its part of the contract.

1:55   The covenant with Israel is rooted in God's promise to Abraham to give him both a people and a land (Gen. 15:1-6; 17:1-8; cf. Mic. 7:20). To narrow that promise to only Abraham's spiritual seed (i.e., Christians), as some commentators do,[32] seems to be too restrictive and is at variance with the eternal nature of God's covenant with Israel which is so concisely and clearly stated in v. 55b.

1:56   Mary stayed with Elizabeth for about three months and, then, prior to the birth of John, returned to her own home (probably to her parents' home, not yet to Joseph's).

THE BIRTH, CIRCUMCISION, AND MANIFESTATION OF JOHN, 1:57-80

1:57   The birth of John is told in 1:57-80. Verse 57 contains a double entendre—the time for Elizabeth to deliver was "fulfilled" (*eplēsthē*). The phraseology, which draws on Genesis 25:24, conveys both a natural meaning (her nine months were complete) and a theological nuance (the divine moment had come for John to be born).

1:58   Apparently, because Elizabeth had isolated herself, her neighbors were not aware of her pregnancy. But upon hearing about the birth of her son, the sign of God's mercy, they rejoiced with her (cf. vv. 46-47). The promise to Zechariah "that many will rejoice at his birth" (v. 14) had truly been fulfilled.

---

30. Luke T. Johnson, *The Literary Function of Possessions in Luke-Acts.*

31. The Greek word used in Luke 1:54, *eleos,* is the same term used in the Septuagint to translate the Hebrew word *chesed.*

32. For example, Marshall, *Commentary on Luke,* 85.

1:59   Luke 1:59-80 relates the circumcision and manifestation (1:80) of John. The episode of the circumcision contains two parts: the narrative of the event (1:59-66) and the hymn of Zechariah, the *Benedictus* (1:67-79). Verse 59 begins the narrative, noting that the parents and family came to circumcise the baby on the eighth day. Circumcision was the sign of the covenant with God and it incorporated the child into the community of Israel (Gen. 17:12; 21:4; Lev. 12:3). Somewhat analogous to a modern christening service, the relatives and friends gathered around the aged couple and wanted to call (*ekaloun*, a conative imperfect) the child by the name of his father, Zechariah. Although the customary procedure was to call a newborn son by the name of his grandfather, there are examples approximate to Luke's day in which the child was named after the father (*Tob.* 1:9; Josephus, *Life* 1.3; *Ant.* 14.10; etc.). It should also be mentioned that, although the naming of a child at circumcision is a custom not attested in Jewish literature until the eighth century A.D. (*Pirqe R. Eliezer* 48), earlier the Greeks practiced such a tradition and it may well have influenced Palestine in the first century A.D.[33]

1:60   Speaking on behalf of her mute husband, Elizabeth shocked the audience when she emphatically said that the child's name would be John, not Zechariah. Even though Luke does not tell us how Elizabeth came to know what the name of the child should be, the reader is obviously to assume that Zechariah had somehow communicated the angelic message to his wife.

1:61   The relatives and friends responded to Elizabeth by saying that there was no one in her family named John. This comment implied they did not agree with the name choice.

1:62   Not content with Elizabeth's answer, the people inquired of Zechariah through the use of signs what the father wanted to name the child. Apparently, Zechariah was both mute and deaf.

1:63   Zechariah asked for a tablet and wrote what the name of the child would be—John. The answer elicited wonder (*ethaumasan*) from the group, probably for a couple of reasons. First, Zechariah agreed with his wife that the name should be John. Second, presumably the father, because he was mute and deaf, did not hear the mother's earlier statement, hence his own reply served as supernatural confirmation that the child should be called John.

33. For further discussion, see Marshall, *Commentary on Luke*, 88.

1:64   Zechariah's muteness and deafness left him immediately (*parachrēma*), a Lucan term often associated with miracles (44:39; 5:25; 8:44, 47, 55; 13:13; 18:43; 22:60; etc.). The verb, his tongue "was loosed," is supplied from the context. Zechariah's obedience to God produced nothing less than a miraculous sign and wonder—his handicap was removed and his faith was restored. Not surprisingly, the elderly father's first words were praise to God, a result often accompanying miracles in Luke-Acts (2:28; 24:53; Acts 2:46; 3:9; etc.). Moreover, if the theory presented earlier in this chapter that Zechariah himself is a divine foreshadowing of Israel's future unbelief turned to belief has credence, then there is warrant for seeing Zechariah's restoration to God here in Luke 1:65 as prophetic of Israel's future restoration (cf. Luke 2:38; 24:21; Acts 1:6).

1:65   Fear, a typical response to the miraculous in Luke-Acts (5:26; 7:16; 8:25, 37; Acts 2:43; 5:5, 11; 19:17), gripped the residents living throughout the hill country of Judea, and everyone was preoccupied with the topic of God's intervention on behalf of Zechariah and Elizabeth.

1:66   The people pondered in their hearts (cf. 2:19, 51; 3:15; 5:22) the significance of the child born to Elizabeth and Zechariah. The statement "for the hand of the Lord was with him" (see Ex. 13:13; 14:8; Isa. 26:11; cf. Acts 11:21; 13:11) is probably Luke's editorial comment. The imperfect tense, *ēn,* denotes continuous action in the past—the hand of the Lord was repeatedly with John.

1:67   Luke 1:67-79 forms the second part of the circumcision episode of John the Baptist—Zechariah's hymn, the *Benedictus.* After the explanatory note in v. 67, the hymn divides into three lines: 68b-71, 72-75, and 76-77. Verses 78-79 serve as the conclusion to the hymn.[34]

The entire hymn seems to evince a chiastic structure (ABCD D′C′B′A′), with the focal point centering on the idea of God's faithfulness to His covenant with Abraham (D, D′):[35]

---

34. Compare Fitzmyer's arrangement in *The Gospel According to Luke I–IX,* 389.
35. For a very similar structure, see Albert Vanhoye's article, "Structure du 'Benedictus,'" 382-89, though I arrived at my arrangement independently of his work.

A   68-69 Redemption/horn of salvation (Messiah)
  B   70   Prophets' prediction (Isaiah?)
    C   71   Salvation of Israel from her enemies
      D   72   Mercy to the patriarchs and the covenant
      D′ 73   Faithfulness to the covenant with Abraham
    C′ 74-75 Deliverance of Israel from her enemies
  B′ 76   Prophet's prediction (Isa. 40:3)
A′ 77-79 Salvation/sunrise on high (Messiah)

Verse 67 attributes the inspiration for Zechariah's hymn to the filling of the Spirit, the logical consequence of which was prophecy. In the Old Testament, being possessed by the Spirit made one a mouthpiece for God (1 Sam. 10:6-13; Ps. 51:10-13; Ezek. 2:1-7; etc.) and the tradition continues in Luke-Acts (Luke 4:14-24; 10:1-14; Acts 2:1-36; 9:17-22; etc.).

1:68   Verses 68-71 comprise the first line of the hymn. The name of the song, *Benedictus,* is taken from the Latin translation of the first word in the hymn, "blessed." The thought-world, however, is Jewish, for the praise formula, "Blessed be the Lord, the God of Israel," is rooted in the Old Testament (1 Kings 1:48; Pss. 41:14; 72:18; 106:48) and developed in early Judaism (*1QM* 14:4; *1QH* 5:20; *Shemoneh Esreh*; etc.). The main point in this opening strophe is that God has visited His people Israel with the salvation that is in Jesus Christ, the descendant of David. Using language reminiscent of the liberation associated with God's presence with Israel in the Old Testament, especially the redemption accomplished at the Exodus, Zechariah saw in the births of John and the coming Messiah (vv. 78-79) a revisitation of divine deliverance (see also 2:38; 21:18; 24:21, where the same word "redemption" [*lytrōsin*] is employed).

1:69   Zechariah's adulation for his son prompted him to praise God for the coming Messiah, expressed in terms of a "horn of salvation" from "the house of David." The oxen's horn was a sign of power and symbolized the strength of God in displaying His salvation on behalf of Israel (Ps. 148:14). The reference to the house of David recalls the dynastic oracle of 2 Samuel 7, which hints at a future messianic figure. Taken together, the two phrases speak of Jesus, the Davidic Messiah, as the occasion for the manifestation of God's power and salvation. The messianic connotation of vv. 68-69 is confirmed by their chiastic counterpart in vv. 77-79.

1:70   The note of promise and fulfillment continues with v. 70, in which Zechariah interpreted the present situation relative to the births of John and Jesus as forecast by the prophet of God. Although v. 70 does not identify which Old Testament prophet or passage is in view, its chiastic complement in v. 76 helps locate one of the referents—Isaiah, especially 40:3.

1:71   The nature of the salvation proclaimed in vv. 68-70 is defined in v. 71—it is deliverance from the enemies of Israel. The idea is a common one in the Psalms (see, for example, Ps. 18), which describes the afflictions and salvation of the righteous from the hands of their oppressors. While it could refer to the political situation of Zechariah's day (especially regarding the Romans), it probably possesses a broader spiritual scope—God will deliver the people of the Messiah from all who oppose them.

1:72   Luke 1:72-75 constitutes the second line of the *Benedictus,* with vv. 72-73 forming the focal point of the chiastic arrangement of the entire hymn. Verse 72 centers on God's faithfulness to His covenant with Israel and indisputably highlights the unconditional nature of that relationship. The two statements in v. 72 are parallel, the one specifying the other: God displays His mercy (*ḥesed*) to the patriarchs by remembering His covenant with them (cf. again Ps. 106:45; Mic. 7:20). Thus, the births of John, the forerunner, and Jesus, the Messiah, are a part of the fulfillment of the promises of the salvation of Israel.

1:73   Verse 73 restates v. 72 by rooting the covenant with Israel in God's promise to Abraham, especially Genesis 22:16-17. While some commentators interpret this verse to be a spiritualization of the covenant with Abraham, the passage itself gives no indication that the people or the land have now been reapplied primarily to the church. The eternal aspect of the divine promise to Abraham continues to be operative, thus holding out hope for the Jewish people in Zechariah's day, and beyond.

1:74   Verses 74-75 return the reader to its chiastic counterpart in v. 71 in delineating the ultimate goal of Israel's hope for deliverance from its enemies—freedom of worship. One cannot but be reminded of Moses' plea to Pharaoh to let the Israelites go free that they might worship the true God without harassment (Ex. 5:1; 8:1; etc.).

1:75   Verse 75 specifies the two-pronged nature of Israel's worship—it is toward God (holiness) and human beings (righteousness), themes characteristic of the preaching of John (Luke 3:3-20) and Jesus

(Luke 4:18-21; etc.). Such worship in truth and Spirit (cf. John 4:23) is everlasting.

1:76 Directly addressing his son in this, the third line of the hymn (vv. 76-77), Zechariah predicted John's prophetic mission, calling him the "prophet of the Most High." Although the same title occurs in *T. Levi* 8:15, probably with reference to the Messiah, the words in their Lucan setting have no intention of presenting John as a rival to Jesus. Rather, they call attention to John's special, albeit subordinate, role to the Messiah (cf. 1:32). That precursor role will involve preparing the way for the coming of the Lord (see Luke 1:70; Isa. 40:3; Mal. 3:1; see also *1QS* 8:13; 9:19). Although the Old Testament passages cited here identify the Lord (*kyrios*) as Yahweh, there can be no serious objection about it as referring to Jesus here in Luke 1:77 (cf. 1:43). That being the case, even from His birth Jesus was equated with God.

1:77 Verse 77 reorients the focus of Israel's salvation; it moves beyond political liberation to include spiritual restoration to God. In other words, Israel's real enemy is itself; Israel's deepest need is to be set free from the enslavement of sin. The statement prepares the audience for John's ministry; it will be a "baptism of repentance for the forgiveness of sin" (Luke 3:3; cf. 1:17).

1:78 Verses 78-79 conclude the *Benedictus.* The occurrence of the unusual word "will visit" (*episkepsetai*) in v. 78 and in vv. 68-69 confirm their chiastic arrangement. Both statements refer, then, not to John, but to Jesus. Whereas Jesus was called the horn of salvation in v. 68, in v. 78 He is referred to as the "sunrise from on high." This chiastic structure helps solve the difficulty of the meaning of the word "sunrise" (*anatolē*, v. 78). While the term is used generically in the Septuagint to translate Mal. 3:20, "for you who fear my name the sun of righteousness shall rise (*anatelei*) with healing in its wings," it was also used to translate the word "shoot" or "branch" with reference to the Davidic messianic heir (Isa. 11:1; Jer. 23:5; Zech. 3:8). Moreover, the verb, *anatelō,* is used of Jacob's seed in Numbers 24:17, which was later interpreted messianically (*CD* 7:18; *1QM* 11:6; *T. Levi* 18:3; etc.). On balance, then, given the messianic connotation of the term in the Old Testament, as well as in early Judaism, along with the chiastic correlation of Luke 1:68-69 and 77-79, *anatolē* most probably should be interpreted messianically as the shoot of David, not just generically for the rising of the sun.

1:79 Jesus' messianic mission is depicted in dualistic terms of light/darkness and death/peace, recalling a conglomerate of Old Testament texts (Ps. 107:10; Isa. 9:12; 42:7; 59:8). As the sun of righteousness, Christ will dispel spiritual darkness and illuminate the path of peace for those who embrace Him (cf. Luke 2:14; 7:50; 8:48; 10:5; 19:38, 42; Acts 10:36; etc.).

1:80 Verse 80 prepares the reader for the public manifestation of the ministry of John the Baptist. John's physical growth and spiritual development ("spirit" probably includes the idea of the Holy Spirit; see vv. 15, 41, 67) parallels the maturation of Samuel, the prophet (1 Sam. 2:26). The significance of John's dwelling in the desert has occasioned a lively debate concerning the question of whether or not he had contact with the Essenes at the Qumran community. There are three possible contacts between the two.[36] Geographically, both resided in the desert, particularly the wilderness of Judea, at the northwest side of the Dead Sea, where it merged with the Jordan River (see Luke 3:2-3). Textually, both regarded Isaiah 40:3 as their key verse (cf. Luke 1:76; 3:4-6 with *1QS* 8:12-16; 9:19). Ritually, one can compare John's baptism of repentance with the Qumran community's mention of its ritual washings (see, for example, *1QS* 5:8, 3), both of which appealed to the need for *Jews* to repent.

The major objection to the proposed connection between John the Baptist and the Qumran community is that the former was associated from birth with the Jerusalem priesthood while the latter held such an office in contempt because they perceived it to be spiritually lax (*1QpHab* 9:4-7; *4QpNah* 3:4, 12). However, the last mentioned point is not an overwhelming argument, for two reasons: First, the Qumran community itself traced its origin to the Zadokite priesthood and thus was open to the priesthood. Second, Josephus tells us that Essenes were known to adopt into their community children still pliable, in order to shape them according to their ways (*J. W.* 2.120). John may well have been one such child who was taken in by Qumran, born as he was to an elderly couple whose death was imminent. It seems, therefore, that a rather convincing case can be made for an association between John and Qumran, though one cannot be dogmatic about it. However, one thing is clear; when the divine call came to John in the desert (cf. Luke 1:80 with 3:2), he broke with his secluded past and began a new, public ministry to Israel.

---

36. Fitzmyer provides a good summary of the issue in *The Gospel According to Luke I–IX*, 389, 453-54. *Contra* William Sanford LaSor, *The Dead Sea Scrolls*, 203-5.

HOMILETICAL SUGGESTIONS

Luke 1, as we have seen in this chapter, is comprised of some five sections: the prologue, 1:1-4; the announcement of the birth of John, 1:5-25; the announcement of the birth of Jesus, 1:26-38; Mary's visit to Elizabeth, 1:39-56; the birth, circumcision, and manifestation of John, 1:57-80. We must admit that most congregations would consider it a challenge to sit through five expository sermons devoted to each respective section, so wisdom might dictate that the minister treat the chapter topically. If so, probably the bulk of the chapter would be best covered by comparing the narratives on John and Jesus, noting the step-parallelism along the way. Obviously, Mary's *Magnificat* stands alone, providing for a touching advent sermon. A different approach to Luke 1, one that should prove both entertaining and inspirational, would be to analyze the chapter from Luke's perspective. One could proceed on the basis that the prologue of 1:1-4 presents Luke as an investigative reporter gathering testimonies about the Christ child. Each character, then (Zechariah, Elizabeth, Mary, John the Baptist, etc.), could be interviewed during the course of a sermon, imagining their own perspectives on the birth of the Messiah.

LUKE
C H A P T E R
TWO

THE BIRTH OF
JESUS CHRIST OUR LORD

Luke 2 is probably the most well-known passage in the entire New Testament. Its Christmas story has been read, sung, and dramatized throughout the history of the church. The nativity narrative is so picturesque and articulate that it seems almost a shame to make comment on it. Yet a consideration of the historical and cultural backdrop makes this text all the more wonderful to behold. The chapter as a whole consists of the following episodes: the birth of Jesus, 2:1-20; the circumcision and manifestation of Jesus, 2:21-40; Jesus in the temple, 2:41-52.

THE BIRTH OF JESUS, 2:1-20

Carl Sandburg's definition of a baby—"God's opinion that the world should continue"—admirably sets the stage for the Christmas story of Luke 2:1-20. The birth of Jesus Christ our Lord accentuates the doctrine of the incarnation, that God has entered the world by becoming human. The humble circumstances surrounding Jesus' birth convey the message that God has identified Himself with the human condition. The nativity drama contains three scenes: the setting of the birth (vv. 1-5), the birth of Jesus (vv. 6-7), the manifestation of the birth to the shepherds (vv. 8-20).

THE SETTING OF THE BIRTH, 2:1-5

2:1   The old adage is true, "History is his story." Luke 2:1-5 illustrates this reality beautifully in the way it juxtaposes the human involvement setting the stage for Jesus' birth (vv. 1-3) with the divine
intent arranging for that event to take place in Bethlehem, the city of
David (vv. 4-5). In doing so, Luke gives the distinct impression that
one king (Caesar Augustus) has given way to another (Jesus). The
phrase, "In those days" refers, in general, to the time of Herod the
Great's reign (1:5) and specifically to 6 B.C., if that is the correct date of
Quirinius's governorship of Syria (2:2). The word *dogma* refers to an
imperial edict, in this case issued by Caesar Augustus. Born Gaius Oc-
tavius on September 23, 63 B.C., and adopted as the son of Julius Caesar in 43 B.C., Octavian was catapulted to fame with his victory over
Cleopatra and Mark Antony at the battle at Actium, 31 B.C. In 27 B.C.,
the Roman Senate bestowed on him the title "Caesar Augustus," and,
with it, undisputed rule over the empire. He ruled from 27 B.C. to his
death in A.D. 14, a period labeled *Pax Augusta* because of its unparalleled peace. The purpose of the imperial fiat was to take a census of
the inhabited world (the land under the control of the Roman empire) which itself would be preparatory for taxation. Although there is
no recorded universal census taken by Augustus, it is well known that
the emperor periodically took provincial censuses for the purpose of
taxation (27 B.C., 12 B.C., A.D. 14, etc.). Luke's account, therefore, should
not be written off as fictitious or erroneous. His accuracy elsewhere
warns against such a cavalier interpretation of his material.

2:2   Verse 2 has been translated in two ways: (a) "This registration
took place before (*prōtē*) Quirinius was governor of Syria," taking
prōtē as a comparative. The advantage of this rendering is that it re-
moves the apparent difficulty posed by Luke's placement of the census
in the governorship of Quirinius (A.D. 6–9). The problem, however,
with this translation is that the following words, "was governor of Syria" (*ēgemoneuontos syrias*), form the genitive absolute construction
(a participle and a noun in the genitive case which sets the resulting
thought apart from the previous words). (b) Accordingly, most scholars today translate v. 2, "This registration was the first, and it took
place when Quirinius was governor of Syria." The historical quandary
that ensues with this rendering has already been dealt with in the
Introduction of this work. We briefly re-enter the discussion here by
observing that the explicit references to Quirinius's legate date his
governorship to the period of A.D. 6–9 (Tacitus, *Annals,* 3:48; Jose-

phus, *Ant.* 18.1.1; 18.26). The historical circumstances were as follows: upon the death of Herod the Great (4 B.C.), the territory over which he ruled was divided among his three sons: Archelaus (4 B.C.– A.D. 6) became the ethnarch over Judea, Samaria, and Idumea; Herod Antipas (4 B.C.–A.D. 39) became the tetrarch over Galilee and Perea; and Philip (4 B.C.–A.D. 34) became the tetrarch over Batanea, Paneas and other regions in the northeast of Palestine, especially east of the Jordan River. However, in A.D. 6 Archelaus was banished to southern Gaul, and his territory was annexed to the imperial province of Syria, which was ruled by Quirinius. At that time, Quirinius conducted a census of the province of Syria, including Judea. That Luke knows of such a census is clear from Acts 5:36. The question is: Is that the census referred to in Luke 2:2? If so, it will have occurred at a date later than the rule of Herod the Great (Luke 1:5), thus creating an apparent contradiction. Though an uncontested answer is still forthcoming, we recall the theory made by some in defense of Luke's historical reliability. Ramsay's suggestion that the *titulus tiburtinus* inscription leaves open the possibility of an earlier "co-legateship" by Quirinius during Herod's reign is helpful and should not be facilely discarded. Because the process of enrollment in a census took a considerable amount of time, it is quite possible that Quirinius instituted the census referred to by Luke at that time, while Josephus refers to the closing stage of it. Or, less likely but possible, is the theory that Quirinius conducted two separate censuses.[1]

2:3   Roman procedure for taxation required people to be registered at their place of residence, not their ancestral home. However, an edict from an Egyptian Greek papyrus discovered in 1904 and dating to A.D. 104 throws light on the Lucan text. The imperial edict of G. Vibius Maximus reads, "Since registration by household is imminent, it is necessary to notify all who for any reason are absent from their districts to return to their own homes that they may carry out the ordinary business of registration and continue faithfully the farming expected of them."[2] H. Braunert has argued that a similar procedure of returning to one's hometown for registration was followed in Palestine.[3]

---

1. Marshall rehearses the various theories put forth relative to this issue and does not find the one advocated here unreasonable in *Commentary on Luke,* 104.
2. The text is included in Adolf Deissmann's *Light from the Ancient East: The New Testament Illustrated by Recently Discovered Texts of the Graeco-Roman World,* 211.
3. Braunert, "Die Römische Provinzialzensus und der Schätzungsbericht des Lukas-Evangeliums," 192-214; 201.

2:4   Though Luke does not mention it, apparently Joseph also had property in Bethlehem while living in Nazareth, hence the human reason for his eighty-five mile trip from the one to the other. It is obvious, however, that Luke wants to emphasize that such a visit was divinely orchestrated to fulfill the prophecy of Micah 5:2 that the Messiah would be born in Bethlehem. "Bethlehem" ("house of bread") was the home of David and it, along with Jerusalem, could be called the city of David (John 7:42; 2 Sam. 5:7, 9; etc.). Thus Jesus' credentials as Messiah are already established on two grounds: First, Jesus was born to a family whose origin could be traced to King David. Second, Jesus the Messiah was born in Bethlehem in accordance with Old Testament prophecy.

2:5   The aorist infinitive, "to register," is dependent on the main verb in v. 4, "went up"; thus, "He went up with Mary, who was pregnant, his fiancée." The verse generates three comments confirming the reliability of Luke's investigative reporting. First, the reference to going "up" from Nazareth (1,830 feet above sea level) to Bethlehem (2,564 feet above sea level) is true to reality. Second, Mary's presence with Joseph is probably accounted for by the fact that Syrian women ages twelve and up were liable to poll tax and thus may have needed to appear in person for enrollment. Third, Luke's statement that Mary was Joseph's pregnant fiancée, though possibly scandalously suggestive to some in his day, accorded with the facts—Mary was found with child before they were married. Later manuscripts tried to smooth this seeming impropriety over by changing the words to, "who was pregnant, his wife" ([A]; etc.). The reader knows, of course, the true nature of things—God was the father of the fetus. Incidentally, as Marshall remarks, the very fact that Joseph as a resident of Galilee had to travel to Judea to be taxed bespeaks against a period *after* Herod's death when his client kingdom was divided up.[4]

THE BIRTH OF JESUS, 2:6-7
2:6   When the holy couple arrived at Bethlehem, the time was fulfilled for Mary to give birth to her child. It should be noted that according to a later erroneous tradition found in the New Testament apocryphal work, *Prot. James,* the birth took place before Joseph and Mary reached Bethlehem, in a cave (17:3; 18:1).

4. Marshall, *Commentary on Luke,* 102.

2:7   The description of the birth of Jesus is as simple as it is beautiful. Three statements are made. First, Jesus was Mary's "firstborn" (*prōtotokon*) "son," signifying the fact that Jesus was the first child to be born to Mary and thus was entitled to the privileges of the firstborn in the Mosaic Law (Ex. 13:2; Num. 3:12-13; Luke 2:23; etc.). Thus Jesus' status as inheritor of the kingdom of God may be hinted at here by Luke (cf. 2 Kings 3:27; 2 Chron. 21:3). It may also be that Luke uses this term to distinguish Jesus from other children that Joseph and Mary would later bear. Second, Mary wrapped the Christ-child in strips of linen cloth. This was customary for newborn babies, because it was felt that tightly wrapped cloth provided both firmness for the bones and emotional security (Ezek. 16:4; *Wis.* 7:4). Third, Jesus was placed in a manger because there was no room in the lodge for the family. As Ellis comments, when Palestinian rooms were filled and the animals were at pasture, an inn or lodge would improvise quarters for the poorer people in the animal courtyard. The placing of Jesus in a manger, a feeding trough, suggests such an environment for His birth.[5] Later tradition identified the place of Jesus' birth as a cave (*Prot. James* 17:3; 18:1; Justin, *Dial.* 78), which apparently helped influence Emperor Constantine's decision to erect a basilica at Bethlehem over a cave, the site of the present-day Church of the Nativity.

THE MANIFESTATION OF THE BIRTH
OF JESUS TO THE SHEPHERDS, 2:8-20
2:8   The introduction of the shepherds into the nativity drama makes both historical and theological statements. The historical verisimilitude of the account is casually brought out by the description of the shepherd's activity. Theirs was the typical behavior of Palestinian shepherds who kept their flocks in the open air and therefore had to rotate their watches in order to protect the sheep. According to Strack and Billerbeck, the activity described here took place from April to November[6] (thus calling into question the later tradition that Jesus was born on December 25). The theological import of the scene is that the birth of the Messiah was first brought to the attention of, not religious or political leaders, but humble people—shepherds.

5. Ellis, *The Gospel of Luke,* 79.
6. Strack and Billerbeck, *Kommentar Zum Neuen Testament Aus Talmud und Midrash, 3, Die Briefe des Neuen Testaments und die Offenbarung Johannis,* 2:114-16.

2:9   The darkness of the night was suddenly dispelled by the appearance of the angel of the Lord (probably Gabriel, 1:19) and the glory of God to the shepherds. The word "glory" (*doxa*) is the Greek translation of the Hebrew word *kabod,* and it refers to the brilliant manifestation of God's presence to His people. The shepherds' fear was a natural response to a supernatural revelation. The two cognate accusatives (a cognate verb and noun in the accusative case) used of the shepherds—"watching their watches" (v. 8) and "fearing with fear" (v. 9)—add a lyrical touch to the narrative.

2:10   The angel allayed the shepherds' fears by announcing that he came as a messenger of "good news" (*euangelizomai*) which would bring great joy to all people. The recipients of this good news obviously included Israel, but did not stop there.

2:11   The reason for the celebrative joy was given by the angel—the messianic age has dawned with the birth of Jesus. The word "today" (*sēmeron*) highlights this eschatological hue of the angel's message (cf. 4:21; 5:26; 19:9; 23:43; etc.), as do the three terms applied to Jesus: Savior, Christ, the Lord. The last two nouns are anarthrous (without the article), posing a difficulty in translation. Is it "Christ Lord" or "the Lord's anointed"? In light of the occurrence of the same two nouns in Acts 2:36, probably the former rendering is to be preferred. Thus, the angelic announcement was that the newborn baby in Bethlehem was none other than a savior of the people, Messiah-Yahweh (cf. *Ps. Sol.* 17:36; *T. Levi* 2:11). It would be hard to imagine a more exalted title for Jesus. Moreover, the term Savior would unavoidably have called to mind the veneration paid to Caesar Augustus by the Greco-Roman world of Jesus' day. Augustus was hailed as "savior" and "god" in many Greek inscriptions.[7] According to the Priene inscription, his birthday on September 23 was celebrated, "the birthday of the god has marked the beginning of the good news through him for the world."[8] But, according to the angel, it was Jesus, not Augustus, who was the real savior and bearer of peace in the world.

2:12   Like Zechariah (1:18-20) and Mary (1:36), the shepherds received a sign confirming the truth of the angelic announcement. The sign was not that the child would be wrapped in linen clothes—that was normal for any newborn. Rather, it was that the shepherds would

---

7. See the discussion by Fitzmyer in *The Gospel According to Luke I–IX,* 393-94, and the pertinent primary texts in Jones, *Documents Illustrating the Reigns of Augustus and Tiberius.*

8. The text and a discussion of it can be found in W. Oittenberger, *Orientis graeci inscriptiones selectae* (Leipzig: Hirzel, 1903–1905), 40-42.

find the baby lying in a manger. Thus, the sign was a paradox; the shepherds would find the Savior, the Messiah-Yahweh (majesty) lying in a feeding trough (humility).

2:13 As if to bolster the shepherds' confidence in the face of this shocking paradoxical news, the angel of the Lord was suddenly joined by the heavenly host praising God and singing.

2:14 The scope of the song of the angels encompassed heaven and earth: "Glory to God in the highest heaven/peace on earth to people of good pleasure." The last word has occasioned a debate in text criticism. The later Byzantine tradition has the nominative, *eudokia* (good will), while the Alexandrian tradition (B, Sinaiticus, A) has the genitive, *eudokias* (of good pleasure). In light of the oldest manuscripts supporting this reading, as well as the parallelism it creates for the verse, the latter seems to be the most accurate. The resulting meaning, then, is, "peace on earth to people whom God has favored"[9] (cf. 3:22; *1QH* 4:32; 11:9; etc.). The implication is that Jesus, not the political structures of the day, would bring true peace because He alone could reconcile humans with God, and only those who embraced Christ would find God's favor.

2:15 Upon the angels' return to heaven, the shepherds determined to see the event (literally, the "word," cf. 1:37) that God had made known to them (cf. 2:17; Acts 7:13; etc.).

2:16 The shepherds hurried to find the baby, undoubtedly with mixed feelings of wonder and confusion. They indeed found the child, precisely as the angel had said. It is interesting that we are not told any details concerning the birth itself. The matter-of-factness and brevity of the account itself speaks of its historicity as well as the normalcy of Jesus' birth. It was His conception that was so unique.

2:17 Discovering the child, the shepherds related the angelic message to others, presumably including Joseph and Mary, and those in the near vicinity.

2:18 In vv. 18-20, three reactions to the miracle of the Christ-child are recorded. First, in v. 18, the inhabitants of Bethlehem responded with wonder, the expected reaction when the human realm encounters the divine.

2:19 Second, Mary's reaction was one of meditative puzzlement. She treasured the words of the shepherds, pondering or trying "to hit

---

9. Fitzmyer provides a thorough investigation of the proposed translations in *The Gospel According to Luke I–IX,* 411-12.

upon their right meaning," as van Unnik defines the term *symbal-lousa*[10] (cf. 2:51). Mary's reflection suggests that her thinking went deeper than the rather external intrigue and merriment of the others.
2:20   Third, the shepherds returned to their work of tending the sheep with a newfound joy as they glorified and praised God because of all they had heard and seen.

THE CIRCUMCISION AND MANIFESTATION OF JESUS, 2:21-40

The infancy narratives continue with the circumcision and mani-festation of Jesus, similar episodes to the narrative about John (1:59-80). Luke 2:21-40 is divided into three major parts: the circumcision of Jesus, vv. 21-24; the *Nunc Dimittis* (the canticle and oracle of Simeon), vv. 25-35; the testimony of Anna, vv. 36-38. The conclusion of the nar-rative is in vv. 39-40, words similarly uttered about the growth of John the Baptist. Two chords are struck in Luke 2:21-40: the piety of Jesus' parents and the ministry of Jesus.

THE CIRCUMCISION OF JESUS, 2:21-24
2:21   The Old Testament background to vv. 21-22 is Leviticus 12. There the Lord prescribed that a woman who bore a son would be ritually unclean for seven days (v. 2). On the eighth day, the male child was to be circumcised (v. 3). The mother remained ritually un-clean for thirty-three days thereafter, not being able to enter the taber-nacle during that time (v. 4). After the completion of the purification period, the mother was to make a sacrificial offering to the Lord in the tabernacle, a lamb for a burnt offering and a pigeon or turtledove for a sin offering (v. 6). If she was poor, two turtledoves or two pigeons would suffice. After the sacrifice, the mother was declared ritually clean (v. 8). Thus, Mary and Joseph's circumcising Jesus on the eighth day demonstrated their piety toward the Old Testament Law. Upon his circumcision, the baby was named Jesus, in obedience to the angel's command before His conception (1:31).
2:22   The piety of Jesus' parents continued in their bringing Him to the temple (presumably from Bethlehem) after the period of purifica-tion in order to make an offering to the Lord. The scene reminds one of Hannah's presentation of Samuel to the Lord (1 Sam. 1:22-24). Two details in the episode have caused some to question Luke's grasp of

---

10. van Unnik, "Die rechte Bedeutung des wortes treffen, Lukas II.19," 72-91.

the facts: the reference to "their" (*autōn*) purification and the lack of documentation in Judaism for the presentation of the firstborn son in the temple. Concerning the first of these, it is argued that in Judaism only the mother was ritually unclean, not the baby, and therefore Luke incorrectly uses the plural pronoun. But Marshall sufficiently answers this criticism by suggesting that the plural refers to both acts of purification and offering, which involved *both* parents[11] ("they" went up to Jerusalem). Regarding the second supposed problem, even though a custom of presenting the child in the temple (as distinguished from the offering made on behalf of the child whose presence at the temple was apparently not required) is not attested in Judaism, there was good precedent for doing so based on Hannah's presentation of Samuel (which, as we just noted, distinctly reminds one of Jesus' presentation).

2:23 Apparently, the consecration of Jesus was intended to be an adaptation of the Old Testament practice of redeeming the firstborn son. That custom was based on the assumption that the firstborn male was the property of the Lord. Since the priestly tribe of Levi had been set apart in their own place, the firstborn sons in other tribes could be "ransomed" through the payment of a redemption price of five shekels which was to be paid to a priest (Ex. 13:1-2; 22:28; Num. 3:11-13, 40-51; Deut. 15:19; etc.). Luke signals this background, especially Exodus 13:2, with his words, "as it is written, every male that opens the womb is to be called holy to the Lord." From the absence of any reference to a ransom price for Jesus, however, it seems that the incident is not to be equated with the custom of the redemption of the firstborn son, but rather it is to be interpreted as a dedication of Jesus to the Lord in a similar manner to 1 Samuel 1:24-28. Is this a subtle hint that Jesus, the sinless one, did not need to be redeemed?

2:24 The offering of the two turtledoves or pigeons was for the purification of the mother, not the redemption of the firstborn, and bespeaks of the inability of Mary and Joseph to afford the one-year-old lamb for the whole burnt offering (see again Lev. 12:8). However, perhaps there is also symbolism here to the effect that Jesus, as the one who would meet with a violent death on behalf of the sins of His people (vv. 34-35), was the true lamb of God to be sacrificed.

11. Marshall, *Commentary on Luke*, 116.

THE *NUNC DIMITTIS*, 2:25-35

Nunc Dimittis is the Latin translation of the two words "now dismiss," the opening words of Simeon's canticle. The episode contains descriptions of Simeon's pious actions (vv. 25-27) and his words of praise, involving the canticle itself (vv. 28-33) and an oracle (vv. 34-35). The *Nunc Dimittis* is similar in nature and function to the *Benedictus* earlier uttered by Zechariah and is the last of the hymns found in the infancy narratives (the others being the *Magnificat*, 1:46-55; *Benedictus*, 1:67-79; Song of the Angels, 2:13-14).

2:25 *Kai idou* ("and behold") introduces a new event in the narrative (cf. 5:12; 10:25; 13:11; 14:2; 19:2; etc.) and gives the upcoming occurrence a supernatural ambiance. Simeon's pious character is described in four editorial comments: (1) He was righteous (*dikaios*; cf. Zech. 1:6). (2) He was devout (*eulabēs*; cf. the characterization of the early Christians, Acts 2:5; 8:2; 22:12). (3) He awaited the consolation (*paraklēsin*; cf. Acts 9:31; etc.) of Israel, which in Jewish thought was based on Isaiah 40:1 and came to mean the comfort that the messianic era would bring.[12] In other words, Simeon longed for the restoration of Israel that was expected to occur with the coming of the Messiah. (4) The Holy Spirit was upon (*epi*) him, thus grounding the words Simeon was about to speak in divine inspiration.

2:26 The same Spirit disclosed to Simeon that he would not die ("see death" means to experience death; cf. Ps. 89:48) until he saw the Lord's Christ. The means of that revelation is not specified. Like God's guidance in the Old Testament, it could have been auditory, or visionary, or by way of inward compulsion, etc.

2:27 The Spirit led Simeon to the temple (*hieron*), probably the court of the women where, with perfect timing, he encountered the parents of Jesus dedicating Him to the Lord.

2:28 With tender care and heartfelt thanks, the aged man took the baby into his arms and blessed God.

2:29 One can almost detect a sigh of relief as Simeon prayed, "Now dismiss your servant, Lord, according to your word, in peace." The first two words, "Now dismiss," provide the title of the hymn (canticle [vv. 29-32]), *Nunc Dimittis*. The present tense of "dismiss" (*apolyeis*) probably indicates that in seeing the Messiah, already Simeon is dying in peace.[13] The two terms, "servant" (*doulous*) and "Lord"

12. Strack-B 2:124-26.
13. So according to Marshall in *Commentary on Luke*, 120.

(*despota*), stand in stark contrast, signifying a servant/master relationship. The latter word is used of God elsewhere by Luke in Acts 4:24. In using these two terms, Simeon acknowledged his service to and dependency on God. The phrase, "according to your word," reveals Simeon's deep-seated trust in his Lord's faithfulness.

2:30   Simeon stated his reason for praise: he had seen for himself the salvation of the Lord, an allusion to Isaiah 40:5, "all flesh will see God's salvation" (cf. 3:6; Acts 28:28). With the mention of God's salvation here in the beginning of the third gospel and at the end of Acts (28:28), an *inclusio* (beginning and ending a passage or a book with the same theme) is formed, thereby accentuating the overriding motif of Luke's two-volume work.

2:31   This salvation had been prepared by God in full view of all people (cf. Isa. 52:10; Ps. 98:1-3; Ezek. 29:27). Luke draws here on Isaiah 52:10 (Septuagint), but changes the word *ethnē* (nations) to *laōn* (peoples). Luke uses the word *laōn* (laity) to refer to the Jews (Acts 26:17, 23), or to the new people of God, including the Gentiles (Acts 15:14). Therefore, there seems to be some overlapping between the terms which encompass both Jew and Gentile. The next verse makes this clear.

2:32   The hymnic quality of the verses surfaces with the occurrence of synthetic parallelism (one line repeats another, but adds a new thought) in v. 32: God's salvation will provide a light which will bring revelation to the Gentiles, and glory to the people of Israel. Thus, the recipients of Christ's divine deliverance will include Gentile and Jew, thereby initiating the fulfillment of the twofold Old Testament promise of salvation for both people groups (cf. Isa. 46:13; 49:6, 9; etc.). In the sequence of things, however, the coming of the Messiah will bring glory to Israel and, consequently, the Gentiles to Jerusalem for salvation (*Ps. Sol.* 17:34). Thus, Luke may well be hinting at the priority of Israel in salvation, an idea he shared with Paul (Acts 13:46; Rom. 1:16; 2:10).

2:33   It is hypercritical to suggest, as some have, that in calling Joseph and Mary Jesus' father and mother, Luke is using a source in Luke 2 that was unaware of the promise of the virgin birth in 1:26-38. Rather, the author presumes the reader's familiarity with chapter 1 and can therefore speak in general terms in the present passage. What amazed Joseph and Mary is not exactly specified, but it surely entailed Simeon's recognition that Jesus was the Messiah, and that God's salvation through Him included both Jew and Gentile.

2:34   Verses 34-35 constitute Simeon's prophetic oracle. After blessing the parents, the sage predicted to Mary that the child was destined for the fall and rise of many in Israel, as well as that He would be a sign of rejection. The language of the oracle is dependent on Isaiah 8:14-15/Isaiah 28:16, the latter of which is utilized in the New Testament as an apologetic explanation for Jesus' rejection, the despised cornerstone (Luke 20:17; Rom. 9:33; 1 Peter 2:6-8). The typical exegesis of Luke 2:34 is that Jesus, as the rejected Messiah, will be the cause for some in Israel to accept Him and for others to spurn Him. That much is certainly true. Yet perhaps Luke would have us probe deeper. Caird has effectively shown that the action of falling and rising probably refers to one group of people, not two. The adverb "many" (*pollōn*), in modifying both verbs—fall/rise—seems to refer to the same entity.[14] Thus, it is the same group who falls and rises. Moreover, J. Jeremias has plausibly demonstrated that the "many" (*pollōi*) is to be taken comprehensively for the whole of Israel.[15] Furthermore, the order of the verbs in v. 34 is significant: fall, then rise. Combining these observations leads one to the following possible interpretation—Jesus, the Messiah who will first undergo suffering before receiving glory (cf. Luke 24:26, 46), is Himself a sign (*sēmeion*) of Israel's fall and rise (restoration). Jesus' own destiny of rejection and exaltation will be representative of Israel's future reversal of fortunes.

2:35   Verse 35a is an interruption in thought in which Simeon predicted Mary's lot: a sword will pierce her soul. Although Fitzmyer interprets the clause to mean that Jesus will bring dissension to Mary's own family (8:21; 11:27-28; 12:51-53),[16] it most probably alludes to her anguish of soul at the rejection of her son which would lead to the cross. Verse 35b resumes the idea of v. 34, that the Messiah would be God's means for revealing the thoughts (cf. Luke 5:22; 6:8; 9:46-47; 24:38) of the many in Israel. There will be no neutral ground concerning Jesus—people will either accept or reject Him.

THE TESTIMONY OF ANNA, 2:36-38

2:36   There was also in the temple a prophetess, Anna, whose name in Hebrew is Hannah (1 Sam. 1:2). She was a daughter of Phanuel

---

14. Caird, *St. Luke*, 64.
15. Jeremias, "*pollōi*," 6:536-545; 541.
16. Fitzmyer, *The Gospel According to Luke I–IX*, 429-30.

(face of God, 1 Chron. 4:4), from the tribe of Asher. She was an elderly woman, having been married only seven years.

2:37 For eighty-four years she had basically lived in the temple, worshiping God day and night with fasting and prayer. Perhaps, as Ellis notes, she belonged to an order of widows with specifically religious functions in the temple.[17]

2:38 At the same time that Simeon uttered his canticle/oracle, Anna went up to the parents and praised God. Thereafter, she continually spread the news about Jesus, linking Him to the redemption of Jerusalem, the consolation of Israel (cf. Luke 2:25; Isa. 52:9). Jerusalem is used by *synecdoche* (the part symbolizes the whole) for Israel. That such a hope was in some sense affiliated with national deliverance is attested to in the Marabba'at texts from Israel's second revolt against Rome (A.D. 132–135). These materials are dated therein to the years of "the Redemption of Israel."[18]

CONCLUSION, 2:39-40

2:39 The holy family's piety is once again stressed as Luke reports that they accomplished all that the Law of the Lord required (relative to circumcision, purification, and dedication). The word Luke uses is *etelesan,* from *telios* ("to finish"), a word employed elsewhere in the third gospel to describe Jesus' death (12:50; 18:31; 22:37). Does the author intend for the reader to make the connection that Jesus fulfilled the Law all the way from birth to death? Having completed their obligations, Mary and Joseph returned to their hometown of Nazareth, in Galilee.

2:40 As John the Baptist grew both physically and spiritually (1:80), so did Jesus. There were two differences between the two, however: First, 2:40 tells us that Jesus was filled with wisdom, something absent in the description of John. This wisdom would be shortly demonstrated by Jesus in the temple with the Jewish teachers (2:41-50). Second, like His mother (1:30), God's grace was upon Jesus in a special way. In this verse, therefore, we can detect a beautiful blending of Jesus' humanity (He grew up and became strong) and deity (He was filled with wisdom and God's grace).

17. Ellis, *The Gospel of Luke,* 83.
18. See Fitzmyer's discusion in *The Gospel According to Luke I–IX,* 432.

JESUS IN THE TEMPLE, 2:41-52

Luke 2:41-52 serves as both a conclusion to the infancy narratives (1:5–2:40) and as a transition to Jesus' public ministry (3:1). The episode itself, especially the theme of the meticulous maturation of a famous person to be, is paralleled, among other places, in Josephus's description of Moses (*Ant.* 2.230), Herodotus's portrayal of Cyrus (*History* 1.21) and Philostratus's writing about Apollonius (*Vita Apollonius* 1.7).[19] However, this fact need not detract in any way from the historical verisimilitude of Luke's account. It should also be remarked that this incident is the only glimpse we have into the silent years of Jesus' childhood. The purpose of the narrative surfaces in Jesus' pronouncement statement in v. 49 in which He highlighted by contrast His obligation to His heavenly Father compared to His earthly familial obedience.

2:41   Jesus' parents' faithfulness to the Law is accentuated again in Luke's comment about them going every year to Jerusalem to observe the Passover. Passover (Heb., *pesaḥ*; Gk., *pascha*) was one of the three feasts all Jewish males were required to observe in Jerusalem annually (the other two were Pentecost [celebrated fifty days after Passover, in the spring] and Tabernacles [a fall feast]; Deut. 16:16). The name, Passover, derives its meaning from Exodus 12 where the Jewish families in bondage to Egypt sacrificed a lamb, placed its blood on the doorposts, and ate unleavened bread in hasty preparation for the Exodus. Those who observed the ritual were the ones the death angel would "pass over," sparing them the judgment that befell the firstborn of the Egyptians. By the time of Jesus, women also attended the feast.[20]

2:42   Jesus' visit to Jerusalem to observe Passover at age twelve is probably informed by the Jewish custom that a Jewish boy became a man at age thirteen from which time on he was obligated to keep the Torah (*m. Niddah* 5:6). This belief was later turned into the ritual of *bar Mitsvah* ("son of the Law"), a rite of passage transitioning the male from adolescence to adulthood and placing him under the Torah. According to the Talmud (*m. Hag.* 1:1; see also Strack-B 2:144–147), the father was to prepare his son for that event by taking him at a younger age to Jerusalem to become accustomed to the feast, as well

---

19. See Rudolf Bultmann's usage of these texts relative to Luke's infancy narrative in *The History of the Synoptic Tradition*, 301.
20. Strack-B 2:141.

as the Law in general. Jesus' journey to Jerusalem at age twelve fits the custom.

2:43   The feast of Passover was celebrated in conjunction with the feast of unleavened bread (Deut. 16:1-4; 2 Chron. 35:17), lasting seven or eight days. After that time, Mary and Joseph headed back toward their home in Galilee. However, Jesus remained behind in Jerusalem, unbeknownst to his parents.

2:44   Jesus' parents traveled a whole day (about twenty miles), mistakenly thinking that he was with the caravan of pilgrims. In pilgrimages to Jerusalem, villagers traveled in large companies in which the women and children preceded the men. Moreover, the incident makes perfect sense against the backdrop of ancient Hebrew society, which was composed of large, extended families. Presumably, the parents' search for Jesus began when they encamped at nightfall.

2:45   When they could not find Him, they returned to Jerusalem in search of Him.

2:46   The three days are probably to be counted as follows: the first day involved the trip away from Jerusalem; the second day transpired on the return trip to Jerusalem; the third day was devoted to the search for Jesus in the city itself. The parents discovered Jesus in the Temple (*hierō*), undoubtedly the outer courts, sitting in the midst of the Jewish teachers (*didaskalōn*). This is the only time Luke applies the term, "teacher," to the Jewish scribes/lawyers. In the rest of the gospel he applies it to John (3:12) and Jesus. This suggests that the encounter between Jesus and the scribes was a positive one and was indicative of the dialogue that often took place between rabbinic teachers and their students in the Temple porticos.

2:47   But what was not ordinary was the repartee which Jesus demonstrated in His conversation with the scribes. The teachers were astonished at His understanding, that is, His answers ("understanding" and "answers" are a *hendiadys*, two ideas stating the same reality) to their questions concerning the Law.

2:48   Though the syntax is loose, it is clear that the unexpressed subject of "seeing" is Jesus' parents. Upon finding Him, Mary expressed both relief at Jesus' safety and reproach at His seeming irresponsibility. She chided Jesus for putting Joseph and herself through the anguish of His disappearance and their subsequent search for Him.

2:49   Verse 49 contains Jesus' first recorded words in all the gospels and it is appropriate that they expressed his desire to do the will of His heavenly Father. With gentle rebuke Jesus countered His parents' question with His own query, "Why are you searching for me; did you not know that I had to be in My Father's house?" Jesus' rhetorical question conveyed a sense of disappointment at His parents' failure to recognize the divine necessity (*dei,* found eighteen times in Luke and twenty-two times in Acts) that propelled His life. The words, *en tois tou patros mou,* have been variously translated as "about my Father's affairs"; "among those things belonging to my Father," or "in my Father's house." The last rendering is preferred, in light of the Temple setting of v. 49, as well as other incidences of a similar construction referring to one's father's house (Gen. 41:51; Est. 7:9; Job 18:19). The point being made by Jesus was that his bond with the heavenly Father transcended the ties with His earthly family. It is clear that, already by age twelve, Jesus' messianic self-consciousness was formed.

2:50 Despite being privy to divine revelation about the ultimate origin of her son, Mary (and Joseph) failed to comprehend Jesus' words about His true Father and His desire to do His will. Mary's understanding of Jesus, like the later disciples (18:34), was in need of refinement. But that maturity would come (Acts 1:14).

2:51 The holy family descended from Jerusalem to return home to Nazareth where Jesus, lest the reader get the wrong impression from the previous verse, was consistently obedient to His parents. As for Mary, she continued to ponder the meaning of her son's words.

2:52 Like Samuel of old, Jesus grew in wisdom, age,[21] and favor before God and humans (see 1 Sam. 2:21, 26; cf. Luke 2:40).

HOMILETICAL SUGGESTIONS

Homiletically, Luke 2 falls naturally into three sermons: the birth of Jesus, 21:1-20; the circumcision and manifestation of Jesus, 2:21-40; Jesus in the Temple, 2:41-52. In preaching 2:1-20, one could treat the text in expository fashion, proceeding according to its threefold division: vv. 1-5, vv. 6-7, vv. 8-20. However, a more creative approach, and one that we have found especially rewarding, is to contrast Christ with Caesar, utilizing the historical backdrop referenced in this chapter. Another approach that we have found strikes a responsive chord in audiences is to compare and contrast Luke's birth narrative of Jesus (2:1-20) with his passion and resurrection narratives (Luke 22-24). We

---

21. See J. Schneider's discussion of the word *ēlikia* as to whether it should be translated "stature" or, more accurately, "age," 2:941-43.

have discovered some ten similarities between the two pieces as presented by Luke. An appropriate title for the sermon would be: "From the Cradle to the Cross: The Birth and Death of Jesus." The similarities are as follows: (1) There were two Joseph's involved in Jesus' birth and death (2:4 and 23:50-52). (2) The issue of taxes impacted Jesus' birth (2:1-3) and was a part of the accusation leading to His death (23:2). (3) Jesus was identified as a king at His birth and death (2:14 and 23:2). (4) The mention of "signs" accompanied Jesus' birth and death (2:12 and 23:8-11). (5) At His birth and death Jesus was wrapped in strips of linen cloth (2:6 and 23:53). (6) In His birth and death Jesus had no place to call his own (2:7 and 23:53). (7) In His birth and death Jesus was the Son of God (2:7 and 23:18 [the latter verse demonstrates Jesus to be the true Son of the Father, in contrast to Barabbas, the false "son of the Father"]). (8) The same pattern occurs at Jesus' birth and resurrection regarding the witnesses: for the shepherds who saw the angels—there was fear, encouragement, and then they became witnesses (2:8-15); for the women at the empty tomb who saw the angels—there was fear, encouragement, and then they became witnesses (24:1-11). (9) At Jesus' birth, Mary "pondered" what this meant (2:19) while at Jesus' resurrection, Peter "pondered" what this meant (24:12). (10) At Jesus' birth, the shepherds praised and glorified God (2:20) while at Jesus' ascension, the disciples praised and glorified God (24:53).

Luke 2:21-40 is perhaps best preached by examining its threefold division: 2:21-24, 25-36, 36-40. All of the hymns of Luke's infancy narratives (*Magnificat, Benedictus*, Song of the Angels, and *Nunc Dimittis*) have been put to music and serve as lovely pieces to be read after working through their respective passages.

Luke 2:41-52 could serve as a relevant text for not only the Christmas season, but also as the basis for a service devoted to a baby dedication or an evangelistic service for children. A catchy opening for examining this passage might include contrasting apocryphal New Testament stories regarding Jesus' silent years with the one canonical account as found in Luke.

LUKE
CHAPTER
THREE

PREPARATION FOR THE
PUBLIC MINISTRY OF JESUS

In chapter 3, Luke's narrative of the life and times of Jesus fast forwards from His childhood to His adulthood. Jesus was born in 6 B.C. and Tiberius became emperor in A.D. 14. Luke 3:1 dates the inauguration of the ministry of John the Baptist and Jesus to the fifteenth year of Tiberius's reign, that is, to A.D. 29. Luke 3:1–4:13 are devoted to four matters that prepare for the public ministry of Christ: the preaching of John the Baptist (3:1-20), the baptism of Jesus (3:21-22), the genealogy of Jesus (3:23-38), and the temptation of Jesus (4:1-13).

THE PREACHING OF JOHN THE BAPTIST, 3:1-20

The preaching ministry of John the Baptist is summarized by Luke under five headings: the setting (3:1-2a), his call (3:2b), his message (3:3-14), the messianic question surrounding him (3:15-18), and his imprisonment (3:19-20).

3:1 Luke pinpoints the beginning of the ministries of John the Baptist and Jesus chronologically by listing a number of political and religious figures who set the stage for the ensuing drama. The first reference is to Caesar Tiberius who, as we just observed, ruled from A.D. 14 to 37. Luke probably reckons the starting point of Tiberius's reign (*ēgemonias*) in August, A.D. 14, the death of Augustus.

The next political figure mentioned is Pontius Pilate, the prefect of Judea, though the term Luke employs is the same generic word for "rule" which he used of Tiberius (*ēgemoneuontos*). The former term, "prefect," was the official name of the Roman governor of Judea from A.D. 6 to 46. A fragmentary inscription discovered in 1961 at Caesarea Maritime contains a dedicatory statement concerning the building, *Tiberieum,* that Pilate built in honor of Tiberius. In that inscription Pilate is called by the Latin title, *praefectus Judaea.* The title, prefect, was changed to procurator in A.D. 46 when Emperor Claudius reorganized the territory, and the title changed again to *legatus* in A.D. 70 and remained so. When Archelaus was deposed from Judea and Samaria in A.D. 6, Augustus installed the office of prefect over that territory; Pilate was the sixth such appointee, ruling from A.D. 26 to 36. He was recommended for the post by Tiberius's advisor, Sejanus, whose anti-Semitism rubbed off on Pilate (see Josephus, *J. W.* 2.169-71, 3; *Ant.* 18:55-59; etc.).

Another political official referred to is Herod Antipas, one of the four sons of Herod the Great, who was in charge of Galilee and Perea from 4 B.C. to A.D. 39. Herod is called tetrarch, one who ruled a fourth part of an area. This is the same Herod referred to in Luke 3:19; 8:3; 9:7, 9; 13:31; 23:7-15; Acts 4:27; 13:11. Two others officials are mentioned: Philip (son of Herod the Great), tetrarch over Iturea and Trachonitus (northeast of Galilee, the capital of which was Caesarea Philippi), who governed from 4 B.C. to A.D. 34; and Lysanias, tetrarch of Abilene (northwest of Damascus, Syria). The identification of the last mentioned person is problematic. There is no official record of a man named Lysanias ruling Syria, except the one Mark Antony had killed in 36 B.C. However, Josephus does refer to "Abila, which belonged to Lysanias" (*Ant.* 19.275; 20.138; etc.) and this is probably the one Luke had in mind.

3:2   Luke concludes his description of the synchronistic setting of the ministries of John the Baptist and Jesus by referring to two religious leaders, the high priests Annas and Caiaphas. Annas was the high priest of Israel from A.D. 6 to 15. After two intervening high priests, one of which was Annas's son, Simon (who ruled A.D. 17–18), Caiaphas, Annas's son-in-law, was appointed high priest by the Roman government (and ruled A.D. 18–36). Even though Annas was not the official high priest at the time of the ministries of John and Jesus, Luke retains the title for him (Acts 4:6), probably for two reasons. First, the Jews apparently still considered him to be the rightful high priest; indeed, the Jews may have continued to call ex-high priests such. Second, according to John 18:13-27, Annas continued to exercise considerable power behind the scenes after being deposed from office by the Romans.

In 3:2b Luke records the call of John the Baptist to the preparatory ministry of Jesus. Like Jeremiah (1:1), the word of the Lord came to John, thus depicting his prophetic role. If John was associated with the Qumran community, then the divine compulsion to preach necessarily entailed the breaking off of that relationship, especially since John would have intimate contact with people. The mention of John's father refers the reader back to chapter 1.

3:3   John's message is related in 3:3-14. Simply stated, the theme of John's preaching was that the messianic age was at hand. John's quotation of Isaiah 40:3-5 signaled to his audience that the Old Testament promise of salvation to Israel was in the process of being fulfilled (Luke 3:4-6). The requirement for receiving that blessing was repentance from sin leading to ethical transformation, not reliance upon physical descent or Jewish ethnicity (3:7-14).

According to v. 3, John conducted his ministry in and around the Jordan River. His clarion call was to preach a baptism of repentance for the forgiveness of sins. The words "baptism of repentance" beautifully combine outward ritual with inward reality. Baptism by water, whether as understood by the Qumran community as applicable to itself (*1QS* 3:3-12; 5:13-14) or as preached by Jewish missionaries to Gentile converts (*b. Yebam.* 22a, 46b), symbolized spiritual cleansing from sin, the result of forgiveness. John's baptism served a transitional purpose: it linked him with the period of Israel, especially the Old Testament prophets' preaching of repentance, while preparing the way for the period of Jesus and His baptism with the Spirit (1:16-17). This transitional role speaks against Conzelmann's relegation of John exclusively to the period of Israel.

3:4   In quoting Isaiah 40:3-5, John revealed his prophetic consciousness with its emphasis on the fulfillment of the Old Testament promise of salvation. Like the Qumran community, John saw himself as a voice crying in the desert, calling people to God. Unlike the people of the Dead Sea Scrolls, however, John's message called for, not separation, but penetration of society; not the meticulous observance of the Law of Moses (*1QS* 8:12-15) but conversion of the heart in preparation for the coming of the Messiah. Such spiritual preparation for the Lord Messiah is depicted in geographical terms—it involved preparing the way for the Lord, making the paths straight. Like the forerunner who cleared away branches, rocks, and any other obstacles on the roads the king would soon travel, John the Baptist admonished the people of Israel to remove the roadblocks of sin from their hearts. Moreover, the combination of the metaphors of baptism and desert, as Ellis notes, may also convey the typological significance that Israel, in repenting of its sin, was about to leave the wilderness, cross the Jordan River, and enter the promised land of the messianic era, by way of an Exodus-like baptism.[1]

3:5   The geographical imagery continues as Luke portrays the preparation for the Messiah in terms of the construction of a level road in the midst of an undulating desert: valleys must be filled, mountains must be razed, the crooked must be straightened, and the rough must be smoothed out. These terms, as Marshall notes, probably possess ethical overtones.[2]

3:6   The words, "and all flesh will see the salvation of God" complete the quotation of Isaiah 40:3-5 and are unique to Luke. The clause reflects the third gospel's concern to demonstrate that the twofold Old Testament promise of salvation to both Jew and Gentile was beginning to be fulfilled in the ministry of John the Baptist.

3:7   The content of John the Baptist's message is detailed in 3:7-14; it was stern and shocking. The old adage of preachers aptly summarizes the intent of John's proclamation, as complemented by Jesus' message (Luke 4:18-19): the one afflicted the comfortable (John), the other comforted the afflicted (Jesus). The sternness of John's message of repentance shockingly targeted Jewish audiences; Israel, like the Gentiles, needed conversion! Verses 7-9 provide the eschatological basis of John's message while vv. 10-14 specify the ethical conduct that should result from it if heeded.[3]

In v. 7, Luke's penchant for generalizing the audiences of John and Jesus comes to the fore with his choice of the word, "crowds" (*ochlois*); see also 3:10; 4:42; 5:1, 3, 15; 7:24; 8:4; 9:11, 18, 37; 11:14, 29; 12:1, 54; 14:25; 22:6; 23:4, 48. This generic term seems to serve Luke's purpose of emphasizing both the universal need and opportunity for salvation. Like the prophets of old, the Baptist preached against the substitution of outward ritual for inward reality, as evidenced in the audience's desire to be baptized without changing their lifestyles (vv. 7-9). John's characterization of his Jewish audience as a generation of

---

1. Ellis, *The Gospel of Luke*, 88.
2. Marshall, *Commentary on Luke*, 137.
3. Fitzmyer points out this connection between eschatology and ethics in *The Gospel According to Luke I–IX*, 465.

poisonous snakes was harsh (cf. *1QH* 3:17). It approximates the modern phrase "snake in the grass" as applied to deceptively destructive people. The Jewish leaders of John's day who taught mere externalism, and not heart transformation, were deadly to both others and themselves. The inflammatory language, therefore, was designed to shock them back to their spiritual senses. The motivation for changing their lives was rooted in divine eschatological judgment, "the wrath to come" (cf. Luke 21:23). Such a concept stemmed from the Old Testament prophets' ironic message that the day of the Lord, mistakenly thought by Israel to signify its coming deliverance, heralded its future destruction because of idolatry (Isa. 13:9; Ezek. 7:19; Zeph. 1:14-16; 2:2). That two-pronged message persisted, and intensified in John's preaching in light of the soon appearance of the Messiah—the day of the Lord will be a day of deliverance or destruction, depending on whether or not one repents before God (see the exposition of the phrase, "baptism in the Holy Spirit and fire" that follows relative to Luke 3:16-17). Luke's words "the coming wrath" (*mellousēs orgēs*) therefore indicate that in the ministry of John the Baptist the eschaton was already in the process of being initiated.

3:8 Genuine repentance will bring forth the fruit of a holy life, preached John. Anticipating his listeners' protest that, because they were physical descendants of Abraham they were thereby the people of God and, therefore, holy, John warned them not to even think about such a notion. The Baptist's audience apparently shared the belief of many Jews that Abraham's merits spared them from the wrath of God (Luke 13:16, 28; 16:22-30; John 8:33-39; Rom. 4:12; Gal. 4:22-31; see also Strack-B 1:116-121). Furthermore, retorted John, God could replace the physical children of Abraham with children raised up from stones. These words are not entirely clear in meaning. Creed thinks Luke records here a play on words from the Aramaic: God is able to raise up "sons" (*benayya*) from "stones" (*abnayya*).[4] Plummer suggests that the terminology draws on Isaiah 51:1-2, a passage that pictures God hewing Israel out of Abraham the rock and that, similarly, John boldly states that God can do the same from stones in the Judean wilderness.[5] Although the specific nuance of v. 8b is not lucid, the general meaning is straightforward—physical ancestry does not ensure spiritual reality. Probably John is preaching the need for a re-

---

4. Creed, *The Gospel According to St. Luke,* 52.
5. Plummer, *A Critical and Exegetical Commentary on the Gospel According to St. Luke,* 90.

constituted Israel, one comprised of a faithful Jewish remnant and responsive Gentile hearers.

3:9   Verse 9 issues an eschatological warning: already divine judgment is falling. Those whose lives are devoid of repentance leading to holiness will be chopped down, like unfruitful trees and rotten wood, and they will be thrown into the fire (cf. vv. 16-17). The metaphor of unfruitful trees would have been especially poignant to John's Jewish audience because in the Old Testament Israel was often symbolized in terms of being God's barren vineyard (Isa. 5:1-7; Jer. 2:21; Hos. 10:1-2).

3:10   Verses 10-14 depict the ethical impact that results when people take seriously the message of eschatological judgment. The question of the crowds, "What shall we do?" attests to conviction of soul that resulted in the realization of their need for salvation (cf. vv. 12, 14; 10:25; 18:18; Acts 2:37; 16:30; 22:10).

3:11   Verses 11-14 prescribe actions becoming of true repentance, all of which involve showing one's love for God by caring for others (see Lev. 19:18). Such acts of social justice and kindness are in keeping with the Old Testament Law itself, according to Micah 6:8. Of all the gospel writers, Luke dedicates his work to this theme of societal righteousness. Some specifics follow: those who had two tunics (*chitnas*; the undergarment worn beneath the outer cloak, *himation*) were to give one to those who had none. Those who had food were to give to those who did not.

3:12   Even (*kai*) the toll-collectors (*telōnai*) were convicted by John's preaching and sought baptism. Such people could be ethically unfair and were considered ritually unclean. The first aspect was so because the system of tax-collecting was subject to abuse and dishonesty. As J. R. Donahue argues,[6] at the time of Jesus Rome divided up the taxation of Palestine into direct and indirect taxes. The former encompassed the poll and the land tax and was taken up by tax-collectors (*dēmosiōnes,* a word never used in the New Testament), people directly employed by Roman officials. The latter involved tolls, tariffs, imports, and customs, and was conducted by toll-collectors (*telōnai,* Luke's word), who reported to the chief toll-collector (*architelōnēs,* cf. Zacchaeus, Luke 19:2). That individual acquired his position by outbidding other aspiring collectors. Since the chief toll-collector had to pay the expected revenue to Rome in advance and then seek to re-

6. See Donahue, "Tax Collectors and Sinners: An Attempt at Identification," 39-61.

coup the amount, the assessment and collection of taxes were open to abuse. The chief toll-collector, working through his agents employed in local tollhouses (*telōnēn,* cf. 5:27), often charged inflated rates, so much so that the government had to impose tariff regulations to control the situation.[7] The other aspect referred to, that toll-collectors were ritually unclean, stemmed from the fact that they were in cahoots with Rome in oppressing the Jews; all the more so in those instances where the toll-collectors were themselves Jews.

3:13 John's message to the seeking toll-collectors was straightforward: collect no more than what is legitimate (cf. 19:8).

3:14 Enlisted soldiers (*strateuomenoi*) also comprised a part of John's audiences, probably Jewish men hired in the service of Herod Antipas (see Josephus, *Ant.* 18.113). This was so because there were no Roman legions assigned to Palestine at that time. The way the soldiers posed the question to John reveals their self-depreciation, "What should we do, even us?" It is difficult to envision a specific situation that prompted John's prohibition of the soldiers' extortion of the people of the land. Perhaps, as Ellis notes, the ones the Baptist addressed were assigned to guard the toll-collectors, thus making them susceptible to the temptation to connive with those they protected.[8] Rather, the soldiers were admonished to be content with their pay, meager though it was.[9]

We may conclude our discussion of John's call to ethical transformation and social justice by offering three qualifications which will help prevent us from misunderstanding Luke 3:11-14: First, unlike the rabbinic teaching that good works merited favor with God, for John, good works were the result, not the means, of conversion. Second, unlike the Qumran people who demanded that their devotees leave society to live in a monastic community, John did not ask people to leave their vocations but, rather, to demonstrate honesty and charity in the midst of them. Third, also unlike Qumran, whose sharing of goods was mandatory of all its members (*1QS* 1:12), John and the early church (Acts 2:44-45) left such giving at the level of voluntary choice.

---

7. For example, see the Palmyrene tariff inscription, i 6-7; iia 46; iib 30; iib 48; iib 127, in G. A. Cooke, *A Text Book of North Semitic Inscriptions* (Oxford: Clarendon, 1903), 313-33.

8. Ellis, *The Gospel of Luke,* 89.

9. Caragounis provides a thorough study of the etymology of the word for "wage" or "provision" in his article, "*Opsōnion.* A Reconsideration of its Meaning," 35-57.

3:15   Verses 15-18 deal with the relationship between John the Baptist and the Messiah. John's phenomenal prophetic ministry piqued the interest of the crowds so that it was only natural that they began to think of him in terms of the Messiah. The definite article (*ho*) before "Messiah" indicates that a specific individual was in view, though it must be said that pre-Christian Jewish messianic expectation was not monolithic.

3:16   John laid to rest the rumor that he was the Messiah by distinguishing his baptism from that of the Messiah. With deep humility and admirable candor, the Baptist acknowledged that there was "one to come" (a messianic title [*ho erchomenos*], see Matt. 3:11; Mark 1:7; Luke 7:19) who would be more powerful than he. Moreover, John did not deem himself worthy even to unlatch the thongs of the sandals of the Messiah, a task so menial that only Gentile, not Jewish, slaves were obligated to perform (*m. Mek. Ex.* 21:2; Strack-B 1:12). The crux of the matter that distinguished John from the Messiah was their baptisms. The former was by water only, while the latter was going to be with the Holy Spirit and fire. This last phrase has occasioned a lively debate, generating at least four interpretations: First, from the time of John Chrysostom on (*Homily on Matt. 11:4*), there have been those who interpret the phrase to mean the "fire of the Holy Spirit," based on Acts 2.[10] Though this is quite plausible and fits nicely with Lucan theology, it is an anachronistic reading of what John said. Second, some view the baptism of the Messiah with the Spirit and fire as exclusively referring to divine judgment.[11] However, this approach attaches too much pessimism to the giving of the Spirit, an event expected by Jews to bring joy. Third, still others divide the Messiah's baptism into one of blessing (the Holy Spirit) and one of judgment (fire).[12] While this perspective is understandable in light of the judgment motif associated with fire in v. 17, it fails to convince because only one baptism is envisioned in v. 16, which is performed on only one group of people ("you," *hymas*). Fourth, the most compelling interpretation is the one which understands that Jesus' baptism will have a dual character—it will dispense the Spirit who, in turn, will purify and refine those who have responded positively to Him. There are a number of Old Testament passages that associate the coming Spirit with refining fire

---

10. Ellis follows this line of thinking in *The Gospel of Luke*, 90.
11. Barrett takes this view in *The Holy Spirit and the Gospel Tradition*, 125-26.
12. For example, Brown, "John the Baptist in the Gospel of John," 132-42; 136.

(Isa. 4:4-5; 32:15; 44:3; Ezek. 36:25-26; Mal. 3:2b-3; cf. *1QS* 4:20-21). The Qumran text just cited enjoys an intriguing parallel with Luke 3:16, "God will purge by his truth . . . some of mankind in order to remove every evil spirit from the midst of their flesh, to cleanse them with a holy Spirit . . . like purifying water." The combination of the elements of water, Spirit, and fire in both texts is remarkable, as is the connection of the Messiah with the outpouring of the Spirit that occurs in another Qumran passage, *CD* 2:12, and here in Luke 3:16.[13]

3:17   But those who reject the Messiah will be judged—the sobering topic of v. 17. The statement is made using the agricultural imagery of threshing, whereby the Palestinian farmer would pummel the grain, and then, using a winnowing fork, would shovel it into the air, letting the wind separate the wheat from the chaff. The one was carried to the barn to be stored, the other was burned. This practice serves as the backdrop for John's eschatological message—those who finally reject Christ will be like the chaff, consumed with an unquenchable (*asbestō*) fire. Such imagery may have been derived from the Gehenna Valley, the continuously burning garbage dump outside the southern wall of Jerusalem. The severity and eternality of the ultimate judgment awaiting those who do not accept Jesus should not be toned down.

Thus, vv. 16 and 17 present a two-pronged message: those who accept Jesus as Messiah will experience the joy and purification of the Spirit (v. 16), but those who reject Him will suffer the eternal consequences (v. 17). For Luke and the other gospel writers, the alternative destinies of blessing for the righteous and judgment for the wicked (assigned by Judaism to the age to come) have already begun in this age depending on one's present response to Christ.

3:18   Verse 18 is a transitional comment, summarizing the ministry of John the Baptist (vv. 3b-17) and, in so doing, prepares the reader for the end of John's career (vv. 19-20). That prophetic vocation consisted of proclaiming the consolation (*parakalōn*) of the good news (*euengelizeto*) of the soon arrival of the messianic era and, with it, a repentant people.

3:19   The final topic of discussion relative to John the Baptist is his imprisonment, vv. 19-20. Luke's emphasis on the imprisonment of John as taking place before Jesus' ministry, even His baptism, has been

---

13. See Fitzmyer, *The Gospel According to Luke I–IX,* 474, and Marshall, *Commentary on Luke,* 147.

explained in a couple of ways. Conzelmann sees Luke making thereby a rigid distinction between the periods of John and Jesus.[14] But we have already observed that John's relationship to Jesus was more transitional than dichotomous. Helmut Flender argues that topical interests guided Luke's arrangement of the material on John and Jesus, especially the parallelism inherent between the two. Thus, Luke presents the narrative of the Baptist, 3:1-20 (his call, 3:1-3; his ministry as fulfillment of Scripture, 3:4-6; his preaching to all classes of society, 3:7-18; imprisonment and suffering, 3:19-20) in symmetrical correspondence with the narrative of Jesus, 4:21–23:56 (His call, 4:1-13; His ministry as fulfillment of Scripture, 4:14-21; His preaching to all classes of society, 4:22-38; His trials and suffering, 23).[15] The latter approach seems to better grasp Luke's purpose.[16]

John's fearless preaching, particularly his denouncement of the sin of Herod Antipas (tetrarch over Galilee and Perea), precipitated his demise. Herod was rebuked by the Baptist because, having dismissed his first wife, the daughter of the Arabian king of Aretas, Herod then married Herodias, his niece and the former wife of one of his brothers (A.D. 26).[17] In light of passages like Leviticus 18:16 and 20:21, which specifically forbid a man having sexual relations with his brother's wife, Herod's actions called for condemnation. The other evils Herod committed are not detailed; they were apparently so well known that they did not require specification.

3:20   The words, "upon all this" (*touto epi pasin*), represent Herod's "crowning achievement"—of all the dastardly things Herod did, his imprisonment of John topped the list. As a fitting conclusion to the account of John's imprisonment, and of his ministry in general, we cite Josephus's testimony about the godly character of John, whose remarks supplement the Lucan narrative:

> Some of the Jews thought that Herod's army had been destroyed by God and that he had been justly punished because of the execution of John, called the Baptist. For Herod put to death this good man who was exhorting the Jews to live upright lives, in dealing justly with one an-

14. Conzelmann, *The Theology of Luke*, 21.
15. Flender, *St. Luke: Theologian of Redemptive History*, 22.
16. The evangelical view of the shaping and topical arrangement that one finds in the gospel material, without in any way taking away from inerrancy, is stated in the ETS Statement on Inerrancy, reproduced in Geisler, *Inerrancy.*
17. According to Matthew 14:3 and Mark 6:17, the brother was Philip.

other and submitting devoutly to God, and to join in baptism. Indeed, it seemed to John that even this washing would not be acceptable as a pardon for sins, but only as a purification for the body, unless the soul had previously been cleansed through upright conduct. When still others joined the crowds around him, because they were quite enthusiastic in listening to his words, Herod became frightened that such persuasiveness with the people might lead to some uprising; for it seemed that they might go to any length on his advice. So before any new incident might stem from him, Herod considered it far better to seize John in advance and do away with him, rather than wait for an upheaval, become involved in a difficult situation, and regret it. As a result of this suspicion of Herod, John was sent as a prisoner to Machaerus . . . and there was put to death. This made the Jews believe that the destruction of Herod's army was a vindication of this man by God who saw fit to punish Herod. (*Ant.* 18.5.2)

THE BAPTISM OF JESUS, 3:21-22

Though brief in description, the baptism of Jesus as presented by Luke is dense in theological terms and ideas. From this one sentence in the Greek, some five purposes for Jesus' baptism emerge which we will take note of in the exposition that follows.

3:21 "All the people" refers to the crowds of v. 7 and, again, reflects Luke's belief that salvation is available to all. The baptism the people submitted to was John's. The compound genitive absolute construction (a noun in the genitive case [*Iēsou,* "Jesus"], and two participles in the genitive case [*baptisthentos,* "baptize" and *proseuchomenou,* "pray"], which somewhat sets the clause apart) is Luke's way of suggesting that the entrance of Jesus into the narrative begins a new dispensation. When Jesus was baptized (by John), and was praying (an element unique to Luke's portrait of Jesus' baptism, a reoccurring theme in the third gospel [1:10, 13; 2:36-38; 5:23; 6:12; 9:18, 28; 11:2; 22:32, 41; 23:46; etc.]), the heavens opened, preparing Him, and the crowds, for a divine revelation. We may interrupt the scene for a moment in order to highlight the first purpose of Jesus' baptism: Jesus' submission to John's baptism (a fact that, though not made explicit by Luke, was well known, see Matt. 1:12; Mark 1:9) showed his approval of John's ministry. The two missions, John's and Jesus', were complementary.

3:22 The Holy Spirit's descent upon Jesus signaled a second purpose of Jesus' baptism: it constituted His prophetic call to the ministry, anointed and empowered by the Spirit. Thus, it is not the case that Jesus' baptism was His first experience with the Spirit. From his conception on, the Spirit superintended His life (1:35, 41; etc.). Rather, the Spirit's presence at Jesus' baptism served as confirmation to both Him and His audience that His public ministry was about to begin.

The reason for the Spirit's descent upon Jesus "like a dove" has eluded commentators. Some think the association of the Spirit with the dove is akin to the rabbinic notion that the *bath-qol* ("daughter of the voice," i.e., since prophecy had ceased in Israel God now revealed Himself by speaking to people from heaven, only the echo of which, not the direct speech, could be heard) was likened to the cooing of a dove (*Tg. Ct.* 2:12).[18] Against this, however, is the fact that God spoke directly from heaven to Jews, and the crowds, according to Luke 3:22b. Others think the Spirit is compared to a dove because of Genesis 1:2, a passage the rabbis interpreted to refer to the Spirit of God hovering over the waters, like a bird fluttering over its young. One Talmudic text, *b. Hag.* 15a, equates that bird with a dove.[19] This view has much to commend it, particularly in light of the reference to Adam in Luke 3:38. If that is so, then a new creation theme is operative in the baptism of Jesus—like the Spirit who hovered over the primeval chaotic waters in order to produce the first creation and humanity, so the Spirit's descent upon Jesus in the waters of baptism was about to produce a new humanity. Yet the fact that the association of the dove with the Spirit is not explicit in Genesis 1:2 permits only a cautious acceptance of this theory. Still others believe the Spirit's descent on Jesus like a dove alludes to Noah's dove (Gen. 8:8-12), thus symbolizing a new era of grace.[20] Some link Luke 3:22a with Hosea 11:11 and thereby see Jesus being presented as the new Israel.[21] The last two mentioned views are possible, but neither Noah nor the new Israel themes seem to be present in the immediate context of Luke 3:21-38. It must be admitted that none of these suggestions is fully convincing, but it appears that the second one mentioned—the new creation theme—has less against it. The description of the Spirit's descent upon Jesus in "bodily form" is more easily explained; it was physical

---

18. So, according to Sjöberg, "*Pneuma*," 6:375-89; 382, no. 260.
19. Keck gives a fine explanation of this angle of interpretation in "The Spirit and the Dove," 41-67; 50-53.
20. Dunn, *Baptism in the Holy Spirit*, 27.
21. Sahlin, *Studien zum dritten Kapitel des Lukasevangeliums*, 103.

proof that the supernatural Spirit had come (cf. the tangible manifestation of the Spirit as cloven tongues of fire in Acts 2:1-4). The "voice from heaven," as we noted, was not the *bath-qol*; rather, it was God's direct revelation (see Deut. 4:10-12; Ps. 18:4; Isa. 30:30-31), signifying the resurgence of the voice of prophecy. The words "you are my son" probably allude to Psalm 2:7. If so, a third purpose behind Jesus' baptism surfaces: He was the Davidic Messiah. Eduard Schweizer states that Luke 3:22 gives to Jesus the messianic title "son" on the occasion of his institution into the office of the eschatological king.[22] The adjective, "beloved," may be an adaptation of Psalm 2:7 or an allusion to Genesis 22:2, 12, thus creating an Isaac typology.[23] Either way, it expressed Jesus' filial relationship with God and may hint at the idea that Jesus' messiahship proceeds from His sonship, rather than the reverse.[24]

The commentators agree that the words "in you I am well pleased" (*en soi eudokēsa*) draw on Isaiah 42:1 and, therefore, depict Jesus as the suffering servant of Isaiah who is endued with the Spirit. That being the case, a fourth purpose of Jesus' baptism can be detected: the Father's words that Jesus, the suffering servant, is well pleasing, provided him with assurance and comfort at the outset of his ministry (cf. Luke 12:50). Similar divine comforting words occur at the Transfiguration (9:28-35), in the face of Jesus' upcoming passion. These two episodes (baptism and transfiguration), then, focus on Jesus' role as the servant: He is to suffer and die, and that according to the will of God.

A fifth purpose of Jesus' baptism can be brought to light: verse 22, with its reference to Jesus as the son, anticipates v. 38 with its reference to Adam as the son of God and, in doing so, associates Jesus with Adam's race. In other words, Jesus' baptism identified Him with the sinful plight of humanity, the remedy for which lies in the cross (cf. 23:43 and its assertion that paradise is now reopened).

22. Schweizer, "*huios*," 8:363-92; 367-68. *Contra* Fitzmyer, who is not convinced that Psalm 2:7 is being alluded to on two grounds: (1) This would be the only New Testament incident which applies Psalm 2:7 to anything other than the resurrection of Christ. (2) There does not seem to be evidence in pre-Christian Judaism that Psalm 2:7 was interpreted messianically. But both of Fitzmyer's arguments labor under the assumption that Luke 3:22 cannot be an exception to the rule.

23. This is Marshall's view in *Commentary on Luke*, 154.

24. See Marshall's development of this point in *Commentary on Luke*, 155-56.

THE GENEALOGY OF JESUS, 3:23-38

Though the genealogies of the Bible may elicit yawns from modern audiences, ancient Judaism was anything but bored with such. Neither was Luke, whose family tree of Jesus calls for four introductory points: the place of genealogical lists in Judaism, the relationship between Luke's and Matthew's genealogies, the structure of Luke's list, the purposes behind Luke's genealogy. After these matters are addressed, we will briefly examine vv. 23-38.

The numerous genealogical lists in the Old Testament attest to their importance in ancient Israel. A high premium was placed on such lists because they demonstrated one's ancestry. Proving one's ancestry was significant for a number of reasons: it determined where one could live, based on tribal allotments (Num. 26:34-35); the transfer of property required accurate knowledge of one's family tree (Ruth 3–4); it served as the basis for taxation (Luke 2:4); the priests needed ancestral proof of their descendancy from Levi (Ezra 2:61-62); it could demonstrate the nobility of one's pedigree (Phil. 3:5); etc.

The relationship between Luke's and Matthew's genealogical lists of Jesus' ancestry is difficult to explain.[25] On the one hand, the two agree on the following points: they trace Jesus' family tree through Joseph (Matt. 1:16; Luke 3:23); they both mention the post-Exilic people, Zerubbabel and Shealtiel (Matt. 1:12; Luke 3:27); and they both trace Jesus' lineage from Abraham to Hezron (Matt. 1:2-3; Luke 3:33-35) and from Amminadab to David (Matt. 1:3-6; Luke 3:31-33). On the other hand, there are differences between the two: they proceed in opposite directions (Luke moves from Jesus to Adam, Matthew moves from Abraham to Jesus); for the corresponding periods from Abraham to Jesus, Luke has fifty-seven names, while Matthew has forty-one; the period from David to Jesus does not appear to coincide, intersecting only with the names of Zerubbabel and Shealtiel; Luke's list is structured along the lines of eleven groups of seven people in each group, while Matthew's list is based on three sets of fourteen generations; etc.

Different solutions have been proposed in an attempt to harmonize the two lists:[26] (1) Matthew lists the royal heirs and Luke provides

25. The classic work on the biblical genealogies is by Marshall D. Johnson, *The Purpose of the Biblical Genealogies with Special Reference to the Setting of the Genealogies of Jesus*; cf. also Fitzmyer, *The Gospel According to Luke I–IX*, 491.

26. For an evangelical point of view, see the discussions by Ellis in *The Gospel of Luke*, 93, and in Marshall, *Commentary on Luke*, 158-59.

the natural descent of Joseph. (2) Matthew follows Joseph's line, while Luke provides Mary's. (3) Although Joseph has an adoptive relation in Luke and a physical descent in Matthew, the lists are compatible because of a Levirate marriage between Jacob (Matt. 1:16) and the supposed widow of Eli (Luke 3:23). However, none of these plausible views is without difficulties. It seems that at this stage in time there is insufficient evidence to reach a firm conclusion on the matter. Therefore, we do well to appreciate the varying presentations of the two writers, for therein lie their special interests. In any event, the two family trees are not intended to be exhaustive, but rather selective lists, thus allowing leeway in their approaches.

Two major items concerning the structure of Luke's list call for brief comment. The first, as already mentioned, is that Luke divides his seventy-seven names (excluding the name of God, 3:38) into eleven groups, with each group comprised of seven names:

Adam	Enoch
Methuselah	Shelah
Eber	Abraham
Isaac	Admin
Aminadab	David
Nathan	Joseph
Judah	Joshua
Er	Salathiel
Zerubbabel	Mattathias
Maat	Joseph
Jannai	Jesus[27]

The numbers are historical, but also seem to convey symbolism. The number seven probably denotes the idea of perfection because it is used of God in the Bible (e.g., Gen. 1; Rev. 21–22). The number eleven took on apocalyptic overtones in early Judaism, symbolizing the eleven weeks of world history which were to be followed by the twelfth week of the messianic era (cf., for example, *4 Ezra* 14:11). Taken together, the two numbers—seven and eleven—are a fitting description of Jesus, the perfect one whose coming initiated the messianic era. Related to this symbolism is the connection between Jesus (3:23) and Adam (3:38). Judaism taught the idea that, with the advent

27. The list is from Marshall in *Commentary on Luke,* 160.

of the Messiah, *endzeit* (the end of time) would recapitulate the *urzeit* (the beginning of time); see, for example, Revelation 21–22 and Genesis 1–3. It looks very much like Luke, in his association of Jesus (*endzeit*, new creation) and Adam (*urzeit*, old creation) plays off that theme in his genealogy.[28]

The Lucan genealogy seems to serve at least two purposes. First, in tracing Jesus' ancestry from His supposed father, Joseph (3:23), back to David (3:31) and Abraham (3:34), Luke establishes Jesus' credentials qualifying Him to be the Messiah of Israel. Second, in taking Jesus' family tree all the way back to Adam, the father of the human race (3:38), Luke shows Jesus to be the savior of the world. Therefore, Jesus is nothing less than the perfect son of God (cf. 3:23 with 3:38; 4:3, 9).

3:23   *Archein*, and its cognates, is the word Luke uses for the "beginning" of Jesus' public ministry (23:5; Acts 1:1, 22; 10:37). The figure of thirty years with reference to Jesus' age is meant to be approximate (cf. 3:1). The words "as it was thought" refer to the people's assumption that Joseph was the father of Jesus; the reader knows better (1:35). Luke proceeds to delineate Joseph's ancestry, tracing it to David, thus establishing Jesus' royal heritage. While Luke names Eli as the father of Joseph, Matthew 1:15-16 lists the father as Jacob. It may be that the theory earlier highlighted about a possible levirate marriage between Jacob and the supposed widow of Eli answers this difficulty. A similar situation seems to pertain to Shealtiel, the "step" father of Zerubbabel (v. 37; see below), thus also making it an option for Eli.

3:24-26   These ancestors are not mentioned in the Old Testament, though they were not uncommon names.

3:27   Jonan may be the son of Zerubbabel cited in 1 Chronicles 3:19 (*'avania*, in Hebrew). Rhesa could be an unmentioned son of Zerubbabel or perhaps, as Marshall notes, it could be a transcription of the Aramaic word, *resa,* meaning "prince" and standing in apposition to Zerubbabel.[29] Zerubbabel was the post-Exilic leader of Israel. Shealtiel is listed as the father of Zerubbabel (cf. 1 Chron. 3:19 [LXX]; Ezra 3:2; Neh. 12:1; Hag. 1:1; Matt. 1:12); however, in 1 Chronicles 3:19 (Masoretic text) Zerubbabel's father is called Pedaiah. The answer to this anomaly, as Machen argues, is probably that, because Shealtiel and Pedaiah were brothers (1 Chron. 3:17), levirate marriage was in-

---

28. Marshall too cavalierly dismisses this notion in *Commentary on Luke,* 160-61. For the important roles that Adam and creation play in Lucan theology, see Neyrey, *The Passion According to Luke. A Redaction Study of Luke's Soteriology,* 165-83.

29. Marshall, *Commentary on Luke,* 163.

volved.[30] Another difficulty emerges with Shealtiel's father's name, Neri, because in 1 Chronicles 3:17 Jeconiah is said to be the father (cf. Matt. 1:12). A number of answers have been proposed for this problem, including the following two: Plummer suggests that Jeremiah 22:30 implies that Jeconiah was childless and from that it can be deduced that Jeconiah adopted the son of Neri, Shealtiel, who was descended through Nathan from David.[31] Years ago, the church historian Eusebius claimed that, because of the curse on the line of Jeconiah (Jer. 22:30), the lineage of Messiah bypassed him.[32]

3:28-31 The list proceeds back to David through his third son, Nathan (2 Sam. 5:14; 1 Chron. 3:5; 14:4), the only name in the group that is known from the Old Testament.

3:32-34 Luke's list from David to Abraham parallels Matthew 1:2-6, except that Luke adds two names—Admin and Arni—that Matthew does not have, neither of which are mentioned in the Old Testament. The others are known from the Old Testament: Jesse, David's father (1 Sam. 16:1); Obed, Jesse's father (Ruth 4:17, 21, 22); Boaz, husband of Ruth (Ruth 2–4); Sala, Boaz's father (1 Chron. 2:11); Nahshon, one of the chiefs of the twelve tribes who helped Moses take the census in the wilderness (Num. 1:7); Amminadab, father of Nahshon (Num. 1:7); Hezron, one of the leaders of the tribe of Judah (Gen. 46:12); Perez, twin brother of Zerah, born to Judah and Tamar (Gen. 38:29); the patriarchs: Jacob, Isaac, and Abraham; Terah (Gen. 11:26, 27) and Nahor (Gen. 11:22), Abraham's father and grandfather, respectively.

3:35-38 Serug is a name probably derived from Sarugi, west of Haran (Gen. 11:20 [LXX]; 1 Chron. 1:26). Reu was a Semite whose name means "friend of God" (Gen. 11:18). Peleg (Gen. 11:16) means "division," undoubtedly with reference to the Tower of Babel (Gen. 11). Heber probably means "Hebrew," making him the father of the Hebrew people (Gen. 10:24; 11:14). Shelah and Arphaxad are found in Genesis 11:10-13; Cainan occurs only in the LXX of Genesis 11:10-13. Noah, Lamech, Methuselah, and Enoch are well-known names from Genesis 5, along with Jared, Mahalaleel, Enosh, Seth, and of course, Adam, who is called "the son of God." But, in light of Luke 3:23 and 4:1-13, Jesus will prove to be the true son of God.

30. J. G. Machen, *The Virgin Birth of Christ* (New York: Harper, 1930), 206-7.
31. Plummer, *A Critical and Exegetical Commentary on the Gospel According to St. Luke,* 104.
32. Eusebius, *Questiones Evangelicae ad Stephanum,* 3.2.

HOMILETICAL SUGGESTIONS

The three major sections of Luke 3: the ministry of John the Baptist (3:1-20), the baptism of Jesus (3:21-22), and the genealogy of Jesus (3:23-38) can produce three powerful sermons. The first section, Luke 3:1-20, could be preached, for example, under the title, "How in This World Can I Be Holy?" and developed in two major points: spiritual reality (3:1-6), and ethical results (3:7-20). The next section, Luke 3:21-22, could be covered by analyzing the five purposes behind the baptism of Jesus enumerated in the commentary. The third section, 3:23-38, could be called "The Roots of Jesus." A couple of approaches could be taken. One might focus on the two purposes of Luke's genealogy which the exposition attempted to make. Or, a more creative attempt might be to single out some of the more well-known persons mentioned and, in soliloquy style, relate their Old Testament setting to the coming of the Messiah. This should work nicely for Adam, Abraham, David, etc. In any case, just having the courage to preach from the genealogy itself will probably capture an audience's attention.

LUKE

CHAPTER

FOUR

THE TEMPTATION OF THE SON OF GOD AND THE INAUGURATION OF THE SERVANT OF THE LORD

Luke 4 highlights two Christological titles: by passing His wilderness temptations, Jesus proved Himself to be the obedient Son of God, in contrast to the failures of Adam and Israel (4:1-13). In preaching His first sermon in Nazareth, Jesus inaugurated His mission as the servant of the Lord (4:14-44). The first episode, the private temptations, amounted to the final preparation for the second episode, the public manifestation of Jesus' ministry.

THE TEMPTATION OF THE SON OF GOD, 4:1-13

Commentators of Luke 4:1-13 have reached an impasse in identifying the Old Testament backdrop for that narrative. Many prefer to view the scene of Jesus' temptation in light of Israel's temptations in the wilderness. This is quite understandable, because of: the desert setting (v. 1); the forty days (cf. the forty years of wilderness wandering, Deut. 8:2); the three quotations from the wilderness wandering setting in Deuteronomy (Luke 4:4/Deut. 8:3; Luke 4:8/Deut. 6:13; Luke 4:12/Deut 6:16); the reference to Jesus as the Son of God, the same title applied to Israel (Deut. 14:1). The interpretation arrived at with the preceding data in mind is that Jesus is the true Son of God, who passed His temptations, in contrast to Israel's failure.[1]

---

1. For this view, see, for example, Fitzmyer, *The Gospel According to Luke I–IX*, 510-12, and Marshall, *Commentary on Luke*, 166-68.

Others play down the wilderness wandering theme and argue for an Adamic context of Luke 4:1-13. They marshal the following pieces of evidence in support of their position: the explicit reference to Adam (3:38) specifies Luke's intended background; Luke's transposition of the genealogy of Jesus from the beginning of Matthew's gospel (Matt. 1:1-17) to its intervening spot between the baptism (Luke 3:28-38) and temptations (4:1-13) of Jesus sheds critical light on how Luke wants it interpreted—Jesus' temptations in the desert are to be perceived against the foil of Adam's temptation in the Garden of Eden; the three temptations of Jesus by the Devil are best grasped by comparing them with Genesis 3 (see the exposition that follows); the reference to Adam as the son of God is the backdrop for understanding Jesus' title Son of God, in Luke 4:3, 9.[2] The interpretation advocated, then, by this school of thought is that Jesus is the obedient Son of God, in contrast to Adam's past disobedience.

We suggest, however, that the aforementioned impasse is removed when one realizes that both the Old Testament and early Judaism cherished the belief that Israel, the true son of God, was intended to be the divine replacement of Adam, the son of God whose sin deprived him of his intimate relationship with God. N. T. Wright has insightfully and thoroughly documented this belief elsewhere,[3] though he does not apply it to Luke 4:1-13. We maintain that such a belief wonderfully furthers our understanding of Luke 4:1-13: Israel, in its disobedience to God in the wilderness, showed itself to still be in Adam, whereas Christ, in His obedience in the desert, showed Himself to the replacement of Adam, who is the true Israel, the son of God. The ensuing exposition of Luke 4:1-13, therefore, draws on both traditions, Adam's temptation in the Garden and Israel's temptations in the wilderness.

4:1 Endued with the Holy Spirit from His baptism at the Jordan River, Jesus was led by the same Spirit into the Jordan wilderness, an area that can still be seen today by looking southwest from Jericho or east from Jerusalem. In light of the reference to Adam in 3:38, it seems that Luke invites the reader to contrast Adam's temptation in the Garden, a perfect environment (but which did not prevent him from succumbing to sin) with Jesus' temptation in the wilderness, a desolate location (but which did not hinder His obedience). Two other pieces

---

2. For this view, see Ellis, *The Gospel of Luke,* 93, and especially Neyrey, *The Passion According to Luke,* 172-79.

3. Wright, "Adam in Pauline Christology," 359-90, 361-65.

of data support this Adamic reading of the text. First, the mention of the Spirit (v. 1) reminds one of Genesis 1:2 and 2:7, references to the Spirit's involvement in the old creation. Jesus, however, filled with the Spirit, launched a new creation. Second, bringing Mark 1:13 and the mention of the wild beasts with Jesus in the desert (undoubtedly one of Luke's sources for the temptation account) to bear on Luke 4:1 is enlightening—as animals in the Garden honored Adam (see Gen. 2:19-20; cf. Gen. 9:1, 2), so even the wild beasts did to Jesus.[4]

4:2 But the background of the temptations of Jesus should not be restricted to Genesis 3. It is clear that the mention of the wilderness (v. 1) in conjunction with the forty days (v. 2) typify Israel's forty years of wilderness wandering and its attendant temptations (*peirasmos*). Furthermore, Jesus' fast of forty days recalls Moses' forty-day fast as he interceded for Israel's sin of worshiping the golden calf (Ex. 34:28; Deut. 9:9). However, the identification of the Devil as the source of the temptation is not similar to the wilderness temptations; it is more reminiscent of Satan's allurement of Eve and Adam in the Garden. Luke's point is that, unlike the parents of the human race who ate the forbidden food and Israel which ate the manna from heaven but still sinned, Jesus, who did not eat, was nevertheless obedient.

4:3 The first of three temptations was posed to Jesus by the Devil. The Devil's temptation did not consist of denying that Jesus was the Son of God (he conceded that, "If you are the Son of God"). Rather, the point of temptation was to get Jesus to use His power as the Son of God for His own purpose (fill His hunger by turning a stone into bread) instead of being obediently dependent on the Father for His needs.

4:4 Jesus resisted the Devil's play by quoting Deuteronomy 8:3, a passage describing God's provision for Israel with manna from heaven while, at the same time, reminding the nation that it should be dependent on the word of God, which alone could ultimately nourish one's life. Alas, however, Israel did not obey God's word. Neither did Adam and Eve heed the warning of the word of God (Gen. 3:1-7). In contrast, Jesus, the Son of God, the replacement of Adam and the true Israel, demonstrated Himself to be totally reliant upon His Father. It was more important to Him to submit to the will of God, even if it entailed hunger and suffering.

4:5 Verses 5-8 constitute the second temptation of Jesus. In v. 5, we are told that the Devil led Jesus up, though the location is not speci-

---

4. Jeremias, "Adam," 141-43.

fied by Luke. According to Matthew 4:8, it was a high mountain from which the Devil showed Jesus all the kingdoms of the inhabited world. This last remark probably infers that it was on a high mountain that Jesus was given a vision of the panorama of the enemy's power and domain, since the world obviously cannot be seen from one mountaintop. Jesus was about to be presented with a choice between two kingdoms, God's or the Devil's.

4:6   The Devil offered to Jesus the authority and glory that accompanied his kingdoms of the world. The meaning of the words "for it has been handed over to me, and I give it to whomever I will" is difficult to pin down, but Neyrey helps clear up the problem with his comparison of this temptation to the Adam/Eve narrative. Adam and Eve were given dominion over all things (Gen. 1:26-30), yet Satan offered them more—they could become like God (Gen. 3:5). But in obeying Satan, the first couple lost their authority and became subject to death. In some way, the dominion of the world devolved onto Satan (John 12:31; 2 Cor. 4), that is, until the seed of the woman, the Messiah, would one day crush the head of the serpent (Gen. 3:15-16; cf. Rom. 16:20; Rev. 12:17).[5]

4:7   The condition for receiving the Devil's kingdom was that Jesus worship him. The strategy was probably to get Jesus to accept the glory of this world without first going to the cross.

4:8   Jesus rebuffed the Devil by again quoting Scripture, this time from Deuteronomy 6:13. Deuteronomy 6 is the classic Old Testament text on monotheism, called the *shemah* (the Hebrew word for "hear"— hear Israel, the Lord our God is one, Deut. 6:4). Jesus affirmed His allegiance to God alone. As Luke's narrative later shows, Jesus obeyed the divine directive to go to the cross and, in so doing, served His God.

4:9   Verses 9-12 describe Jesus' third temptation, which is placed last in the list by Luke because of its locale in Jerusalem, the divine destiny of Jesus (9:51); in Matthew it is listed as the second temptation. The Devil led Jesus to the pinnacle of the temple, identified variously as the royal colonnade of the temple on the south side of the outer court (Josephus, *Ant.* 15.410-20) or as the southeast corner of the temple mound, which overlooked the Kidron Valley (a tradition dating back to Byzantine times; see Appendix C). From the pinnacle, the Devil presented his greatest challenge yet—"if you are the Son of God, throw yourself off of here." It may be that the later rabbinic text, *b. Peshim* 36(32a),

5. Neyrey, *The Passion According to Luke,* 174.

informs the Devil's temptation. It reads, "Our teachers have taught, 'When the king, the Messiah, reveals himself, he will come and stand on the roof of the temple.'" If so, then the Devil's temptation consisted of enticing Jesus to cater to popular messianic expectations.

4:10   The Devil's bait included an appeal to Scripture. He quoted Psalm 91:11-12 in vv. 10-11, respectively. If Jesus truly was the Son of God, then the angels would protect Him during His fall.

4:11   Continuing his quotation of Psalm 91, now v. 12, the Devil assured Jesus that the angels would undergird His body with their own hands so as to prevent Him from being hurt by the stones on the ground.

4:12   Jesus' reply to the Devil was quick and decisive, as He countered the enemy's perversion of Scripture by quoting Deuteronomy 6:16—you shall not tempt the Lord your God! Jesus would not presume on His Father's power, nor would He swerve from His will. He will go to the cross; first suffering, then glory (cf. Luke 24:26, 46). In the third temptation, we hear the echo of ancient Israel's putting God to the test by its murmuring disobedience (cf. Deut. 6:12-16). As Neyrey notes, we also hear therein the Serpent's temptation to Adam that he will not die if he eats of the forbidden fruit (Gen. 2:17; 3:3-4, 9). Jesus, too, was tempted to defy the sure death that would result from leaping off the temple. His gallantry would be rewarded with angelic protection. Behind this temptation, then, lay the subtle suggestion that Jesus need not die in Jerusalem in order to be proclaimed the Son of God.[6] Unlike Israel and Adam, however, Jesus obeyed God; He chose the way of the cross.

4:13   From Luke's words "all temptations," we are apparently to gather that the three recorded were illustrative of others that occurred during the forty-day span. Jesus successfully withstood all such diabolic schemes. As a result, the Devil left Him until an opportune time. Comparing this statement in v. 13 with 22:3 (see also 10:18) led Conzelmann to theorize that the period of Jesus was, therefore, "Satan-free."[7] But this is to miss the fact that, although Satan is only explicitly mentioned in those verses, his behind-the-scene activity very much influenced Jesus' opponents, and even His disciples in their attempts to keep Him from going to the cross.

6. Ibid., 174-76.
7. Conzelmann, *The Theology of Luke,* 27.

THE INAUGURATION OF THE PUBLIC MINISTRY
OF THE SERVANT OF THE LORD, 4:14-44

With the preparatory work complete, Jesus now stepped into the spotlight of public ministry, a major portion of which would be conducted in Galilee (4:14-9:50). Chapter 4:14-44 provides a description of the inauguration of that mission, focusing on Jesus' role as the Servant of the Lord (cf. 4:16-21 with Isa. 61). Three topics arc addressed: the summary report of the Galilean ministry, vv. 14-15; Jesus' programmatic sermon in the synagogue at Nazareth, 4:16-30; Jesus' visit to Capernaum 4:31-44.

THE SUMMARY REPORT OF
THE GALILEAN MINISTRY, 4:14-15

4:14 After His temptation in the desert, Jesus returned to His home province of Galilee, empowered by the Spirit. Jesus' notoriety quickly spread throughout the entire area, a remarkable feat since, as Josephus observes, there were 240 cities and villages in Galilee (Josephus, *Life* 235).

4:15 Jesus began teaching in the Galilean synagogues. The synagogue most likely came into existence during the Babylonian Captivity, after the Jerusalem temple was destroyed. Its purpose was to encourage the studying of the Law. By the time of Jesus, the synagogue had spread throughout the Jewish dispersion and, unavoidably, had basically replaced the temple's place in worship. The content of Jesus' teaching is not yet specified; it will be detailed in vv. 18-19. Initially, the crowds responded very favorably to Jesus' message. The power of the Spirit through His teaching evoked the praise of all the people.

JESUS' PROGRAMMATIC SERMON
IN THE SYNAGOGUE AT NAZARETH, 4:16-30

4:16 Jesus came to Nazareth, His hometown (see 2:39-51). Following His customary procedure, Jesus went to the synagogue on the Sabbath. Luke 4:16-30 is the oldest account of a synagogue service. From later Jewish sources, we can reconstruct the probable order of a synagogue service in the first century.[8] It proceeded as follows: the recitation of the *shemah* (Deut. 6:4-9) and the *Shemoneh Esreh* (eighteen benedictions); set readings from the Pentateuch and the Prophets;

---

8. Schürer, *The History of the Jewish People in the Age of Jesus Christ*, 2:447-54; 452.

prayer; a sermon by a competent individual, especially visiting priests and rabbis; concluding Aaronic benediction (Num. 6:24-26). The reader/expositor for the day was appointed by the president of the synagogue before the service began.[9] There was probably some freedom on the part of the reader concerning which prophetic passage could be chosen. Jesus, at the right time, stood in order to read.

4:17 Jesus was handed the scroll of Isaiah. It is debatable whether or not a fixed reading of the prophets was operative in first-century Palestine, so it is unclear whether the reading from the prophet Isaiah was scheduled or not. In any event, Jesus turned to the passage He wanted to read.

4:18 That text was Isaiah 61:1-2/58:6b. Only two phrases of the Old Testament texts are omitted—Isaiah 61:1c, "to heal the broken-hearted," and 61:2b, "the day of vengeance of our God" (excluded from Luke 4:19). The first omission is of no significance, but the second is; Jesus did not include the negative remark in His inaugural sermon. The original setting of Isaiah 61:1, 2/58:6b pertained to the divine promise that the Hebrews would return to Israel from exile in Babylon. Jesus selected that theme as an appropriate précis of His own mission, which began at His baptism, with its attendant filling of the Spirit. Like the prophets of old, he was anointed for service. Such empowerment, like the servant of Isaiah, resulted from the Spirit.

Jesus' ministry is encapsulated in four statements: First, He was sent to preach the good news to the poor. The words "preach the good news" (*euangelizesthai*) could modify the preceding verb "anointed," but are more likely based on the order of the words as found in Isaiah 61:1, and are therefore to be taken with the verb which follows, "sent." Thus, Jesus was "sent to preach the good news" to the poor. The "poor" denotes economic deprivation (see 4:18; 6:20, 24; 7:21-22) but, in light of the possible background of the *anawim* community (see Luke 1–2), probably includes spiritual poverty as well, i.e., the recognition of one's sinfulness before God. Second, Jesus was sent to preach release for prisoners and sight for the sightless. The two complements are parallel: release for prisoners, sight for the sightless, and are governed by the one verb preach (*kēruzai*). The term "release" (*aphesin*) for prisoners refers to the year of Jubilee (cf. with Lev. 25:30 [LXX])

9. Schürer describes the three officers of the synagogue: the ruler, the receiver of alms, and the servant who brought out the Torah scroll for reading in the service and then returned it to its chest in *The History of the Jews,* 2:433-39.

every fiftieth year, during which fields were not used, debts were dismissed, people returned to their homes, and slaves were set free (cf. Luke 4:19). The term probably also has a spiritual overtone—release from the debt of sin (cf. 1:77; 3:3; 24:47; Acts 2:38; 5:31; 10:43; 13:38; 26:18). Jesus' restoration of sight to the blind will also be physical (18:35-43) and spiritual (24:13-35). Third, Jesus was sent for the release of the downtrodden. The meaning is at least spiritual (forgiveness for those downtrodden by sin, cf. again 1:77; 3:3; 24:47), but may also imply an eschatological reversal of roles for the oppressed and their oppressors (cf. 6:20-26).

4:19   The fourth mission statement summarizes the preceding three —Jesus came to preach the Lord's acceptable year, a reference to the year of Jubilee. It is just possible that the reason Jesus returned to His hometown was because it was a Jubilee year.[10] In any event, the economic significance of the celebration took on eschatological meaning with the coming of the Messiah—He announced the arrival of the age of salvation (cf. 2 Cor. 6:2).

4:20   Two more glimpses into the nature of the synagogue are provided in v. 20. First, after closing the scroll, Jesus handed it to the attendant (*hypēretēs*), one of the three synagogue officials in ancient Judaism (the other two were the president [*archisynagōgos*] and the elders [*presbyteroi*]). The attendant was a kind of sexton. Second, the reading of the Scripture in the service was done standing, whereas the sermon was uttered while the speaker sat down, which explains Jesus' actions. The congregation's attention was riveted (cf. 22:56; Acts 1:10; 3:4, 12) on Jesus.

4:21   Jesus introduced His homily with an arresting thought, "Today this scripture is fulfilled in your hearing" (literally, "in your ears," cf. Deut. 5:1; 2 Sam. 3:19). That is, the consolation of Israel foretold in Isaiah 61:1-2 is now beginning to be fulfilled in Jesus, the Servant of the Lord. Luke 4:21 is basically a restatement of Mark 1:15, "And Jesus said the time is fulfilled (*peplērōtai*) and the kingdom of God has drawn near and believe in the gospel (*euangeliō*)." In other words, in the person of Jesus Christ, the good news of the kingdom of God had arrived.

4:22   The meaning of *emartyroun autō* ("witnessing of Him") turns on whether the pronoun is a dative of advantage or disadvantage. If it

---

10. For a fascinating interpretation of Jesus' ministry in terms of the year of Jubilee, beginning with Luke 4:14, see Yoder, *The Politics of Jesus.*

is the former, then the meaning is positive—the people bore witness to, or agreed with, Him. If it is the latter, then the meaning is negative—they bore witness against Him. This last interpretation would be consistent with the violent response by the people recorded in vv. 28-29. However, the positive rendering seems to be the right view because: (1) it is hard to see how Jesus' words of grace (v. 22) would have elicited a hostile reaction at that point, and (2) the crowd's volatile action stemmed from Jesus' criticism of Nazareth (v. 24), implicating it with those Jews in the Old Testament God bypassed in order to reach the Gentiles.

Similarly, "astonished" (*ethaumazon*) can mean admiration (7:9) or opposition (11:38). Yet, once again, it appears a positive sense is intended—the people regarded Jesus' words with admiration and amazement. The former resulted because of His words of grace, with reference in all probability to His divine message of salvation. The latter resulted from their assumption that Jesus was just a "hometown boy," the son of Joseph. Here was one of their own proclaiming the dawning of the messianic era.

4:23   But Jesus was not swayed by His compatriots' initial positive response; instead He removed their facade and proceeded to the heart of the matter. Jesus verbalized their thoughts when He uttered the proverb (*parabolēn*) "physician heal yourself" (cf. *R. Gen.* 23[15c]), which identified the real motive of the people—they wanted Him to perform miracles for them, His friends and neighbors, like He did[11] for Capernaum, an old rival to Nazareth. Moreover, Jesus' words undoubtedly pinpointed His listeners' desire to see Him prove His claim that the era of salvation had indeed come, by performing miraculous signs; seeing is believing.

4:24   Jesus countered with His own proverb, "Truly I say to you, no prophet is acceptable in his own country." The word *truly* is the translation of the Hebrew *amen,* the only Semitic word Luke does not translate (cf. 12:37; 18:17, 29; 21:23; 23:43). This in itself speaks of the fact that the word goes back to Jesus Himself and, as Jeremias argued, is a word that introduces an authoritative prophetic statement.[12] The idea expressed in the proverb—that a famous man is often not welcomed by his homeland—was well-known in the first century, though

---

11. This presumes prior activity by Jesus in Capernaum, which Luke chose not to include in his narrative at this point.

12. Jeremias, *The Prayers of Jesus,* 112-15.

without specific parallel in Judaism. A contemporary proverb could easily have applied to the situation at hand, as well: criticism often reveals more about the critic than the one being criticized. Their criticism of Jesus' failure to perform miracles was actually an indictment of the unbelief of the inhabitants of Nazareth (see the parallel passage in Mark 6:3-6/Matt. 13:54-58).

4:25   Jesus illustrated His point by implicitly comparing His prophetic role with the careers of Elijah and Elisha (vv. 25-27), two prophets who, because of divine judgment upon Israel at the time, were sent by God to help Gentiles. That pattern was soon to be repeated in the mission of Jesus and the church. The opening remark by Jesus, "In truth I tell you," asserted the accuracy of His forthcoming statement—although there were many widows in Israel during the time of Elijah, a period of some three and one-half years without rain and a great famine.[13]

4:26   The phrase "was not sent" (*epemphthē*) is an instance of the "divine passive," a passive verb which has as its understood subject, God. Thus, Elijah was sent by God not to the widows in Israel, but rather to a widow in Zarephath near Sidon. Zarephath was a Phoenician town on the Mediterranean coast between Tyre and Sidon. Jesus alluded here to 1 Kings 17:8-16, the touching story of God's provision for a Gentile widow through Elijah. Luke's construction, *pros oudemian autōn . . . ei mē,* is striking by way of contrast—Elijah was not sent to any of the widows of Israel but only to one widow—and a Gentile at that.

4:27   Jesus drove home His point with a second illustration of God's aid to Gentiles, the story of the cleansing of the leper Naaman. In that delightful account as recorded in 2 Kings 5:1-19, Naaman, the commander of the Syrian army, reluctantly bathed in the Jordan River seven times at the command of Elisha, the prophet. He was miraculously healed for doing so. The irony is clear: though there were many Jewish lepers at the time (see 2 Kings 7:3-10; cf. 2 Chron. 26:19-21), the one who was healed was a Gentile.

4:28   The audience got the point; unlike Jesus' works outside His hometown, no miracles would be performed in Nazareth. Hearing Jesus' words and realizing their import, the people in the synagogue were filled with fury.

---

13. The time of three and one-half years is a round number (cf. James 5:7 and 1 Kings 18:1).

4:29   Rising up, the crowd in lynch mob fashion threw Jesus out of the town. They then took Him to the top of a hill with the purpose of throwing Him off of it. Although modern-day Nazareth is located on the side of a valley, then, and now, it was surrounded by hills. The fact that the term "brow" or "top" (*ophruos*) is indefinite suggests it may have been one of those surrounding hills outside the town to which Jesus was taken. The whole scene was a foreshadowing of the coming crucifixion of Christ, in which His own people rejected Him. Like the servant of Isaiah, Jesus was despised of men.

4:30   But Jesus passed through the midst of the crowd and went on His way. It is not clear that Jesus' escape was the result of miraculous intervention. Such a demonstration would have given the crowd what it wanted—a divine sign. However, two circumstances about the incident suggest that supernatural forces were at work, albeit in secretive fashion. First, the ultimate source of the peoples' diabolic desire to kill Jesus sounds suspiciously satanic (cf. 4:13). Second, the reason the crowd did not bring about Jesus' demise was that it was not the time yet for Him to be killed. The occurrence, however, marked the beginning of His divinely appointed end.

JESUS' VISIT TO CAPERNAUM, 4:31-44

4:31   Luke's comment about Jesus descending from Nazareth to Capernaum is accurate; the former is nestled in hills more than twelve hundred feet high whereas the latter, located on the northwest corner of the Sea of Galilee, is 686 feet below sea level. Jesus apparently had a rather lengthy stay in Capernaum (which means "village of Nahum"), as the words "was teaching on Sabbath days" suggest. This is corroborated by Mark's gospel, which indicates that Jesus made Capernaum the headquarters of His Galilean ministry (Mark 1:14–5:43). It was a logical choice because Capernaum rested astride the Great Trunk Road, the international road of trade that proceeded along the Coastal Plain, connecting Egypt with the Levant and Mesopotamia. Stationing His ministry there, Jesus would not have to travel great distances to get the good news out, because those who heard His message would do so naturally in conjunction with their travels.[14]

4:32   Jesus' teaching (*didachē*) amazed the people because His words were authoritative. In light of 4:14, we are to understand that that authority resulted from the power of the Spirit which filled Him.

---

14. See the discussion by Beitzel in *The Moody Atlas of Bible Lands,* 171.

Like the Old Testament prophet, imbued with the divine Spirit, Jesus proclaimed the word of the Lord to His contemporaries.

4:33   The site of the synagogue of Capernaum in which Jesus taught may be the basis of the one excavated there today, dating back to the third century A.D. While Jesus was teaching there, a demoniac ("a man having an unclean demonic spirit") cried out with a loud voice. From passages such as Genesis 6:1-4, 1 Peter 3:19, and Jude 6 it may be surmised that demons were a type of fallen angels that desired to inhabit humans and gave them supernatural, albeit evil, power. Whereas it used to be fashionable to accuse the Bible of confusing tormenting demonic activity with cases of mental disorder, in this modern day when even scientists accept the reality of the paranormal, such a cavalier attitude no longer seems to be as widespread. Moreover, the ancients knew the difference between psychological disorder and demonic activity (see Herodotus, *History* 2:173).

4:34   The word *ea* is translated as an exclamation, "Ha!" expressing, in this case, displeasure (cf. Job 15:16; 25:6; LXX). The words "what to us and to you" form a rhetorical question by which the demoniac asks Jesus what He and the demons have in common. The second question, "Have you come to destroy us?" reflects the belief that the advent of the kingdom of God would spell the demise of demonic control over the world (cf. Luke 8:31; 10:19; 11:18-22; Rev. 20:2, 9-10; *1QM* 1:10-14; 14:10-11), knowledge shared by the evil spirits themselves. The demoniac's erratic speech moved from exclamation to statement to question and then back to statement, "I know who you are, you are the holy one of God." In saying that, the demon displayed its recognition of Jesus as being associated with God and, therefore, as holy (cf. Ps. 106:16), in contrast to its own evil nature (see v. 33). It may also be that the demon thought that in saying the name of Jesus, it might gain mastery over Him. Such hope, as the story reveals, proved futile.

4:35   Jesus commanded the demon to be silent and to leave the man. The word "command" (*epetimēsen*) has been shown by Howard Clark Kee to be a technical term denoting the subjection of evil spirits[15] (cf. Zech. 3:2; *Jub.* 10:5-9; *1QM* 14:10). It is a word of exorcism. Jesus muffled the babblings of the demon, then expelled it by His authoritative word. The evil spirit left the man at Jesus' command and, undoubtedly in a fit of rage, threw him into the midst of the assembled people. Miraculously, the man was unharmed and the demon was gone.

15. Kee, "The Terminology of Mark's Exorcism Stories," 232-46.

4:36   The audience was filled with wonder at the authority and power of Jesus' word which, at His command, dismissed even demons. This may have distinguished Jesus from the "ordinary" exorcist's fanfare of incantations, charms, and superstitions. Thus Jesus' Spirit-empowered ministry manifested itself through word and deed (cf. v. 32).

4:37   The news about Jesus spread like wildfire throughout Galilee (cf. v. 14).

4:38   For the first time, one of the disciples of Jesus is mentioned, Simon (Heb. *Simeon*). The narrative of the healing of Peter's (cf. 6:14) mother-in-law serves as a prelude to his call to follow the Lord (5:1-11). After leaving the synagogue, Jesus entered Simon Peter's house. It is interesting that facing the synagogue in Capernaum today remains a house purported by some archaeologists to be Peter's home, over which a church was later built. Entering into that disciple's house, Jesus was informed that Peter's mother-in-law had a very high fever, a symptom that did not escape the eye of Dr. Luke. Two casual observations impress the reader at this point which have rather profound significance. First, Peter was married (cf. 1 Cor. 9:5). Second, Peter owned property. But he would soon be called upon to reprioritize those responsibilities under the lordship of Christ (cf. 5:11).

4:39   Jesus stood over the woman and commanded the fever to leave, which it immediately did. The command was similar to the word spoken to the demon (v. 35) and may suggest the idea that Satan ultimately is behind sickness and, hence, infirmity, in one sense, is satanicly inflicted (cf. 13:16), though he obviously must receive God's permission to do so (cf. Job 2:6; 2 Cor. 12:7). With heartfelt gratitude for her miraculous and instantaneous cure, the woman began to serve the guests.

4:40   No doubt hearing about the miracles performed by Jesus, all the people of the area brought their sick loved ones to be healed by Him by day's end. Jesus laid His hands on each one of them, a practice only attested in Judaism in *1 Qap. Gen.* 20:28-29 (a Qumran text describing Abraham's healing of Pharaoh by the laying on of hands). The act itself conveyed the divine power of Jesus to the ailing person. All were healed (*etherapeuen*).

4:41   Jesus exorcised many demons at that time, who loudly expressed their recognition of Jesus as the Son of God. This was so probably because they, being supernatural in nature, knew the presence of their supernatural counterpart. By way of a modern illustration, one thinks of Darth Vader in the film *Star Wars,* who detected the presence of "the force" in Luke Skywalker. However, Jesus silenced the outcry of the demonic confessions of His messiahship. Such action on Jesus' part has been called the "Messianic Secret" and has generated a number of theories to explain the prohibition. First, there is the theological theory popularized by W. Wrede. Wrede argued that Jesus did not, in fact, ever claim to be the Messiah. Rather, the church fabricated that claim and then put the Messianic Secret prohibitions into Jesus' mouth in order to tone down His lack of acceptance of the title.[16] In response to this once popular view, more recent scholars have carefully shown that such statements undeniably go back to the historical Jesus and, therefore, give clear evidence that He perceived Himself as the Messiah.[17] A second theory is the magical view, which says that Jesus silenced the demons' proclamations of Him as the Son of God and Messiah because the demons thought that in pronouncing His name they could gain mastery over Him. Yet, the magical view is more akin to the stories about Hellenistic wonder workers than it is to the exorcisms by Jesus, which evince more of a Jewish setting.[18] Third, there is the polemical theory, which states that Jesus would not permit the demons to confess Him publicly as Messiah because they, as unclean spirits, were not fitting creatures to utter such holy things. Yet, it seems that the New Testament witness is uniform in its testimony that all will one day pay homage to Jesus (cf. Phil. 2:9-11; 1 Peter 3:19; Rev. 20:11-15), beginning with Jesus' earthly career (cf. Luke 11:17-20), and this would include demons. Fourth, the most reasonable explanation behind the Messianic Secret seems to be the political reality that Jesus in general did not want to be labeled the Messiah because it would send the wrong message to the civil leaders of His day. Jesus came not to be the political, but the suffering, Messiah. He therefore wisely prevented the demons' confession from fueling the fires of an already excited populace. When the moment was right, there would be time for an enthusiastic response from the crowds, when Jesus' journey to the cross was no longer in jeopardy (see Luke 19:28-44).

4:42   Seeking a respite from the crowds as well as a quiet place in which to seek divine guidance for His next mission site, Jesus retreated

16. Wrede, *The Messianic Secret.*
17. Marshall, *I Believe in the Historical Jesus.*
18. See Kee's refutation of the proposed Hellenistic background to Jesus' miracles in "The Terminology of Mark's Exorcism Stories."

to a deserted spot. However, the crowds sought Him out and tried to prevent Him from going on His way.

4:43 Jesus, however, would not be detracted by the Capernaum crowd from His divinely ordained mission of preaching the good news of the kingdom of God to others. A word about the kingdom of God is in order at this juncture. The scholarly consensus is that the theme of the kingdom of God was the major message of Jesus. The term itself means God's rule over His people's lives and draws its inspiration from the Old Testament idea that Yahweh is king (1 Sam. 6:5; 12:12; 33:22; 43:15; Jer. 8:9; Dan. 7:11; Mic. 2:13; Zeph. 14:9, 16). As Fitzmyer notes, even in the Old Testament the words "kingdom of God" expressed an eschatological hope for a period when God's salvation would be realized, and His dominion over the whole earth would be accomplished. That aspiration began to be realized in the life of Christ.[19] The idea of the kingdom of God in Luke, like Mark and Matthew, has two time frames: it is both spiritually present (4:43; 6:20; 7:28; 8:1, 10; 9:2, 11, 27, 60, 62; 10:9, 11; 11:20; 13:18, 20; 16:16; 17:20, 21; 18:16, 17, 24, 25, 29; Acts 28:31) and physically future (13:28, 29; 14:15; 19:11; 21:31; 22:16, 18; 23:51; Acts 1:6). That is, in the first coming of Christ the kingdom of God was revealed, but not until His return will it be fulfilled.[20]

4:44 Jesus, then, continued on with His itinerant preaching in the synagogues of Judea, a term sometimes used in Luke generically for Israel as a whole, not just the province (1:5; 6:17; 7:17; 23:5; Acts 10:37).

HOMILETICAL SUGGESTIONS

Luke 4 nicely divides into two sermons. The first sermon could be entitled "The Temptations of Christ." As a catchy opener, the preacher might consider referring to the controversial film *The Last Temptation of Christ* by Martin Scorsese, and then proceed from there to discuss the three temptations Jesus faced in the desert. Perhaps 1 John 2:16 could be used in conjunction with Luke 4:1-13 in order to personalize Jesus' temptations. If so, the outline might be:

---

19. Fitzmyer, *The Gospel According to Luke I–IX,* 155.
20. Ellis, "Present and Future Eschatology in Luke," 27-41.

I. Passion: The Lust of the Flesh

This point would deal with Luke 4:1-4 and Jesus' submission of His passion to turn stones into bread. All of us are confronted by our passions and drives, whether they are material, sexual, vocational, or whatever. We could learn a lesson from Jesus in this matter.

II. Possessions: The Lust of the Eyes

This point would deal with Luke 4:5-8 and Jesus' refusal to be enticed by this world's possessions which Satan offered to Him.

III. Position: The Pride of Life

The third point is based on Luke 4:9-13 and Jesus' rejection of the suggestion to achieve the ultimate position in the eyes of humans—to be publicly proclaimed the Messiah in dramatic fashion by descending from the pinnacle of the temple unscathed.

All of those temptations still face us today in one way or another. But we are reminded that Jesus, our High Priest, was tempted in every point as we are, yet without sin. Therefore, we can find grace in time of need (Heb. 4:15-16).

The second sermon could deal with Luke 4:14-44 and be called "A Tale of Two Cities." The brunt of the message could be to contrast the villages of Nazareth and Capernaum concerning their relationship to Jesus. At the same time, the speaker might suggest that the two towns represent two types of churches. The possible contrasts between the two cities are provided here in chart form:

Nazareth	Capernaum
Rejected Jesus, their own (vv. 24, 28-30)	Accepted Jesus, who was not from there (vv. 32, 36, 40)
No faith/no miracles (implied in vv. 22-23)	Faith/miracles (implied in vv. 37, 40, 42)
Not open to missions (vv. 25-27)	Open to missions (v. 40)

LUKE
CHAPTER
FIVE

JESUS: FRIEND OF SINNERS

Luke 5 provides five vignettes from the ministry of Jesus: vv. 1-11, the call of Simon Peter; vv. 12-16, the healing of a leper; vv. 17-26, forgiveness and cure for a paralytic; vv. 27-32, the call of Levi, a toll collector; vv. 33-39, Jesus and fasting. The composite impression Luke leaves with the reader is one of Jesus ministering to the outcasts and the needy of society, an example all disciples of Christ should emulate.

THE CALL OF SIMON PETER, 5:1-11

The call of Simon Peter in Luke 5:1-11 is a transposition of Mark 1:16-20 and is reminiscent of John 21:1-11.[1] It introduces the reader to Simon Peter, soon to become the leading disciple (6:14; 9:20, 33; 18:28; 22:31-32; 24:34). Luke 5:1-11 contains the account of the miracle of the big catch of fish and concludes with a pronouncement by Jesus that forever changed Simon Peter's life, "Henceforth you will be catching men."

5:1 The construction *egeneto* plus the verb *epikeisthai,* "It happened that the crowds pressed him," is loosely related to what precedes it. Luke selects this particular incident from the Galilean ministry because of its relevance to the call of Simon Peter. The crowds sur-

---

1. For further discussion of the relationship between Luke 5:1-11 and Mark 1:16-20, and John 21:1-11, see Fitzmyer, *The Gospel According to Luke I–IX,* 559-64.

rounded Jesus to hear the "word of God," a subjective genitive indicating that it was God's word that Jesus preached (cf. 8:11, 21; 11:28; Acts 4:31; 6:2, 7; 8:14; 11:1; 12:24; 13:5, 7, 44, 46, 48; 16:32; 17:13; 18:11). The phrase reminds one of the word of the Lord that came to the prophets of the Old Testament, thus authenticating both Jesus and the early church as God's messengers. Jesus was standing along the shore of Lake Gennesaret. Although that body of water was also called the Sea of Galilee, the name Gennesaret was also appropriate because it signified the land immediately south of Capernaum, the village on the northwest tip of the lake. Moreover, though others refer to the water as the Sea of Galilee, Luke properly labels it by its more specific title, lake.

5:2 Jesus spotted two boats moored along the shore, whose owners had departed in order to wash their nets. Much of the fishing done on Lake Gennesaret would be done at night, following which the fishermen would wash out their nets and then hang them up to dry.[2]

5:3 Jesus entered into one of the boats, an open craft probably twenty to thirty feet in length, which belonged to Simon. Jesus asked him to put out to sea a little off the shore, intending to use the boat as His pulpit from which to teach the crowds. Jesus' teaching was done sitting, in keeping with the rabbinic custom of the day.

5:4 When He finished teaching, Jesus commanded Simon to take the boat into the lake's depths, and then to let down the nets for a haul of fish. Two observations combine to suggest that other people were in the boat with Peter. First, the imperative "let down your" nets (*chalasate*) is in the second person plural. Second, the nets Simon used were the seine net, which required more than one person to operate. Perhaps the companions were James and John (v. 10) or Andrew. It should also be noted that Jesus' command to catch the fish possibly stemmed from His desire to remunerate the fisherman for the usage of his boat, though, of course, the incident would serve an even more noble purpose—to call Simon to be a follower of Jesus.

5:5 Peter addressed Jesus as "master" (*epistata*), a title used only by disciples in Luke's gospel (8:24, 45; 9:33, 49; 17:13) as distinguished from "teacher" (*didaskalos*), a term used therein by non-disciples (7:40).[3] The title "master" reflects Peter's obedient attitude toward Jesus, as did his willingness to let down the nets into the water despite

---

2. See Gower, *The New Manners and Customs of Bible Times*, 128-30.

3. Glombitza, "Die Titel *didaskalos* und *epistates* für Jesus bei Lukas," 275-78.

having toiled all night at the task to no avail. He was willing to obey Jesus' word, even during the daytime when fishing was not at its best.

5:6   Peter did what the Lord commanded, the result of which was that the nets almost broke because of the heavy haul of fish.

5:7   Because of the huge catch, Peter and his companions summoned their partners in the other boat, presumably still moored at the shore, to come and help. The word for "partners" is a more specific term (*metochois*) than the later word used, "companions" (*koinōnoi*), v. 10, and suggests a business partnership. The people in the other boat responded and filled their boat, so much so that both boats were in danger of sinking.

5:8   When Simon Peter saw what had happened, he fell on his knees before Jesus and told Him to depart from him for he (Peter) was a sinful man. Three observations can be made from this. First, Peter's full name is identified, "Simon Peter." Matthew 16:18 relates the specifics of how the apostle came by that name and Luke, writing after the event, presumes that tradition (cf. Luke 6:14), something Matthew also did (Matt. 16:16). Second, in response to those skeptics who wonder how Peter could fall on his knees and carry on a conversation with Jesus while the boat was sinking or how Peter expected Jesus to depart from the boat while still at sea, a couple of comments can be made: (a) in dire circumstances, people tend not to react in a cool and calm manner, and Peter was no exception (cf. Luke 9:33; 22:33); (b) in any case, it may be that from v. 11a we are to gather that the conversation took place on shore (cf. John 21:7-11). Third, to the question "What prompted Peter's confession of sin in the wake of the miracle?" the answer seems to be that the numinous presence and power of God through Jesus stirred within Peter fear and a sense of sinfulness. One thinks of other biblical confessions of sin resulting from encountering the divine (Isa. 6:5; Dan. 10:8-11; Rev. 1:17).

5:9   Verse 9 confirms the previous interpretation; Peter and those with him were gripped with wonder and fear at the huge catch of fish. The only explanation was that Jesus had performed a miracle.

5:10   James and John, the sons of Zebedee and companions (*koinōnoi*) of Peter, were also amazed at the supernatural occurrence. Whether the two men were in the second boat or on the shore is not clear (cf. Mark 1:16-20). The three would later become the inner circle of Jesus' disciples (Luke 6:14; 8:51; 9:28, 54; Acts 1:13; 12:2). Jesus singled out Peter, however, telling him not to be afraid, a word of comfort needed in the presence of divine epiphanies (cf. 1:13, 30).

Jesus' statement about Peter catching men alive (*zōgrōn*) from now on is made against the backdrop of the large catch of fish. Peter is about to undergo a change in careers—from fisherman to fisher of men for the kingdom. Jesus' words to Peter served as both assurance of forgiveness and promise of service.

5:11   When they reached shore, they (Peter and his companions, probably James and John) left everything—boats, nets, careers, all of it—and followed Jesus. The word "follow" (*akolouthein*) is a technical term in Luke for discipleship (9:23, 49, 57, 59, 61; especially 18:22, 28). As such, it is similar in nature to his term in Acts for following Christ, the "way" (Acts 9:2, 19:9, 23; 22:4; 24:14, 22). In later rabbinical understanding, "following" was used of the relationship between students and their rabbis.[4]

THE CLEANSING OF A LEPER, 5:12-16

We have in the cleansing of the leper one of a number of messianic miracles, supernatural acts Israel expected its Messiah to perform when He came (cf. Luke 7:19-22). Although those miracles had a positive effect on the people (5:15, 26), they stirred controversy between Jesus and the Jewish authorities (5:21, 30; 6:11).

5:12   "One of the towns" is probably to be located in the area of Gennesaret (5:1; cf. also 4:43). In one such town, a man filled with leprosy came to Jesus, undoubtedly believing that, based on past performance (4:37), Jesus could heal him (v. 12). Four aspects of the dreaded disease of leprosy require comment at this point. Medically, leprosy, as it is called in the Bible, may not be the equivalent of modern-day leprosy, Hansen's disease. The Old Testament uses various terms to describe dry, crusty patches on the skin, none of which are sufficient to identify the exact disease. For example, the features described in Leviticus 13–14 more likely describe erysipelas next to a boil, ringworm or dermatitis than leprosy. That is not to belittle, however, the suffering that accompanied skin diseases in the Bible nor the extreme difficulty of curing them.[5] Socially, victims of "leprosy" in Judaism were quarantined, relegated to live outside of towns (Ex. 4:6; Num. 5:2, 3; 2 Kings 5:27). Such isolation was tantamount to being

---

4. See Fitzmyer, *The Gospel According to Luke I–IX*, 242-569.
5. For a good discussion that helps to clarify the issue, see Thompson, *Handbook of Life in Bible Times*, 269-71.

ostracized by society. Spiritually, because ancient Israel believed that there was a causal relationship between good health and a life of obedience to God, a theological interpretation was often attached to sickness in general, and leprosy in particular (cf. Job). Thus leprosy, as a physical blotch on the skin, was thought to be the result of spiritual uncleanness; hence the need for the Old Testament priest to offer a sacrifice for the cleansing of the leper (Lev. 14; cf. Luke 5:14). Eschatologically, the healing of leprosy was expected to be performed by the Messiah at the coming of the kingdom of God (Luke 7:22; see also Strack-B 1:593-596). In fact, the cure of a leper was considered to be as difficult as raising the dead, something only God could do. This particular leper approached Jesus and bowed before Him with his face to the ground, which indicated both his pitiful condition and his respect for Christ. Perceiving that Jesus had divine power, the leper said that, if Jesus wanted to, He could cleanse the man.

5:13   Stretching out His hand, Jesus touched the leper, a risky gesture for any ordinary person susceptible to infectious contamination. With authority and compassion, Jesus pronounced His intention, "I will," and then commanded the man to be cleansed (*katharistheti*). Miraculously, the leprosy immediately departed from him.

5:14   Jesus' command for the man not to tell anyone probably stemmed from a couple of factors: First, Jesus did not want the word of His healing activity to get out of hand and cause a commotion, which, in fact, is what transpired according to Mark 1:45 (cf. Luke 5:15-16). Second, at the social level, Jesus wanted the man to first go to the priest, offer the appropriate sacrifice prescribed by Leviticus 14, and then be ritually declared clean. That official pronouncement would have served to incorporate the former leper back into the mainstream of society. The words "as a witness to them" (*autois*) are ambiguous in their reference point. The antecedent of "them" could be the priest(s) in the temple or the crowds of people. Two points tip the scale toward the priests being the referents of "them." Geographically, Jesus told the man to go show himself to the priest, which obviously was to be done in the Jerusalem temple. Had the man obeyed the command, he would have had to travel some sixty miles, thus separating himself from the people of Gennesaret in time and distance. Contextually, v. 15 begins with an adversative statement, "But the news about Him spread," an event sparked by the cured lepers' testimony to the crowd (Mark 1:45). Thus, Jesus' command to the man not to tell anyone before going to the priest apparently did not accomplish its intent, instead the man told the people, something Jesus did not want done. The nature of the testimony to the priest(s) consisted of at least the fact that the leper was cured. It may also have signified to the priest(s) that a messianic miracle had been performed.

5:15   The news about Jesus escalated, thanks to the leper's healing. Great crowds flocked to hear Jesus' word and to be healed of their infirmities.

5:16   Jesus, however, was not at the beck and call of the crowds. He often left them to go into the desert and pray. His reason for doing so probably was that He sought God's strength in private in order not to succumb to the temptation to become the people's popular hero (cf. the temptations in the desert).

THE HEALING OF A PARALYTIC, 5:17-26

The next five passages (5:17-26, 27-32, 33-39; 6:1-5, 6-11) consist of controversy stories telling of Jesus' conflict with the Jewish religious leaders of His day. There is a basic threefold pattern in all of them: Jesus performs a controversial action; the Jewish leaders protest His action; Jesus silences His critics with a pronouncement statement.[6] These controversy accounts were part of a collection of such narratives in the early church, not only reporting the conflict setting of Jesus' day but applying the principles emerging from those events to the church's controversy with Judaism.[7]

5:17   The structure of vv. 17-26 is as follows: vv. 17-20—Jesus' controversial or revolutionary action; v. 21—the protest by the Jewish leaders; vv. 22-26—Jesus' pronouncement statement and miracle which backed up His divine claim. Verse 17 is a flashback to one of those days when Jesus taught and ministered in the villages near Capernaum (vv. 12-16; cf. 7:1). Luke's mention of the Pharisees and teachers of the Law gathering from all over Galilee, Judea, and even Jerusalem itself to hear Jesus prompts several remarks about these religious leaders: their name, origin, and teaching. The name "Pharisees" means "separated ones," probably with reference to their aloofness toward other Jews less meticulous about the Law than they, based on Leviticus 10:10. The "teachers of the Law" were undoubtedly included among

---

6. The outline is Ellis's in *The Gospel of Luke*, 104.

7. For an excellent consideration of this topic, see Guelich, *Mark 1:1–8:26*, 81-84, and the commentary that follows.

the Pharisees and were probably synonymous with the scribes or lawyers (5:21), Jewish experts in interpreting the Law (7:30; 10:25; 11:45, 46, 52; 14:3). The origin of the Pharisees goes back to the Maccabean period, according to Josephus (*Ant.* 13.171). By that author's time (ca. A.D. 90), the Pharisees formed one of the three prevailing "philosophies" among Palestinian Jews (the other two being the Sadducees and the Essenes, *Ant.* 13:171). The Pharisees' and scribes' teaching involved a strict adherence to the Mosaic Law, along with the oral law (traditions ascribed to Moses and the elders). The purpose of the latter was to build "a fence around the Torah"; that is, to protect the written Law from being broken by promulgating hundreds of minute applications of the Law designed to cover every area of life (*Pirqe Abot* 1:1 [Sayings of the Elders]; cf. Mark 7:3). The Pharisees viewed their mission in life as stirring Israel on to obey God's Law. Their beliefs included human freedom balanced with the sovereignty of God, the resurrection of the body, angels, the coming of the Messiah (*Ps. Sol.* 17:23–18:14), and the restoration of Israel to its land at the end of time (Josephus, *Ant.* 13.172). Luke's mention of the gathering of these religious leaders gives the impression that they were sitting around (*ēsan kathēmenoi*) waiting for something miraculous to happen. They were not disappointed, because the power of God (*kyriou* without the article refers to God) came upon Jesus to empower Him to heal.

5:18   At that time, some men, carrying a man who was paralyzed on a pallet, attempted to enter into Jesus' presence and lay the man down before Him. The parallel passage in Mark 2:1-12 adds the details that there were four men (Mark 2:3) and that Jesus was teaching in a house (Mark 2:1).

5:19   Not being able to get through the crowds, the men went up onto the roof, pulled off some of the tiles, and lowered the paralytic on the pallet through the hole into Jesus' presence. Fitzmyer thinks Luke has rewritten the story in terms of his own acquaintance with Hellenistic architecture, because Palestinian roofs were made of beams, covered with reeds, matted layers of thorns, and a deposit of clay, not tile.[8] In point of fact, however, Morris correctly observes that tiled roofs were in use in Israel by the time of Jesus.[9]

5:20   Jesus saw the faith of the men, evidenced by their determination to find a way to get their friend to Him. Jesus' response to the

---

8. Fitzmyer, *The Gospel According to Luke I–IX,* 582.
9. Morris, *The Gospel According to St. Luke,* 116-17.

man, "Your sins are forgiven," indicated the intimate association that exists between sickness and sin (cf. 1 Sam. 16:14; John 5:14; 9:2; James 5:15). In this particular case, it is not clear whether that association was specific (the man had committed sin that caused his sickness) or generic (the man was sick, one of the unfortunate consequences of being a member of fallen humanity); probably the former. Either way, Jesus forgave the man of his sin which, itself, was an act restricted to God alone.

5:21   Verse 21 contains the protest by the Pharisees and scribes, who said to themselves that Jesus' claim to forgive sins amounted to blasphemy against God. The definition of blasphemy emerges from Leviticus 24:10-23, where it refers to abusing the name of Yahweh. In New Testament times, a more general definition prevailed to the effect that blasphemy consisted of denying God's power (2 Kings 19:4, 6, 22) or His glory (Ezek. 25:12). Later, in rabbinic writings, blasphemy became more restrictive in nature—pronouncing the name of Yahweh (*m. Sanh.* 7.15).[10] The connotation of the accusation against Jesus involved His apparently equating Himself with God. This nuance is brought out in the next clause, "for only God can forgive sins." The notion seems to be that since sin ultimately offends God, only He can forgive it. Thus, for Jesus to assert that He could forgive sin was tantamount to making Himself God's equal.

5:22   Verses 22-26 form the third component of the controversy story—Jesus' pronouncement statement and miracle backing up His divine claim. Jesus perceived that the Pharisees and scribes were reasoning among themselves about His bold claim. Such knowledge on His part quite possibly should be attributed to supernatural insight.

5:23   Jesus posed a counterquestion which asked the Jewish religious leaders which of the two was easier to say, "Your sins are forgiven?" or "Arise and walk?" The first would have been easier because it required no outward proof that it had been accomplished. The latter was therefore the more difficult because it demonstrably required the supernatural power and authorization of God. In essence, then, to perform the latter entailed doing the former.

5:24   In order to show that He, the Son of Man, had the power to forgive sins, Jesus chose the more difficult option—He commanded the paralytic to get up, pick up his pallet, and go home. Two questions arise concerning this verse, particularly with regard to the identifica-

---

10. See Beyer, "*Blasphemia*," 1:621-25; 622.

tion of Jesus as the Son of Man. First, who identified Jesus as the Son of Man, Jesus Himself or the third evangelist? The answer depends on the referent of the word *eidēte*—but in order that "you may know." If it is Luke who makes the statement then his editorial comment—"that the Son of Man has power on earth to forgive sins"—is directed toward his audience. However, because the title "Son of Man" was used of Jesus almost exclusively by Himself (it is not a title employed much by the early church), then it is most likely the case that the third evangelist is quoting Jesus' words to the Jewish leaders, the referent of the word *eidēte*.[11]

A second question concerns the definition of the title "Son of Man." At least four answers have been put forth. First, the title has been thought by some to refer to the Gnostic redeemer myth, a pre-existent figure who descended to earth with the ultimate purpose of enlightening people with the knowledge of their true destiny—the spirit, not the physical, world. Knowledge of one's innate spiritual nature, not forgiveness of sins, was the message of such a personage. But besides the obvious fact that Jesus' message was one of forgiveness (vv. 20, 23, 24), the cavalier assumption that a Gnostic system existed at the time of Jesus has rightly been discarded by many present generation scholars. Second, some have argued that the phrase "Son of Man" is a generic description of Jesus' humanity. However, the context militates against that viewpoint; the point of the healing will be precisely to show that Jesus is no mere mortal. Third, some have suggested the title is Adamic in meaning (cf. Ps. 8:4-8 with Gen. 1:26-28); Jesus is the new man, the true Adam. While this is plausible, especially in light of the influence of Adam theology on the genealogy and temptation narratives (3:23–4:13), an Adamic connotation shows no sign of directly influencing this particular passage. Fourth, the most probable meaning of the title is that it is to be identified as the apocalyptic heavenly Son of Man of Daniel 7:13. This figure derived His authority from God (His deity) and also represented the saints of the kingdom of God (His humanity). He will be revealed in the end times. In that term, therefore, we find the seedbed for the later coalescence of the ideas of deity and humanity, admirably lending itself to a messianic interpretation (see also *1 Enoch* 37–71). This seems to be what Jesus had in mind; as the heavenly Son of Man, He had the power to forgive

11. See Ellis's discussion in *The Gospel of Luke,* 106.

sins (His deity) on earth (His humanity).[12] The apocalyptic rendering is confirmed by Jesus' application of the title Son of Man to His *Parousia* (coming again) in glory (Luke 22:69).

5:25   Upon Jesus' command, the paralytic miraculously rose up immediately in the presence of the people, especially Jesus' critics, picked up what he had been lying on, and went home glorifying God. This was "in your face" testimony to the Pharisees and scribes, and it silenced them, for the time being.

5:26   The effect of the miracle on the general populace was one of wonder and fear. They glorified God (cf. 4:21), saying that "today" they had seen paradoxical (*paradoxa*), or remarkable, things.

THE CALL OF LEVI AND THE BANQUET, 5:27-32

Luke 5:27-32 is the second conflict story in this section (5:17–6:11), and it also follows the threefold pattern found in the previous narrative: vv. 27-29, Jesus' revolutionary action; v. 30, the protest of the Pharisees and scribes; vv. 31-32, Jesus' pronouncement statement.

5:27   After the healing of the paralytic, Jesus went out of the house. Upon doing so, He spotted a toll collector named Levi in his tollhouse. The toll collector, as noted earlier, collected taxes for the Roman government. Capernaum, the probable location of this incident, was a toll post and Levi, like other toll collectors there, collected customs due on goods arriving in Judea. This same Levi was probably also called Matthew (Matt. 9:9; 10:3). Both names, Levi (one of the names of the twelve patriarchs) and Matthew ("the gift of Yahweh"), were Hebrew and, although normally a Palestinian Jew had two names (one Hebrew and the other Greek or Latin [see Acts 1:23; 12:25; 13:9]), there were instances when a Jew possessed two Hebrew names (Joseph Barnabas [Acts 4:36], Joseph Caiaphas [Josephus, *Ant.* 18:35]). Amazingly, Jesus called a toll collector, not usually known for their integrity, to follow Him.

5:28   Without giving it a second thought, Levi left his toll collector career behind ("he left everything") and took up a new occupation—following Jesus.

5:29   That he did not necessarily leave behind all of his possessions is indicated by the fact that Levi still had the wherewithal to throw a

---

12. It is here that the Adamic interpretation becomes more convincing, for the Son of Man figure is quite plausibly portrayed as the replacement of Adam. If so, then Adam theology influenced Daniel 7:13 directly, but only indirectly Luke 5:24.

big banquet for Jesus. Many toll collectors and others (cf. v. 30, "sinners") came to Levi's house for the party, undesirables as far as the Pharisees and scribes were concerned. It may be that, as Ellis observes, the party also served as a farewell dinner for Levi, sponsored by his colleagues.[13]

5:30   The Pharisees' and scribes' protest against Jesus' revolutionary action—associating with sinners—occurs in v. 30. The words "Pharisees and their scribes" are similar to those in Mark 2:16, a companion text: "the scribes of the Pharisees," indicating that scribes were a part of the Pharisaic movement. They grumbled at the disciples for eating and drinking with sinners. Such criticism was in keeping with the Pharisaic aloofness to non-observant Jews, all the more so with toll collectors. Together—nonobservant Jews, toll collectors, Gentiles, and so on—were all considered sinners. It is doubtful that the Pharisees and scribes were at the banquet, for to attend would have been beneath their dignity. In complaining about the disciples' behavior, the religious leaders were actually criticizing Jesus' actions, for, in early Judaism, the rabbi was held responsible for the demeanor of his pupils.

5:31   Jesus' pronouncement statement comes in vv. 31-32. Jesus provided a twofold response to His critics. The first half was a truism, "The healthy do not have need of a physician but the sick do."

5:32   The first half of Jesus' reply, which drew from the physical realm, prepared the way for the second half of the statement, which was aimed at the spiritual level—Jesus came, not to call the "righteous" to repentance, but to call sinners. The correlation is clear: healthy/righteous; sick/sinners. Jesus' response was calculated to be ironic and convicting. It was ironic because, as it turns out in God's program of salvation, it is the sinners who can come to the place of repentance. The so-called righteous ones, like the Pharisees and scribes, are not invited to enter the kingdom of God, apparently because they think they are already in it. In reality, the religious leaders were desperately in need of divine forgiveness, but they first had to admit it. That would have involved conviction and humility. And so it goes today; whoever would be saved must first admit they are lost, religious though they may be.

13. Ellis, *The Gospel of Luke*, 107.

JESUS AND FASTING, 5:33-39

The controversy about Jesus and fasting comprises the third conflict story in Luke 5. The threefold pattern associated with such accounts recurs in 5:33-39, though the revolutionary action of Jesus is more presumed in v. 33 than recounted. The protest of the Pharisees is related in v. 33, as well, while Jesus' pronouncement statements are recorded in vv. 34-39.

5:33 This verse contains both Jesus' revolutionary action and the resulting protest by His critics. The antecedent of the phrase "they said to him" presumably is the Pharisees and the scribes mentioned in v. 30. Their accusation was directed against Jesus' disciples who, unlike those of John the Baptist (cf. 7:18-19; 11:1) and the Pharisees (18:12), did not fast and pray. Rather, so it was said, they ate and drank. This "party animal" label undoubtedly emerged because of incidents like the one in vv. 27-32. It would later be applied to Jesus as well (7:33-34). Jewish fasting as a religious behavior goes back to Exodus 34:28; Leviticus 16:29-31; Deuteronomy 9:9, where it meant abstention from eating food and drinking water. It was to be expected that John the Baptist would have a penchant for fasting, ascetic that he was (7:33; cf. Mark 1:6). So would his disciples. It is well known that Pharisees practiced fasting on Mondays and Thursdays (Strack-B 4:1, 77-114). Apparently, however, Jesus and His students broke with this tradition, though Jesus did engage in the vigil when preparing for His temptations in the wilderness (4:2) and for His coming passion (22:16, 18). Moreover, Jesus was certainly devoted to prayer (3:21; 6:12; 9:18, 28; 11:2; 22:32, 41; 23:46). Therefore, the criticism of the Pharisees and the scribes was not really accurate. Their problem, as the next verses show, was that they did not know what the occasion was that precipitated the disciples' festive spirit.

5:34 In vv. 34-35, Jesus clarified the situation for the Pharisees and scribes. He raised a rhetorical question, "You cannot make the attendants of the bridegroom fast while he is with them, can you?" The question may presuppose a custom reflected in the popular rabbinic text *Megillat Taanit* (Scroll of Fasting) to the effect that fasting was forbidden on certain specified days devoted to joyous celebration of Israel's blessings from God.[14] Be that as it may, the general tone of Jesus' comment is perspicuous—the bridegroom's wedding is an occasion of joy for both his attendants and himself, not sorrow. It may

14. See also Fitzmyer, *The Gospel According to Luke I–IX*, 598.

also be the case that, because the figure of the bridegroom was used in the Old Testament to represent Yahweh's relationship to His people (Isa. 54:5-8; 62:5; Jer. 2:2; Ezek. 16; Hos. 2:18, 21), by extension Jesus intended that it be applied to Himself in a messianic sense. At the very least, we can say that the joy surrounding Jesus and His disciples was the delightful consequence of the revelation of the kingdom of God.

5:35   But the time will come, remarked Jesus, when the bridegroom will be taken away and then the attendants will have occasion to fast. With this comment, Jesus was making a veiled reference to His forthcoming death, which would temporarily disorient and even disillusion His disciples; that is, until they witnessed His post-resurrection appearances (24:1-53).

5:36   Verses 36-39 contain three short parables furthering the discussion of the present joy of the messianic era, and illustrating the basic incompatibility of Christianity with Judaism. The Greek word *parabolē* translates the Hebrew Old Testament word *mascal* and has a variety of nuances: "maxim" (the title of Proverbs), "proverb" (1 Sam. 10:11, 12; 24:14), "vague prophecy" (Num. 23:7), "parable" (2 Sam. 12:1-6), "allegory" (Ezek. 17:2-24), "riddle" (Prov. 1:6). With its usage by Jesus, *parabolē* takes on the classic meaning of parable (2 Sam. 12:1-6), consisting of illustrations from Palestinian daily life which conveyed spiritual truths. Usually, a parable is concerned to make one major point, often in a surprising or intriguing way. The point of the first parable is that no one tears a patch off a new garment and sews it onto an old garment, because both pieces will be ruined. The new garment will be ripped, and the old garment will not match the patch of the new garment. In saying this, Jesus was contrasting Christianity and its newness of life with Judaism and its worn-out traditions.

5:37   The second parable (vv. 37-38) conveys a message similar to that of the first, but using a different metaphor—new wine in old wineskins. In the ancient Near East goats and other animals would be killed, their skins scraped of hair, cleaned, and sewed up to form containers for liquids: water (Gen. 21:15), milk (Judg. 4:19), and wine (Josh. 9:4, 13). In the latter case, for someone to pour new wine, which by nature had not yet fully fermented, into old, inflexible wineskins would spell disaster. The pressure from the swelling that results from further fermentation of the new wine would burst the old wineskin. Both would be destroyed: the wineskin would break and the new wine would spill onto the ground. Once again, Jesus' message was the incompatibility of Christianity and Judaism. The metaphor of wine was appropriate to the scene depicted in vv. 29-32.

5:38 On the contrary, new wine should be placed in new wineskins. The added message here was that Christianity should be allowed to express itself in a new way for a new day of salvation.

5:39 The third parable continues the thought of the two previous ones and, together, the three parables constitute Jesus' pronouncement statement, the effect of which silences His opposition temporarily. The metaphor of wine is the same as that in vv. 37-38, but the illustration is different. Like the man who, having become used to old wine, does not desire new wine, the Judaism of Jesus' day was complacently satisfied with its old traditions, which prevented it from desiring the new message of the gospel.

HOMILETICAL SUGGESTIONS

Luke 5 can be covered in four self-contained sermons, which generally address the theme of evangelism. First, 5:1-11 could be entitled, "Fishermen and Fishers of Men," and could discuss the topic of evangelism, using the imagery of fishing. Two broad points could be made: (a) human techniques, vv. 1-5: go where the fish (v. 4)/people are; use the proper equipment (boat, bait, rods—vv. 3-4)/training (different methods of evangelism suited to various peoples' needs); persistence (v. 5); (b) divine guidance, vv. 6-11, will ultimately ensure the catch/results.

Luke 5:12-16 is a powerful section on reaching the marginal people and outcasts in our society, just as Jesus healed the leper. The sermon could be entitled, "When AIDS Comes to Church." Three points may be made: (a) v. 12, Jesus' compassion for the leper; (b) v. 13, Jesus' contact with the leper; (c) vv. 14-16, Jesus' command to the leper to tell others what God had done for him.

Luke 5:17-26 and the healing of the paralytic beautifully illustrate what it means to bring our friends to Christ. Just like those who brought the paralytic to the Lord, we need: (a) vv. 17-18a, concern for our lost friends; (b) vv. 18b-19, commitment to bringing our friends to Christ; (c) vv. 20-21, to expect conflict in bringing our friends to Christ; (d) vv. 22-26, to enjoy the results of bringing our friends to Christ.

Luke 5:27-39 could be the basis of a delightful sermon entitled, "The Church's Seven Last Words: We Never Did It That Way Before!" The focus of the message would center on evangelism for a new day: (a) vv. 27-32b, reaching nontraditional people; (b) vv. 33-39, using nontraditional methods.

LUKE
CHAPTER
SIX

JESUS AND THE DISCIPLES

The theme that ties together the three sections of Luke 6 is Jesus and His disciples. In 6:1-11, one finds a carryover of the controversy setting of 5:12-39, this time involving an incident in which Jesus defends the behavior of His disciples concerning Sabbath keeping. The second section, 6:12-19, relates Jesus' prayerful selection of twelve apostles from the larger group of disciples. Finally, the longest section of Luke 6 is the Sermon on the Plain, 6:20-49, which is devoted to Jesus' teaching on true discipleship.

MORE CONFLICT STORIES, 6:1-11

Two more conflict stories are recorded by Luke in Luke 6:1-11, each of which follows the threefold pattern earlier identified: a revolutionary action of Jesus, criticism from the Jewish leadership, Jesus' pronouncement statement. Both of these accounts deal with Jesus and Sabbath keeping.

6:1   The first of these stories is described in vv. 1-5. The opening words of v. 1 have occasioned a text critical debate. Some important manuscripts read "one" (*en*) Sabbath (p75, Sinaiticus, B). Others have the strange words "second first" (*deuterō protō*) Sabbath (A, C, D). The latter rendering would refer, then, to the second Sabbath after the first Sabbath, which recalls the second Sabbath after the Feast of Unleavened Bread (the first Sabbath being the one that fell during the week of the feast). But it is more likely that Bruce M. Metzger is correct in suggesting that the two terms are a combination of glosses: "first" was inserted by a scribe to contrast it with the other Sabbath mentioned in 6:6; another scribe deleted it, however, and inserted "second" in view of 4:31; and a third scribe mistakenly combined the two glosses into one.[1] Therefore, the original reading was probably "one Sabbath."

On that particular Sabbath when Jesus and His disciples were walking through a grain (corn) field, the disciples plucked the ears of grain, rubbed them in their hands to separate the kernels from the chaff, and ate the kernels. Gleaning in the fields was an action permitted by the Law, according to Deuteronomy 23:25, as long as one did not use a sickle to do so. But plucking grain on a Sabbath, an action associated with harvesting, was forbidden, according to the rabbinic tractate *Shabbat* 7:2, 9. That passage proscribes thirty-nine categories of work on the Sabbath. These requirements were thought to put a "fence around the Torah," and thus protect it from disobedience. Harvesting was one of the taboos. Even the modern tourist in Israel can appreciate the specificity of regulations that still govern the Sabbath. For example, on the Sabbath, one must eat leftover food, drink day-old coffee, and take the Sabbath elevator (an elevator that automatically stops on every floor so that the residents will not have to work by pushing the floor number!). In Jesus' day, according to another rabbinic tractate, *Pesahim* 8:7, in order to prevent the very sort of thing Jesus' disciples did—harvest on the Sabbath—Jews were required to prepare a meal in advance in the event that a traveler stopped at their house. Jesus' disciples' behavior, then, was revolutionary.

6:2 Verse 2 contains the Pharisees' criticism of Jesus' disciples, who accused them of breaking the Sabbath by reaping on it (Ex. 34:21). The Pharisees' interrogation of Jesus regarding His disciples' behavior probably stemmed from the idea that the rabbi was responsible for his student's actions.

6:3 Jesus responded to the criticism in authoritative fashion, countering His opponents' appeal to Scripture with a quotation of His own from 1 Samuel 21:1-7, implying their ignorance of that passage. The Old Testament text records the story of David and his men eating the holy bread from the sanctuary at Nob.

6:4 According to 1 Samuel 21:1-7, when David fled from Saul, he entered into the sanctuary at Nob and asked for food to curb his hunger.

---

1. Metzger, *A Textual Commentary on the Greek New Testament,* 139.

After confirming David's sexual purity, the priest, having no other food available, gave David the showbread to eat (bread of the Presence/Presentation, the latter being the Septuagint rendering). The showbread consisted of twelve loaves of bread placed on a golden table situated in the Holy Place (Ex. 25:30; 35:13; 39:36; 40:23; Num. 4:7; 1 Kings 7:48; 2 Chron. 4:19). It was set out every Sabbath, with the bread from the week before then made available to the priests, who alone were to eat it (Lev. 24:9). Later rabbinic interpretation placed this incident about David on a Sabbath (Strack-B 1:618-19). R. T. France makes the plausible suggestion that Jesus appealed to this event because it grounded His own reinterpretation of the Law with reference to Sabbath keeping in David's unprecedented action. Just as David possessed the divine authority to reinterpret the Law, so did Jesus, one greater than even David.[2] If so, then, as Ellis remarks, here we have an instance which places Sabbath observance in the category of ceremonial rather than moral law.[3]

6:5   Verse 5 seems to confirm the interpretation of v. 4 just offered. If a human being such as David could dispense with Sabbath regulations, certainly the Son of Man could do the same. We earlier suggested that the Son of Man title implied Jesus' heavenly origin and deity. As the living representative of God, He had the authority to reinterpret the Law. The parallel text in Mark 2:27 specifies the purpose for such revamping of the meaning of the Sabbath—the Sabbath was made for the benefit of humans, not the reverse. There is an interesting addition to Luke 6:5 in Codex D (Bezae, the western text), "Man, if you know what you are doing, you are blessed; but if you do not know, you are cursed and a transgressor of the Law." However, this saying is surely not original to Luke, but rather originated in an apocryphal gospel like the third century A.D. writing *Gospel of Thomas*.

6:6   Verses 6-11 relate another Sabbath controversy story, this one concerning the healing of a man with a paralyzed hand. Jesus entered the synagogue, possibly the one at Capernaum, for the purpose of teaching. This added comment by Luke sets the stage for the upcoming Sermon on the Plain, 6:20-49. On this particular Sabbath, Jesus encountered a man whose right hand was paralyzed. It may be that, with this last remark, Dr. Luke highlights the difficulty of the man's situation— his right hand, the one he needed for work, was the one impaired.

---

2. France, *Jesus and the Old Testament*, 46-47.
3. Ellis, *The Gospel of Luke*, 109.

6:7 Luke registers the suspicious, condemnatory attitude of the scribes and the Pharisees. They watched Jesus carefully to see if He would heal the man on the Sabbath. It may even be that they purposely set Jesus up by bringing the man into the synagogue. Their point of accusation, should Jesus heal the man, would be that Jesus had broken the Sabbath by healing on it. Only in life-threatening circumstances could the ban against healing on the Sabbath be lifted. Thus, the rabbinic tractate *Shabbat* 8:6 reads, "Whenever there is doubt whether life is in danger this overrides the Sabbath." Obviously, the Jewish religious leaders did not consider the plight of the paralytic man as life threatening.

6:8 Verses 8-11 combine Jesus' revolutionary action and pronouncement statement. In v. 8 Jesus, fully aware of His critics' thoughts, commanded the man to rise up and come and stand in the middle of the people, in full view of all.

6:9 Jesus posed a twofold rhetorical question that penetrated to the heart of the issue, "Is it lawful on the Sabbath to do good or evil, to save or destroy life?" Jesus' point was that to fail to do good and save life was tantamount to doing evil and destroying life. In stating the issue that way, Jesus was doing a couple of things: First, He was restoring the Sabbath to its original purpose—to bring benefit to the worshiper of God (cf. again Mark 2:27). Second, in effect, Jesus was elevating Himself to the level of God, who had the authority to reinterpret the Sabbath.

6:10 In an almost defiant manner, Jesus stared at His audience, then commanded the man to stretch out his hand. The man complied and Jesus miraculously restored the hand.

6:11 The scribes and Pharisees were filled with anger toward Jesus and debated among themselves what they should do with Him.

THE CHOOSING OF THE TWELVE, 6:12-19

Although many disciples followed Jesus, He singled out twelve to be His special emissaries and eventual leaders of the early church. Luke 6:12-19 is one of four New Testament passages listing the twelve apostles: Matthew 10:2-4; Mark 3:16-19; Luke 6:12-19; Acts 1:13. Jesus' time on the mountain, and calling of the twelve disciples (6:12-16), the Sermon on the Mount (6:20-49), and the subsequent miracles (7:1-17) have been compared to the formation of Israel into twelve tribes, Moses' time on Mt. Sinai and descent with the Law, and subsequent wilderness miracles, respectively.

6:12 During one of those days, Jesus sought solitude before God on a mountain, where He observed an all-night prayer vigil.

6:13 It is implied that the purpose for the night of prayer was to seek God's guidance in choosing the apostles. When daybreak came, Jesus called His band of disciples together and chose twelve of them to be His apostles (cf. 9:10; 11:49; 17:5; 22:14; 24:10). The term "apostle" calls for three comments: First, the Greek word is *apostolos*, which means "sent one." So significant is the word that it has been left in its original Greek form in subsequent translations. Second, the origin of the term has been hotly debated. Some, like Walter Schmithals, argued that the later church borrowed the term from Gnosticism (with reference to special people enlightened by spiritual knowledge) and then anachronistically read it back onto the lips of the Lucan Jesus.[4] However, Karl Heinrich Rengstorf was surely more correct to trace the word to the Palestinian Jewish institution of *shaliah,* an Aramaic term meaning "sent ones," with reference to those representatives commissioned by the Sanhedrin or rabbis to represent them and act in their name with authority to settle fiscal and legal matters. The term, then, goes back before the time of Jesus and provides a suitable historical antecedent for Jesus' choosing and commissioning of His own representatives.[5] Third, the qualifications for becoming an apostle are later set down by Luke in Acts 1:21-22: (a) they had to be men who accompanied the historical Jesus from John's baptism forward, and (b) they had to have seen the resurrected Jesus.

6:14 Verses 14-16 contain the names of the twelve apostles. First in all the apostolic lists is Simon Peter (cf. 5:8). The surname Peter (*petros*) means "Rock" and originated with his confession that Jesus was the Christ (Matt. 16:16-19). Regardless of one's church tradition, it can be agreed upon by all that Peter was the dominant apostle of the historical Jesus. Andrew (cf. Acts 1:13) was Peter's brother, a Galilean fisherman like Peter (Mark 1:16, 29). The two probably formed a partnership. James, called "the Great" (contrast James the Less of Mark 15:40), was, like John his brother, a Galilean fisherman, whose martyrdom is recorded in Acts 12:1-2. The two were companions of Peter. The next pair were Philip and Bartholomew (cf. Acts 1:13). Philip plays a prominent role in the gospel of John (1:43-48; 6:5-7; 12:21; 14:8). Bartholomew is traditionally identified with Nathanael (John 1:45).

---

4. Schmithals, *The Office of Apostle in the Early Church.*
5. Rengstorf, "Apostolos," 1:398-447; esp. 414-20.

6:15 Matthew is to be equated with Levi (5:27). Neither he nor Thomas (see John 11:16; 20:24) occur again in Luke. Next is James the son of Alphaeus, about whom we learn virtually nothing in the gospels. Simon the Zealot has traditionally been associated with the zealot party, a group of Palestinian Jews who opposed the Roman occupation of Israel (c.f. possibly Josephus, *Ant.* 18.23-25). This group officially emerged right before the first Jewish revolt against Rome in A.D. 66–70. It was they who probably instigated the rebellion, thinking that God's hand could be manipulated to defend them if they engaged the enemy in conflict. Unofficially, there seems to have been a long history of Jewish people of such persuasion, going back to the Maccabean period (second century B.C.).

6:16 Next is Judas, the son of James (cf. Acts 1:13). However, Mark 3:18 and Matthew 10:3 identify him as Thaddeus. Joachim Jeremias suggests that Luke preserved the disciple's first name whereas Mark and Matthew use his second name, Thaddeus, the name preferred in the early church in order to distinguish him from the other Judas, the betrayer.[6]

Judas Iscariot is the last named disciple, for obvious reasons. But what is not clear is the meaning of the name "Iscariot." Three views have been proposed. First, the most common interpretation is that Judas Iscariot means the man from Kerioth, a town mentioned in Joshua 15:25 (near Hebron) and Jeremiah 48:24 (near Moab). But second, because that town has not yet been located in modern times, Bertil Gartner suggested the term means "liar," based on an Aramaic word, *sakar.* However, this view labors under two assumptions: (1) the Hebrew word (Iscariot) is a mistranslation of the Aramaic term (*sakar*),[7] something hard to imagine in view of the fact that the nomenclature, "Judas Iscariot," was so well known in the early church; and (2) that because Iscariot has not yet been located means it did not exist in Jesus' day. Third, Oscar Cullmann, following the variant reading, *zkapiōth,* interpreted the word to mean *sicarius* (assassin), thus making Judas a zealot (cf. Simon the Zealot).[8] But the problem here is that that variant reading is too poorly attested (only in D). Therefore, the traditional view that Iscariot refers to the town of Judas' origin is to be preferred. An ominous chord is struck in this list of disciples—Judas of Iscariot will be the one who will betray Jesus.

6. Jeremias, *New Testament Theology,* 232-33.

7. Gartner, *Iscariot,* 6-7.

8. Cullmann, *The State in the New Testament,* 15-16.

6:17   Three groups of people are mentioned relative to Jesus' descent from the mountain to a plain level: His twelve apostles who came down the mountain with Jesus; a large number of other disciples (probably from whom He had earlier chosen the Twelve); a great throng of people from all over Israel—as far south as Jerusalem and northwest as the coastal cities of Tyre and Sidon (which are located today near Beirut, Lebanon).

6:18   The latter group came to Jesus in order to hear His words (a sampling of which Luke will recount in the Sermon on the Plain, vv. 20-49) and to experience His miraculous works, in terms of both healings and exorcisms.

6:19   The throngs of people were clamoring to touch Jesus, for those who did so were healed by the supernatural power exuding from His body.

THE SERMON ON THE PLAIN, 6:20-49

Luke 6:20-49 contains Jesus' Sermon on the Plain. Before analyzing the sermon, we offer three introductory comments on its relation to the Matthean Sermon on the Mount (Matt. 5-7), its interpretation, and its structure. Concerning the first of these comments, two basic stances have been taken: the Sermon on the Plain is a different message from the Matthean Sermon on the Mount; or the two are different renditions of the same sermon, stemming from the "Q" (*Quelle*, source) document. Those arguing for the first alternative point out the following differences between the two: (1) There is an apparent geographical difference, Matthew's sermon is on the mountain, Luke's is on a level plain. (2) There is a difference in content between the two, notably Luke's absence of the material occurring in Matthew 5:17, 19-20, 21-24, 27-28, 33-39a, 43; 6:1-8, 16-18; 7:15-16. On verse count alone, Luke's sermon has 30 verses to Matthew's 107 verses. (3) The structures of the pieces are different: Matthew's is more tightly arranged, centering on the concept of righteousness: 5:3-16, beatitudes and similitudes and true righteousness; 5:17-20, the central importance of true righteousness; 5:21-48, the contrasts between outward and inward righteousness; 6:1-18, the false righteousness of the Pharisees; 6:19–7:27, the righteousness of the citizens of the kingdom of heaven. Luke's sermon, however, is more loosely composed, with no seeming overarching theme tying it together: 6:20-26, beatitudes and woes; 6:27-36, love for one's enemies; 6:37-49, the good deeds of the righteous.

These differences, however, need not suggest that we are dealing here with two separate sermons by our Lord. These variations are rather easily explained: First, the geography of the two settings is not really different. This particular observer noticed that, when standing on the traditional site of the Sermon on the Mount (near Capernaum on the Sea of Galilee), the terrain looks like a level plain on a hill, but from the vantage point of the Sea of Galilee, it looks like a mountain. Second, the reason for the difference in the content of the two sermons is not difficult to grasp. The material unique to Matthew just cited deals almost exclusively with the Old Testament Law and accords well with the Jewish setting of the first gospel, whereas Luke's Gentile outlook precluded the need to incorporate that material. Furthermore, we must grant the gospel authors the freedom to have chosen their material from the life of Christ in accordance with their individual Spirit-guided purposes. Third, the last point also helps to explain the different structures of the two gospels' presentation of Jesus' sermon.

On the other hand, the undeniable similarities between the Sermon on the Mount and the Sermon on the Plain strongly suggest that the same material has been adapted by both writers. Fitzmyer conveniently summarizes those parallels:

subject-matter	teaching about conduct expected of disciples (or following crowds)
exordium	the beatitudes
content	almost all of the Lucan sayings are found in the Matthean sermon; also an eschatological dimension of Jesus' words; and above all, the teaching about love of one's neighbor and even of one's enemies
conclusion	the parable of the two houses, challenging listeners to become doers
occasion	early in Jesus' one-year ministry and preceding the cure of a centurion's servant
relation to a common place	in Matthew 5:1, on the "mountain"; in Luke, after descent from "the mountain" (6:12, 17)[9]

9. Fitzmyer, *The Gospel According to Luke I–IX,* 628.

In interpreting the Sermon on the Plain/Mount, three observations need to be made. First, its interpretation has been controversial. Numerous views have arisen in connection with the sermon. The old liberal viewpoint of the nineteenth century basically said one had to keep the ethics of the sermon in order to truly be a Christian. The Lutheran tendency has been to interpret the sermon through the Law/gospel dialectic. Because its demands are impossible to keep, the sermon functions as the Law, with all its convicting power. But because the sermon thereby drives the reader to God's grace for forgiveness and power for obedience, it is gospel. Early in this century, Albert Schweitzer proposed the "interim ethic" interpretation of the sermon. Jesus' teachings were designed for the short period immediately before the coming of the kingdom of God on earth. But because the kingdom did not come at the death of Christ, so Schweitzer argued, the ethics of the kingdom were thereby rendered unattainable and impractical.

We will conclude the previous point after briefly noting the second observation about the sermon—it is paradoxical in nature. This is especially the case in Luke 6:20-49. Thus, the poor are blessed and the rich are cursed (vv. 20-26), which is nothing less than a reversal of roles. The persecuted are to bless their enemies (vv. 27-38). It is inward, not just external, obedience that Christ expects of His disciples (vv. 39-49). The function of these paradoxical aspects of the sermon is to challenge the disciple to trust in the ethics of Jesus and not in the values of this age.

Third, and this observation resumes the discussion of the first point regarding interpretation, the best approach to the sermon is an eschatological one.[10] Insofar as the kingdom of God was present in the ministry of Jesus, already the people of God can enjoy the blessings of the age to come, by faith. That being the case, the ethics of the Sermon on the Plain pertain to Christians and are, therefore, attainable. Yet, because the kingdom of God has not been consummated, still awaiting the return of Christ and His earthly reign, the standards cannot be realized in their full measure in this age. Therefore, the overlapping of the two ages—the kingdom of God has been revealed but has not been fulfilled—seems to be the best frame of reference for interpreting the sermon.

---

10. See the discussion by George Ladd in *A Theology of the New Testament,* 120-34. Also see a similar approach in Charles C. Ryrie, *Dispensationalism* (Chicago: Moody, 1995), 97-101.

Regarding the structure of the Sermon on the Plain, as mentioned before three themes seem to surface: vv. 20-26, the eschatological reversal of the fortunes of the poor and rich; vv. 27-38, the merciful behavior of the disciples of Jesus; vv. 39-49, inward obedience to the word of Christ.

THE ESCHATOLOGICAL REVERSAL OF
THE FORTUNES OF THE POOR AND RICH, 6:20-26

Guelich captures the eschatological, or end time, ambiance of the Beatitudes:

> They address those who already are what they are identified as being. The identity of the Beatitudes' subjects first comes into being in the encounter with God through Jesus' ministry in which God's redemptive initiative in history confronts the individual and calls for a decision to surrender, to yield one's all to God. To those who so respond out of desperation, the subjects of the Beatitudes, the various promises of the future are given. These promises are given as assurance rather than as reward. . . . The promise is future but not exclusively. The future consummation of God's reign is still to come but it also has made its impact in the present. . . . The "eschatological blessings" of the promises are both present and future.[11]

6:20 Jesus fixed His eyes on His disciples, the primary audience of the Sermon on the Plain. But the crowd of people also formed the larger audience (vv. 17, 24-26, 7:1). From this it may be surmised that the sermon served a twofold function: to encourage faithfulness among Jesus' disciples and to challenge non-disciples to follow Him.

The Beatitudes and their counterparts, the Woes, require introductory comments concerning their form and function. Regarding the form of the Beatitudes and the Woes, each includes a pronouncement in the present tense[12] and a promise in the future tense. The pronouncement begins with the word "blessed" or "woe," whereas the promise (or warning) begins with a *hoti* ("because") clause. Luke's statements are in the second person plural (cf. Matthew's usage of the third person singular, Matt. 5:1-12). In order to appreciate the function of the Beatitudes and the Woes, one needs to contrast their usage in Greek and Jewish literature. In Greek literature, the Beatitude

---

11. Guelich, *The Sermon on the Mount,* 111.
12. The following discussion is based on Guelich's material in *The Sermon on the Mount,* 63-72.

("blessed," *makarios*) in particular was used to express the happy, untroubled state of the gods, and then extended to depict the happiness of the rich who were free from care. In the Old Testament, however, a reversal of such values is recorded. There, especially in the Psalms and Isaiah, those who were physically poor, and therefore utterly dependent on God for their defense (the *anawim,* cf. Luke 1:46-55), were the ones blessed of God (Pss. 14:6; 22:24; 25:16; 34:6; 40:17; 69:29; 82:13; 86:1; 88:15; Isa. 51:21; 54:11; 61:1-2), whereas their persecutors, the rich and the powerful, were the ones destined to be judged (Pss. 7; 10; 35:10; 37:14-15; Isa. 3:14-15; 10:2; 32:7). Failure to grasp this Old Testament background will result in restricting Luke's declarations in the Sermon on the Plain to the literal, physical level. The Psalms and Isaiah, however, encompass both physical and figurative/spiritual definitions of what it means to be poor, hungry, sad, and persecuted (cf. the Matthean formulations, 5:1-12).

Thus Jesus' blessing on the poor should be understood in the light of the *anawim* of the Psalms and Isaiah. That is, those who recognize their spiritual bankruptcy before God and throw themselves upon His mercy are the real citizens of His kingdom. As a matter of fact, the physically poor do seem to have a greater openness to this quality of humility before, and dependency upon, God, because of their destitute condition, more so than the rich who are tempted to be self-sufficient and therefore self-reliant. There are, of course, wonderful exceptions to this last pattern. The promise to the poor is in the present tense, "because yours is (*estin*) the kingdom of God." The present tense, however, is a timeless construction pertaining to both the present and future. As such, therefore, it refers to God's present reign in the heart of the humble, dependent disciple of Jesus, as well as to the future consummation of that kingdom when Christ will return to establish His earthly reign, the Millennium.

6:21 The second Beatitude, "Blessed are those who hunger now, for you will be filled," logically follows the first Beatitude; hunger and poverty go together. The hunger here, as in Matthew 5:6, should not be restricted to the physical level; it also involves a deep spiritual appetite for God (cf. Isa. 55:1; Amos 8:11). Leonard Goppelt expressed this association well: "The hungry are men who both outwardly and inwardly are painfully deficient in the things essential to life as God meant it to be, and who, since they cannot help themselves, turn to

God on the basis of his promise."[13] The assurance to such an individual is that he or she will one day be filled, probably a reference to the coming messianic banquet (see Isa. 25:6, 8; 49:10-13; Ps. 107:3-9; cf. in Luke, 12:37; 13:29; 14:14-15, 16-24).

The third Beatitude, "Blessed are those weeping now, for you will laugh," connotes the twofold theme of oppression by persecutors and sin, the result of which is mourning. But the promise to those people is that their sorrow will be transformed into joy, a characteristic of the coming kingdom of God (cf. Ps. 126:2, 5; Isa. 60:20; 61:3; 65:16-19; 66:10; Jer. 31:13; Matt. 5:4; Luke 2:25; Rev. 7:17; 21:4).

6:22 The fourth Beatitude is in vv. 22-23. Verse 22 contains the present pronouncement, and v. 23 gives the future promise. Four invectives can be expected by the disciples of Jesus, according to v. 22: First, they will be "hated" (*miseō*), a term used elsewhere of the attitude of the opponents of God's people (Isa. 66:5; Luke 1:71; 21:17). The second and third maledictions, "ostracize" (*aphorisōsin*) and "denounce" (*oneidisōsin*), quite possibly refer to the Jewish leaders' practice of expelling Jewish Christians from the synagogue. That practice is reflected in the twelfth benediction of the *Shemoneh Esreh* (the Eighteen Benedictions), a curse that was designed to weed out the *minim* or the heretical "Nazarenes" (Jewish Christians) from synagogue worship. Although the text dates to the late first century, it probably goes back to an earlier time. The twelfth benediction reads, "For the renegades let there be no hope, and may the arrogant kingdom soon be rooted in our days, and the Nazarenes and the *minim* perish as in a moment and be blotted out from the book of life and with the righteous may they not be inscribed. Blessed art Thou, O Lord, who humblest the arrogant."[14]

The procedure for banning Christians from the synagogue has been discussed by Louis Martyn. He observed that how they are to be separated is not said either in the benediction or in the Talmudic passages in which it is mentioned. Martyn observed, however, that we are not left wholly to our imagination. We need only to place ourselves for a moment in the ancient synagogue service. There we find ourselves face-to-face with three persons whose roles were probably central to the working out of the Benediction Against Heretics: the

---

13. Goppelt, "*Peinaō*," 6:12-22, 18.

14. The "Benediction" is found in Barrett's collection of primary texts, *The New Testament Background. Selected Documents,* 211.

president of the synagogue (*Rosh ha-Keneset* = *archisynagōgos*), the overseer (*Chazzan* = *ypēretēs*), and the delegate of the congregation (*Sheliach Zibbur*). The last of these is not an official of the synagogue, but rather any adult male selected by the president and then actually invited by the overseer to lead the congregation in the recitation of the Eighteen Benedictions. A number of rabbinic passages enable us to surmise that for detecting heretics the twelfth benediction was employed in the following manner:

1. A member of the synagogue does something to arouse suspicion regarding his orthodoxy (cf. John 3:2; 7:52a).
2. The president instructs the overseer to appoint this man to be the delegate of the congregation, i.e., to lead in the praying of the Eighteen Benedictions.
3. Unless the man has a means of avoiding the appointment, he must go before the Ark (*Torah Nitch*) and recite aloud all of the Eighteen Benedictions, pausing after each to await the congregation's Amen. All listen carefully to his recitation of Benediction number 12.
4. If he falters on number 12, the Benediction Against Heretics, he is removed from his praying (cf. *b. Ber.* 28b-29a). He is then, presumably, drummed out of the synagogue fellowship.[15]

The fourth invective the disciples of Jesus should expect is to have their name rejected as evil for the sake of the Son of Man, undoubtedly with reference not to individual names, but to the name of "Christian" (see Acts 11:26; 26:28; 1 Peter 4:14).

6:23   Jesus predicted that His disciples will jump for joy one day because they have been persecuted for His name's sake. Joy amid persecution is a theme that occurs elsewhere in Luke (Acts 5:41; 16:25; 21:13). The reward for such behavior will be greatness in heaven, a motivation apparently not thought by Jesus to be crass. Disciples should not be surprised by their tribulation for the cause of Christ. The same thing happened to the Old Testament prophets, thus placing Jesus' disciples in very good company.

6:24   The theme of the eschatological reversal of roles continues in vv. 24-26, where the Woes are given. The first Woe, "But woe to you who are rich because you have already received your consolation,"

---

15. Martyn, *History and Theology in the Fourth Gospel,* 58-60.

points to the deeper reality of the problem with riches—they tempt one to forget about the coming kingdom of God. Enjoying the amenities and luxuries of this life can also detract one from caring for the needy of this age. Such people, as the old adage goes, had better enjoy their wealth while they can for it will be gone tomorrow. The term "consolation" is the same word used in Luke 2:25 ("the consolation of Israel") and paints an ominous picture of the rich that is in stark contrast with the bright future of the poor. Jesus' audience probably included wealthy people who needed to be jarred from clutching their possessions, in order to place their trust in God (cf. 6:46-49).

6:25   Two Woes antithetical to the Beatitudes occur in v. 25. The result structurally is a striking parallelism between the four Beatitudes and the four Woes:

A   v. 20—poor now/kingdom of God later
  B   v. 21a—hungry now/filled later
    C   v. 21b—weep now/laugh later   Beatitudes
      D   vv. 22-23—ill received by men/
                    well received by God

A'   v. 24—rich now/poor later
  B'   v. 25a—filled now/hungry later
    C'   v. 25b—laugh now/weep later   Woes
      D'   v. 26—well received by men now/
                  ill received by God later

To those who are "stuffed" from overindulgence in food, their lot one day will be the pangs of hunger (cf. Isa. 65:13; James 4:9). Similarly, those who laugh now will weep later. The laughter referred to by Jesus may be the derisive/mocking attitude of the fool (Eccl. 7:6). The word can also indicate scorn at others (Ps. 126:2; James 4:9). Theirs is a sad fate.

6:26   The fourth Woe matches the structure of the fourth Beatitude (v. 23b) except that it replaces the word "prophet" with "false prophet." It warns against gauging one's character by the standard of reputation. People who enjoy the widespread praise of men may find themselves in the same company of the Old Testament false prophets who, because they told the people what they wanted to hear, experienced great popularity (Isa. 30:10-11; Jer. 5:31; 6:14; 23:16-17; Mic. 2:11). Probably Jesus intended to place the rich in that category.

LOVE YOUR ENEMIES, 6:27-38

Marshall divides this section into three paragraphs: 6:27-31, showing love to one's enemy, the Golden Rule; 6:32-36a, the reward of such love and its contrast with the "love" of sinners; 6:36b-38, imitating God's love and mercy.[16] Yet many commentators do not think there is a logical connection between this and the previous section (6:20-26) or even within the section itself. However, the idea of the reversal of roles attendant with the arrival of the kingdom of God seems to be the point of connection for all of vv. 20-38. Thus, citizens of the kingdom love their enemies (vv. 27-31), in contrast to what their enemies do to them (cf. v. 22), or even in distinction from the mutual love shown between sinners (vv. 32-36), and thereby imitate God's love, which is merciful and does not give us what we deserve (vv. 36-38).

6:27   This section begins with an introductory statement designed to get Jesus' audience to listen for the purpose of obeying, "But to those who listen" (cf. v. 47). Afterward come four imperatives in vv. 27-28 which are stated without a conjunction (an asyndeton): love, do good, bless, pray. Jesus' command to love your enemies was without parallel in the thought world of His day. Contrast His bold injunction with the Greek writer Lysias, who makes a rather typical comment, "I considered it established that one should do harm to one's enemies and be of service to one's friends" (*Pro milite* 20). Or compare Luke 6:27 with the Jewish Qumran community's attitude toward its enemies, "Hate all the sons of darkness" (*1QS* 1:10; 9:21). About the closest one comes to Jesus' radical statement is the appeal by some ancient writers to turn one's enemies into friends (Thucyides 419, 1-4; Diogenes Laertius 8:1, 23; *T. Ben.* 4:3; *T. Jos.* 18:2). But even that conduct falls short of Jesus' command to love someone while he is still an enemy. That Jesus was not engaging in sentimental talk is shown by the term He uses, *agapē,* the highest form of love. The second command, "Do good to those who hate you," also confirms that Jesus was not talking ethereally; His disciples should demonstrate the highest regard for their enemies by performing tangible deeds of kindness toward them. This kind of behavior is in utter contrast to that described in v. 22 and can only be accomplished by those over whom the kingdom of God rules.

16. Marshall, *Commentary on Luke,* 257.

6:28 Furthermore, disciples of Christ are to bless those who curse them. This exhortation may have a specific situation in mind—those who were banned from the synagogue and underwent a curse for being identified with Christ were to bless their opponents. It probably also has a more general background in view; the thought of returning blessing for cursing was an advancement beyond the *lex talionis* (law of retaliation) attitude of the Old Testament covenant (Gen. 12:3; 27:29; Num. 24:9). Moreover, disciples of Jesus are to pray for those who abuse them (cf. Matt. 5:11; Rom. 12:14), something the Lord Himself did (Luke 23:34).

6:29 The directives in vv. 29-30 are in the second person singular, contrasted with the plurals used previously in 27-28 and to follow in vv. 31-36, probably because here specific occasions are mentioned, whereas in the other verses general circumstances are in view. The injunction to turn the other cheek when slapped once again exceeds the old principle of retaliation (Ex. 21:24; Lev. 24:20; Deut. 19:21). It may be that Ellis is correct in suggesting that the command is connected with the ritual slap on the cheek given a Jewish Christian upon being excommunicated from the synagogue.[17] When one considers the practice of administering thirty-nine lashes for a synagogue offender (cf. Acts 5:40; 2 Cor. 11:24), such a suggestion is in no way implausible. The other command in v. 29, giving one's tunic to someone who was in the process of taking the cloak, refers to the outer garment and inner garment, respectively (cf. Matt. 5:40), and truly constitutes a radical reversal of values.

6:30 Following Jesus is not a give-and-take relationship. It is, as the next commandment indicates, a matter of giving born out of self-denial for the sake of Christ. Disciples are to give to all who ask of them, and they are not to ask for the things taken from them to be returned. This type of commitment cuts against the grain of today's "me-ism" generation.

6:31 The "golden rule," and "just as you wish men to treat you, treat them likewise" were probably not unique to Jesus. Rabbi Hillel (ca. 10 B.C.) stated it earlier, but in a negative form: "What is hateful to you do not to your neighbor: that is the whole Torah, while the rest is commentary" (*b. Shab.* 31a; cf. *Tob.* 4:15; *Letter of Aristeas* 207; Manuscript D of Acts 15:29; *Didache* 1:2; *Targum Jerusalem I* on Lev. 19:18). Jesus, however, accentuated the command by putting it in a positive fashion and by associating it with loving one's neighbor (v. 27).

---

17. Ellis, *The Gospel of Luke*, 115.

6:32   Verses 32-36 contrast this love of one's enemies with the reciprocal, and therefore conditional, "love" shown between sinners. The golden rule of v. 31 is deepened here; Christians should treat others the way they are not treated. For Christians to love those who love them evokes no praise from God, for even sinners demonstrate that kind of conditional love. Rather, disciples of Christ are to emulate unconditional love by caring for those who have no intention of ever loving them in return.

6:33   The challenge is restated by Jesus in terms of His followers doing good to those who will never reciprocate by doing good to them.

6:34   The command is restated again, this time with reference to loaning something. Christians who lend to only those who will return the favor have no thanks from God, for even non-Christians do that.

6:35   Verse 35a encapsulates the previous three commands: "Love your enemies, help people, lend to them, but with no thought of return."[18] This is altruism at its best. Two blessings accrue to the disciple of Jesus for doing so. First, their reward will be great. Inherent to this promise is the concept of rewards for faithful service rendered to the Lord (cf. Luke 19:17, 19; 22:29-30). Second, to ensure proper motivation, Jesus pronounced the ultimate blessing on disciples who love unconditionally—they will be known as the sons of the Most High (1:32), because showing kindness to the ungrateful and wicked is consistent with God's character.

6:36   Verse 36 is a bridge statement, concluding vv. 32-35 and introducing vv. 37-38. The admonition "to be merciful because God is merciful" is an apt summary of vv. 32-35, because it exhorts disciples to go above and beyond the call of duty. Their conduct toward others should be merciful; that is, they should treat others positively even when dealt with negatively. In so doing, they mimic God. The word "show mercy" (*oiktirmōn*) is used in the Septuagint of God's actions toward others (Ex. 34:6; Deut. 4:31; Joel 1:13; Jonah 4:2) and is a fitting term for the behavior of His children. Showing mercy also serves as the basis for not judging others, as well as giving to them, according to vv. 37-38.

6:37   Verses 37-38 contain two negative commands ("do not judge; do not condemn") and two positive commands ("forgive; give"), actu-

---

18. The word *apelpizontes* normally means despair, but it is translated by Chrysostom as "hoping for some return." That is the preferred meaning here; see Marshall, *Commentary on Luke,* 264.

alizing the mercy of God in the believer's life. The usage of the passive voice in all four cases (you: will not be judged; will not be condemned; will be forgiven; will be given to) is what theologians often call the "theological passive," an action referring indirectly to God. The statement that believers are not to judge is not an endorsement of naïveté, rather it is a charge to live a life free of fault finding. Those who live thus will in no way (*ou mē*) be judged by God. The next command specifies the first: believers are forbidden to condemn others, probably with regard to their sins—something Jesus Himself refused to do (cf. Luke 5:27-32). If His disciples follow His example, they will not be condemned. The third injunction is in keeping with the second: disciples are to forgive others; in turn they will be forgiven.

6:38   Fourth, disciples are to give to others, and then God will give to them. The resulting generosity to God's children is spelled out in an asyndeton, drawing on the Palestinian custom of filling a measuring jar with a superabundance of grain. The grain was pressed down into a jar until it held as much as possible, shaken to settle every space. Then more grain was poured into the jar until it overflowed into the lap of one's garment. For effect, Jesus concluded the illustration with a tongue twister: "For the measure with which you measure others will be measured in return to you."

At least three principles of application emerge from vv. 37-38. First, it is a psychological fact that the most contented people in the world are those who do not judge and condemn others and who forgive and give. Conversely, people who have critical and condemnatory spirits and who harbor bitterness and hoard their resources are emotionally unhealthy. Second, from a sociological perspective, people who emulate the four qualities delineated here attract others to them, and thereby live full and meaningful lives. The Scrooges of the world do not. Third, and most important, the preceding characteristics function as a barometer of one's spirituality. It is likely that the people who do not judge and condemn others, who forgive others of their sins, as well as provide for the needs of their fellow human beings, are those who have truly experienced the mercy and grace of God, in contradistinction to those who have not.

INWARD OBEDIENCE TO THE WORD OF CHRIST, 6:39-49

This section can be divided into three parts: vv. 39-42, the need for the disciples to imitate Jesus' nonjudgmental attitude; vv. 43-45, the fruit of inward obedience; vv. 46-49, obedience as the test of true discipleship.

6:39   Jesus addressed His disciples by employing a commonly known proverb, "Can the blind lead the blind?" (cf. Plato, *Rep.* 8:554b; Philo, *Virt.* 7). Two questions are utilized to make His point. The first uses a subjunctive interrogative (*mēti*) which requires a "no" answer. Can the blind lead the blind? No. The second uses an indicative interrogative (*ouchi*) which requires a "yes" answer. Will they not both fall into a ditch? Yes. The point is difficult to comprehend, but it seems to be that the leader's ability and character should be superior to his or her students. The sightless leader has no advantage over the sightless student. Rather, it is the sighted who should lead those who are without vision.

6:40   On the contrary, what should happen is that the leader, being fully trained, will be such a role model that the student will desire to be like him or her. Therefore, as Marshall puts it, the meaning of vv. 39-40 seems to flow out of v. 37—the disciples must behave like Jesus, who did not judge others.[19]

6:41   The aforementioned interpretation is confirmed in v. 41, where there occurs a warning against falsely evaluating others. The aphoristic nature of Jesus' saying is clear—before one criticizes the splinter of wood in another person's eye, let him first remove the beam out of his own eye. In modern parlance the saying would be, "People who live in glass houses ought not to throw stones." Jesus' words find a parallel in rabbinic tradition. R. Tarphon (ca. A.D. 100) said, "I should be surprised if there were anyone in this generation who would accept correction. If one says to a man, 'Remove the speck from your eye,' he will reply, 'Remove the beam from yours!'" (Strack-B 1:446).

6:42   The first part of v. 42 expresses the ludicrousness of trying to remove the speck out of someone else's eye when not seeing the beam in one's own eye. The second part of the verse pinpoints the hypocrisy of it—the one who criticizes his brother in Christ regarding some minor matter had better first get his own act together. The term used for such inconsistent behavior is "hypocrite" (*hypokrisis*), a word originally referring to a play actor in Greek drama but later developing into its commonly understood meaning of pretender. Jesus' message was lucid—disciples need to practice self-criticism before censuring others.

---

19. Marshall, *Commentary on Luke*, 269-70.

6:43   Verses 43-45 deal with the topic of the fruit of inward obedience. The old adage captures the logical connection between vv. 37-42 and vv. 43-45: the heart of the problem is the problem of the heart. The problem with judging and criticizing others is an impure heart. Just as a good tree does not yield rotten fruit nor conversely a rotten tree produce good fruit, neither can a person of bad character produce fruit of righteousness. What is needed is a transformation of the heart.

6:44   Verse 44 continues the agricultural analogy by introducing the theme that kind produces kind. Every tree is known by its fruit. For example, figs are not generated by thornbushes; grapes are not picked off of brambles. The implication is that good and bad words proceed from righteous and unrighteous hearts, respectively.

6:45   Verse 45 makes explicit what was implicit in v. 44: good people speak the good that resides in their hearts; bad people speak the bad that resides in their hearts. The verse concludes with the proverbial statement that people speak only what is in their hearts. The obvious intent of Jesus' comments in vv. 43-45 was to inculcate obedience in the hearts of His disciples so they would produce the fruit of righteousness, both in word and deed.

6:46   Verses 46-49 continue in the same vein as vv. 43-45, calling for obedience, the true test of discipleship. Jesus spelled out what He expected from all would-be followers—they should be doers, not just hearers, of His word. Merely listening to Jesus' teachings without acting on them entitles no one to call Him Lord. The double vocative, "Lord, Lord," conveys the futility of lip service to Jesus, however deferential it may be. It is obedience that is required.

6:47   In contrast to the mere hearer of Jesus' words is the obedient follower, who is described by three participles: coming, hearing, doing. This person becomes the point of the object lesson which follows.

6:48   Luke probably adapts Jesus' saying to a non-Palestinian setting (cf. Matt. 7:24-27) of a man building a house well, by digging deep and laying the foundation on solid rock. When a river flooded and beat against the house, it could not shake it loose because the house was well built. The innuendo is unmistakable—whoever hears and obeys Jesus' word is like that house.

6:49   Verse 49 provides the counterpart of the analogy. Whoever does not act on Jesus' teachings is like a man who does not lay a good foundation for his house which, when the flood comes, will collapse and bring disaster.

HOMILETICAL SUGGESTIONS

The three sections that comprise Luke 6 make for great preaching. Because the first section, 6:1-11, deals with Sabbath controversies, one message could be devoted to the topic of "Sabbath, Sunday, and Service: Worshiping in Spirit and in Truth." A number of points should be addressed, including the observance of Sabbath in the Old Testament, the change to Sunday worship in the New Testament, and the proper observance of the Lord's Day in contemporary society, based on Luke 6:1-11.

The second section of Luke 6, vv. 12-19, could be cared for by doing a short series on the twelve apostles, touching on their backgrounds, strengths and weaknesses, and fate. There are excellent books available that do such.

The third section of Luke 6, vv. 20-49, is simultaneously the most difficult and rewarding one to expound. It is difficult because of the controversy in interpretation it generates, but it is immensely rewarding because of the power its teachings unleash in the church when obeyed. Three sermons would nicely cover the material: "The Beatitudes and Woes," vv. 20-26; "Love Your Enemies," vv. 27-36; "Obedience—the Mark of True Disciples," vv. 37-49. Again, there are helpful resource materials available for the preacher courageous enough to tackle "the greatest sermon ever preached" which, by the way, would be an appropriate title for the series on the Sermon on the Plain.

LUKE
CHAPTER
SEVEN

THE MIRACLES OF THE MESSIAH

Luke 7 focuses on the miracles of Jesus the Messiah. Verses 1-17 record two of the more "phenomenal" wondrous works of Jesus: the healing of the centurion's servant and the raising of the widow's son. Verses 18-35 provide Jesus' response to the question of John the Baptist concerning Jesus' messiahship, especially v. 22. Christ's answer is unmistakable; He is the long-awaited Messiah. The episode also includes a refrain to be heard throughout the rest of the third gospel—the opposition of Jewish religious leaders to Jesus' mission. Finally, vv. 36-50 delineate the greatest messianic miracle of all, the forgiveness of sin.

THE HEALING OF THE CENTURION'S SERVANT
AND THE RAISING OF THE WIDOW'S SON, 7:1-17

The account of the healing of the centurion's servant occurs here in Luke and probably is paralleled in Matthew 8:5-13 and possibly also in John 4:46-53. The highlight of the episode is the faith of the centurion, who is representative of the Gentile audience that will eventually receive the gospel of Christ (cf. especially Cornelius's conversion in Acts 10:1-23).

7:1 Upon completing His teaching to the crowds (i.e., the Sermon on the Plain, 6:20-49), Jesus entered Capernaum, probably because it served as the headquarters of His Galilean ministry.

165

7:2 Because Galilee did not become a part of the Roman province until A.D. 44, the centurion, a captain of one hundred men, probably served in Herod Antipas's military. His assignment may have involved guarding and enforcing the toll tax there at Capernaum.[1] This particular centurion had a servant (*doulos*) who was sick to the point of death, whom he deeply respected.

7:3 Having heard about Jesus' miraculous power (cf. 4:37), the centurion sent some of the Jewish elders of the city (cf. 20:1; 22:52; Acts 4:5, 8, 23)[2] to ask Jesus to come and heal the servant. Because the centurion was a Gentile (see v. 9), it was natural that he would send a Jewish delegation to Jesus, a Jew.

7:4 The high esteem of the Jewish elders for the centurion is apparent from their earnest request of Jesus, "He is worthy, to whom you should grant this," and is in contrast to the man's own humble attitude, "I am not fit" (v. 6), "I did not think myself worthy" (v. 7).

7:5 The reasons for the delegation's high regard for the centurion are listed: he loved the Jewish nation, and he built the local synagogue. These considerations suggest that the captain was a God-fearer, a Gentile who embraced Israel's God but who did not undergo circumcision (cf. Acts 10:2).

7:6 Jesus willingly and immediately went with the Jewish embassy to the centurion (unlike, we might add, Peter's reticence to go to Cornelius's house, Acts 10:20, 23). When they were not far away from their destination (such a litotes construction [stating an affirmation in the negative] is characteristic of Luke in Acts, where it occurs eleven times[3]), some of the friends of the centurion intercepted Jesus, delivering the message that He should not trouble Himself any further. The reason the centurion conveyed for this was that he was unworthy of Jesus' presence in his house. Two factors probably informed that evaluation: First, the centurion may not have wanted Jesus, a Jew, to risk defiling Himself by entering a Gentile home (cf. Acts 10:28; 11:12; *m. Oholot* 18:7, "The dwelling-places of Gentiles are unclean"). Second, from the honorific language he applied to Jesus ("Lord," "sir," v. 6), it is clear that the centurion genuinely felt himself to be beneath Jesus' dignity and was thereby deeply humbled.

1. Sherwin-White, *Roman Society and Roman Law in the New Testament* (Oxford: Univ. Press, 1963), 123-24.

2. Schürer, *The History of the Jewish People in the Age of Jesus*, 2:1, 150-54.

3. So, according to Haenchen, *The Acts of the Apostles*, 78.

7:7   Verse 7 gives the impression that the centurion was actually in the presence of Jesus but the language is that of direct speech relayed by his friends. The message continued; it was because the centurion felt too abased before Jesus that he did not go to meet Him, but rather sent his friends to make the request of Him. As far as the centurion was concerned, Jesus could just as well speak the word from a distance and the son would be healed. The term for son here, *pais,* can be documented from Hellenistic Greek as referring to a slave or servant and need not attribute a youthful age to the ailing man.[4]

7:8   The centurion knew that Jesus had the power to heal from a distance, comparing His authority derived from God to his own authority delegated to him from his superiors, "I too am a man under authority." Within his own sphere of command, the centurion too could give orders from a distance and have them obeyed. If he told a soldier to go, he would go; if he told another to come, he would come; if he told his servant to do this, he would do it.

7:9   Jesus was amazed at the centurion's comments and, turning to those who had followed Him, declared that He had yet to find in Israel such a demonstration of faith as that displayed by the Gentile centurion. Inherent in Jesus' pronouncement was a rebuke of His Jewish audience's lack of faith.

7:10   When the party sent to Jesus returned to the house of the centurion, it found the servant well; the Master's word had cured him.

7:11   Verses 11-17 report the miraculous resuscitation of the widow's son of Nain. Luke's customary introductory words to a new narrative, "and it happened" (*kai egeneto*), loosely connect this particular story to the preceding events. Thus, after the healing of the centurion Jesus went to Nain, a town today located in the Jezreel Plain, six miles southwest of Nazareth. He was accompanied by His disciples and a great crowd, undoubtedly due to the spreading report of His miraculous power.

7:12   As Jesus and the crowd drew near to the gate of Nain, they encountered a funeral procession leaving the town. Burial in ancient Israel was done outside of the city in order to maintain ritualistic purity. The deceased were buried quickly because of the hot climate and because embalming was not practiced. The poorer folk were buried in the ground, and rocks were piled on the spot to warn passersby. The well to do were buried on ledges that had been carved out in

4. See Bauer-Gingrich-Danker, *Greek-English Lexicon of the New Testament,* 604.

caves. Over time, after the body dematerialized, the bones were then put into an ossuary, a stone box, in order to create more room for the dead. This particular funeral involved the only son of a woman, compounded by the sad fact that she was a widow. The lady therefore faced both emotional and financial trauma. The gathering of the people of the city with the woman was typical of the ancient Near East, where neighbors rallied around their grief-stricken friends, freely expressing their mourning. Often professional "mourners" accompanied a funeral in order to aid in the process of expressing one's sorrow.

7:13 Luke uses the absolute form of Lord, "the Lord" (*kyrios*), which emphasizes Jesus' deity. Seeing the bereaved woman, Jesus felt compassion for her, the sole motivation for this particular miracle; faith does not seem to have been a factor. In telling her not to continue to weep, Jesus was not short-circuiting the grief process; He did so in light of the miracle He was about to perform.

7:14 Jesus touched the bier in which the man's body lay and in doing so ignored the ritual uncleanness of the dead body. Telling the procession to stop, Jesus said to the young man, "Arise!"

7:15 At Jesus' word, the dead man sat up (cf. Acts 9:40 and the raising of Tabitha) and, as proof that he was now alive, began to speak. Jesus then gave the young man back to his mother, which is distinctly reminiscent of 1 Kings 17:23 and Elijah's raising of the widow's son of Zarephath and subsequent giving him back to his mother. In fact there are a number of striking parallels between Luke 7:11-16 and 1 Kings 17:8-24: Jesus came to a town, Nain, as did Elijah to Zarephath (Luke 7:11; 1 Kings 17:10); both Jesus and Elijah met widows at the gates of the towns (Luke 7:12; 1 Kings 17:10); both raised the widows' sons from the dead (Luke 7:15; 1 Kings 17:22); both gave the sons back to their mothers (Luke 7:15; 1 Kings 17:23); both were recognized as true prophets of God (Luke 7:16; 1 Kings 17:24). It is this background, rather than the supposed Hellenistic miracle workers like Apollonius of Tyana, that casts light on this, and other miracles of Jesus.[5] At this point, a famous anecdote comes to mind from the life of D. L. Moody. Mr. Moody was asked to conduct a funeral service, so he decided to study the gospels to find a funeral sermon delivered by Jesus. How-

---

5. The reader is referred to Fitzmyer's excellent discussion of the supposed similarities and essential differences between the miracles of Jesus and ancient Hellenistic wonder workers, including Apollonius of Tyana, in *The Gospel According to Luke I–IX*, 656-58.

ever, Moody searched in vain, because every funeral Jesus attended He broke up by raising the dead!

7:16   Luke records that the watching crowd was filled with awe and glorified God. Using indirect speech (note the two *hoti* clauses), the evangelist records the people's responses—they identified Jesus as a great prophet raised up among them and they saw in Jesus' mighty works the visitation of God upon Israel. The first statement recalls 1 Kings 17:24 and is informed by an Elijah typology (cf. also 9:8, 19). The second acclamation is a direct fulfillment of the promise to Zechariah about the coming Messiah (1:68).

7:17   The word about the resuscitation of the young man from the dead spread like wildfire throughout all of Judea (the generic name for Israel) and even in the adjacent countryside outside Israel.

JESUS AND JOHN THE BAPTIST, 7:18-35

This section consists of three parts: John the Baptist's question about Jesus' messiahship, vv. 18-23; Jesus' praise of John the Baptist, vv. 24-30; Jesus' judgment on His generation's evaluation of John the Baptist and Himself, vv. 31-35.

JOHN THE BAPTIST'S QUESTION
ABOUT JESUS' MESSIAHSHIP, 7:18-23

7:18   The disciples of John the Baptist informed him about Jesus' teaching and miracles. Because the Baptist was in prison (see 3:20), he called two of his disciples unto himself.

7:19   John the Baptist sent the two disciples to Jesus with a question, "Are you the one who is to come, or should we wait for another?" In light of 3:16, it is almost certain that John the Baptist was entertaining second thoughts about Jesus being the long-awaited Messiah (cf. Luke 13:35; Ps. 118:26). That verse clues the reader in on John's expectation of the nature of Jesus' messiahship—he would baptize with the Spirit and fire. But things had apparently not materialized as planned; John the Baptist was in prison, and Jesus was not performing great acts of fiery judgment. All of this gave John cause for concern; hence his query of Jesus. Perhaps the real Messiah had not yet arrived on the scene.

7:20   Verse 20 repeats verbatim John's question of v. 19, as the two disciples delivered it to Jesus.

7:21 The two disciples received their answer that very hour because Jesus healed many people of their ills—diseases, plagues, demonic spirits. Moreover, Jesus restored sight to the blind (cf. Isa. 61:1 with Luke 4:18).

7:22 The disciples therefore were to go back to John and declare to him what they had seen and heard. What they were to report is summarized in six clauses, most of which fulfill, in some way, Isaianic promises: the blind were recovering their sight (cf. Isa. 61:1; 35:5); the lame were walking (cf. Isa. 35:5); the deaf were hearing (cf. Isa. 35:5); the dead were being raised (cf. Isa. 26:19); the poor were hearing the good news of the gospel (cf. Isa. 61:11). The only activity not paralleled in Isaiah is the cleansing of lepers but, as Marshall notes, the cleansing of Naaman during the ministry of Elisha the prophet serves as an appropriate backdrop for that miracle, especially since there appears to be an Elijah typology at work in Luke 7.[6]

7:23 Jesus concluded His response to the query of the Baptist by asserting a beatitude, "Blessed is the one who is not scandalized at me." Part of the meaning of this statement is to be found by comparing John the Baptist's assessment of the coming Messiah, according to Luke 3:16, with Jesus' own understanding of His mission, according to the programmatic sermon in 4:16-22. John, as we said before, expected the Messiah to do wonderful miracles, including administer fiery judgment, like Elijah and Elisha of old. However, the works of Jesus were of a more positive nature—the healing of hurts and ills and the forgiveness of sins—not the calling down of fire on nonspiritual religious leaders or Roman officials (something perhaps John could have wished for, imprisoned as he was). It is interesting, as Fitzmyer notes, that none of the Isaiah passages dealing with vengeance are applied to Jesus' ministry by Luke (i.e., Isa. 29:20; 61:2b).[7] This lack of judgmental action on Jesus' part may well have contributed to John the Baptist's apparent disillusionment. And perhaps, too, John was disappointed at the seeming failure of the kingdom of God to have appeared on earth. It was a misunderstanding in which the disciples too would soon share (Luke 9:3-29).

6. See Marshall's comments in *Commentary on Luke,* 292.
7. Fitzmyer, *The Gospel According to Luke I–IX,* 667-68.

JESUS' PRAISE OF JOHN THE BAPTIST, 7:24-30

7:24 Verses 24-28 record Jesus' praise of John the Baptist. It can be outlined as follows: vv. 24-27, rhetorical questions about John; v. 28, an antithetical statement concerning John and the believer; vv. 29-30, an editorial comment regarding John. Verses 24-27 contain three rhetorical questions raised by Jesus about John the Baptist. There is a bit of a debate as to whether the interrogative beginning each question, *ti,* should be translated as "what" or "why" and also as to the resulting punctuation. If the former is right, then the translation would be, for example, "What did you go out into the desert to see? A reed blowing in the wind?" If the latter is more correct, then the translation would be, "Why did you go into the desert? To see a reed blowing in the wind?" Although there is no material difference between the two translations, the United Bible Society's Greek text is to be preferred, which opts for the former view.

Jesus raised the questions after the disciples of John the Baptist had left. Speaking to the crowds, He asked, "What did you go out into the desert to see? A reed blowing in the wind?" The reference to the desert obviously recalls the habitat of the Baptist (1:80; 3:2, 7). It is probably the case that Herod served as a foil to Jesus' questions about John. The first, then, would contrast the Baptist with Herod. The former was no ordinary sight, like a frail reed shaken by the wind, an apt metaphor for Herod's acquiescence to the wish of Herodias's daughter (see Matt. 14:1-12; Mark 6:14-29; Luke 3:19-20). Not so John; here was a man of integrity, one who did not compromise his convictions.

7:25 Jesus raised and answered a second rhetorical question, "But what did you go to see? A man dressed in fine clothes?" Here Jesus was possibly contrasting the fashionable attire of the wealthy with the tradition that John the Baptist dressed meagerly and ruggedly—a garment of camel's hair and a leather belt about his waist (see Matt. 3:4). Not so with the wealthy, who were clothed with soft raiment and lived securely in royal palaces. Perhaps the reader is also invited to see here a criticism of King Herod's royal apparel (cf. his son, Herod Agrippa I's, kingly attire in Acts 12:21).

7:26 Jesus' third question intensified the discussion and expected a positive reply, "What did you go to see? A prophet?" The Greek word *nai* affirms what has been said (as distinguished from *amen,* which affirms what will be said).[8] Yes, indeed, John was a prophet. But John

---

8. See Marshall's remarks in *Commentary on Luke,* 295.

was not just an "ordinary" prophet; he was greater than a prophet. The next verse spells out how this was so.

7:27   Quoting Mal. 3:1, Jesus cast John the Baptist in the supreme prophetic role of Elijah, the forerunner of the Messiah. In this way, John was the greatest of the prophets. Jesus' wording of the Old Testament almost certainly identifies Himself as the object of John's ministry, thereby attributing messianic proportions to His mission, "Behold I send my [God's] messenger [John] before your [Christ's] presence, who will prepare your [Christ's] way before you [Christ]." This understanding is to be preferred to the other alternative, that Jesus was conflating Malachi 3:1 with Exodus 23:20 (a text referring to the angel of the Lord preceding Israel in the wilderness). Even if, as some commentaries maintain, there was no pre-Christian Jewish expectation that Elijah would precede the Messiah per se, that does not preclude the possibility that Jesus was the first to make such a connection, just as He may have done in equating Himself with the suffering Messiah (an idea not present in intertestamental Judaism either).

7:28   Verse 28 relates Jesus' antithetical statement concerning John the Baptist and the believer. On the one hand, John the Baptist was greater than any other human being, because he was the Elijah-type prophet who served as the forerunner of the Messiah. But on the other hand, the one who is the least in the kingdom of God is greater than John. Although *mikroteros* is a comparative, it can be translated as a superlative, because of the waning influence of the latter in koine Greek. Thus the translation "least" is to be preferred. If so, the view that the lesser being compared here is Jesus to John (i.e., Jesus was younger than John) would be inaccurate. What is being said, then, is that the least prominent believer in the kingdom of God is superior in status to John. But we should not interpret Jesus' statement to mean, as Conzelmann does, that John the Baptist was therefore to be relegated exclusively to the period of Israel.[9] Rather, the fact that he was the forerunner of the Messiah placed him in a transitional stage, between the period of Israel and the period of Jesus.

7:29   Verses 29-30 constitute Luke's editorial comment on the ministry of John the Baptist. It is a bittersweet evaluation. Positively, the people hearing Jesus (toll collectors included) acknowledged God, having been baptized (the aorist passive participle is antecedent in

---

9. See Marshall's critique of Conzelmann's exegesis of Luke 7:28 in *Luke: Historian and Theologian,* 146-47.

action to the verb "acknowledged") with the baptism of John. The sense is that the listening audience acknowledged Jesus' statement to be true that John was a prophet of God, having themselves earlier submitted to the latter's baptism.

7:30   Negatively, the Pharisees and the lawyers (the experts in the Mosaic Law; cf. 10:25; 11:45-46, 52; 14:3; similar to the scribes) nullified God's will concerning themselves. The prepositional phrase *eis heautous* could go either with the noun "God's will" ("the will of God concerning themselves they nullified") or with the verb "nullified" ("the will of God they nullified concerning themselves"). Our translation reflects the latter. The Pharisees and lawyers did this when they refused to submit to John's baptism. In rejecting John, therefore, they rejected God. They would soon do the same to Jesus (cf. v. 31-50).

JESUS' JUDGMENT ON HIS GENERATION'S
EVALUATION OF JOHN THE BAPTIST AND HIMSELF, 7:31-35

7:31   This paragraph can be broken down into three parts: a simile, vv. 31-32; the interpretation of the simile, vv. 33-34; a wisdom saying, v. 35. Jesus introduced His simile with a twofold question, "To what shall I compare the men of this generation? What are they like?" The questions expects a pejorative evaluation, especially the words "this generation" (cf. Luke 11:29-32; Deut. 32:5; Judg. 2:10; Jer. 7:29).

7:32   The simile ultimately compares sulking, noncooperative children with the opponents of John and Jesus. Jesus' imagery of children sitting in the marketplace (*agora*) calling to one another (*allēlois*) imagines the two groups of children arguing with each other about what to play. The one group invited the others to join with them in playing the flute and dancing, but they would not. The other group invited the others to join them in imitating professional mourners at a funeral procession, but they would not.

7:33   The interpretation of the simile is provided in vv. 33-34. Those children imitating a funeral dirge represent the ascetic lifestyle of John the Baptist. But, like the other children who refused to join in the play acting of professional mourners, the Jewish backers rejected John, passing him off as a demoniac. They thought that his mad asceticism was due to demon possession.

7:34   Those children playing and dancing represent the joyful lifestyle of Jesus the Son of Man. But, like the other children who did not join the merrymaking, the Jewish leaders rejected Jesus, accusing Him of being a glutton and a drunkard, and surrounding Himself with such lowlifes as toll collectors and sinners. Either way, John and Jesus could not win the approval of the religious establishment.

7:35   The third component of this paragraph is a wisdom statement by Jesus, "And yet [the *kai* is best taken in an adversative sense] wisdom is justified [*edikaiōthē*] by all her children." The identification of wisdom in light of the parallel comment in v. 29 must be a circumlocution for God. The children are not Jesus and John, but the followers of Jesus and John, who are the envoys of God. What the verse means, therefore, is that, while the Jewish leaders have rejected Jesus and John, the general populace has accepted them, showing them and God to be right after all. Similar descriptions of the rejection of wisdom by some and the acceptance by others occur in the Old Testament (Job 28; Prov. 1; 8) and in noncanonical Jewish literature (*Sir.* 1:24; *Bar.* 3:9–4:4; *1 Enoch* 42; *4 Ezra* 5).

We take this opportunity to recall our earlier proposal that there are certain persons in Luke's writings whose partial comprehension of Christ typifies Israel's incomplete grasp of her Messiah. We suggested that Zechariah was one such person. We now propose another example—John the Baptist. This is not nearly as improbable as it first sounds. Actually, one can detect some seven parallels between Luke 7:18-35 and Romans 11 concerning the typology that may exist between John the Baptist and Israel. The deduction to be drawn from these similarities is that the one, John the Baptist, foreshadows the other's restoration, Israel. Both John the Baptist and Israel experienced a temporary lapse in faith (cf. Luke 7:19-20 with Rom. 11:25). Only a suppression of the data can tone down John's struggle over the issue of whether Jesus was really the Messiah or not. If we take his question in a straightforward manner, the evidence overwhelmingly suggests that the prophet was in a state of disillusionment bordering on disbelief, however temporary it may have been.

It is remarkable that the same word is predicated of John the Baptist and Israel concerning their response to Jesus—scandalized (*skandalisthē*; cf. Luke 7:23 with Rom. 11:9 [cf. 9:33]). Israel was scandalized by Jesus, and we must take Jesus' words seriously in Luke 7:23 that it was possible for His audience to be offended at His nontraditional role, including John the Baptist.

Both settings draw on Isaiah in reporting the fact that in Christ the good news of the gospel has arrived (cf. Luke 7:22 with Isa. 66:1; cf. Rom. 10:15 with Isa. 52:7). Both passages draw on the Old Testament background of the prophet Elijah and connect his ministry to preparing a righteous remnant before God (cf. Luke 7:27 with Rom. 11:4-5). In both texts, an appeal is made to the audience to see and hear the good news of Christ (cf. Luke 7:22 with Rom. 11:8, albeit with contrasting tones), drawing again on Isaiah the prophet (cf. Luke 7:22 with Isa. 61:1; cf. Rom. 11:8 with Isa. 29:10). According to Luke 7:28, John the Baptist's ministry was preparatory for the kingdom of God; in Romans 11:7, 11-16, Israel serves the divine purpose of paving the way for the formation of the church, even if unknowingly. Both passages close with a statement about the wisdom of God being vindicated (cf. Luke 7:35 with Rom. 11:33-36). These parallels are too numerous and specific to be coincidental and are well explained as Luke's allusion to the temporary unbelief of Israel through the mirror image experience of John the Baptist, as well as their future restoration.

FORGIVENESS OF SIN, THE GREATEST MIRACLE, 7:36-50

Verses 36-50 relate the story of Jesus' pardon of a sinful woman. It was the greatest messianic miracle of all because, whereas the effects of the physical miracles were temporary, the result of forgiveness of sin is eternal. The episode can be outlined under three headings: the act of the woman washing Jesus' feet, vv. 36-39; the analogy of the woman washing Jesus' feet, vv. 40-43; the application of the woman washing Jesus' feet, vv. 44-50.

THE ACT OF THE WOMAN WASHING JESUS' FEET, 7:36-39

7:36   A Pharisee invited Jesus into his home to dine with him. It may have been a meal following a synagogue service. The fact that the participants reclined suggests it was a festive occasion.[10] At such gatherings, people normally lay on their sides on divans (Near Eastern couches without backs or sides). It is interesting that Jesus showed no hesitation in accepting the Pharisee's invitation. After all, He came to be the Savior of all—toll collectors, sinners (v. 34), and religious leaders.

7:37   A certain woman of ill repute, probably a prostitute, learned that Jesus was in the Pharisee's home; so she went there with an alabaster, or a long-necked, glass bottle of perfume.[11]

---

10. See Jeremias's excellent study on the customs of Jesus' day regarding meals, especially the Passover, *The Eucharistic Words of Jesus,* 20-21.
11. Marshall provides a thorough examination of the relationship between this episode and the one in Matt. 26:6-13; Mark 14:3-9; and John 12:1-8 in *Commentary on Luke,* 304-7.

7:38   In all probability, the woman intended to anoint Jesus' head with her perfume. But, because Jesus, like the other participants, reclined with His head toward the table, the closest the woman could get to Jesus was His feet. Standing at His feet, she was overwhelmed with a mingled sense of conviction of sin and love for Jesus, so much so that she began to weep. One action led to the next. Undoubtedly embarrassed at shedding tears on Jesus' feet, she then proceeded to loosen her hair (a socially improper act) and wipe them dry. Overwhelmed in His presence, she then began to kiss His feet and anointed them with perfume. In light of vv. 48-50, it is probably the case that the woman's actions are best explained as an expression of gratitude to Jesus for forgiving her sins at an earlier time. If so, her actions bespeak of her sense of conviction of sin and concomitant love of Jesus, which together produced a spiritual catharsis. Such moments are often too wonderful to explain logically.

7:39   Meanwhile, the Pharisee who invited Jesus to his house said to himself that if Jesus were really a prophet He would know that the woman who was touching Him was a sinner. The conditional sentence is contrary to fact (*ei* and the indicative in the protasis and *an* and the indicative in the apodosis) and therefore indicates that the Pharisee did not believe that Jesus was in fact a prophet. Two insults are implied in the statement: first, Jesus did not know that the woman was a sinner, thus revealing His lack of prophetic insight; and second, Jesus allowed a sinful, unclean woman to touch Him.

THE ANALOGY OF THE WOMAN
WASHING JESUS' FEET, 7:40-43

7:41   Verses 40-43 provide an analogy of the woman's washing of Jesus' feet. In response to the musings of the Pharisee (now addressed as Simon) and in confirmation of His own prophetic knowledge, Jesus told the host that He had something to say to him. It is hard to be sure if Simon's subsequent acknowledgment of Jesus as teacher (*didaskalos*; cf. 3:12, a revered title) was sincere or hypocritical, especially since he doubted Jesus' prophetic character. The analogy or parable begins in v. 41. A moneylender had two debtors. The first owed him five hundred denarii (a denarius was the equivalent of a day's wage) and the other owed him fifty denarii.

7:42   Because the two debtors were not able to pay the moneylender back, he graciously canceled their debts. Jesus asked Simon, "Which of them would love the moneylender more?"

7:43   Simon replied that the one whose canceled debt was the most would presumably love the moneylender the most. Simon's hesitation reflected his awareness that he was about to be caught in a trap. Jesus declared that His host's answer was right.

THE APPLICATION OF THE INCIDENT
OF THE WOMAN'S WASHING JESUS' FEET, 7:44-50
7:44   Verses 44-50 press home the lesson to be learned from the woman's demonstration of profound gratitude toward Jesus. Beginning in v. 44, the Lord proceeds to contrast the woman's actions point by point with Simon's hospitable actions, or rather non-actions. Jesus pointed out to Simon that he had not performed the expected courtesy of washing his guest's feet, a custom necessitated by the dusty roads in ancient Israel (cf. Gen. 18:4; 19:2; 24:32; 43:24). On the contrary, the woman bathed Jesus' feet with her tears and dried them with her hair.
7:45   Whereas Simon did not greet Jesus with the customary kiss on the cheek, the woman, from the time she entered the house, had repeatedly kissed Jesus' feet.
7:46   Simon did not freshen Jesus' head or face with olive oil, but the woman went so far as to anoint His feet with costly perfume.
7:47   The point of application now became clear—the woman represented the debtor who had the greatest bill and consequently loved the moneylender the most for canceling the debt. Her unusual display of love for Jesus testified to the depth of her appreciation for His forgiveness. But Simon represented the debtor who had the lesser bill and therefore the lesser love for the moneylender. The point here seems not so much to be that the Pharisee had fewer sins to be forgiven but rather that he was not acutely aware of his own great need of forgiveness, hence his minimal show of affection for Jesus. It is also important not to misconstrue the basis of the woman's forgiveness. The *hoti* conjunction is not causal; i.e., the woman's sins were not forgiven, "because she has loved greatly." Instead, it is logical, i.e., the woman's sins were forgiven, "as is evidenced by the fact that she has loved greatly."
7:48   Jesus then confirmed to the woman that her sins were forgiven. The perfect tense of the verb *apheōntai* indicates a past action that continued in the present tense. Thus the woman had been earlier forgiven of her sin, the result of which continued up to that very moment (cf. v. 47 for the same verb).

7:49   The other guests at the meal began to ask themselves, "Who is this one who even forgives sins?" The story thereby has come full circle. It began with Simon questioning Jesus' prophetic character because He supposedly did not know that a sinful woman was touching Him. However, Jesus showed that He clearly knew what manner of person the woman was. Furthermore, even the guests began to realize that Jesus was more than a prophet; He was divinely able to forgive an unclean woman.

7:50   Jesus affirmed His earlier statement to the woman; her faith had saved her. So, then, faith was the real basis of her forgiveness and love was its evidence. Her salvation was complete (note the perfect tense of the verb "save," *sesōken*). She could now depart in peace.

HOMILETICAL SUGGESTIONS

As it seems to happen often in Luke's gospel, the chapters nicely divide into three sermons. Such is the case for chapter 7. The title of the mini-series could be "The Miracles of the Messiah," of which there are three types: physical miracles, vv. 1-17; an emotional "miracle," vv. 18-35; a spiritual miracle, vv. 36-50.

The first message would deal with the healing of the centurion's slave and the raising of the widow's son, obviously physical miracles. This would be a good sermon in which to survey Jesus' miracles as a whole: the purposes of miracles (a point extending beyond Luke 7 itself but nonetheless pertinent to it)—verification of Jesus' credentials, alleviation of human suffering, inauguration of the kingdom of God; the classification of miracles—healings, exorcisms, nature miracles; and the instances of miracles. Here the preacher could focus on the two miracles specified in Luke 7:1-17: the healing of the centurion's slave, with its emphasis on faith (v. 9) and the raising of the widow's son, which does not, in fact, mention faith but rather highlights Jesus' love (v. 13). The point to be made from this last observation is that miracles are not easily explained and are certainly not at the beck and call of humans. Rather, they are sovereignly effected according to God's wise and loving plan.

The second sermon would cover vv. 18-35, an emotional "miracle," with reference to John the Baptist. The sermon could center on the doubt of John the Baptist concerning Jesus Christ. Three points emerge from the text, the first being the trials of faith, vv. 18-20. Here we should let the text speak candidly about the doubt that trials produced in John the Baptist's life, and our own as well. Second, is the anchor of faith, vv. 21-23. Perhaps the lesson to be learned from these verses is that we, like John the Baptist, should not let present difficult moments cause us to forget the workings of God for us in the past nor dim the prospects of His interventions on our behalf in the future. The third point is the development of faith, vv. 24-35. These verses are eloquent about the character of John the Baptist, not to mention Jesus, and they assure the reader of God's positive evaluation of the Baptist's life and all who permit trials to mature their faith.

The third sermon could be entitled, "The Greatest Miracle of All," vv. 36-50. It would treat the topic of the spiritual miracle of forgiveness of sin. The message could be delivered in two points: (1) the woman as an example of those who acknowledge the greatness of their sin and thereby encounter Christ's forgiveness; (2) the Pharisee as an example of those who do not recognize the greatness of their sin and therefore lack genuine pardon.

LUKE
CHAPTER
EIGHT

MORE WORDS AND WORKS OF JESUS

Luke 8 may be entitled "More Words and Works of Jesus," a chapter that intermingles parables uttered and miracles performed by Jesus in the vicinity of the Lake of Galilee. After an introductory comment about some of the women who followed and supported Christ's ministry (vv. 1-3), Luke records two parables, the sower and the seed, and the lamp (vv. 4-18), both themes being that the kingdom of God, though starting small, will one day have great impact upon humanity. The parabolic section concludes then with a definition of what it means to be a part of the family of Christ (vv. 19-21). The next major section is devoted to some of the miracles of Christ (vv. 22-56). One of the connecting themes of the three miracles (the healing of the Gerasene demoniac, the resuscitation of Jairus's daughter, which frames the account of the cure of the woman with a hemorrhage) is that Jesus cleansed those who were ritually unclean.

WORDS OF JESUS, 8:1-21

At this juncture in the travel narrative of Jesus, Luke includes a few comments about some of the women who followed and supported the ministry of Christ (vv. 1-3). Then the third evangelist spells out the nature of that ministry, recalling two significant parables Jesus used to illustrate the kingdom of God: the parable of the seed (vv. 4-15) and the parable of the lamp (vv. 16-18). Luke concludes the section with a short episode which equates the true family of Christ with those who respond obediently to His words (vv. 19-21).

WOMEN WHO SUPPORTED
CHRIST'S MINISTRY, 8:1-3
8:1   Luke resumes the travelogue of Jesus, reporting that He journeyed from "town to town and village to village" (the *kata* is distributive). In other words, Jesus continued His itinerant ministry in the region of Galilee. The message of Jesus is conveyed by use of a hendiadys—"proclaiming the good news of the kingdom of God." The twelve disciples accompanied Jesus, not only to be witnesses of His ministry but also to receive training for their upcoming mission (9:1-11; cf. 10:1-24).

8:2   A band of women also traveled with Jesus, the highlighting of which flows from Luke's concern to show that the message of Christ is a gospel for all people, women included. The three women singled out for identification are those who found in Christ the answer to their dire situations, especially the need to be exorcised of demons. The first was Mary called Magdalene. Magdala (today called Migdal, "tower") is a town located three miles from Tiberias. Josephus seems to have identified it as Tarichaeae (*J.W.* 2.252). Mary's situation was especially severe, such that Jesus expelled seven demons out of her. Here is truly a "worst to first" case scenario in that Mary, through the power of Christ, was transformed from a demoniac to become one of the first witnesses of the resurrection (24:10).

8:3   The second woman mentioned is Joanna, the wife of Chuza. This man is not otherwise known, but the word *epitropou* suggests that he enjoyed a high position in Herod Antipas's court. The term can mean manager or even procurator; probably the former is intended. Marshall makes the plausible suggestion that this official was Luke's source of information about Herod's court. The fact that Joanna was also one of the first witnesses of the resurrection of Christ (24:10) suggests that the two were well-known personalities in the early church.[1] The third woman mentioned, Susanna, is otherwise unknown. These three women were only a few among many others who served Jesus by supporting Him out of their possessions.

This last comment generates a number of observations. First, the term used of the women's support of Jesus' mission is *diakonia,* prob-

---

1. Marshall, *Commentary on Luke,* 317.

ably because it anticipated the office of deacon, especially deaconess, created in the early church (Acts 6; Rom. 16:1; 1 Tim. 3:11). Second, the remarks about women following Jesus and about their support of Him out of their financial wherewithal attest to the historical reliability of Luke's reporting. The one, women students of a rabbi or philosopher, was unheard of in the ancient world; thus its very uniqueness bespeaks of its historicity. The other, the financial means of the women, was not unusual in antiquity, a further mark of authenticity of the account.[2] Third, the relationship between the Lord Jesus and the women specified was that of a reciprocal ministry—Jesus ministered to them spiritually; they served Him financially (cf. Rom. 15:25-27).

THE PARABLES OF
THE SEED AND THE LAMP, 8:4-18

8:4   Jesus used two parables to illustrate the progress of the word of the kingdom, beginning with the metaphor of the seed, vv. 4-15. The illustration of the seed sown appears in vv. 4-8, while the explanation follows in vv. 9-15. The situation which occasioned Jesus' usage of parabolic teaching was the gathering of great multitudes of people to Him from the surrounding towns, a fact expressed in two appositional genitive absolutes ("a great multitude was coming" and "those from the cities were journeying to Him"). Presumably, the large crowd corresponds in some way to the large-scale rejection which the gospel would soon encounter (cf. vv. 9-14).

8:5   The parable begins with alliteration, "a sower sowed . . . seed," undoubtedly catching the attention of the audience. In order to appreciate the story, one has to understand first-century Palestinian farming techniques. Joachim Jeremias aids us with that by showing that sowing preceded plowing in Palestine at the time of Jesus (cf. *Jub.* 11:11; *m. Sabbat* 7:2; *b. Sabbat* 73b; *t. Berakot* 7:2). The farmer moved over an unplowed field, broadcasting the seed so that the seed fell on the footpaths, rocky soil, into the thornbushes, and onto good soil. All of it would then be plowed, awaiting rain and growth.[3] Some of the seed fell beside the road onto the footpaths, where the birds quickly devoured it.

8:6   Other seed fell on the rocky soil, a thin layer of dirt on rocks which prompted a quick spurt of growth but, because of the lack of depth to the soil and accompanying moisture, it dried up.

2. See Ferguson's discussion in *Backgrounds of Early Christianity,* 57-58.
3. Jeremias, *The Parables of Jesus,* 9-10.

8:7   The third part of the seed fell among the thorns which grew up with the seed and choked its life away.

8:8   Some of the seed, however, fell onto good ground and produced a hundredfold return. Jesus punctuated His analogy with emphasis by calling out to the audience, "He who has ears to hear, let him hear." The challenge served to cause the listening crowds to rivet their attention on the deeper significance of the parable.

8:9   Verses 9-15 contain Jesus' explanation of the parable to the disciples. Verses 9-10 reveal the true purpose behind Jesus' parabolic teaching, which was twofold: to reveal the kingdom of God to the disciples (vv. 9-10a), but to conceal it from nonbelievers (v. 10b). The first purpose is accentuated in vv. 9-10a, where the disciples, apparently in a more private setting and including more than the twelve apostles (cf. 8:1-3), inquired of Jesus about the meaning of the parable of the seed. The fact that they did not fully comprehend the parable's meaning suggests that their own knowledge of Jesus and the kingdom was incomplete. Only supernatural revelation would fully enlighten them. That implies that divine election was involved in both the disciples' reception and the crowd's rejection (v. 10) of the message of Christ.

8:10   The inclusion of the disciples on the secret of the mystery of the kingdom of God is stated explicitly by Jesus in v. 10a. The term "mystery" is based on the Old Testament idea of the secret plan of God and is translated from the Aramaic *raz* in Daniel 2:18-19, 27-30, 47. The latter word recurs in the Qumran scrolls for God's eternal, hidden plan now revealed to His faithful servants (*1QpHab* 7:8; *1QS* 3:23; *1QM* 3:9; 16:11), analogous to His revelatory work through Daniel. The mystery revealed to the disciples of Jesus is specified in vv. 11-15—the kingdom of God, though invisible and apparently ineffective, will ultimately prevail. The verb "to you has been given" is a theological passive indicating that the source of the information is God. The second purpose for Jesus' employment of parables is boldly stated in v. 10b—they conceal the truth of the kingdom from unbelievers. The election purpose of God is explicit—to the rest (unbelievers), parables cloud the message in order that (*hina* introduces a purpose clause) "seeing they will not see and hearing they will not hear." These words are taken from Isaiah 6:9-10, a pronouncement of divine judgment upon unbelieving Israel. The verbs in Luke 8:10 are probably the equivalent of the Hebrew infinitive absolutes used in Isaiah 6:9-10, "You can look and look and hear and hear, but to no avail."

8:11   Verses 11-15 record Jesus' explanation of the parable. Thanks to Adolf Jülicher, it was once popular among scholars to posit a clear-cut distinction between a parable and an allegory; the former was thought to teach only one point in contrast to the latter which makes a number of points.[4] Based on that supposed literary distinction, many New Testament scholars went on to say that the parables proper belonged to the actual words of Jesus whereas the allegorical interpretations of them were created by the early church and then placed back on the lips of Jesus.[5] A number of commentators today, however, demur from such a facile view, rightly claiming that Jesus added the interpretation Himself, an explanation fully in keeping with the intent of the parable proper.[6] According to v. 11, Jesus revealed the meaning of the parable to the disciples by identifying its central theme—the seed sown by the farmer is a metaphor for the Word of God and its ultimate progress.

8:12   The four types of soil, according to vv. 12-15, represent four types of "hearts" relative to the reception, or lack thereof, of the Word of God. First, the seed of the Word falling along the footpaths and eaten by the birds stands for the devil who quickly comes and snatches the gospel from the hearts of some, before it germinates in faith and produces salvation. In other words, these people did not believe the gospel, due to the destructive work of Satan.

8:13   Second, the seed that fell onto the rocky soil represents those who receive the gospel with initial enthusiasm but, because they have no root (i.e., no depth to their faith), they do not last when the time of "trial" (*perasmos*) comes. They fall away. The connection between faith and trials is obvious: the latter tests the former (cf. James 1:2-15). When trials are not responded to in faith, they become a temptation. Put another way, trials reveal whether or not a person has genuine faith.

8:14   Third, the seed choked by the weeds refers to those people who, having heard the gospel, are detracted from continuing in it by the anxieties, riches, and pleasures of this life.

8:15   Fourth, some of the seed did find a lodging place in a noble and good heart. These people are the ones who held fast to the Word and bore fruit with "perseverance" (*hypomonē*) in the face of adversity.

---

4. Jülicher, *Die Gleichnisreden Jesu I*, 203-322.
5. Jeremias's work in *The Parables of Jesus* is a typical example of this approach.
6. See the bibliography in the excellent work by Blomberg, *Interpreting the Parables,* an advocate of this view.

This last word is the key to resolving an age-old debate with regard to these verses (and in the New Testament)—is Jesus saying that Christians can lose their salvation if they do not continue in faith in the midst of the trials of life? There are two extreme answers to this question. One extreme is "easy-believism," the notion that a person's profession of faith, though it is without true commitment to the gospel, suffices for salvation. The other extreme is "lordship salvation," the idea that, if a person does not accept the total lordship of Christ over his or her life at the moment of conversion, that person is not saved. On this reading, receiving Jesus as Savior and not as Lord is a contradiction in terms. The answer to the problem, however, seems to lie between these polarized responses—genuine Christians will grow in their development of Christ's lordship over their lives. The operative word here is "perseverance" (*hypomonē*), from which we get the doctrine of the "perseverance of the saints." Such is the belief that true believers will persevere in their faith, despite failures along the way. On this reading, the three types of soil represent the nonbeliever who, though having entertained the thought of receiving Christ and the gospel, for one reason or another did not genuinely receive Him into his or her heart. The fourth soil stands for those who did and who consequently experienced a spiritual bumper crop (cf. v. 8). As Fitzmyer effectively argues, the probable underlying message of the parable of the seed is that, though it often meets with apparent failure, the word of the kingdom of God will ultimately prevail and enjoy a great spiritual harvest.[7] The very audience of Jesus illustrates this principle: while many of His hearers fell away from following Christ, the disciples, motley and (at times) disappointing group that they were, genuinely believed and later produced great fruit for the kingdom (cf. Acts 2).

In concluding our discussion of this passage, it might be helpful to compare this particular parable with Paul's remarks in Romans 9–11. In fact, there are intriguing similarities between the two that call for comment. The following connections can be identified: (a) Both passages are preoccupied with the outcome of the word of the gospel, especially its ultimate triumph despite rejection along the way (cf. Luke 8:12 with Rom. 9:6). (b) Both texts draw on Isaiah 6:9-10 to explain the large-scale Jewish rejection of Jesus Messiah (cf. Luke 8:9-10 with Rom. 11:8-10). Note also Acts 28:26-27, which is Luke's report of Paul's

7. Fitzmyer, *The Gospel According to Luke I–IX*, 712-13.

testimony before the Jews, one that also appealed to Isaiah 6:9-10. This last passage shows that there was a definite link between Luke and Paul on the matter of the Jews' rejection of their Messiah based on the statement by Isaiah. (c) The wording of Luke 8:12 about the Devil taking away "the word from their heart, so that they may not believe and be saved," except for the negative formulation, is remarkably similar to Rom. 10:9, "Believe in your heart . . . be saved." Both verses are concerned about a proper response to the word of the Lord from the heart in order to be saved. (d) Ellis correctly observes that both passages are concerned to show that there is a faithful remnant of Jews who do respond positively to Jesus Messiah (cf. Rom. 9:27; 11:1-5 with Luke 8:8, 15).[8] (e) In both texts, a divine mystery is revealed to true believers about the working of God in history through the word of His gospel (cf. Luke 8:10 with Rom. 11:25). (f) Both passages highlight the divine purpose of God through election of some for Himself and not others (cf. Luke 8:9-10 with Rom. 9:6-29; 11:28-32). However, missing in Luke 8:4-15 is Paul's assurance in Romans 11 that God has not finished with Israel. Or is it? The next parable suggests otherwise.

8:16 Verses 16-18 contain the parable of the lamp. At first glance, v. 16 seems to break the flow of thought of the context. Jesus made an obvious statement—no one lights a lamp in order to cover it with a vessel or to put it under a bed. The typical Palestinian oil lamp was circular, spouted, and partly covered. To put a pot over it would extinguish it; to put it under a bed would conceal its glow. Rather, one lights an oil lamp and puts it on a stand, visible to all who come into the house. The intent of the verse, therefore, as Marshall and Fitzmyer have noted, was to challenge Jesus' disciples and all believers to be a witness to the light of the gospel to those in spiritual darkness.[9] Those two authors go on to make the plausible suggestion that "those who come in" to see the light refers to those Jews who, though initially rejecting Jesus, later came to embrace Him.[10]

8:17 Verse 17 confirms the previous hypothesis. Jesus uttered two synonymous statements: that which is presently hidden will in the future be revealed, and that which is currently unknown will eventually come to light. Marshall catches the significance of the statements: "The context refers to the disciples making known publicly what Jesus

---

8. Ellis, *The Gospel of Luke,* 126-27.
9. Marshall, *Commentary on Luke,* 328; Fitzmyer, *The Gospel According to Luke I–IX,* 718.
10. Marshall, *Commentary on Luke,* 329; Fitzmyer, *The Gospel According to Luke I–IX,* 719.

has told them secretly . . . and the principle appears to be applied to the present secrecy and future manifestation of the message of the kingdom."[11] Thus, vv. 16-17 leave the door open for a future turning of the Jews to Jesus, even though they initially rejected Him. This is not unlike Paul's teaching in Romans 11:25-27 about the future restoration of Israel.

8:18   Verse 18 records Jesus' summary statement about the two parables He has just uttered, and His teaching in general. The audience should pay careful attention to *how* it hears the word of Christ; that is, it needs to take seriously the gospel and obey it. If it does, it will receive more truth; if it does not, the truth will be removed from it. The old adage puts it well, "Truth received brings more light; truth refused brings the night."

THE TRUE FAMILY OF JESUS, 8:19-21

8:19   While Jesus was teaching, His mother and brothers came to Him but could not get into the house because it was crowded (cf. v. 20). Two incidental details are generated by Luke's comment here. First, Joseph is not mentioned, presumably because he had died by now. Second, Mary had other children, called the "brothers" (*adelphoi*) of Jesus. Only with great difficulty can one avoid the conclusion that these were "blood brothers," not cousins of Jesus. Even the erudite Catholic scholar Fitzmyer concedes this point. He writes about the supposed perpetual virginity of Mary, "There is no indication in the New Testament itself about Mary as *aei parthenos,* 'ever virgin.' This belief in one form or another can only be traced to the second century A.D."[12]

8:20   It was reported to Jesus that His mother and brothers were outside, wanting to see Him. Conzelmann is surely in error in interpreting the words "outside" and "see you" to mean the members of the family of Jesus were outsiders to the kingdom of God and were desirous only to see Him perform miracles, respectively.[13] Rather, Luke's comment is straightforward, with no hidden meaning.

8:21   Jesus responded that His mother and brothers were those who heard and obeyed the Word of God (cf. 11:27-28). In saying this, the Lord was redefining, not necessarily rejecting, His family (*contra*

11. Marshall, *Commentary on Luke,* 330.
12. Fitzmyer, *The Gospel According to Luke I–IX,* 724.
13. Conzelmann, *The Theology of Luke,* 48.

Ellis).[14] Later, Jesus' family would come to faith in Him (Acts 1:14). The theme with which Luke 8 began, the followers of Jesus obeying His word (vv. 1-4), and further illustrated through parables (vv. 4-18), now concludes the section by identifying the requirement for entrance into the family of Jesus—genuine faith in the Word of the Lord. Being physically related to Christ, whether Jewish (vv. 4-18) or even one of His family members (vv. 19-21), was insufficient for salvation. One needed to be spiritually related to Him.

THE WORKS OF JESUS, 8:22-56

Luke's gospel moves from the topic of the words of Jesus to that of His works, with the latter giving credence to the former. It is one thing to make great statements, it is something else to back them up with action. Jesus' miraculous works (8:22-56) reinforced His words (8:1-21). More specifically, the miracles of Jesus which displayed the powerful presence of the kingdom of God guaranteed the ultimate triumph of the kingdom of God as predicted in the parables. The miracles included in chapter 8 are the calming of the storm (vv. 22-25), the cleansing of the Gerasene demoniac (vv. 26-39), the cure of the woman with a hemorrhage (vv. 40-48), the raising of Jairus's daughter (vv. 49-56). This miracle complex encompasses all three types of miracles recorded in the gospels: nature miracles (the calming of the storm); exorcism (the cleansing of the Gerasene demoniac); healing (the cure of the woman with a hemorrhage/the raising of Jairus's daughter).

THE CALMING OF THE STORM, 8:22-25

8:22 Though Luke's phrase "one of those days" only loosely connects the upcoming narrative chronologically with the foregoing section, there is a definite thematic association between the two—Jesus' parabolic words are about to be confirmed by His powerful works. On one of those days, Jesus entered a boat with His disciples and told them to sail across to the other side of Lake Galilee, which they began to do. No reason for the trip is explicitly offered in the account, but we will not be off the mark to understand this foray as a divinely planned event to display the power of Jesus which, in turn, will help buttress the disciples' faith.

14. Ellis, *The Gospel of Luke,* 129-30.

8:23   As they were sailing along, Jesus fell asleep, a matter-of-fact remark that bespeaks of His humanity. Suddenly a whirlwind descended upon the boat. Such disturbances quite often happen on Lake Galilee because it is surrounded by hills with gorges funneling into the water. Western winds, then, from the Mediterranean Sea sweep down these gorges, creating storms on the lake.[15] The abrupt squall began filling the boat with water to the point that the disciples' lives were in jeopardy.

8:24   The disciples awoke Jesus, calling Him "Master, Master," thereby expressing both their panic about the situation as well as their deference to His divine ability to deliver them. Immediately Jesus commanded the wind and the water to be silent, and a calmness returned to the lake. Here in vv. 23-24 we see a perfect blending of Jesus' humanity and deity. Because He was human, He was in need of sleep (v. 23), but because He was deity, like Yahweh of old, He demonstrated mastery over the seas (cf. v. 24 with Pss. 18:16; 29:3-4; 107:23-32).

8:25   Jesus then chidingly asked the disciples where their faith was, suggesting that their panic-stricken action was not becoming of mature trust in Him; though at least they did turn to the right person for help. The disciples, still quaking with fear from the shock of the moment, were awestruck at Jesus' mastery over the elements. They queried, "Who is this one whom wind and water obey?"

THE EXORCISM OF THE
GERASENE DEMONIAC, 8:26-39

8:26   They then came to shore in the land of the Gerasenes, opposite to Galilee. The mention of this place calls for two comments, one theological, the other textual. From a theological perspective, the disciples and Jesus were probably blown off course by the storm, but by divine design. Someone was in great need of a powerful work by Jesus—the Gerasene demoniac. Their paths were destined to cross. Furthermore, the fact that the land was Gentile anticipates Luke's concern to track the impact of the gospel on the Gentile world (see Acts).

From a text critical point of view, the manuscript evidence in Luke has three variant readings for the name of the land. Manuscripts p75 and B (Vaticanus), and so on read "Gerasenes." Gerasa (modern Jerash) is in the Transjordan area, about thirty miles southeast of the

---

15. Finegan, *The Archeology of the New Testament,* 47-48.

Sea of Galilee. The mention in v. 33 of the pigs running so far from Gerasa to the lake has caused some to discount this reading as the most original. Manuscript A (Alexandrinus) has "Gadarenes." Gadar (modern Umm Qeis) is also in the Transjordan area and is located about six miles southeast of the Sea of Galilee. Manuscript Sinaiticus reads "Gergesenes." Gergesa (modern Kersa) is near the lake's eastern shore. About a mile south of the town there is a steep bank leading into the water. It is difficult to reach a decision among these variant readings. The least likely reading is Gadarenes, because it is not as well attested as the other two. Gergesenes, while better explaining the pell-mell rush of the swine into the water, is not quite as well supported as the reading Gerasenes. The fact that the latter is the most difficult reading seems to tip the scales in its direction. On the other hand, one gets the impression from the story to follow that the town is close by the lake. Perhaps, however, v. 26 is only indicating that Jesus and His disciples entered the "region of the Gerasenes," not the town itself. This would account for their encountering the demoniac in the wilderness and near the shore. It is quite possible that this region was understood to extend to the very edge of Lake Galilee.

8:27   Upon reaching the shore, Jesus was met by a man who for some time had been possessed by demons. Three dire consequences attended the man's situation: he did not wear clothes; he did not live in a house; he lived in the tombs. The latter would have been especially despicable to a Jew, for contact with a dead body would have been considered ritually unclean (Num. 19:11, 14, 16; Ezek. 39:11-15). In the land of Israel, tombs were to be whitewashed so that passersby would be aware of their uncleanness (Matt. 23:27). These tombs probably were not.

8:28   Seeing Jesus, the demoniac fell down before Him. His loud voice resulted from the control of the demonic forces. The man, empowered by demons, addressed Jesus as the Son of the Most High God and asked what He wanted with him. He begged Jesus not to torment him. Two observations emerge in this dramatic scene. First, supernatural recognized the presence of supernatural; the demons knew Jesus' heavenly origin. Second, the man's request for Jesus not to torment him was tragically ironic, for in light of the harm the demons had perpetrated upon the man (see v. 29), it was they, not Jesus, who had tormented him.

8:29   Luke provides an explanation for the demoniac's request not to be tormented—Jesus had commanded the unclean spirits to leave the man. The influence of the demons over their victim was powerful and pathetic. Many times they seized him, which necessitated the villagers' restraining him with chains and fetters. But, empowered by the evil spirits, the man broke the chains and fetters and was driven into the desert. Who was tormenting whom?

8:30 Jesus asked the man what his name was and he responded "Legion," because many demons inhabited him. The Greek term *legiōn* is based on the Latin *legio,* a Roman regiment of six thousand soldiers. The demonic force within the man was incredible. No wonder he was demented. An interesting cat and mouse tactic seems to have attended this incident. The demons uttered Jesus' name (v. 28), probably thinking that by doing so they could exercise control over Him. Now, when requested by Jesus to give their names, the demons withheld them, providing their number instead, probably thinking that Jesus therefore would have no power over them.

8:31 The demons begged Jesus not to send them into the abyss, the final abode of Satan and his demons (Rev. 20:3). Even now, some of those spirits are incarcerated (see Jude 6; 2 Peter 2:4). In other words, they begged Jesus not to judge them before Judgment Day. It should also be noted that the word *abyss* is used in the Septuagint for the Hebrew term *tehom,* the name for the watery depth under the earth, according to Hebrew cosmology (see Gen. 1:2).

8:32 There was a large herd of pigs feeding nearby on the hill (Mark 5:13 says there were two thousand). The demons asked Jesus for permission to be sent into the swine. Pigs were considered ritually unclean by Jews because they did not "chew their cud" (Lev. 11:7; Deut. 14:8), even though they did meet the other requirement of clean animals—they had cloven hooves. The request, therefore, of the "unclean" spirits to enter the pigs, unclean animals, is understandable from a Jewish point of view. It may also be that the demons, not being permitted to continue to reside in the man, had to fill their restless desire to inhabit a living being somehow, even if by possessing pigs.

8:33 When Jesus expelled the demons from the man, they entered into the pigs which, with uncontrolled behavior, ran down the steep slope into the lake and drowned. The violent incident suggests a number of things. First, the destructive nature of the demons is highlighted. Be it man or beast, their residence within only brought harm and loss of life. Second, the destruction of the pigs confirmed that the demons had been cast out of the man. Third, powerful though they were, the demons were subject to Jesus Christ, the Lord of all. Fourth, if the abyss, the final abode of the Devil and his angels, is a symbol of the Old Testament notion of the watery depth under the earth, then the situation turns out to be a poignant illustration of irony. The demons begged Jesus not to torment them by sending them prematurely to the abyss and asked, instead, that they be sent into the swine, one presumes, because they wanted to remain in the body of a living being. Upon entering the pigs, however, the unexpected occurred; the pigs rushed to their destruction, and the demons' as well, in the water/abyss.

8:34 Verses 34-39 record the townspeople's response to Jesus' miracle. The herdsmen of the swine saw the event and, undoubtedly frightened, ran back to the town to tell the people.

8:35 The people came out to see what had happened; they were in for a surprise. The demoniac they once knew was sitting quietly at the feet of Jesus, instead of roaming in the tombs; he was clothed, not naked; mentally sound and serene, no longer deranged and driven. This man who formerly was controlled by the demonic spirits was now a disciple of Jesus.

8:36 The townspeople became afraid, hearing the testimony of the herdsmen who were eyewitnesses of the demoniac's healing. The word Luke uses for the man's recovery, "saved" (*esōthe*, from *sōsō*), is one of his favorite words to describe the holistic salvation that Jesus and the gospel brought to its recipients.

8:37 Rather than thank Jesus for healing one of their own, the people from the Gerasene countryside focused on their fear, begging Jesus to depart from them. The source of their fear was probably mixed: the numinous power of the exorcism and the possibility of a future display of "destructive" miracles affecting their possessions and livestock, if Jesus stayed. Jesus complied with their request and entered the boat and departed. Like His own people, the Jews, the Gentiles rejected the Christ (cf. Luke 4:25-30).

8:38 In stark contrast to the general populace's reaction to Jesus was that of the delivered demoniac, who begged Jesus to let him stay with Him. But Jesus sent the man off, as the next verse indicates, to evangelize his community.

8:39 Jesus told the man to go back to his home and tell the people what God had done for him. The man did what Jesus said and more; he went throughout the whole town preaching what Jesus had done. Two comments are in order here. First, Jesus' ministry is identified as the work of God, thus accentuating Jesus' deity. He is on par with

God. Second, one finds in the healed man's response a model for Christian witness—we should spread the good news of what God has done for us in Christ to all around us, so that they, too, can encounter Him.

THE RESUSCITATION OF JAIRUS'S DAUGHTER
AND THE CURE OF THE WOMAN WITH A HEMORRHAGE, 8:40-56

The next section contains two miracles by Jesus widely recognized by interpreters to be arranged in a "sandwich," or framing, construction. Such a technique begins one story, in this case the request to heal Jairus's daughter, interrupts it at a crucial point with another story, in this case the healing of the woman with a hemorrhage, and then returns to the conclusion of the original story, the resuscitation of Jairus's daughter. The hermeneutical value of this literary device is that the outer story (Jairus's daughter) framing the inner story (the woman with a hemorrhage) throws light on the meaning of the latter. We will develop the theme in the exegesis that follows that the fact that Jairus's daughter who died, therefore becoming ritually unclean, was raised by Jesus and made clean, duplicates the experience of the woman with the hemorrhage who, though ritually unclean, was made clean by Jesus. The similarities between the two episodes are best explained by this shared pattern of a female being transformed from the status of unclean to clean, thanks to Jesus. We begin with a chart that identifies those similarities.

Similarities Between

Jairus's Daughter	The Woman with a Hemorrhage
v. 41—Jairus fell at the feet of Jesus	v. 47—The woman fell before Jesus
v. 42—Daughter	v. 48—Daughter
v. 42—Twelve year old	v. 43—Twelve years of illness
v. 50—Believe and she will be made well	v. 48—Faith made you well
vv. 54-55—Jesus' touch raises Jairus's daughter; she was clean	vv. 44-47—Touching Jesus made the woman well; she was clean
v. 55—She was healed immediately	v. 47—She was healed immediately

8:40   When Jesus returned to the west side of the lake of Galilee the crowds welcomed Him, for they had been awaiting His return. Their reception of Jesus was in contrast to the Gerasenes' rejection of Him and probably proceeded from their desire for Him to perform miracles on their behalf.

8:41   Luke begins this episode with a typical Septuagint description, "and behold." The story then relates how Jairus approached Jesus for help. The name Jairus is the Greek form of the Hebrew name *Yair* (Num. 32:41; Deut. 3:14; Josh. 13:30) and probably means, "he will enlighten." Fitzmyer makes the observation that the leader of the Jews against Rome at Masada was called *Elazar ben Yair* (see Josephus's account, *J. W.* 2:447).[16] Jairus was a leader of the synagogue, whose job it was to arrange for the worship services. Jairus, too, had joined the crowd awaiting Jesus' return, and when He came the synagogue ruler fell at His feet, pleading with Jesus to come to his house. The depth of Jairus's need prompted him to cast aside the dignified demeanor that was typical of such a respected religious office.

8:42   The reason for Jairus's coming to Jesus is now given. His only daughter, a twelve-year-old child, was dying. The commentators rightly note how Luke has brought forward the detail that the girl was twelve years old from Mark 5:42 in order to set the stage for the next story about the woman who had been sick with a hemorrhage for twelve years (v. 43). We suggest that another reason was also at work. Luke places the two numerical references exactly side by side in order to emphasize the fact that the little girl was ritually clean whereas the sick woman was not. It is easy to overlook the significance of the description of Jairus's daughter; she was his "only daughter, who was twelve years old." These words are more than intimate terms of endearment. They point to the fact that the little girl (compare Mark's diminutive *thugatrion,* "little" daughter, as well as Jesus' reference to the girl as a "child," Luke 8:54) was not yet a woman. As such, she had not yet experienced the menstrual cycle and therefore had not yet fallen under the category of ritual uncleanness; see Leviticus 15:19-24. This, as we will see in v. 43, was not so for the woman with a hemorrhage who had been continuously ceremonially unclean for twelve years. If we are accurate in this suggestion, then the reason the story of Jairus's daughter encases the account of the woman with a hemorrhage is to illustrate how the latter will experience a change of status from un-

16. Fitzmyer, *The Gospel According to Luke I–IX,* 745.

cleanness to cleanness, like the little girl. After stating the girl's age, Luke then interrupts the narrative of Jairus's daughter with the story of the woman with a hemorrhage. He introduces it by noting that crowds of people pressed in on Jesus as He made His way to the synagogue ruler's house. This sets the stage for what follows.

8:43 Among the crowd was a woman who had a flow of blood, a hemorrhage, for twelve years. Dr. Luke observes that no one had been able to heal her (he omits the Marcan phrase criticizing physicians [Mark 5:26]). Some manuscripts add the phrase "though she had spent all her livelihood" no one had been able to heal her (Sinaiticus, A). Others, however, omit it (p75, B), making a firm conclusion on its originality untenable. The commentators rightly recognize that the condition of the woman most probably stemmed from a uterine hemorrhage, which perfectly explains her desire to touch Jesus in a crowd, a situation that would not call attention to her ritual uncleanness. Leviticus 15:25-31 makes clear that a woman with this condition was to be separated from Israel because of ceremonial uncleanness.

8:44 The afflicted woman, under the covering of the crowd, slipped up behind Jesus and touched the fringe of His garment. The word "fringe" is the Greek word *kraspedon,* the Septuagint term for the tassel which male Jews were to wear on the corners of their outer garments (see Num. 15:38-39; Deut. 22:12). The woman undoubtedly thought that if she touched only the edge of Jesus' garment, along with the diversion of the pressing crowds, no one would know that she, an unclean person, had touched Christ. The moment she touched Jesus she was healed; the hemorrhage ceased.

8:45 Instantly, Jesus surprisingly asked who it was that touched Him. While the people denied having done so, Peter pointed out to the master the obvious—it was unavoidable that the crowding and pressing multitude would have brushed up against Him and therefore no individual could be singled out.

8:46 Jesus replied that someone indeed did touch Him, because He recognized that power had been released from His body. Two aspects of Jesus' deity are thereby highlighted: His supernatural knowledge (He knew that one woman in the midst of a huge crowd had touched Him) and His divine power (the woman's touching of Jesus' garment brought miraculous healing).

8:47 The woman realized that she was not going to escape unnoticed; Jesus knew that it was she who had touched Him. Therefore she came trembling before Jesus and fell down at His feet. She then confessed in the presence of all what had happened; she had touched Jesus' garment hoping to be healed, and it was so. Our theory that the woman was ritually unclean explains her fear and embarrassment. The source of her consternation was probably twofold: she was socially humiliated by having her uncleanness manifested to all, and she was fearful that Jesus would be angry with her because her touching Him may have rendered Him unclean too. No doubt she expected Jesus to now rebuke her for her action.

8:48   Instead, Jesus pronounced a blessing upon her, "Daughter, your faith has saved you; go in peace." Like the Old Testament priest who declared the unclean person clean and then sent the individual away with God's blessing (cf. Lev. 15:30), Jesus cleansed the woman, sending her on her way with a new status, wholeness. The very name, "Daughter," signified that she had now reentered fellowship with Israel and was no longer a marginal member of society. This was possible because the woman had exercised faith in Jesus. Accepting the outcast and mainstreaming them into the people of God was a theme Luke was fond of, and the evangelist was quick to recognize its presence in this episode—hence his placing of it at this particular point. The resumption of the story of Jairus's daughter in the next verse confirms this interpretation.

8:49   Even while Jesus told the woman to depart in peace, a messenger from Jairus's house brought the sad news that the synagogue leader's daughter had died. There was no need to trouble Jesus with the matter any longer. If we have been on the right track in our interpretation thus far, then there is an added nuance to the report of the girl's death—her body was now ritually unclean according to the Mosaic Law (Num. 19:11, 14, 16). This consideration will factor into the interpretation of the rest of the story.

8:50   Upon hearing the tragic news, Jesus consoled Jairus by telling him not to be afraid but to have faith and his daughter would be saved. These very words had been previously uttered by Jesus to the woman with a hemorrhage with miraculous results, and they were directly relevant to Jairus's situation.

8:51   When Jesus came to Jairus's house, He would not permit anyone to go in with Him except the inner circle of His disciples (Peter, John, James) and the girl's parents. Probably two reasons explain the exclusion of any of the others. First, as v. 53 makes clear, the mourners did not have faith in Jesus' power; therefore, they would not be granted the privilege of seeing Him raise the girl from the dead. Second, in keeping with our theory, the house, because of the presence therein of a dead body, was now ritually unclean, and all who entered would be ceremonially contaminated.

8:52   The others excluded from the house no doubt included relatives, friends, and official mourners, all of whom were deeply grieving over the girl's death. To this group Jesus said, "Do not cry, for she is not dead, but asleep." The word "sleep" was used by Jesus as a euphemism for death, intimating that the girl was about to be awakened unto life.

8:53   The crowd responded to Jesus' statement with scornful laughter, for they knew the girl was dead, not sleeping. They obviously missed the point.

8:54   At that, Jesus took hold of the girl's hand and spoke to her, "Child, get up." Jesus' compassion for the girl manifested itself in the very fact that He touched her, and in His willingness to have contact with a dead body, which was ritually unclean.

8:55   Jesus' touch restored the girl immediately even as it did the woman with the hemorrhage (v. 47). In both cases, Jesus' power dismissed their uncleanness. The girl's life returned to her; she stood up, and Jesus ordered that food be given to her. The last piece of information served two functions. It proved the girl was alive; she could eat. And it foreshadowed the means Jesus would utilize to prove the reality of His own resurrection (see Luke 24:36-43).

8:56   The parents were beside themselves with amazement and joy, but Jesus commanded them not to divulge the event to anyone. The injunction was undoubtedly designed to prevent the incident from exciting the crowds.

HOMILETICAL SUGGESTIONS

Luke 8 can be effectively dealt with in two sermons: "The Parables of the Kingdom of God (8:1-21)," and "The Miracles of the Kingdom of God (8:22-56)." The first sermon breaks down into three points: the recipients of the kingdom, vv. 1-3 (a paragraph that relates especially to women who follow Jesus); the revelation of the kingdom, vv. 4-18 (the two parables reveal the mystery of the growth of God's kingdom—it started small but, despite obstacles, will one day have a great impact upon this world); the requirement of the kingdom, vv. 19-21 (obedience to the will of God proves one to be a member of the family of Christ). The second sermon, "The Miracles of the

Kingdom," could be treated as illustrative of how Jesus makes us whole, proceeding from a right relationship with Him. Each of the mighty deeds recorded in 8:22-56 could be applied to an area of human need. Thus the calming of the storm (vv. 22-25) can be seen to depict our *emotional* healing, the replacement of fear with faith (v. 25). The exorcism of the Gerasene demoniac can illustrate Jesus' power to heal us *mentally* (v. 35). The cure for the woman with a hemorrhage (vv. 42b-48) speaks to our need for *social* restoration. Just as the woman was delivered from the ostracism that accompanied continuous ceremonial uncleanness and integrated into society, so can we. Finally, the raising of Jairus's daughter (vv. 40-42a, 49-56) assures believers that Jesus has the power to ultimately deliver them *physically*, by the resurrection of the body at the end of history.

LUKE
CHAPTER
NINE

THE CONCLUSION TO THE GALILEAN MINISTRY

The bulk of the material in Luke 9 is devoted to concluding the Galilean ministry, vv. 1-50. The following episodes are recorded: the mission of the twelve disciples, 9:1-9; the feeding of the five thousand, 9:10-17; Peter's confession, 9:18-20; the first passion prediction and explanation, 9:21-27; the Transfiguration, 9:28-36; the cure of the boy possessed with a demon, 9:37-43a; the second passion prediction and illustration, 9:43b-48; the outsider exorcist, 9:49-50. The journey to Jerusalem, the central section of Luke's gospel, begins at 9:51 and ends at 19:44. Luke 9:51-62 contains two episodes: the Samaritan reaction to Jesus (9:51-56) and challenges to would-be followers of Jesus (9:57-62).

THE CONCLUSION OF THE GALILEAN MINISTRY, 9:1-50

This section witnesses a major shift in the ministry of Jesus Messiah. His purpose for coming to earth is expressed—it is not to set up an earthly kingdom in Jerusalem but rather to go there to suffer and die on the cross. The crowds, as the plot thickens, show themselves to be inept at grasping this truth, the disciples included.

THE MISSION OF THE TWELVE DISCIPLES, 9:1-9
9:1 Jesus began to multiply His ministry by sending His twelve apostles/disciples on a missionary foray into the region of Galilee. He gave them power and authority over demons and to heal diseases.

9:2   Alluding to a play on words, Luke mentions that Jesus "sent" (*apostellō*) the "apostles" to preach the kingdom of God and to heal illnesses; the latter (power to heal) was proof of the spiritual presence of the kingdom of God.

9:3   Verses 3-5 provide Jesus' "rules of the road" for His traveling missionaries. Verse 3 lists items excluded on the journey: walking stick, bag for storing small objects, bread, money, two tunics (outer garments), bringing along only one. Two remarks need to be made about these prohibitions. First, they are historically accurate, a point confirmed by other testimonies at the time. For example, Josephus writes something similar about the Essenes of his time, "They enter the houses of men whom they have never seen before as though they were their most intimate friends. Consequently they carry nothing whatever with them on their journeys except arms as a protection against brigands." (*J.W.* 2.124-25, as quoted in Ellis, *The Gospel of Luke,* 137) One could also compare in this regard the rabbinic prohibitions concerning those Jews traveling to the temple. They were not to take staff, sandals, or money (*m. Berakot* 9:5). Second, the reason for traveling light was to teach the disciples to trust in God's provision, not their own ingenuity.

9:4   Two types of responses to the disciples are envisioned by vv. 4-5. One is a positive reception. To those who welcomed the disciples, the apostles were to remain in their houses, using them as the home base for their ministry in that particular town. One sees from this the necessity of hospitality for the spread of the gospel in the early church. There were no hotels as such, only brothels. Hence the spread of the gospel was dependent on open homes and hearts.

9:5   The other response to the mission of the Twelve was rejection. For those towns that rejected the disciples' message, they were to shake the dust off of their feet as they departed from the village. The practice informing this action was the custom of the Jews' shaking the dust off their feet when leaving a Gentile town so as not to return to Israel and defile it with uncleanness (Strack-B 1:571). For Christians to do so to Jews was tantamount to accusing them of not being truly Jewish, but pagan and hostile to God (cf. Acts 13:50-51).

9:6   Having been commissioned by Jesus, the disciples preached the good news of the kingdom and healed everywhere they went.

9:7   The account of Herod Antipas's response to Jesus' and His disciples' activity in vv. 7-9 amounts to an interlude in the narrative of the mission of the Twelve. It seems to serve a couple of purposes. First, Herod raised a question about Jesus that will preoccupy the majority of Luke 9, "Who is this man?" (v. 9; cf. v. 18). Second, Herod's fixation on Jesus anticipated his later hostility and rejection of Him (see 13:31 and 23:6-12, respectively). The report about Jesus reached Herod and piqued his curiosity. More than that, the crowd's attempts to identify Jesus especially confused the tetrarch, whose territory encompassed Galilee, the main center of Jesus' ministry. Perhaps Herod was concerned about the possibility of the people switching their allegiance from him to Jesus. One is reminded of John 6:15 where, after Jesus miraculously fed the multitudes, the crowds tried to install Him as their king (cf. Luke 9:12-17). The crowds themselves were confused about the identification of Jesus. Three of their explanations were relayed to Herod. First, some said that Jesus was John the Baptist raised from the dead. Herod, of course, was responsible for the Baptizer's death (cf. 7:18-24; Mark 6:14-32).

9:8 Second, others said Jesus was the manifestation of Elijah (cf. 7:24-27). Third, still others equated Jesus with an Old Testament prophet who had come back to life. No name is given, but perhaps it was Moses (cf. Deut. 18:18).

9:9 Herod discounted the first possibility because he himself had had John killed earlier. He obviously ruled out the possibility of John's resurrection. So if it was not John, who then was Jesus? Herod deeply desired to see Jesus and find out for himself who He was.

THE FEEDING OF THE 5,000, 9:10-17

9:10 Luke provides the conclusion of the mission of the twelve disciples in v. 10. A simple synopsis is given—the apostles told Jesus what they had done. Having received their report, Jesus withdrew with His disciples to a more private place, Bethsaida. Some manuscripts read "into a place into the desert" (for example, the Curetonian Syriac Version), probably in order to harmonize an apparent contradiction between Luke 9:10 and the other synoptic gospels (Matt. 14:13; Mark 6:31). However, the best reading in Luke is Bethsaida (Sinaiticus, B, p75). But there is no real contradiction inherent in the Lucan reading, for the evangelist undoubtedly names Bethsaida as the nearest well-known town to the private spot to which Jesus retired. The town itself is located on the north side of the Sea of Galilee. It was built by the tetrarch Philip, one of the sons of Herod the Great, who ruled over the Transjordan area in which Bethsaida was located. It may be that Jesus picked that spot so that He would not be under the watchful eye of Herod Antipas.

9:11   However, when the crowd of people learned of where Jesus was, they followed Him. Jesus welcomed them and performed the same twofold ministry He had earlier commissioned His disciples to do—He preached the kingdom of God and cured all who had need of healing.

9:12   As the day reached its end, the disciples approached Jesus and asked Him to send the people away so that they could find lodging and food in the surrounding areas. The place they were in was too desolate for such.

9:13   Jesus' reply startled the disciples, "You feed them!" The disciples replied that they were unable to do so because they only had five loaves of bread (probably barley) and two fish. John 6:9 supplements the account by noting that the disciples had collected the meager amount from a young lad. As far as the disciples were concerned, the only way they could feed the crowd was to go to all the surrounding towns and buy food. The dialogue between Jesus and His disciples is reminiscent of 2 Kings 4:42-44, where a man came to Elisha the prophet, bringing twenty loaves of barley and some ears of grain. The man told the prophet to use the food to feed the men who accompanied Elisha. Elisha's attendant, however, protested that the small amount would not be sufficient to feed so large a group. Nevertheless, the Lord multiplied the food through Elisha to the point that, after all ate, there was some left over. The possible allusion to this Old Testament story in Luke's version may serve to portray Jesus as a type of Elisha.

9:14   The number of men alone in the group, not counting women and children, was about five thousand. Jesus then ordered the disciples to divide the crowd up into groups of fifty. Some have seen here an allusion to Exodus 18:21, where Moses divided up Israel into groups of thousands, hundreds, fifties, and tens (cf. *1QS* 2:21; *1QSa* 1:14-15). But the correspondence is not exact enough to establish the connection.[1]

9:15   The disciples obeyed Jesus' command, no doubt without full knowledge of why they were doing it.

9:16   Five actions of Jesus are recounted by Luke which describe the miracle of the multiplication of the loaves of bread and fish. It is difficult to miss the allusion to the institution of the Lord's Supper as recorded in Luke 22:19 regarding four of those actions. As such, the meeting of the physical hunger of the five thousand foreshadowed the filling of the need of spiritual hunger symbolized in the

1. *Contra* Ellis, *The Gospel of Luke,* 138.

Lord's Supper.[2] First, Jesus "took" (*labōn*) the loaves and fish in His hands (cf. Luke 22:19, "Jesus took [*labōn*] the bread"). Second, Jesus lifted His eyes toward heaven, an obvious sign of His attitude of prayer and dependence on God. Third, Jesus "blessed" (*eulogēsen*) them, the bread and fish (cf. Luke 22:19, Jesus "blessed [*eucharistēsas*]" the bread). Perhaps intermingled with Jesus' blessing of the food was a prayer of grace uttered by Jews before meals, "Blessed be you, O Lord our God, King of the world, who causes bread to come forth from the earth" (*t. Berakot* 6:1). Fourth, Jesus "broke" (*kateklasen*) the bread and fish into pieces (cf. Luke 22:19, Jesus "broke [*eklasen*]" the bread). Fifth, Jesus "kept giving" (*edidou*, imperfect tense) the food to the disciples (cf. Luke 22:19, Jesus "gave [*edōken*] the bread to His disciples), who kept passing the food to the crowds. The last action almost certainly captures the miracle—Jesus kept producing the bread and fish in His hands by the supernatural power of God.

9:17 Luke emphasizes the fact that all the people ate and were filled. So much was the abundance that twelve baskets full of leftovers were collected. Undoubtedly each of the twelve disciples collected a basketful.

PETER'S CONFESSION, 9:18-20

9:18 Verses 18-20 record Peter's confession that Jesus was the Christ. Luke, who has been following Mark's narrative, now omits Mark 6:45–8:26, in effect fast-forwarding to Mark 8:27-30, the story of Peter's confession. The result of this "Big Omission," as scholars call it, is that Luke presents Peter's confession against the backdrop of the feeding of the five thousand, and especially in close contact with 9:9 and Herod's query about Jesus' identification. In fact, the answers provided in v. 19 repeat those reported to Herod in v. 9. The difference is that whereas Herod was left perplexed about the identity of Jesus, Peter was not; Jesus was the Christ.

Luke omits the reference to the location of Peter's confession; it was in Caesarea Philippi (see Mark 8:27, modern-day Banyas, which is northeast of Lake Galilee). The site was just about as far as one could go before leaving Israel proper, and Galilee in particular. Perhaps Jesus chose this location for the revelation of His messiahship because it was far enough away from the Jewish religious leadership in Jerusalem, thus preventing any confusion associated with the name of Messiah from

2. See Fitzmyer's discussion on this point in *The Gospel According to Luke I–IX*, 767-68.

reaching their ears. In any event, Jesus was alone there with the disciples, praying. Prayer is a favorite motif of Luke and his reference to Jesus praying prepares the way for the divine revelation that is about to be given to Peter (cf. Matt. 16:17). Jesus opened the discussion by inquiring of the disciples with whom the crowds were equating Him.

9:19 The crowds' answers match those reported to Herod (vv. 7-8): John the Baptist, Elijah, the prophet of old to arise (cf. Deut. 18:18, Moses?).

9:20 Jesus personalized the question for the disciples, "Who do you say that I am?" thereby pressing them for a decision, as well as exposing the inadequacy of the crowds' reaction. Peter acted as spokesman for the Twelve, answering that Jesus was the "Christ of God" (cf. 2:26; 23:35; Acts 3:18; 4:26). Peter's confession identified Jesus as the long-awaited Messiah, the divinely anointed deliverer of Israel.

THE FIRST PASSION
PREDICTION AND EXPLANATION, 9:21-27

9:21 Jesus censured Peter and the disciples from telling others that He was the Messiah, most probably to prevent the people from equating Him with a political deliverer.

9:22 Verse 22 contains the first of three passion predictions by Jesus; the other two are in 9:44 and 18:31. Before analyzing the prediction itself, we need to briefly address two matters relative to Jesus' self-designation in the passion statements, the Son of Man: the topical arrangement of the title and the historical criticism of the title. We draw here on the excellent study of George Ladd.[3] Regarding the topical arrangement, the Son of Man title falls into three distinct categories in the synoptic gospels: (1) the earthly Son of Man (authority to forgive, Matt. 9:6/Mark 2:10/Luke 5:24; Lord of the Sabbath, Matt. 12:8/ Mark 2:27/Luke 6:5); (2) the suffering Son of Man (Mark 8:31/Matt. 9:22; Mark 9:12/Matt. 17:12); (3) the apocalyptic Son of Man (He will come in glory, Matt. 16:27/Mark 8:38/Luke 9:26).

The other consideration regards whether or not the Son of Man statements go back to the historical Jesus. Many scholars of an earlier generation argued that the Son of Man statements are examples of *vaticinia ex eventu* (pronouncement after the event). They claimed that the early church created the sayings and put them into the mouth of Jesus. Their basis for saying so was the criterion of dissimilarity, a

---

3. Ladd, *A Theology of the New Testament*, 145-58.

principle that assumed that anything Jesus said or did that was parallel to what Judaism or the early church did or said, rendered it inauthentic.[4] One gets the distinct impression that, on this reading, next to nothing from the recorded life of Christ stands a chance of being genuine in the hands of the critic!

In any case, Ladd turns the principle against its users concerning the authenticity of the Son of Man statements. He registers three facts about the appellative: (1) in the gospel tradition the Son of Man was Jesus' favorite self-designation (sixty-five times); (2) the title is never used by anyone else to designate Jesus; (3) there is no evidence in Acts or the epistles that the early church called Jesus the Son of Man.[5] Ladd's conclusion from this data is devastating for the historical critic:

> We maintain that the one solid critical position is the fact that in all our New Testament sources, Jesus and Jesus alone used the term Son of Man to designate himself. Form critics emphasize the criterion of dissimilarity; i.e., only those sayings can be surely reckoned authentic which have no parallel either in Judaism or in the early church. If this principle is applied to the Son of Man saying, the idea that the Son of Man would appear on earth in humiliation to suffer and die has no parallel in Judaism or in the early church. The church often spoke of the sufferings of the Christ or of Jesus Christ, but never of the Son of Man. The fact that the Son of Man appears only in Jesus' own words, "seems to prove conclusively that the title Son of Man must have been truly and incontestably Jesus' own designation of himself." This is bedrock, although the majority of critics, including Bornkamm, fail to recognize the force of it. If Jesus did speak of himself as the Son of Man in his earthly activity, then the only compelling argument against the authenticity of the eschatological sayings is their alleged incompatibility with the earthly sayings. Furthermore, it fits the criterion of dissimilarity to apply the idea of an eschatological Son of Man to one already on earth in humiliation. There is, therefore, good critical reason for an open-minded inductive approach to accept all three classes of sayings as authentic.[6]

Toward the end of the Galilean ministry, it became clear to Jesus that His role as the Messiah was to go to Jerusalem and suffer and die at the hands of the religious establishment (delineated along the lines

---

4. This criterion is exploited by Perrin in *Rediscovering the Teaching of Jesus*, 39-43.

5. Ladd, *A Theology of the New Testament*, 146.

6. Ibid., 153.

of the three groups of the Sanhedrin: elders, chief priests, scribes). The notion of a suffering Messiah would have taken the disciples, and Israel, by surprise because there is no clear-cut evidence that pre-Christian Judaism expected anything other than a political deliverer.[7] The only significant personage understood by Jews at the time of Christ to suffer was the servant of the Isaiah prophecies (Isa. 53), but Israel applied that passage to itself, not the Messiah.[8] However, Jesus attempted to correct His audience's misconceptions by showing that He was the fulfillment of the prophecy of Isaiah 53 (see Mark 10:45; 14:24; Luke 22:37; Acts 3:13; 8:32-33). He was the Suffering Servant, Messiah.[9] As such, He must (*dei*) fulfill the divine plan (cf. 2:49; 4:43; 13:33; 17:25). But the reward for His passion will be the resurrection on the third day.

9:23   Verses 23-27 broaden the scope of the suffering of the Messiah to include His followers as well, setting forth the demands of discipleship in four radical statements. However, the conditions are but differing facets of the same reality—self-denial for Christ's sake. First, the person who wishes to follow after Jesus must deny himself and take up his cross daily and follow Him. The audience envisioned for this challenge is the crowd of people (cf. 9:17) and anyone who is a would-be disciple. That person is to follow after Jesus, which entails denying himself and taking up the cross daily, in imitation of Christ. The obvious referent of "taking up the cross" is crucifixion, a hideous form of capital punishment practiced by Persians, Greeks, and Romans. That Jesus' reference should be taken metaphorically and not necessarily to literal martyrdom, is made clear by the word "daily." Obviously one cannot be killed on a daily basis. The summons, then, is for the disciple of Christ to emulate the self-denying activity of his Lord.

9:24   The self-denial theme extends to the second condition, which is expressed chiastically: whoever saves his life will lose it, but whoever loses his life will save it. The seriousness of this challenge is evidenced in the words employed: "save" (*sōsai*); "soul/life" (*psyche*); "lose, destroy" (*apolesei*). The principle being stated by Jesus was a paradoxical one—to live for oneself in this age is to lose out on the

---

7. For the documentation on this point see, for example, Ladd, *I Believe in the Resurrection of Jesus*, 60-73.
8. See Klausner's discussion in *The Messianic Idea in Israel*, 163.
9. See Ladd's treatment of Jesus' usage of these various titles in *I Believe in the Resurrection of Jesus*, 62-72.

salvation of the age to come. But the one who denies himself by following Christ, though he or she may appear to give up plans, possessions, and even existence for the cause of Christ in this world will, in fact, gain the bliss of the afterlife. Furthermore, such a person will actually live a more meaningful life here and now. Jim Elliot, martyred missionary by the Auca Indians, once encapsulated this truth well, "He is no fool who loses what he cannot keep to keep what he cannot lose."

9:25 The third admonition is put in the form of a rhetorical question, "What profit is it to gain the whole world but to lose one's soul?" The contrast is between the brevity of this world and the eternality of the human soul. To strive after the goods of this world to the neglect of the values of eternity is no profit; it is only a tragic loss (cf. Luke 12:13-34 and Ps. 49). In other words, to follow the way of the world, instead of the footsteps of Jesus, is to invite the judgment of God.

9:26 The fourth radical statement of discipleship touches the motivational level of living. The real issue is, Will a person be ashamed, or not ashamed, to follow Christ? The person in this life who is scandalized and embarrassed by the suffering associated with Christ's first coming will not share in the glory of His second coming (cf. Rom. 1:16; 2 Tim. 2:12). The positive side is expressed in Luke 12:8. The motif of the coming of the Son of Man in glory with the Father and the holy angels has its origin in Daniel 7:13-14, and is applied to the *Parousia* of Jesus, the Son of Man. The response that is called for in all four of these calls to commitment is one of faith, for faith does not focus on that which can be seen (the embarrassment and rejection attached to the crucifixion of Christ) but on that which cannot be seen (eternal glory). True faith is willing to lay one's life down daily in service to Christ.

9:27 In contrast to those who might be ashamed of Jesus in this life were those who would not experience death before they saw the kingdom of God, presumably because they were not ashamed of Jesus but publicly followed Him. The claim is emphatic; they would "in no way see death" (*ou mē geusōntai thanatou* [emphatic negative statement]) before they would see the kingdom of God. Basically three views have been taken toward this promise of Jesus to His disciples. First, some understand the promise to refer exclusively to the future, particularly the Parousia of Christ; compare v. 26. In other words, some of the disciples would not experience death before the return of Christ to earth to establish His kingdom.[10] The obvious problem with this viewpoint is that such a statement would be historically inaccurate, because the disciples have since died and the Parousia has not yet come. Second, others believe the promise referred almost exclusively to the present day of Jesus, particularly the upcoming Transfiguration episode, vv. 28-36. Thus, some disciples (Peter, James, and John) did not experience death before they saw the kingdom of God —the Transfiguration of Jesus.[11] This view is closer to the truth, but it does not do justice to the preceding context of v. 27 which specifically refers to the second coming of Christ in glory, v. 26. Third, others perceive that the eschatological tension between the present and the future best explains the text.[12] That is, the Transfiguration episode immediately to follow in Luke's narrative is proof that the kingdom of God has entered into human history through Jesus Christ. It is indeed present, but only to the eye of faith, like that of the disciples. However, the Transfiguration is not the ultimate expression of the kingdom of God; the Parousia will be. Taking these two perspectives together—the kingdom of God is spiritually present but is not fulfilled—we see then that the Transfiguration served as a proleptic experience of the Parousia.

THE TRANSFIGURATION, 9:28-36

Before analyzing the Transfiguration[13] verse by verse, it would be helpful to take notice of Evans's insightful overview of the underlying Lucan motif.[14] Evans rightfully recognizes that we must begin with the most original account, Mark 9:2-8, and then proceed from there to Luke 9:28-36. Concerning the Marcan passage, according to Evans we find therein a typological connection with Exodus 24 and 33-34, passages which describe Moses' ascent up the mount where he meets God and then descends with a shining face. The following specific parallels between Mark's account (9:2-8) and Exodus are evident: the reference to "six days" (Mark 9:2; Ex. 24:16); the cloud that covers the mountain

---

10. See, for example, E. Lohmeyer, "Die Verklärung Jesu nach dem Markus-Evangelium," *ZNW* 21 (1922), 185-215.

11. Walvoord, for example, approaches this perspective in *Matthew: Thy Kingdom Come*, 126-27.

12. See Ladd, *A Theology of the New Testament*, 209.

13. For the view that the Transfiguration is a misplaced resurrection narrative, see the critique of Robert H. Stein, "Is the Transfiguration (Mark 9:2-8) a Misplaced Resurrection-Account?" *JBL* 95 (1976), 79-96.

14. Evans, *Luke*, 150-51.

(Mark 9:7; Ex. 24:16); God's voice from the cloud (Mark 9:7; Ex. 24:16); three companions (Mark 9:2; Ex. 24:1, 9); a transformed appearance (Mark 9:3; Ex. 34:30); the reaction of fear (Mark 9:6; Ex. 34:30); and in Exodus 24:13, Joshua is singled out and taken up the mountain with Moses. Since "Joshua" in the Greek Old Testament is "Jesus," the early church may have seen in Exodus 24:13 a veiled prophecy, or typology, that came to fulfillment in the Transfiguration, where once again Moses and Jesus are together.

From the Marcan account, Evans proceeds to observe several noteworthy modifications in Luke's version of the Transfiguration, modifications which only enhance and strengthen the connection between the Transfiguration and Moses. (1) In v. 30 Luke reverses the order of the names of the two heavenly visitors by mentioning the name of Moses first. This reversal is likely designed to place more emphasis upon the Law-giver. (2) That Luke intends such emphasis is confirmed when he notes in v. 31 that the two visitors speak with Jesus of "His departure." The word "departure" translates the Greek word *exodos,* the very word that gives the Book of Exodus its name. (3) Only Luke mentions Jesus' "glory" seen by His disciples (v. 32). Luke may very well intend this to recall Moses' request to see God's glory (Ex. 33:18-23). Also, in Exodus 24:16 we read that the "glory of the Lord rested on the mount." This glory not only looks back to the glory manifested upon the mount in Exodus, but also anticipates the glory into which the Messiah will enter at His resurrection (see Luke 24:26). (4) Luke notes in v. 29 that Jesus' face was changed, which may recall more specifically the change in Moses' face (Ex. 34:30, 35). (5) Luke introduces the episode by saying "about eight days after" (v. 28), instead of Mark's "six days later" (9:2). There is seemingly only one plausible explanation for this alteration. The rules for observing the Feast of Booths are laid down in Leviticus 23:33-44c. According to Leviticus 23:36 there are to be offerings for seven days and then on the eighth day there is to be "a holy convocation" or gathering. During this time the people are to dwell in booths (tents or tabernacles, Lev. 23:42), the purpose of which is to remind the people of the Exodus long ago (Lev. 23:43). (6) Finally, Luke has slightly modified the wording of the heavenly voice in v. 35. Instead of Mark's "My beloved Son" (9:7), Luke has "My chosen Son." This modification is likely meant to recall the chosen servant of Isaiah 42:1.

Evans concludes from this that Luke has taken the raw materials that he found in the Marcan version of the Transfiguration and has enriched the parallels in such a way as to enhance the presentation of Jesus as God's Son (and Servant) whose authority and significance greatly surpass those of Moses and Elijah. Luke shows his readers that the two greatest Old Testament figures appeared in order to discuss with Jesus His own impending "exodus." Moses, who may represent the Law, and Elijah, who may represent the prophets, bear witness to Jesus' identity and to His destiny awaiting Him at Jerusalem. Even the heavenly voice is probably meant to allude to both major parts of the Old Testament. The first part of the voice's declaration, "This is my Son whom I have chosen," echoes Isaiah 42:1 and so represents the prophets. The second part, "listen to him," is a phrase taken from Deuteronomy 18:15 (where Moses commands the people to listen to the great prophet that God would some day raise up) and so would represent the Law. This idea of the "Law and the Prophets" bearing witness to Jesus is seen explicitly in Luke 24:27 and 24:44. Moses and Elijah bear witness to Jesus and then fade away from the scene, leaving Jesus "alone," because of the era of the "Law and the Prophets" is over (Luke 16:16a). Now it is the era of the "good news of the kingdom of God" (Luke 16:16b). Just as God's glory appeared on Mount Sinai, so now God's Son, in all of His glory, has appeared on the mount (cf. John 1:14-18). Whereas only the face of Moses shone, Jesus' entire personage is transfigured. Finally, because the disciples wish to build "three shelters" (i.e., "tents" or "booths") for Jesus and the two visitors, Luke has likely seen the connection with the Feast of Booths, a festival in commemoration of the Exodus. Hence, Luke begins his episode on the eighth day, the day on which a "holy convocation" was to take place (Lev. 23:36, 42). Undoubtedly, in the evangelist's mind there could be no holier convocation than the meeting of Moses, Elijah, and Jesus; God's Law-giver, Prophet, and Son.

9:28 We leave Evans's comments and move to examine the details of vv. 28-36, the major theme of which is that Jesus' suffering will lead to glory (cf. vv. 21-26). Three disciples, Peter, James, and John, were made privy to that last theme, however momentary it may have been. The opening phrase, "and it came to pass after these words about eight days," locates the timing of the heavenly vision; it situates the scene during the Feast of Tabernacles (cf. Lev. 23:36 with Luke 9:33). Peter, James, and John, having emerged as the inner circle of Jesus' disciples, accompanied Him up a mountain for the purpose of prayer. Although Luke does not name the mountain, ever since Origen some have identified it as Mt. Tabor, which is west of the Sea of Galilee.

Others, however, equate it with Mt. Hermon, north of Caesarea Philippi, the place of Peter's confession.

9:29   While Jesus was praying, His face changed and His clothing became brilliantly white. The Marcan term well describes what happened to Jesus—He underwent a *metamorphosis*. That is, His inward supernatural glory transformed His outward natural body into brilliant light. It may be that Luke omits the word because his Greek audience might have confused Jesus' transformation with Greco-Roman myths of humans undergoing a metamorphosis and becoming divine (cf. *Apel. Met.* 11.23; *Corp. Herm.* 13.3). For Luke, however, Jesus' Transfiguration is more akin to the Old Testament, particularly at two points. It reminds one of the historical event of Moses' encounter with Yahweh and the resulting change of complexion it produced (Ex. 34:30). It also recalls Judaism's eschatological hope of the future resurrection of the righteous, which will entail being clothed with a glorious body (Dan. 12:3; *1 Enoch* 38:4; 104:2; *4 Ezra* 8:88; 1 Cor. 15:44-55; Rev. 2:7; 20:11).[15]

9:30   The preceding proposed Old Testament background is confirmed by the appearance of Moses and Elijah. Three comments can be derived concerning the presence of these two men on the mountain with Jesus. First, the two men's presence make a canonical statement. That is, Moses and Elijah summarize the Law and the prophets, respectively, and thus represent the Old Testament's witness to Jesus as the Christ (cf. Luke 24:27a, 44). Second, both Moses' and Elijah's departures from this earth were mystical in nature, shrouded in the supernatural. Therefore, their appearance with Jesus would not have been a surprise. Third, based on the previous connotation, these two men of God became eschatological figures. Moses was understood to be the prototype of the prophet God would raise up in the last days (Deut. 18:18), and Elijah was associated with the forerunner of the Messiah (3:1-2; 4:5-6; cf. Rev. 11:1-10).

9:31   Luke observes that Moses and Elijah appeared in glory, indicating their heavenly origin. Glory in the Bible refers to God's brilliant presence which evokes the awe of humans (Ex. 23:17; 40:34). The quality itself encompasses the story of the whole Bible, progressing somewhat along the following trajectory: God, in His essence, is glorious (Ps. 8:4; Isa. 6:3). He manifested that glory to Israel in the wilderness via the pillar of fire by night and the cloud by day (Ex. 13:21). Moses

15. See Behm, "*Metamorphoō*," 4:755-59.

participated in that glory on the mount (Ex. 34:29-35); and the tabernacle, too, was enveloped with it (Ex. 40:34-38). During Solomon's reign, God's glory filled the newly constructed temple (2 Chron. 7:1-3), only to leave it during Ezekiel's day, because of the nation's idolatry (Ezek. 10). The next time we read of the divine glory in the Bible, it is with reference to Jesus, the tabernacle of God (John 1:14). Though that glory was veiled in His flesh during His time on earth, at the resurrection Jesus' body exuded the divine glory, Philippians 3:20-21. Christians, too, possess God's glory in their hearts (2 Cor. 3:18), which at the return of Christ will transform their bodies (Phil. 3:20-21).

Juxtaposed to the topic of glory is the subject of Jesus' suffering, depicted in the word "departure" (*exodon*). The term, in large part, portrayed Jesus' suffering and death as the means to His receiving divine glory. The appointed place for Jesus to meet that destiny would be Jerusalem. There He would die and be raised to glory.

9:32 In the meantime, Peter, James, and John had been weighed down with sleep, probably because it was late at night (9:37). Unfortunately, they would find themselves "sleeping on the job" on another significant occasion (see Luke 22:45). The disciples awoke from their slumber and saw Jesus in His glory, as well as Moses and Elijah.

9:33 The construction "while departing," *en tō diachōrizestha*, expresses contemporaneous action (*en tō* with an infinitive). Thus, it was while Moses and Elijah were beginning to depart from Jesus that Peter spoke up. In other words, the two heavenly guests' exit prompted Peter's subsequent remarks. Peter impetuously tried to prevent the heavenly scene from coming to an end. He said to Jesus that it was good that the three disciples were present, for each one could build a tent for each of the heavenly beings: Jesus, Moses, and Elijah. The term for tent is *skēnas,* which was probably a reference to the Hebrew word *sukkah,* the word used for the temporary tents or booths built to house the Israelites during the seven-day Feast of Tabernacles (Deut. 16:13; cf. Ex. 23:16; 34:22). The feast commemorated Israel's wanderings in the wilderness after the Egyptian Exodus, and it anticipated the nation's entrance into the Promised Land. By the time of Jesus, it had become a pilgrimage feast. The editorial comment that Peter did not know what he was saying undoubtedly refers to the apostle's misplaced desire to capture the moment of glory and prolong the experience. It may even be that Peter believed that the heavenly scene anticipated Jesus' soon arrival in Jerusalem when He would be enthroned in glory and Israel's enemies would be defeated. Thus, Peter's error was to assume that Jesus could enter His kingly glory, along with the disciples, without having to first suffer.

9:34   While Peter uttered these things, a cloud came and enveloped them. The cloud surely represented the glorious presence of God, even as it did in the Old Testament (Ex. 16:10; 19:9; 24:15-18; 40:34) and will at the return of Christ (Mark 13:26; 14:62; Rev. 1:7; 14:14-16). It also accompanied Jesus at His ascension (Acts 1:9). It is difficult to know the antecedent of "them" (*autous*). At the very least, the heavenly cloud covered Jesus, Moses, and Elijah. Two considerations suggest that the three disciples were enveloped as well. First, being caught up into the cloud would explain the ensuing fear that gripped the disciples. Second, the phrase "while they entered," *en tō eiselthein* (again, *en tō* with an infinitive indicates contemporaneous action), suggests that the moment of fear came while the *disciples* were entering into the clouds for, according to v. 33, the disciples were not afraid earlier when Moses and Elijah were being withdrawn. The point of fear came when they literally got caught up in the scene. The fact that the divine voice came out of the cloud, according to v. 35, does not rule out this interpretation because one can imagine that the disciples, along with the three heavenly beings, were surrounded by the cloud, from which the voice came.

9:35   The voice of God came from the cloud, reminiscent of Jesus' baptism (3:22), except that here the voice was directed more to the onlookers (the disciples), than to Jesus. Three things were said about Jesus, each of which identified Him with an Old Testament title indicative of His intimate relationship with God. First, the divine voice called Jesus "My Son," a reference to Psalm 2:7. The title as applied to Jesus communicated His heavenly origin and deity. Second, God announced that Jesus was His "chosen one," an allusion to the Suffering Servant of Isaiah 42:1. G. Schrenk rightly recognizes that this appellation signified the path Jesus must take in order to achieve heavenly glory; He had to go the way of the cross. Schrenk writes, "He is the elect, not merely in or in spite of His passion, but in His appointment thereto."[16] Luke's later references to Jesus as the servant who suffered in order that He might attain heavenly glory confirm the interpretation of the title "servant" here in v. 35: Acts 3:13, 26; 4:27, 30. Third, the heavenly voice commanded the disciples to "hear Him," with reference to Jesus. The words echo Deuteronomy 18:15 and its charge to Israel to listen to

---

16. Schrenk, "*Eklektos*," 4:144-92; 189.

the prophet-like Moses that God would raise up in the latter times. The divine command for the disciples to listen to Jesus accomplished two tasks: it challenged them to recognize that Jesus, as the Son and Servant, was greater than Moses and Elijah, and it reinforced Jesus' earlier words to the disciples to take up their crosses and follow Him (vv. 22-26).

9:36   While the voice spoke, Jesus alone was left, the significance of which must be that Moses, representing the Law, and Elijah, representing the prophets, gave way to Jesus Christ. The disciples, understandably overwhelmed by the event, said nothing of it to anyone during the days that followed. Later, however, after the resurrection of Jesus, Peter broke his silence and declared the Transfiguration to all who would hear, in 2 Peter 1:17-19.

THE CURE OF THE BOY
POSSESSED WITH A DEMON, 9:37-43a

9:37   Luke's reference to the next day suggests that the Transfiguration occurred at night. As Jesus, Peter, James, and John descended from the mountain, a large crowd of people met them, presumably accompanied by the remaining disciples (v. 40).

9:38   Suddenly, a man began shouting at Jesus, calling Him teacher and begging Him to look upon his needy son. The word "look upon" is *epiblephai,* the same word used in the Magnificat of God's mercy on the afflicted (1:48). Moreover, the son was the father's only child, thus making the situation all the more touching.

9:39   The father then described the pitiful condition of the boy. A demonic spirit would seize him, and the child would scream. The boy would then go into convulsions, foaming at the mouth. The demon would leave only after a great struggle, inflicting bad bruises on the boy before it left. The description fits an epileptic seizure, in this case brought on by a demonic force.

9:40   The father had begged the remaining disciples to exorcise the demon, but they were not able to do so. One is reminded of Gehazi, Elisha's apprentice, who was unable to resurrect the Shunammite's son, a feat that only Elisha could perform (2 Kings 4:18-37).

9:41   Jesus' first reaction was one of rebuke. He called the audience, including both the disciples and the father, a faithless and crooked generation, a statement hearkening back to unbelieving Israel in the wilderness (Deut. 32:5). Jesus further vented His frustration with the people by expressing the wish not to be with them any longer.

Such an emotional response from Jesus was probably due to a couple of factors. First, He was in the presence of the demonic, which He hated. Second, the people's lack of faith in the power of God to heal, especially on the part of the disciples and the father's confidence in the disciples, contributed to Jesus' anger. Had the disciples not just successfully completed a healing and exorcising mission (Luke 9:1)? Jesus' second reaction was to command the father to bring Him the boy.

9:42 Even as the father brought the child to Jesus, the demon initiated an epileptic fit. It threw the boy to the ground and threw him into a convulsion. At that, Jesus rebuked the unclean spirit, casting it out and thereby healing the boy. He then compassionately gave the child back to his father. According to Mark 9:24, Jesus performed the exorcism in response to the father's faith, small as it might have been.

9:43a Witnessing the miracle, the crowd was astonished at the majestic power of God, not unlike the three disciples at the Transfiguration.

THE SECOND PASSION PREDICTION, 9:43b-48

9:43b The crowd's reaction to Jesus' miracle was one of wonder, but probably not yet based on genuine faith in Jesus the suffering Messiah. Thus Jesus clarified the picture again for His disciples.

9:44 Verse 44 contains Jesus' second passion prediction in which He once more stated that He, the Son of Man, would be handed over to men, the Jewish rulers in Jerusalem, for the purpose of dying. His prophecy was in stark contrast to the expectation of the throngs of people.

9:45 But the incomprehension of Jesus' purpose was not restricted to the crowds; the disciples also unfortunately were party to the same error. In fact, Luke notes that the disciples' misunderstanding of Jesus' suffering ministry was part of the divine plan—"its meaning was hidden from them so that they could not comprehend it." Consequently, they were afraid to ask Him what His statement meant. Here one seems to be in the presence of the motif earlier identified in Luke with regard to Zechariah and John the Baptist—Israel's partial spiritual blindness leading to full restoration. This time it is the disciples who embody this theme. We suggest that some five connections exist between the disciples' misunderstanding of Jesus and Romans 10–11. First, both the disciples and Israel are characterized as an obstinate people. Luke 9:41 includes the disciples along with the nation of Israel as an unbelieving and crooked generation. Romans 10:21 labels disobedient Israel something very similar: Israel "is a disobedient and obstinate people." Second, neither the disciples nor Israel comprehended the purpose of God in Christ. Luke 9:45 asserts that the truth of Jesus' suffering Messiahship was concealed from the disciples whereas Romans 11:7, 25 claims that Israel is spiritually callous toward God in Christ, not understanding His purpose. In fact, the very word Luke uses of the disciples' incomprehension (*kalyptō*) in v. 45 is the same word used in a passage related to Romans 10–11, namely, 2 Corinthians 3:14. That passage speaks of Israel's incomprehension of Jesus.

Third, both the disciples' and Israel's incomprehension of Jesus was by divine design. The *hina* clause in Luke 9:45 makes clear that the disciples' unbelief was a part of God's plan. Romans 11:8, in its quotation of Isaiah 6:10, does the same thing in that it places Israel under God's judgment. Thus in both cases the divine judgment motif is operative. Fourth, it is interesting that the term "mystery" is applied to both the disciples and Israel. Luke 8:10 relates that Jesus granted to the disciples the mystery of the kingdom of God, which ironically seems to backfire in Luke 9:41, 45 with the disciples' unbelief. In Romans 11:25, Paul declares that Israel's partial spiritual hardening toward God is a mystery revealed to him. Fifth, and this completes the previous point, both the disciples and Israel, though at present partially blind to the purpose of God, will one day be restored to full spiritual sight. Romans 11:26-27 asserts that in the future Israel will embrace her Messiah and be saved. If we jump ahead in Luke's gospel to Luke 18:35-43, the same thing occurs with regard to the disciples. There Jesus restores the sight of a blind man which, according to many recent scholars, is a real miracle that also serves as a parable of the disciples' future coming to sight concerning Jesus' true identity.[17] If these five points have validity, then the theory that the disciples, in their development from partial to full comprehension of Jesus, represent the future restoration of Israel, is reinforced.

9:46 That the disciples did not fully understand Jesus' suffering mission is illustrated by their argument over which of them was the greatest. The disciples' rivalry stemmed from their mistaken assumption that Jesus was headed to Jerusalem to be enthroned as the glorious Messiah of Israel. Naturally, they wanted in on the ground floor. Consequently, a dispute arose among them as to which of them would be the highest ranking officials in the kingdom of God.

---

17. For its Marcan context, see Guelich, *Mark 1:1–8:26,* 428-36.

9:47   It is important to note that Jesus did not dismiss the disciples outright; He took the time to attempt to correct their misunderstanding. This action, as recent commentators remark, serves to show that there was hope for the disciples. Jesus' teaching would eventually sink in, after the resurrection (Luke 24:25-35). We might add that, if the aforementioned theory has merit, then the hope for the disciples' mirror images the hope for a restored Israel one day. In the present setting, Jesus, knowing what the disciples were thinking, used a child as an object lesson of true greatness. Jesus proceeded to take a child and place him by His side. In doing so, Jesus was using the smallest, weakest member of human society as an example of what it means to have great stature in the kingdom of God.

9:48   The principle being established by Jesus was that in the kingdom of God there is a reversal of values involved. The last will be first; the least will be the greatest. Such a reversal in thinking calls for humility, repentance, and faith, requirements for entrance into God's kingdom. Jesus illustrated this truth by setting forth a child as the hallmark of greatness. Whoever receives a child, receives Jesus. Whoever receives Jesus, receives God. The concept underlying these statements is the Jewish institution of *Shaliah* (see the Greek counterpart which is used, *apostellō*, v. 48), a practice by which a man's representative is like the man himself (*m. Berakot* 5:5). In other words, to receive the "lowliest" member of society is to receive Jesus, which is simultaneously to receive God.

THE OUTSIDER EXORCIST, 9:49-50

9:49   The following two verses extend the previous lesson of receiving the least valued in society to include the disciples' need to accept an outsider into their circle of ministry. The link word between vv. 46-48 and vv. 49-50 is the "name" of Jesus. John spoke up that they (the disciples) had seen a man exorcising demons in the name of Jesus, but that they tried to stop him because he was not one of their group. What John probably had in mind was the fact that the exorcist was not commissioned to serve Christ like the disciples had been for their recent mission (9:1-11).

9:50   Jesus responded to John in proverbial fashion, "Do not stop him, for whoever is not against you is for you." The point of the maxim was to forbid a spirit of exclusivity among the disciples. Jesus, however, took a more inclusive view of those who wished to serve Him; He welcomed outsiders. The saying has an interesting parallel in one of Cicero's speeches addressed to Caesar, *Pro Quinto Ligario* 33 (46 B.C.), "Though we held all to be your opponents but those on our side, you counted all as your adherents who were not against you." Some have thought Luke 9:50 contradicts Luke 11:23, "Anyone who is not with Me is against Me." However, the contradiction is only apparent. Luke 9:50 speaks against a spirit of *exclusivity* among *believers* whereas Luke 11:23 speaks against a spirit of *neutrality* among *nonbelievers* when it comes to their decision to follow Jesus (cf. Luke 9:57-62).

THE BEGINNING OF THE
JOURNEY TO JERUSALEM, 9:51-62

9:51 Verse 51 records the beginning of Jesus' journey to the city of His destiny, Jerusalem. As such, it marks the opening of the central section of Luke's gospel, which runs from 9:51 to 19:44. The "travelogue" motif recurs throughout the entire narrative (9:51-57; 10:1, 38; 11:53; 13:22, 33; 17:11; 18:31, 35; 19:1). However, Luke's concern in this unit is more on the teachings of Jesus about the nature of His messiahship and discipleship than it is with the geographical locale along the way. Thus, the ultimate location is Jerusalem, which imprints the narrative with its theme of suffering. Luke begins the section by relating Jesus' upcoming journey to Jerusalem to the divine plan. Two words convey the idea that Christ is in sync with God's plan. First, the days were being "fulfilled" (*symplērousthai*) for Jesus to go to Jerusalem, a term suggesting the completion of the divine purpose. Second, in arriving at Jerusalem, Jesus would experience His "ascension" (*analēmpseōs*). The word, at the very least, refers to Jesus' death in Jerusalem. But two factors militate against restricting the word to that sense only: (a) the Elijah motif in 9:52-56 (calling down fire on the non-respondent Samaritans, 2 Kings 1:10, 12) reminds one also of Elijah's assumption to heaven, 2 Kings 2:1-14; and (b) a near relative term of *analempseōs, analambanō* (taken up) refers to Jesus' ascension into heaven after His death, in Acts 1:2, 11, 22. Thus, Jesus' ascension in Jerusalem refers to the totality of God's plan for Him there; He will die, be raised, and then ascend to the Father. For His part, Jesus resolutely and obediently set His face toward Jerusalem to fulfill His destiny.

9:52 As Jesus began the trip, He sent ahead messengers to prepare the way. They came to a Samaritan village and desired to make lodging arrangements for Jesus and His apparently large band of disciples. This is the first mention of the Samaritans in Luke's gospel, but here, and elsewhere (10:30-37; 17:11-19; Acts 1:8; 8:1-13, 14, 25; 9:31; 15:3), it fits in with His theme that the gospel is universal in scope. The origin of the Samaritan people seems to have been the intermarrying of Jews from the Northern Kingdom with imported non-Jewish colonists after the conquest of 722 B.C. (2 Kings 17:24). These mixed Jews-Gentiles developed their own translation of the Pentateuch (Samaritan Pentateuch), built their own temple of worship on Mt. Gerizim (see John 4:20), which was later destroyed by John Hyrcanus (128 B.C.), and celebrated their own Passover (a practice which continues to this very day in modern-day Nablus [ancient Shechem] on Mt. Gerizim).

9:53   However, the Samaritans would not welcome the disciples, and indirectly Jesus, because they were headed to Jerusalem. Two observations are in order here. First, the Samaritan rejection of Jews passing through their country to go to Jerusalem reflects the historical tension between the two races at the time of Jesus. Because of that, Galilean Jews often bypassed Samaria by crossing the Jordan River and traveling to Jerusalem by way of Perea (cf. Josephus, *Ant.* 20.118). Second, Luke records this event because it was Jesus' first experience of opposition on His way to Jerusalem. It thus has great theological value in that it foreshadows His coming conflict in the Holy City. It also reminds one of the incident at Nazareth when, having just announced the inauguration of His ministry as the Servant of the Lord, Jesus was rejected by His hometown (4:14-30).

9:54   Upon hearing the unwelcome response, James and John asked if the Lord wanted them to call down fire from heaven and destroy the Samaritans, like Elijah of old (2 Kings 1:10, 12). No wonder they were elsewhere called "the sons of thunder" (*Boanērges,* Mark 3:17)!

9:55   Jesus turned to James and John and rebuked them. In doing so, He disassociated Himself from the image of Elijah, the fiery reformer. Rather, Jesus was practicing what He preached (6:29) by not engaging in retaliatory action to those who spurned Him, like the Suffering Servant of Isaiah (53:7; cf. 1 Peter 2:23).

9:56   Jesus quietly moved on to another village.

9:57   Verses 57-62 highlight three encounters with Jesus illustrating His stringent demands for discipleship. The opening phrase reminds the reader that Jesus was on the "way" (*hodōs*) to Jerusalem. The term "way" later became a synonym for early Christianity (Acts 9:2; 19:9, 23; 24:22). It was similar in some respects to the Qumran community's usage of the term for a devoted follower of God.[18] Along the way, someone told Jesus that he wanted to follow Him wherever He would go.

9:58 Jesus' reply to the man underscored the radical lifestyle that must characterize one of His disciples. Like Jesus the Son of Man, His followers will experience homelessness and rejection. Even animals like foxes with their holes and birds with their nests have more security. One must therefore count the cost before deciding to follow Jesus.

9:59 A second encounter ensued when Jesus challenged a man to follow Him. The man asked Jesus to first let him go and bury his father, a sacred duty of the Jews (Strack-B 1:487-89).

9:60 Jesus' response was twofold. First, the man should let the dead bury the dead. Undoubtedly, what Jesus meant was that the spiritually dead (the ones who had not followed Christ but stayed behind) should bury the physically dead. Tragically, both groups had something in common. Jesus' command challenged the very fabric of society—He would tolerate no rival priority from His disciples, not even one's own family (cf. Luke 14:26). Second, let the would-be disciple follow Jesus by proclaiming the kingdom of God.

9:61 A third episode occurred when another man stated that his intention was to follow Jesus, but first he had to say good-bye to the people at his home, a customary courtesy that even a prophet-to-be practiced (cf. 1 Kings 19–21).

9:62 Jesus responded to the man using agricultural imagery; no one who plows a furrow will look back, because it would obviously produce crooked rows. Rather, a person must look forward. So it is with the kingdom of God. One must not turn back from following Jesus, but resolutely move ahead (cf. Phil. 3:13-14).

HOMILETICAL SUGGESTIONS

An apt title for a series of sermons devoted to Luke 9 would be, "I Have Decided to Follow Jesus." The major points could basically follow the sections delineated in the exposition espoused in this chapter, over a series of two or three messages (pardon the alliteration!).

18. See the study by McCasland in "The Way," 222-30.

I. 9:1-11: Engage in Christ's Power

II. 9:10-17: Expect Christ's Provision

III. 9:18-36: Evaluate Christ's Passion (First Suffering, Then Glory)
   A. Vv. 18-27: The Confession of Christ
   B. Vv. 28-36: The Transfiguration of Christ

IV. 9:37-62: Emulate Christ's Principles
   A. Vv. 37-45: Faith
   B. Vv. 46-48: Humility
   C. Vv. 49-50: Openness
   D. Vv. 51-56: Mercy
   E. Vv. 57-62: Commitment

LUKE
CHAPTER
TEN

THE KINGDOM OF GOD HAS COME

Most of Luke 10 is not paralleled in the other gospels. Its very uniqueness reveals a major concern of the third evangelist—the kingdom of God has appeared in word and deed. The episodes in this chapter contribute in one way or another to that theme. The mission trip of the seventy (-two) disciples (vv. 1-24) served the purpose of announcing that the kingdom of God had indeed come, one of the proofs of which was the defeat of Satan and his denizens by the word of Christ through the apostles. In the parable of the Good Samaritan (vv. 25-37), Jesus emphasized that the kingdom of God consists of loving one's neighbor, one of the two great deeds performed by citizens of the kingdom of God. The other is to love the Lord with all one's heart. Finally, in the contrast between Mary and Martha (vv. 38-42), we see that a significant expression of serving in the kingdom of God consists of listening to the word of Christ. We pursue these matters below.

THE MISSION OF THE SEVENTY (-TWO) DISCIPLES, 10:1-24

Jesus' dispatching of a larger band of disciples for mission work in Luke 10:1-24, in addition to the earlier one detailed with regard to only the twelve disciples in 9:1-11, is unique to Luke.[1] For Luke, such a missionary endeavor was filled with eschatological meaning. Ellis pinpoints this perspective well. Concerning Luke 10:1-24, he writes:

> The setting of the mission is the messianic salvation, i.e., the eschatological consummation, already in process. The "harvest" even now is being gathered (2), time is pressing (4), and rejections final and damning (11, 13-16). The messianic peace is bestowed (5), and the powers of the coming age are manifest in driving back the powers of death and the devil (9, 17f.). Not only in the work of Jesus himself ... but also in the works of his disciples the kingdom of God is being actualized.
>
> The lordship of Satan and of death yields to the in-breaking powers of the new age. Yet, as King Belshazzar's guests continued to feast unaware that his kingdom had fallen and his doom had been sealed, so the present age is unaware that Satan's reign is broken. It sees only a writing on the wall, and it cannot read what it sees. For Luke the mission of the Seventy is the continuing task of the Church. As Jesus' empowered representatives Christians have a twofold task. First, they are to make the kingdom present in healing, in exorcism, in the bestowal of the messianic peace. As it was in the days of the pre-resurrection mission, this presence is sporadic, partial, veiled. It is a writing on the wall occurring only as the Spirit actualizes it. It is only a token, a minute foretaste of the universal revelation of the kingdom at the glorious *parousia* of Jesus. Thus, secondly, Christians, like the Seventy, must explain the writing on the wall. The present manifestation of the powers of the new age proclaims that Jesus is Lord (17) and that the public revelation of the kingdom of God is impending (12). Cf. Jn 5.25, 28f.[2]

We will treat this pericope under three headings: the regulations for the disciples on the mission (vv. 1-16); the report of the disciples as a result of the mission (vv. 17-20); the revelation to the disciples in light of the mission (vv. 21-24).

---

1. There are two broad theories concerning the relationship between Luke 10:1-24 and 9:1-11. The first is that 10:1-24 is a doublet of 9:1-11 created by Luke for the purpose of showing that witnessing about Jesus was a task not restricted to the twelve apostles but open to all disciples; see Fitzmyer, *The Gospel According to Luke X–XXIV*, 844. The second theory differs from the first in that it argues that Luke 10:1-24 was an actual historical mission in the life of Jesus that, indeed, served the purpose of expanding the task of ministry beyond the twelve apostles; see Marshall, *Commentary on Luke*, 412-14. We side with the latter viewpoint.

2. Ellis, *The Gospel of Luke*, 153.

THE REGULATIONS FOR THE
DISCIPLES ON THE MISSION, 10:1-16

10:1   Some time after the events of chapter 9, Jesus appointed seventy (-two) other disciples (different from the twelve apostles) to do
His work. Because the manuscript evidence is so evenly divided in its
testimony between the numbers seventy (Sinaiticus, A, C) and seventy-
two (p75, B, D), it is virtually impossible to determine the most accurate reading. Hence, we leave the number inconclusive—seventy
(-two). In any case, the commentators rightly perceive that the intent
of the number of disciples commissioned was to recall the table of
nations in Genesis 10:2-3, which, by the way, is identified as seventy by
the MT and seventy-two by the Septuagint. Jesus' purpose, therefore,
in choosing seventy (-two) disciples will have been to symbolize the
upcoming evangelization of the Gentiles and Diaspora Jews, a task to
be continued later by the church. The group of disciples were sent
out two by two on their mission, most probably because two witnesses were required to establish a testimony (Num. 35:30; Deut. 19:15).
The "buddy system" no doubt also provided moral support along the
way. These disciples were to go ahead of Jesus, preparing the villages
and towns for His arrival.

10:2   Before they embarked, the disciples received guidelines for
their journey. First, Jesus exhorted them to pray that the Lord of the
harvest would raise up laborers, because the harvest was great and the
workers were few. Ellis accurately calls attention to the eschatological
connotation of the metaphor of harvest in the Bible (Isa. 27:11-12;
Matt. 13:39; John 4:36-38; Rev. 14:15). In effect, what Jesus was saying
was that the end of the age had begun in His ministry and in His
envoys' message.[3] God was bringing into the kingdom of God the
souls of people. The abundance of the harvest and the urgency of the
moment called for God to stir up others, along with the disciples, to
labor in the divine vineyard.

10:3   There was also a sense of danger which would accompany the
disciples' mission. Like sheep, they were being sent into the midst of
wolves. In this they symbolized the destiny of their master. A later
rabbinical tradition approximates Jesus' statement here about sending
His disciples into harm's way. Emperor Hadrian (ca. A.D. 135) is reported to have said to Rabbi Yehoshua (ca. A.D. 90) that Israel was the
sheep in the midst of seventy wolves, the Gentile nations. Rabbi Yeho-

---

3. See again ibid., 153.

shua replied, "Great is the Shepherd who delivers it [Israel] and watches over it and destroys them [the wolves] before them [Israel]."[4] The disciples, too, could expect similar protection from their Great Shepherd.

10:4 The prohibitions of verse 4 indicate that the disciples' mission was to be conducted with a sense of dependency and urgency. Regarding the former, because the disciples were not permitted to take a purse with money, a knapsack with provisions of food, or more than one pair of sandals (cf. 9:3), they would necessarily be dependent on God for their needs (cf. 22:35). Regarding the latter, because Oriental greetings were time-consuming, the disciples were to avoid customary chitchat because of the sense of urgency of their mission (cf. 2 Kings 4:2a). This, too, had eschatological implications—the ordinary customs of their world were secondary compared to the importance of the arrival of the kingdom of God (cf. 9).

10:5 In contrast to nonchalant greetings on the way, when the disciples entered into a house they were to utter a special greeting of peace on its inhabitants. Such a word was not the mere formality that occurred when a guest came into a home but, rather, an announcement of salvific blessing upon those who received Christ's messengers, and by extension, Christ Himself. It was, in effect, the conveyance of messianic peace.

10:6 If a peaceful person dwelled there (that is, if the person received the message of Christ's peace and salvation), then the messianic blessing will rest upon that house. If not, then the offer of salvation will be withdrawn and, with it, peace.

10:7 Jesus further instructed His disciples that they were to eat and drink that which their hosts provided them. Furthermore, they were not to feel uncomfortable about accepting such gifts to the point that they felt they had worn out their welcome and thus needed to move from house to house. They should accept their hosts' graciousness because they, the workmen, were worthy of their hire (cf. Matt. 10:10; 1 Cor. 9:14; 1 Tim. 5:8).

10:8 Jesus broadened the scope of His guidelines to encompass the whole town; whenever a town welcomed the disciples, they were to eat what was put before them. As Marshall notes, this statement may have taken on wider significance later in the church when Paul admonished Christians who were being entertained in the house-

---

4. See Jeremias, "*Arēn*," 1:340.

holds of pagans not to raise scruples about the food put before them (cf. 1 Cor. 10:27).[5]

10:9   In those towns receptive to Jesus' messengers, they were to heal their sick and announce that the kingdom of God had appeared. The connection between healings and the kingdom of God is obvious—the former was proof of the presence of the latter. What is not so clear, however, is the meaning of the word *ēngiken*. Does it mean, as C. H. Dodd argued, "arrived," thus stating that the kingdom of God was already present?[6] Or, as W. G. Kümmel countered, does it mean "drawn near," thus stopping short of saying that the kingdom of God was actually present?[7] The word itself can convey either meaning; only the context can distinguish between the two. But two verses tip the scales toward "arrived" here in Luke 10:9. First, Mark 1:15 contains the same word which, with the occurrence of the phrase, "the time has been fulfilled," suggests that the kingdom of God was actually present in the ministry of Jesus. Second, Luke 11:20 is very clear to say that Jesus' exorcisms demonstrated that the kingdom of God had come (*ephthasen*) upon His audience. Marshall's conclusion concerning the issue (with which we concur) deserves quoting. He argues that Luke 10:9 and 11:20 make essentially the same point:

> In 11:20 the presence of the kingdom is attested by the exorcisms and its power is available for the hearers, whereas here the power of the kingdom has drawn near to those to whom it is being preached and may be received by them if they respond to the message. Attempts have been made to elucidate the texts by distinguishing between temporal and spatial nearness. In Mk. 1:15 the nearness is more temporal, whereas here it is more spatial. But this distinction should not be pressed. It is the presence of Jesus (or that of his commissioned disciples) which brings the kingdom near, and this presence is both temporal (it is here now, but it was not before), and spatial (it is near to those who are reached by the mission). The kingdom of God is not therefore a timeless reality, . . . but it comes near to men in and through Jesus and his disciples.[8]

However, the nature of the kingdom that Jesus revealed was spiritual, not physical.

5. Marshall, *Commentary on Luke,* 421.
6. Dodd, *The Parables of the Kingdom,* 28-30.
7. Kümmel, *Promise and Fulfillment: The Eschatalogical Message of Jesus,* 24.
8. Marshall, *Commentary on Luke,* 422.

10:10   Verses 10-16 indicate that the disciples would not only meet with positive reactions; there would be rejection of their message, as well. This, too, possessed an eschatological overtone—the end-time judgment of those who rejected God during their lives had already begun to happen in this age in accordance with their present rejection of Messiah. If a town refused to accept the disciples' messianic message, then the disciples were to enter into the streets of that town and pronounce judgment upon it.

10:11   The judgment Jesus' messengers were to announce was that the very dust they collected on their feet while traveling through that particular town was to be shaken off as a parable of the town's fate. We recall from 9:5 that shaking the dust off of one's feet was something Jews did upon leaving Gentile territories so as not to carry it home to Israel and thus pollute the land. In effect, the symbolic, prophetic action of the disciples shaking off the dust from their feet relegated the Jewish town that rejected Jesus to the category of being pagan. The kingdom of God had been offered to the people, but they rejected it.

10:12   In vv. 12-16, some of the most notoriously sinful Gentile cities are mentioned—Sodom, Tyre, Sidon. But the judgment of those cities will pale in significance compared to those Jewish towns that rejected their own Messiah will incur. The first infamous Gentile city mentioned by Jesus was Sodom. When the day of the Lord's wrath comes, it will be more tolerable for Sodom (Gen. 19:24-28) than for those Jewish cities who rejected the messianic offer of salvation.

10:13   Two of the Galilean cities Jesus pronounced woes upon were Chorazin and Bethsaida. The location of Chorazin is not exactly known; perhaps it is to be equated with modern Kerazeh, three miles northwest of Tell Hum.[9] For Bethsaida, a city on the northeast side of the Sea of Galilee, see 9:10. Because of these two towns' rejection of Jesus via His messengers, their fate was worse than the Phoenician trade cities of Tyre and Sidon. The Old Testament describes the last two cities' destruction because of their wickedness (Isa. 23:1-18; Jer. 25:22; 47:4; Ezek. 26-28; Amos 1:9-10). But, said Jesus, if they would have had the opportunity to witness the miracles that Chorazin and Bethsaida saw, then they would have long since repented of their sins, clothing themselves in sackcloth (rough goat skins; cf. Isa. 58:5; Dan. 9:3 [Septuagint]; Jonah 3:6-8) and sitting upon ashes (cf. Job 2:8; Jonah 3:6).

---

9. See Finegan, *The Archeology of the New Testament,* 57-58.

10:14 On the day of judgment, Tyre and Sidon will be better off than Chorazin and Bethsaida, because the latter two towns saw Jesus' miracles and had the opportunity to repent, but they did not. To whom much is given, much is required.

10:15 Jesus continued heaping invectives upon those towns which rejected Him, especially Capernaum. He applied Isaiah 14:15 and the taunt uttered there at Babylon to Capernaum. Instead of being exalted, that town would be cast down to *hades*. Jeremias has conducted a fine word study of the last term. In Greek mythology *hades* was the god of the underworld, the place of the dead. In time, the word became more generic in meaning, referring to the abode of the dead. In the Septuagint, *hades* translates the Hebrew word *sheol* (cf. Eccl. 9:10; Isa. 14:9, 11, 15), meaning the place of shadowy existence after death where humans were but a pale image of themselves while alive (Pss. 6:6; 89:49). In postexilic Judaism, *hades* took on moral overtones. It became a place compartmentalized into the abode for the righteous and the sinful (cf. Dan. 12:2). Luke 16:22-26 envisions those places as Abraham's bosom and gehenna, respectively.[10]

10:16 Verse 16 brings the mission charge to a close by encapsulating the audience's twofold response—those who listen to the disciples listen to Jesus. Those who do not hear the disciples refuse to hear Jesus, the one who sent His envoys to preach. But to reject Jesus is tantamount to rejecting God the Father who sent Him. The underlying notion informing this power of representation is the Jewish institution of *Shaliah*.

THE REPORT OF THE DISCIPLES AS
A RESULT OF THE MISSION, 10:17-20

10:17 Verses 17-20 contain the elated report of the disciples as a result of their mission. Jesus greeted them with a threefold response. According to v. 17, the seventy (-two) returned from their mission trip filled with joy because of the success they encountered. They discovered that even the demons were subjected to their commands (contrast Luke 9:40) through the name of Jesus (cf. Acts 3:6; 4:10, 17-18, 30; 5:40; 9:27 and, by way of contrast, Acts 19:13-14).

10:18 Verses 18-20 record Jesus' three replies to the disciples upon their return. The first is here in v. 18. Jesus asserts that He saw Satan fall like lightening from heaven. This is Luke's first usage of the term

10. Jeremias, "Hades," 148.

Satanas (a Hellenistic form of the Hebrew *Satan*), but the name is synonymous with the malevolent supernatural being he earlier called the "devil" (4:2-13; 8:12). Jesus' statement about the fall of Satan seems to contain a number of nuances. First, Jesus, as the preincarnate second member of the Trinity, witnessed the *primeval* fall of Satan; compare Luke 10:18, "fall like lightening from heaven" with a similar remark about Lucifer in Isaiah 14:12 ("How are you fallen from heaven, O Day Star, son of dawn"). Second, in light of v. 19 and the reference to the disciples treading upon serpents, it may be that Luke has in mind the *historical* promise of Genesis 3:15 that the seed of the woman will trample upon the serpent. Third, when a passage such as Revelation 12:7-12 is brought to bear on Luke 10:18, then we are perhaps justified in seeing an *eschatological* orientation to Jesus' pronouncement of victory. That is, the day is coming when Jesus Christ will ultimately defeat Satan. In any event, the expression gives evidence that the kingdom of God confronted Satan and spelled the beginning of the end of his reign of terror on earth. As an illustration of such, one might compare Jesus' first coming with D-Day during World War II and His return with V-Day, the conclusion of that war.

10:19 Jesus' second response reminded the disciples that He had indeed given them authority to trample upon scorpions and snakes as well as power over their spiritual enemies, especially Satan and the demonic hosts. He added the assurance that nothing would harm them. The claim reminds one of Genesis 3:15. The Jewish intertestamental writing *T. Levi* 18:2-14 is interesting in this regard:

> Then the Lord shall raise up a new priest. And his star shall arise ...lightening up the light of knowledge...He shall shine forth as the sun...and from the temple of glory shall come upon him sanctification ...And he shall give the majesty of the Lord to his sons...forevermore. ...In his priesthood shall sin come to an end; and the lawless shall cease to do evil...and he shall open the gates of Paradise, and shall remove the threatening sword against Adam. And he shall give to the saints to eat from the tree of life, and the spirit of holiness shall be on them and Beliar shall be bound by him, and he shall give power to his children to tread upon the evil spirits....And all the saints shall clothe themselves with joy. (18:2-14)

10:20 Jesus' third response to the disciples put things in their proper perspective. The real cause for celebration among His followers should not be their power to cast out demons (as wonderful as that may be), but rather that their names are written in heaven. The background for this statement is the Old Testament practice of registering the citizens who belonged to a particular city. The idea developed to express the idea of the heavenly book which contains the names of the righteous (Ex. 32:32-33; Pss. 69:28; 87:6; Isa. 4:3; Dan. 12:1). One might compare this with Revelation 3:5; 13:8 (cf. *1 Enoch* 47:3; 108:3; *Jub.* 19:9). In other words, the disciples should rejoice because they were members of the kingdom of God that they preached. A negative counterpart to Jesus' encouraging words here can be found in Matthew 7:22-23 (cf. Luke 13:22-27).

THE REVELATION TO THE DISCIPLES
IN LIGHT OF THE MISSION, 10:21-24

10:21 Verses 21-24 have been called "a meteorite fallen from the Johannine sky,"[11] because the language of the revelation of truth used therein is so reminiscent of John's gospel. In the Lucan setting, these verses group together three sayings of Jesus which respond to the report of the disciples' mission trip. The first saying is in v. 21; it is an exclamation of praise because of God's revelation. The statement is thoroughly eschatological in perspective, as Ellis remarks.[12] The reference to that "moment" (*hora*) indicated that the hour of the kingdom of God had come. The manifestation of the powers of the new age had broken in through the ministry of Jesus, and now, through His disciples (cf. 10:17, 19). The expression that Jesus rejoiced in the Holy Spirit signified the joy of messianic redemption.

Next, Jesus' praise to God the Father, Lord of heaven and earth, for hiding (*apekrypsas* [apocrypha]) His truth from the wise and intelligent (cf. 1 Cor. 1:18-25) and for revealing (*apekalypsas* [apocalypse]) it to children (in this case, the disciples) was akin to Jewish apocalypticism's belief that God disclosed His secret, eternal plans about the end times to His special messengers (cf. Dan. and Rev.). The antecedent of "these things" (*tauta*) probably refers back to vv. 17-20 and the invasion of this world controlled by demons by the kingdom of God. The disciples, like Jesus, were God's children, knew divine secrets, and were well pleasing to the Father.

---

11. See Fitzmyer's discussion in *The Gospel According to Luke X–XXIV,* 866.
12. Ellis, *The Gospel of Luke,* 157.

10:22   The second saying pertained to Jesus' intimate association with God the Father. Two points are made. First, Jesus' revelation from God was inclusive. All things, especially the divine power and knowledge, were delivered to Jesus. The term "deliver" (*paradidonai*) was often used of passing on traditional teaching (1 Cor. 11:23; 15:3). Second, Jesus' relationship to God was exclusive. Three times in this verse Jesus is referred to in the absolute form, "the Son," denoting His position of supremacy before God. Furthermore, so unparalleled was Jesus' relationship to God that only the one could reveal the other— only the Father knew the Son and only the Son knew the Father. Therefore, others could only know God if Jesus disclosed Him to them.

10:23   Verses 23-24 give the third saying of Jesus, a pronouncement of blessing upon the disciples. Turning to the disciples, Jesus privately announced a beatitude upon them because of what they had witnessed on the mission trip.

10:24   The privileged position of the disciples is stressed against the backdrop of the Old Testament prophets and kings. The latter had longed for the day of the arrival of the kingdom of God (see Luke 24:25, 44; 1 Peter 1:10-12 for the expectations of the prophets and perhaps Isa. 52:15; 60:3 for the hopes of the kings), but they did not live to see or hear it. By way of contrast, the disciples, humble lot though they were, were chosen by God to experience the dawning of the age to come in the ministry of Jesus.

THE CHARACTERISTICS OF DISCIPLES, 10:25-42

Luke 10:25–11:42 deals with what it means to be a follower of Jesus. First, real disciples love the Lord God and their neighbors (10:25-37). Second, true disciples serve Jesus (10:38-42).[13]

DISCIPLES LOVE THE LORD GOD
AND THEIR NEIGHBORS, 10:25-37

10:25   Verses 25-37 present a bold contrast between the desire to be a disciple (the lawyer, vv. 25-28) and truly being a disciple (the Good Samaritan, vv. 29-37). In a sense, the two people illustrate v. 21: the lawyer is an example of one who is wise and intelligent but who does not know the truth of God, whereas the Good Samaritan is an

---

13. Compare the similar comments by Marshall in *Commentary on Luke*, 439.

example of a child (actually an outcast) who does know God's revelation. As the scene begins, the lawyer (*nomikos*, a teacher of the Law [*nomos*]) tempted Jesus (*ekpeipazōn*; cf. 4:12) with a question, "Teacher, what must I do to inherit eternal life?" The question was one that occupied people's attention at the time (cf. *b. Ber.* 28b where someone asked Rabbi Eliezer, "Rabbi, teach us the ways of life so that by them we may attain to the life of the future world"). Two words accentuate the eschatological underpinning of the question. First, the lawyer desired "eternal life" (*zōē aiōnios*) which meant the life of the age to come (cf. 18:18, 24; Dan. 12:2). Second, the term "inherit" (*klēronomeō*) was associated with the future kingdom of God (Gal. 5:21; cf. 1 Cor. 6:9).

10:26 Jesus responded to the lawyer's question with a counterquestion in two parts. The first part seemed mildly sarcastic, "What does the Law say?" In other words, "You are the lawyer who interprets the Law; you tell me what it says." The second part is somewhat debated. Do the words *pōs anaginōskeis* mean, "How do you *read* (the Law on this point)?" Or do they mean, "How do you *recite*?" Jeremias makes a good case for the second rendering, arguing that it refers to Jewish methods of interpretation. In particular, Jesus was soliciting from the lawyer the recitation of the *shema* (Deut. 6:4-5, "Hear [*shema*] Israel, the Lord our God is one. And you shall love the Lord your God)," which was repeated by the Jews twice a day, which the lawyer proceeded to do (see v. 27).[14]

10:27 The lawyer provided a twofold reply to Jesus, combining two classic Old Testament passages on the subject of obeying the Law: Leviticus 19:18 and Deuteronomy 6:4-5—love the Lord your God with the totality of your being (heart, soul, might, mind) and love your neighbor as yourself, respectively. It may be that the two Old Testament verses were joined in pre-Christian times (see *T. Iss.* 5:2; *T. Dan.* 5:3; Philo, *De spec. leg.* 2:15). These two texts were considered to be the heart of Jewish religion and were of the same piece of cloth as Micah 6:8. However, although the two verses were quoted in Judaism, the fact that Lev. 19:18 was interpreted as referring to fellow Israelites, not one's enemies, necessitated the broadening of its parameter. This Jesus earlier did in His teaching (Luke 6:27-28) and would soon illustrate through the parable of the Good Samaritan (10:29-37).

14. Jeremias, *New Testament Theology,* 187.

10:28   Jesus affirmed the lawyer's answer in principle. Now he must practice what he just preached, namely, love God and love others. Only in doing that would the lawyer find eternal life.

10:29   Now comes the classic example of loving one's neighbor, the parable of the Good Samaritan. The lawyer who raised the issue, apparently feeling uncomfortable about his own efforts (or lack thereof) to love God by loving his neighbor tried to rationalize Jesus' command, and thereby justify (*dikaiōsai*) himself. He did so by trying to put a limit on Jesus' ethic of loving one's neighbor, "But who is my neighbor?"

10:30   The word *hupolabōn* probably does not refer to Jesus literally "taking up" the lawyer with him to, say, some podium. Rather it is an idiom, Jesus "took up his offer." Jesus spoke of a certain man left unnamed who traveled from Jerusalem to Jericho, a distance of seventeen miles on a road which descends from 2,500 feet above sea level to 770 feet below sea level (Jericho, an oasis town, is the lowest city in the world). That road was famous for its lurking dangers, especially robbers (see Josephus, *J. W.* 2.451-75). This particular man was attacked by some robbers and beaten, robbed, stripped of his clothes, and left for dead.

10:31   The story continues and builds with interest, as three individuals are brought separately on the stage, a typical Near Eastern storytelling device. The first was a priest who, by coincidence, happened to come upon the victim. The remark heightens the drama; the man in need, deserted on a dangerous, lonely road, was accidentally discovered by a priest. But instead of helping the man, the priest crossed to the other side of the road and deliberately passed him by. The priest's motive for doing so may have stemmed from fear for his own safety. It may also have been that the priest thought the man was dead and therefore he would not touch him and thereby defile himself as a priest (see Num. 5:2; 19:2-13).

10:32   A second individual, a Levite, passed by the same spot, another comment indicating the fortuitousness of the discovery. The Levites were descendants of Levi, a son of Jacob (Gen. 29:34). Although they were not related to Aaron, like the priests, they were nevertheless a privileged group, having charge, among other things, over the liturgy of the temple services. But, alas, this particular Levite repeated the action of the priest before him, probably for similar reasons.

10:33   The third individual, a Samaritan, is introduced by Luke with emphasis and with an adversative in order to contrast him with the preceding two characters—"But a Samaritan." This man, whose ethnic background would have been despised by a Jewish audience, would have come as a shock to the listeners. They probably expected the third individual, the normal spot for the hero of a story, to be an Israelite. Not so. The man who showed mercy to the victim was an outcast. No ritual observance of the Law prevented this Samaritan from loving his neighbor.

10:34   The Samaritan applied first aid to the victim, putting wine on the wounds as an antiseptic, olive oil to soothe them (for the medicinal usage of wine and oil, see *b. Shab.* 14:21), and bandages to stop the cuts from further bleeding. He then put the man on his own mount and transported him to an inn, making provision for him there.

10:35   The next day, the Samaritan took out two denarii (one denarius amounted to a day's wages at that time) and gave them to the innkeeper. The Samaritan told the owner to care for the injured man and whatever expenses might exceed his payment he would reimburse on his return trip. A couple of observations are in order concerning the compassion of the Samaritan. First, he delayed his trip in order to help the victim; he waited until the next day before setting out again for his destination. Second, if Jeremias is right that a day's board then cost one-twelfth of a denarius,[15] then the Samaritan's two denarii constituted a rather large amount of money, sufficient enough to care for the man for several days.

10:36   Jesus' counterquestion, "Which of the three men appeared to be a good neighbor to the man who fell among thieves?" changed the question of the lawyer. H. Greeven captures the significance of the change, "One cannot define one's neighbor; one can only be a neighbor."[16]

10:37   The lawyer, apparently wishing to avoid saying the name, "Samaritan," replied that the neighbor was the one who showed mercy. Jesus then told the lawyer to go and do likewise.

DISCIPLES LOVE THE WORD OF JESUS, 10:38-42

10:38   If people aspire to be disciples of Jesus, they are to be neighbors to others by loving them; they must also love the Lord their God. The account of Martha and Mary illustrates this necessity, demonstrating the importance of loving Jesus by listening to His word with undivided

---

15. Jeremias, *Jerusalem in the Time of Jesus,* 123.
16. Greeven, "*Plesion*," 317.

attention. On His way to Jerusalem, Jesus entered a village where a woman named Martha welcomed Him into her home. This was undoubtedly the same Martha who, along with Mary, was the sister of Lazarus. They lived in Bethany (see John 11:1; 12:1-3).

10:39   Martha's sister, Mary, sat at the feet of Jesus, the position of a listening disciple (see Luke 8:35; Acts 22:3), hearing His word.

10:40   But Martha, though surely desiring to listen to Jesus herself, became distracted from doing so by all of the preparations for the meal. In frustration she told on her sister to Jesus; she asked Him if He cared that she was left alone to do all the work and would He please tell Mary to give her a helping hand.

10:41   Jesus gently chided Martha, calling her name twice and telling her that she was unduly worried and disturbed about the details of the meal. Although some manuscripts read "worried and troubled" (*tyrbazein*, A, K), the best attested reading is the one we have followed "worried and disturbed" (*thorybazē*, p75, Sinaiticus, B).

10:42   From a text critical point of view, there are three possible readings of the beginning of this verse: (1) "But of a few things there is need" (38; Sy; Arm), referring to a few dishes; (2) "But of one thing there is need" (p75, A), referring to one dish; (3) some manuscripts combine both readings, "but of a few things there is need, or of only one" (Sinaiticus, B). Although the last reading is well supported, it looks to be a later, conflated reading of the other two. The first reading is too poorly supported to have been the original text. Thus the second reading is probably the most accurate.[17] Jesus told Martha, therefore, that there was really only one need—to love Him by listening to His word. This is what Mary chose to do. Martha should not, therefore, take that from her sister by involving her in unnecessary food preparations. No doubt Martha, too, was being reminded by Jesus to set her own priorities straight and take the time to love the Lord, not just by serving Him but also by listening to Him. Understood properly, this account need not be interpreted the way the patristic church later understood it, that the contemplative life is superior to the active lifestyle.

17. See Fee, "One Thing Is Needful? Luke 10:42," 61-76.

HOMILETICAL SUGGESTIONS

It seems that Luke 10 lends itself to two sermons. The first, vv. 1-24, is an excellent text on missions. It could be entitled, "Laborers for the Harvest," addressing three points. The first, vv. 1-16, is The Requirements of Missions. There are two such requirements of citizens of the kingdom of God relative to missions: either go yourself to the mission field (like the seventy [-two] disciples), or help send a missionary to the field (like those in the mission trip who hosted the disciples and supplied their needs for the work). We can all do the second alternative, and more of us than realize can choose the first option, especially in this day of short-term missionary activity. The second point covers vv. 17-20, The Results of Missions. Because Jesus has defeated Satan and his cohorts at the cross and thereby sealed their doom, Christians can confidently invest their time, talents, and treasures in the work of world evangelization, knowing that the spiritual harvest will be bountiful, even if it is at times imperceptible. Third, vv. 21-24, The Reward of Missions: Like the disciples of old, contemporary Christians need to realize their privileged place in the plan of God. Their part in the spread of the kingdom of God, like ours, was the envy of Old Testament prophets and kings. Great is the reward for those who labor in the vineyard of the Lord.

The second major section of Luke 10 to be expounded is vv. 25-42. The two episodes included there, the parable of the Good Samaritan (vv. 25-37) and the story of Mary and Martha (vv. 38-42), present the two commandments that members of the kingdom of God should observe: loving one's neighbor and loving God (Christ), respectively. The former involves demonstrating the kingdom of God in deed; the latter involves showing the kingdom of God by quietly meditating on Jesus' word. The two actions, however, are obviously not mutually exclusive.

LUKE

CHAPTER

ELEVEN

KINGDOMS IN CONFLICT

We begin Luke 11 with a quote by Ellis that helpfully identifies the twofold theme of this chapter. Speaking of the conflict between the kingdoms of God and Satan therein, he says that the central part of Luke addresses two audiences: Jesus' disciples and His opponents. In this section of the gospel, Luke tells us that the Spirit is intimately related to the kingdom.

> The two elements, "spirit" and "kingdom," form one theme virtually throughout the section. Disciples who are taught to pray "thy kingdom come" realize in the pentecostal gift of the Spirit a (partial) fulfilment of their prayer (11.1-13). The same working of the Spirit in Jesus' healings and exorcisms (11.14-28) is the real sign of the impending kingdom. It is "the greater thing" that is present in his pre-resurrection ministry (11.29-36). But the leaders of Israel dissuade and divert the people from this reality. Thus they take from them the "key of knowledge" and become liable to God's judgment (11.37-54).[1]

Two themes, then, will occupy our attention in this chapter: the kingdom of God (vv. 1-13) versus the kingdom of Satan (vv. 14-54).

1. Ellis, *The Gospel of Luke,* 161.

241

THE KINGDOM OF GOD, 11:1-13

The kingdom of God is the basic subject of vv. 1-13, which is actualized by prayer, a favorite topic of Luke. Three aspects of prayer are detailed there: principles of prayer, vv. 1-4; determination in prayer, vv. 5-8; encouragement for prayer, vv. 9-13.

PRINCIPLES OF PRAYER, 11:1-4

11:1 Luke begins this narrative with one of his famous introductory statements, "and it came to be" (*kai egeneto*). The incident Luke records concerned Jesus' custom of praying. On one such occasion, while Jesus was praying, one of the disciples (whom Luke does not name) asked Jesus to teach them to pray. Two factors seem to have motivated the request. First, no doubt Jesus' prayer life whetted the disciples' spiritual appetite. Jesus' intimate communion with God created a hunger for the same on the part of the disciples. Second, the disciples wanted Jesus to teach them to pray like John the Baptist taught his followers to pray. Jeremias is probably correct to suggest that the disciples of Jesus wanted a prayer that would be characteristic of their particular spiritual community.[2] Possibly John's group did, too, as did the Qumran community (see the *Hodayot,* or the *Thanksgiving Psalms*). Such a custom seems to have culminated in the formation of the Eighteen Benedictions, a distinctive prayer of the Jewish synagogue of the first century.

11:2 Jesus' response to the disciples' request (vv. 2-4) has become immortalized in the hearts of God's people throughout the centuries. It is variously called the Lord's Prayer, the disciples' prayer, or the Our Father. Its structure consists of an address to God and five requests of God (Matt. 6:9-13 has seven requests). The point we wish to make in the following exposition is that all six of the components (including address and requests) touch on the subject of the kingdom of God. Ellis comments on the eschatological impact of these points, noting that "the focus of the prayer is the time of salvation . . . in which men

---

2. Jeremias, *Abba: Studien zur Neutestamentlichen Theologie und Zeitgeschichte,* 161. Concerning the text critical question on Luke 11:2, the oldest manuscripts read, "Father, sanctify your name" (p75, Sinaiticus, B). This reading is to be preferred to that which is found in other manuscripts, "Our Father who is in heaven, sanctify your name" (A, C, D). The latter text is due to a later scribe's assimilation of Matt. 6:9 to Luke 11:2.

will stand in a new relation to one another and to God."³ We propose the following six points: (1) "Father" (v. 2)—the intimacy of the kingdom of God; (2) "sanctify your name" (v. 2)—the sanctity of the kingdom of God; (3) "your kingdom come" (v. 2)—the imminence of the kingdom of God; (4) "give us bread for the coming day" (v. 3)—the sufficiency of the kingdom of God; (5) "forgive us our sins" (v. 4)—the mercy of the kingdom of God; (6) "lead us not into temptation" (v. 4)—the victory of the kingdom of God.

Jesus told the disciples that when they prayed they should address God as their Father. This is the same title Jesus used for God (10:21; 22:42). The Greek word is *pater,* from which the Latin phrase is derived, *pater noster* (our Father). But, as Jeremias has carefully demonstrated, underlying the Greek word is the Aramaic word *Abba.*⁴ This term was the most intimate name by which children would address their father; it meant "Daddy." This author has heard for himself the same term used in the streets of Jerusalem. Children running and playing in the Muslim quarter on the east side of the city can be heard to say *Imma* (Mommy) and *Abba* (Daddy). When Jesus granted His disciples the permission to use such a term of endearment, He was acknowledging the newfound intimacy of the kingdom of God. That which the Jew had longed for in the Old Testament and in early Judaism was now a reality for those who believed Jesus—they could now be called the individual children of God. Heretofore, the recognition that God was their Father was applied only to the Jews as a whole (Deut. 14:1; Ps. 89:27). Jeremias's evaluation still stands, before Christ *"there is as yet no evidence in the literature of ancient Palestinian Judaism that 'My Father' is used as a personal address to God"* (italics his).⁵

Ellis has not missed the significance of the title "Father" for the reality of the presence of the kingdom of God: "The name 'Father' is both a Christological sign of Messiah's unique relation to God and an eschatological sign to his followers of their sonship."⁶ The intimacy and the simplicity of the title "Father" stands in contrast with typical Jewish prayers of Jesus' day. Rudolf Bultmann contrasted

> the ornate, emotional, often liturgically beautiful, but often overloaded forms of address in Jewish prayers with the stark simplicity of "Father"!

3. Ellis, *The Gospel of Luke,* 162.
4. Jeremias, *Abba,* 160.
5. Jeremias, *The Prayer of Jesus,* 29.
6. Ellis, *The Gospel of Luke,* 162.

The "Prayer of Eighteen Petitions," for instance, which the devout Jew is expected to say three times daily, begins, "Lord God of Abraham, God of Isaac, God of Jacob! God Most High, Creator of heaven and earth! Our Shield and the Shield of our fathers!" The "Lord's Prayer" stands out above Jewish prayers not only in its simple address but in its direct simplicity throughout. . . . God is near; He hears and understands the requests which come thronging to Him, as a father understands the requests of his own child.[7]

The first request, "Let your name be sanctified," speaks of the sanctity of the kingdom of God. The desire to hallow God's name originated in the Old Testament (see Isa. 8:13; 29:23; Ezek. 36:23). Ezek. 36:23 accentuates the eschatological aspect of sanctifying God's name. Ezekiel predicted that the day would come when the name of God would be profaned among the nations no more because of Israel's sin and subsequent exile. Rather, when Israel is restored in the future to her land and to her Lord, God will thereby vindicate the holiness of His name. The Jewish *Qaddish* (holy) prayer approximates this concern: "Exalted and hallowed be his great name in the world which he created according to his will." For the disciples to pray that God's name would be sanctified, therefore, was to acknowledge the arrival of the kingdom of God. With the birth of Jesus, the hallowing of God's name began (1:32).

The second request, "Let your kingdom come," bespeaks the imminence of the kingdom of God. This statement, along with 11:20, attests to the fact that the kingdom of God was spirituallly present in the ministry of Jesus but would not be physically realized until His second coming. The statement in v. 20, "the kingdom of God has come upon you," emphasizes the first aspect. The request in v. 2 that the kingdom of God come emphasizes the second aspect. Once again, the Jewish *Qaddish* prayer approximates the sentiments of v. 2: "May he let his kingdom rule in your lifetime and in your days and in the lifetime of the whole house of Israel, speedily and soon." The difference between the *Qaddish* prayer and the Lord's Prayer, however, is that in the ministry of Jesus that kingdom was a present, spiritual reality.

11:3   Verse 3 contains the third request of the Lord's Prayer, and with it a notoriously difficult word to translate. The controversy cen-

7. Bultmann, *Theology of the New Testament*, 23-24.

ters on the term *epiousion.* Three major views have been generated by this word. First, there is the *sacramental* view. Influenced by Origen's explanation of the word as allegorically referring to the Lord's Supper, the Eucharist, Jerome, in the Vulgate, translated the term as "supersubstantial." In other words, the daily bread was interpreted as the daily mass; hence the reason for calling this approach "sacramental."[8] But, as the Catholic scholar Fitzmyer rightly points out, this interpretation reflects a later usage of the term, not its biblical connotation.[9] Second, there is the *natural* interpretation of this word; it refers to God's provision of food for His children on a daily basis. Like the divine sustenance of manna in the wilderness for the Israelites which was gathered "a day's portion for this day" (Ex. 16:4), so Christians may trust God to provide for their everyday food. This may well be the case, but there were other words at Jesus' disposal for referring to the "daily" bread—*hemnerinos* and *ephēmerios,* for example. If that is what He had in mind, it seems Jesus would have used those terms, not *epiousion.* The best answer appears to be the third view, the *eschatological* interpretation. This perspective translates *epiousion* as bread for "the coming day" or "for tomorrow." With this in mind, Jeremias argues that the idea latent in the phrase is that God is requested to give today the bread which belongs to the kingdom of God in the age to come. On this reading, the bread encompasses both physical and spiritual food and, as such, attests to the sufficiency of the kingdom of God.[10] Thus the prayer asks God to permit His disciples to enjoy now the blessings of the end times.

11:4 Verse 4 records the fourth request of the Lord's Prayer, and it touches on the mercy of the kingdom of God. Jesus' disciples are to ask God to forgive them of their sins, for they also forgive all who wrong them. In Judaism, ultimate forgiveness of sin was thought to await God's decision on Judgment Day. If a person's good deeds outweighed his or her bad deeds, that person would be forgiven. Here, however, Jesus observed that forgiveness of sins is a present experience for those who are citizens of the kingdom of God. Given that fact, God's end-time decision at the Last Judgment has already happened now in this life for those who embrace Jesus Christ. Such forgiveness, therefore, rests solely on the grace and mercy of God, for

---

8. Fitzmyer, *The Gospel According to Luke X–XXIV,* 900, 905.
9. Ibid.
10. Jeremias, *Abba,* 165-67.

Christians have not yet completed their lives. Thus their forgiveness cannot be based on works. This truth is similar to Paul's doctrine of justification by faith. The next qualifying comment, "for we also forgive all those who have wronged us," does not negate the preceding grounds of mercy. It is not that a disciple secures God's forgiveness by forgiving others. Rather, disciples show that they have already been forgiven by God by demonstrating the same mercy toward those who have wronged them.

The fifth request of the Lord's Prayer is that Jesus' followers will not be led into temptation. This, too, possesses eschatological import and pertains to the kingdom of God. The word for temptation, *peirasmos,* can mean trial or temptation. The former can lead to the latter if not responded to in faith. In the setting of the Lord's Prayer, *peirasmos* conveys, at the very least, a general meaning of temptation or trial. Marshall correctly argues that the words "not enter into temptation" mean not to yield or succumb to temptation.[11] But there is more to the word *peirasmos.* Jeremias shows that the term also conveys an eschatological nuance. It refers to the temptation that will accompany the great tribulation, which, itself, precedes the full arrival of the kingdom of God.[12] In any event, both shades of meaning—general and eschatological—ensure victory over temptation for those who are members of the kingdom of God.

DETERMINATION IN PRAYER, 11:5-8

11:5 In addition to the principles of prayer delineated in the Lord's Prayer in vv. 1-4, vv. 5-8 enunciate an important factor in effective prayer—determination and persistence (cf. 18:1-8). It is illustrated by a story whose setting was typical of a first-century Palestinian village. Jesus told the disciples to imagine having a friend who comes to them at midnight with a minor emergency on his hands. He needs food to feed an unexpected guest who has just arrived. The story would be typical of life in Bible times. The traveler would have journeyed by night to avoid the heat of daylight. The friend-host felt obligated to observe the laws of ancient Near Eastern hospitality and care for the man's needs, even though it was late.

11:6 In attempting to do so, he discovered to his chagrin that his cupboards were bare.

11. Marshall, *Commentary on Luke,* 462.
12. Jeremias, *Abba,* 170.

11:7   He then approached his nearby neighbor's house. The man inside the house replied that he did not want to be bothered because he had bolted the door some time before and, also, to get up and open the door would wake up his entire family. The setting envisioned here was typical of the one-room peasant's cottage. All the family slept on mats. For one to get up and walk across the floor would have disturbed the whole household. Jeremias has offered an alternate reading of v. 7—rather than being a real reply by the man awakened from his sleep, v. 7 is actually a rhetorical question which continues the thought of vv. 5-6. According to Jeremias's interpretation, then, v. 7 is contrary to fact and should be translated thus, "Can you imagine the man inside the house saying that he cannot help his friend because he cannot open the door or disturb his family?" According to the unwritten rules of ancient Near Eastern hospitality, whereby one was obligated to help another regardless, such flimsy excuses for not doing so would be unthinkable.[13] On this reading, the man becomes a paradigm of hospitality, not a foil for the gracious God who is ever willing to meet the needs of His own (which the traditional interpretation requires).

Jeremias's interpretation is intriguing, but it is negated by two points. First, to arrive at this viewpoint, Jeremias posits that the traditional interpretation (the man is a bad example designed to accentuate God's willingness to provide for the needs of His own) was added/edited by Luke to the latter interpretation (the man is a paradigm of hospitality) which was originally spoken by Jesus. But such a methodology seems speculative and, ultimately, cannot be proved. Second, the immediate and larger contexts of v. 7 contradict Jeremias's approach. In the immediate context, vv. 9-13 clearly illustrate the need for determination in prayer, the point of v. 7, as does the larger setting of Luke 18:1-8.

11:8   "I say to you" applies the parable to Jesus' audience (cf. v. 5). The next clause is concessive. We may translate it thus, "even if the man [the owner of the house] will not get up and answer the request of the seeker because they are friends, yet because of his friend's shamelessness, or determination [*anaideian*], he will get up and give him whatever he needs." Though some take the antecedent of the word *anaideian* to be the houseowner, the *autou* clearly modifies the seeker friend, "*philon autou*." Therefore, it is the seeker's shame-

13. Jeremias, *The Parables of Jesus,* 157-58.

lessness of not being afraid to wake up his neighbor at midnight to make a request of him that is referred to, not the houseowner's shamelessness of not being willing to provide the need. In light of the illustration to follow in vv. 9-13, the truth of the parable becomes clear—the seeker's shamelessness and determination in asking his friend for help function as an example for disciples to persevere with their prayer requests before God. In effect, the houseowner, in his initial unwillingness to respond to his friend's need, serves as a foil to the open ear and loving heart of God who provides for His children. The next paragraph expands upon this theme.

ENCOURAGEMENT FOR PRAYER, 11:9-13

11:9 Verses 9-13 offer encouragement for the disciples' prayer life—because their God loves them, their perseverance in prayer will pay off. The paragraph itself divides into parts: vv. 9-10—a challenge to persevere in prayer; vv. 11-13—a comparison of earthly fathers with the heavenly Father, which, in turn, motivates the believer to pray to God.

Jesus introduced the illustration with the solemn words "So I tell you." What follows in vv. 9-10 are two synonymous statements which contain three parallel descriptions of prayer, each of which is expressed with a present imperative. Thus in v. 9 Jesus challenges His audience to ask, and it would be given to them. The term for "ask" is *aiteite*; it is a present imperative. Christians are commanded to continuously ask God to supply their needs. The word, therefore, highlights the persistence that is called for in one's prayer life. In fact, the term "ask" is a catchword that bonds together vv. 9-13, thereby accentuating the theme of prayer: v. 9—*aiteite*; v. 10—*aitōn*; v. 11—*aitēsei*; v. 12—*aitēsei*; v. 13—*aitousin*. The word "will be given," *dothēsetai,* is a divine passive. That is, the verb in the passive voice implies that God is the one performing the action, in this case, granting the believer's request. A second description of prayer parallel to the first is "seek and you will find." The term "seek," *zēteite,* is also a present imperative, once again emphasizing the diligence required for effective prayer. If believers do that, God will enable them to find what they are looking for relative to their needs. The third parallel description of prayer Jesus uttered was, "Knock and it (the door) will be opened." Again, the verb is a present imperative—continuously knock, *krouete*—and the answer is in the form of a divine passive, "it will be opened," *anoigēsetai.*

11:10   Verse 10 provides the second part of the synonymous statement—ask, seek, and knock and, in doing so, provides assurance that believers' prayers will be answered. What Jesus did, in effect, was to assert a spiritual fact of life: the one who asks, receives; the one who seeks, finds; for the one who knocks, the door is opened. The last word creates a text critical problem. The manuscript evidence is divided. Is the accurate reading, "is opened" (*anoigetai*, p75, B) or, "will be opened" (*anoichthēsetai*, A)? Neither does the context clarify the situation. Is the present tense an assimilation of the other present tense verbs in v. 10, or is the future tense an assimilation to the future tense of v. 9? Fortunately, however, both renderings make basically the same point, so that a final choice between the two is not necessary. The point is, those who continuously knock are the ones for whom God opens the door.

11:11   Verses 11-13 contain a comparison Jesus made between earthly fathers and the heavenly Father with regard to providing for their children. It is a statement based on an argument that moves from the lesser to the greater—if earthly fathers, who are evil, care for the requests of their children, how much more will the heavenly Father care for His own. Three pairs are used to illustrate the point: fish/serpent; egg/scorpion; good gifts/Holy Spirit.

The first pair, fish/serpent, occurs in v. 11. Jesus asked the rhetorical question, "Who of you as a father will your son ask for a fish, and instead of a fish, you will give him a serpent?" The query is based on the general similarity that exists between a fish and a serpent, especially the eel. The point is, therefore, would a father answer the request of his son for a fish to eat by deceiving him and potentially harming him with the giving of a serpent instead? To raise the question is to answer it; no!

11:12   Jesus illustrated the point with another pair: egg/scorpion, "Would a father give to his son a scorpion instead of an egg for food?" This pair also assumes similarity between the two objects. A scorpion with claws and tail rolled up resembles an egg. Again, the message is clear—it would be unthinkable for a father to deceive his son by providing him with something harmful instead of something helpful.

11:13   Jesus drove the point home to His audience with a third pair of objects: good things/Holy Spirit. "If earthly fathers, who are evil by nature, give good things to their children, how much more will the heavenly Father, implied—who is holy by nature—give the Holy Spirit to those who ask Him?" Though the contrast is not as stark here as in the other two pairs, there is still a significant difference implied based on the minor to major argument—human fathers give good things, but the divine Father gives the Holy Spirit. The reference to the Holy Spirit reflects the Lucan penchant for emphasizing the role of the Spirit in the life of Jesus (see Luke 1:35, 41, 67; 3:22; 4:1, 18), and it anticipates His gift to the disciples at Pentecost (Luke 24:49; Acts 1:4, 7, 8). As such, it indicates that the messianic age has begun in Christ.

THE KINGDOM OF SATAN, 11:14-54

Luke 11:1-13 presents the kingdom of God, particularly as it is present in prayer. Its counterpart, the kingdom of Satan, occupies the rest of the chapter, vv. 14-54. We suggest that the theme which holds together the sections to follow is characteristics of the citizens of the kingdom of Satan, of which three are developed: they maligned Jesus' authority, vv. 14-22; they opted for neutrality toward Jesus, vv. 23-26; they emphasized externality, instead of inward spirituality, vv. 27-54. The last point can be further developed into three subpoints: the human family versus the divine family, vv. 27-28; unbelief versus belief, vv. 29-36; religion versus relationship, vv. 37-54. In essence, what Jesus talked about in Luke 11 was nothing short of two kingdoms in conflict—the kingdom of God (vv. 1-13) versus the kingdom of Satan (vv. 14-54). And although the former will encounter temporary setbacks along the way, it will ultimately prevail over the latter.

THEY MALIGNED JESUS' AUTHORITY, 11:14-22

11:14 Verses 14-22 record the famous Beelzebul controversy, whereby some of the people blasphemed Jesus by accusing Him of exorcising demons by the power of Beelzebul or Satan. In actuality, however, the crowds showed themselves to be the ones who were under the influence of Satan, because they maligned Jesus' divine authority. The account is couched in terms of a controversy story. All three attendant circumstances can be identified: Jesus performed a controversial action, v. 14; He was criticized for that action, vv. 15-16; Jesus made a pronouncement statement (in this case an extended pronouncement statement) which silenced the opposition, vv. 17-22. The action performed by Jesus in this particular setting was the exorcising of a demon. There is a text critical issue in v. 14. One reading is, "and He was casting out a demon, and he was mute" (A, C). The other major reading omits *kai auto ēn,* "and He was casting out a mute demon" (p45, p75, Sinaiticus, B). Probably the latter reading is to be preferred, though the meaning is the same in either case. The point being made is that the man was mute because he was possessed by a demon. But upon Jesus' exorcism of the demon, the man was able to speak. As a result of the miracle, the crowd was amazed.

11:15 One would assume that all of the people should have been overwhelmed with praise for God's working through Jesus. Such was not the case, however, for some of the crowds took offense at Jesus' actions, believing that He had performed the miracle by the power of Satan. Their accusation literally reads, "by Beelzeboul the prince of the demons He cast out the demon." The term "Beelzeboul," like "Belial" (*1QS* 1:18, 24; 2:5, 19; 2 Cor. 6:15), became an alternate name for Satan. Its earliest attestation occurs in the Canaanite Ugaritic texts and meant "Baal, the prince" of the Canaanite deities[14] (see the name "Beelzebub" in 2 Kings 1:2-3, 6, 16, which meant "lord of the flies," which was a polemical distortion of Beelzeboul, "Baal the prince"). The name "Beelzeboul" became associated with the demonic realm because of texts like the Septuagint of Psalm 96:5, "All the gods of the nations are demons." That is, Baal, the god of the Canaanite nations, was considered to be a demon. Given this background, one can detect the play on words, "Beelzeboul" (Baal, the prince), "the prince of the demons." Thus some accused Jesus of being in cahoots with Beelzeboul; the reason Jesus could cast out a demon was because He Himself was a demon.

11:16 Others tempted Jesus by seeking from Him a more sure indication—a heavenly sign—that He was indeed from God. The very word Luke uses of these people, "tempt" (*peirazuntes*), points to the satanic influence on the crowds (cf. 4:2). In other words, their request of Jesus for a sign to vindicate Him of satanic collusion ironically demonstrated that they were the ones who were partners with Satan.

11:17 Verses 17-22 record Jesus' extended pronouncement utterance. We follow Marshall's fourfold delineation of that reply.[15] First, Jesus observed that Satan/Beelzeboul was unlikely to be responsible for exorcising his own agents, since that would imply a serious weakness in his rule, vv. 17-18. According to v. 17, Jesus sensed that the crowds were suspicious of the source of His power. He responded with two illustrations, both of which pertained to civil war: a kingdom

14. Gordon, *Ugaritic Textbook,* 1:14-15, 49; 3:3, 9, 21.
15. Marshall, *Commentary on Luke,* 471.

divided against itself is destroyed and a house or family, in times of internecine strife, will fall upon one another.

11:18 Jesus made the obvious application: if Satan were divided against himself, how would his kingdom stand? For Satan to oppose himself by empowering Jesus to exorcise demons would be self-defeating. Such would be the case if the crowds were right in saying that Jesus, by the power of Beelzeboul, cast out demons.

11:19 Second, in v. 19 Jesus replied that for the Jews to ascribe His exorcisms to Satan was tantamount to ascribing the exorcisms their people performed to Satan. In other words, Jesus turned His opponents' argument against them by asking them what was the source of the power of their own people for exorcising demons. It is well known that exorcisms were conducted by the Jews (see Acts 19:13-16; Josephus, *Ant.* 8.45-48; Strack-B 6:1, 527-35). Therefore, for the Jews to attribute the source of those exorcisms to Satan was to implicate themselves as partners in crime. But Jesus warned that on Judgment Day those very exorcists who (it is implied) operated by the power of God, not Satan, would stand as judges over Jesus' critics.

11:20 Third, by a process of elimination, then, the only power at work in Jesus' exorcisms was God's. Jesus expressed this notion by use of a first-class conditional sentence (*ei* [if] in the protasis, an indicative verb in the apodosis, *ephthasen*, "has come"), which should be translated not "if," but "since," affirming the reality of the statement. Thus, "*since* by the finger of God I cast out demons, *then* the kingdom of God has come upon you." Two observations may be made concerning this comment by Jesus. First, the phrase "by the finger of God" echoes Exodus 8:19 and the recognition therein that Moses was performing the plagues by the miraculous power of God. Even so Jesus, like Moses, was delivering God's people from evil, in this case demons. Second, though some would contest it, there is little doubt that the verb *ephthasen* should be translated, "the kingdom of God *has come* upon you" (see again the discussion of 10:9). The very context suggests this to be the case; the power of God through Christ which cast out demons was proof of the presence of the kingdom of God.

11:21 The fourth aspect of Jesus' pronouncement is in vv. 21-22—the release of Satan's victims suggests that their master has been overcome. Jesus appealed to the common sense of His audience; as long as a strong man, fully armed, guards his courtyard (of his castle), his possessions are safe.

11:22   Jesus continued His illustration, noting that when a man stronger than the lord of the castle attacks and overcomes him, the victor takes for himself the panoply, keeping the spoils for himself. Obviously, the story of the strong man illustrated Christ's defeat of Satan and the rescue (exorcism) of those held in bondage to him. The latter presupposes the former.

THEY SIDED WITH NEUTRALITY, 11:23-26

11:23   We prefer to take vv. 23-26 together, believing that v. 23 provides the key to the interpretation of the enigmatic story of the return of the evil spirit, vv. 24-26. Verse 23 contains the theme of the paragraph—those who attempt to be neutral in their stance toward Jesus, in fact, have sided against Him and are therefore citizens of the kingdom of Satan. We earlier compared v. 23 with 9:50. The former emphasizes the fact that when it comes to serving Christ, Christians should not harbor a spirit of exclusivity. He who is not against Jesus is for Him. Verse 23 makes a different point, however—when it comes to accepting Christ, non-Christians cannot hide behind the veneer of neutrality. To do so is to reject Christ. Jesus made two parallel statements expressing this truth. First, whoever is not with Jesus is against Him. Second, using shepherd imagery appropriate to Himself, the "good shepherd," Jesus asserted that he who does not gather a flock with Him, scatters them. The message to His critics was poignant— they could not objectively and smugly call His motives and mission into question without being liable to divine judgment.

11:24   Jesus illustrated this truth with an analogy about a man out of whom a demon was exorcised, comparing him to a house that has been cleaned. The story begins with Jesus' mentioning an unclean spirit, a demon, which had been cast out of a man. The exorcist is not named. It could have been Jesus, one of His disciples, or one of the Jewish exorcists referred to in v. 19. The lack of reference to the individual does not impair the interpretation of the text. Having been expelled from the man, the demon roamed through the desert in search of a resting place. The idea here could be that the deserted cities were thought to be a "suitable" abode for demons (see Isa. 13:21; 34:14; Rev. 18:2). Or it might be that, as Marshall notes, the point is more the absence of people from desert regions so that the demon could not find anywhere to rest, given demons' proclivity to inhabit human bodies.[16] Failing to find a resting place in the desert, the demon determined to return to the house that he left, that is the body of the man whom he had earlier possessed.

11:25 Upon its return, the unclean spirit found the house swept and set in order. It is probably implied that the house was unoccupied. Three reasons suggest this to be the case. First, some ancient manuscripts add the phrase "being unoccupied" (Sinaiticus[2], B, C) to v. 25. Second, the parallel passage in Matthew 12:44 has the word "unoccupied." Third, the context of Luke 11:25 seems to assume that the reason the demon could return to the house was because it was vacant. If these reasons are sound, then the house, since the exorcism of the demon, had not been utilized. It served no real purpose or, at best, a neutral one. But neutrality is, in fact, a decision. Some proverbial phrases come to mind at this stage of the story: "an idle mind is the devil's workshop"; "a double-minded man is unstable in all his ways"; "you can't straddle the fence."

11:26 Because the house was vacant, the demon went away and brought back seven other demons more evil than himself and entered the man. Consequently, the last state of the man was worse than the first state. An analogy comes to mind, like a vacant house which is vulnerable to vandalism, the person with an undecided heart concerning Christ, neutral though he may try to be, is subject to Satan's control. Such was the case with Jesus' audience. Though the people had witnessed His power in exorcising demons, they attempted to remain neutral in their posture toward Jesus. In reality, however, they opened up their hearts to the habitation of the very demons that had been cast out of others.

THEY EMPHASIZED EXTERNALITY, 11:27-54

The Human Family Versus the Divine Family, 11:27-28

11:27 The record of the woman in the crowd blessing Jesus' mother is unique to Luke. Given its context, the response is certainly an improvement on the earlier reactions of those who maligned Jesus' authority, vv. 14-22. Nevertheless, from Jesus' correction of the woman we learn that her response was still sub-Christian. The woman confused the human family of Jesus with the family of God. In effect, she emphasized external appearance (rather than inward obedience), an-

16. Ibid, 479.

other characteristic of the kingdom of Satan. While Jesus was talking, a woman in the crowd cried out with a loud voice, saying to Jesus, "Blessed is the womb that bore you and the breasts that nourished you." The manner of expression employed by the woman was synecdoche (using the parts for the whole). In this case, parts of the body referred to the whole person. Thus, the woman was praising Mary. Undoubtedly, the saying recalls Luke 1:48, where Mary prophesied, "From now on all generations will count me blessed."

11:28 Jesus immediately replied, "Rather blessed are the ones who hear the word of God and observe it." The opening word in Jesus' response, "*menoun*," is critical to interpreting His comment. M. E. Thrall delineates three different senses of the word:[17] (1) It is adversative, i.e., "nay, rather," "on the contrary" (cf. Rom. 9:20; 10:18). On this reading, Jesus would be contradicting the woman's blessing upon His mother. But, as Thrall rightly observes, when Luke wants to express contradiction, he uses *ouchi, legō hymin* ("No, I say to you"; see 12:51; 13:3, 5), not *menoun*. (2) It is affirmative, i.e., "indeed." According to this viewpoint, Jesus would be agreeing with the woman. But there are two difficulties with this rendering. First, as Thrall remarks, when Luke wants to express affirmation, he uses *nai* (7:26; 10:21; 11:51; 12:5). Second, the context of v. 28 (before it, vv. 14-26, and after it, vv. 29-54) obviously does not convey a sense of affirmation. Rather, it is critical of Jesus' opponents. So is v. 28. (3) *Menoun* is corrective, i.e., "Yes, but rather," meaning what the woman said was true as far as it goes, but it did not proceed far enough. This is the best rendering. Thus, what Jesus said was to first agree with the woman's praise of His mother who nursed Him as a child (cf. 1:48). But He went on to add that it is not physical descent that pleases God with regard to Mary or, for that matter, any other would-be disciple. Rather, it is obedience to Jesus, God's final revelation, that God approves. It is that which incorporates one into the "holy" family.

Unbelief Versus Belief, 11:29-36

11:29 In vv. 29-36, Luke interweaves two themes: unbelief and belief. The former is recognizable in the way Jesus castigated the growing crowds' desire for Him to perform spectacular miracles. Such a curiosity was indicative of their unbelief. This was in contrast to the pagan Ninevites in Jonah's day, along with the heathen queen in Solomon's day,

17. Thrall, *Greek Particles in the New Testament,* 34-35.

who embraced the God of the Jews by faith (vv. 29-32). The intertwined themes of unbelief and belief continue in vv. 33-36 with Jesus' illustration of the power of spiritual perception (belief) or lack thereof (unbelief).

The numerical growth of the crowds prompted Jesus to label them "an evil generation." This was the case because their purpose for following Him was not sincere; rather they sought from Him a spectacular sign to prove His messiahship. But Jesus adamantly refused to give them anything of the sort. The only sign they would get would be the "sign of Jonah," the identification of which begins to unfold in v. 30 and comes to full explanation in v. 32.

11:30   What Jesus meant by the sign of Jonah begins to unfold with His comparison between Jonah, the prophet, and Himself. Just as Jonah was a sign to the Ninevites, so Jesus, the Son of Man, would be a sign to His evil generation. Although it is quite possible that the sign of Jonah referred to the miraculous deliverance of the prophet from the great fish, the book of Jonah itself does not suggest the Ninevites were cognizant of that supernatural event. This observation, together with Jesus' reference to the preaching of Jonah in v. 32, suggests, therefore, that the sign of Jonah was his preaching of the message of repentance. Furthermore, for Jesus to portray His resurrection against the backdrop of Jonah's divine deliverance from the fish as the only sign the Jews would get (as many commentators think He is doing here), for all practical purposes, contradicts His refusal to utilize the miraculous in order to establish His credibility. In other words, it would be to grant them the very thing He said He would not give them.

11:31   Jesus introduced another illustration into the discussion, calling forth the story of the Queen of Sheba (Ethiopia?; see Isa. 43:3) who traveled from far to the south to learn of the wisdom of Solomon (1 Kings 10:1-13). On Judgment Day, she will raise up in condemnation of the Jews in Jesus' day. Two contrasts between the Queen of Sheba and the people of Jesus' generation explain the forthcoming judgment. First, the Queen of Sheba was a pagan, yet she believed in the God of Solomon (1 Kings 10:9). However, the Jews, the supposed people of God, were in the process of rejecting someone greater than Solomon, Jesus Christ, wisdom incarnate. Second, the Queen of Sheba traveled a long distance to embrace Solomon's wisdom and his God. But the Jews of Jesus' day had God's greatest envoy, the Son of Man, in their very midst yet failed to take advantage of the situation.

11:32   Returning to His first illustration, Jesus prophesied that joining the Queen of Sheba on Judgment Day in condemnation of the Jews would be the Ninevites of Jonah's day. This will be so because, whereas the Ninevites repented at the preaching (*kērygma*) of Jonah, the Jews in Jesus' presence did not respond to Him who was greater than the prophet Jonah. Thus, Jesus' audience, in rejecting Him, was spurning one who was greater than king (Solomon) and prophet (Jonah). In effect, they rejected God Himself. The irony is biting: the Ninevites and the Queen of Sheba accepted the messengers of God. But Jesus' audience rejected God Himself.

11:33   The intertwined themes of unbelief and belief continue in vv. 33-36, this time using the metaphors of darkness and light. The section begins with an obvious point—no one lights a lamp in order to put it in a crevice or under a measuring vessel.[18] On the contrary, an oil lamp is lit and placed on a stand for the purpose of shedding light for all who enter the room. Though Jesus does not explicitly apply the metaphor to Himself, its relevancy to Him would be difficult for His audience to miss—He is the light of the world, whose light is not hidden but clear to all who believe in Him.

11:34   Jesus furthered His point by providing a lesson in spiritual anatomy. The eye is the lamp of the body. If the eye is healthy, then the body has light. If the eye is evil, then the body gropes in darkness.

11:35   Jesus then gave the moral of the story for the audience, using an oxymoron—"see" to it that the light that you receive does not turn out to be "darkness." That is to say, if the crowds do not believe in Jesus, the light of the world, then their unbelief will blind them spiritually.

11:36   Jesus concluded the illustration by stating that the person who is full of light, with no part of darkness within him, is the one who will have light as bright as the rays of a lamp. Though the statement is not entirely clear, J. M. Creed probably has best captured its meaning, "If the heart is truly receptive of light, it will receive light from the true light when it shines, that is from Christ."[19]

Religion Versus Relationship, 11:37-54

11:37   Jesus' theme in vv. 27-54 was that citizens of the kingdom of Satan are people who wrongly emphasize the external instead of the

18. The phrase "under a bushel-measure" is omitted in p45 and p75 but retained in Sinaiticus, B, etc. The evidence is so divided that retaining the phrase seems the best choice.
19. Creed, *The Gospel According to St. Luke,* 164.

spiritual. Two of the three contrasts delineating that point have been addressed: natural family versus divine family (vv. 27-28) and unbelief versus belief (vv. 29-36). The third contrast follows—citizens of the kingdom of Satan, especially the Pharisees and the scribes, promote a hypocritical religion before men instead of developing a genuine relationship with God. Ellis provides a penetrating précis of the section:

> Foregoing the ceremonial washing was like omitting the blessing. It arched the eyebrows of the Pharisee. By his calculated action Jesus sets the stage for the question he desires to answer. What really makes a man religiously clean? It is not the externals, "the cup and the platter," that are important but rather the inward man's actions, "justice and the love of God" (41). Cf. Mk. 7.14ff.; Ps. 51.17ff.; . . . The sin that brings Christ's startling rebuke is hypocrisy. Outwardly religious, the Pharisees at heart are full of greed "and wickedness." In short order they verify Jesus' charge, "laying snares to catch him with his own words" (54, . . .).
>
> The six woes (Matthew 23 has seven) reveal the appalling condition of many religious leaders of the time. The churchmen observe only the forms of religion and itch for the praise of men. By their example they succeed only in defiling men who, not aware of their deceit, emulate them (cf. Mt. 23.15). Equally guilty are the religious lawyers or theologians. By false interpretations of Scripture they create intolerable religious burdens. They honour the dead prophets but "kill and persecute" the "prophets and apostles" now among them. Luke climaxes the series with the most damning indictment: their perverse influence has led the people to reject Jesus' message and, thereby, has deprived them of the "knowledge" of salvation (52). Cf. Mt. 23.13; Mt. 16.19.[20]

After Jesus spoke to the audience, a Pharisee invited Jesus to his home for a meal. Jewish people in Palestine ate two meals a day, a light brunch midmorning (*aristan*) and the main meal late afternoon (*deipnon*). The meal Jesus participated in was the *aristan* (v. 37). The reference to reclining suggests that the meal took place around a triclinium (a three-sided table with an opening on one side to allow the attendant to serve the meal; the participants reclined on couches with their heads toward the table).

11:38 The Pharisee was shocked that Jesus ate without washing (*ebaptisthe*). The ceremonial custom of washing one's hands before a meal was a practice rigorously followed by the Pharisees (see Mark

20. Ellis, *The Gospel of Luke*, 169.

7:1-5; Josephus, *J. W.* 2.129), though it was not demanded by the Old Testament. Jesus ignored the rule, and that in a Pharisee's home!

11:39   The Pharisee's shock elicited a series of stinging remarks from Jesus aimed at the religious pretense of the Pharisees and scribes. Three woes are hurled at each, beginning in v. 42. Verses 39-41, though not labeled a woe, serve, in effect, as such (cf. Matt. 23:25). Addressing the Pharisees directly, Jesus accused them of hypocrisy, likening them to someone washing only the outside of a cup and platter but leaving the inside unclean and filthy. Lest they missed the message, Jesus exposed the hearts of the Pharisees—consisting of greed and evil. No doubt such condemnation further shocked Jesus' host, for the Pharisees as a whole were considered to be outstanding religious leaders at the time of Christ.

11:40   Jesus called the Pharisees "foolish people," pointing out the folly of cleaning the outside and not the inside of dishes. The reference to the one who made both the outside and inside is a double entendre—the human who made the vessel intended it to be clean on the outside and inside, just as the God who made humans intends them to be clean outwardly (physically) and inwardly (spiritually).

11:41   Jesus prescribed the cure for the Pharisees' greedy and evil hearts; let them give away their possessions as alms for the poor, and that action will purify and cleanse their motives from within. It will be recalled that the emphasis on helping the poor is a favorite Lucan theme.

11:42   Verse 42 contains the first woe Jesus uttered against the Pharisees. They were sticklers for observing religious ceremonial details, but they neglected the important matters of the heart, such as justice toward others and love for God. With a sweeping statement, Jesus criticized the Pharisaic penchant for meticulous observance of the tithe. The Old Testament required the payment of tithes of farm and garden produce (Deut. 14:22-29; 26:12-15; Lev. 27:30-33; Mal. 3:8-10). But the rabbinic tradition greatly expanded the law of tithing (see the Talmudic tractate *Maaseroth*). Jesus mentioned three objects relative to tithing: mint (a condiment for food), rue (a plant about three feet high with gray-green foliage and yellow flowers also used as a condiment), and vegetables in general.[21]

The first of these, mint, was not specifically listed as tithable, but dill, a similar plant mentioned in connection with mint in Matthew

---

21. See Fitzmyer's discussion of the topic in *The Gospel According to Luke X–XXIV,* 948.

23:23, was. Rue was not a plant to tithe. This observation, taken with
the next terms "all eatable herbs," i.e., vegetables, suggests that Jesus'
criticism moved from the specific to the general. Thus, not only did
the Pharisees tithe mint (which was tithable), but they went so far as
to tithe plants not tithable, like rue, and, for that matter, any edible
plant! But despite their meticulous observation of the law of the tithe,
the Pharisees neglected the weightier matters of the heart—justice to
others and love for God. They should have paid as much attention to
those concerns as they did to the others.

11:43   The second woe pronounced upon the Pharisees was because they loved the praise of men. Jesus gave two examples: The
Pharisees loved to sit in the front seat in synagogues, a place of honor.
Furthermore, they loved to be greeted in the marketplaces. According
to later tradition, it was a sign of respect to a superior if that person
was greeted first by another person in the streets (Strack-B 1:382).

11:44   The third woe was that the Pharisees were like unmarked
graves over which people unknowingly walked. Marking a grave (by
whitewashing it; see Matt. 23:27) was necessary because people needed to avoid the ritual defilement that resulted from touching the dead
(cf. Lev. 21:1-4, 11; Num. 19:11-22). But in the case of the Pharisees,
their hypocritical religion of externals, rather than bringing godliness
to people, actually defiled them. The people who admired and adhered to the Pharisaic tradition, therefore, were being spiritually contaminated without knowing it. The implication was clear—the Pharisees
were devoid of the life of God.

11:45   The scribes fared no better under Jesus' scrutinizing finger,
as vv. 45-52 indicate. They, too, received their share of woes from
Him. When Jesus finished His invectives against the Pharisees, a scribe,
or lawyer (*nomikōn*), complained that for Jesus to criticize the Pharisees was tantamount to criticizing the scribes. This was so because
most scribes were members of the Pharisaic party. The scribes were
the ones who meticulously interpreted the Old Testament Law, codify-
ing their traditions, which numbered into the thousands. This body of
interpretation, then, became the basis of the Pharisees' practice.

11:46   Jesus' first woe against the scribes was occasioned by their
expansion of the Old Testament Law into excessive regulations (some
six thousand of them!) that weighed down the people. Thus, the

scribes, rather than offering a helping hand to the people, in effect pointed a condemnatory finger at them.

11:47   The second woe against the scribes pinpointed their hypocrisy—they built tombs in honor of the prophets, a characteristic of Judaism,[22] when, in fact their fathers were the ones who killed them. In essence, the scribes, despite the outward pretense of honoring God's messengers of old, were actually partly to blame for their deaths.

11:48   Verse 48 restates v. 47. The scribes' fathers killed the prophets, and they are no better, even if they build tombs in their honor.

11:49   Jesus followed the second woe with an enigmatic statement, "Wisdom of God said, 'I will send them prophets and apostles, some of whom they will kill and persecute.'" Two questions arise from this comment. First, who is the "wisdom of God"? One answer is that wisdom is here understood in terms of the Old Testament preexistent figure of wisdom personified (cf. Prov. 8). This is true as far as it goes, but in light of 7:35 we should probably go further and equate wisdom with Jesus Christ (cf. 1 Cor. 1:30; Col. 1:15-20). Second, who are the prophets and apostles? In light of vv. 47 and 50-51, certainly the prophets at least refer to the Old Testament messengers of God. But that group may also include early Christian prophets, especially since the next term, "apostles," undoubtedly refers to the apostles of Jesus. Therefore, the statement appears to be a prophecy of Jesus about the future persecution of His disciples, based on the Jews' past treatment of the Old Testament prophets.

11:50   As a result of such behavior, Jesus predicted that the blood of the prophets shed from the beginning of time would be required of Jesus' generation. Ellis interprets this judgment as having occurred at the fall of Jerusalem; it is "a saying from [Jesus'] pre-resurrection ministry [interpretation] given detailed application by a Christian prophet to the judgment on 'this generation' in the siege and destruction of Jerusalem (A.D. 66–70)."[23]

11:51   Jesus delineated the parameters of the persecuted prophets; they extended all the way from Abel to the blood of Zechariah, who perished between the altar and the sanctuary. The reference to Abel is understandable as he, though not technically a prophet, did suffer, like the Old Testament prophets, for righteousness' sake. But the ref-

---

22. See Jeremias, *Heiligengräben in der umwelt Jesu.*
23. Ellis, *The Gospel of Luke,* 172.

erence to Zechariah is not clear. At least three possible identifications present themselves. First, Jesus referred to Zechariah the priest, the son of Jehoiada, who was stoned by the people in the court of the temple (2 Chron. 24:20-22). If so, then the scope of Jesus' reference extended from the beginning of the Old Testament (Gen. 4, Abel) to its close (2 Chron. 24:20-22; Chronicles is the last book in the Hebrew canon). Second, the Matthean parallel in Matthew 23:35 identifies the person as Zechariah, the son of Berechiah. Many take this to be a confusion on Matthew's part who supposedly mixed up Zechariah the prophet, the son of Berechiah (Zech. 1:1, whose murder is nowhere mentioned) with Zechariah, the son of Jehoiada. Third, others provide a way out of the impasse by suggesting that the Zechariah in view is another Zechariah, son of Barischiah (Baris), who was murdered in the temple courts (A.D. 68–70; see Josephus, *J. W.* 4.335).[24] The last suggestion seems to best account for the data, especially if the destruction of Jerusalem is meant by the words "the blood of all the prophets will be required of this generation" (cf. 50). If so, Jesus' reference encompassed God's prophets all the way from the beginning of time up until His own generation.

11:52   Jesus summed up the scribes' activity in a third and final woe; they take away the key of knowledge from the general populace, and do not ever use it themselves. The idea is that the scribes' encrustation of the Word of God with the traditions of men keeps people from encountering the revelation of God. This is so because they themselves do not know the living God (cf. Mark 7:8-13).

11:53   When Jesus left the home of the Pharisee in which He was dining, the Pharisees and scribes joined forces in expressing their anger against Him. They reacted violently to what He said, carefully examining His words.

11:54   Their purpose was to catch Him in something He might say, in order to hold it against Him.

HOMILETICAL SUGGESTIONS

Perhaps Luke 11 should be covered in broad strokes. Two sermons would probably be sufficient to accomplish that task. If so, the outline offered in the exposition would well suit that purpose:

---

24. Ibid.

I. Citizens of the Kingdom of God—They Develop Inwardly through Prayer, vv. 1-13
   A. Principles of Prayer, vv. 1-4
   B. Determination in Prayer, vv. 5-8
   C. Encouragement of Prayer, vv. 9-13

II. Citizens of the Kingdom of Satan—They Parade Outward Religion, vv. 14-54
   A. They Malign Jesus' Authority, vv. 14-22
   B. They Side with Neutrality, vv. 23-26
   C. They Emphasize Externals, vv. 27-54
      1. Natural Family Versus Spiritual Family, vv. 27-28
      2. Unbelief Versus Belief, vv. 29-36
      3. Religion Versus Relationship, vv. 37-54

LUKE
CHAPTER
TWELVE

HINDRANCES TO HOLINESS

In Luke 12, Jesus' preaching to the crowds intensifies as He calls His audience to genuine commitment to Him. What He challenged them to do, in essence, was to live holy lives before God. One can detect three hindrances to holiness addressed by Jesus in this chapter. For each hindrance, the problem is identified and its solution is given: (1) fear of man, the solution to which is fear of God, vv. 1-12; (2) love of money, the solution to which is trust in God, vv. 13-34; (3) dullness of perception, the solution to which is anticipating the return of Christ, vv. 35-59.

FEAR OF MAN, 12:1-12

Verses 1-12 challenge the disciples, and the crowds as well, to learn from Jesus' previous criticism of the Pharisees and scribes. Marshall captures the connection of thought in the section:

> The passage begins with a comment addressed to the disciples which sums up the teaching of the previous section directed against the Pharisees. Hypocrisy is ultimately futile, for the secret thoughts of men will one day be revealed (12:1, 2f.). The connection of thought in Luke's mind appears to be: disciples too may be tempted to conceal the real allegiance of their hearts before men, but they should not fear what

men may do to them. Let them rather fear God who has the ultimate power of life and death. They can be sure that he will remember and care for them in the midst of persecution, just as he cares even for birds. Whoever is faithful to Jesus before men will be upheld by the Son of man before God, but whoever denies him will face ultimate rejection (12:4f., 6f., 8f.). Similarly, anyone who sins against the Spirit will suffer condemnation, but the person who speaks against the Son of man will be forgiven. Hence, when the disciples face persecution and are tempted to forswear their allegiance, let them not be afraid, for the Holy Spirit will direct them what to say (12:10, 11f.).[1]

12:1 Verse 1 sets the stage for Jesus' comments by recalling His previous criticisms of the Pharisees, in general, while specifically contrasting the negative reaction of the Jewish leadership (11:54) with the positive response of the masses. The scene begins with Luke's notation that the crowds increased in number so much that people were pressing each other in order to get closer to Jesus. He then took the occasion as an opportunity to focus on teaching His disciples. There is a question about whether "first" (*prōton*) refers to the preceding clause or to the following clause. If the former, then Luke is saying that Jesus taught His disciples "first" (then the crowds) or, more likely, Jesus "above all" taught His disciples. If the latter, then Luke is saying that the disciples should "above all" beware of the leaven of the Pharisees. Probably the former construction is more accurate (cf. Luke 21:9; Acts 3:26; 7:12; 13:46 for similar constructions using the word *prōton*). Jesus' challenge to His disciples, and also to the crowds which overheard His conversation, was to avoid the leaven of the Pharisees' hypocrisy. Just as leaven permeates bread making it rise, so pharisaic hypocrisy could creep into the lives of the disciples, if they were not on their guard. The specific nature of that hypocrisy will be spelled out in vv. 2-12—it is an inordinate concern for what others will say and do to a person. Such preoccupation with what others think can lead one to following their dictates, rather than being a disciple of Jesus.

12:2 Verses 2-3 contain a principle—the truth will eventually get out. Jesus expressed it in four synonymous statements, two of which occur in v. 2; the other two statements occur in v. 3. The first two statements are given in negative form:

1. Marshall, *Commentary on Luke*, 509-10.

Now	**Later**
Nothing is covered	that will not be uncovered
Nothing is secret	that will not be known

12:3   The second two parallel statements occur in v. 3; they are given in positive form:

Now	**Later**
What was said in the dark	will be heard in daylight
What was whispered behind closed doors	will be preached from the housetops

The obvious message behind the synonymous statements is that a person's true character will come to light on Judgment Day. At that time all hypocrisy will be exposed. Far better, therefore, to live a life of consistency now, in which one's inward spirituality manifests itself in a holy lifestyle.

12:4   Jesus then pinpointed the problem—hypocritical living stems from the fear of others. But Jesus diffused the fear by reminding His disciples, His friends, that humans can take the life of a Christian, but that is all. They cannot touch the believer's soul and afterlife in eternity.

12:5   The solution to the problem of fearing others is to fear God. God is the one who, after the person has been killed, has the authority and power to consign that person to Gehenna. The name "Gehenna" is derived from the words, "valley of Hinnom" (*ge* = valley, *hinnom*), which is located today on the south and west sides of Jerusalem. In Old Testament times it was a place where Jews followed the hideous Canaanite practice of offering their children to Baal-Molech as a burnt offering (2 Kings 16:3; 2 Chron. 28:3; Jer. 7:32; 19:4-6; 32:34-35). After the reform of King Josiah, Gehenna became a continuously smoldering garbage dump (2 Kings 23:10). By Jesus' day, Gehenna had become associated with the place of fiery, eternal punishment in the afterlife (cf. Rev. 9:1-2, 11; 19:20; 20:1-3). In other words, what Jesus was saying was that the fear of man pales in significance next to the fear one should have of God.

12:6   Jesus offered a word of encouragement to temper the previous minatory assertion. He appealed to the common knowledge that sparrows (food for the poor) sold so cheaply, five for two *assariōn*

267

(an *assarion* was a Roman copper coin worth about one-sixteenth of a *denarius*). And yet, insignificant as sparrows appeared to be, not one of them was forgotten by God.

12:7 Jesus continued His encouraging comment by reminding His disciples that the number of hairs on their heads was known by God. Therefore, they should not be afraid because they were worth far more than sparrows to God. The logic moves from the minor argument (sparrows' worth before God) to the major argument (humans' worth before God).

12:8 Jesus' words now return to a somber tone in vv. 8-9, employing antithetical parallelism:

Now	**Later**
Positive, v. 8—whoever confesses Me before men	the Son of Man will confess him before angels
Negative, v. 9—whoever denies Me before men	will be denied before God's angels

Thus vv. 8-9 amount to a conditional statement; according to v. 8, if a person confesses (*homologēsē*, says the same thing) Jesus before others in this life, then Jesus, the Son of Man,[2] will confess that person as a disciple of His before the angels in the next life.

12:9 Conversely, if a person denies Jesus before men in this life, then Christ will deny that person before God and the angels in the next life.

12:10 Verses 10-12 need to be viewed together. Verse 10 contains Jesus' enigmatic statement about the peril of blaspheming against the Spirit. Verses 11-12 assure the disciples that the Holy Spirit will empower them to be articulate witnesses for Christ despite persecution. Verse 10 reads, "Everyone who speaks a word against the Son of Man will be forgiven, but whoever blasphemes against the Holy Spirit will not be forgiven." What does this mean? Fitzmyer delineates five views that have emerged in the interpretation of this text:[3] (1) In light of Mark 3:22-29, which combines the Beelzebul controversy (cf. Luke 11:14-22) with the reference to the blasphemy against the Spirit, one should equate the blasphemy against the Spirit with the Pharisees' ac-

---

2. See Marshall's discussion on the title "Son of Man" as Jesus' circumlocution for Himself in ibid., 376, 515-16.
3. Fitzmyer, *The Gospel According to Luke X–XXIV,* 964.

cusation that Jesus was empowered by Satan to cast out demons. That being the case, the blasphemy against the Spirit was restricted to the Jewish leadership in Jesus' day and therefore is not repeatable. (2) The Patristic interpretation was that speaking against the Son of Man referred to non-believers' maligning Jesus whereas blaspheming against the Holy Spirit refers to believers who, having the Holy Spirit, apostatize from the faith, never to be restored to God again (cf. Heb. 6:1-6?). (3) The blasphemy of the Son of Man was the sin of Jesus' contemporaries who rejected Him before His resurrection, but the blasphemy against the Spirit was their rejection of Him after His resurrection, once the Spirit had come at Pentecost (cf. Acts 13:45; 18:6; 26:11). (4) Similar to this viewpoint is the interpretation that Luke 12:10 is connected to vv. 11-12 so that the blasphemy against the Son of Man (v. 10a) refers to the Jews' rejection of Jesus before His resurrection. The blasphemy against the Holy Spirit, then, refers to the Jews' rejection and persecution of the disciples' post-resurrection ministry, one empowered by the Spirit. (5) Fitzmyer's view is a more general interpretation, the unforgivable sin is not a one-time rejection of Christ, but the persistent, obdurate opposition to the influence of the Spirit which animates the preaching of the gospel. In our opinion, if v. 10 is properly kept in the context of vv. 11-12, then the fourth view is to be preferred.

12:11   Jesus' tone changes in vv. 11-12 so that He now offers comfort to His disciples regarding future persecution. He forecasts the fact that they would be taken into the Jewish synagogues in order to be interrogated for their faith. The reference to rulers and authorities suggests that His followers would also be brought before the Gentile magistrates (cf. Paul the apostle's experiences, Acts 9:15; 21:11; 24:10; 26:1). The disciples, however, were not to worry about what they would say at their defense (*apology*).

12:12   The reason the disciples should not have anxiety regarding their defense before the rulers was because the Holy Spirit would empower them to articulate their faith in Christ at that time (cf. Luke 21:12-15).

LOVE OF MONEY, 12:13-34

A second hindrance to holy living identified by Jesus is the love of money, vv. 13-34. The contents of the section are twofold: the parable of the rich fool (vv. 13-21) and the teaching on earthly possessions and heavenly treasure (vv. 22-34). The solution offered therein to the problem of the love of money is for one to trust in God to provide one's needs. The result is that that person, because he or she is liberated from being preoccupied with material things, can serve the Lord with single-mindedness.

THE PARABLE OF THE RICH FOOL, 12:13-21

12:13 Jesus' instruction of the disciples was interrupted by a man from the crowd who wanted Jesus to settle an inheritance dispute between him and his brother. The Old Testament background is helpful for understanding the situation. From Psalm 133:1 it can be surmised that the heirs of a piece of property were expected to live together and keep the land intact. In this case, apparently the man appealing to Jesus was the younger brother who wanted his portion of the land, but his older brother refused to give it to him. The younger brother's reason for coming to Jesus was that in the Old Testament, and at the time of Jesus, religious leaders were asked to settle such disputes (Num. 27:1-11; Deut. 21:15-17; *m. B. Bat.* 8:1–9:10).

12:14 Jesus dismissed the man's request with a rhetorical question, "Man, who appointed me as a judge or arbitrator over you?" Two things are probably implied in Jesus' reply. First, he disassociated Himself from the religious legal profession. He was no rabbi or scribe who deciphered casuistic laws. Second, as Ellis so well puts it, the action requested of Jesus was not commensurate with His mission: "Jesus is not a social reformer nor an arbiter of personal disputes. For his society he has only one word: 'repent and follow me.'... Even for his followers he enunciates ethical principles more often than he gives rules for specific situations."[4]

12:15 Jesus then addressed the crowds, warning them against greed. In doing so, He put His finger on the real problem of the man's request—it was born out of materialism. Then Jesus offered a moral maxim: a meaningful life does not depend on one's possessions, even if those possessions are abundant. Rather, it was implied, real living comes from walking with God and trusting Him for one's every need.

12:16 Jesus illustrated that truth by means of a parable. There was a rich man who had a farm that produced abundant crops. It can be assumed that the former proceeded from the latter.

4. Ellis, *The Gospel of Luke*, 176.

12:17   In soliloquy style the man pondered to himself about how to find space to store his abundant harvest.

12:18   Thus far, the story envisions a "bigger and better" scenario. The farmer mused to himself that what he should do is tear down his present barns and build bigger ones to store his grain and goods.

12:19   Further engaging himself in conversation, the man expressed his intention of, after having stored his harvest, relaxing and taking life easy for years to come. In good, hedonistic style, he planned to eat, drink, and be merry.

12:20   But, alas, the farmer did not reckon with the possibility of his own death. Accordingly, God branded the man a fool (cf. 11:40; Ps. 14:1). That very night the man's life would be taken from him, and who would get all he had prepared? Certainly not the farmer. One might invoke at this point another statement by Jesus as an editorial comment on the fate of the farmer, "What shall it profit a man if he gain the whole world, but lose his own soul?"

12:21   Jesus concluded the parable by giving the moral of the story— the farmer had hoarded up things for himself and, in so doing, neglected to become rich toward God and, one might add, failed to provide for the needs of those less fortunate than himself. This concluding comment enables the reader to grasp what Jesus wanted to communicate. The parable of the rich fool is not against prayerful and careful investment in the future. Rather, it serves as a warning not to squander one's resources by living selfishly and hedonistically.

TEACHING ON EARTHLY POSSESSIONS
AND HEAVENLY TREASURE, 12:22-34

12:22   In verses 22-34 Jesus re-focuses His attention on His disciples, providing for them teaching on the divine perspective toward material possessions. That viewpoint can be expressed in terms of a modern-day song title, "Don't Worry, Be Happy," except that, in light of vv. 22-34, we would be more accurate to change the title to read, "Don't Worry, Be Holy." The key to living a worry-free lifestyle is to seek first the kingdom of God, v. 31. Jesus instructed His disciples about their relationship to possessions by giving them some don'ts. They should not worry about their lives (*psychē*), about what they would eat, or about what clothes they should wear.

12:23   Verse 23 contains the rationale for the preceding remark: life is more than food, and body is more important than clothing. That is to say, there is more to life than the physical—feeding and clothing the body. There is also the spiritual.

12:24 Using a minor to major argument in vv. 24-28, Jesus compared/contrasted God's care of the birds of the air and the lilies of the field with His provision of His children. With His first illustration, Jesus invited His disciples to look at the crows. Such creatures do not sow or reap, neither do they have storerooms or barns to keep their food. Yet how much more does God love His children? Will He not surely care for them?

12:25 Jesus concluded His illustration by asking a rhetorical question which was designed to expose the futility of worrying over one's possessions: "Which of you by worrying can add time to his life?" The words *hēlikian pēchyn* literally read, "cubit to his stature." Most commentators, however, prefer to translate the words figuratively, as we have done, "time to his life." The question refers back to the rich farmer who, though taking great pains to plan his financial future, died that very night.

12:26 Jesus raised another rhetorical question which reiterated the first: "If you cannot accomplish the least thing, then why worry about the rest?" The message is, if we cannot control the length of our lives, even to adding a brief moment, then why should we be obsessed with material things that cannot add to our lives either?

12:27 Jesus provided a second illustration of God's care, calling His disciples to look at the lilies. The term *krina* was a generic term that could encompass lilies, the anemone, daisies, and so on. In any event, the beauty of the flowers growing alongside the well-watered Galilean hillsides is the point of Jesus' illustration. Such flowers grow effortlessly, neither laboring nor spinning. Yet even Solomon's royal wardrobe (1 Kings 10:4-5, 21, 23; 2 Chron. 9:4, 20, 22), which undoubtedly required much toil and work to make, could not compare to the beauty of the flowers.

12:28 Jesus pressed home the illustration to His disciples. If God so beautifully clothes the grass today, only to throw it into the furnace tomorrow, how much more will He clothe His children? The labeling of the flowers as mere grass heightens the contrast between shrubbery (cf. the temporary nature of grass, Pss. 37:2; 90:5; Isa. 40:6-8; 1 Peter 1:24) and God's children. Not to realize as much is to demonstrate little faith.

12:29   Jesus summarized His instruction thus far by challenging His disciples not to be obsessed with finding food and clothing. The word *meteōrizesthe* can mean "to raise up" or "to worry."

12:30   Jesus gave another contrast; pagans continuously seek after material things because they do not have God in their lives, but Christians need not live frantically, because they have a heavenly Father who is more than willing, and able, to care for them.

12:31   The solution to the problem of the love of money is to seek the kingdom of God above all else in one's life. Jesus assured His disciples that if they would do that, God would provide all their needs. In other words, if the disciples of Jesus will submit to God's rule in their lives and seek to advance His spiritual kingdom on earth by propagating the gospel, then God will care for their physical necessities.

12:32   Jesus allayed the fears of His disciples by promising them the kingdom. Their fear stemmed from the fact that they were a small, unassuming group compared to, say, the mighty Roman empire or even the powerful Jewish religious leadership. Ultimately, however, the kingdom of God entrusted to them, and to all Christians (cf. Dan. 7:13-14), will prevail over all its enemies. The usage of the flock metaphor may come from the influence of Zechariah 11:11 (cf. Zech. 13:7), which compares Israel to a scared, scattered flock of sheep. If so, there is a hint in Luke 12:32 of the coming crisis that would result for the disciples because of the death of Jesus (cf. Matt. 26:31). But Jesus' resurrection would dispel their fears (see Matt. 26:32).

12:33   Jesus concluded the topic of possessions by making three concluding remarks in vv. 33-34. First, He prescribed radical action by challenging His disciples to sell their material things and give them away as alms, v. 33a. Is this counsel to be taken literally or figuratively? Peter Liv has taken up this question and provided some helpful information in arriving at an answer by summarizing some of the key Lucan passages on the renunciation of wealth, 12:33-34 included. He argues that Jesus' demand for renunciation functions as a *test* of discipleship. It is a test of true repentance, as in the cases of Levi and Zacchaeus. It forces one to examine one's values and priorities (Luke 14:26, 33). It reveals the object of one's ultimate allegiance (Luke 18:22; 19:1-10). It differentiates the person who truly recognizes the urgency and radicalness of the message of the kingdom (Luke 5:11, 28; 9:3-4) from the one who remains in the service of mammon.

The demand for renunciation is also a *tool* in the discipleship training process. It provides a context whereby the disciples can learn to be totally dependent on God (Luke 12:33a) and be single-minded in purpose (Luke 18:22). In drawing the disciples' attention to the poor, this demand trains them to be in right social relationships, to be in harmony with the kingdom's ideals for society.

Liv goes on to argue that the call of Jesus to renunciation is a demand for undivided loyalty from His would-be followers, even in the face of crisis. Riches are enticing, and they turn people away from Jesus and the reality of the kingdom. People are called to take decisive action in the face of the eschatological crisis. The force of Jesus' demand on the rich ruler (18:22) should not be attenuated. However, the call to the rich ruler cannot be applied to every bystander without qualification. When applied to bystanders, the demand for renunciation can mean the requirement for *readiness* or *willingness* to surrender all. Such application does not necessarily entail a literal abandonment of possessions, though in some cases it may. This understanding of the teaching on renunciation would seem to be much more compatible with the teaching on the right use of possessions, which allows for owning possessions.

Liv continues, noting that, however, as a test and a tool in the discipleship training process, renunciation can be applied to all, be they leaders or new Christians. Sometimes Jesus used this test and tool; at other times He did not. To those who were already loyal to the Lord, as in the cases of Levi and Zacchaeus, the abandonment of all possessions is not necessary. But they must show genuine signs of discipleship; they are not to be attached to their possessions, nor should they neglect the poor. One's horizontal relationship is often indicative of the state of one's vertical relationship with God. In this vein, the story of Zacchaeus (Luke 19:1-10) serves as a yardstick for genuine conversion and discipleship.

Liv concludes his article by observing that readiness to respond to the call of renunciation is a sign of genuine conversion, a sign of undivided loyalty to Jesus, a sign of unwavering faith in Him. It shows that the person has turned from self-reliance on God, that he or she has changed from self-centeredness to God-centeredness and other-centeredness. Readiness to renounce reveals that there is genuine repentance, a transformation from getting to giving for the cause of the kingdom. The readiness to renounce one's possessions discloses the object of a person's ultimate allegiance and the reality of his or her relationship with God.[5]

5. Liv, "Did the Lucan Jesus Desire Voluntary Poverty of His Followers?" 291-317.

Second, leaving Liv's comments, we suggest that Jesus gave the eschatological motivation for selling one's possessions: in doing so one will store up heavenly treasure, vv. 33b. To seek first the kingdom of God and thereby place spiritual values at the top of one's priorities will ensure eternal wealth. It will be like making purses that do not wear out, or treasure that will not be stolen or destroyed by moths. The last metaphor refers to the fact that one form of ancient wealth was expensive clothing which, when stored in closets, could be destroyed by moths.

12:34 The third comment offered by Jesus concerning possessions was a practical explanation: where a person's treasure is, there will be that person's heart, v. 34. The message is eminently reasonable: if a person's primary interests are earthbound, that is where his or her commitment will be. If a person's interests are spiritual and therefore heavenly in nature, that is where his or her commitment will be. Obviously, disciples should choose the latter alternative.

DULLNESS OF PERCEPTION, 12:35-59

A third hindrance to holy living, in addition to fear of men (vv. 1-12) and love of money (vv. 13-34), is dullness of perception (vv. 35-59). If one focuses merely on this present age, spiritual myopia will set in, dulling the sense of one's eternal values. The solution to this problem, as offered by Jesus, is an acute anticipation of the return of Christ. Jesus expressed this truth by employing a number of negative images: unfaithful stewards (vv. 35-48); a divided household (vv. 49-53); inept meteorologists (vv. 54-56); unforgiven debtors (vv. 57-59).

UNFAITHFUL STEWARDS, 12:35-48

12:35 Jesus used two introductory pictures to challenge His disciples to be ready for service to the Lord. The first was girding the loins, a practice whereby the men would tie their flowing garments around the waist with a belt. It symbolized readiness for work (Ex. 12:11; 1 Kings 18:46; 2 Kings 4:29; Eph. 6:14; 1 Peter 1:13). The second was keeping the lamp burning, suggesting alertness of mind for a task.

12:36 The imagery now switches to servants watching for their lord's return from a wedding. The reference to the "lord" (*kyrion*) is a double entendre, signifying both the master of the servants and Jesus. The uncertainty surrounding the man's return from the wedding celebration is true to life since wedding celebrations in ancient Israel could last up to seven days. But the ultimate significance of the illustration surely is to be found in the call to watchfulness in anticipation of the Lord's second coming. The picture of the master arriving at his home and knocking, seeking entrance, reminds one of Revelation 3:20.

12:37   Those servants who are alert to their master's return will be blessed. So blessed are they, in fact, that the lord will reverse the roles and serve them by girding up his loins and seating them at the table and serving them. This action is reminiscent of John 13:5. It also envisions the return of Christ and His inclusion of His followers in the messianic banquet (Rev. 19:7).

12:38   The reference to the lord returning at the second or third watch seems to reflect the Roman reckoning of nighttime, which was divided into four equal lengths (6:00 P.M.–9:00 P.M.; 9:00 P.M.–12:00 A.M.; 12:00 A.M.–3:00 A.M.; 3:00 A.M.–6:00 A.M.). Thus the time indicated is somewhere between 9:00 P.M. and 3:00 A.M. Those who await their lord's return at the wee hours of the night will be most blessed people.

12:39   Jesus' emphasis now shifted from the servants to the master. The houseowner who knew when a thief planned to break into his house would prevent that possibility. Breaking into a house in ancient Israel would have involved breaking through the mud walls.

12:40   Jesus applied the story to the disciples by reminding them that, because they did not know the hour of Christ's return, they should be ready at all times, for the Son of Man would come like a thief in the night.

12:41   Peter interrupted Jesus and asked Him if the call to readiness applied just to the disciples or to all people, i.e., the crowds.

12:42   Jesus couched His answer in terms of a servant being placed over other servants of a household. The one appointed to the task of meeting the needs of the other servants is characterized by faithfulness and wisdom. The allusion to the disciples who were chosen by Jesus for the purpose of caring for the spiritual welfare of the members of the household of faith is easily detectable in this illustration.

12:43   The servants of the Lord who faithfully discharge their responsibilities in this matter will be blessed.

12:44   That servant will be put in authority over all the householder's belongings. Marshall puts it well: the servant "moves from being temporarily in charge to being permanently in control of all his possessions."[6]

---

6. Marshall, *Commentary on Luke*, 541.

12:45   However, it is possible that that servant will convince himself that his lord will be delayed and take the occasion to mistreat the other servants and maids, and to eat and drink and get drunk.

12:46   But if the servant does that he will only have himself to blame for the ensuing punishment. The lord will return at an expected time and will cut the servant off from the faithful. There are two sets of parallel phrases in this verse: "at a time when he does not expect him"/"at an hour he does not suspect"; will "cut him into two"/"assign him the lot with the faithless." The word *dichotomēsei* means cut in two and seems to be an unusually harsh response from the returning lord. However, the word is best understood as a hyperbole expressing severe punishment. Thus the translation "cut off" best captures the meaning (cf., for example, *1QS* 2:16, "he will be cut off from all the sons of light"). Jesus is probably making an allusion here to the delay of the Parousia (the return of Christ). The warning, then, is directed to disciples who should remain vigilant in the anticipation of Christ's return. If they "slack off," however, they might find themselves unprepared for that eventuality.

12:47   Verses 47-48 specify the judgment that will be meted out upon unfaithful servants (of the Lord). Two scenarios are envisioned. The first is the punishment that will be executed upon the servant who knew his master's desires but did not prepare for, or act upon, them. That servant will receive many blows, that is, great punishment.

12:48   The second scenario is that the servant who does not know the master's will, and therefore does not do it, will be punished less severely than the first servant. As the commentators rightly remark, the proportionate judgment referred to by Jesus was based on the Old Testament contrast between deliberate sins (those committed with "a high hand") and those done in ignorance (Num. 15:27-30; Deut. 17:12; Ps. 19:13). But in either case, the warning is designed to elicit continual faithfulness from the disciples of Jesus. It is just as applicable to those outside of Christ. People who do not accept Christ will be judged. However, those who heard the gospel but rejected it will be more severely punished than those who did not accept Christ because they never heard the gospel. The principle is profound: to whom much is given, much will be required.

DIVIDED HOUSEHOLDS, 12:49-53

12:49   A second negative image illustrating spiritual dullness is that of divided households relative to the cause of Christ. Two related ideas surface in vv. 49-53: the twofold desire of Jesus, vv. 49-50, and the discord that results because of Jesus, vv. 51-53. First, Jesus expresses His twofold desire in vv. 49-50. He came to cast fire on the earth, which He wished had already happened (*ti thelō ei ēdē anēphthē* is a contrary-to-fact statement). The nature of the "fire" is debated. Is it a symbol of the refining work of the Spirit? Or is it a figure of speech for judgment? The verses that follow, vv. 51-53, with their themes of division and persecution, at the very least support the second option. But in light of Luke 3:16 and the reference there to the Spirit and fire, perhaps the two interpretations are not mutually exclusive. Marshall states it well:

> It is more probable that the saying in its present context should be understood with reference to judgment (cf. Acts 2:19; Rev. 8:5, 7; 20:9). . . . But this process of judgment works by way of the separation of good from evil, and hence leads to the persecution of the righteous and division among men; fire is therefore taken to be a symbol of strife and division. . . . This interpretation fits in with 3:16 where the coming One is to baptize with the Spirit and with fire, the fire being expressive of the judgment that falls upon the wicked. At the same time, however, the fire also falls upon the righteous, and it may be right to see it as affecting both Jesus and his disciples who must submit to the baptism described in the next verse. Consequently, it may be possible to bring the two main interpretations together by identifying the fire as the Spirit who will mediate the "judging" message of the kingdom.[7]

12:50   The parallel desire of Jesus is formulated by a cognate accusative: "I have a *baptism* with which to be *baptized*." In light of v. 49 and a passage such as Mark 10:38-39, we are surely on the right track to understand the phrase to be an allusion to Jesus' upcoming death on the cross, together with the judgment He endured at the hands of God for the sins of the world. For Jesus' part, He could wish that that event had already been fulfilled. The word "fulfill" (*telesthē*) indicates that Jesus' upcoming death is according to the divine plan.

12:51   Verses 51-53 present the stark reality that Jesus' mission will divide families, a chord struck in the infancy narrative (2:34). Although Jesus did come to bring peace among men (2:14), His message would inevitably cause internecine strife, as well.

7. Ibid., 547.

12:52   Verses 52-53 bear out the preceding warning. A family of five will be divided over the claims of Christ, three members pitted against two, and two against three.

12:53   Chiastic structure governs v. 53, which delineates the five members of the family envisioned in v. 52: father against son/son against father, mother against daughter/daughter against mother, mother-in-law against bride/bride against mother-in-law (cf. Mic. 7:6). The whole family was disrupted over Christ: father, mother, daughter, son, and the son's wife. Many Christians today can attest to this truth. But, thankfully, those believers who are opposed by their natural family because of their faith in Christ have a spiritual family upon which to rely as support (cf. Luke 8:19-21).

INEPT METEOROLOGISTS, 12:54-56

12:54   A third negative image illustrating insensitivity to the things of God is drawn upon in vv. 54-56—the Jews of Jesus' day were inept at forecasting the spiritual climate of their day. Fitzmyer perceptively catches the import of Jesus' words here:

> Jesus turns to the crowds and continues his remarks with ominous words. As weatherwise Palestinian farmers, they had learned to read the face of nature, with its clouds and winds. They should, then, be able to assess the critical moment in which they exist. He thus contrasts the people's "meteorological sensitiveness" with the "religious sensitiveness." . . . Without referring directly to himself or his message . . . , Jesus upbraids his audience for their lack of comprehension. Coming on the heels of sayings concerned with judgment, this aspect of judgment underlies the present set of sayings too. What the audience fails to notice is the critical import of his appearance and message about God and his kingdom (see 7:22-23; 11:20).[8]

Jesus' audience rightly recognized that clouds forming in the west from the Mediterranean Sea would soon bring rain.

12:55   Similarly, when they felt the wind blowing from the south from the Arabian desert, Jesus' contemporaries knew a heat wave would soon be upon them.

12:56   Jesus called such people hypocrites because, if they possessed the ability to interpret meteorological matters, they should also have been able to interpret the spiritual significance of Jesus' pres-

---

8. Fitzmyer, *The Gospel According to Luke X–XXIV,* 999.

ence among them. His presence among them should have signaled to them that the kingdom of God was a spiritual reality. But their unwillingness prevented them from doing so.

UNFORGIVEN DEBTORS, 21:57-59

12:57   The final negative image exposing Jesus' contemporaries' failure to perceive spiritual truth is that of unforgiven debtors, vv. 57-59. The point of the parable is not entirely clear, but Ellis seems to be correct to relate the incident of a debtor settling with his accuser out of court to the need for the sinner to seek forgiveness before God before Judgment Day, when it will be too late.[9] Jesus began the illustration by rebuking the crowds for their lack of prudence in assessing their relationship to God.

12:58   Jesus' audience well knew that the sensible thing for a man to do who was in debt to another was to be reconciled to that person before he took the debtor to court. If the debtor does not make every effort to avoid the situation, then his adversary will drag him before the judge who, in turn, will hand the debtor over to the bailiff, who will then throw the man into prison.

12:59   That being the case, the debtor will surely stay in prison until he repays every cent (*lepton*) he owes. The point of the parable seems to be that the Jews listening to Jesus' voice needed to wake up to the spiritual reality that they were sinners before God. The wise thing for them to do would be to seek God's forgiveness for that debt, for to wait until Judgment Day would be too late. Only by trusting in Christ could they be spared from that fate.

HOMILETICAL SUGGESTIONS

The three divisions in this chapter could conveniently form a three-sermon series entitled, "Hindrances to Holiness." The first hindrance would be "The Love of Men: Blaspheming the Spirit or Confessing Christ?"—vv. 1-12. The sermon can be broken down into two major points: blaspheming the Spirit and confessing Christ. Under the first heading (vv. 1-3, 8-10), the different interpretations of this enigmatic topic should be explained. Under the second heading—confessing Christ—two items would need to be addressed, which can help motivate the believer to not be ashamed of Christ: the judgment of

9. Ellis, *The Gospel of Luke,* 183.

God (vv. 4-5) and the provision of God (vv. 6-12). The second sermon could be entitled "The Love of Money," vv. 13-34. Two points could be developed. The first would be the parable of the rich fool, vv. 13-20. The second would be teaching on wise living. It comprises two items: trust in God, vv. 21-28, and commitment to God, vv. 29-34. The third sermon, "Dullness of Perception," vv. 35-59, could be expounded by simply covering the negative images detailed in the commentary: unfaithful stewards, vv. 35-48; divided households, vv. 49-53; inept meteorologists, vv. 54-56; and unforgiven debtors, vv. 57-59.

LUKE

CHAPTER

THIRTEEN

A SYNOPSIS OF THE KINGDOM

The central theme in Luke 13 is the kingdom of God. What Luke provides the reader is basically a synopsis of the kingdom. Four points are detectable: entrance into the kingdom, the main requirement for which is repentance (vv. 1-9); opposition to the kingdom, manifesting itself, as usual, through the Jewish religious leaders (vv. 10-17); the growth of the kingdom, the pattern of which moves from small influence to great impact (vv. 18-21); the triumph of the kingdom, the basis of which is the death and resurrection of Jesus (vv. 22-35).

ENTRANCE INTO THE KINGDOM, 13:1-9

The first point summarizing the kingdom of God in Luke 13 is in vv. 1-9, and it is the need for repentance in order to enter the kingdom of God. Jesus utilized three illustrations to emphasize that point, two of which were historical incidents and the third of which was a parable.

13:1 The first illustration emphasizing the need for repentance was the incident between Pilate and the Galileans. The incident was referred to by some of the people in the crowd listening to Jesus. Apparently, what transpired was that some Galileans (probably less than eighteen; otherwise the next story would lose its force, v. 4) who were offering sacrifices in the temple of Jerusalem were killed by Pilate's soldiers. The phrase "whose blood Pilate had mingled with their sacrifices" is probably figurative, signifying the fact that the Galileans

283

were killed at the same time they offered sacrifices. The story itself is not attested in extrabiblical sources and is unique to Luke. But that it was historically accurate can be ascertained from three observations. First, that Galilean laymen were offering sacrifices was typical of the feast of Passover, the only time laymen could slaughter the animal sacrifices themselves. Normally that task was reserved for the priest.[1] Second, the Galileans had a reputation for rebelliousness against Rome.[2] Third, according to Josephus, Pilate was a brutal man.[3] These observations bespeak of the verisimilitude of the incident.

13:2   Jesus replied with a question which exposed a false assumption on the part of the crowd: "Do you think that these Galileans were greater sinners than other Galileans?" The assumption of the Galilean audience was that calamity was divine punishment for sin (cf. Job 4:7; 8:20; 22:4-11; John 9:1-2).

13:3   Jesus emphatically negated His own question, "No, I tell you! (*ouchi, legō hymin*) unless you repent, you will be destroyed in a similar way." The reference is to spiritual judgment before God, not necessarily a life shortened by tragedy.

13:4   Jesus used a second historical illustration to emphasize the need for repentance, the story of the eighteen Jerusalemites killed by the collapse of the tower in Siloam. Siloam was the name of the water supply at the juncture of the southeast walls inside the city, fed by the Gihon Spring outside the east wall. An underground tunnel connecting the two was cut through the rocks in the days of King Hezekiah.[4] It may be that when Pilate built an aqueduct to improve the water supply the project caused the tower at the juncture of the southeast walls to fall. Though the incident is not recorded elsewhere, it matches the situation at the time of Jesus. Jesus' point was that those eighteen people killed in the tragedy were no more sinful than all the rest of the inhabitants of Jerusalem at the time.

13:5   For a second instance Jesus answered His own question with emphatic negation, "No, I tell you! If you do not repent, you will be destroyed in similar fashion." Although it is possible that Jesus anticipated the coming fall of Jerusalem in A.D. 70 with these words, they more probably refer, once again, to judgment before God.

---

1. Jeremias, *The Eucharistic Words of Jesus*, 207.
2. See Marshall, *Commentary on Luke*, 553.
3. See Josephus, *Ant.* 18.55-59; 60-62; 85-87.
4. The Siloam inscription records the point at which workers met each other after tunneling through the stone.

13:6   The third illustration used to emphasize the need for repentance was agricultural in nature, the parable of the unfruitful tree, vv. 6-9. A man had a tree planted in his vineyard, a common practice (cf. Luke 17:6; 28; 20:9). When the owner checked the tree for fruit (presumably at a later time when it should have been ripe, see v. 7), he found none.

13:7   For three years the owner had been checking for fruit on the tree, but with no success. Disappointed, the man told the gardener to cut the tree down so that it would no longer sate the soil and space.

13:8   But the gardener interceded on behalf of the fig tree, asking that it be granted one more year to bear fruit. The gardener hoped that loosening the soil around it and putting fertilizer on it might help the fig tree to produce fruit.

13:9   The gardener left the option open, so that if, after one more year the fig tree did not produce fruit, the owner could cut it down. The meaning of the parable is rather straightforward. Jesus' audience had the opportunity then to repent of their sin and thereby enter the kingdom of God. If they did so, their lives would become fruitful unto God. But that offer would not last forever. The time of grace would one day come to an end and then judgment would fall.

OPPOSITION TO THE KINGDOM, 13:10-17

The second point summarizing the kingdom of God in Luke 13 is in vv. 10-17. It is a familiar one—opposition to the kingdom. And, as often was the case, that resistance occurred in the context of Jesus' healing on the Sabbath, in this situation a crippled woman. From a literary point of view, the account is a pronouncement story, precipitated by a miracle. Verses 10-13 record Jesus' controversial action. Verse 14 contains the synagogue official's criticism. Verses 15-17 provide Jesus' authoritative pronouncement.

13:10   The setting of the incident was an occasion on which Jesus was teaching in one of the synagogues.

13:11   At that time a woman afflicted with an infirmity for eighteen years was in the audience. The physical cause of her inability to straighten up has been examined by J. Wilkinson, who identified the paralysis as the result of *spondylitis ankylopoietica,* which produces the fusion of spinal bones.[5] The spiritual cause, however, is attributed by Luke to a spirit, probably a demonic spirit (cf. v. 16).

5. Wilkinson, "The Case of the Bent Woman in Luke 13:10-17," 195-205.

13:12   When He saw her, and without being asked to do so, Jesus told the woman that she was liberated of her infirmity. The perfect tense *apolelysai,* "liberated," indicates that the woman's ensuing cure would be permanent.

13:13   With that, Jesus placed His hands upon her and she was immediately healed, now able to straighten her back. The force of the imperfect tense of the verb "was glorifying" (*edoxazen*) God, indicates the woman's heartfelt thanks to Jesus.

13:14   Verse 14 contains the complaint of the ruler of the synagogue to the crowd. He was angry that Jesus had healed the woman on the Sabbath, retorting that there were six other days to perform such activity. Jesus should choose one of those days to work a miracle, not the Sabbath (cf. Ex. 20:9; Deut. 5:13).

13:15   Verses 15-17 record Jesus' authoritative pronouncement in response to the criticism. He utilized a minor to major argument—if it was permissible to care for livestock on the Sabbath, then surely the caring for a needy human being, especially an Israelite, would meet with divine approval. In v. 15 Jesus accosts the hypocrisy of the synagogue leader by pointing out that Jewish custom allowed the loosing or untying of the ox and ass from the feeding trough on the Sabbath for the purpose of leading it to water (see *b. Shab.* 5:1-4; 7:2; 15:1-2; *b. Erub.* 2:1-4). The word "loose," as referring to the untying of the livestock, anticipates a play on words in v. 16; the woman "was loosed" (*lythēnai*) from her sickness.

13:16   Jesus called the woman a daughter of Abraham, signifying that she was a part of the people of God and therefore most definitely deserved, at the very least, the attention animals received on the Sabbath. For eighteen long years Satan had prevented her from being loosed (*lythēnai*) from her illness. In fact, as Marshall perceptively observes, Satan continued his work of preventing healing even on the Sabbath.[6] Should not Jesus do as much and cure the woman?

13:17   Jesus' pronouncement silenced His critics, convicting them with shame (cf. Isa. 45:16). On the other hand, the rest of the synagogue crowd rejoiced at what God was doing through Jesus (cf. Ex. 34:10).

---

6. Marshall, *Commentary on Luke,* 555.

THE GROWTH OF THE KINGDOM, 13:18-21

The next aspect of the kingdom of God surveyed in Luke 13 is the growth of the kingdom, vv. 18-21. Two parables illustrate its progress: the parable of the mustard seed, vv. 18-19, and the parable of the leaven, vv. 20-21. Both of these similes demonstrate that the kingdom of God as present in the life of Jesus began small but one day will end up big, making a lasting impact on the world.

13:18   Jesus introduced the first parable with a two-pronged question: What is the kingdom of God like? To what should it be compared?

13:19   Jesus answered His questions by comparing the kingdom of God to a man who planted a mustard seed in his garden and then watched it grow into a tree big enough to house the birds of the sky. The point was that the kingdom of God, like the mustard seed, begins small but will grow into a large plant capable of housing many birds (cf. Dan. 4:9-18 and Ps. 104:12). Some interpret the birds to be a symbol of evil and that therefore Jesus was making a negative point about the church. They argue that the truth being communicated is that the church began with purity but one day will grow into a large, compromising religious institution, housing evil people. But this reading of the parable of the mustard seed is surely allegorical and incorrect. Rather, Jesus was alluding to the fact that, although His spiritual kingdom began in an insignificant way (it was initiated with a few motley disciples), nevertheless it took hold of this world and, through the preaching of the gospel, transformed the lives of many. It will continue to do so until Jesus returns and sets up His physical kingdom on earth (cf. Rev. 10:1-6), which will consummate the invisible, spiritual kingdom already present.

13:20   Jesus introduced a second parable by again raising the question, "To what should I compare the kingdom of God?" As a further illustration, He compared the kingdom to a woman taking leaven and mixing it with three measures of flour until it all was leavened, or fermented. The point of the description is to highlight the great influence of a small amount of leaven which, in this instance, caused the rising of bread sufficient enough to feed 160 people. Some interpreters wish to view this parable negatively (compare the previous parable) by taking the leaven as a symbol of evil (as it customarily is in the Bible). It is more likely that the leaven possesses a positive meaning here. It typifies the powerful influence of the kingdom of God which, though having begun small, will one day change the world.

THE TRIUMPH OF THE KINGDOM, 13:22-35

Verses 22-35 consist of three instances which depict the rejection of Jesus, as well as His ultimate triumph. The first instance, vv. 22-30, contrasts those who will not enter the kingdom of God with those who will. The point in time that will mark the demarcation between the two will be the return of Christ, the event that will publicly vindicate Jesus. The second instance, vv. 31-33, recalls Herod Antipas's desire to kill Jesus, along with Jesus' prophecy of His resurrection and subsequent victory. The third incident, vv. 34-35, reports Jesus' lament over Jerusalem's upcoming rejection of Him, together with His prediction of His triumphant entry into the city which itself anticipates His glorious second coming.

13:22 Verses 22-30 comprise the first instance which highlights the triumph of Christ and His kingdom. With v. 22 the reader is reminded that Jesus was en route to Jerusalem, teaching along the way in the towns and villages.

13:23 On one occasion while on that journey, someone asked Jesus, "Sir, are only a few people going to be saved?" The question seems to reflect a debate that existed among Jews at the time of Christ. Some believed all Jews would be saved on Judgment Day: "All Israelites have a share in the world to come" (*m. Sanh.* 10:1). Others thought that only a minority of Jews would be saved in the end: "This age the Most High has made for many, but the age to come for few" (*4 Ezra* 8:1; cf. 7:47 and 9:15). Jesus responded to the man.

13:24 Marshall's analysis of Jesus' response to the question is superb:

> The question is not answered directly (cf. Acts 1:6-8) although an answer is implicit in the second clause. Instead the point is applied existentially to Jesus' hearers: rather than speculate about the fate of others, let them make sure now that they enter by the door, however narrow and difficult it is, rather than put off decision, because at the last day many people who want to enter will find that they have left it until too late.[7]

Jesus used two metaphors to get His point across: the narrow door (v. 24) and the closed door (v. 25). According to v. 25, people should strive to enter the narrow door of the kingdom now, not later.

---

7. Ibid., 564-65.

Later will be too late, even though many may try. The word "strive" (*agōny*, "agonize") captures the struggle involved in denying one's self and taking up the cross to follow Jesus. Part of that struggle stems from the fact that the doorway to the kingdom of God is narrow (cf. Matt. 7:13-14). In other words, one needs to repent of sin and embrace Jesus as Savior. Not many seem to be willing to do that. They appear to prefer the broad road of destruction.

13:25   The second metaphor is the closed door, which is introduced in v. 25 by the phrase "from the time which." These opening words provide further rationale for the inability of many people to enter the door of the kingdom of God—the master will eventually lock the door, closing it to late seekers despite the pleas of those standing outside begging for admission. Tragically, the only reply they will solicit from the master is, "I do not know who you are or from where you have come." There is an end to God's grace. Therefore, it is incumbent upon people to respond while they have time.

13:26   Verses 26-30 envision the stark contrast in destinies that await those who reject Christ, compared to those who accept Him. According to v. 26, those outside the kingdom of God will desperately appeal to their past contacts with the master. They will invoke their casual friendship with Jesus: they ate and drank with Him and were taught by Him. It is clear that the story singles out for criticism the Jews who were contemporaries of Jesus. To have only been nominally associated with Jesus will not bode well for a person's eternal destiny. What is required is heartfelt devotion to Him, the master and Lord.

13:27   In a vein similar to Psalm 6:8, Jesus the master's only response to the plea of those found outside the kingdom on Judgment Day will be, "I do not know you; depart from me all you who work evil." Not to trust Jesus and thereby enter in His kingdom is to align oneself with the evil of this world.

13:28   To add insult to injury, not only will Jesus' Jewish contemporaries not enter the kingdom of God; they will have to endure the sight of those heroes of their religion, such as Abraham, Isaac, Jacob, and the prophets, enjoying the blessings of the kingdom. Those people who do not accept Jesus will be on the outside looking in. Such separation will cause weeping and gnashing of teeth, indications of how great will be their sorrow.

13:29   If that were not bad enough, such Jews will also have to watch from a distance as people from the four corners of the world, Gentiles included, enter the kingdom of God and enjoy the messianic banquet (see also Isa. 25:6-8; 54:13-14; 55:1-2; Luke 14:15; 22:16; Rev. 3:20; 19:9).

13:30   The inclusion of people outside Israel, along with Gentiles, in the kingdom of God while excluding many of the Jews of Jesus' day inside Israel will be nothing less than an eschatological reversal of roles: the last will be first; the first will be last. We also meet here again the Lucan emphasis on the universal nature of the gospel (cf. Acts 1:8).

13:31   Verses 31-33 record the second instance which highlights both the rejection and triumph of Christ's kingdom. It involved Herod Antipas's reaction to Jesus. According to v. 31, on that occasion when Jesus was talking about those of His contemporaries who would be excluded from the kingdom, word came to Jesus from the Pharisees that Herod Antipas wanted to kill Him. The motive of these particular Pharisees seems to have been pure—because Herod desired to kill Him, Jesus should quickly leave Galilee, the province of that tetrarch. This was the same Herod who earlier had killed John the Baptist (cf. Mark 6:14-28).

13:32   Jesus was unflappable in His mission. He called Herod a fox, insinuating that he was crafty and devious. But Jesus refused to be intimidated by that politician. Rather, He had a task to perform—He would continue to exorcise demons and heal illnesses, for "today and tomorrow and on the third day" He would reach His goal. The quoted phrase is a Semitic idiom for a short, indefinite period of time followed by an imminent and certain event (Strack-B 2:203). The "goal" referred to by Jesus comes from the word *telos*. The idea behind the term is the upcoming death and resurrection of Jesus, which was God's will, and the vindication of His life.

13:33   But Jesus, in fact, would leave Galilee, not because He was afraid of Herod but because He was moving according to a divine schedule. The reference to "today, tomorrow and the next day" corresponds to the words in v. 32, "today and tomorrow, and on the third day." Both sets of words anticipate Jesus' death and resurrection. This is confirmed by the next words which assert that Jesus will arrive in Jerusalem in order to die. In other words, Jesus knew that He was scheduled by divine appointment to die in Jerusalem, the place where a number of prophets of the Lord had been killed in the past (2 Kings 21:16; 24:4; 2 Chron. 24:20-22; Jer. 26:20-23; 38:4-6).

13:34   Verses 34-35 give the third incident which focuses on the rejection and acceptance of Christ and His kingdom. Verse 34 begins with an apostrophe to Jerusalem, which will lead to a lament over the city (see v. 35), "O Jerusalem, Jerusalem." The words of Jesus contained two points. First, Jerusalem has rejected, and will continue to reject, God's prophets sent to her, including the greatest of them all, Jesus. She goes so far as to murder and stone them. Second, by contrast and to no avail, Jesus often desired to shelter the city like a hen gathers her brood under her wings (cf. Deut. 32:11).

13:35 According to v. 35, Jesus seems to have made two future prophecies about Jerusalem. First, the words "Behold your house is forsaken" seem to predict the coming destruction of Jerusalem by the Roman army in A.D. 70 (cf. Matt. 24:2; Luke 21:20). Second, the words "You will not see me until the time comes when you say, 'Blessed is the one who comes in the name of the Lord'" probably merge two prophecies into one. The first one predicted the acclamation of Jesus by the Jews at the triumphant entry (Luke 19:37-38), itself a commonly accepted messianic interpretation of Psalm 118:26. The second prediction emerges out of the first—it envisioned Israel's acceptance of Jesus as Messiah at His second coming. It is interesting that Marshall thinks that these words may well afford a last hope of salvation for the Jews at the Parousia, and he invokes Acts 3:19 and Romans 11:26 as support for that view.[8] If so, this interpretation correlates with our theory that Luke believes that Israel will be restored to Messiah Jesus at His return.

HOMILETICAL SUGGESTIONS

The outline presented in this chapter should preach itself:

Luke 13: Synopsis of the Kingdom

I. Entrance into the Kingdom, vv. 1-9
   A. The Galilean Incident, vv. 1-3
   B. The Jerusalem Tragedy, vv. 4-5
   C. The Parable of the Fruitless Fig Tree, vv. 6-9

II. Opposition to the Kingdom, vv. 10-17
   A. Jesus' Controversial Action, vv. 10-13
   B. Opposition from the Synagogue Leader, v. 14
   C. Jesus' Authoritative Pronouncement, vv. 15-17

8. Ibid., 577.

III. The Growth of the Kingdom, vv. 18-21
  A. The Parable of the Mustard Seed, vv. 18-19
  B. The Parable of the Leavened Bread, vv. 20-21

IV. The Triumph of the Kingdom, vv. 22-35
  A. The Challenge to Jesus' Audience, vv. 22-30
  B. Herod's Desire to Kill Jesus, vv. 31-33
  C. Jesus' Prophecies over Jerusalem, vv. 34-35

LUKE
CHAPTER
FOURTEEN

DYNAMICS OF DISCIPLESHIP

The thematic tie that seems to bind the pericopes in Luke 14 is the dynamics of discipleship, concerning which three can be identified. First, discipleship elicits criticism, vv. 1-6. Second, discipleship emulates humility, vv. 7-24. Third, discipleship requires commitment, vv. 25-35.

DISCIPLESHIP ELICITS CRITICISM, 14:1-6

The first episode in Luke 14 is a pronouncement story, which is comprised of the three typical components—Jesus performs a controversial miracle; the Jewish religious establishment criticizes Him; Jesus silences His critics with an authoritative utterance. However, in this particular instance, the components do not follow the preceding order; the criticism comes first. The overall message of the section is that Jesus, and His followers, can expect criticism for the good they do.

14:1 The setting of the chapter is in the house of a ruler of the Pharisees. The reference to "ruler" probably means a prominent member of the Pharisaic party. Jesus had been invited there on a Sabbath to eat a meal. It was customary for the guest speaker in the synagogue on the Sabbath to be invited for a meal after the service. But at this particular dinner, the people in the house were scrutinizing Jesus' behavior to see if He would break any more laws regulating the Sabbath. In effect, v. 1 records the criticism of Jesus by the religious establishment, characteristic of pronouncement stories.

14:2 The people were not disappointed, for there happened to be a man in front of Jesus who was suffering from dropsy, a disease that swells up the body due to fluids forming in the cavities and tissues. Verse 2 sets the stage for the controversial miracle that follows in vv. 3-4.

14:3 Seeing the afflicted man, Jesus asked the scribes and the Pharisees whether or not it was lawful to heal on the Sabbath. In raising the question, Jesus shifted the attention from Himself to His critics.

14:4 The critics were quiet because they were now the ones who were in a dilemma. If they said no, they would reveal themselves for what they really were—inhumane religious leaders. If they said yes, they would be breaking their own laws governing the Sabbath. Hearing no objection, then, Jesus took hold of the man, healed him, and sent him away whole. The description of the miracle is as simple as it is beautiful.

14:5 Jesus then probed His critics with a further question, "If a son or an ox falls into a well, would you not immediately pull it out, even on the Sabbath?" Although some manuscripts have "ox" (*onos*), not "son" (*huios*) in order to alleviate the incongruity of the value between a child and an ox, the best reading is "son." This is so because it is well attested (Sinaiticus) and it is the most difficult reading. The two are, in fact, incomparable in worth. The sense, then, is as follows: despite the Sabbath, the Pharisees would surely rescue a child, or even an ox, which had fallen into a well.

14:6 Jesus' pronouncement silenced the critics. They were not able to answer His question. Their inability to do so spoke for itself.

DISCIPLESHIP EMULATES HUMILITY, 14:7-24

Verses 7-24 specify one of the great marks of discipleship—humility. The section can be divided into two parts: the principle of humility, vv. 7-15, and the parable on humility, vv. 16-24.

14:7 Verses 7-15 explain the principle of behavior that should characterize disciples—they should be humble, not status seekers. The setting of the scene was still the home of the head Pharisee, especially the festive meal to which Jesus and others had been invited. While there, Jesus noticed that some of the guests were seeking the seats of honor at the banquet table. Marshall notes that prominence at such occasions depended on one's rank and distinction. The most important guests arrived late for banquets. The top place at a Jewish meal was at the head of the table or the middle of the middle couch (see *Sir.* 3:17; Strack-B 1:774, 914).[1] To those seeking places of honor, Jesus crafted a parable designed to expose their selfishness.

14:8 Jesus said to them that if they have been invited to a banquet (*gamos*), they should not recline in the seat of honor, for it may be that the host has already invited someone else who is more prestigious to sit there.

14:9 That being the case, the host would have to request the person to give up his seat of honor to the late arriving, more prominent person. How embarrassing that would be to have to get up and give up the first seat while moving down to the last seat.

14:10 Far better for the guest to choose the last place in which to sit. Then, when the host comes and asks that person to move to a more prominent place, he or she will be honored before all at the banquet table. These words echo Proverbs 25:6-7, "Do not put yourself forward in the presence of a king or stand in the place of the great; for it is better to be told, 'Come up here,' than to be put lower in the presence of the prince." *R. Lev.* 1 has a similar statement: "Stay two or three seats below your place and sit until they say to you, 'Go farther up.' Do not begin by going up because then they may say to you, 'Go down.' It is better that they should say to you, 'Go up, go up,' than that they should say to you, 'Go down, go down!'"

14:11 A divine principle is stated in v. 11 in chiastic fashion: "Everyone who exalts himself will be humbled; everyone who humbles himself will be exalted." Two observations can be made concerning this spiritual axiom. First, the two key words—"exalt" (*hypsōn*) and "humble" (*tapeinōthēsetai*)—occurred earlier in Luke 1:52 with reference to Jesus (cf. Phil. 2:5-11). Jesus humbled Himself by becoming a servant. But one day God will exalt Him by bestowing on Him a name above every name. This principle is extended to all disciples of Jesus. Second, the verbs in Luke 4:11, "will be humbled" and "will be exalted," are theological passives, meaning that God is the unnamed subject of the action. It is God who will humble those who try to exalt themselves or vice versa.

14:12 In vv. 12-14, Jesus illustrates the principle of humility and servanthood, marks of a true disciple. He challenged the host not to

1. Marshall, *Commentary on Luke,* 581.

invite his friends, brothers, relatives, and rich neighbors to a luncheon or a dinner, for they would be able to repay the favor.

14:13 Rather, the host should invite to his meal the poor, the crippled, the lame, and the sightless. The contrast in vv. 12-13 between the sets of four guests is striking.

14:14 Jesus pronounced a beatitude upon that host who does the latter because his motivation for inviting those incapable of returning the favor would be pure. But even if those unfortunate people are not able to repay the kindness, God will do so by resurrecting the host along with the righteous at the end of the age (cf. Dan. 12:2-3; Acts 24:15). The principle enunciated by Jesus obviously is applicable to all who will follow His dictates.

14:15 In vv. 15-24 Jesus provides a parable on humility—the parable of the great dinner. The parable was prompted by a remark made by one of the guests eating with Jesus at the Pharisee's house. The eternal and eschatological significance of Jesus' challenge was not lost to this particular guest who exclaimed his own beatitude, "Blessed is the one who will eat in the kingdom of God!"

14:16 In response, Jesus told the story of a man who invited many people to a great dinner. In ancient Israel, the wealthy first sent invitations to their well-to-do guests, announcing the time of the upcoming meal. When the time of the meal came, the host would summon the guests to the meal.

14:17 At the proper time, the servant of the host went to the guests announcing that the meal was now ready and summoning them to come. Ellis puts it this way, "To require repeated invitations was a status symbol in Jerusalem society."[2] If so, the upcoming turn of events whereby the rich refuse the invitation to the meal while the poor accept it, symbolizes the reversal of roles that will occur on Judgment Day.

14:18 The Greek phrase *apo mias* should probably be translated as "unanimously" or "with one accord." Thus, with one accord the invited guests declined to come. Typical of ancient Palestinian stories, three illustrations are given. The first example was that of a farmer who had purchased some land. His rather flimsy reason for not attending the meal was that he had to go out to the land and inspect it. He therefore asked to be excused from the meal.

---

2. Ellis, *The Gospel of Luke,* 194.

14:19   The second illustration was that of a man who had bought five yoke, or pairs, of oxen. He asked to be excused from the meal because he needed to inspect his newly purchased livestock.

14:20   The third illustration was that of a man who had just been married and therefore could not attend the meal (cf. Deut. 20:7; 24:5).

14:21   When the servant reported the results to the host, the latter was furious. Already the reader is alerted to the divine symbolism of the owner with Jesus' choice of words, *oikodespotēs*—house lord. That is, the "despot" represents God. In response, then, the owner commanded the servant to go out quickly (because the meal was ready) to the streets and lanes of the town and invite the poor, the crippled, the sightless, and the lame (cf. v. 13). Undoubtedly the contrast intended by Jesus' illustration of the rich and the poor was that between those Jews who rejected Him, especially the religious establishment, and those Jews who accepted Him, especially the outcasts of society.

14:22   The servant did as he was commanded, but he reported back to the owner that there was still room for more at the meal.

14:23   The master then told the servant to go outside of the town into the highways and alongside the fences and compel people to come so that the banquet hall could be filled. The reference to compelling the people to come reflects the Oriental courtesy in which the invited guests at first politely refused to come until they were pressed to do so. As the commentators well recognize, the veiled reference is to the Gentiles who would soon be invited to enter the kingdom of God through faith in Christ (cf. Acts. 13:46; 18:6; 28:23-28).

14:24   Jesus concluded the parable with an ominous statement that signified the reversal of fates that would occur on Judgment Day— those who were originally invited to the messianic banquet (the Jewish religious leaders) will not be admitted into the kingdom of God. The poor and the outcasts (those Jews and Gentiles who accept Jesus) will.

DISCIPLESHIP REQUIRES COMMITMENT, 14:25-35

The last section of Luke 14 describes the commitment that is necessary to be a disciple of Jesus. Two points are made relative to the topic: the challenge to commitment, vv. 25-27; the cost of commitment, vv. 28-35.

14:25   Verses 25-27 contain Jesus' challenge to discipleship. According to v. 25, the growing number of crowds following Jesus on the way to Jerusalem prompted Him to issue a charge to them.

14:26   As the shadow of the cross loomed large in Jesus' life, it was no time for halfhearted devotion on the part of would-be disciples. If anyone wanted to follow Jesus, he or she must hate or renounce family—father, mother, wife, children, brothers, sisters—and his/her own life. Not that Jesus was suggesting that His disciples should mistreat their families or themselves. Rather, in terms of comparison, all other people and priorities must pale in significance compared to the Christian's allegiance to Christ.

14:27   Whoever is not willing to take up the cross and follow Jesus cannot be His disciple.

14:28   In vv. 28-35, Jesus gives three illustrations of what it means to count the cost in following Him. The first is in vv. 28-30—the tower builder. Jesus raised the question, "Who plans to build a tower of defense for a house or town without first sitting down and calculating the expense to see if there are enough resources to complete it?"

14:29   The person who does not count the cost might not get past laying the foundation. Moreover, in addition to the financial loss, that person will experience the emotional embarrassment of being ridiculed by others.

14:30   That person will have to endure the taunting criticism of the neighbors, "Here is a man who could not finish what he started!"

14:31   Jesus' second illustration of counting the cost concerned a king figuring the logistics of the size of his army compared to that of his enemy. Would he enter into battle with a force of ten thousand soldiers against an army of twenty thousand?

14:32   The king who wisely counted the cost beforehand, discovering his army to be insufficient to fight an approaching enemy, would send a delegation of peace to meet the enemy before it was too late.

14:33   Jesus pressed home the application by challenging those who desired to follow Him to renounce their possessions and priorities in order to make Him Lord of all. Only then would they be His disciples.

14:34   The third illustration used by Jesus of the need to count the cost in order to be a disciple was salt. Like the previous two illustrations, the point of the metaphor of the salt was that lack of total commitment nullifies discipleship. Salt that retains its saltiness is good. But if salt loses its saltiness, it is good for nothing. "Half-saltiness" does not fulfill the purpose of salt. The word for tasteless is "moronic" (*mōranthē*). For a chemical explanation of how Palestinian salt like that found in the Dead Sea can become insipid, see Marshall's explanation.[3]

14:35   Insipid salt serves no purpose. It would not benefit the ground, as salt normally did when used as a fertilizer for soil. Without saltiness, salt would not even be helpful for a dung heap. Instead people would just throw it out. Jesus challenged His audience to get the point—discipleship requires wholehearted devotion to Him.

HOMILETICAL SUGGESTIONS

Luke 14 can be nicely treated in three sermons, following the theme and outline presented in this chapter. The first sermon, "Discipleship Elicits Criticism," would cover vv. 1-6. The sermon itself would address the reality that following Jesus will invoke difficulties, often generated by the religious establishment. The three points offered in this chapter—Jesus' controversial action of healing the man with dropsy, the criticism of the Pharisees, and Jesus' pronouncement statement—adequately cover the text. The second sermon, "Discipleship Emulates Humility," vv. 7-24, can be dealt with in storytelling fashion. Karen Mains has a wonderful chapter in her book *Open Heart, Open Home* which can be used to dramatize the parable of the great supper.[4] It envisions the dialogue of the poor and needy outside of the gates of a mansion looking in on a sumptuously prepared meal. The story concludes with a powerful challenge to the church to go out into the highways and byways of life in order to bring people to Christ. The third sermon, "Discipleship Requires Commitment," vv. 25-35, can be expounded using the two major points we suggested: the challenge and cost of discipleship. The last point could utilize the three illustrations found therein: the tower builder, the warrior-king, and tasteless salt.

3. Marshall, *Commentary on Luke,* 596.
4. Mains, *Open Heart, Open Home,* 123-31.

LUKE

CHAPTER

FIFTEEN

THE GOSPEL OF THE OUTCAST

T. W. Manson insightfully introduces Luke 15, and the unit in which it occurs, 15:1–19:27, as the

"Gospel of the Outcast" . . . for here Luke's use of his "L" material seems to reveal a deliberate attempt to show God's concern for those human beings whom people tend to despise or condemn. This is evident not only in the parables of chap. 15 (dealing with a shepherd, a poor [perhaps miserly] woman, and a prodigal son), but in other episodes later on (the dishonest manager [16:1-8a], the dishonest judge [18:1-8], the rich man and Lazarus [16:19-31], the ten lepers [17:11-19], the Pharisee and the toll-collector [18:9-14], and even in the story of Zacchaeus [19:1-10]). It thus introduces into the end of the travel account a note of importance for the Lucan portrait of Jesus; it prepares (indirectly) for the ministry in Jerusalem and the passion narratives.[1]

THE PARABLE OF THE LOST SHEEP, 15:1-7

According to vv. 1-2, the setting for the three parables in Luke 15—the lost sheep, vv. 3-7; the lost coin, vv. 8-10; the lost, or prodigal, son, vv. 11-32—was the criticism of Jesus by the Jewish religious estab-

---

1. T. W. Manson, *The Sayings of Jesus as Recorded in the Gospels According to St. Matthew and St. Luke arranged with Introduction and Commentary* (London: SCM, 1971), 282.

301

lishment because sinners were coming to Him. The theme of the three parables is the joy of God at the repentance of a sinner.

15:1   On the way to Jerusalem, the tax collectors and sinners were drawing near to Jesus to hear Him (cf. 5:29). Coming on the heels of chapter 14, this episode of the outcasts from the religious society coming to Jesus exposes the ironic contrast between them and the Pharisees' rejection of Jesus.

15:2   The Pharisees and scribes grumbled about Jesus' association with the sinners. The very thought of welcoming, and eating with, non-religious Jews was unthinkable for the religious leaders. The later rabbinic document *m. Mek. Ex.* 18:1 reinforced that belief: "Let not a man associate with the wicked, not even to bring him the law."

15:3   As He often did in the face of criticism, Jesus responded by telling a parable. The singular "parable" is probably to be taken generically, "a parabolic discourse."

15:4   Jesus began by asking what man who owns one hundred sheep would not search for a lost sheep until he finds it. The size of the flock signifies a moderate-sized herd. The identification of the lost sheep would have been discovered by the shepherd at night as he counted his sheep as they entered the sheep's gate. The reality of the shepherd leaving the sheep in the desert while searching for a stray sheep continues to this very day with the Bedouin shepherds who roam along the Dead Sea on the border of Israel and Jordan. The idea of the love of the shepherd for the sheep echoes God's love for Israel (Ezek. 34:12, 23).

15:5   Verses 5-7 record the joy of the shepherd finding his one lost sheep, comparing it to the joy of God over a repentant sinner. According to v. 5, upon finding the sheep, the shepherd joyously lifts the lamb upon his shoulders.

15:6   When he arrives home, the shepherd would then call together friends and neighbors, inviting them to celebrate with him over his newly found sheep.

15:7   Similarly, there will be more joy in heaven over one repentant sinner than over ninety-nine righteous people who do not need to repent. The future tense "there will be" probably refers to the coming Judgment Day. The words "joy in heaven" probably refer to the celebration of the angels (cf. v. 10), or perhaps they are a circumlocution for God. It is a matter of debate as to whether or not Jesus' mention of ninety-nine who need not repent is ironic. If so, it would have been a veiled criticism of the Pharisees' and scribes' perception of themselves as righteous. If not, it would be a matter-of-fact comment.

THE PARABLE OF THE LOST COIN, 15:8-10

Fitzmyer beautifully catches the significance of the parable of the lost coin:

> The parable of the lost coin makes almost the same point as that of the lost sheep, but now, instead of a moderately rich shepherd, the main figure is a poor woman who has lost one of her ten drachmas. Luke may intend to depict her as miserly. In any case, she serves to portray divine initiative in seeking out what was lost, again the sinner, as the introduction suggests (v. 2). The appended application allegorizes the sense of the parable in stating that the joy is limited not to earth, but is found even "before God's angels" (v. 10). The paired parables thus insist that, through the preaching of Jesus, God's initiative and grace are extended in boundless fashion; they pass over the defection of the sinner and seek out instead such a one for reform. If a human being will exert such effort to recover her property, how much more will God himself expend? This is the Lucan Jesus' answer to the criticism of the Scribes and the Pharisees, the reason why he consorts and dines with such sinful people.[2]

15:8 Jesus introduced the parable of the lost coin with a question, "What woman who has ten silver coins, and loses one of them, will not light a lamp and sweep her house until she finds the coin?" The coinage mentioned, the *drachma,* was a Greek silver coin, basically equivalent to the Roman *denarius.* About 300 B.C. it represented the value of a sheep, but by the first century A.D. it was greatly devalued. The ten silver coins may, as Jeremias argues, refer to the woman's dowry, in this case worn on a string as a headdress.[3] This might explain her deep desire to find a coin missing from it. The actions the woman performed—lighting a lamp and sweeping the floor—indicate that her house was a typical poor Palestinian dwelling with a low door and no windows.

2. Fitzmyer, *The Gospel According to Luke X–XXIV,* 1080.
3. Jeremias, *The Parables of Jesus,* 133.

15:9   Like the shepherd in the previous parable, the woman in this parable, upon finding the lost coin, will invite her friends and neighbors to celebrate with her.

15:10   As in the case of the lost sheep, so now in the incident of the lost coin, the message is that there will be joy among the angels in heaven over the repentance of one sinner. That is, the angels will rejoice with God over the repentance of a lost soul.

The Parable of the Lost Son, 15:11-32

Regarded as perhaps the greatest of all Jesus' parables, the parable of the prodigal son has become the topic of painters, dramatists, musicians, literature, philosophers, and, of course, preachers.[4] Fitzmyer summarizes its meaning:

> As it now stands in the Lucan Gospel, the parable presents the loving father as a symbol of God himself. His ready, unconditioned, and unstinted love and mercy are manifested not only toward the repentant sinner (the younger son) but toward the uncomprehending critic of such a human being. The parable portrays the message of Jesus, the kingdom-preacher, especially with the Lucan stress on the divine willingness to accept the repentant sinner into that kingdom. This parable probes the human psyche and touches it deeply in the cry of the young son, "Father, I have sinned against heaven and before you. I no longer deserve to be called your son." In the Lucan Gospel as a whole the story exemplifies the proclamation of the Lord's year of favor, which Jesus was sent to announce to the downtrodden (4:18-19). As the Son of Man who has come to seek out and to save what was lost (19:10), he will not be deterred from such a proclamation by the attitude of those who might prefer their own sense of uprightness to joining in joy and love for those who react with repentance to such a proclamation.[5]

On the one hand, the experience of the prodigal son is altogether too common. F. W. Danker cites an ancient Greek papyrus letter that reminds one of the parable of the lost son:

> Greetings: I hope you are in good health; it is my constant prayer to Lord Serapis. I did not expect you to come to Metropolis, therefore I

---

4. The words are Fitzmyer's in *The Gospel According to Luke X–XXIV*, 1083; see his amplification of the comment.

5. Fitzmyer, *The Gospel According to Luke X–XXIV*, 1085-86.

did not go there myself. At the same time, I was ashamed to go to Kanaris because I am so shabby. I am writing to tell you that I am naked. I plead with you, forgive me. I know well enough what I have done to myself. I have learned my lesson. I know I made a mistake. I have heard from Postumus who met you in the area of Arisnoe. Unfortunately he told you everything. Don't you know that I would rather be a cripple than owe so much as a cent to any man? I plead, I plead with you . . . (Signed) Antonios Longus, your son.[6]

On the other hand, the message of the parable of the prodigal son is not commonly known—the love of God for His wayward children. Such a theme is rooted in the Old Testament (Jer. 31:18-20; Hos. 11:1-9; Isa. 63:15). Perhaps no contemporary preacher has better captured the picture of God as presented in the parable than H. Thielicke's famous sermon about God as "the waiting father." In that sermon he wrote:

> In our lives we may have squandered what we would. Perhaps we have squandered and mismanaged our marriage. We may have squandered away our good reputation. We may have ruined our bodies or our imaginations. Perhaps our thinking has been corroded by envy and the heat of harmful passions. Perhaps we have dragged the faith of our childhood in the gutter and become nihilists and cynics. All this may be true. But right here comes the great surprise: God has not given me up. He still counts me his child. He tells me that he cannot forget me. When anybody has done as much for me as my Father in heaven has done, when he sacrifices his best beloved for me, he simply *cannot* forget me. And therefore I can come to him. God pays no regard to what I have *lost*; he thinks only of what I *am*: his unhappy child, standing there at his door again.[7]

15:11 Jesus introduced the parable by calling attention to a man who had two sons. The stories of these two sons provide the outline of the parable as a whole: the younger son (vv. 11-24) and the elder son (vv. 25-32). The message will become clear in the telling of the parable: the former represents non-religious Jews, sinners, and outcasts. The latter represents the Jewish religious crowd.

15:12 It can be deduced that the younger son was about seventeen years old because no mention is made of his being married, which

6. Danker, *Jesus and the New Age,* 170.
7. Thielicke, *The Waiting Father. Sermons on the Parables of Jesus,* 38-39.

often took place between the ages of eighteen and twenty. The younger son requested that the father give him his portion of the property falling (*epiballon*) to him. According to ancient Jewish customs in Israel, a father could dispose of his inheritance to a child in one of two ways: either by a will to be executed at his death (see Num. 36:7-9; cf. 27:8-11) or as a gift while he was still alive (see *Sir.* 33:19-23 for a common warning against doing such). In the latter case, the usufruct, or interest, on the property would continue to go to the father until his death. If the son sold the property, the purchaser could only take possession of it after the father's death.[8] The reference to the father dividing his inheritance up between the sons reminds the reader of Deuteronomy 21:17 and its regulation that the elder son should receive a double portion of the father's possession. Thus, in the parable of the prodigal son, the younger received one-third of the father's inheritance whereas two-thirds of it was reserved for the elder son.

15:13 "Not many days after" is a litotes (expressing something positive in a negative way). Creed has shown that the words "gathered together" referred to the younger sons' action of converting the property into cash.[9] Having done so, the son moved away to a distant country, probably a land outside of Israel. There he squandered away his possessions with reckless abandon. According to v. 30, part of his inheritance was wasted on prostitutes.

15:14 When the young man had spent his money, a severe famine came upon that country and the lad found himself destitute.

15:15 In order to subsist, the younger son joined up with a citizen of the land. The employer, a Gentile who owned pigs, hired the Jewish lad to feed the swine. The description bespeaks of the low point the young man had reached. Jewish abhorrence of pigs, unclean animals according to the Old Testament (Lev. 11:7; Deut. 14:8), was proverbial. A later rabbinic saying encapsulates that disgust, "Cursed be the man who raises pigs, and cursed be the man who teaches his son Greek wisdom" (*b. B. Qam.* 82b).

15:16 The young man was so famished that he desired to eat the carob pods that were the pig's food. Nobody would feed him anything else.

15:17 In such dire straits, he came to his senses. Speaking to himself in soliloquy fashion, he realized that his father's hired hands had

8. See Derret's analysis of the legal situation in *Law in the New Testament,* 107.
9. Creed, *The Gospel According to St. Luke,* 199.

far more to eat than he did. His destitute situation began to bring him to the place of repentance.

15:18   The lad determined to leave the situation he was in and go back to his father, saying, "Father, I have sinned against heaven and before you." The words "against heaven" are a circumlocution for God. The young man's confession pinpoints the twofold reality of sin—it offends God and humans.

15:19   The son's recognition that he no longer deserved to be called his father's son attests to the depth of his repentance. He knew that both financially and emotionally he was disinherited from his father. He deserved to be treated as one of his father's servants.

15:20   Then the young man got up and started home toward his father. The depth of the son's repentance is matched only by the depth of the father's love. His actions touch the heart. The father saw the young man while he was still a long way off. This suggests the father longed and looked for his son's return one day. Then, he had pity on his son by running to meet him. This indicates that the father took the initiative in being reconciled to his son. Next the father threw his arms around the son's neck, repeatedly kissing him. This shows that the father forgave the son (cf. 2 Sam. 14:33), even before he asked it.

15:21   The lad began to utter his predetermined confession that he had sinned against God and his father and no longer deserved to be called his son (cf. vv. 18-19). Some manuscripts add the words "Treat me as one of your hired hands" (Sinaiticus; B; etc.). But the shorter reading (see manuscripts p75; A; etc.) is the preferred one because the longer reading is most probably a scribe's harmonization of v. 21 and v. 19.

15:22   The father's response probably surprised the young man. The father told his servants to quickly bring three articles of clothing to the lad, each of which signified the son's authoritative status. First, he was to be clothed with the "best robe" (*stolēn tēn prōtēn*), that is, the robe of finest quality (cf. Gen. 41:42). Second, he was to have the ring of authority (cf. *1 Macc.* 6:15). Third, sandals were given him. Sandals were worn by a free man, not a slave, thus further signifying the son's exalted position.

15:23   Next the father commanded that the "fattened calf" be killed and eaten. The custom informing the statement was that of specially feeding an animal, saving it to be slaughtered for a festive occasion. Obviously, the father considered his wayward son's return as a time to celebrate and rejoice.

15:24   The father stated the cause of the celebration: his son was spiritually dead but had now come back to life; he was lost but was now found. The last description recalls the theme of chapter 15. At the father's words, the family began to celebrate.

15:25   Verses 25-32 introduce the older son, whose reaction to his brother's return was less than joyful. If the younger son who was lost but now found symbolized the non-religious Jews who repented of their sin and embraced Jesus, then the elder son symbolized the religious Jewish leadership who rejected Jesus, and who opposed His ministry to sinners and the outcasts. The elder son was out in the fields. When he drew near his home, he heard music (*symphōnias*) and dancing.

15:26   The elder son inquired of one of the servant boys what was happening.

15:27   The servant replied, "Your brother has come, and your father has killed the fattened calf, because he has received him back healthy." The last word refers to both the younger son's physical and spiritual well-being.

15:28   The elder son became angry, undoubtedly fueled by jealousy. He refused to go into the house and join the party. The father became aware of the situation and, as he did with the younger son, took the initiative to restore the elder son, asking him to join the celebration in the house.

15:29   The elder son replied to his father that he had served him like a slave for many years, not once breaking his commands. And yet the father had not even given the son a goat (much less a fattened calf) to eat and celebrate with his friends. The pouting son obviously symbolized the Pharisees and scribes, who thought that God owed them something for their scrupulous obedience to the divine law.

15:30   The elder son scornfully called the younger son "that son of yours." How could the father kill a calf and celebrate the return of a person who had spent his father's estate on "prostitutes" (*pornōn*)?

15:31   The father's soft reply to his "son" (*teknon*) reminded him of two things. First, he, the elder son, had always been with the father, which stressed their continuing intimate association. Second, the father reminded his eldest son that he still owned all that the father had, i.e., the two-thirds of the remaining inheritance.

15:32   The father concluded his comments to the elder son by saying to him that they had to rejoice and be merry about the return of the younger son ("this your brother," cf. v. 30) because, whereas he was once spiritually dead, now he was alive. Once he was lost, but now he was found. Two distinctive Lucan ideas surface here: First, the word "had" (*edei*) to rejoice and be merry refers to the necessity of accomplishing the divine plan. Second, the theme of the lost being found ties together the three parables of Luke 15: the lost sheep, the lost coin, and now the lost son.

HOMILETICAL SUGGESTIONS

It is hard to improve on perfection, and that is how the three parables of Luke 15 should be described. Their story plots, their historical-cultural backdrop, and their timeless message that God rejoices over the lost who are found, provide all the material one needs in preaching them. In other words, one can do no better, it seems, than to repeat their stories. We would add that when preaching the parable of the prodigal son one consider reading the sermon by Helmut Thielicke, "The Waiting Father," perhaps the greatest sermon ever preached on that parable.[10]

---

10. Thielicke, *The Waiting Father*, 38-39.

LUKE

CHAPTER

SIXTEEN

THE USE AND ABUSE OF MONEY

Luke 16 in general deals with the use and abuse of money. The parable of the dishonest steward (vv. 1-13), though difficult to fully understand, at least is clear in its message that disciples should wisely use their money. The parable of the rich man and Lazarus (vv. 19-31) serves as a stark reminder that one's possessions can be squandered selfishly rather than used for the benefit of others. Coming between these two parables is a series of sayings of Jesus basically treating the subject of the Mosaic Law (vv. 14-18). No noticeable connection can be made between those remarks and the theme of money that dominates the two parables. This lack of thematic connection actually speaks well of Luke's reporting ability, for it demonstrates his faithfulness to the sources before him.

THE PARABLE OF THE DISHONEST STEWARD, 16:1-13

The meaning of the parable of the dishonest steward has puzzled many of its interpreters. Two broad viewpoints have been proposed.[1] First, there are those who interpret the steward's actions of reducing the amount of debts owed to his master as falsification of the records. Second, others see the reduction of the debts as a cut in the steward's commission, which was ethically acceptable. As we will see, the evidence seems to support the second interpretation.

1. See Fitzmyer's excellent survey of the issue in *The Gospel According to Luke X–XXIV*, 1096-99.

16:1   Jesus' primary audience in Luke 16 was the disciples, though the Pharisees overheard the conversation (cf. v. 14). The parable centered on the steward or manager (*oikonomon*) of a certain rich man's estate. The latter received word that his steward had been cheating him in the handling of his financial affairs. The economic setting presupposed here has been analyzed by two authors, M. D. Gibson[2] and J. D. M. Derrett.[3] They have shown that the rich man was typical of an absentee landlord, the owner of a Galilean *latifundium* (a large land estate), who entrusted the transaction of his business to a steward. This person was properly trained and given great authority, able to represent his master in significant financial matters (e.g., the renting of land to tenant-farmers, the making of loans against a harvest, the liquidation of debts, the keeping of all financial accounts). In this particular case, however, the steward was unfaithful to his master. The specifics are not given in the parable.

16:2   Upon hearing the accusations, the owner called the manager before him and commanded him to make an inventory of his financial dealings. That list would accomplish two things: First, it would expose the steward's dishonesty. Second, it would facilitate the steward's replacement, serving as a record for the next manager. The master then summarily dismissed the steward.

16:3   In soliloquy fashion the steward expressed his quandary, "What am I going to do? My master is taking my job away from me. I am not strong enough to dig, and I am ashamed to beg!" The steward found himself in a dilemma. He was not physically capable of handling the former, and he was not emotionally able to deal with the latter.

16:4   The aorist *egnōn* (know) expresses sudden knowledge—suddenly the steward came up with an idea for persuading people to accept him into their homes once he lost his job.

16:5   The steward called each of his master's debtors to come to him. Two examples follow. Of the first debtor the steward asked how much he owed the overlord (*kyrios*).

16:6   The man replied that he owed one hundred baths (*batous*) of olive oil. A bath was about nine gallons (see Josephus, *Ant.* 8.57). Thus the man owed about nine hundred gallons of oil. The steward told the man to sit down and quickly change the bond (*grammata*) to fifty baths of oil.

---

2. Gibson, "On the Parable of the Unjust Steward," 334.
3. Derrett, *Law in the New Testament*, 48-77.

16:7   The second example involved a man who owed one hundred *korous,* or bushels, of wheat (see Josephus, *Ant.* 3.321). The steward gave him similar instructions, giving him the bond and telling him to change it to eighty bushels of wheat.

16:8   Because of the dishonest steward's wise actions, the lord (*kyrios*) praised him. Two questions emerge from this statement: First, why did the lord praise the steward? Here the research of Gibson and Derrett referred to earlier helps us. They have shown that in the ancient Near East, it was a common and acceptable practice for a financial agent such as the steward in this parable to lend his master's property out to others at a commission or interest fee which was added to the principal in promissory notes or bonds. The notes or bonds often only mentioned the total amount owed, without differentiating the principal and interest. On this reading, the steward's reduction of the debt was neither a cancellation or falsification of the accounts. Rather, it was a reduction of the steward's commission. Thus, the one debtor only owed the master fifty jugs of oil whereas the other fifty was the steward's commission. The second debtor owed eighty bushels of wheat and the twenty other bushels were the steward's commission. The high interest rates (50 percent for the oil and 25 percent for the wheat) were not exorbitant for that day. The reason, then, for the lord's praise of the steward was that he acted prudently in eliminating his commission in order to win the favor of the master's debtors. The second question that emerges from v. 8a concerns the identification of the lord. That answer depends on where the parable proper ends. If it ends at v. 8b, then the lord is Jesus. But if the parable ends at v. 8a, then the lord is the master (cf. vv. 1, 3, 5), with v. 8b constituting Jesus' application of the story. This last proposal seems to be the most correct.[4]

Verses 8b-13 can be viewed as Jesus' threefold application of the parable to His disciples. First, vv. 8b-9 elevate the dishonest servant as an example of one who wisely uses money, something which the disciples could stand to learn. Two points are made. Verse 8b contains a practical lesson; v. 9 provides the eschatological motivation for doing so. According to v. 8b, the wise use of money by the sons of this age (in this case the dishonest steward) is a lesson the sons of light could learn. The underlying concept informing the two phrases, "sons of this age" and "children of light" (cf. John 12:36; Eph. 5:8; 1 Thess. 5:5;

4. See Dodd, *The Parables of the Kingdom,* 17.

1QS 1:9; 2:16), is the Jewish idea of the two ages—this evil age and the righteous age to come. The word introducing the contrast "for" (*hoti*) could either be viewed as indicating indirect speech or, more likely, as a simple consecutive further explaining the behavior of the wise steward. Fitzmyer well summarizes v. 8:

> Why does the master praise the manager? Though the master may not have known the amount of commission that his manager was acquiring, he must be presumed to have known about the customary practice. There was no "agency for wrongdoing" (i.e. no legal system in which an agent's evil conduct would become the responsibility of the master), and the master would scarcely have approved of the manager's falsification of accounts (or probably even any direct violation of the Torah). The master praises the manager for his prudence, because he realizes that the manager has eliminated his own commission from the original usurious bonds.[5]

16:9   The eschatological motivation for using one's possessions wisely is that it prepares an eternal dwelling for those who so use it. Jesus' words run as follows: "And I tell you, make for yourselves friends out of the mammon of unrighteousness in order that when it runs out you will be received in eternal dwellings." Five observations can be made from this statement. First, the preposition *ek* should be translated literally, "make for yourselves friends *out* of the mammon of righteousness." That is, through the wise use of money (possibly alms giving; see below), disciples can make friends of others. Second, the word "mammon" is from the Aramaic word *mamon*, which originally meant, "that in which one puts one's trust," hence wealth.[6] Third, the phrase "mammon of unrighteousness" probably means mammon leading to unrighteousness. At the very least, the idea latent in the phrase highlights the tendency of mammon to lead to ill-gotten gain.[7] Fourth, the antecedent of "receive you" is indefinite. It may refer to angels, God, or those people/friends who are benefited by the disciple's wise use of money, probably in the form of alms. The last suggestion seems most plausible. Fifth, the eternal dwellings refer, in general, to heaven and perhaps more specifically to the heavenly mansions that await the righteous (cf. John 14:2; *4 Ezra* 2:11; *1 Enoch* 39:4). The meaning of

---

5. Fitzmyer, *The Gospel According to Luke X–XXIV*, 1098.
6. Friedrich Hauck, "Mammon," 4:390-412; 391.
7. Fitzmyer, *The Gospel According to Luke X–XXIV*, 1109.

vv. 8b-9, therefore, can be expressed thus: similar to the dishonest steward, disciples of Christ should use money to help others, for in doing so they will increase their rewards in heaven. However, this understanding of vv. 8b-9 should not be misconstrued to mean that Luke understands Jesus to be teaching that salvation results from one's merits.

16:10   Verses 10-12 give the second application of the parable of the dishonest servant to disciples of Jesus. It contrasts faithfulness and unfaithfulness with regard to possessions. The principle is straightforward: the one who is faithful in little things will be faithful in more important things; the one who is dishonest in little matters cannot be trusted with greater responsibility. It seems that this axiom is a commentary on the dishonesty of the steward (cf. vv. 1b-2). Wise though he was in preparing for his future, still the steward lost his job because of unfaithfulness. So, then, disciples of Christ can learn a couple of lessons from the dishonest manager. Positively, like him, they can prepare for their heavenly future by helping those in need today. Negatively, the unethical behavior of the steward should motivate disciples to be dependable in all God has entrusted to them.

16:11   The application continues in interrogative form: "If therefore in dishonest mammon you are not faithful, who will trust you in the true things?" That is, if a person cannot be trusted with worldly wealth, how can they be trusted with spiritual realities?

16:12   Jesus posed a second question by way of application, "And if you cannot be trusted with someone else's possessions, who will give you your own?" "Your own possessions" could either refer to material things or to spiritual realities. Either way, faithfulness is the key to the proper use of one's material and spiritual possessions.

16:13   In v. 13, Jesus summarized a general attitude toward material things by giving a third application of the parable of the dishonest steward: no servant can serve two masters wholeheartedly, for he will hate one and love the other or cling to one and look down on the other. In other words, a servant by definition is one who is enslaved to the will of another. So it is with God and money. A person must choose between them. The obvious application to be drawn from Jesus' statement is that disciples should commit themselves unreservedly to God alone.

SAYINGS ABOUT THE MOSAIC LAW, 16:14-18

Verses 14-18 do not seem to fit in with the theme of money, though v. 14 does appear to point somewhat in that direction. But the theme that does give coherence to the paragraph is the Law of Moses. Thus, vv. 14-15 contrast the Pharisees' (meticulous interpreters of the Mosaic Law that they were) proclivity to emphasize the outward things of the Law with the divine emphasis on the heart. Verses 16-17 stress both the discontinuous and continuous relationship between the kingdom of God and the Law, respectively. Verse 18 uses divorce as an illustration of the continual validity of God's law for disciples of Christ. As mentioned earlier, the fact that the theme of money does not extend to vv. 14-18 is actually a testimony to Luke's faithfulness in recording his sources.

16:14   Verse 14 contains Luke's editorial comment, listening to Jesus' talk about possessions were the "money-loving" Pharisees, who sneered at Him. The greed of the Pharisees was apparently well-known (cf. Strack-B 1:937; 2:222; 4:1, 336-39).

16:15   Jesus returned the compliment by pointing out that the Pharisees were inordinately concerned to justify themselves before others. But God will not be fooled by such external boasting; He looks on the heart. While meticulous observance of the Law and the public esteem that money brings may cast the Pharisees in a good light, such things do not impress God. The things that are exalted by human beings are an abomination to Him. The rabbinic parallel says it well, "One who is proud of heart is designated an abomination, as it is said, 'Everyone that is proud in heart is an abomination to the Lord,'" Proverbs 16:5 (*m Mek. Ex.* on Ex. 20:18). It may be that Jesus' criticism of the Pharisees stemmed from their tendency to say that their wealth was a result of their piety and therefore confirmed God's blessings on them.

16:16   This verse is a *crux interpretum*. Every clause requires comment. The first clause is, "up until John (were) the Law and the prophets." The Law and the Prophets signify the Old Testament (cf. Luke 24:44). The question is, Was John's ministry restricted to that period of time, as Conzelmann argued?[8] That is, does "until" (*mechri*) include or exclude John? Although the grammar alone cannot settle the issue, the larger context of Luke's gospel can, for 3:1-17; 7:26 show that John was a part of that new era of salvation. Thus, it is more accurate to say

---

8. The following discussion of v. 16 is indebted to Marshall's analysis in *Commentary on Luke,* 628-30.

that John the Baptist was a *transitional* person between the period of Israel and the period of Jesus. The second clause, "from that time on the kingdom of God has been preached," also requires comment. Do the words "from that time on" (*apo tote*) include or exclude John the Baptist in, or from, respectively, the preaching of the kingdom of God? Again, in light of 3:1-17 and 7:26, John seems to have been a transitional figure in the era of salvation.

The third clause is difficult, "and everyone forcefully enters it." The term *biazetai* is a deponent verb (middle in form, active in function) and should be translated, "forcefully enters." But what does it mean? Ellis summarizes the three main possibilities: "(1) The demonic powers (or Jesus' opponents) oppress it. (2) The Zealots seek to 'force' it to birth through violence. (3) The believing 'press' into it."[9] We agree with the first interpretation, as does Ellis, except that those who opposed the kingdom in Jesus' day involved more than the supernatural sphere of demons; they also included humans, especially Jesus' opponents. Two clues in Luke 16:14-16 show this to be the case. First, v. 14 indicates that the Pharisees, in effect, tried to hinder the working of the kingdom of God in the life of Christ. Second, v. 16, with its mention of John the Baptist, recalls the opposition of Herod and the Jewish leaders. These, too, attempted to thwart the progress of the kingdom. Matthew 11:12 seems to support this interpretation.

16:17   If v. 16 indicates that there was a certain amount of discontinuity between Jesus and the Mosaic Law, vv. 17-18 indicate that there was also continuity between the two. Verse 17 reads, "But it is easier for the sky and the earth to pass away than for one stroke of the Law to fall." The meaning of "stroke" (*keraian*) is debated. It could be: the smallest Hebrew letter (the *yod*), the tittle distinguishing similar Hebrew letters, or the scribal ornaments added to various letters. Whichever is the most accurate, the meaning is the same for all three proposals—the most insignificant detail of the Law will not pass away. R. J. Banks puts it well in his monumental work on Jesus and the Law in the Synoptics, "The Law has lost none of its validity despite the coming of the kingdom. It is, however, in the demands of the kingdom, not in its own continued existence, that the Law is validated."[10]

16:18   Verse 18 provides an illustration which indicates the continuing validity of the Law—the Old Testament teaching on divorce. Jesus in

9. Ellis, *The Gospel of Luke*, 203.
10. Banks, *Jesus and the Law in the Synoptic Tradition*, 218.

this statement absolutely forbids divorce. Whoever divorces his wife commits adultery. Whoever marries a divorced wife commits adultery. Whereas the Mosaic Law reluctantly permitted divorce (Deut. 24:1-4), the original divine intention prescribed that husband and wife live together harmoniously until death (Gen. 2:23-24). It was such intention that Jesus undoubtedly appealed to here (cf. Matt. 5:32; 19:3-10; Mark 10:2-12). Though this injunction may raise the eyebrows of moderns or fall on deaf ears, still its truth is the prescription for a healthy, stable society. Though there may be exceptions to this rule (see the qualifying clauses in Matt. 19:9 and 1 Cor. 7:15), adherence to its general truth is expected among disciples of Christ.

THE PARABLE OF THE RICH MAN AND LAZARUS, 16:19-31

In vv. 19-31 Luke returns to the theme of possessions. In the parable and application of the dishonest steward (vv. 1-13) the theme addressed was the proper use of money. Now, in the parable of the rich man and Lazarus, vv. 19-31, the accent falls on the abuse of money, particularly the rich man's callous insensitivity to a beggar man. There are two parts to the parable. The first, vv. 19-26, deals with the theme of the reversal of the fortunes in the next life for the rich and the poor (cf. 1:53; 6:20-26). The second part, vv. 27-31, deals with the inability of the Law and the Prophets, and even the resurrection, to motivate the rich to repent. Purported extrabiblical parallels to the parable of the rich man and Lazarus are thoroughly critiqued by Marshall[11] and Fitzmyer,[12] and are found wanting.

16:19 Jesus began the parable by calling attention to a certain rich man. All manuscripts leave the individual unnamed, except p75 (the second-century Greek manuscript of Luke). It has a shortened form of the Egyptian word *Nineuēs—Neues.* The meaning of the name is debatable, but it may refer to Nineveh, in an attempt to spell out the fact that both entities, the rich man and the city, suffered the judgment of God. The Vulgate translates the name as *Dives,* which means rich. Most probably, the name did not originally occur in Luke's gospel. This rich man lived luxuriously. He dressed in purple and fine linen. The purple coloring came from the fish *murek,* which inhabited along the Phoenician coast. The inside of it was used to dye linen purple, a

---

11. Marshall, *Commentary on Luke,* 633.
12. Fitzmyer, *The Gospel According to Luke X–XXIV,* 1126-27.

sign of royalty (see Mark 15:17, 20; Rev. 18:12). The man ate sumptuously on a daily basis.

16:20   In dire contrast to the rich man was a poor beggar named Lazarus, who was thrown at the gate of the wealthy man. The implication is that he was ill or crippled. The name "Lazarus" is an abbreviation of the Old Testament name Eliezer, which means "God has helped," a fitting description of the destiny of this particular man in the afterlife (v. 22). This is the only time a character is given a name in Jesus' parables. This could signify that the story was a true life experience. Some have thought that this Lazarus was the brother of Mary and Martha, especially since in both scriptural instances a resurrection did not convince Jesus' opponents (cf. Luke 16:27-31 with John 11:39-46). But the similarities probably are coincidental rather than actual correspondences. In any event, this Lazarus was a beggar and was covered with sores.

16:21   Lazarus longed to be fed (cf. the same expression used of the prodigal son, 15:16) with the scraps that fell from the rich man's table. To make matters worse, the dogs licked Lazarus's sores. The point is obvious—the rich man could have cared less about Lazarus's needs.

16:22   The day came when the beggar died. At death he was carried by the angels to the bosom of Abraham. The thought of angels accompanying the souls of the righteous to heaven seems to first occur here. It is later attested to in rabbinic sources (Strack-B 2:223-25). The idea of Abraham's bosom can be explained in one of three ways. First, it might derive its explanation from the Old Testament concept of the righteous being gathered at death to the fathers, such as Abraham (Gen. 15:15; 25:8). Second, it could suggest the tender thought of a child lying on its parent's lap (cf. John 1:18). Third, it can be understood as sitting at the place of honor at the messianic banquet (see John 13:23). The context of Luke 16:22 tips the scales in favor of the third view: Because Lazarus was consigned to the temporal status of being a beggar at the rich man's table, in the afterlife his fate was reversed such that now he was seated at the place of honor in the messianic banquet. It may be that Abraham's bosom is to be equated with Paradise (cf. Luke 23:43). The rich man, too, died and was buried, undoubtedly with pomp and ceremony.

16:23   The destiny of the rich man was *hades* (the abode of the dead) and, in particular, the place of judgment or hell therein. The deceased man was in torment. He turned his eyes and saw at a distance Abraham and Lazarus at his side.

16:24   The rich man called out to father Abraham, probably thinking himself to be a good abiding Jew. He requested mercy of Abraham, even though he himself never showed such to Lazarus. In fact, the rich man presumptuously asked that Abraham send Lazarus to serve him! The rich man wanted Lazarus to dip the tip of his finger in water to temporarily soothe his thirst and the agony of his pain resulting from the flames of hell. What horrible imagery!

16:25   Abraham's response pinpointed the reversal of fates that occurred for the rich man and Lazarus. The rich man received the good things during his life on earth, while Lazarus experienced only the bad things. Now the tables were turned. Lazarus received divine comfort and bliss while the rich man greatly suffered.

16:26   *Kai en pasi toutois* literally means, "in all these things," but idiomatically it means "besides all this." Thus, besides the rich man's moral culpability preventing him access to Abraham's abode was an unbridgeable chasm separating the two parties (cf. *1 Enoch* 18:11-12 for a similar description of the separation of hell and heaven). There is no hint here of purgatory or remedial cleansing. The chasm was fixed, it is assumed, by God.

16:27   That request failing, the rich man then implored Abraham to send Lazarus (probably via a dream or vision) to his father's household, to warn them of impending doom. Apparently the man was still under the mistaken impression that Lazarus was at his beck and call.

16:28   The rich man had five brothers still living in his father's house. He begged Abraham to send Lazarus to testify and warn them of the torment they too faced, if they did not change.

16:29   Luke uses the historic present tense for Abraham's reply: "Abraham *says*, 'They have Moses and the prophets. Let them listen to them.'" In other words, the five brothers had ample testimony in the Law and the Prophets without needing a miraculous sign in order to change their behavior.

16:30   The rich man pathetically disagreed, arguing that they would only repent if someone came back from the dead to warn them. The rich man knew from personal experience that his family did not take seriously the Law and the Prophets.

16:31   Abraham countered by responding that if the brothers would not listen to Moses and the prophets, then they would not be persuaded by even someone who arose from the dead and appeared to them. Luke's allusion to those who failed to be convinced by the truth of Jesus' resurrection is unmistakable (11:29-32; 13:32; cf. also 18:34).

HOMILETICAL SUGGESTIONS

Three sermons could be devoted to Luke 16. The first one could be entitled "Stewardship Sunday," and it would treat vv. 1-13. Two broad points could be made, the first being the interpretation of the parable of the dishonest steward. Here the preacher could perhaps use the interpretive suggestions offered in this chapter as a means of covering the broad strokes of the parable, especially the cultural background. The second point is the application of the parable of the dishonest steward. Here preachers should avail themselves of the practical and insightful principles of stewardship as expounded, for example, by Larry Burkett in his book *The Coming Economic Earthquake*.[13]

The second section of Luke 16, vv. 14-18, is admittedly difficult. The theme of the paragraph is the Law of Moses. A popular title for the message dealing with the passage could be, "The Long, Long Arm of the Law." The sermon itself would delineate two points: discontinuity with the Law of Moses (vv. 14-16); continuity with the Law of Moses (vv. 17-18). The major concern of the preacher treating this passage would be to discuss the role of the Law for Christians. An informative illustration introducing the sermon would be to describe the heretic Marcion's contempt for the Old Testament as a bad example for Christians *not* to follow.[14]

The third sermon devoted to Luke 16 should analyze vv. 19-31: "The Parable of the Rich Man and Lazarus: The Horrors of Hell." The sermon, obviously arresting and alarming in nature, should probably be preached in an evangelistic setting. We learn at least six disturbing truths about hell from this parable: (1) Hell is *corporeal* in nature—the rich man possessed a body subject to agony (v. 23, "he lifted up his eyes and saw"; v. 24, he was thirsty). (2) Hell is *terrible* in nature—the rich man experienced tormenting pain from the flames of judgment (vv. 24, 25, 28). (3) Hell is *juridical* in nature—the rich man was consigned to hell by a holy God because he did not repent of his sin (vv. 25, 30). (4) Hell is *eternal* in nature—there is an unbridgeable chasm between hell and heaven (v. 26). (5) Hell is *emotional* in nature—the rich man recognized Abraham and Lazarus, and he still knew about his living brothers (vv. 23, 24, 28, 30). Such memory and

---

13. Larry Burkett, *The Coming Economic Earthquake* (Chicago: Moody, 1991).

14. Marcion, a second-century heretic, denied the validity of the Old Testament, as well as the Law's continuing relevance for the New Testament.

recognition surely contributed to his torment. (6) Hell is *spiritual* in nature—the rich man wanted Abraham to have mercy on him (v. 24), and he deeply desired for his brothers to repent lest they join him in his agony (vv. 28, 30). The rich man was spiritually repentant, but too late.

LUKE

CHAPTER

SEVENTEEN

CONTINUING THE JOURNEY TO JERUSALEM

For the third time Luke explicitly mentions Jesus' journey to Jerusalem (17:11), the place of His destiny (v. 25). The reader will note that the travel account (9:51–19:27) is appropriately divided into three parts, each one beginning with a reference to Jesus' journeying to Jerusalem: (1) 9:51–13:21; (2) 13:22–17:10; (3) 17:11–19:27. Luke 17 begins the third section of the travel narrative. The chapter itself breaks into three divisions, with no real connecting theme discernible. They are matter-of-fact statements describing Jesus' progress to the Holy City: The Instruction of the Disciples, vv. 1-10; The Illustration of the Ten Lepers, vv. 11-19; The Inquiry about the Kingdom of God, vv. 20-37.

THE INSTRUCTION OF THE DISCIPLES, 17:1-10

In vv. 1-10, Jesus communicates four instructions to His disciples: (1) He warned them not to be stumbling-blocks to others, vv. 1-3a; (2) He admonished them to show unlimited forgiveness to others, vv. 3b-4; (3) He challenged them to grow in their faith, vv. 5-6; (4) He reminded them that they were indebted to God's grace, vv. 7-10.

17:1 The first instruction of Jesus was a warning to His disciples, and surely to all Christians as well, not to cause others to "stumble" (*skandala*). The word "scandal" refers to causing others to fall into sin, perhaps even to sway others from their allegiance to Christ (cf. Matt. 18:6, 7; Mark 9:42; Rom. 14:13). Jesus acknowledged the inevita-

323

bility of such incidents, but He warned that those who perpetrated scandals will heap upon themselves woe and disaster.

17:2   The judgment pronounced against the person causing others to stumble into sin is frightening: "It would be better for that person to be hurled into the sea with a millstone around his neck than to cause a little one to stumble." The indictment raises two questions. First, how are we to understand the severity of the judgment? The millstone was a large, heavy basalt stone, like those near the Qumran site today. According to Judges 9:53 and Revelation 18:21, a millstone was an instrument of death or destruction. Thus Jesus' invective against people who cause others to sin was tantamount to saying that it would be better for such people to die before they commit such offenses.

Second, who are the "little ones" who are tempted to embrace sin? Some might identify these people as little children, as happens, for example, in the case of child abuse. Although one can certainly sympathize with this interpretation, in light of Luke 10:2 (cf. Matt. 18:6), it is more probable that Jesus had in mind adult Christians. It is possible that in recording these words of Jesus, Luke also remembered the warning of Paul, his companion, about false teachers entering the flock of God and destroying them by their doctrines (see Acts 20:29-30).

17:3   Jesus fittingly concluded His first piece of instruction to His disciples by telling them to be on guard among themselves. While the command could be taken to introduce the second set of instructions, it seems more appropriate to group it with the previous challenge, given the hortatory tone of vv. 1-2. Thus, the disciples are commanded to be on guard that they do not turn out to be the ones who precipitate the spiritual demise of others.

The second instruction of Jesus is given in vv. 3b-4—He admonished His disciples to show unlimited forgiveness to others. Jesus' advice was straightforward: if your brother sins, rebuke him; if he repents, forgive him. The instruction itself relates to internecine strife among Christians. Three comments quickly come to mind regarding this teaching. First, disagreements and arguments are inevitable, even among believers. Second, when they come, Christians should have the courage to deal forthrightly with one another. In the case of a sinning brother or sister, one should confront him or her, speaking the truth in love. Disciples should not have to "walk on eggshells around each other." Third, forgiveness should always be offered, but it should come *after* the erring believer has repented. Otherwise, the repair in the relationship will not be complete and lasting.

17:4   The question might be raised at this point, How often should believers forgive other believers who sin against them? Jesus gave a hypothetical situation that provides the answer to that question: "If a brother sins against you seven times in one day and seven times says to you, 'I repent,' then you are to forgive him." In other words, Christians are to forgive each other indefinitely, without limit. After all, does not God do the same for us (cf. 11:4)?

17:5   In vv. 5-6, Jesus issued a third set of instructions: disciples are to grow in their faith. This teaching was initiated by the disciples' request of Jesus to increase their faith. Luke calls them the "apostles," which prompts the question, Was the faith that the twelve disciples requested apostolic faith, restricted to them to work more signs and miracles (cf. Luke 9:1-11; Acts 3:1-10; 5:12-16), or, for lack of a better term, "generic" faith for all believers? Perhaps one does not have to choose between the two alternatives.

17:6   Jesus replied with a condition—if the disciples had faith only as small as a mustard seed, they would be able to command a large mulberry tree to be uprooted and be planted in the sea, and it would obey. The particular form of the conditional sentence is puzzling. It approximates the second-class contrary to fact condition. In such a construction, the protasis contains *ei* ("if") plus an indicative whereas the apodosis contains *an* ("then") plus the indicative verb. The indicative verbs are expressed by the secondary tenses. The statement should be translated, "if the disciples had faith (and they do not), then." But the second-class condition breaks down in v. 6 because there is a present indicative in the protasis (*ei*, "if," *echete*, "you have") but an imperfect indicative in the apodosis (*an*, "then," *elegete*, "you could say"). The mixed condition is probably designed to affirm that the disciples did have faith, but that it required growth. Regardless of the technicalities of the grammar involved, however, the verse is clear in its focus—the smallest amount of faith in God can produce miracles.

17:7   Verses 7-10 give the fourth set of instructions Jesus communicated to His disciples—He reminded them that they were indebted to God's grace. He did so by raising a rhetorical question that introduced a parabolic-type story: Which of you having a servant plowing the fields or tending the sheep would say to that person when he comes to the house after work, "Sit down quickly and eat"? The implied answer is, no one.

17:8   Quite the reverse. The master would tell the servant to fix his meal and serve him first. Then, after waiting on his master, the servant could eat and drink his meal.

17:9   Having done that, should the master then thank the servant for performing his tasks? The negative, *mē* ("not"), expects a "no" answer.

17:10   Verse 10 applies the teaching to the disciples of Jesus. In a similar way to the servant, believers should recognize that, after having performed the Christian tasks expected of them, they are still unworthy and do not merit God's favor. Both their salvation and service are because of divine grace. An old rabbinic saying reveals a similar thought, "If you learned much in the Torah, claim not merit for yourself; for this purpose were you created" (*m. Abot* 2:8).

THE ILLUSTRATION OF THE TEN LEPERS, 17:11-19

The recounting of Jesus' healing of the ten lepers is unique to Luke's gospel. To be sure, it is a miracle, an account of the supernatural healing of, not one leper, but ten; and that from a distance (v. 14). But it is more than a miracle, it is a parable. It is an illustration of Jesus' offer of salvation to Jews and non-Jews like Samaritans. The parable fits therefore with the Lucan emphasis on the gospel as salvation for all humanity.

17:11   As indicated earlier in this chapter, v. 11 marks the beginning of the third section of the travelogue of Jesus' journey to Jerusalem. In making His way toward Jerusalem, Jesus passed along the border between Samaria and Galilee. The words *dia messon* are best translated "through the middle of," or "between," referring to Jesus' travel along the border between Samaria and Galilee. Samaria is probably mentioned first, even though it is south of Galilee, because of the emphasis in the story on the Samaritan, not because Luke's geography was erroneous (as Conzelmann claimed[1]).

17:12   In one of the villages Jesus entered on His way, He encountered ten lepers. The lepers kept their distance from Him, in keeping with the Old Testament law (Lev. 13:46; Num. 5:2-3).

17:13   The lepers, undoubtedly having heard of Jesus' power to heal, cried out to Him, asking Him to have mercy on them.

17:14   Jesus looked at the lepers and told them to go show themselves to the priests. Such was the regulation a leper was to follow, especially if he or she had been cured (see Lev. 13:49; 14:2). For the ten lepers to obey Jesus before being healed took great faith on their

---

1. Conzelmann, *The Theology of Luke,* 60-62.

part. As they proceeded toward the priest, they discovered themselves to be clean, i.e., healed.

17:15   One of the lepers, seeing that he had been healed, spontaneously turned back toward Jesus, glorifying God in a loud voice.

17:16   He prostrated himself before Jesus, thanking Him. Luke concludes the verse with dramatic flair—the man was a Samaritan.

17:17   Luke records three rhetorical questions that Jesus raised in reaction to the Samaritan's gratitude, the first two being: "Were not ten cleansed?" "Where are the other nine?"

17:18   Jesus' third question was the most penetrating of all, "Was no one found to give glory to God except this foreigner?" It was sadly ironic that the nine Jewish lepers expressed no thanks to God for their healing yet the Samaritan did. It is important not to miss the interchanging of praise to Jesus (v. 16) and to God (v. 18). The deity of Jesus is signified thereby.

17:19   Jesus told the Samaritan to get up and go on his way, for his faith had saved him. Here we detect a distinction in the types of faith people placed in Jesus during His earthly ministry (and perhaps today as well). The nine Jewish lepers had faith for miraculous healing (v. 14), but apparently not for spiritual salvation. The Samaritan had both. Ellis appropriately concludes the account, "The ungrateful 'nine' exemplify the general attitude of the Jewish people toward Jesus' mission; the 'Samaritan' is prophetic of the future response of non-Jews to the gospel (Ac 8:5f.; 11:18)."[2]

THE INQUIRY ABOUT THE KINGDOM OF GOD, 17:20-37

Ellis's introduction to Luke 17:20-37 is insightful:

> The episode consists of an oracle (20f.), peculiar to Luke, followed by a series of apocalyptic sayings (2-37). Matthew places the sayings in the Olivet Discourse (Mt. 24). By appending them here Luke creates a thematic setting in which the present [spiritual] manifestation of "the kingdom of God" is set in relation to the future glorious revelation of "the Son of man.". . . This alternating present/future perspective of the kingdom is found earlier. Cf. 3.16 (present) with 3.17 (future); 9.26b (future) with 9.27 (present); 11.2 (future) with 11.3, 13, 20 (present); 11.31f. (power present and judgment future); 12.37-46 (future reward and judgment) with 12.49, 52 (immediate judgment); 16.16 (present)

---

2. Ellis, *The Gospel of Luke,* 209.

with 16.19-31 (future reward and judgment). This feature has affinities
with the Fourth Gospel. . . . Elsewhere (12.35-48; 19.11-27) Luke points
out that Jesus anticipated a considerable and incalculable lapse of time
before his return. Here he teaches, from selected words of Jesus, that
the coming will be unexpected (26, 28). The kingdom appeared in the
Lord's pre-resurrection mission without "signs" for the curious (21). So
also there will be no preliminary signs, "see here, see there," to herald
him as the revealed "Son of man" (23f. . . .). The appearance of the
kingdom in Jesus' mission was evident to believers by his acts. How
much more will his glorious and public *parousia* be self-validating.[3]

That is to say, vv. 20-21 attest to the *present, spiritual* aspect of the
age to come, namely, the kingdom is here, whereas vv. 22-37 bespeak
the *future, physical* aspect of the age to come, the kingdom of God has
not yet been consummated. The former occurred with the first coming of Jesus; the latter will transpire at the second coming of Jesus.

17:20   On one occasion, the Pharisees asked Jesus when the kingdom of God would come. Luke had already addressed the subject of
the kingdom of God in 9:27; 10:9, 11; 11:2, 20. Jesus replied that the
kingdom of God will not come by observation. The word *observation*
(*paratērēsis*) admits to a number of possible meanings, as Marshall
notes:[4] (1) concrete observation of signs on earth and in heaven (cf.
Matt. 24:36; Mark 13:32; 1 Thess. 5:1; cf. Acts 1:7); (2) the Pharisaic
expectation that the Messiah would come on the night of the observation of the Passover (Ex. 12:42; cf. the Greek translation of Aquila of
Ex. 12:42); (3) religious observances (such as Pharisaic ritual rules)
which would hasten the coming of the kingdom of God; (4) the words
meta paratērēsis ("with observation") are the Greek equivalent of the
Aramaic word for "secret" (*bintir*). Thus the kingdom of God will
come not secretly but publicly. In assessing these possible meanings,
the second view is artificial because the belief it is based on cannot be
tracked back to the time of Jesus. The fourth view is, at best, hypothetical, as its proponents concede.[5] The third view is possible but is not
substantiated by the context of Luke 17. Therefore, the first view is the
most accurate. Indeed, the idea upon which it is based—there will be
certain signs of the times that will herald the kingdom of God—is
commonplace in the New Testament (see Matt. 24; Mark 13; Luke 21;

3. Ibid., 209-10.
4. Marshall, *Commentary on Luke,* 654.
5. Beasley-Murray, *Jesus and the Future,* 172.

Rev. 6–19). On this reading, then, Jesus was saying to the Pharisees that the kingdom of God would not necessarily be preceded by certain long-awaited signs of the times (cf. our discussion of Luke 21).

17:21   Using the third person indefinite plural, Jesus continued, "no one will say, 'Behold it is here or behold it is there.'" The thought is that because the kingdom of God will not necessarily be attested to by visible signs, people will not be able to point it out as here or there. These words are similar to Mark 13:21 and its injunction to disciples not to be tricked into following false messiahs. Rather than looking to miraculous signs to validate the presence of the kingdom of God, the Pharisees should realize that the kingdom of God is *entos* them. Various meanings have been proposed for the rare preposition *entos*: (1) "Within you," that is, the kingdom of God is in your hearts. *Entos* is rendered as "within you" in the Septuagint of Psalms 103:1; 109:22; Isaiah 16:11. The problem with this translation, however, is that it would seem inappropriate to say that the kingdom of God is within the Pharisees. Thus the context seems to rule out this first view. (2) "Within your grasp," that is, the kingdom of God is within the grasp of the Pharisees, if they humble themselves to receive it. This meaning of "within your grasp" for *entos* can possibly be found in some extrabiblical papyri texts. However, that meaning has been disputed for those texts by H. Riesenfeld.[6] (3) "Among you; in your midst," that is, the kingdom of God is present among the Pharisees in the person and work of Christ. The translation of *entos* as "among you" is attested to in the Sinaitic Syriac version of Luke 17:21; cf. a similar rendering of the word by Herodotus, *History*, 7.100.3. The problem with this meaning, however, is that if Luke had wanted to say "among you," he could have used the word *en mesō*, which he does elsewhere (2:46; 8:7; 10:3). Despite this objection, two factors suggest that "among you" is the preferable translation. Grammatically, *entos* with a plural noun (in this case, *hymon*, "you" plural) can mean "among you." Contextually, Luke 11:20, a parallel passage to 17:21, conveys the idea that the kingdom of God is among men in the person and work of Jesus.

17:22   If vv. 20-21 emphasize the already aspect of the kingdom of God, then vv. 22-37 highlight the not yet aspect of the kingdom of God, especially the coming revelation of Jesus, the Son of Man, at His Parousia. In vv. 22-37, Jesus shifted his attention from the Pharisees to the disciples. He told them that the days were coming when they

6. H. Riesenfeld, *"Emboleuein-Entos," Nuntius* 2 (1949), 11-12.

would long to see one of the days of the Son of Man, but they would not. The phrase in v. 22, "one of the days of the son of Man," is peculiar, especially since the normal expression is "the *day* of the Son of Man" (see 17:24, 30). Numerous attempts have been made to explain this oddity, the most compelling of which are the following: (1) The phrase "one of the days of the Son of Man" has been formed in comparison with the phrase the "days of the Messiah" (see Strack-B 2:237; 4:2). The problem here, however, is that the words "day of the Messiah" may not go back to the time of Jesus. (2) The phrase may refer to the earthly days of the Son of Man for which the disciples, when they encounter a future time of tribulation for the sake of the gospel, will long. (3) However, the context of v. 22 provides a better explanation—the plural "days of the Son of Man" have been created analogously to the plural "the days of Noah" (v. 26) and "the days of Lot" (v. 26). On this reading, Jesus was alerting the disciples to the eventuality that they would one day, in the heat of spiritual battle, long for the return of Jesus, the Son of Man. The words "but you will not see it" do not rule out the possibility that the disciples will live long enough to see that day. Rather, they refer to the fact that the coming of the Son of Man will not be by observation and sign, a similar thing said to the Pharisees (v. 20).

17:23 In their longing for the return of the Lord, the disciples should not be misled by messianic pretenders. That is what Jesus meant when He warned the disciples not to believe people who said, "Look, there or here it [the Messiah and the kingdom] is" (cf. again Mark 13:21). For similar messianic claims before the destruction of Jerusalem in A.D. 70, see Josephus, *J. W.* 6.288-315.

17:24 The reason no one will need to tell the disciples, or any Christian for that matter, that the Son of Man is coming is because His return will speak for itself. Like lightning flashing from one end of the sky (heaven) to the other, so the Parousia will be visible for all to see. There are two technical difficulties in this verse. First, the phrase *ek tēs hypo ton ouranon eis tēn hypo ouranon* is difficult to translate. Literally, it should be rendered, "from under the heaven to under the heaven." Idiomatically, it seems to mean, "from one end of the sky to the other." Second, the best manuscripts do not have the words "in his day" (with reference to the Son of Man [p75, B, D]). But because of homoioteleuton (a case where a scribe inadvertently skipped one of two words having the same ending, in this case a scribe's eye apparently jumped from the ending *ou* of "man" [*anthrōpou*] to the ending of *ou* of "his" [*autou*]), the words are probably original to the text.

17:25 However, before the return of the Son of Man in glory, He must first undergo the suffering resulting from the rejection of His generation. Jesus obviously alluded here to His crucifixion. Two comments are in order at this point. First, in light of a statement such as Luke 24:26-27, Luke's recording of Jesus' prediction about His upcoming death in 17:25 was apologetic in purpose—Jesus died and was then raised to glory to fulfill the Old Testament prophecies about Him. The word *dei* ("must") capitalizes on this perspective. Second, the sequence Jesus was about to experience—suffering then glory—is apocalyptic in nature. That is, Judaism firmly believed that before the righteous experienced the glory of heaven they must first go through trials and tribulations on earth (cf. Acts 14:22).[7]

17:26 Verses 26-30 contain two Old Testament illustrations with which the return of Christ, the day of the revelation of the Son of Man, is compared. The point of comparison is the suddenness with which God's judgment falls, almost without notice. The first analogy is in v. 26, the days of Noah. Just as it was in the days of Noah, said Jesus, so it will be in the days of the Son of Man. The reader will recall the plural usage of "days" in both instances (cf. v. 22).

17:27 During the time of Noah people were oblivious to the approaching judgment of God. A series of asyndetic imperfect verbs conveys the nonchalance with which people treated God: they ate, drank, married, were given in marriage. All things continued as normal, that is until Noah and his family entered the ark, at which time the Deluge (*kataklysmos*) came and destroyed all the people (see Gen. 7:7, 10, 21; 1 Peter 3:20).

17:28 The second analogy with the days of the Son of Man Jesus used was the incident at Sodom. At the time of Lot, people also treated God with benign neglect, as the asyndetic imperfect verbs relate: they ate, drank, bought, sold, planted, built.

17:29 But when Lot left the city, fire and brimstone rained down from heaven, destroying all the inhabitants of the city.

17:30 It will be like that on the day when the Son of Man will be revealed (*apokalyptetai*) from heaven.

17:31 The theme of impending judgment continues in vv. 31-37. Jesus got the point across by drawing on ancient Palestinian customs, two of which occur in v. 31. The first dealt with the Palestinian house. Jesus said that anyone who was on the roof of the house, on the day of

---

7. See my discussion in *The Glory of Adam and the Afflictions of the Righteous*, 1983.

the return of the Son of Man, must not descend and go into the house to gather together his or her possessions before fleeing. Ancient Palestinian houses had flat roofs, the access to which was by an exterior staircase. People often rested on their roofs, from which vantage point they might catch a gentle breeze on a hot day. The admonition, then, was that, when the person realized the return of the Lord was near, he or she must descend the steps and run. They should not take the extra time to enter their houses and pack their belongings (cf. Mark 13:15). The second custom was agricultural. Anyone out in the field working should not return back home to get any possessions that had been behind (cf. Luke 9:62).

17:32   As a poignant reminder, Jesus recalled for His audience the incident with Lot's wife, who in her flight from Sodom stopped to look back (cf. Gen. 19:26). The human-like formations of crystalline rock salt dotting the desert around the Dead Sea would serve as an apt reminder to the Jews of her fate. The word Jesus used for "remember" was *mnēmoneuete* (mnemonic). It means to pay heed to; to learn a lesson from.

17:33   There follows, then, a spiritual maxim, "Whoever seeks to save his life to preserve it will lose it; but whoever loses (his life) will keep it alive"; cf. also Luke 9:24-25. The contexts of both passages, 17:31-33 and 9:24-25, suggest that what Jesus had in mind was the need to let go of this world's possessions so that one could put one's full trust in Him. On the day of the return of the Son of Man, such things will not profit the soul.

17:34   The thought of the return of the Son of Man prompted Jesus to say that on that day there will be a division among people between those who are prepared and those who are unprepared for His coming. For example, two (men) will be in bed, and one will be taken while the other will be left. It is not clear which destiny is conveyed by which verb. The one "taken" could be from judgment and the other "left" could be for destruction; or vice versa. However, the references to Noah and Lot in the context might tip the scale toward the first possibility. Noah and Lot were taken and, therefore, saved from judgment while the rest were left for destruction.

17:35   Now comes another Palestinian custom taken from domestic activity. Two women will be grinding meal, and one will be taken while the other will be left behind. The saying reflects the ancient practice of two women grinding meal, one to pour out the grain and the other to grind it with the stone. Again, the idea is probably that one will be taken and therefore spared judgment while the other one will be left behind to face destruction. The criterion for distinguishing the two, like v. 34, will be the spiritual principle delineated in v. 33. That is, those who have trusted Christ and served Him will be saved from the coming destruction, while those who have not will be judged.

17:36   Verse 36 is not in the best Greek manuscripts (p75, Sinaiticus, A, B) and is an addition to the biblical text. It was probably added by a scribe because of Matthew 24:40.

17:37   The disciples, pressing Jesus for more information, asked Him when all these things would occur. They had apparently forgotten the injunction of v. 23. Jesus' answer made clear that the disciples would not need someone to tell them when or where the Son of Man would return. His coming will be clearly indicated, just as the presence of the eagles circling in the sky indicate the locale of the corpses below. The reference to the eagles has been variously explained. Some think Jesus confused the eagle with the scavenger, the vulture, because in flight both birds look the same. Others think the reference to the eagle is an allusion to the Roman Empire, especially the image of the eagle attached to the Roman flag or standard, which preceded the army in battle. More probably, the eagle, as Ellis notes, was a proverbial symbol of judgment, in this case, the Last Judgment (cf. Rev. 4:7; 8:13; 12:14).[8]

HOMILETICAL SUGGESTIONS

Although we have divided Luke 17 into three sections (the instructions of the disciples, vv. 1-10; the illustration of the ten lepers, vv. 11-19; the inquiry about the kingdom of God, vv. 20-37), it seems preferable to preach the chapter in two sermons. The first sermon should extend from v. 1 to v. 19 and could be entitled, "Calling All Disciples." The four points developed in the commentary proper would nicely cover the appropriate material, except that the fourth point should also draw on the story of the ten lepers as an illustration, vv. 11-19. Thus Jesus: (1) warned the disciples not to be stumbling blocks to others, vv. 1-3a; (2) admonished them to show unlimited forgiveness to others, vv. 3b-4; (3) challenged them to grow in their faith, vv. 5-6; and (4) reminded them that they were indebted to God's

---

8. Ellis, *The Gospel of Luke,* 212.

grace, vv. 7-10, an illustration of which is the Samaritan leper who demonstrated deep gratitude to Jesus, vv. 11-19.

The second sermon would deal with Luke 17:20-37. An apt title for the passage is, "Living between the Times," with reference to the spiritual and physical aspects of the kingdom of God. The passage naturally lends itself to two broad points: (1) the first coming of Christ and the revelation of the kingdom, vv. 20-21; and (2) the second coming of Christ and the consummation of the kingdom, vv. 22-37. This last point can be subdivided into three points, each of which accentuates an aspect of the return of Christ, the thought of which should govern the behavior of Christians until that event: (a) the discernment needed concerning Christ's return (vv. 22-25); (b) the imminence of Christ's return (vv. 26-30); (c) watchfulness in light of Christ's return (vv. 31-37).

LUKE

CHAPTER

EIGHTEEN

RADICAL FAITH

To be an effective Christian, one must have a radical faith in Christ. In one way or another, each of the episodes in Luke 18 touches upon the topic of faith. Verses 1-8 and the parable of the unjust judge conclude with a description of the *persecuted* faith of disciples of Jesus. The parable of the Pharisee and the tax collector, vv. 9-14, calls attention to the need for a *repentant* faith. Verses 15-17 profile the importance of *childlike* faith. The incident of the rich ruler tragically reveals the significance of *unreserved* faith, vv. 18-30. Finally, the contrast between the disciples' misunderstanding of Jesus' passion prediction, vv. 31-34, and the healing of the sightless man, vv. 35-43, points out the need for a *developing* faith on the part of followers of Christ. These various aspects of faith, then, will form the outline of our exposition of Luke 18.

A PERSECUTED FAITH, 18:1-8

The parable of the unjust judge is similar in message to the parable of the importunate friend at midnight, vv. 5-8. They both illustrate the open ear and the loving heart of the heavenly Father by way of contrast to a less than cooperative human being. The flow of thought consists, therefore, of a minor to major argument. In the parable of the unjust judge, the contrast is between a judge who finally acquiesces to the plight of a woman in need and a loving God who

335

promptly responds to His children's calls for help. The story itself is comprised of an introduction (v. 1), the parable proper (vv. 2-5), and the application of the parable (vv. 6-8). As we will see in the exposition itself, v. 1 enlightens the meaning of v. 8, a difficult remark to comprehend. Though it does not use the word, the application section highlights the theme of faith, especially concerning Christians who suffer persecution for their testimony.

18:1 Jesus introduced the parable of the unjust judge by challenging his disciples to always pray and not to lose heart in doing so (cf. 11:5-13). With this opening comment, the reader is already being clued in on the key to acquiring faith—continual prayer.

18:2 Jesus spoke of a judge in a certain town who neither feared God nor respected people. The unjustness of the judge is signaled by the fact that he did not care for God or people. As the parable unfolds, it will become clear that Jesus chose this worst-case scenario in order to demonstrate that if such a person as this will answer the pleas of those in his jurisdiction, then how much more so will the loving, righteous Judge over all the earth answer the prayers of His children.

18:3 In that same town there was a widow who repeatedly came (*ērcheto*, an imperfect verb) to the judge, seeking vindication against her opponent. She had apparently been wronged by this individual and wanted just compensation. As Fitzmyer remarks, this story about a helpless widow is one of a number in Luke-Acts (2:37; 4:25-26: 7:12; 20:47; 21:2-3; Acts 6:1; 9:39, 41), undoubtedly expressing the third evangelist's concern for the "outcasts" of society. Widows unfortunately fit into that category in ancient Israel.[1]

18:4 After repeatedly refusing her pleas, the judge reasoned with himself, in soliloquy fashion, that, even though he did not fear God or respect humans . . .

18:5 Yet because the widow would become a nuisance by continually coming to him, he decided to vindicate her. Otherwise, she would wear him out. Although the word *hypōpiazē* literally means "to give a black eye" (cf. 1 Cor. 9:27), the figurative rendering is preferable here.

18:6 Verses 6-8 contain the application of the parable. In v. 6 the Lord (Jesus) admonished His audience to pay attention to what the unjust (*adikias*) judge said.

18:7 Jesus continued the application by raising a twofold question: "Will not God vindicate His chosen ones who cry out to Him day and

---

1. Fitzmyer, *The Gospel According to Luke X–XXIV,* 1178-79.

night?" "Will He delay over them?" The emphatic negative, *ou mē,* in the first question expects an affirmative answer. The "chosen ones" (*eklektōn*) is a term taken from the Old Testament for the people of God (Isa. 42:1; 43:20; 65:9, 15; Ps. 105:6, 43) and applied to Christians in the New Testament (Mark 13:20, 22, 27). The second question is introduced by an indicative verb, "delay," whereas the first question was introduced by a subjunctive verb, "bring vindication." The meaning of the Greek word *makrothumei* is debated, but Marshall, who lists as many as nine possible renderings, seems to be accurate in assigning the meaning of "delay" to the word, as we have adopted here.[2] The twofold question serves to make a twofold contrast between the unjust judge of the parable and God. First, if the unjust judge who did not fear God or respect humans answered the woman's petition, how much more so will God respond to the needs of His children who suffer for their faith. Second, unlike the unjust judge who answered the woman's pleas only after many entreaties, God will not delay in responding to His own. Verse 8a makes this clear.

18:8 Verse 8a gives the answer to the last question of whether God will quickly vindicate His children. To the chosen ones, it may seem like a long time before God answers their prayers, but afterward they will realize that it was a short time after all. With Jesus' question in v. 8b the topic seems to suddenly shift, "But when the Son of Man comes, will he find faith on the earth?" Actually, however, the question is intimately related to the preceding verses. The question of whether or not there will be faith on the earth when the Son of Man returns logically flows from the fact that Christians will experience persecution before that event transpires, vv. 2-7. Although they may be tempted to give up their faith because their prayers to God for deliverance are apparently not being heard, they should persevere in prayer and faith before Him, v. 1. The parable of the unjust judge, therefore, can encourage them to trust in God's ultimate vindication on their behalf.

A REPENTANT FAITH, 18:9-14

The parable of the Pharisee and the toll collector presses home the need for faith born out of genuine repentance. The former personage represents a religious system based on human merit and the

2. Marshall, *Commentary on Luke,* 674-75.

pride it breeds. The latter character stands for all time as the epitome of repentance from sin and faith in God's mercy alone. The two people in this parable also symbolize the two types of responses Jesus encountered from His audiences.

18:9 Jesus addressed the parable to those who regarded themselves as righteous and accordingly treated others with contempt. The "us against them" mentality that Jesus pinpointed here was typical of the Pharisaic condescending attitude toward non-pious Jews, the *am ha-aretz* (people of the land); see *b. Sanh.* 101a; *b. Sukka* 45b; Phil. 3:4-6.

18:10 Two men ascended up the temple mound to pray in the sanctuary (*hieron*, cf. 1:9). Public prayer was offered in the temple at Jerusalem two times a day—at 9:00 A.M. (see Acts 2:15) and at 3:00 P.M. (see Acts 3:1). The one man was a Pharisee. The Pharisees were known for their scrupulous fidelity to the Law. Josephus expressed it well when he described them as "a body of Jews known for surpassing the others in the observances of piety and exact interpretation of the laws" (*J. W.* 1.110, as quoted in Fitzmyer, *The Gospel According to Luke*, 1186). The other man was a toll collector, a notoriously dishonest profession (see 5:30; 7:34; 15:1).

18:11 The actions and words of the Pharisee betrayed his arrogance. The place he positioned himself depicted his pompous attitude, standing far to the front of the court of Israel (cf. v. 13). His prayers about himself do nothing to diminish the impression that he was thoroughly enamored with his spirituality. He began his prayer with thanks to God, but as the prayer continues, not for who God was but rather for who he was! The prayer itself separates the "holier than thou" Pharisee from the rest of humanity, which he brands as robbers (see Ex. 20:14-15), evildoers, adulterers, and, yes, "this" toll collector. The demonstrative pronoun "this" (*houtos*) pejoratively distinguishes the Pharisee from his counterpart in the temple. That Jesus' depiction of the Pharisee as contemptuously self-righteous was not a caricature can be seen by comparing the Pharisee's prayer with other self-laudatory comments made by contemporary Jewish religious leaders. For example, see again Galatians 1:14; 2:15; Philippians 3:4-6; *b. Sukka* 45b. The last reference illustrates the point. In that Talmudic work, one rabbi was reported to be confident that his righteousness was sufficient to spare his whole generation from judgment. If the saved numbered only "a hundred, I and my son are among them; and if only two, they are I and my son." However, we must not generalize Jesus' statement to mean that all Pharisees and Jewish religious leaders were so arrogant; see, for example, the Qumran document's contrite confession, *1QS* 11:2-3, 5 and Rabbi Hillel's humble remarks in *m. Abot* 2:5.

18:12 The Pharisee's prayer went on to specify two of his religious observances. First, he fasted twice a week. Fitzmyer provides a rather comprehensive note on Jewish fasting:

> Fasting was prescribed in the OT for the Day of Atonement in postexilic times (Lev 16:29, 31 [*RSV*: "you shall afflict yourselves" = you shall fast]; 23:27, 29, 32; Num. 29:7) and possibly for some other occasions (Zech 8:19; cf. 7:3, 5; Esth 9:31; Neh 9:1). Fasting by individuals in OT times was an expression of mourning (2 Sam 12:21), ... [repentance] ... (1 Kgs 21:27; Ezra 10:6), supplication (Neh 1:4; Dan 9:3). That Pharisees and disciples of John the Baptist fasted in NT times is known from elsewhere in the NT (Luke 5:33). This passage is the earliest attestation of the custom of Jews fasting twice a week. *Did.* 8:1 instructs Christians that they are not to fast "with the hypocrites" on the second and fifth days of the week, but on the fourth day and on the parasceve (= day of preparation for the Sabbath). This probably reflects a Christian tradition of about A.D. 100. The days thus mentioned for Jewish fasting, Mondays and Thursdays, are attested in *b. Ta'an.* 12a (final redaction ca. A.D. 450). There the days are explained as the day on which Moses ascended Mount Sinai (Thursday) and that on which he came down from it (Monday) after forty days; but see Str-B 2.243 n. 2 for a more probable reason: Two days not contiguous with a Sabbath and themselves as far apart as possible, hence Monday and Thursday. The Pharisee's mention of fasting twice a week indicates his sense of pride of meticulously keeping the Law.[3]

The second religious observance the Pharisee boasted in was tithing. He tithed to God all that he acquired. The giving of 10 percent of one's income was prescribed in Deuteronomy 14:22-25. Two options are delineated there. If the person lived close to Jerusalem, once a year at harvest time that person was obligated to offer in the temple a tithe of all his produce—seed, grain, wine, oil, firstlings of the flock. But if the person lived too far from Jerusalem, he could convert the produce into money and offer that instead. Tithing continued in Jesus' day, and the Pharisee was quick to point out that he faithfully followed the regulation.

18:13 What a contrast between the actions and words of the Pharisee and those of the toll collector! The latter stood far off from the

---

3. Fitzmyer, *The Gospel According to Luke X–XXIV,* 1187.

temple, probably just within the court of Israel. He dared not even raise his eyes toward heaven, much less his hands, which was customary in public prayer. That the man possessed genuine faith was demonstrated in his repentant and contrite heart. He beat his breast, a sign of deep sorrow (cf. Luke 23:48; Josephus, *Ant.* 7.252). His prayer was simple but profound, "O God, be merciful to me a sinner." The toll collector's prayer was a confession of sin, unlike the Pharisee's prayer of thanksgiving for himself. The term "mercy" (*hiastheti*), according to David Hill, can be traced back to the idea of propitiation,[4] which means to satisfy the holiness of God. It reminds one of the mercy seat on the ark of the covenant in the Holy of Holies in the temple. The same Greek word is used twenty-one times in the Septuagint for the lid of the mercy seat.[5] All of this bespeaks of the fact that the toll collector was acutely aware that he was devoid of righteousness and solely dependent on the mercy of God for forgiveness.

18:14   The words "I tell you" were Jesus' way of driving home the point of the parable—this one (the toll collector) went to his house justified rather than that one (the Pharisee). The divine rationale for such a decision follows, namely, "whoever exalts himself will be humbled, but whoever humbles himself will be exalted." The key to righteousness is humility expressing itself in repentance toward God and casting oneself solely upon the mercy of God. It is interesting that four of the pivotal terms Luke uses in vv. 13-14 also occur in Pauline literature: "propitiation/mercy" (*hiastheti*; cf. v. 13 with Rom. 3:25); "righteousness" (*dikaios*; cf. v. 14 with Rom. 3:21 and also Phil. 3:6, 9); "humble" (*tapeinothesetai*; cf. v. 14, and also 1:48, with Phil. 2:8); "exalted" (*hypson*; cf. v. 14, and also 1:52, with Phil. 2:9). This is to be expected of a man who was a companion to the great apostle Paul. One wonders if Paul himself, according to his testimony in Philippians 3:4-9, did not once fit into the category of the self-righteous Pharisee, that is until he was humbled, like the toll collector, before God, on the road to Damascus.

A CHILDLIKE FAITH, 18:15-17

Luke's propensity for emphasizing Jesus' love for the outcasts of society extends to children, as vv. 15-17 reveal. The ironic thing about

4. Hill, *Greek Words and Hebrew Meanings,* 23-48.
5. See the discussion in Cranfield, *The Epistle to the Romans,* 214-15.

this episode is that the ones who regarded the children as unworthy of Christ's attention and affection were not the Jewish leaders, but the disciples! Not only did Jesus welcome these little human beings as members of the kingdom of God; He also extolled them as model citizens of the same, because of their capacity to trust and to love. From a literary point of view, the incident of Jesus blessing the children is a pronouncement story, comprised of: a controversial action of Jesus (v. 15a); criticism from the disciples (v. 15b); and Jesus' pronouncement utterance which silenced the critics, disciples included (vv. 16-17).

18:15 Verse 15 records, in effect, Jesus performing a controversial action—welcoming even the babies brought to him by their parents. Luke uses the term *brephos*, i.e., babies (but "child" [*paidia*] in vv. 16-17). The word "hold" or "touch" (*aptētai*) could also involve the act of blessing a person (cf. 5:13; Gen. 48:14). Probably, therefore, Jesus was praying a blessing over the little ones as He held them in His arms. Verse 15b amounts to a criticism raised regarding Jesus' conduct, in this case coming from the disciples, though the rebuke itself was directed more toward the parents than toward Jesus. The disciples probably thought the children were wasting Jesus' time.

18:16 In vv. 16-17 Jesus made an authoritative pronouncement that silenced the criticism against the children. The utterance made two points. First, children are welcomed members of the kingdom of God. Jesus expressed this truth by calling for the children. He then commanded that the children be permitted to come to Him, forbidding anyone to hinder them. Oscar Cullmann argued that these words "do not hinder" (*mē kōluete auta*) were used by the later church to defend the practice of infancy baptism (cf. also Acts 8:36 and 10:47).[6] The phrase "for of such is the kingdom of God" refers to children in general, not just the ones Jesus was holding. The quality being lauded here was that of simple trust, without appeal to one's own merit. This is the entrance requirement into the kingdom of God.

18:17 The second point reflected in Jesus' pronouncement statement was that children are model citizens of the kingdom of God. Jesus said, "Truly, I say to you, whoever does not receive the kingdom of God as a child will never enter it." If one does not become like a child, then one will be emphatically denied entrance into the kingdom. Fitzmyer captures the spirit of the pronouncement, "Here the

---

6. Cullmann, *Baptism in the New Testament,* 73.

child's qualities of openness, lowliness in society, minority, helpless-
ness, without claim of achievement, and in need of constant maternal
or paternal attention are what is being alluded to."[7] What is needed,
then, on the part of would-be disciples of Jesus is a childlike faith.

AN UNRESERVED FAITH, 18:18-30

If, according to vv. 15-17, children illustrate how to enter the
kingdom of God, the rich ruler, vv. 18-30, shows how not to enter the
kingdom. What the latter lacked, and what is abundantly found in the
former, is unreserved faith. Verses 18-30 deal with that topic by relating the story of the rich ruler who sought Jesus for eternal life. The
paragraph can be broken into two parts: the incident of the rich young
ruler, vv. 18-23; the commentary on the rich young ruler, vv. 24-30.

18:18   The incident itself of the rich ruler occurs in vv. 18-23.
Though Luke does not specify when the rich ruler came to Jesus, we
know it happened on the journey to Jerusalem. It may owe its present
position to its thematic contrast with the preceding story. Verse 18
calls the man a "ruler" (*archōn*; cf. 8:41; 11:15; 12:58; 14:1; 23:13, 35;
24:20). We cannot tell whether he was a religious or civil magistrate.
That he was rich is clear from v. 23. The ruler addressed Jesus as
"good Teacher." Calling a rabbi "good" was almost never done.[8]
There is no reason to doubt the sincerity of the ruler's compliment.
But the real concern of the magistrate resided in the question he
posed to Jesus, "What must I do to inherit eternal life?" (cf. 10:25).

18:19   Jesus' response, "Why do you call me good?" has been variously explained. Fitzmyer's summary serves the interpreter well:

> (a) The question is intended to bring the man to perceive that
> Jesus was divine: ". . . that he may believe in the Son of God, not as a
> good master, but as the Good God.". . . (b) Jesus rejects the epithet
> "good" from the questioner's point of view and seeks to correct the
> magistrate's flattery. . . . (c) Jesus implicitly acknowledges his sinfulness.
> . . . (d) The adj. *agathos* should be understood in the sense of "gra-
> cious, kind.". . . (e) Jesus is saying nothing about his own person, but
> directing the man's attention to God and his will as the only prescrip-
> tion for pleasing him.[9]

---

7. Fitzmyer, *The Gospel According to Luke X–XXIV,* 1194.
8. The only recorded instance is *b. Ta'an* 24b, a fourth century A.D. text.
9. Fitzmyer, *The Gospel According to Luke X–XXIV,* 1199.

That last view is probably the most accurate though, in our view, it need not be pitted against the first interpretation. The words "No one is good except God alone" acknowledge the inherent goodness of God (see 1 Chron. 16:34; Ps. 34:8; Nah. 1:7) as well as His exclusive claim to it. Therefore, what Jesus meant by His remark was that any goodness residing in Him was derivative from God. A. Plummer captures the idea: "His [Jesus'] goodness is the goodness of God working in Him."[10]

18:20   Jesus amplified His response, stating that, in effect, if the man wanted to have eternal life, he should keep God's commandments which, of course, as a Jew he knew. Then Jesus listed the second tablet of the ten commandments: do not commit adultery; do not kill; do not steal; do not bear false witness; honor your father and mother. Jesus' enumerating of these five commandments prompts several observations, as the commentators are quick to mention. First, the four negative commands are formed with *mē* ("not," a subjunctive) plus an aorist subjunctive, which is different from the Septuagint, which uses *ou* ("not," in the indicative). Second, Luke's list of the commandments is out of order: 7, 6, 8, 9, 5. It may be that these two observations indicate that Luke is using an early church catechetical pattern (cf., for example, the Nash papyrus which inverts the sixth and seventh commandments[11]). Third, Jesus may have quoted the second tablet of the Decalogue (the "ten words") because the rich ruler needed to be shown that he lacked love for people (see vv. 22, 24), which is the heart and soul of the second tablet. If so, then his assumption that he could inherit eternal life based on his obedience to the Law would be demonstrated to be wrong.

18:21   The ruler replied in rather grandiose fashion that he had kept the commandments from his youth. The time span involved in the ruler's mind may have begun with his *bar mitsvah* ("son of the Law"), the time when a youth became an adult at the age of thirteen, and therefore obligated to fulfill the Mosaic Law.

18:22   Jesus gave the man a tall order, "Yet the one thing you lack is to sell all that you have and distribute it to the poor; then follow me." The reader gathers from Jesus' response that the "one" thing the ruler lacked was all-encompassing—to stop trusting in his wealth and give

---

10. Plummer, *A Critical and Exegetical Commentary on the Gospel According to St. Luke,* 422.
11. The Nash Papyrus is one of the oldest fragments of the Hebrew Old Testament, dating to the first century B.C. It contains the ten commandments as found in Deut. 5.

it to the poor. Having given it all away, the only one left for the ruler to trust would be Jesus. Then, and only then, would he be ready to follow Him. As we have noticed before, the command to distribute one's wealth to the poor is a favorite Lucan theme (cf. Acts 2:44-45). Moreover, in requesting the man to give his wealth to the needy, Jesus was undoubtedly seeking to discover if the ruler really did keep the second tablet of the ten commandments, which is concerned with how a person treats others. Only in doing that can one receive true riches in heaven.

18:23   Upon hearing this the ruler became very sad, because he was very rich. The depth of his sadness matched the breadth of his possessions. According to Matthew 19:22 and Mark 10:22, the rich ruler left without following Jesus. Ellis's evaluation of the situation is apropos. Speaking of the ruler he says, "Suddenly, he discovers 'sadly' that for him life's first priority is not God's kingdom but his riches. Jesus always requires from one just that earthly security upon which one would lean. Only in the context of abandonment to Christ's demand can one's basic life motivation really be 'for the sake of the kingdom of God.'"[12]

18:24   The words "becoming very sad," although in numerous Greek manuscripts, including (A, K, P), are not in two of the oldest manuscripts (Sinaiticus, B). They were probably added by a later scribe who borrowed it from v. 23. The rich ruler's dejected departure elicited from Jesus a searching statement, "How difficult it is for those who have riches to enter the kingdom of God." The explanation was left unsaid, but it is not hard to articulate: the rich are tempted to trust their money, not God.

18:25   Jesus furthered His comment with a hyperbolic comparison, "It is easier for a camel to pass through the eye of a needle than for a rich person to enter the kingdom of God." Three explanations have been offered for this statement. First, to tone down the impossibility and even absurdity of a camel passing through the eye of a needle, some equate the "eye of the needle" with the name for a small entrance in a city wall through which a camel could squeeze only with great difficulty. The problem with this view is that no one knows of the existence of such a name for that kind of entrance in Palestine. Second, some church fathers, such as Origen and Cyril of Alexandria, suggested the word for "camel," *kamēlon,* was a misspelling of the

---

12. Ellis, *The Gospel of Luke,* 217-18.

word, "rope," *kamilos.* Thus, the saying should read, "It is easier for rope to pass through the eye of a needle." But there is no text tradition confirming such a misspelling. Furthermore, this hypothesis looks very much like an attempt to water down the impossibility of Jesus' comment. Third, the most feasible explanation of the phrase is that Jesus was making a hyperbolic statement designed to show the impossibility of the rich entering the kingdom of God. It would be easier for the largest of Palestinian animals (the camel) to pass through the smallest of openings (the eye of the needle) than for the rich to enter the kingdom of God (cf. 6:24). Verses 26-27 confirm this interpretation.

18:26 Those hearing Jesus were shocked by the unfeasibility of His statement. If the rich, whose prosperity was regarded as a sign of God's acceptance and blessings, cannot be saved (that is, enter the kingdom of God; cf. v. 25), then who can be saved?

18:27 Jesus' reply has become proverbial, "What is impossible for man is possible for God." Although the rich, and for that matter all people, are not able in and of themselves to let go of material things and trust in God, God is able to persuade and empower them to do so (cf. 1:37).

18:28 Apparently feeling unrecompensed for their sacrifice and concerned for their heavenly reward, Peter acted as the spokesman for the disciples, reminding Jesus that they had left all that they had to follow Him (cf. 5:11).

18:29 Jesus assured Peter and the disciples that whoever leaves household or wife or brothers or parents or children for the sake of the kingdom of God will be recompensed. The severed relationships could be taken figuratively with reference to someone replacing them with top priority to Christ in their hearts. Or, more likely it is literal in the sense of leaving one's family ties for the sake of spreading the kingdom of God. Such a response could be blessed or cursed by one's family, depending on whether or not they are walking with Christ. In the case of the former response, one thinks of all the families who have approvingly released their loved ones to the service of the Lord, for example on the mission fields. In the case of the latter response, one thinks, for example, of those Jews who become Christians who are then renounced by their families and considered no longer to be alive.

18:30 Verse 30 helps to specify the nature of the reward for such self-sacrificing disciples—they will receive many times as much in the age to come than in this age, i.e., eternal life. The recompense is two-fold: First, in this time (*kairō*), or this present age, disciples will receive "many times as much" (*pollaplasiona*), probably an allusion to the spiritual family of God that will replace one's earthly family. (Not that one's earthly family cannot also become one's spiritual family.) Second, in the age to come, disciples will receive eternal life. This idea of the two ages (this age and the age to come, which is based on the Hebrew words *ha-olam hazzeh* and *ha-olam-habba*) also occurs in Luke at 20:34-35. It seems to be the substructure of the entire New Testament.[13]

A Developing Faith, 18:31-43

The contrast between the disciples' misunderstanding of Jesus' third passion prediction (vv. 31-34) and the faith of the healed sightless man points out the need for a developing faith on the part of the followers of Christ. More than that, the miracle of the healing of the sightless man serves as a prophetic parable of the partial to full development of the disciples' faith and, perhaps, also as a picture of Israel's future restoration to her Messiah.

18:31 Verses 31-34 record Jesus' third passion prediction. The recipients of the announcement were the twelve disciples, Jesus' inner circle. These Jesus took to Himself and for a third time reminded them that they were going "up" to Jerusalem (Jerusalem is situated in the mountains). Upon reaching the Holy City, all that was written by the prophets about the Son of Man would be fulfilled. Two comments are in order here. First, the phrase "about the Son of Man" should be taken with the verb "was written"; the dative *tō hiō* functions as *peri* ("concerning") with the genitive and thus modifies *gegrammena*. Thus, the wording should be, "all that was written about the Son of Man will be fulfilled" (cf. 22:37, 46; Acts 13:29; 24:14). Second, "will be fulfilled" (*telesthēsetai*) is a theological passive; that is, God is the understood subject. Thus, God is the one who will bring all things to pass concerning the Son of Man, especially His death and resurrection (see vv. 32-33). We see in this reference, then, Luke's salvation history theme at work.

18:32 Jesus, the Son of Man, will be delivered over (*paradidonai*; cf. Matt. 20:18-19; Mark 10:33) to the Gentiles, undoubtedly an allusion

---

13. See George Ladd, *A Theology of the New Testament* (Grand Rapids: Eerdmans, 1974).

to the Roman authorities (cf. 20:20, 23). The handing over was done by the Jews (23:1). Jesus will suffer at the hands of the Gentiles by being ridiculed, insulted, and spit upon by them (cf. 22:63; 23:11, 36). **18:33** Worse than that, He will be flogged and killed. The flogging or scourging was the "preliminary" punishment of criminals before crucifying them. It consisted of whipping the victim thirty-nine times, with some nine ropes attached to which were bones, glass, and nails for the infliction of pain (cf. Isa. 50:6 with Mark 10:34 and Luke 22:63). The "killing" comprised the crucifixion itself (cf. 23:33). However, Jesus' death will not be the end of the story. He will rise again on the third day (cf. 9:22).

18:34 Three times in this verse Luke emphasizes the incomprehension of the disciples with regard to Jesus' passion prediction: "they did not comprehend these things"; "the message was hidden from them"; "they did not understand the things being said." What Luke meant was probably that the disciples failed to understand why Jesus, the Christ, needed to die and then be resurrected. Their theology did not have room for a suffering and dying Messiah (see 24:25-27; 44-46).

18:35 Verses 35-43 record the miracle of the healing of the sightless man at Jericho. The incident occurred as Jesus was nearing Jericho, a town not far from Jerusalem (cf. 10:30).[14] There at Jericho He encountered a sightless man (Bartimaeus, according to Mark 10:46-52) alongside the road (probably near the gate of the town) begging. Tragically, in the ancient world, as today, blindness often goes hand in hand with begging, because of the destitute situation of the person.

18:36 Hearing a crowd passing by, the sightless man asked what was going on.

18:37 Someone told him that Jesus the Nazarean was passing by. The word *nazōraios* has been variously identified. Raymond Brown lists the possibilities:

> The main interpretations are: *Nazōraios* is a Greek proper adj. formed from: (a) Greek *Nazara,* a variant of the village name *Nazaret, Nazareth . . .*, hence "a person from Nazareth, a Nazarene." Appeal to this form, however, does not explain the long ō, which cannot be ignored. (b) Hebrew *nāzîr,* "one consecrated by vow" . . . , hence "one consecrated," a designation which would fit Jesus as one set apart for God's service. Yet it still does not explain the presence of the long ō. . . .

14. On the literary relationship of this miracle with Mark 10:46-52, see Marshall, *Commentary on Luke,* 692-93.

(c) Hebrew *nēser,* "shoot sprout," as in Isa 11:1, "A twig will come forth from the stump of Jesse, and a shoot (*nēser*) will blossom from its roots," said of a descendant expected to sit on the Davidic throne. In Aramaic targums of the Byzantine period *nēser* was given a clear messianic sense; and under the influence of Rev. 22:16 ("I am the root and the offspring of David") patristic writers applied the Isaian term and idea to Jesus. . . . But it is still a problem to explain the long *ō* nor can the shift from *s* to *z* be accepted without further ado. (d) Aramaic *nāsōrayyā',* allegedly "observers," a name found in later Mandean writings for a group related to John the Baptist. But there is no evidence for the use of such a name in first-century Palestine. . . . (e) Probably the best explanation of *Nazōraios* at the moment is to regard it as a gentilic adj. meaning "a person from Nazara/Nazareth," but with the possible added nuance of either *nāzîr,* "consecrated one," or *nēser,* "sprout, scion" of Davidic lineage. The "scion of David" is found in Qumran literature (*4QFlor* 1:11; *4QPBless* 1:3-4), used of a messianic figure.[15]

18:38 At that, the sightless man cried out, "Jesus, Son of David, have mercy on me." Already Luke has identified Jesus as a descendant of David (1:27, 32; 2:4; see also 20:41, 44). The title "Son of David" seems to have been associated in Judaism with the Messiah (see *4 Ezra* 12:32; *4QFlor* 1:11; *Ps. Sol.* 17:23). It is difficult to escape the conclusion, therefore, that the usage of the title by the sightless man indicated his belief that Jesus, the Son of David, was the Messiah. Indeed his call for mercy, i.e., healing, confirms this suggestion (cf. v. 42).

18:39 The crowds rebuked the man in order to keep him from crying out. However, the man intensified his effort, crying out all the more for Jesus, the Son of David, to have mercy on him. Like the disciples who earlier tried to prevent the children from coming to Jesus, so now the crowds tried to do the same with the sightless man.

18:40 Jesus intervened, stopping when He heard the cries of the man and ordering the people to bring the man to Him. The sightless man drew near to Jesus, and Jesus asked him a question.

18:41 "What do you want me to do?" The question was designed to elicit faith. The man called Jesus "Lord" (*kyrie*). In light of his earlier title for Jesus, "Son of David," the word surely meant more to the sightless man than just a term of respect, i.e., master or rabbi. It conveyed his sense that Jesus was the Lord; He was deity. Having addressed Him thus, the man asked Jesus to restore his sight.

15. Brown, *The Birth of the Messiah,* 209-13, 223-25.

18:42 At that, Jesus commanded that the man be restored to his sight. On the basis of his faith the sightless man was then able to see. The term "salvation" is used by Luke in a holistic way—the man was healed both physically and spiritually (cf. 5:20; 7:50; 8:48; 17:19).

18:43 Immediately, the man's vision was restored, and he began to follow Jesus (probably as a new disciple), glorifying God (see 2:20; 5:25, 26; 7:16; 13:13; 17:15; 23:47). In response to the miracle they witnessed, the people (*laos*) gave praise to God. Fitzmyer remarks that from this passage on, until the end of the gospel, the word *people* (*laos*) occurs nineteen times, signaling its importance to Luke. The people's positive attitude is often used in contrast to the Jewish leaders' criticism of Jesus.[16]

We should like to conclude the exposition of this chapter by returning to a theme we earlier suggested influences Luke's portrait of Jesus, namely, that a particular person's, or group of persons', partial faith leading to full faith in Jesus is viewed by the third evangelist as a picture of the future restoration of Israel. It is commonplace among scholars to view the miracle of the healing of blind Bartimaeus as also a parable of the disciples' faith.[17] Just as Bartimaeus's faith in Jesus brought him physical sight (Luke 18:35-43), so the disciples were in need of spiritual sight concerning the suffering nature of their Lord's messiahship (18:31-34). That spiritual vision came to them after the resurrection of Christ; cf. Luke 24:13-53; Acts 1:1-8. These two scriptures are interesting relative to this point. In both instances, the disciples are reported to have finally come to understand the suffering nature of Jesus' messiahship as prophesied in the Old Testament (see Luke 24:26-35, 44-49; Acts 1:2-3). It is also the case that in both settings, the disciples asked questions about the restoration of Israel to God (see Luke 24:21; Acts 1:6). It is difficult thereby to miss the connection between the faith of the disciples and the restoration of Israel. The development of the disciples' faith from partial to full understanding corresponds to Israel's future restoration to Jesus, her Messiah.

HOMILETICAL SUGGESTIONS

It is quite possible to compress the entire chapter of Luke 18 into one sermon, entitled, "Radical Faith." The outline offered in this com-

---

16. Fitzmyer, *The Gospel According to Luke X–XXIV,* 1217.
17. See, for example, ibid., 1214.

mentary should easily facilitate that task, because each point emerges out of biblical illustrations. We suggest, therefore, the same threefold outline for each episode: explanation, illustration, application.

I. Vv. 1-8:   A Persecuted Faith
   A. Explanation: The Reality of Persecution
   B. Illustration: Parable of Unjust Judge
   C. Application

II. Vv. 9-14:   A Repentant Faith
   A. Explanation: The Meaning of Repentance
   B. Illustration: The Pharisee and the Toll Collector
   C. Application

III. Vv. 15-17: A Childlike Faith
   A. Explanation: The Qualities of Childlike Faith
   B. Illustration: Jesus and the Children
   C. Application

IV. Vv. 18-30: Unreserved Faith
   A. Explanation: Define Total Commitment to Christ
   B. Illustration: The Rich Ruler
   C. Application

V. Vv. 31-43: A Developing Faith
   A. Explanation: The Growth of Faith
   B. Illustration: The Disciples' Spiritual Sight and the Blind Man's Physical Sight
   C. Application

LUKE

CHAPTER

NINETEEN

COMPLETING THE JOURNEY
TO JERUSALEM

Luke 19:1-44 completes the travelogue of Jesus' journey to Jerusalem. It consists of the following episodes: the conversion of Zacchaeus, vv. 1-10; the parable of the pounds, a response Jesus made to overtly enthusiastic expectations about the coming of the kingdom of God, vv. 11-27; the Triumphant Entry, vv. 28-44. Verses 45-48 serve as a transitional paragraph which introduces Jesus' temple ministry, beginning with His cleansing of the temple.

THE CONVERSION OF ZACCHAEUS, 19:1-10

The episode of the conversion of Zacchaeus, a chief toll collector who resided in Jericho, is structured as a pronouncement story, technically called an *apopmthegms,* in this case a biographical *apopmthegms.* It is composed of the three typical parts we have come to expect of Jesus' pronouncement stories: a controversial action by Jesus, vv. 1-6; criticism of Jesus by the Jewish leadership, vv. 7-8; Jesus' authoritative pronouncement, vv. 9-10.

19:1 The opening verse geographically links the aforementioned episode of the healing of the sightless man just outside Jericho (18:35) with the upcoming incident with Zacchaeus. Jesus was passing through the city.

19:2 In that city was a man named Zacchaeus, probably an abbreviation of "Zachariah," meaning the "righteous one" (cf. Ezra 2:9;

351

Neh. 7:14; *2 Macc.* 10:19). Two things are said about this person. First, he was a chief toll collector. As such, Zacchaeus was quite possibly head of a group of toll collectors who were responsible for customs due in the area on goods passing from Peraea into Judea.[1] Second, he was rich, which undoubtedly stemmed from his dishonest and exorbitant taxes on goods (see v. 8). Yet, as the story progresses, Zacchaeus becomes an example of God's power to save the rich and therefore accomplish the impossible (cf. 18:27).

19:3   Zacchaeus sought to see Jesus. For what reason, we do not know. Curiosity? Sincerity? In any event, he was not able to see Jesus because he was too short and could not see over the crowds.

19:4   In order to catch a glimpse of Jesus, Zacchaeus ran ahead of the crowds and climbed a sycamore tree. Archaeologist J. Finegan has plausibly identified the type of sycamore tree that Zacchaeus will have climbed, located in the Herodian section of Jericho, the place where Herod the Great built a winter resort. Comparing Herodian Jericho to such cities as Rome and Pompeii, Finegan writes, "Like such cities NT Jericho undoubtedly had its parks and villas, avenues and public squares, where fine trees grew."[2] Zacchaeus climbed one such tree in order to see Jesus as He passed by.

19:5   Jesus came to the spot, looked up, and saw Zacchaeus. Jesus told him to come down quickly, for today He must stay at his house. Three supernatural occurrences marked Jesus' encounter with Zacchaeus. First, Jesus went to the exact spot where Zacchaeus was, thereby suggesting divine knowledge on His part. Second, Luke uses a favorite word expressing the need for the divine plan to be accomplished—"must" (*dei*). Third, another of Luke's favorite words, "day" (*sēmeron*), conveys the idea of the fulfillment of God's plan of salvation (cf. v. 9). In other words, Zacchaeus's salvation was a part of the divine agenda, if for no other reason than he represented God's love to the outcasts of Jewish society (see v. 7), a theme dear to Luke's own heart.

19:6   Zacchaeus did what Jesus asked, and he joyously welcomed Him into his home. This statement concludes the first part of the pronouncement story, Jesus' controversial action of visiting with a toll collector.

---

1. Otto Michel, *"Telōnēs,"* 8:88-105; 97-99.
2. Finegan, *The Archeology of the New Testament,* 85.

19:7   The second part of the *apopmthegms* is the criticism of Jesus' actions by the onlookers. The people began to object to Jesus' involvement with a sinner, even to the point of lodging with him. The same word for "criticize" (*diegognuzon*) was used earlier of the Pharisees and scribes in 5:30 and 15:2.

19:8   But Zacchaeus responded to the Lord Jesus (apparently there on the road) that he would give half of what he owned to the poor. And those from whom he had extorted money he pledged to pay back four times over. This is the typical interpretation of v. 8. However, Fitzmyer demurs from this viewpoint when he argues that that verse is not a confession of Zacchaeus's repentance of sin and resolve to provide restitution to those he cheated, but rather it is his testimony to Jesus that he is, in fact, not a sinner. On the contrary, "he gives" (present tense) to the poor and, should he discover that he has defrauded others, will pay that back too.[3] Fitzmyer's suggestion is creative, but it does not hold up under closer examination, for four reasons: First, grammatically, the present tense verb "I give" (*didōmi*) is best taken as a futuristic present, "I will give," and thus to be taken as a statement of resolve—"I hereby determine to give half of what I own to the poor." Second, again from a grammatical perspective, the clause "*if* I have extorted anything from others, *then* I will pay it back four times over" is a first-class conditional statement expressing reality. In other words, the clause should begin, "*since* I have extorted." On this reading the chief toll collector was confessing the reality of his sin. Third, contextually, the accusation that Zacchaeus was a sinner in v. 7 looks to be met with Zacchaeus's acknowledgment and repentance of that sin in v. 8. Fourth, again taking the context into consideration, according to v. 9, Jesus' pronouncement that salvation had come to Zacchaeus's home would not seem to be compatible with a positive reading of v. 8. If Zacchaeus was indeed giving to the poor and willing to compensate those he had wronged *before* he met Jesus, then one wonders why he ever needed the Lord in the first place.

19:9   In response to Zacchaeus's confession of sin prompted by his faith in Jesus, the Lord declared that salvation had come to the toll collector's house that day (cf. Acts 10:2; 11:14; 16:15, 21; 18:8). Because of this, the sinful Jew, an outcast in the eyes of the religious crowd, had become a son of Abraham. He was an illustration of 1:55, 72-79.

---

3. Fitzmyer, *The Gospel According to Luke X–XXIV,* 1220-21, 1225.

19:10   Jesus then gave the divine rationale behind Zacchaeus's, and all sinners', salvation, "For the Son of Man has come to seek and to save what was lost." The reference to the Son of Man seeking and saving the lost draws on the shepherding imagery of Ezekiel 34:11-31; 36:14, the context of which God promises to re-gather Israel, His scattered people, like a shepherd who finds his lost sheep (cf. Luke 15:1-7). It might also have had a direct bearing on Zacchaeus for, as the story of his conversion unfolds, his seeking Jesus (v. 3) turned out to be the result of Jesus' first seeking him (v. 10).

THE PARABLE OF THE POUNDS, 19:11-27

The parable of the pounds (vv. 11-27) is actually the product of the interweaving of two parables: the parable of the pounds proper (vv. 13, 15b-26) and the parable of the rejected king (vv. 12, 14, 15a, 27). The first of these parables is similar, though not identical, to the parable of the talents (Matt. 25:14-30).[4] The second is unique to Luke. It undoubtedly was a story Jesus adapted from an incident in the life of Archelaus, applying it to His own ministry.

19:11   The opening genitive absolute, "As they were listening to these things He went on to tell a parable," is Luke's editorial comment roughly connecting the previous narrative with what is to come. Luke gives the reason for the parable, "Because they were near Jerusalem, it seemed to the people that the kingdom of God was going to appear immediately." The belief informing this comment was the Jewish conviction that the Messiah's earthly kingdom would appear in Jerusalem (see Zech. 14; Acts 1:6; Strack-B 2:300). Naturally, then, the people, disciples included, assumed that Jesus, the Messiah, was about to begin His kingly reign upon reaching Jerusalem. But Jesus' twofold parable to follow will serve to correct that misunderstanding, teaching that there will be an interval of time elapsing between His first and second comings. Basically, three points will be made: First, Jesus' first coming will end in rejection (vv. 12, 14). In effect, the kingdom of God has not yet arrived visibly on earth. Second, at His return, however, Jesus will arrive as king over the earth, and He will judge His enemies, including those who persecuted Him (vv. 15a, 27). Third, in the interval, disciples must be vigilant and faithful in his service (vv. 13, 15b-26).

---

4. See ibid., 1228-33; Marshall, *Commentary on Luke,* 701-2.

19:12   This verse introduces the parable of the rejected king by referring to a certain man who was of noble birth (*eugenēs*). This man traveled to a distant land to acquire for himself a kingship and then to return. Two points emerge from the verse. Historically, as the commentators recognize, the story resembles the account of Archelaus who, upon the death of his father Herod the Great in 4 B.C., traveled to Rome in order to confirm his kingship bestowed on him in his father's will. The area involved Judea, Samaria, and Idumea. However, a delegation of some fifty Jews were sent by the people of the land to oppose his appointment by Emperor Augustus, arguing instead for autonomy for the region. Augustus somewhat compromised by awarding Archelaus only the title of ethnarch (Josephus, *Ant.* 17.206-23, 299-314; cf. Luke 19:14). Theologically, the story of the nobleman going to a far country to receive the title of king and then returning alludes to the experience of Jesus, in a number of ways: (1) Jesus was born of noble birth in that He was divinely conceived (cf. Luke 19:12 with 1:31-33). (2) After Jesus' death and resurrection, He ascended to heaven for His appointed kingship (cf. Luke 19:12 with 24:50-51; Acts 1:9-12). (3) After an interval, Jesus will return to make visible that kingship (cf. Luke 19:12 with 21:27; and again Acts 1:9-12).

19:13   Before he left, the nobleman called ten of his servants to him and gave them collectively ten pounds (*minas*). The Greek word for "pound" is *mina,* the equivalent of about twenty dollars, or in those days, approximately three months' wages. The small amount of money (ten *minas* to be distributed among the ten servants = one *mina,* or pound, apiece) involved a test of faithfulness. Whoever is faithful in little will be faithful and blessed with much (cf. Luke 8:18 with 19:13, 17, 19, 26). The nobleman commanded the servants to do business with the pounds until he returned.[5] Hence the title of the parable—"The Parable of the Pounds."

19:14   Jesus interrupted the parable of the pounds by resuming the story of the parable of the rejected king. The nobleman's fellow citizens, the ones over whom he was to rule, disliked him and sent a delegation after him to persuade the ruler of the distant country not to authorize him to rule over them. Like v. 12, two points emerge from this verse: First, historically the story alludes to the delegation of Jews

---

5. On the issue of whether or not *erchesthai* means "come" or "return," see Fitzmyer, *The Gospel According to Luke X–XXIV,* 1235. His reluctance to allow for the second possibility seems to be unfounded. The word probably should be taken more figuratively ("return"), thus alluding to Jesus' second coming.

that followed Archelaus to Rome, requesting Augustus not to confirm his kingship over them. Second, theologically, the story matches Jesus' experience of being rejected as Israel's king (cf. Matt. 22:6 and Acts 17:7).

19:15 Verse 15 seems to merge together the two parables: the parable of the rejected king in v. 15a is combined with the parable of the pounds in v. 15b. Verse 15a alludes to the second coming of Christ to earth, at which time He will be enthroned as visible king over the earth. No longer will He be the rejected king, much to the chagrin of His enemies (see v. 27). Verse 15b picks up the story of the parable of the pounds. The nobleman summoned his servants to whom he gave the money in order to give an account of how they had used it.

19:16 The spotlight falls on three of the servants. The first came to his lord and told him that his one pound had earned ten pounds. Derrett has shown that such a large increase was not out of line for the then known Palestinian economy, especially with its exorbitant interest rates.[6]

19:17 The nobleman responded, "Well done, good servant; because you were faithful in a little thing, you will have authority over ten towns." Because the servant was trustworthy and enterprising in his usage of the one pound, now he will rule ten towns of the nobleman's newly acquired kingdom.

19:18 Then the second servant came, telling the nobleman that the one pound he was given he had made into five pounds.

19:19 The nobleman responded to that servant in fashion similar to the way he had replied to the first, giving him authority over five towns in his kingdom.

19:20 The words "the other servant" pose a difficulty in light of the fact that the parable of the pounds refers to ten servants, not three (as does the parable of the talents in Matt. 25:14-30). Perhaps, as Ellis theorizes, the three reporting servants in Luke's accounts represent the three types of responses from the ten servants.[7] In any case, this servant's actions were in contrast to the other two servants. He took the master's pound and stored it away in a handkerchief (scarf or neckcloth) used to protect the back of the head from the sun. Although the practice of keeping money in this manner is attested to in rabbinic writings (*b. Ketubot* 67b; Strack-B 2:252), it was regarded as unsafe

6. Derrett, *Law in the New Testament,* 17-31.

7. Ellis, *The Gospel of Luke,* 224; *contra* Marshall, *Commentary on Luke,* 706.

(Strack-B 1:970). The servant's actions revealed sloth and disobedience on his part.

19:21　Verse 21 reveals the disobedient servant's shallow motivation for not using his master's resources industriously. He was afraid of his austere (*austēros*) master, who carried off what he did not deposit and reaped what he did not sow. The first clause in the preceding sentence draws on a banking metaphor and is used to describe a person who sought disproportionately high returns from his investments (see Josephus, *Ag. Ap.* 2.216). The second clause draws on agricultural imagery, noting the master's savvy ability to capitalize on the harvest of the land without having had to sow the seed. With these metaphors in mind, Marshall expresses the gist of the fear of the servant, "The servant appears to have feared that he would get no return for his work: all the profit would have been taken by the master. At the same time, he may have feared that if he incurred a loss on the capital he would have to make it up to the master."[8]

19:22　Using the historic present tense, Luke provides the master's response, "He says, 'By your own mouth, wicked servant, I will judge you. You knew that I carry off what I do not deposit and reap what I do not sow?'" Instead of letting fear paralyze his actions, the servant should have let fear motivate him to act wisely.

19:23　At the very least, said the master, the servant could have put the money into the bank so that it would have collected interest.

19:24　In response, the master ordered his attendants (perhaps these are the remaining seven servants, cf. v. 13) to take the pound away from the unproductive servant and give it to the one with the ten pounds. The idea informing this decision was probably the principle that whoever is faithful in a few things will be faithful in many things and will be rewarded accordingly. Perhaps also the master was influenced in his action by the truth that if we do not use our talents we will lose them. This servant could tragically testify to that reality. The next verses amplify these concepts.

19:25　The attendants protested the master's decision, pointing out that the one awarded the pound already had ten pounds.

19:26　The master solemnly pronounced his judgment, asserting that whoever has, to him will be given more and whoever does not have, from him will be taken away. The paradoxical, almost oxymoronic, statement reflects the spiritual axiom earlier recorded in 8:18:

8. Marshall, *Commentary on Luke*, 707.

Whoever is faithful to the Lord will be rewarded and whoever is not will suffer loss. Light received brings more light; light refused brings the night.

19:27 Verse 27 concludes the parable of the pounds by returning to the parable of the rejected king. Even though the action taken toward the disobedient servant was severe (even as it will be on Judgment Day for the unfaithful Christian), there is no hint in the text that the salvation of the faithless servant of the Lord was in jeopardy. Not so for the enemies of the nobleman, i.e., Christ, according to v. 27. The strong adversative "however" (*plēn*) seems to contrast the punishment of the unprofitable servant with that of the master's enemies (cf. v. 14) who did not want him to rule over them. He commanded that they be brought before him and slaughtered. The language of slaughtering one's enemies occurs in both the Old Testament (1 Sam. 15:33, where Samuel had Agag, king of the Amalekites, slaughtered at Gilgal) and the New Testament (Rev. 14:10, Christ the Lamb-Lion will slaughter His enemies at His return). In Luke's context, it probably had two focuses—historical and eschatological. Historically, Jesus' enemies (i.e., the Jewish people who crucified Him) were indeed destroyed by the Roman army at the fall of Jerusalem in A.D. 70 (cf. Luke 21:6, 20-24; 23:28-31). Eschatologically, Jesus' enemies, those who reject Him, will be consumed at His return (cf. Luke 21:25; 22:66-70; cf. Rev. 19).

THE TRIUMPHANT ENTRY, 19:28-44

The Triumphant Entry of Jesus into Jerusalem both concluded His journey to the city of His destiny as well as initiated the passion narrative proper. In effect, the Triumphant Entry in all the gospel accounts began Jesus' Passion Week. Therefore, it seems appropriate at this junction to provide a chronological frame of reference for charting the events of that week. We do so by following Harold Hoehner's synopsis. Having done that, we will proceed to analyze the Triumphant Entry pericope itself, beginning with an investigation of its literary genre. Hoehner's suggested synopsis of Jesus' Passion Week runs as follows:

> A few days before the final Passover, Jesus drew near to Jerusalem (Jn. 11:55), arriving at Bethany six days before the Passover (Jn. 12:1), namely the Saturday before the Passion Week. That evening, Jesus was

anointed at Simon the leper's house (Matt. 26:6-13; Mk. 14:3-9; Jn. 12:1-8). On the next day (Sunday), there was a great crowd that came to Bethany to see Jesus (Jn. 12:9-11).

Monday

The next day (Jn. 12:12), Monday, was Jesus' triumphal entry into Jerusalem (Matt. 21:1-9; Mk. 11:1-10; Lk. 19:28-40; Jn. 12:12-19), His visit to the temple (Matt. 21:10-11; Mk. 11:11), and then His return to Bethany. The day of the triumphal entry would be Nisan [April] 10 when the lamb was selected for Passover. Hence, the triumphal entry was the day when Christ presented Himself as Israel's Paschal lamb.

Tuesday

On Tuesday on the way from Bethany to Jerusalem, Jesus cursed the fig tree (Matt. 21:18-19; Mk. 11:12-14), and then He went to Jerusalem to cleanse the temple (Matt. 21:12-13; Mk. 11:15-17; Lk. 19:45-46). The religious leaders began to seek how they might destroy Him that evening, and that evening Jesus left Jerusalem, presumably returning to Bethany (Mk. 11:18-19; Lk. 19:47-48).

Wednesday

On the way to Jerusalem on Wednesday, the disciples saw the withered fig tree (Matt. 21:20-22; Mk. 11:20-26). At the temple in Jerusalem, Jesus had a day of controversy with the religious leaders (Matt. 21:23–23:29; Mk. 11:17–12:44; Lk. 20:1–21:4). That afternoon Jesus went to the Mount of Olives and delivered the Olivet Discourse (Matt. 24:1–25:46; Mk. 13:1-17; Lk. 21:5-36). Two additional things occurred on that day: (1) Jesus predicted that in two days He would be crucified at the time of the Passover (Matt. 26:1-5; Mk. 14:1-2; Lk. 22:1-2); and (2) Judas planned the betrayal of Christ with the religious leaders (Matt. 26:14-16; Mk. 14:10-11; Lk. 22:3-6).

Thursday

On this day, He had His disciples prepare the Passover lamb (Matt. 26:17-19; Mk. 14:12-16; Lk. 22:7-13), and Jesus and His disciples had their Passover meal in the Upper Room (Matt. 26:20-30; Mk. 14:17-26; Lk. 22:14-30; Jn. 13:1–14:31). Leaving the Upper Room, Jesus had a discourse with His disciples and offered an intercessory prayer in their behalf (Matt. 26:30-35; Mk. 14:26-31; Lk. 22:31-39; Jn. 15:1–18:1). They arrived at the Garden of Gethsemane, and it was here where Jesus suffered in agony (Matt. 26:36-46; Mk. 14:32-42; Lk. 22:39-46; Jn. 18:1). Later that night Jesus was betrayed and arrested (Matt. 26:47-56; Mk. 14:43-52; Lk. 22:47-53; Jn. 18:2-12). During the rest of that night Jesus was tried first by Annas and later by Caiaphas with the religious leaders (Matt. 26:57-75; Mk. 14:53-72; Lk. 22:54-65; Jn. 18:13-27).

Friday

Early in the morning, Jesus was tried by the Sanhedrin, Pilate, Herod Antipas, and Pilate again (Matt. 27:1-30; Mk. 15:1-19; Lk. 22:66–23:25; Jn. 18:28–19:16). Jesus was then led to the cross and crucified at 9:00 A.M. and died at 3:00 P.M. and was buried later that day (Matt. 27:31-60; Mk. 15:20-46; Lk. 23:26-54; Jn. 19:16-42). Christ the Paschal Lamb (1 Cor. 5:7) died at the time when the Israelites were sacrificing their Passover lambs.

Saturday

Jesus was lying in the tomb during the Sabbath, and the Pharisees secured Roman guards to keep watch of the tomb (Matt. 27:61-66; Mk. 15:47; Lk. 23:55-56).

Sunday

Christ was resurrected from the dead (Matt. 28:1-15; Mk. 16:1-8[9-13]; Lk. 24:1-35). He is a type of the offering of the first fruits which was offered the day after the Sabbath (Lev. 23:9-14; 1 Cor. 15:23).

Conclusion

The week of the Passion was filled with many events, beginning with the Saturday before the Passion Week and ending with the crucifixion of Christ on Friday and the resurrection on Sunday.[9]

Before turning to a detailed analysis of the Triumphant Entry (Luke 19:28-44), we must first identify its literary genre. In doing so, we will be in a better position to interpret its meaning. The consensus among scholars today for conducting this investigation is that one must begin with the Marcan account, 11:1-14, the basis of the synoptic tradition of that pericope. Recently, Paul Brooks Duff has provided an insightful treatment of the literary genre of Mark 11:1-13, finding an admixture of two major ancient motifs: the Jewish Divine Warrior and the Advent of the Greco-Roman King.[10] Duff then goes on to show that the Marcan Triumphant Entry utilizes those motifs ironically. In effect, what Duff demonstrates is that the Divine Warrior/Greco-Roman King themes are given an ironic twist by Jesus in order to accentuate His true mission—He is a suffering Messiah, a humiliated king.

9. Hoehner, *Chronological Aspects of the Life of Christ,* 90-93. For a map of Jerusalem at the time of Jesus, see Appendix C.
10. Duff, "The March of the Divine Warrior and the Advent of the Greco-Roman King," 55-71.

We will briefly summarize Duff's findings below, noting the four similarities emerging between the Divine Warrior motif (based on Zech. 9, 14), the advent of the Greco-Roman King (based on ancient literature ranging from Josephus to Plutarch), and the Marcan Triumphant Entry, 11:1-14. However, in the Marcan narrative it is the fourth correspondence which displays Jesus' ironic twist to the other two motifs, not to mention the expectations of the crowds: (1) The conqueror/ruler is escorted into the city by the citizens or the army of the conqueror (see Zech. 14:4-5; Josephus, *J. W.* 7.132-57; Mark 11:1-7). (2) The triumphant procession into the city is accompanied by hymns and acclamations to the conqueror (see Zech. 9:9; Plutarch, *Aem.* 34.7; Mark 11:9-10). (3) Various elements in the procession symbolize the conqueror's/ruler's authority (see Zech. 9:9b; 14:1-3; App. *Wars* 66; Mark 11:7-8). (4) The procession concludes at the temple, where a sacrificial offering of some sort is made, which symbolizes the conqueror's enthronement over the temple (religion) and city (state) (see Zech. 14:20-21; Josephus, *J. W.* 7.153; Mark 11:11-14). It is in this last correspondence that Jesus introduced an ironic twist to the Jewish/Greco-Roman Triumphant Entry motifs for, according to Mark 11:11-14 (cf. Luke 19:45-46), Jesus cleansed the temple, disassociating Himself from any connotation of setting Himself up as king over the city. Duff's conclusion concerning the Marcan narrative, in our estimation, essentially applies to the Lucan portrayal of the Triumphant Entry,[11] and therefore merits quoting:

> But what at first glance seems to be a story of a triumphal entry and Temple cleansing is broken up and hence transformed by the second evangelist. By breaking up the narrative in the manner in which he does, the evangelist gives his "triumphal entry" an ironic twist. The echo of . . . Zechariah 14 . . . [overlaid] . . . with elements of Greco-Roman entry processions manifests this irony for the march of the divine warrior and the entry of the Greco-Roman king providing a stark contrast with the Marcan account of Jesus' entry into Jerusalem. For example, in Zechariah 14, the divine warrior appears on the Mount of Olives, enters Jerusalem in procession with his holy ones, appropriates the Temple, and inaugurates a new age of blessedness centered on the Jerusalem Temple, a transformed age in which the distinction between

11. The only major difference between the Lucan and Marcan Triumphant Entry accounts, especially the cleansing of the temple narrative, is that the former is not sandwiched into the incident of the cursing of the fig tree whereas the latter is.

sacred and profane has lost all meaning. Similarly, a conquering ruler from the Greco-Roman milieu would enter his city amid acclamations of his entourage, accompanied by various symbolic depictions of his authority, and immediately upon entering that city would symbolically take possession of it. On the contrary, in Mark's story, the entry parade—because of the interruption of vv. 11-14—abruptly and anticlimactically ends, and Jesus simply leaves the Temple and the city. The "appropriation" of the Temple on the following day is not really an appropriation at all but a disqualification, a fact made all the more apparent by Mark's structure, a structure that connects Jesus' entry and activity in the Temple with his cursing of the fig tree. As we have seen, the cursing of fig tree and the subsequent "lesson" (i.e., the mountain-moving logion) suggest to the reader the condemnation of the Temple.

In short, the evangelist teases his readers with what seem to be triumphal allusions but never satisfies their expectations which might have been built up by those allusions. In fact, by his careful arrangement of the text and by the insertion of the fig tree episodes, Mark subverts those triumphal allusions. . . . Consequently, those readers who have not really grasped the significance of Jesus' suffering messiahship and the true nature of the kingdom—that is, those readers who expect Jesus to inaugurate the kingdom of God in a manner resembling that of a warrior-king—will, like the characters of the disciples in Mark's Gospel, have to revise their expectations.[12]

19:28   The words "After saying these things Jesus kept proceeding ahead, going up to Jerusalem" connect with the parables of the pounds/rejected king and the nobleman who traveled to a distant land, thereby clarifying the purpose of Jesus' journey to Jerusalem. To avoid any misunderstanding about Jesus' ascent to Jerusalem, Luke intends that the preceding parables guard against the expectation that Jesus was about to set up His physical kingdom when He arrived there. He first had to suffer and die, go to heaven, and then, and only then, return from the "distant country" before setting up the kingdom of God in Jerusalem (see v. 11). The words "ascent (*anabainōn*) to Jerusalem" are to be taken literally and figuratively. Literally, the road from Jericho to Jerusalem proceeded upward thousands of feet. Figuratively, Jerusalem, the city of Jesus' destiny, was to be the place He would be "lifted up" on the cross and, from there, ascend to the Father (24:50-53; Acts 1:9-11).

12. Duff, "The March of the Divine Warrior and the Advent of the Greco-Roman King," 70-71.

19:29   Jesus, leading the way with His disciples, drew near to Bethphage and Bethany. The location of the first of these towns, Bethphage (Heb., house [*bet*] of unripe figs [*paggē*]), is uncertain. Perhaps it is to be equated with modern-day *Kefr-et-Tur*, a village about one mile east of Jerusalem, on the eastern side of the Mount of Olives. The other town, Bethany (Heb., house [*bet*] of *Nniyah* [dates]), is located two miles east of Jerusalem, also on the eastern slope of the Mount of Olives. It is called today *El Azariyeth*. It was regarded as the home of Lazarus, Mary, and Martha (John 11:1). The order in Luke (based on Mark 11:1) is surprising, giving the impression that, going westward, Bethphage comes before Bethany, when just the opposite is true. It may be that, however, as Marshall suggests, Bethany, the better known place, was added as an afterthought to elucidate the situation of Bethphage.[13] Both towns are located on the east side of the Mount of Olives, a hill that is part of a range of low-lying mountains overlooking Jerusalem to the east across the Kidron Valley. The range extends about two and one-half miles from north to south and has three main summits. The highest summit is modern-day Mount Scopus (2,690 feet above sea level), the northern mountain. The Mount of Olives (2,660 feet above sea level) is the central summit, facing directly across the Kidron Valley from the temple mound area. The southern summit is the Mount of Corruption or Offense (see 2 Kings 23:13).[14] Approaching Bethphage and Bethany, Jesus sent away two of His disciples.

19:30   The destination of the two disciples is identified as "the village opposite," referring to Bethphage. There the disciples were to find a colt (*pōlon*)[15] which was unbroken/had never been ridden. The disciples were to untie it and lead it to Jesus. The reference to the colt is reminiscent of Zechariah 9:9, "a new foal," and gives a messianic sense to the upcoming event. Some commentators have argued that Jesus' instructions in vv. 30-31 only imply that He had made prior arrangement with the colt's owner.[16] However, this is to overlook the fact that Jesus' divine foreknowledge was at work, evidenced in the reference to Him as "Lord" (v. 31), as well as the crowd's recognition of Jesus' miraculous power (v. 37).

13. Marshall, *Commentary on Luke*, 712.
14. See Finegan, *The Archeology of the New Testament*, 88-90.
15. On the relationship between Luke 19:30/Mark 11:2 and Matt. 21:2, see Evans, *Luke*, 293. It may be that Matthew's mention of two animals (instead of Mark's and Luke's mention of one) was because a colt, young and unbroken as it was, was accompanied by its mother.
16. See, for example, Marshall, *Commentary on Luke*, 713.

19:31   If the disciples should be asked why they were taking the animal, they were to answer, "The Lord (*kyrios*) has need of it."
19:32   The two went their way and found things to unfold precisely as Jesus said.
19:33   As the disciples untied the colt, its owners inquired why they were doing so. Normally, animals such as donkeys (for the poor) and horses (for the wealthy) were made available by their owners for travelers for a price or, at times, to be borrowed.
19:34   It may have been the latter occasion that informed the disciples' response, "The Lord has need of it." No mention is made of the colt's owner's permission to take the animal, but that is obviously what transpired. He may have been familiar with Jesus, perhaps understanding Him to be a rabbi with the authority to make such a request. Be that as it may, ultimately it was Jesus' supernatural word conveyed by His disciples that secured the right to use the animal.
19:35   Verse 35 describes the disciples' subsequent actions. They led the colt to Jesus. They then tossed their cloaks (*himatia*) on the colt and set Jesus upon the animal. Their action meant more than just providing a saddle for Jesus to ride on a hitherto unridden colt. It signified homage to Him. In light of similar statements made about Jehu in 2 Kings 9:13 and the coming deliverer in Zechariah 9:9, the disciples' action was tantamount to proclaiming Jesus as the Messiah King. Verse 38, with its threefold designation of Jesus as "King," "the one who comes in the name of the Lord," and the object of peace and glory in heaven confirms this interpretation.
19:36   Like a snowball effect, others, too, along the way to Jerusalem began to spread their cloaks on the road before Jesus. Like the "red carpet" treatment showed to the newly appointed king, Jehu (2 Kings 9:13), the followers of Jesus paid their homage to Him.
19:37   By the time the entourage began the descent down the western slope of the Mount of Olives, crowds of disciples had begun to praise God with a loud voice, rejoicing over the miracles they had seen Jesus perform in the past. Marshall aptly comments that this verse is reminiscent of the praise which greeted Jesus on His entry into the world at Bethlehem from the angels and the shepherds (2:13, 20).[17]
19:38   Verse 38 records the threefold acclamation of the crowds in their praise to Jesus. First, they applied to Jesus the words of Psalm

17. Marshall, *Commentary on Luke,* 715.

118:26, "Blessed is the one who comes in the name of the Lord." Whereas this part of the Hallel ("praise," Pss. 113-118) could be interpreted generically in the sense that festive pilgrims sang it to one another upon their arrival to Jerusalem to celebrate Passover and Tabernacles, it could also convey a messianic connotation. The crowds' reaction to Jesus obviously indicates the latter sense here. Second, Jesus was proclaimed the "king," which underscores the fact that the crowds believed Jesus' arrival in Jerusalem was the fulfillment of Zechariah 9:9, "Behold your king is coming to you." Third, the crowds announced that Jesus' arrival brought "peace in heaven and glory in the highest," honorific terms that echo Luke 2:14. In other words, the crowds recognized in Jesus their long-awaited Savior.

However, this is not all there is to the story, for Luke introduces into the Triumphant Entry two reservations about Jesus' purpose for coming to Jerusalem. These reservations, like the irony we noted earlier in the Marcan parallel account (11:1-14), serve to correct any misconceptions regarding Jesus' mission. He did not come to be enthroned as king over Israel, nor would He set up His kingdom in Jerusalem at that time, as the crowds hoped. The cleansing of the temple would make that clear (see vv. 45-46). But even in the present passage there are two factors which curtail unbridled enthusiasm about the soon coming of the visible kingdom of God to earth (cf. 11). First, Luke omits the words in Mark 11:10, "Blessed is the coming kingdom of our father David." Evans writes of this:

> By omitting this exclamation, Luke is careful to convey the idea that what has arrived is not the "kingdom," but the "king." Saying that the kingdom is coming could leave the impression that the kingdom of God should have been inaugurated with Jesus' arrival at Jerusalem (or shortly thereafter). This idea Luke is careful to avoid. This may explain why Luke omits mention of the palm branches (see Mark 11:8), which signify political ideas (see 2 Macc. 10:7). . . . As the man of noble birth in the parable above (19:11-27), Jesus arrives in Jerusalem to be made king, but soon he will depart and remain absent for a period of time. Only when he returns will the kingdom be established.[18]

Second, the words "peace in heaven," though reminding one of the angelic promise at the birth of Jesus, because He will bring "peace on earth" (2:14), actually change the nuance of the meaning. Ellis

18. Evans, *Luke,* 289.

writes of this change, "The messianic peace is realized now only 'in heaven,' that is, in the realm to which the resurrected Jesus goes. 'Peace on earth' (2:14) is rejected by Jerusalem (19:42) and must await the Parousia for its fulfillment."[19]

19:39   Not all responded so positively to Jesus' entry into Jerusalem. The Pharisees were disturbed by the commotion of the crowds and told Jesus to rebuke His disciples. Perhaps the Pharisees feared for Jesus' safety, and their own, if such fervor should lead to a messianic revolt against Rome. Or possibly they felt that Jesus should not tolerate the unwarranted praise of the people (cf. Matt. 21:14-16)— praise that should have been reserved only for God.

19:40   Luke oddly combines *ean* ("if") with a future indicative, *siōpēsousin* ("will grow silent"); usually *ean* goes with a subjunctive verb to form a third-class conditional sentence. The resulting words, "if the people should grow silent, then the stones will cry out," are not clear. Marshall lists as many as four possibilities:

> 1. It is not more possible for the disciples to keep silent than it is for stones to speak. 2. If the disciples keep silent, the stones will be forced to proclaim the mighty acts of God instead of them. . . . 3. Hab. 2:11 was taken up in the Targum and rabbinic writings to indicate that the stones could cry out against those who do evil (SB II, 253). This may be taken to refer to the stones crying out against the disciples who would sin by keeping silent . . . , or 4. to the stones crying out against the people who rejected Jesus and silenced the disciples (. . . the reference is not to the stones speaking, but to the testimony of their being overthrown in A.D. 70).[20]

It seems that the fourth view is what was intended by Luke, especially in light of the verses that immediately follow, vv. 41-44. If the inhabitants of Jerusalem do as the Pharisees command—refuse to recognize Jesus as Messiah king—then the very stones of which the city was built would. Actually, as the gospel of Luke unfolds, the crowds will ironically do what the Pharisees ordered by changing their tune from, "Blessed is He who comes in the name of the Lord" to, "Crucify Him" (23:21). And, in fact, the stones of Jerusalem would vindicate Jesus, when the city was destroyed by the Romans in A.D. 70 (see 21:20-24).

19. Ellis, *The Gospel of Luke*, 227.
20. Marshall, *Commentary on Luke*, 716.

19:41   Verses 41-44 record Jesus' lament over the coming destruction of Jerusalem in A.D. 70, confirming our interpretation of v. 40. Jesus' lament over Jerusalem, together with the incident of the cleansing of the temple (vv. 45-46), reinforce the reality that His purpose in entering Jerusalem was not to be enthroned as its king. On the contrary, His mission for coming to the Holy City was to die, a purpose soon to be perpetrated by the unwitting Jewish leaders (vv. 47-48).

Verse 41 dramatically portrays Jesus' weeping over the city against the backdrop of the rejoicing of the crowds as they approached Jerusalem. As He drew near the city, He wept at the sight of it (cf. 13:34; Jer. 9:1; 14:17).

19:42   Verse 42 records the tragedy and irony in Jesus' Triumphant Entry into the Holy City. Jesus expressed a deep desire for Jerusalem to experience the peace that He offered to her that day. The tragedy of the situation is obvious—Jerusalem, not many days from thence, would reject the prince of peace. The irony of it is reflected in the fact that Jerusalem, which means "city of peace," would not live up to its name. The one hiding this truth from Jerusalem's eyes is probably to be understood as God.

19:43   Alas, rather than experience peace, Jerusalem was about to be destroyed by war. What follows in vv. 43-44 are five hostile actions predicted by Jesus that would accompany the Roman destruction of Jerusalem in A.D. 70. The first is that Jerusalem's enemies would throw an embankment against the city. The reference may be to the earthworks constructed by the Roman soldiers of General Titus's army (see Josephus, *J. W.* 5.466). Second, the enemies would encircle the city, laying siege to it (see Josephus, *J. W.* 5.502-11). Third, the result would be that Jerusalem would be hemmed in on every side.

19:44   Fourth, Jerusalem's enemies, having overrun the city's defenses, would dash both city ("you") and its citizens ("your children within you") to the ground, signifying their utter defeat. Fifth, the destruction would be complete; not one stone will be left on another. Josephus describes the fulfillment of this dire prediction:

> Caesar ordered the whole city and the temple to be razed to the ground, leaving only the loftiest of the towers, Phasael, Hippicus, and the Mariamme, and the portion of the wall enclosing the city on the west: the latter as an encampment for the garison that was to remain, and the towers to indicate to posterity the nature of the city and of the strong defences which had yet yielded to Roman prowess. All the rest

of the wall encompassing the city was so completely levelled to the ground as to leave future visitors to the spot no ground for believing that it had ever been inhabited. Such was the end to which the frenzy of revolutionaries brought Jerusalem, that splendid city of world-wide renown. (*J. W.* 7.1.)[21]

The reason for the calamity that will one day befall Jerusalem is that it did not recognize and take advantage of the time of divine visitation offered to it by Jesus (cf. Ex. 3:16; 1 Sam. 1:19-21; Luke 1:68, 78; 7:16).

Our interpretation of Luke 19:41-44 has proceeded along the lines of a prophetic approach to Jesus' words concerning the fate of Jerusalem. That is, vv. 41-44 were predicted by Jesus ca. A.D. 33 and were supernaturally fulfilled in A.D. 70. However, two other viewpoints of this passage should be documented here. The first is Rudolf Bultmann's theory that vv. 41-44 were not uttered by Jesus, but rather by the early church, *vaticinium ex eventu* ("pronouncement after the fact"), subsequent to the fall of Jerusalem.[22] His belief is that Luke gives the impression that Jesus spoke these words when it was actually the later church that did so. But, despite its unnecessary skepticism toward the supernatural ability of Jesus to predict the future, such a view overlooks the fact that extrabiblical sources record similar predictions of the fall of Jerusalem to the Romans made by individuals before the actual event occurred. Compare, for example, the Qumran community's pesher on Hab. 2:8; 3:5-7 (*1QpHab* 2:8; 9:5-7), applying the Old Testament prophet's prediction of the coming fall of Jerusalem to the Babylonians in 587 B.C. to the Jerusalem of its day, *before* the Roman destruction. Or compare Josephus's account in *J. W.* 6.288-309 of a man named Jesus, the son of Ananias (not to be confused with the Jesus of the gospels), who predicted the fall of the temple to Rome before A.D. 70.[23]

A second approach to Luke 19:41-44 is one that is more hospitable to the prophetic view we have followed. In a fascinating study, C. H. Dodd tried to show that Luke's passages predicting Jerusalem's destruction (19:42-44; 21:20-24) derive from an early oracle, pre-dating the destruction itself in A.D. 70, and were not written after the destruc-

---

21. See also Fitzmyer's excellent treatment of Luke 19:43-44 in *The Gospel According to Luke X–XXIV*, 1259.

22. Bultmann, *History of the Synoptic Tradition*, 123, 127.

23. See the superb discussion of this issue in Fitzmyer, *The Gospel According to Luke X–XXIV*, 1254-55.

tion, as is often supposed. Dodd pointed out that the language describing the destruction is borrowed from the Greek translation of the OT. Dodd identifies five distinct descriptions of hostile action taken against Jerusalem that reflect this OT language: (1) *your enemies will build an embankment against you*: A phrase which may have been borrowed from Isaiah 29:3, "I will encircle you Ariel [a name for Jerusalem], throw up an embankment, and set towers about you" (see also Isa. 37:33; Jer. 6:6-21; Ezek. 4:1-3). (2) *and encircle you*: This may also echo Isaiah 29:3: "I will encircle you" (see also 2 Kings 6:14). (3) *and hem you in on every side*: This phrase may echo parts of the following passages: "Put siege works against it, and build a siege wall against it" (Ezek. 4:2; 21:22); "Nebuchadrezzar king of Babylon came with all his army against Jerusalem, and they laid siege to it" (Jer. 52:4). (4) *They will dash you to the ground, you and the children within your walls*: In reference to the hope of judgment against Babylon, Psalm 137:9 proclaims: "Happy shall he be who takes your little ones and dashes in pieces with their children." In reference to the fall of Nineveh, Nahum 3:10 states that "her little ones were dashed into pieces" (see also 2 Kings 8:12). (5) *They will not leave one stone on another*: possibly an echo of 2 Samuel 17:13: "so that not even a stone will be left there" (see also Ezek. 26:12 where the prophet predicts that the stones and timbers of Tyre will be picked up and thrown into the sea). Jesus' oracle concludes with a reference to Jerusalem's failure to "recognize the time of God's coming to you" (lit. "recognize the time of your visitation"), which is probably an allusion to Jeremiah 6:15 in the LXX: "in the time of their visitation they will perish." Dodd states:

> It appears, then, that not only are the two Lucan oracles composed entirely from the language of the Old Testament, but the conception of the coming disaster which the author has in mind is a generalized picture of the fall of Jerusalem as imaginatively presented by the prophets. So far as any historical event has coloured the picture, it is not Titus' capture of Jerusalem in A.D. 70, but Nebuchadrezzar's capture in 586 B.C. There is no single trait of the forecast which cannot be documented directly out of the Old Testament.[24]

Dodd, however, believes that the oracles were uttered and circulated in Judaea before Titus's siege of Jerusalem, but at a time when a

24. Dodd, "The Fall of Jerusalem and 'the Abomination of Desolation,'" 52.

war with Rome was a menacing possibility and that in Christian circles the oracles were believed to go back to Jesus. But because the actual language of the oracles is derived from the Septuagint, Dodd does not believe the Lucan form of the oracle goes back to Jesus. However, we would respond, with Evans, that there is no compelling reason to "conclude that Jesus did not predict Jerusalem's destruction. It is highly probable that he did and that his prediction of the destruction of the city and its temple was a major factor in the religious establishment's turn against him. . . . Luke has apparently obtained a tradition of such a prediction that, in passing from Aramaic (the language of Jesus) to Greek (the language of the LXX), has been worded in terms of the vocabulary and imagery of the LXX."[25] Though we cannot agree with Dodd in full, we see no reason why Jesus did not supernaturally predict the coming fall of Jerusalem by the Romans in A.D. 70, using the Old Testament language of the fall of Jerusalem to the Babylonians, in 587 B.C.

THE CLEANSING OF THE TEMPLE, 19:45-48

Luke 19 ends with a transitional paragraph which, on the one hand, concludes Jesus' journey to Jerusalem and, on the other hand, begins the passion narrative. The paragraph is comprised of three parts: the cleansing of the temple, the major incident recorded in the paragraph (vv. 45-46); Jesus' teaching ministry in the temple (vv. 47a); the Jewish leaders' attempts to kill Jesus (vv. 47b-48).

19:45 Jesus' entrance into, and cleansing of, the temple (vv. 45-46) completes Luke's commentary on the Triumphant Entry, in particular, and the journey to Jerusalem, in general. Jesus did not come to Jerusalem to be enthroned as a political messiah. He came, like an Old Testament prophet, to announce judgment and then pay for His faithfulness to God with His life.

The cleansing of the temple[26] served two purposes: Positively, Jesus' purging of the temple prepared it as a place where He could teach the crowds about the things of God (v. 47), and negatively, Jesus cleansed the temple because of His objection to the mercantile activities going on there (vv. 45-46). According to v. 45, upon entering the city Jesus went into the temple and started to drive out those who were selling there. Ellis enlightens the reader about such activity:

---

25. Evans, *Luke*, 295.
26. On the issue of the relationship between the cleansing of the temple accounts in John and the Synoptics, see the helpful discussion by Evans in *Luke*, 295-96.

The temple tax, required of all Jews, had to be paid in special Jewish coinage. At certain times money-changers set up counters for this purpose in the courtyards of the temple. In the same "court of the Gentiles" the temple administration handled the sale of offerings and sacrifices. The high priest's family seems to have shared the profit of this trade. . . . These practices and the profiteering involved in them created great resentment among the visiting pilgrims. Jesus' action and teachings against the traders doubtless contributed to his popularity among "all the people."[27]

19:46 As Jesus drove out the merchants, He quoted two Old Testament passages: Isaiah 56:7, "My house will be a house of prayer," and Jeremiah 7:11, "you have made it a den of robbers." The first quotation specified the divine purpose of the temple whereas the second quotation castigated the human perversion of that purpose. Evans amplifies the context of those two Old Testament quotations. He observes that Isaiah 56:7 is part of a passage that anticipates the day when salvation will come and when the Lord's deliverance will be revealed (56:1); it will be a time when forgiveness will be offered (56:3, 6), and eunuchs will be welcomed into God's house (56:4). Because of the acceptance of foreign peoples, God's "house [or temple] will be called a house of prayer for all nations" (56:7). Ironically, at the Passover, Jews and proselytes from many nations came to the temple in Jerusalem, but instead of entering a house of prayer, as the Isaianic passage describes, they entered a place of business.

Evans notes that the second part of Jesus' statement is taken from Jeremiah 7:1-15, a passage where the sixth-century prophet condemned those who had desecrated the first temple with their idolatry and crimes (among which is stealing; Jer. 7:9). Passover celebrants were almost surely being overcharged for sacrificial birds and animals, and were perhaps even being cheated when money was exchanged for the shekels needed to buy these animals.[28]

Jesus' expulsion of those who were selling (and exchanging) would have been viewed by the temple leaders as contempt for their authority and possibly as contempt for the religion itself. It is sometimes wondered how Jesus could have gotten away with this action, for temple police were always present to prevent just such an occurrence. Although speculative, a plausible answer has been put forth by

27. Ellis, *The Gospel of Luke*, 230.
28. The following explanation derives from Evans in *Luke*, 291-92.

Victor Eppstein,[29] who argues that the year in which Jesus cleansed the temple was the first year that sellers of animals were permitted into the temple precincts. If this is the case, then Caiaphas would hold the dubious distinction of being the first high priest to authorize this business activity in the temple. (The custom of exchanging money within the temple's precincts had apparently been established earlier.) Opinion regarding the appropriateness of such a new policy would have been sharply divided. It may be that many priests, Levites, and temple guards were looking on sheepishly when Jesus strode boldly into the temple and began driving out the sellers and money changers. Indeed, quite possibly Jesus' action not only did not provoke antagonism from most of the religious figures (although His action surely was upsetting to the merchants), but it may have actually been looked upon with secret approval. Seen in this light, it becomes understandable how Jesus could assault the temple and not only escape arrest but continue teaching in the temple precincts.

19:47   Luke writes in v. 47a that Jesus taught daily in the temple (cf. 21:37). The subject matter of Jesus' teaching is recorded in Luke 20–21 and is summarized in 20:21—Jesus taught the way of God. The site of His teaching was the temple precincts, the outer court area. Included in Jesus' audience were the chief priests, the scribes, and the leaders of the people. These plotted how they might "do away" with Jesus (cf. 6:11; 11:53, 54). The chief priests (cf. 3:2; 9:22) will increasingly appear as Jesus' opponents as the Passion Week progresses (20:1, 19; 22:2, 4, 50, 52, 54, 66; 23:4, 10, 13; 24:20). Many of the chief priests were wealthy and powerful in Jerusalem, but with its destruction in A.D. 70 their influence disappeared. The scribes were mentioned earlier in 5:21. The leaders (*prōtos*, "first" or "priority") of the people were comprised of both religious leaders and non-clergy members of the Sanhedrin (the ruling body of Israel at the time [see 22:66]).

19:48   But the evil triumvirate could not carry out its evil machinations because the general populace (*laos*, "laity") hung on to what Jesus was saying.

HOMILETICAL SUGGESTIONS

Luke 19 could be handled as a two-part mini-series entitled, "The Road to Jerusalem." The messages would cover the three major episodes

---

29. Eppstein, "The Historicity of the Gospel Account of the Cleansing of the Temple," 42-58.

delineated in this chapter: the conversion of Zacchaeus (vv. 1-10), the parable of the pounds (vv. 11-27), and the Triumphant Entry (vv. 28-48). The first sermon should treat the first two episodes. The conversion of Zacchaeus could be well served by outlining it as a pronouncement story: vv. 1-6, Jesus' controversial action; vv. 7-8, the criticism of Jesus; vv. 9-10, Jesus' authoritative pronouncement. Perhaps the episode itself could be introduced by quoting the children's song, "Zacchaeus was a wee little man. . . ." The second sermon could be dealt with as we have suggested here by mingling together the two parables: the parable of the pounds (vv. 13, 15b-20) and the parable of the rejected king (vv. 12, 14-15a, 27). Perhaps the best way to preach these parables would be to offer two broad points: the interpretation of the parables and the application of the parables. The interpretation of the parables would follow the explanation offered in the commentary. The general application is rather simple—to accept the kingship of Jesus over one's life (the parable of the rejected king) is to utilize one's talents in His service (the parable of the pounds); to reject the kingship of Jesus is not to use those talents for Him. The specific application would surely touch upon the basic aspects of living: the need to employ one's time, treasure, and talent in the service of Christ.

The second part of the mini-series, entitled, "The Road to Jerusalem," should analyze the Triumphant Entry, including the scenes of Jesus' cleansing of, and teaching in, the temple (vv. 28-48). We suggest that, rather than proceeding through the passage verse by verse, the speaker consider using Duff's four major points offered in our analysis of this section: (1) the conqueror/ruler is escorted into the city; (2) the procession is accompanied by hymns to the conqueror; (3) various elements symbolize the conqueror's authority; (4) the procession concludes at the temple. The fourth point delivers the punch line, containing Jesus' ironic twist to the Triumphant Entry. It consists of His entering the temple and cleansing it (contrary to Jewish and Greco-Roman expectations) and thereby sealing His destiny to die.

LUKE

CHAPTER

TWENTY

TEACHING IN THE TEMPLE

Chapter 20 is devoted to Jesus' teaching in the temple precincts of Jerusalem. The atmosphere was tense as the Jewish leaders attempted to trip up Jesus and precipitate His downfall. But on each occasion Jesus eluded their verbal traps. Some six skirmishes ensue as the plot thickens: the question over Jesus' authority, vv. 1-8; the parable of the wicked tenant farmers, vv. 9-19; the conflict over Caesar, vv. 20-26; the issue of the resurrection, vv. 27-40; the question about the son of David, vv. 41-44; the denunciation of the scribes, vv. 45-47.

THE QUESTION OVER JESUS' AUTHORITY, 20:1-8

The first volley of words between Jesus and the Jewish leaders in the temple area concerned the source of Jesus' authority. The conflict setting amounts to a pronouncement story, comprised of the three typical elements we have come to expect from such encounters: v. 1, Jesus' controversial act; v. 2, the Jewish leaders' criticism of Jesus; vv. 3-8, Jesus' authoritative pronouncement.

20:1   On one of the days Jesus was teaching and preaching in the temple (cf. 19:47), the chief priests, scribes, and elders were standing by, undoubtedly watching Him. The three groups formed the Sanhedrin, so their presence signaled both religious and political motives. In effect, Jesus' teaching, preaching, and surely His cleansing of the

375

temple (19:45-46), were viewed by the officials as highly controversial, if not adversarial.

20:2   The Jewish leaders' criticism of Jesus came in the form of a twofold question: "By what authority do you do these things? Who is the one who gave you this authority?" The Jewish authorities knew that Jesus was not trained as a rabbi. So who gave Him the right to teach about God and to cleanse His temple? The words "do these things" refer to both Jesus' words and actions.

20:3   Verses 3-8 provide Jesus' authoritative pronouncement which, for the moment, silenced His critics. Verse 3 records Jesus' response, a counterquestion: "I will ask you a 'word' [question]." The device of a counterquestion frequently occurred in rabbinic debates.

20:4   Jesus' question was poignant, "Was the baptism of John from heaven or from men?" Since John, like Jesus, was not a rabbi, the authorities' response to the one would affect their response to the other.

20:5   Verses 5-7 allow the reader to eavesdrop on the conversation of the Jewish leaders, revealing the horns of a dilemma that Jesus' question created for them. According to v. 5, they reasoned that if, on the one hand, they admitted that John the Baptist's ministry was of heavenly origin, then Jesus would ask them why they did not believe John and submit to his message of repentance.

20:6   But, on the other hand, the leaders reasoned that if they said that John's ministry was merely of human derivation, without divine backing, then the Jewish populace would stone them, for they were persuaded that he was a prophet from God (1:76; 3:2-20; 7:26-30). The authorities' fear probably stemmed from the practice of stoning false prophets (Deut. 13:1-11) which, in their case, would be reversed. They were afraid the same penalty would be inflicted on them for not accepting John as a true prophet.

20:7   Having no other recourse, the leaders feigned ignorance saying that they did not know the origin of John's baptism/ministry.

20:8   The leaders' refusal to answer the origin of John's authority prompted Jesus to decline from divulging the source of authority for the things He did. The implication, however, of His heavenly authority was clearly communicated.

THE PARABLE OF THE WICKED TENANT FARMERS, 20:9-19

Although the parable of the wicked tenant farmers (vv. 9-19) does not follow the threefold pattern of a conflict pronouncement story, it nevertheless pits the Jewish leaders against Jesus and forecasts the latter's death at the hands of the former.

20:9   Subsequent to the question regarding His authority, Jesus proposed a parable to the people listening to Him. He told of a certain man who planted a vineyard. The reference to the vineyard would immediately bring to the audience's minds the words of Isaiah 5:1-7, Isaiah's Song of the Vineyard (cf. Mark 12:1-12, which makes the reference more explicit). In this parable the Old Testament prophet tells of God's loving care for Israel, His "vineyard." But when harvest time came, the vineyard yielded sour, not good, grapes. According to the prophet Isaiah, God will abandon His vineyard, allowing it to be trampled underfoot. Later Jewish interpretation came to understand Isaiah 5:1-7 as a prophecy of the destruction of the temple by the Babylonians in 587 B.C. In employing the language of this parable, therefore, Jesus could not fail to have signaled the theme of judgment to His listeners except that, as the story progresses, it is more the Jewish leaders, than the people, who will receive the brunt of the message (v. 19).

This particular man went on to lease his vineyard out to tenant farmers, and then left the country for some time. Jeremias has shown that the general background "of the story fits in with known conditions in Palestine. Many estates were lent out by absentee landlords, and in certain circumstances the tenants might attempt to take possession of the property for themselves by fair means or foul. Even the sending of the son, which is the most obviously allegorical feature in the story, will fit into this framework. Accordingly, what we have is a true-to-life story, but one that could easily lend itself to allegorisation."[1] The reference in the parable to "a long time" does not allude to the delay of the Parousia. Most likely, it envisions the long time that God dealt particularly with Israel in sending His prophets to her.

20:10   After a while, the absentee landlord sent one of his servants to the tenant farmers to collect a share of the vineyard's produce. The servant met with rude treatment, as the farmers beat him up and sent him away empty-handed.

20:11   The owner proceeded to send another servant. But the farmers beat him, too, dishonored him, and sent him away empty-handed.

20:12   The owner proceeded to send a third servant, but the farmers wounded him (*traumatisantes*) and threw him out.

---

1. Jeremias, *The Parables of Jesus,* 175.

20:13   In soliloquy fashion, the owner said, "What shall I do? I shall send my beloved son; perhaps they will treat him with respect." The modern-day reader already knows where the parable is going by this point. The three servants sent and rejected represent the Old Testament prophets sent by God to Israel but who were unheeded, and even maligned. The son can be no other than Jesus, God's beloved Son (3:22; 9:35; 22:70), who was crucified.

20:14   When the farmers saw the son, the heir of the vineyard, approaching they deliberated among themselves, premeditating his murder in order to receive the inheritance. Jeremias surmises that the farmers may have assumed from the arrival of the son that the owner had died. So if they killed the sole heir, the vineyard would pass into their hands as first claimants.[2]

20:15   The farmers carried out their evil plan. They cast the son out of the vineyard and killed him. Their order of action—casting out, then killing—anticipates what the Jewish leaders would do to Jesus—cast Him out of the city of Jerusalem and then kill Him. At that point in the story, Jesus asked the audience a question, "What will the owner of the vineyard do?"

20:16   Jesus answered His own question, asserting that the absentee landowner would come and destroy the farmers and give the vineyard to others. It is important to observe, with Evans, that "the others" does not mean that Jesus was intimating that God's kingdom would be taken from the Jews and given to the Gentiles. Rather the words were Jesus' attack on the religious bureaucracy and therefore a veiled warning that they as leaders would be replaced (see v. 19).[3] The people responded to Jesus' announcement with horror, "May it never be!" (*mē genoito*; cf. Rom. 3:4, 6, 31; 6:2, 15; 7:7, 13; 9:14; 11:1, 11; 1 Cor. 6:15; Gal. 2:17; 3:21). This is the only time this expression occurs in the four gospels. Is it a sign of Paul's influence on Luke's reporting? Perhaps the people's reaction was to the fate of their leaders, or possibly to the eventuality of their city's destruction. But in light of v. 17, the populace's shock seems to have been a general reaction to the way the farmers treated the landowner's son.

20:17   Looking at the people, Jesus responded to them, "Then what is that which is written, 'The stone which the builders rejected has become the cornerstone'?" Jesus' connection of the rejected son and

2. Ibid.
3. Evans, *Luke*, 303.

the rejected stone seems to suggest that He is explaining the people's query about the treatment of the son. The scripture Jesus quoted was Psalm 118:22. Fitzmyer comments that

> the rejected stone becomes the cornerstone, symbolizing Jesus rejected and crucified, who becomes the risen Lord. The stone that did not measure up to the expected estimate of the builders becomes instead the most important stone in the edifice; it is accorded the place of honor by the function that it plays in the whole structure. "Cornerstone" should not be misunderstood. It does not mean cornerstone as we frequently use the word in modern English (to designate the stone of a principal angle of a building, usually laid at its formal inauguration, with a date on it and often some inscription, and a hollowed-out recess for holding documents relating to the history of the structure—thus a principal stone of the building). Rather *kephalē gōnias,* lit. "(the) head of (the) corner," designated in antiquity the stone used at a building's corner to bear the weight or stress of the two walls. It would have functioned somewhat like a "keystone" or "capstone" in an arch or other architectural form. It was the stone which was essential or crucial to the whole structure. In this sense, Jesus is the "beloved son," rejected by builders (another image for the leaders of contemporary Judaism), i.e. put to death by them. By his resurrection he becomes the key figure in God's new building, the reconstituted Israel, or the chief stone of the heavenly sanctuary (to borrow a motif from Hebrews).[4]

20:18   Jesus added two comments. First, whoever trips over that stone will be shattered into pieces, an allusion to Isaiah 8:14-15 (cf. Luke 2:34). As Evans observes,

> This saying is reminiscent of the "stumbling-stone" passages found in the NT. In Rom. 9:32-33 Paul alludes to and quotes parts of Isa. 8:14 and 28:16. The idea is that Jesus is both a precious foundation stone (for him who has faith, Isa. 28:16) and a stone of stumbling (to the one who has no faith, Isa. 8:14)…. See also 1 Pet. 2:6-8 where Ps. 118:22 is quoted along with and between the two passages from Isaiah. In one rabbinic text, which is apparently messianic … Ps. 118:22 is cited along with a saying that parallels Luke's unique saying about the stone that crushes: "[The Israelites] are compared to stones, as it says, 'From thence the shepherd of the stone [i.e., Messiah] of Israel' (Gen. 49:24); 'The stone which the builders rejected' (Ps. 118:22). But the other

---

4. Fitzmyer, *The Gospel According to Luke X–XXIV,* 1282.

nations are likened to potsherds, as it says, 'And he shall break it as a potter's vessel is broken' (Isa. 30:14). If a stone falls on a pot, woe to the pot! If a pot falls on a stone, woe to the pot! In either case, woe to the pot! So whoever ventures to attack [the Israelites] receives his desserts on their account" (*Esther Rabbah* 7.10). . . . This midrash also cites Dan. 2:34.[5]

Second, whomever the stone falls on it will crush, probably an allusion to Daniel 2:34-35, 44-45 and the stone (the kingdom of God) that smashes the statue in Nebuchadnezzar's dream (the kingdoms of the earth).

20:19   The scribes and the chief priests listening to Jesus knew that He had directed the parable toward them. Consequently, they wanted to lay their hands on Jesus and arrest Him that very hour, but they feared the people. The reaction to Jesus was truly mixed: the people accepted Him as the cornerstone, but the leaders, the "builders" of Israel, rejected Him. To them He was a stumbling stone.

CONFLICT OVER CAESAR, 20:20-26

More conflict ensued between Jesus and the religious establishment, this time over the relationship between one's allegiance to Caesar and to God. The episode is cast in the form of a pronouncement story. The three ingredients are: Jesus' controversial action (vv. 19-20); the Jewish leadership's criticism of Jesus, veiled as it was behind flattery (vv. 21-22); and Jesus' authoritative pronouncement which, once again, silenced His critics (vv. 23-26).

20:20   Verse 20 logically comes on the heels of v. 19. Because Jesus deliberately directed the parable of the wicked tenant farmers at the Jewish religious leadership in v. 19 (a controversial action, to say the least), they determined to catch Him in a mistake which they hoped would bring about His demise, v. 20. The ones who watched Jesus closely (*paratērēsantes*) were the Jewish leaders. Part of their surveillance involved sending out spies to monitor Jesus' words and actions. These people pretended to be righteous, that is, they acted as if they were adherents to God and His law. Their purpose was to catch Jesus in a mistake, in order to deliver Him up (*paradounai*; cf. 18:32) to the rule and the authority of the Roman governor (prefect). With these

---

5. Evans, *Luke*, 303.

words, Luke exposes the nature of the spies' hypocrisy: they aimed to use the law of God to pit Jesus against the state.

20:21 Verses 21-22 focus on the Jewish leadership's criticism of Jesus, via the spies. The spies began the conversation with Jesus by flattering Him, praising Him for the accuracy and orthodoxy of His speaking and preaching and acknowledging that He was impartial ("you do not lift up the face") and sought only to teach the truth of the way of God. For the words "the way of God" as a phrase denoting a lifestyle of obedience to God, see 1:79; 3:4; Acts 18:25; cf. Acts 9:2; 19:9.

20:22 The spies' fulsome praise ended with a loaded question, "Is it lawful to pay tribute to Caesar or not?" The question raised an inflammatory issue because, since the time of the Roman general Pompey (63 B.C.), the Romans required the Jews of Palestine to pay taxes to Rome. In fact, the very word Luke uses for tribute, *phoron,* is the one used by Josephus with reference to the Roman tribute (*J. W.* 2.117-18). In Jesus' context, it referred to the direct poll tax levied on the inhabitants of Judea (cf. Luke 2:1). The allocation of Jewish money for a foreign ruler met with stiff resistance in the first century A.D., sparking revolts by the Jews in Palestine from time to time. For example, Josephus tells of Judas the Galilean who taught that one must not pay tribute to Caesar, which resulted in an unsuccessful attempt by some of the Jews to oust the Romans from their land (*J. W.* 2.117-18; Acts 5:37). The title for the Roman emperor, "Caesar," was a name adopted by the Romans under Julius Caesar (assassinated in 44 B.C.) and carried on in practice. In Jesus' day, the emperor was Tiberius Julius Caesar Augustus (see Luke 3:1).

20:23 Verses 23-26 constitute Jesus' authoritative pronouncement. His divine fiat ended the conversation (v. 26). According to v. 23, Jesus perceived the spies' trickery. That is, He recognized that they were trying to embroil Him in controversy, hoping that He would mistakenly pit the one (Caesar) against the other (God). The question apparently presented Jesus with a no-win situation.

20:24 Jesus' recourse was to respond with a counterquestion. He requested the spies to produce a denarius, which ironically enough they had in their possession. He then asked them, "Whose image and inscription does it have?" They answered, "Caesar's." Fitzmyer discusses the silver denarius, noting that it had been in use in the Roman world since the third century B.C. and continued to be used into the third century A.D. He further observes that denarii bore the head of Tiberius and the inscription *TI. CAESAR DIVI AVG. F. AVGVSTVS* (Tiberius Caesar, son of the divine Augustus, Augustus). The image and in-scriptions on ancient coins would have been understood as a property seal; the coins *belonged* to Caesar. Part of the background of Jesus' question was that for an "upright" Jew the image of Caesar on a coin was an abomination. It was, in effect, proscribed by Exodus 20:4, because it referred to Tiberius as the son of "divine Augustus."[6]

20:25 Jesus introduced His thoughts with the word *toinyn,* "Well, then," which conveyed an air of authority and finality. We might translate it, "There you have it!" He then uttered the pronouncement, "Pay to Caesar what is Caesar's and to God what is God's." Straightforward as Jesus' quip was, it has generated at least three interpretations. Fitzmyer conveniently summarizes those views:[7] The first is the two-kingdoms interpretation, a sense given to it since patristic times. According to this view, Jesus was not only recommending the payment of the imperial tribute, but He was also inculcating a proper attitude toward political authority or the state which also affects human life. He was thus aligning himself with older Jewish ideas (cf. Dan. 2:21, 37-38; Prov. 8:15-16; *Wis.* 6:1-11). Thus, the kingdom of God is present, indeed, but it does not suppress or supplant the political kingdoms of this world. According to this interpretation, Jesus was manifesting a sovereign liberty toward the political authority, but He was not advocating revolt against its legitimate claim on human subjects. This interpretation may be right in seeing a germinal appreciation of the role of the state in Jesus' thinking, but it tends to equate what is due to God with what is due to Caesar—on a more or less equal plane.

The second view is the ironic interpretation. To avoid the stress on the political which the first interpretation would propose, some commentators have understood the words of Jesus as irony. Jesus was not really interested in the tribute to Caesar, so His recommendation, "Pay to Caesar what is Caesar's," is a flash of wit, devoid of any serious import. One gives to Caesar what belongs to him, but of what importance is that in relation to the kingdom of God? However, this interpretation pits the second part of the pronouncement against the first, whereas the conjunction that separates them is *kai,* "and," not an adversative *alla,* "but."

6. Fitzmyer, *The Gospel According to Luke X–XXIV,* 1296.
7. Ibid., 1292-94.

The third view is the anti-Zealot interpretation. On this reading, Jesus was openly opposing the refusal to pay the Roman tribute, but His pronouncement had no real bearing on the problem of the state. He was telling His critics that they were trying to bring to the fore a question which was only secondary and that they were downplaying a real human concern: the coin belongs to Caesar, but you to God. The coin, which bears the image of Caesar, we owe to Caesar. We, however, as men who bear the image of God, owe ourselves to God.

Fitzmyer believes the third view tends in the right direction. Jesus' pronouncement presupposes a comparison of what is marked with Caesar's image and what is marked with God's image (see Gen. 1:26-27). The kingdom which Jesus preaches does not call into question Caesar's rightful kingship, but that is not the all-important aspect of human life. A human being belongs to God, whose image he/she bears; God has not only a right of possession over human beings, but also a claim to a basic recognition of His lordship. We concur with this interpretation.

20:26 The spies' mission failed. They were not able to catch Jesus in a mistake in the sight of the people. There were no grounds for political insurrection. Only by trumping up the charges later could the Jewish leadership use the present incident as evidence against Jesus (see Luke 23:1-5). In fact, Jesus' words were so convincing that the spies themselves were amazed at His teaching and their accusations fell silent.

THE ISSUE OF THE RESURRECTION, 20:27-40

A fourth controversy dialogue between Jesus and the Jewish leadership found in Luke 20 concerns the matter of the future resurrection (vv. 27-40), an issue debated by the Sadducees and Pharisees. The former group attempted to embroil Jesus in the controversy. The episode itself follows the threefold pattern of the *apophthegms,* or conflict story: v. 27, Jesus' controversial action (according to the Sadducees)—He believed in the future resurrection; vv. 27-33, the Jewish leadership's criticism of Jesus, which was couched behind the Sadducees' apparently sincere inquiry; vv. 34-38, Jesus' authoritative pronouncement.

20:27 It was a matter of record that Jesus believed in the future resurrection of the body (see Luke 9:22; 14:14; 18:33). More than that, Jesus inaugurated the end-time resurrection through His raising of the dead

(Luke 7:11-17; 8:40-56), which would soon include Himself (24:1-7). However, such a belief was not shared by the Sadducees. According to Fitzmyer, the Greek name *Saddoukaioi* is to be related to the Hebrew proper name *Sādôq,* "Zadok," which appears in Greek in the Septuagint as *Saddouk* (2 Sam. 8:17; Ezek. 40:46; 43:19) and in Josephus as *Saddok* or *Saddouk* (see *Ant.* 18.4-10). The descendants of Zadok were granted the privilege of officiating as priests in the temple after the return from the Babylonian Captivity. These "Zadokites" formed the nucleus of the priesthood staffing the Jerusalem temple. First Chronicles 6:1-8 traces the lineage of Zadok back to Eleazar, elder son of Aaron (cf. *Sir.* 51:12). The Sadducees of first-century Palestine were related to this Zadokite priestly line, but they had become a tightly closed circle, no longer exclusively a priestly group. They were priestly and lay aristocrats, considerably Hellenized. Of them Josephus writes, "The Sadducees having the confidence of the wealthy alone but no following among the populace" (*Ant.* 13.298); "There are but few men to whom this doctrine [of the Sadducees] has been made known, but these are men of highest standing" (*Ant.* 18.17). Though they appear only here in the Lucan gospel, they emerge again in Acts 4:1; 5:17; 23:6-8. Like the Essenes, they practically disappeared from history with the destruction of Jerusalem, though references to them do occur in the Talmud.[8]

One of the cardinal doctrines of the Sadducees was their disbelief in a future resurrection of the body and, for that matter, their denial of any form of life beyond the grave. The Sadducees based their belief on what they perceived to be the total absence of any teaching on the afterlife in the Pentateuch—according to them, the only inspired part of the Old Testament.[9] Josephus writes of the Sadducees, "As for the persistence of the soul, penalties in death's abode, and rewards, they do away with them" (*J. W.* 2.165); "The Sadducees hold that the soul perishes along with the body" (*Ant.* 18.16). In opposition to the Sadducees who denied the "resurrection" (*anastasis*), the Pharisees defended its accuracy on the basis of certain Pentateuchal passages such as Exodus 6:4; 15:1; Numbers 15:31; 18:28; Deuteronomy 31:16. It is this particular debate which the Sadducees wished to foist onto Jesus. Their ensuing question, therefore, though on the surface sincere, was a veiled criticism of Jesus' belief, not to mention an attempt to expose the absurdity of a cherished Pharisaic creed.

8. Ibid., 1302.
9. For further discussion on this point, see ibid., 1303.

20:28   The Sadducees addressed Jesus as "teacher," apparently acknowledging His divine authority. Using the Old Testament, especially Deuteronomy 25:5 (cf. Gen. 38:8), the Sadducees began to formulate a question about "levirate" (from the Latin, *levir,* "husband's brother, brother-in-law") marriage: "If a man's brother dies and leaves a wife but has no children, his brother is to take the wife and raise up offspring for his brother." The Mosaic provision served a couple of important functions. First, it ensured that the deceased brother's family name would continue. Second, it protected the widow and provided for her future. Such a marriage was not considered a violation of Leviticus 18:16; 20:21 because the brother was dead. Though there is some debate as to whether the custom existed at the time of Jesus, Josephus speaks of the practice as still current in his day (*Ant.* 4.254; ca. A.D. 90). The Sadducees' comment confirms that assumption.

20:29   The question of the Sadducees begins to take shape in v. 29. Envisioning a hypothetical situation, the Sadducees imagined that there were seven brothers, the first of whom married a woman, but who died childless. Why the number seven? Marshall's answer is as good as any. He observes that the round number "seven" appeared in the context of repeated marriages in the apocryphal work, *Tobit* 3:8, and that the idea of levirate marriage is likewise present in that story (*Tob.* 6:9-12; 7:12). This suggests that we have here in Luke (cf. Matt. 22:23-33; Mark 12:18-27) a popular theme in folklore about a story of seven brothers, each of whom married the same wife in turn, and died childless.[10] According to Ellis, it was probably the case that the story itself was often used by the Sadducees in an attempt to ridicule the Pharisees.[11]

20:30   The Sadducees continued their question, feigning sincerity: "Then the second" (married her, dying childless).

20:31   "Then the third took her, and likewise all seven left no children and died." The question of the Sadducees presupposes that the seven brothers successively married the same woman.

20:32   "Finally," said the Sadducees, "the woman died."

20:33   Then came the point of the Sadducees' question, "At the resurrection, whose wife will this woman be, since all seven had her?" The logic of the opponents' query masked their skepticism. Behind the Sadducees' question was their attempt to show, not only what they

10. Marshall, *Commentary on Luke,* 739-40.
11. Ellis, *The Gospel of Luke,* 235-36.

perceived to be the ludicrousness of the situation, but also the immorality that such a scenario would entail. After all, so they may have reasoned, if all seven brothers and the one wife were alive in heaven in resurrected form, would not a marital relationship implicate them in adultery?

20:34 In vv. 34-38, Luke provides Jesus' reply, which consisted of two arguments: one theological, vv. 34-36; the other exegetical, vv. 37-38. The reply constituted Jesus' pronouncement utterance. Theologically speaking, He reminded the Sadducees that the existence of marriage, like all human institutions, is restricted to this age. Such structures, as viable and wonderful as they may be, will not continue into the age to come, i.e., heaven. In v. 34, Jesus acknowledged that marriage and the giving of marriage was a normal part of this age. The reference to "this age" was a typical Jewish expression for "this life." It, and its counterpart, "the age to come" (cf. v. 35), formed the very theological foundation of the Old Testament's and Judaism's view of history, and also the New Testament.[12]

20:35 The Semitic contrast of the two *aeons* (ages) continues in v. 35. Jesus said three things about the age to come: (1) To enter it, one must be "counted worthy" (*kataxiōthentes*). The last word is a theological passive, i.e., counted worthy *by God*. Though Jesus did not specify the grounds for being reckoned so, we have a good indication as to its meaning in the publican's repentant attitude of total dependence on God's mercy (18:14). (2) The age to come will be characterized by both continuity and discontinuity with this age—it will involve the resurrection of the dead. There will be continuity between the two ages because heaven will witness a resurrection of the earthly body. But the two ages will also be marked by discontinuity because the believer will have a resurrected and glorious, not temporal and mortal, body. (3) The discontinuous aspect of the age to come is attested to by the fact that the earthly institution of marriage will not continue into it.

20:36 The point of discontinuity is expanded upon in v. 36, where three additional comments are made. (1) The righteous in the age to come will not die; they will be immortal. (2) As such, they will be like the angels in heaven, a belief not shared by the Sadducees either (see Acts 23:8). Angels, too, are immortal and do not marry. (3) More than that, believers will be the sons of God because they share in the resurrection. This statement by Jesus served two functions. First, it indicated

---

12. See Ladd, *A Theology of the New Testament.*

that believers will be superior to angels in that they will be called the children of God. Second, because Christians are children of God, they partake of His divine nature, the proof of which will be their resurrection bodies (cf. 2 Peter 1:4).

20:37 Verses 37-40 provide Jesus' second argument in reply to the Sadducees' question, the exegetical proof of the future resurrection of the righteous. Here Jesus turned the tables on His opponents by appealing to the Pentateuch itself in support of the doctrine of the resurrection. In v. 37, Jesus noted the fact that the dead are raised was disclosed by Moses in light of his experience with God in the burning bush (Ex. 6:2-6). Jesus quoted the last verse, observing that Moses called the Lord "the God of Abraham, the God of Isaac, and the God of Jacob." The point of the scriptural argument is that Yahweh identified Himself to Moses as the God of the patriarchs long after they died. Marshall puts it well, "The timing of the statement shows that God is still the God of the patriarchs after their death, and therefore they either must be still alive in some way and/or can confidently expect that he will raise them from the dead."[13]

20:38 Verse 38 accentuates the last statement as it concludes Jesus' exegetical argumentation defending the resurrection of the body: God is "not the God of the dead but of the living, for all are alive to Him." The first part of Jesus' remark highlights the fact that only living people can have a God, and therefore God's promise to the patriarchs that He is/will be their God requires that He maintain them in life, which obviously assumes that they continued to exist beyond the grave.[14] The second part of the comment is, relative to the gospels, distinctively Lucan. It is probably an allusion to *4 Macc.* 7:19, "they [i.e., the martyrs of the faith] believe that unto God they die not, just as not even our patriarchs, Abraham, Isaac, and Jacob, but live unto God." The phrase is an expression of the immortality of the patriarchs. The "all" extends the promise of the resurrection beyond the patriarchs to encompass the righteous. The uniquely Lucan words, "all are alive to him," then, are the evangelist's attempt to clarify the idea of life after death to his predominantly Gentile audience. The point of Jesus' answer, at least as it should be understood in the context of the whole passage, is that at death the righteous are in some sense alive to God and yet await the resurrection. Jesus' teaching, as Fitzmyer has

13. Marshall, *Commentary on Luke*, 742.
14. See again ibid., 743.

shown, was in keeping with those first-century Palestinian Jews who believed that the soul was immortal and so at death would enter the presence of God, and that at some future time there would be a resurrection which would bring about the reunion of soul and body (cf. 2 Cor. 5:8 and 1 Thess. 4:13-17).[15]

20:39 Jesus' argument for the resurrection was so convincing that even the scribes, normally His critics, had to agree that He answered the question of the Sadducees correctly.

20:40 In light of Jesus' authoritative response to the controversial questions put to Him in the temple area, no one (neither Sadducee and Pharisee) dared to publicly ask Him any more questions.

JESUS' QUESTION ABOUT THE SON OF DAVID, 20:41-44

Verses 41-44 are transitional in nature. They continue the air of tension surrounding Jesus' teaching. More particularly, as we will shortly see, they assume the theme of the resurrection found in vv. 27-40. But vv. 41-44 also move the story along, applying the notion of the resurrection specifically to Jesus and thereby proving Him to be both David's son and David's lord. Because vv. 41-44 are difficult to grasp, it would be wise to survey the passage before examining it verse by verse. We offer three broad points at the outset of the discussion: the riddle posed by Jesus' twofold rhetorical question; Jesus' implied answer to the riddle; the purpose of the riddle.

1. Jesus went on the offensive in His debate with the Jewish authorities by raising a twofold rhetorical question, which forms a riddle:
   a. V. 41—How can *you* say that the Messiah will be David's son?
   b. Vv. 42-43—But *David* himself said the Messiah would be David's lord.
   c. V. 44—I ask you, then, which is it? Is the Messiah David's son or David's lord?

2. Jesus' answer, though not explicitly given, is definitely implied: It is not a matter of either/or, but of both/and. The Messiah is both David's son and David's lord. From that, Jesus

15. Fitzmyer, *The Gospel According to Luke X–XXIV,* 1301-2.

intended that the audience recognize that He was the Messiah. As such, He was both David's son (see Luke 1:32; 3:31; 18:38-39) and, at His coming resurrection, David's lord, and thus the fulfillment of Psalm 110:1.

3. The purpose, then, of Jesus' question about the son of David was, in general, to once again defend the truth of the resurrection (cf. vv. 27-40) which would be required for Him to experience in order to be recognized as David's lord. But, more specifically, Jesus' twofold question was designed to show His hearers that indeed He was the Messiah, in birth as David's son, and in death and resurrection as David's lord. The three preceding remarks should better expedite the exegesis of vv. 41-44.

20:41   Verse 41 raises the first part of Jesus' rhetorical question, thereby initiating the riddle, "How do they say that the Messiah is the son of David?" J. Klausner is surely wrong to suggest that the interrogative "how" (*pōs*) indicates that Jesus was denying the commonly held opinion that the Messiah would be the son of David.[16] Quite the contrary, Jesus' question was affirming such a belief. There is ample evidence showing that Jews believed that Messiah would be David's son, as the scribal interpretation of 2 Samuel 7; Psalm 89:20-37; Isaiah 9:2-7; 11:1-9; Jeremiah 23:5; 33:14-18; Ezekiel 34:23; 37:27; *Ps. Sol.* 17:21; *4QFlor* 1:11-13; *Shemoneh Esreh* 14 (see Strack-B 1:11-14) makes clear.

20:42   Verses 42-43 expose Jesus' real concern. He was not denying that Messiah would be David's son. Rather, what He questioned was how could the Messiah be David's son when, according to Psalm 110:1, David himself said the Messiah was his lord? The first portion of Psalm 110:1 reads, "The Lord said to my lord, sit at my right hand. . . ." The history of the interpretation of this verse in Jewish and Christian circles is too complex to broach here.[17] Our purpose is to catch Jesus' view of it which, simply put, was messianic. He interpreted the speaker of Psalm 110:1 as David. The "Lord" is God. The "lord" (small "l") is the Messiah. Jesus' interpretation of Ps. 110:1 runs therefore as follows: David says in Psalm 110:1, "The Lord (God) said to my (David's) lord (Messiah)—sit at my (God's) right hand until I make your (Messiah's) ene-

16. Klausner, *Jesus of Nazareth: His Life, Times, and Teaching,* 320; *contra* Fitzmyer, *The Gospel According to Luke X–XXIV,* 1312, and Marshall, *Commentary on Luke,* 744.

17. For a full treatment, see Hay, *Glory at the Right Hand: Psalm 110 in Early Christianity.*

mies a footstool for your (Messiah's) feet." The upshot of the statement, then, was to affirm that the Messiah was David's lord ("my lord") and that one day He (the Messiah) would be raised to the right hand of God. The reference to the Messiah being "raised" to the right hand of God signifies His exalted place in the universe. Jesus obviously understood its ultimate significance in terms of His imminent resurrection.

20:43   Verse 43 quotes the second portion of Psalm 110:1, "until I make your enemies a footstool for your feet." The imagery comes from the practice of the ancient Near East whereby the conquered leaders would be forced to kneel on the platform before the victorious king. In effect, they became the ruler's footstool. Little wonder then that Luke applied Psalm 110:1, with its imagery of the Messiah emerging victorious over His enemies, to Jesus' resurrection and subsequent exaltation to heaven; see Luke 22:69, where Psalm 110:1 and Daniel 7:13 are conflated and applied to Jesus' resurrection and return; see also Acts 2:34-36.

20:44   Jesus formulated His riddle: "David calls him lord; then how can he be David's son?" The rhetorical question presupposed a patriarchal society where the son was subordinate, not dominant, over the father. The answer Jesus intended to elicit from His critics, as we suggested earlier, is both/and. Jesus, as Messiah, was both David's son and, by His resurrection, David's lord.

THE DENUNCIATION OF THE SCRIBES, 20:45-47

Jesus continued His teaching in the temple with a warning against the scribes, vv. 45-47. These minatory sayings exposed their ostentation, deceit, and greed. This hypocritical way of life should not characterize the Christian disciple.

20:45   Luke introduces the paragraph with a genitive absolute, "While all the people were listening, Jesus spoke to the disciples."

20:46   The content of Jesus' speech to the disciples consisted of a barrage of severe criticisms aimed at the scribes, the teachers of the Law. The tirade began with a word of warning, "Beware of the scribes." Then followed some five verbal attacks on them: (1) The scribes liked to walk about in long robes (*stolē*). The robes have been traditionally identified with the long, flowing garments of the learned (the *tallith*), according to Strack-B 2:31-33. Others think the robes Jesus referred to were the festal garments worn on the Sabbath. Either way, it was the ostentation of the scribes which was being attacked. (2) They loved to be greeted, and basked in the spotlight of popularity and to have the front seats in the synagogues (cf. Luke 11:43). (3) They craved the attention of having the first places at dinners (cf. 14:7).

20:47   (4) The scribes devoured the houses of widows, revealing their deceit and greed. Fitzmyer summarizes the different interpretations this accusation has generated:[18] (a) Scribes accepted payment for legal aid to widows, even though such payment was forbidden. (b) Scribes cheated widows of what was rightly theirs; as lawyers, they were acting as guardians appointed by a husband's will to care for the widow's estate. (c) Scribes sponged on the hospitality of these women of limited means, like the gluttons and gourmands mentioned in *Ass. Mos.* 7:6 ("devourers of the goods of the poor, saying that they do so on the basis of their justice"). (d) Scribes mismanaged the property of widows like Anna who had dedicated themselves to the service of the temple. (e) Scribes took large sums of money from credulous old women as a reward for the prolonged prayer which they professed to make on their behalf. (f) Scribes took the houses as pledges for debts which could not be paid.

It is difficult to know which of these views best expresses Jesus' meaning. But in light of the incident about the poor widow in the temple who gave all she had that directly follows in Luke 21:1-4, as well as criticism number 5 below, view (e) above might help explain the accusation. (5) The scribes were guilty of praying long prayers to impress people with their "spirituality." This criticism may be linked to the fourth criticism, i.e., the devouring of widows' houses. Perhaps the long prayers were said publicly in order to give an impression of piety and trustworthiness and so to induce widows to entrust the scribes with their possessions. For these scribes, the most severe judgment from God awaited them.

HOMILETICAL SUGGESTIONS

One effective way to handle Luke 20, Jesus' Teaching in the Temple, would be to tell the story behind each conflict setting and then expound upon Jesus pronouncement statement. Using this approach, one could preach the whole chapter in one or two sermons. To take longer might make the chapter monotonous for the listener. The six

18. Fitzmyer, *The Gospel According to Luke X–XXIV,* 1318.

skirmishes between Jesus and the authorities would follow, then, as we treated them in the commentary:

1. Vv. 1-8: The Question over Jesus' Authority
   a. Vv. 1-2: The Story
   b. Vv. 3-8: The Pronouncement

2. Vv. 9-19: The Parable of the Wicked Tenant Farmers
   a. Vv. 9-18: The Parable
   b. V. 19: The Application

3. Vv. 20-26: The Conflict over Caesar
   a. Vv. 20-22: The Story
   b. Vv. 23-26: The Pronouncement

4. Vv. 27-40: The Issue of the Resurrection
   a. Vv. 27-33: The Story
   b. Vv. 34-40: The Pronouncement
      1.) Vv. 34-36: The Theological Argumentation
      2.) Vv. 37-40: The Exegetical Argumentation

5. Vv. 41-44: The Question about the Son of David
   a. V. 41: How Can the Messiah Be David's Son?
   b. Vv. 42-43: David Said the Messiah Was His Lord
   c. V. 44: The Messiah Is Both and Jesus Is the Messiah by Virtue of His Resurrection

6. Vv. 45-47: The Denunciation of the Scribes
   a. V. 45: They Love to Walk in Long Robes
   b. V. 45: They Crave Greetings of Respect and the Chief Seats
   c. V. 45: They Desire the First Places at Dinners
   d. V. 47: They Devour Widows' Houses (cf. Luke 21:1-4)
   e. V. 47: They Pray Long Public Prayers to Parade their Piety

LUKE

CHAPTER

TWENTY ONE

THINGS TO COME

Luke 21 concludes Jesus' teaching ministry in the temple area of Jerusalem, the city of His destiny. It does so by including two dispro-portionate episodes: the brief comments on the widow's minuscule offering (vv. 1-4), and the lengthy discourse on things to come relative to Jerusalem and its temple (vv. 5-38). The former of these topics basi-cally serves as a commentary on Jesus' earlier castigation of the scribes (20:45-47). The latter topic is developed by Luke at length and, as we hope to show, remarkably supports one of the theses with which this commentary began—that certain persons and places (in this case, Je-rusalem) foreshadow the coming restoration of Israel, both spiritually to her Messiah and physically to her land. This second subject, then, will occupy most of our attention in the exegesis of Luke 21.

JESUS' COMMENTS ON THE WIDOW'S OFFERING, 21:1-4

Jesus' comments on the widow's offering in the temple (21:1-4) serve as an apt commentary on His previous criticism of the scribes (20:45-47), especially v. 47; the scribes "devour the houses of wid-ows." As such, Jesus' words function more as a lament over the wid-ow's situation than as praise for her naive self-sacrifice. Because of the religious authorities of her day, the poor widow gave up her last penny and so was victimized for the profit of an oppressive religious system

393

(unfortunately, such injustices continue today). Her "house" was indeed devoured by the religious establishment. That being the case, Luke has not placed the incident of the widow's offering before the prediction of the fall of the Jerusalem temple (vv. 5-38) haphazardly. It was the temple's religious system in the hands of the Jewish authorities which treated the poor unjustly that contributed to its demise in A.D. 70.

21:1 Having just uttered His scathing criticism of the scribes' exploitation of the possessions of the widows (20:47), Jesus looked up and saw the rich dropping their contributions into the temple treasury. The word for "treasury," *gazophylakion,* refers to the treasure chambers in the temple at Jerusalem, mentioned in Neh. 12:44; *1 Macc.* 14:49; *2 Macc.* 3:6, 24, 28, 40. These objects were receptacles for collecting contributions and taxes brought to the temple. According to *m. Segalim* 6:15, there were thirteen of these shofar-chests (that is, trumpet/shaped containers) which stood in the forecourt of the temple. They were variously called "New Shekel Dues," "Old Shekel Dues," "Bird Offerings," "Young Birds for the Holocaust," "Wood," "Frankincense," "Gold for the Mercy Seat," and six of them were labeled, "Free Will Offerings."

21:2 In stark contrast to the contributions of the wealthy, Jesus noticed a needy widow dropping into the depositories two *lepta.* The *lepton* (cf. 12:59) was the smallest coin of the day in Palestine, worth only a fraction of a denarius, itself worth a day's wage. It was truly a small contribution.

21:3 Yet, according to Jesus, although the widow's offering was the smallest contribution, she actually gave more than the others.

21:4 Jesus' explanation followed: the rich gave proportionately, "out of their abundance"; the widow gave totally, "she in her need has given all her livelihood." But what did Jesus mean by this comment? Various attempts have been made to explain it. In a study on the episode, A. G. Wright gives five of them:[1] (a) The true measure of gifts is not how much is given but how much remains behind, or the percentage of one's means (the cost to the giver). (b) It is not the amount that one gives but the spirit in which the gift is given. The "spirit" is, however, variously explained (e.g., self-offering, self-forgetfulness, unquestioning surrender, detachment). (c) The true gift is to give everything one has. (d) Alms and other pious gifts should correspond to one's

---

1. Wright, "The Widow's Mites: Praise or Lament? A Matter of Context," 256-65.

means. (e) The story expresses Jesus' mind on the subject of almsgiving. Wright correctly notes that all the explanations apart from the first have no basis in the gospel text itself. Nothing is said about the inner "spirit" of the widow. Again, the contrast in the story is between "more" and "less" not between a "true gift" and a "non-authentic gift." There is no basis in the text for giving according to one's means; the widow gives all that she has! She gives beyond her means. To reduce the point of the story to a counsel about almsgiving is to miss its main thrust; certainly almsgiving to the poor is out of question here. Thus, the first theory best explains Luke 21:1-4, especially its relationship to Luke 20:45-47.

THE FUTURE OF JERUSALEM, 21:5-38

Luke devotes the bulk of chapter 21 to Jesus' discourse on the future of Jerusalem and her temple. The scholarly discussion of Luke 21:5-38 is both challenging and a bit confusing. Assuming the basic conclusion reached in that body of literature, our purpose here is to attempt to move the discussion along by offering three contributions to the subject. The consensus reached in recent analyses of Luke 21:5-38 is that vv. 8-24 speak of the coming fall of Jerusalem (A.D. 70), whereas vv. 25-36 predict the return of Christ. The former forms the backdrop for the latter, and the two should not be confused. We envision our contribution to the topic to be threefold: First, Luke focuses upon a significant sign which will respectively precede these major events. The sign occurring before the fall of Jerusalem will be the surrounding of that city by the Roman armies (under General Titus in A.D. 70), v. 20. The other important sign predicted by Luke is the return of Christ, which, in effect, will surround the city of Jerusalem (v. 27), and which itself will signal the arrival of the kingdom of God (v. 31). Concerning the last event, the commentators we have read do not seem to notice where Luke's emphasis lies here—on the arrival of the kingdom of God, which is precipitated by the return of Christ. The former of these happenings—the arrival of the kingdom of God—is Luke's major interest, perhaps even more so than the event of the return of Christ. The reason for this becomes clear with our second suggestion.

Second, just as the surrounding of Jerusalem by the Roman armies in A.D. 70 will signal her destruction (vv. 20-24), so the "surrounding" of Jerusalem by Christ at His second coming will signal her restoration (vv. 27-36). In other words, from Jesus' perspective, the future fall of Jerusalem will be a foreshadowing (negative though it will be) of the coming restoration of Israel in the indefinite future. This is in keeping with our suggestion that certain persons in the third gospel, and now places (Jerusalem), are recognized by Luke as predictive of the future recovery of Israel. We will corroborate this theory by comparing Luke 21 with Romans 11:25-27.

That being the case, our third point is that Luke 21:5-38 can be seen to be heavily influenced by the Jewish two-age structure, though modified in light of the Christ event. On the one hand, the age to come (the spiritual kingdom of God) has been revealed in the person of Jesus and will continue to influence His people, even in the divine display of judgment on Jerusalem, the city of the Messiah's crucifixion. But on the other hand, the age to come (the physical kingdom of God) still awaits consummation. That will happen at the return of Christ and the subsequent restoration of the Holy City. At that time, the kingdom of God will be near (v. 31), and then the Lord will restore the kingdom to Israel (see Acts 1:3, 6). The preceding remarks will become more clear as we proceed through the text of Luke 21:5-36. We suggest the following outline:

I. Vv. 5-6:   Jesus' Prediction of the Destruction of Jerusalem

II. V. 7:   The Disciples' Question about the Destruction of Jerusalem

III. Vv. 8-36: Jesus' Reply: The Destruction of Jerusalem Will Come Long before the Arrival of the Kingdom of God and the Restoration of Jerusalem
  A. Vv. 8-24: The Destruction of Jerusalem
     1. Vv. 8-19:   Signs *Not* Pointing to the End (the Fall of Jerusalem)
     2. V. 20a: The Sign Pointing to the End (the Fall of Jerusalem) = The Surrounding of the City by the Roman Armies
     3. Vv. 20b-24: The Destruction of Jerusalem
       a. V. 20b: Recognize the Destruction Is at Hand
       b. Vv. 21-23: Escape from the City
       c. V. 22b: Distress on the Land
       d. V. 23b: Fulfillment of Jesus' Words
       e. V. 24b: Restoration of Jerusalem

B. Vv. 25-36: The Kingdom of God and the Restoration of
Jerusalem
  1. Vv. 25-26: Signs *Not* Pointing to the End (the Arrival of the
     Kingdom of God and the Restoration of
     Jerusalem)
  2. Vv. 27-30: The Sign Pointing to the End (the Arrival of the
     Kingdom of God/Restoration of Jerusalem) =
     The Return of Christ
  3. Vv. 31-36: The Restoration of Jerusalem
     a. V. 31:   Recognize the Arrival of the Kingdom
     b. Vv. 34-36: Escape from the Earth
     c. V. 35:   Distress on the Earth
     d. V. 36b: Fulfillment of Jesus' Words
     e. Vv. 32, 33: Restoration of Jerusalem

The above outline will better facilitate our exegesis of vv. 5-38.
The reader will note the remarkable correspondences that we suggest
exist between the two events of the destruction of Jerusalem (vv. 8-24)
and the arrival of the kingdom of God and restoration of Jerusalem
(vv. 25-36). We now embark on our verse-by-verse analysis of the text.

THE DESTRUCTION OF JERUSALEM, 21:5-24

Again, vv. 5-24 can be outlined as follows: vv. 5-6, Jesus' prediction of the fall of Jerusalem; v. 7, the disciples' question about that fall;
vv. 8-24, Jesus' reply—the city will be destroyed long before the coming of the kingdom of God.

21:5   Verses 5-6 contain Jesus' prediction of the destruction of the
Jerusalem temple. The prophecy was occasioned by some people, apparently in the temple area, praising its magnificent structure. The history of the temple is as follows: After the Jews returned from the
Babylonian Captivity, they reconstructed the second temple under
Zerubbabel as a replacement of Solomon's temple destroyed by Nebuchadnezzar in 587 B.C. The new structure was built on the old site
and completed about 515 B.C. (see Hag. 1:4-15). It was less finely made
than Solomon's structure, and Herod the Great was later motivated to
refurbish it in the fifteenth year of his reign (20–19 B.C.), "erecting
new foundation-walls, enlarging the surrounding area to twice its former dimensions" (Josephus, *J. W.* 1.401, as quoted in Fitzmyer, *The
Gospel According to Luke X–XXIV*, 1330). Work on the reconstruction
of the temple continued for decades. The gospel of John alludes to

Jesus' purging of the temple in its forty-sixth year of building (2:20). The reconstruction continued until about A.D. 63, a mere seven years before it was destroyed (see Josephus, *J. W.* 5.184-227; *Ant.* 15.1-7).[2]

The bystanders praised the temple because of its fine stones and votive offerings. Concerning the former, Josephus said that the temple was built of "hard, white stones, each of which was about twenty-five cubits in length, eight in height, and twelve in width" (*Ant.* 15.392). Of the temple Josephus writes elsewhere:

> The exterior of the building wanted nothing that could astound either mind or eye. For, being covered on all sides with massive plates of gold, the sun was no sooner up than it radiated so fiery a flash that persons straining to look at it were compelled to avert their eyes, as from the solar rays. To approaching strangers it appeared from a distance like a snow-clad mountain; for all that was not overlaid with gold was of purest white. From its summit protruded sharp golden spikes to prevent birds from settling upon and polluting the roof. Some of the stones in the building were forty-five cubits in length, five in height and six in breadth. (*J. W.* 5.222-24)[3]

Concerning the votive offerings, the Greek word *anathema* means "that which is set up" and was often used of ornaments set up in temples. "Josephus (*J. W.* 5.210; *Ant.* 15.394-95) speaks of a gate of the Temple, completely overlaid with gold, with gold vines above it, from which hung grape clusters as tall as a man, and of fine Babylonian tapestries. The luxurious trappings stand in contrast to the destruction to be mentioned."[4] To these people Jesus had something to say.

21:6   Jesus said, "As for these things you are staring at—the days are coming when not one stone will be left upon a stone that will not be destroyed." Although the antecedent of the nominative pronoun opening the sentence, *tauta,* is not identified, it is surely to be understood as referring to the magnificent structure of the temple. So complete will be the destruction of the shrine, predicted Jesus, that not one stone would be attached to another. That prophecy was literally fulfilled in late August/early September A.D. 70 when the Roman army, led by General Titus, Emperor Vespasian's son, ransacked Jerusalem and

---

2. See Fitzmyer's description in *The Gospel According to Luke X–XXIV,* 1330.

3. See again Fitzmyer for more discussion on the temple in *The Gospel According to Luke X–XXIV,* 1330.

4. See the comments of Fitzmyer in *The Gospel According to Luke X–XXIV,* 1331.

burned it to the ground. Of that burning, Josephus wrote, "God, indeed long since, had sentenced [the temple] to the flames; but now in the revolution of the years had arrived the fated day, the tenth of the month of Lous [= 29 August A.D. 70], the day on which of old it had been burnt by the king of Babylon [= tenth day of Hebrew month of Ab, Jer. 52:12-13]" (*J. W.* 6.250). Josephus goes on to say that Titus so destroyed Jerusalem that, except for certain towers and wall portions deliberately left, one would scarcely have guessed that it had been inhabited (*J. W.* 7.376-79).

21:7 Verse 7 records the disciples' question about Jesus' prophecy. That it was the disciples who raised the question is clear from Matthew 24:3; Mark 13:1; cf. also Luke 21:12-19. They asked Him, "Teacher, when will these things happen, and what will be the sign when these things will take place?" It is pretty clear that the antecedent of "these things" is the destruction of the temple. The second part of the disciples' question asks for a sign (*sēmeion*) heralding the event.

21:8 Verses 8-24 records Jesus' reply to the question. It consisted of a three-part answer: (1) There will be signs that do *not* yet point to the fall of Jerusalem (vv. 8-19). Therefore the disciples should not overreact when such events occur. (2) However, there will be one sign that will signal the destruction of the city—the Roman armies surrounding Jerusalem (v. 20). (3) Then Jesus provided a prophetic glimpse of the destruction itself, which consisted basically of a fivefold description.

Verses 8-19 delineate four general signs that will show that the destruction of Jerusalem is coming, though it will not yet be imminent. First, there will arise those who will falsely claim to be the Messiah, incorrectly saying that the time of the kingdom of God has fully arrived. Jesus warned His disciples not to be misled by such people and not to follow after them. These phrases of Jesus are pregnant with historical meaning. His warning not to be misled by false prophets would find its fulfillment at the fall of the temple. Jesus' prediction that many would come, claiming to be Him, i.e., the Messiah, came to pass many times over (see Acts 5:36-37; Josephus, *Ant.* 20.97-99, 167-72). Jesus further warned that these pseudo-messiahs would proclaim that "the time has drawn near." This statement may well have applied to the messianic claimants who arose just prior to the Jewish war with Rome (A.D. 66–70) or to various religious frauds who, during the war with Rome, promised miraculous deliverance, claiming that God's kingdom was near. Jesus' disciples, however, must not be duped by such end-time sensationalism and apocalyptic fervor.

21:9   Verses 9-10 record a second sign that would not yet point to the destruction of Jerusalem—there will be wars (vv. 9-10). According to v. 9, when the disciples hear about wars and rebellions, they are not to be disturbed. These things must happen first, but they do not signal that the end has come. Speaking of these words, Marshall writes:

> These may be interpreted in terms of the Roman civil war or of internecine struggles in Palestine. War is a standard topic in apocalyptic (cf. Is. 19:2; 2 Ch. 15:6; Dn. 11:44; Rev. 6:8; 11:13; 4 Ez. 13:31), and such disturbances could lead to a belief that the end was at hand and perhaps fill men's hearts with fear that they would not live to see it or make them believe that evil had the upper hand and the end would never come. So the disciples are warned not to be terrified.... Such events are in God's plan; they must happen as his plan unfolds (cf. Dn. 2:28; Rev. 1:1; 4:1; 22:6; ...), but they do not signify that the end will follow immediately.[5]

It is important to note here that the "end" (*telos*) to which Jesus referred at this particular point was most probably the destruction of Jerusalem, not the end of the age and the time of the return of the Son of Man (cf. 21:25-28). There are two reasons for this: First, grammatically, the end refers back to "these things" (*tauta*) of vv. 6-7, i.e., the fall of Jerusalem. Second, historically, the signs delineated in vv. 8-19 were fulfilled in and around the events of the Jewish War with Rome (A.D. 66–70). Indeed, as we will soon see, the predictions by Jesus in vv. 12-19 were fulfilled in the days of the book of Acts (A.D. 33–66).

21:10   Verse 10 expands upon the eventuality and reality of war, "Nation will rise against nation and kingdom against kingdom."

21:11   Verse 11 lists a third sign—there will be disturbing signs on earth and in the heavens. In place after place on earth there will be great earthquakes (*seismoi*), plagues, and famines (cf. Acts 16:26 and 11:28, respectively.) In the sky there will be dread portents (*phobēta*) and great signs (*sēmeia*). Such happenings were associated with Antiochus Epiphanes' invasion of the Jerusalem temple in 167 B.C. (see *2 Macc.* 5:2, 3; *Sib. Or.* 3.796-808). Closer to Jesus' time is Josephus's description of the star and comet at the burning of the Jerusalem temple itself in A.D. 70. Josephus, the Jewish commander turned Roman historian, writes of this time, "Many who were emaciated and tongue-tied

---

5. Marshall, *Commentary on Luke,* 764.

from starvation, when they beheld the sanctuary on fire, gathered strength once more for lamentations and wailing. Peraea and the surrounding mountains contributed their echoes, deepening the din" (*J. W.* 6.274). Josephus tells, too, of six thousand refugees who perished in the flames of the temple porticos, deluded by a "false prophet, who had on that day proclaimed to the people in the city that God commanded them to go up to the temple court, to receive there the tokens of their deliverance" (*J. W.* 6.285). They were deluded by charlatans and would-be messengers of God and believed not "the manifest portents that foretold the coming desolation. . . . So it was when a star, resembling a sword, stood over the city, and a comet which continued for a year" (*J. W.* 6.288-89). Josephus goes on to tell of omens (lights seen in the sanctuary, a cow giving birth to a lamb) that attended the destruction.[6]

Fitzmyer, rightly in our opinion, concludes about the signs of vv. 8-11:

> When one considers such false prophets, portents, and ominous signs associated with the historic destruction of the Jerusalem Temple, it makes it plausible to think that "the end" (v. 9) could well be in Luke's view that of Jerusalem and its Temple. For this reason we see no need to import reference to the end of the world at this point in the Lucan eschatological discourse—which is the custom of the majority of commentators upon it.[7]

21:12   Verses 12-19 describe a fourth sign preceding the destruction of Jerusalem—persecution of Jesus' disciples. Verse 12 makes clear that before the end the disciples will have to undergo suffering for the cause of Christ, enduring numerous acts of harassment. Much of what Jesus predicted was fulfilled in the book of Acts.[8] People would lay their hands on the disciples and persecute them (see Acts 4:16-18; 8:1-3; 12:1-5). The disciples would be delivered over to synagogues and prisons (i.e., Jewish persecutions; see Acts 12:1-11; 25:13–26:32); They would be led off to kings and prefects (i.e., Gentile persecutions; see Acts 23:24–24:27; 24:27–26:32) for the name of Christ.

---

6. See also Fitzmyer, *The Gospel According to Luke X–XXIV,* 1335.

7. Fitzmyer, *The Gospel According to Luke X–XXIV,* 1335.

8. The following threefold summary is indebted to Evans, *Luke,* 308-9.

21:13   The disciples' appearance before the ruling authorities would lead to their (the disciples') giving testimony (*martyrion*) of their allegiance to Christ.

21:14   Jesus instructed the disciples to determine in their hearts not to prepare beforehand their defense (*apologēthēnai*). The Greek word for "to prepare beforehand," *promeletan*, was a technical expression for practicing a speech in advance (see Aristophanes, *Ecclesiazusae* 117). The Greek word for "defense," *apologia*, came to mean in early Christian circles "defense for the Christian faith" (cf. Luke 12:11; 1 Peter 3:15). Examples of this occur in Acts, i.e., Acts 4:8.

21:15   The reason the disciples should not prepare beforehand their testimonies is because Jesus Himself will give them words and wisdom such that their adversaries will not be able to withstand or contradict what they say. Jesus' promise was that He Himself (*egō*) would provide the disciples the mouth (*stoma*) or words they needed. In Luke 12:12, it is the Holy Spirit who will supply the disciples with the much needed assistance to testify of their faith in Christ. In these two passages we see, therefore, an intimate association between Christ and the Spirit (cf. 1:35; 4:1, 14; see also Acts 2:33). The assurance that the disciples will be enabled to give irresistible testimony to their faith in Christ reminds one of Stephen's defense (Acts 6:10; 7:2-53), as well as Peter's and John's testimonies (Acts 4:13).

21:16   Not only will the disciples face harassment from the courts, but they will also encounter betrayal from their parents and brothers, relative and friends. The consequence will be that some of the disciples will be put to death, as was the case for Stephen (Acts 7:54-60) and James, the son of Zebedee (Acts 12:1-2).

21:17   Jesus forecast that His disciples would be hated by all because of His name.

21:18   However, using a proverbial statement, Jesus promised His disciples, "Not a hair of your head will be lost" (cf. 1 Sam. 14:45; 2 Sam. 14:11; 1 Kings 1:52; Luke 12:7; Acts 27:34). This utterance by Jesus appears to stand in contradiction to v. 16. Marshall lists the possibilities of interpretation: (1) It has been suggested that the saying simply means that no harm would occur to the disciples without the Father's permission. (2) Others suggest that v. 16 refers to only a few martyrs, whereas this verse refers to the safety of the church as a whole. (3) Most commonly it is argued that the verse is referring to spiritual safety.

The disciples may suffer injury and death, but nothing can harm their essential being. Probably the third view is the most accurate.[9]

21:19 Jesus concluded His challenge to the disciples by telling them that it would be their perseverance (*hypomonē*, "to remain under") which would procure for themselves their lives (*psychas*, "soul"). What Jesus seemed to be saying was that those who faithfully endured their persecution would win for themselves eternal life. Perhaps we are not far off the mark to suggest that the verse teaches that steadfastness demonstrates the authenticity of one's profession of faith and, thereby, one's possession of eternal life.

21:20 We began this section of vv. 8-24 by suggesting that Jesus gave a threefold reply to the disciples' question about the coming destruction of Jerusalem. The first aspect of Jesus' response dealt with signs not yet pointing to the end (vv. 8-19). Verse 20a constitutes the second part of that reply—*the* sign immediately preceding the fall of Jerusalem will be the surrounding of the Holy City by the Roman legions. The word Jesus used for armies, *stratopedōn,* is the very word Josephus used of General Titus's army camps encompassing Jerusalem (*J. W.* 5.47-97; 6.97, 149-56). It is this event that will be the sign that the temple will soon be destroyed (Luke 12:7).

With v. 20b, the third part of Jesus' reply to the disciples began— the destruction of the city. Luke records basically five components of that ensuing carnage (vv. 20b-24). First, according to v. 20b, when the disciples see this happening, they should know (*gnōte*) that the desolation is near (*ēggiken*). The term for "desolation" (*erēmōsis*) comes from the Marcan parallel, 13:14, where the phrase "abomination of desolation" occurs. That phrase is taken from the Septuagint of Daniel 9:27; 11:31; 12:11 (cf. *1 Macc.* 1:54), an allusion to the desecration of the temple caused by the statue of Zeus Olympus erected by Antiochus IV Epiphanes in 167 B.C. in the Jerusalem temple. The new desolation will be seen in the encircling of Jerusalem by the camps of the Roman army.

21:21 Verse 21 gives a second attendant circumstance of the fall of Jerusalem: the need for people to escape from the city before it is too late. In this connection, Jesus issued a number of warnings tantamount to saying, "Everybody run for cover!" At the outbreak of the siege those in Judea must flee to the mountains, i.e., those chains of mountains to the east, north, and south of Jerusalem. We can only

9. Marshall, *Commentary on Luke,* 769.

speculate if this saying is to be identified with the oracle mentioned by Eusebius, the effect of which prompted the Christian church to flee Jerusalem into the Transjordan city of Pella, "People of the church in Jerusalem were commanded by a certain oracle before the war to those in the city who were worthy of it to depart and dwell in one of the cities of Perea called Pella" (*Ecclesiastical History* 3.5.3). Next, Jesus warned that those who lived in the city should get out of it. One is reminded here of the many who tried to escape Jerusalem at the time, but were not successful in doing so. A notable exception was the daring escape of Rabbi ben Zakkai who hid himself in a coffin that was being taken out of the city. It is this same man who later convened the council of Jamnia (in Galilee) in A.D. 90 for the purpose of reconstituting Judaism in the aftermath of Rome's defeat of Israel. Then, Jesus warned that those in the open fields outside Jerusalem should not go back into the city. Incidentally, that Jesus was not yet talking about His return and the end of history can be seen from the fact that the point of His warning was to flee Jerusalem. As Ellis remarks, "How does one escape the final apocalyptic catastrophes by fleeing Judea?"[10] To do so one would have to flee the whole earth.

21:22   A third component of the fall of Jerusalem is that it will be the fulfillment of God's divine plan of judgment: "For these are days of vengeance, to fulfill all that has been written." The oracle of condemnation recalls similar statements of the Old Testament prophets about the ominous fate of Jerusalem (cf.: v. 22 with Hos. 9:7; v. 24ab with Deut. 28:64; *Sir.* 28:18; v. 24c with Zech. 12:13, a prophecy of the restoration of Jerusalem which first presupposes its fall, 8:1-8). The reference to the fulfillment of Scripture, "to fulfill all that was written," reinforces that theme and one again recalls Old Testament oracles of the fall of Jerusalem that came to pass (Jer. 6:1-8; 26:1-9; Mic. 3:12; Zech. 8:1-8). So will it be with Jesus' words.

21:23   Fourth, there will be great distress (*anagkē*) on the land and wrath upon the people. Marshall notes that *gē* must refer to Judea, not to the world.[11] Thus the judgment envisioned will fall on the land of Judea and its people, a detail once again distinguishing the fall of Jerusalem (cf. v. 9) from the return of Christ and the end of history. A number of woes would befall Jerusalem at the time of its destruction

10. Ellis, *The Gospel of Luke,* 244.
11. Marshall, *Commentary on Luke,* 773.

in A.D. 70, according to vv. 23-24a. Pregnant women and nursing mothers would especially feel the brunt of war. To illustrate this woe uttered by Jesus over women with children, one can point to Josephus's story about Mary, a woman from Perea (the Transjordan area), who was among the Jews starving in Jerusalem at the time of Titus's siege and who seized her child, an infant she nursed, killed it, and roasted it for food for herself (*J. W.* 6.201-13). Parenthetically, Luke omits in v. 23 the Marcan parallel about women praying that their flight not be in winter (Mark 13:18). This is probably so because he writes *after* the fall of Jerusalem.

21:24   The catastrophes continue in v. 24a. Many Jews, said Jesus, will fall by the edge of the sword (cf. *Sir.* 28:18; Luke 2:34). Josephus estimated that one million Jews died in the war against Rome and that thousands who unsuccessfully tried to escape were crucified outside the city walls during the siege (*J. W.* 6.271, 420-27). Moreover, Jesus prophesied that many would be carried off captive to all the nations (cf. Deut. 28:64), a prediction fulfilled when Titus took ninety-seven thousand Jewish exiles to Rome, parading them as a part of his triumphal procession at Rome (see Josephus, *J. W.* 7.118-22, 132-62; 6.420-27). Finally, Jesus noted that Jerusalem was destined to be trampled on by the Gentiles (cf. Rev. 11:2). This warning became a reality after A.D. 70. But in v. 24b Jesus predicts that one day there will be an end to Jerusalem being trodden down by the nations, "until the times of the Gentiles are fulfilled." It is highly likely that Jesus intended by this phrase to suggest that the moment will come when Gentiles will no longer possess Jerusalem and that when such a time (*kairoi*) is fulfilled (*plērōthōsin*), the nation of Israel will repossess her land (cf. Dan. 2:44; 8:13-14; 12:5-13; *1QS* 4:18-19; Rom. 11:25).

This hope for the restoration of Israel to her land constitutes a fifth component of the description of the fall of Jerusalem. The Lucan oracle, then, contains a double message: the coming destruction of Jerusalem (vv. 20-24a) and the coming restoration of Jerusalem (v. 24b). The former occurred in connection with Jesus' first coming (the fall of Jerusalem occurs ultimately because of the divine word); the latter will transpire at Jesus' second coming and the visible establishment of the kingdom of God on earth (cf. v. 24b with vv. 27-30 and Acts 1:3-6). Therefore, the fall of Jerusalem serves as a foreshadowing of the coming restoration of Israel.

We conclude our discussion of this section by recording Fitz-myer's assessment of Dodd's theory mentioned earlier in connection with Luke 19:41-44:

> In discussing Luke 19:41-44, Jesus' lament over Jerusalem, we referred to C. H. Dodd's contention that that passage and this one depend far more on the description of the destruction of Jerusalem under Nebuchadnezzar in the sixth century B.C. than on Titus' capture of it in A.D. 70. . . . That may be, as far as the terminology is concerned, for Luke likes to make his accounts echo similar OT stories. But the question remains, Why has he substituted these covert references to the destruction of Jerusalem under the Romans for the Danielic "abomination of desolation"? Luke never names the Romans any more than Mark names either Antiochus IV Epiphanes or the Romans—saying only, "Let the reader understand." Though Luke does not follow Mark in using such indirection, he knows that, since he writes after the event, he will be understood.
>
> No one will contest that Luke has overlaid his form of Jesus' utterances about Jerusalem's coming desolation with various OT allusions, some of them more explicit than others (e.g. Hos 9:7 in v. 22; Sir 28:18 and Deut 28:64 in v. 24ab; and Zech 12:3 in v. 24c). The effect of this is to present the destruction of Jerusalem as an event in Lucan salvation-history. The "end" of v. 9 is now seen as "the time of vengeance," when "all that stands written will see fulfillment" (v. 22). "All that stands written" refers at least to the four allusions to OT writings mentioned above, which, though they are not all prophetic in themselves, are regarded by Luke . . . not only as prophetic, but even as predictive.
>
> Moreover, Jesus' words against Jerusalem not only have to be understood in terms of prophetic utterances of the OT against Jerusalem (e.g. Mic 3:12; Jer 7:1-14; 22:5), but also have to be related to his utterances against the Galilean towns of Bethsaida and Chorazin (10:13-15), where eschatological judgment was also pronounced.
>
> However, what Jesus says here about the coming desolation of Jerusalem forms a springboard for a wider development, for this pericope brings to an end the first part of the eschatological discourse, and now Jesus will move on to speak of what is coming upon the world.[12]

THE KINGDOM OF GOD AND
THE RESTORATION OF JERUSALEM, 21:25-38

The reader will recall the outline for this section (vv. 24-36); it consists of a threefold reply by Jesus to His disciples, which corre-

---

12. Fitzmyer, *The Gospel According to Luke X–XXIV,* 1343-44.

sponds to vv. 8-24: (1) there will be signs not yet pointing to the end (of history), vv. 25-26; (2) there will be a singular sign pointing to the arrival of the kingdom of God—the return of Christ to Jerusalem, vv. 27-30; (3) at that time the kingdom of God will be established on earth and Jerusalem will be restored (vv. 31-36).

21:25   The first part of Jesus' explanation of the coming of the end of history dealt with the signs of the end times. These signs are usually associated in the Bible with the Great Tribulation, a period of unprecedented affliction on the earth and which precedes the visible arrival of the kingdom of God (cf. vv. 25-26 with Dan. 12:1-2; Joel 3:3-4; Matt. 24:29; Mark 13:24-25; Rev. 6–20). It is important to note that though the signs delineated in Luke 21:25-26 correspond to vv. 8-19, they have not yet occurred and find no correspondence in history. They await the time immediately before the Parousia.[13] Verse 25 mentions signs (*sēmeia*) in the heavens and on the earth. The cosmic catastrophes in the heavens will affect the sun, the moon, and the stars. Joel 3:3-4 expresses it well: "There will be portents in the heavens and on the earth, blood and fire and columns of smoke; the sun will be turned to darkness and the moon to blood" (cf. also Isa. 13:10; 34:4; Ezek. 32:7; Hag. 2:6, 21; 2 Peter 3:10-13; Rev. 8:7-13). The terrestrial catastrophes follow on the heels of the cosmic portents, including the roaring and surging of the seas (see Ps. 46:4). The consequence will be that there will be great distress among the nations.

21:26   Fear and foreboding of what will happen to the inhabited earth will leave people breathless. The powers of heaven will be shaken such that the created order will seem to revert back to primeval chaos (cf. Isa. 34:4).

21:27   Verses 27-30 contain the second part of Jesus' explanation of the end of history—the singular sign of the approaching of the kingdom of God (v. 31) will be the return of Jesus Christ, the heavenly Son of Man. According to v. 27, out of the shaken heavens will emerge the Son of Man coming on a cloud with power and great glory. The description of Jesus' second coming is portrayed against the backdrop of

---

13. We should mention at this point that evangelical Christians tend to view the return of Christ in one of two ways. Dispensationalists believe that Christ will come first for His church and rapture it away before the seven-year tribulation period occurs on earth (1 Thess. 4:13-18) and then, at the conclusion of the tribulation period, return to earth in power and glory to establish His physical kingdom (cf. Luke 21). In other words, the church will not go through the tribulation period. Non-dispensationalists, however, merge the rapture of the church with the second coming of Christ (1 Thess. 4:13-18 = Luke 21). In other words, the church will go through the tribulation period.

Daniel 7:13 and symbolizes the handing over of the kingdoms of this world to God's Messiah. Daniel 7:13-14 was widely interpreted as messianic in early Judaism (*1 Enoch* 69:29; *R. Num.* 13:14; *R. Pss.* 21:5; *b. Sanh.* 96b-97a), and it is a fitting description of Jesus' Parousia. Christ will visibly return to earth with power and great glory (the motif of clouds comes from Dan. 7:13 and symbolizes the *shekinah* glory of God; cf. also Ex. 13:21-22; 1 Kings 8:10-11; Ezek. 10:4, 18-19; Luke 9:32-35). We suggest that the descent of Christ to Jerusalem (cf. Luke 21:27 with Zech. 14:3-4) is the heavenly counterpart to the earthly scene of v. 20a. If the latter describes the surrounding of Jerusalem with the earthly armies of Rome (and thereby signifies the Holy City's destruction), then the former describes the surrounding of Jerusalem with Christ and His heavenly armies (cf. 2 Thess. 1:7-10; Rev. 19:11-16), that will signify the restoration of the Holy City.

21:28 At that moment, and in contrast to the people of the earth who quake with fear at the cosmic and terrestrial upheavals coming upon them (vv. 25-26), the followers of Jesus should stand tall, holding their heads up high, because their redemption (*apolutrōsis*; cf. 1:68; Rom. 8:23; Eph. 1:14; 4:30) is near (cf. also Acts 1:9-11).

21:29 Next, Jesus used a parable to illustrate the close proximity of the kingdom of God. Jesus told the disciples to look at the fig tree, and all trees for that matter. Jesus included the last phrase because the lesson to be learned from the fig tree can be learned from all trees.

21:30 When trees put forth their leaves, even the casual observer knows that summer and its fruit is not far away.

21:31 Verses 31-36 comprise the third, and final, part of Jesus' explanation about the things to come—the consummation of the kingdom of God and the restoration of Israel. Five circumstances will accompany that event, which remarkably correspond to the five elements accompanying the fall of Jerusalem earlier identified in vv. 20b-24. The only major difference between the parallels is that vv. 20b-24 are historical in nature, occurring around A.D. 70, whereas vv. 31-36 are eschatological in nature, occurring at the end of the present age.

According to v. 31, just as one can tell that summer and its fruit are near with the appearance of leaves on trees, so it is with the signs of the end time (vv. 25-26) in general and the return of Christ specifically (vv. 27-30). Those events, especially the latter sign, will demonstrate that the kingdom of God is near. We have already met with the all-important topic of the kingdom of God in Luke, noting its twofold perspective: the kingdom of God as spiritually present in the first coming of Christ (see 10:9, 11; 17:20, 21), but not until the second coming of Christ will it come visibly to earth (see 11:2; 19:11; Acts 1:3-6). Luke 21:31 fits into the latter category. Thus, v. 31 constitutes the first, and climactic, circumstance of the end of human history—the consummation of the kingdom. Jesus' admonition to His future followers to "recognize" from the sign of His return that the kingdom of God is "near" corresponds to v. 10b, "recognize" that these things are "near." The one refers to the destruction of Jerusalem (v. 20b); the latter to its restoration (v. 31).

21:32 We suggest vv. 32-33 form the second attendant circumstance of the coming of the kingdom of God and, as such, correspond to v. 24b, which alludes to the future restoration of Jerusalem (Israel). Though one cannot be dogmatic about it, we believe that v. 32, a very difficult verse to interpret, also assures Israel as a nation that she will not pass away; that is, she will be restored to God despite intense suffering along the way. Verse 33 contains Jesus' promise that this will be so. We translate v. 32 thus: "Truly I say to you that this nation (*genea*) will never ever (*ou mē*) pass away until all these things happen." The meaning of *genea* is considerably debated, generating three major translations: (1) the generation in which Jesus lived; (2) the generation of the end-time events; (3) the nation or people of Israel. Some who take the first view connect the "all these things" of v. 31 with the fall of Jerusalem (vv. 6-24). But if that is the case, then why has Luke placed v. 32 here, after passages concerning the coming of the Son of Man (vv. 25-28) and the coming of the kingdom of God (vv. 29-31)? Others who take the first view say that Jesus predicted that the end of history would occur in His generation and that He was wrong. But Marshall has convincingly refuted the latter position by showing that Jesus in fact expected an interval time between His generation and the fall of Jerusalem and the return of the Son of Man and the end of history.[14]

The second view is the one adopted by most commentators, and understandably so. On this reading, the generation alive at the occurrence of the end-time events will not pass away before the coming of Christ and His kingdom, so quick will be the transaction of events. However, this view assumes that the word *genea* means generation. In fact, the word is flexible in meaning and is best determined by the context. *Genea* can mean three things: (1) the descendants of a common

---

14. Marshall, *Commentary on Luke,* 752, 758; cf. Ellis, *The Gospel of Luke,* 246-47.

ancestor; (2) a set of people born at the same time; (3) the period of time occupied by such a set of people, often in the sense of successive sets of people.[15] It cannot be said without further ado, therefore, that *genea* necessarily means generation.

We suggest that the term in Luke 21:32 more properly refers to the Jewish race (number 1 definition above). We believe the context points to this definition, on two counts. First, few commentators recognize the importance of the emphatic negation (*ou mē*, "never ever") that precedes the term *genea*. It would be odd for Jesus to utter such an emotionally charged statement about a generation. It is better suited to be said about a people—God's chosen people, the Jews. Actually Jesus' strong statement sounds like an oath, similar to the one God swore to Abraham about preserving His people (1:54-55, 73-74). Second, if we are correct in our suggestion that v. 32 corresponds to v. 20b, then we meet in this statement the divine promise that God will one day restore His people.

21:33   Jesus' guarantee in v. 33 that heaven (the sky) and the earth will pass away, but His words will not pass away, can be seen, then, to refer to His oath to restore His people. These words of Jesus remind one of the power and efficacy of God's word through His prophet Isaiah, 40:8; 55:10-11—passages, by the way, which predict the future restoration of Israel to her land after her exile in captivity to Babylon.

21:34   Verse 34 gives a third circumstance attending the arrival of the kingdom of God: spiritually alert people will escape the coming judgment. This is similar to what the Lord said in vv. 21-23. Verse 34 issues a warning for the last days. People need to be on guard for the return of Christ by not letting their hearts be spiritually dulled by carousing, drunkenness, and worldly cares. If they are not alert, that day will surprise them (cf. Matt. 24:36-51; Mark 13:32; 1 Thess. 5:2).

21:35   For those who are distracted and unprepared, that day will suddenly catch them like a trap (see Isa. 24:17; cf. Rev. 3:10). It will snare all those who dwell upon the earth. This idea of judgment and duress that is to come upon all the earth constitutes a fourth happening associated with the end of history, and it corresponds to v. 23, except that in v. 35 it encompasses all the world, not just Judea, as it did in v. 23.

21:36   In order to avoid the eventuality of these things, Jesus' followers should be on the alert, praying for strength to survive the

15. So according to Marshall, *Commentary on Luke,* 780, who takes the second view.

things to come. The reference to the "things to come" amounts to a fifth component of the end of history in that it is a testimony by Jesus that what He said will surely happen. It corresponds to v. 22. Having prepared themselves spiritually, Jesus' followers will be able to stand in the presence of the Son of Man at His return and meet His approval.

We may conclude Jesus' eschatological discourse, with its emphasis on the future restoration of Israel, by offering the following parallels between Luke 21:20-36 and Romans 11:25-27. These specific resemblances highly suggest that Luke, as he recorded Jesus' prophecy of things to come (especially the future re-gathering of Israel), had Paul's teaching on the same in mind. We briefly call attention to four uncanny correspondences between them: (1) Both texts acknowledge that Israel will suffer God's judgment because she is spiritually blind to Jesus, the Messiah (cf. Luke 21:20-24a with Rom. 11:25a). (2) Both passages contain the idea of "the fullness of the Gentiles," a remarkable parallel (cf. Luke 21:24b with Rom. 11:25b). (3) Both writers pin their hopes for the future on the return of Christ (cf. Luke 21:25-27 with Rom. 11:26b). (4) Both authors envision the future restoration of Israel (cf. Luke 21:24b, 31-33; Acts 1:3-6 with Rom. 11:26a-27).

21:37   Verses 37-38 give Luke's editorial summary of Jesus' teaching ministry in the temple at Jerusalem. According to v. 37, in the day Jesus taught in the temple area while at night He lodged on the hill called the Mount of Olives.

21:38   In the morning all the people would get up early to come to listen to Jesus in the temple. Here ends Jesus' teaching ministry in the temple.

HOMILETICAL SUGGESTIONS

In preaching through Luke 21, we suggest that the opening episode about the widow's offering (vv. 1-4) is best cared for by including it in the sermonic material dealing with 20:47, especially since 21:1-4 seems to serve as a commentary on "devouring the houses of widows" (20:47). Therefore, the bulk of Luke 21, vv. 5-38, should be treated under the title of "Things to Come." This chapter obviously lends itself to a series on prophecy and the detailed outline presented in our commentary on those verses would be an effective way to cover the material carefully. Thus, we will only make general suggestions here about preaching the material.

First, the section on the signs *not* pointing to the end (vv. 8-19, 25-26) can be easily illustrated by using the daily newspaper. But, it should be added, a proper interpretation of those verses should be adhered to in order to help prevent the usual fanfare and sensationalism often associated with things to come. This sane approach will become more and more important as the year 2000 draws near, for apocalyptic expectations will certainly intensify.

Second, vv. 20-24 and the fall of Jerusalem can be dealt with from a historical perspective, especially using the quotations of Josephus's description of that event. The point of application of vv. 20-24 is pure and simple: if Jesus correctly predicted to the minute detail the fall of Jerusalem in A.D. 70, one can depend on the reliability of His prophecies about His own return.

Regarding the actual return of Christ and the coming of the kingdom of God, one could treat vv. 27-33 in conjunction with Luke's parallel text on the subject, Acts 1:3-11. Both passages emphasize the public, powerful, and personal aspects of Christ's second coming. Verses 34-38 would serve, then, as an apt application of the topic: be spiritually ready for Christ's return.

LUKE

CHAPTER
TWENTY TWO

THE PASSION NARRATIVE

Luke 22–23 is devoted to the passion narrative, the story of Jesus' celebration of Passover, His betrayal and arrest, His trial and crucifixion. Luke 22, which occupies us in this chapter, deals with the preliminary events leading up to the passion itself. But before analyzing the chapter, we will cull together a few comments about the passion narrative as a whole, remarking on three matters in particular: its genre, sources, and purpose. Concerning the first of these, like the infancy narrative and the resurrection narrative, the passion narrative is a sub-form in the literary genre of gospel. Scholars have long believed that the passion story was the first part of the gospel tradition to attain the form of a connected narrative. In fact, it is not unusual for interpreters of the gospels to call the gospels "passion narratives with extended introductions." Accordingly, Fitzmyer writes that all four gospels

> have a passion narrative with a certain striking similarity (betrayal of Jesus by Judas, Last Supper with the disciples, arrest in an outdoor area outside the city, Peter's denials, an interrogation before a high priest, an appearance before P. Pilate, being led off to death, crucifixion, title on the cross, death, burial)—a similarity which...suggests that the Evangelists had access to a relatively fixed complex of accounts.[1]

1. Fitzmyer, *The Gospel According to Luke X–XXIV,* 1360.

The earliest attestation to the story of Jesus' death and resurrection occurs in Paul's writings, who makes countless allusions or references to Jesus' passion, death, and burial: His Last Supper and His betrayal (1 Cor. 11:23-25), His "sufferings" (Phil. 3:10), His "cross" (Phil. 2:8), His "crucifixion" (Gal. 2:20; 3:1; 1 Cor. 1:23; 2 Cor. 13:4), His being "hung on a tree" (Gal. 3:13), His "death" (1 Thess. 5:10; 1 Cor. 11:26; 15:3; Rom. 4:25; 5:8-10; 6:3), His "burial" (1 Cor. 15:3; Rom. 6:4); even to "the Jews who killed the Lord Jesus" (1 Thess. 2:14-15) or to His being "crucified" by the "rulers of this age" (1 Cor. 2:8). Even though these allusions are isolated in Paul's writings and often made in a context more theological than historical, they reveal that Paul was aware of a "story of the cross" in the sense of a connected narrative.[2]

The need for a continuous or connected account of Jesus' passion undoubtedly arose, as Fitzmyer observes, "from the experience of early Christian preachers or missionaries confronted with the objection, 'Well, if he [Jesus] were God's Messiah, then why did he end up crucified? If he were God's agent for human salvation, why did God allow him to die a criminal's death on a cross?' As such, he quickly became 'a stumbling block to Jews, and to Gentiles foolishness' (1 Cor. 1:23)."[3]

The second item to be addressed briefly is the matter of Luke's sources for the passion narrative. No scholar today seriously questions that the third evangelist draws extensively on Mark's passion narrative. Of the twenty-one episodes occurring in Luke 22–23, fourteen of them correspond to Mark in almost the same order. In other words, the continuous thread of Luke's passion narrative is based on Mark.[4] In addition to Mark, Luke uses other sources in his passion narrative. Marshall summarizes this material:

> Although the story is essentially the same as that in Mk., Luke has added material from other sources, and has so arranged it that various distinctive motifs stand out. The precise extent of non-Marcan source material is disputed, but there can be no doubt of its presence. As a result of it, we have a fuller elaboration of the farewell sayings of Jesus at the Last Supper, a shift of the Jewish trial from the night to the early morning, various new details in the crucifixion, and new appearance stories. Throughout the section the death and resurrection of Jesus are depicted

---

2. The summary is Fitzmyer's in *The Gospel According to Luke X–XXIV,* 1360.
3. Fitzmyer, *The Gospel According to Luke X–XXIV,* 1361.
4. For the specifics, see ibid., 1365.

in terms of the death of a righteous man suffering as a martyr. But above all Jesus is presented as going through suffering to glory, following the path marked out for him by the will of God, prophesied in the OT and foretold in his own teaching to his disciples. It is the end of the Gospel, but at the same time it points forward to the new beginning in the Acts of the Apostles.[5]

The third matter calling for comment concerning the Lucan passion narrative is its purpose, or rather, purposes. We suggest that some four motifs emerge relative to Luke 22–23, and also 24.

There is a *political* perspective evident in Luke's account of Jesus' passion. The vindication of Jesus' innocence by Governor Pilate (23:4, 14-15, 22) and the Roman centurion at the cross (23:47) served Luke's concern to demonstrate that Christianity was no insurrectionist religion against the Roman empire.

Second, Luke highlights the *sacrificial* aspect of Jesus' passion, especially in presenting Him as a righteous sufferer, in general (cf. 23:34b-35 with the psalm of the righteous sufferer, Ps. 22:8, 19; see also Luke 23:50; Acts 3:14; 7:52; 22:14 regarding the theme of Jesus the righteous one). More particularly, Jesus is portrayed in Luke's passion narrative as the suffering servant who sacrificially atones for the sins of others (cf. Luke 22:37 with Isa. 53:12; see also Luke 22:19-20; 24:26-27, 44-46).

Third, Luke, aware as he was of Greek thinking, sees in Jesus' passion a *philosophical* perspective as well. Like the philosopher Socrates,[6] Jesus faces death with the Hellenistic (Greek) moral ideals of self-control (22:51) and freedom from fear (22:45; 23:28-31). He, like Socrates, prepares His followers for the future (22:35-38). Moreover, Jesus arose from the dead and ascended to the Father in a way superlative to the *apotheosis* (translation into heaven and deification) of any Greek hero or philosopher (Luke 24). Luke's portrayal of his Lord in such a philosophical manner undoubtedly appealed to Hellenistic audiences.

But, in our estimation, it is the *eschatological* motif that dominates Luke's passion narrative. Several end-time themes surface in Luke 22–24. (a) There is much concern about the coming of the kingdom of God to earth at the end of this age (22:16-18, 29-30; 23:51; cf. Acts 1:3, 6). (b) Jesus' suffering on the cross, which leads to the glory

5. Marshall, *Commentary on Luke*, 785.

6. See Plato's *Apology* for a description of Socrates's courage and integrity in the face of death.

of His resurrection (24:26-27, 46; cf. Acts 1:3), echoes a theme dear to the heart of Jewish apocalypticism—suffering in this age leads to the glory of the age to come.[7] (c) The text about Jesus opening Paradise (23:43) draws upon another Jewish eschatological axiom: the end of time (paradise regained) will restore the beginning of time (paradise lost; see Isa. 65:17-25; Rev. 21–22). (d) The occurrence of the resurrection of Jesus (Luke 24) is itself the inbreaking into history of an event normally associated in Judaism with the climax of history (see Dan. 12:2-3; Ezek. 37). In other words, what Judaism expected to happen at the end of time (a general resurrection of all humanity) has already begun in the resurrection of Jesus (see also 1 Cor. 15:20-28). (e) Jesus' promise to fill His disciples with the Spirit (cf. Luke 24:49 with Acts 1:8) would have been interpreted by Jews as a sign of the promise of the dawning of the age to come (cf. Joel 2:28-32 with Acts 2:14-21). We now proceed to analyze Luke 22, taking up each episode occurring therein.

THE PLOT OF THE JEWISH LEADERS, 22:1-2

The first episode in the Lucan passion narrative is the observation about the conspiracy of the Jerusalem leaders against Jesus, vv. 1-2. It sounds an ominous note for the drama that will soon unfold.

22:1 The drama of Jesus' passion began with the approach of the Feast of Unleavened Bread, called the Passover. The feast originated with the events surrounding Israel's Exodus and was held from Nisan (April) 15 to 21, during the barley harvest (Ex. 12:1-20; 23:15; 34:18; Deut. 16:1-8). By New Testament times the feast was closely connected with the Passover, held on Nisan 14–15. The latter term derived from the Hebrew word *pesaḥ*, which means "to jump over," an appropriate name because the angel of death "passed over" those who spread the blood of the sacrificial lamb upon the doors of their homes back in Egypt. The Greek transliteration of *pesaḥ* is *pascha* which, in the course of things, became associated with the Greek word *paschein*, "to suffer." It was the Christian community, then, that made the connection between "passover" and the "passion."

22:2 At that time, the chief priests and the scribes sought how they might destroy Jesus. The religious leaders tried to devise a secret plot to kill Jesus because they were afraid of the people, who, at the time

---

7. See Pate, *The Glory of Adam and the Afflictions of the Righteous.*

of Passover in Jerusalem, would have numbered into the hundreds of thousands. With these words the reader is introduced to a favorite Lucan theme in the passion narrative—the relative innocence of the general populace compared to the guilt of the leaders (see 22:6, 47, 52; 23:1-2; 23:27, 35, 48; 24:20-21; cf. 19:45-48; 21:38). Such a concern on Luke's part surely delivers him of any charge of being anti-Semitic.

The Betrayal of Jesus by Judas, 22:3-6

Luke moves immediately from the notice that the religious authorities were trying to do away with Jesus secretly to the account of Judas's betrayal. An important Lucan element that one finds in this episode is the satanic influence behind Judas's machinations.

22:3   The early church attributed Judas's betrayal to more than one motive: he was a thief (John 12:4-6); perhaps he was a zealot who became disenchanted with Jesus' peaceful mission (*if* the name Iscariot is to be linked etymologically to the word *sicarius,* "assassin," with respect to the Jewish zealots' terrorist attacks on the Romans who occupied their land); he was divinely predestined for the role of traitor (Mark 14:21; Acts 1:18-25). In an attempt to explain Judas's despicable behavior, Luke adds one more motive—Judas was empowered by Satan (cf. John 13:2, 27). Ultimately, only this could explain Judas's defection from the ranks of the twelve apostles.

22:4   Judas provided the solution to the problem of the chief priests and the temple police. It is interesting that the last mentioned group (*stratēgois*; cf. Acts 4:1; 5:24, 26) were also identified in Judaism as the persons who handled the temple funds (Josephus, *Ant.* 20.131; *m. Abot* 3.2; *m. Yoma* 2:1.9). These people, then, along with the chief priests, may have conspired with Judas not only for the purpose of knowing when and where to arrest Jesus in private, but also to make the financial arrangements with the betrayer.

22:5   The bargain was struck. The religious authorities rejoiced at Judas's offer, and they gave him a sum of money for his part in the plan (cf. see Matt. 26:15 for the amount—thirty pieces of silver).

22:6   Judas agreed with the deal and sought to find an occasion to hand Jesus over to the leaders, when the crowds of people were not around. Knowing where Jesus and the disciples met in the evenings and when they might be alone afforded Judas an opportunity for betraying his master.

PREPARATION FOR THE PASSOVER MEAL, 22:7-14

This episode serves to prepare for the following episode, the Passover meal (vv. 15-20). Luke records how Jesus took the initiative on *parasceve* (the day of preparation) to celebrate the Passover with His disciples. There can be no doubt that the meal was indeed a Passover meal (see v. 15); however, that may compare with John's gospel.[8]

22:7 Luke records in v. 7 that the day of unleavened bread arrived when the Passover lamb was to be slaughtered. The phrase "the day of unleavened bread" is a generic description of the week-long feast celebrated from Nisan 15 to 21. It originally celebrated the beginning of harvest, but later was combined with Passover. The eating of unleavened bread commemorated the haste with which the Jews in captivity in Egypt ate their bread before their Exodus. Because it takes time for leaven to cause bread to rise, the Jews ate unleavened bread, so that they could be ready for a quick escape from Pharaoh. The idea of unleavened bread later took on spiritual connotations—it represented the purging of sin from one's life (see 1 Cor. 5:7-8). To this day orthodox Jews celebrating Passover participate in a ceremony on *parasceve* in which, with candle and spoon, they find and remove any leaven present in the house.[9]

The additional phrase, "when the Passover lamb was to be slaughtered," specifies more exactly the date involved, which was Nisan 14. The instructions for the Passover were given at the time that the Israelites were leaving Egypt (Ex. 12; cf. also Lev. 23:4-8; Num. 9:3-14; Deut. 16:1-8). On the tenth day of the first month (Nisan = March/April), a lamb was selected for each household (Ex. 12:3). On Nisan 14 the lamb was slain "between the two evenings" (Ex. 12:6; Lev. 23:5; Num. 9:3-5), which, according to Josephus, was between the ninth and eleventh hours. In other words, the lamb was slain on Nisan 14 in the temple court area, between 3:00 and 5:00 P.M. At 6:00 P.M., when the new day began for the Jews, Nisan 15, the Passover meal was eaten, which also began the week of the Feast of Unleavened Bread (Nisan 15–21).

22:8 Jesus sent Peter and John, instructing them to make the necessary preparations to eat the Passover supper. Literally, the text reads,

---

8. The reader is referred to Fitzmyer's superlative discussion of this issue in *The Gospel According to Luke X–XXIV,* 1379-82.

9. The ritual is called *b'dikas bometz* (Hebrew for "searching for leaven").

"to eat the pascha," a customary Jewish expression (Ex. 12:11, 43-46; Num. 9:11). A great deal of effort was involved in the preparation of the Passover:[10] (1) The site had to be selected, no small chore in Jerusalem, an overly crowded city with pilgrims at Passover. (2) Once the site had been chosen, it was necessary to purge the house of any ritual impurities: leaven was removed, vessels were cleansed, and so on. (3) On the afternoon of Nisan 14, the Passover lamb had to be inspected by the priest and then slaughtered in the forecourts of the temple. As many as 265,000 lambs were killed for the Passover, in the last hours of the day. The traffic would have been incredible. (The writer can attest to this fact, having once gotten caught up in holy day traffic in Jerusalem at the Damascus gate, a trying situation.) Then the blood of the lamb had to be poured out at the altar, and a certain part of the lamb was reserved for the priestly sacrifice; the rest would be wrapped in skin and taken home for the meal. (4) The rest of the meal had to be cared for as well: the wine, unleavened cakes, bitter herbs, mixed fruit and vinegar, and so on.

22:9 The two disciples naturally wanted to know what room Jesus intended for them to prepare for the Passover.

22:10 Jesus gave a sign that would show the disciples which room to prepare. When they entered the city, the disciples would be met by a man carrying a jar of water. They were to follow him into the house he entered. A man carrying a jar of water would have been an unusual sight in a culture in which the women performed such tasks (cf. John 4:7). The occurrence of a man doing that job would clue Peter and John in on who they were to follow. Whether the rendezvous with the man was prearranged by Jesus or whether it was an act of Jesus' divine foreknowledge is not clear. Either way, however, it is clear that Jesus was in control of the situation, as well as His approaching destiny.

22:11 Upon encountering the man, the disciples were to follow him to the designated house. There they were to inquire of the housemaster where the guest room was in which Jesus and the disciples would eat the Passover meal. The reference to "teacher" (*didaskalos*) may identify the owner of the house as one of Jesus' followers.

22:12 The owner of the house would then show the disciples the room, a large guest room (probably an exterior room built on the flat roof). It would already be furnished. The Greek word for "furnish," *estrōmenon,* suggests that cushions for reclining at the meal (a prac-

---

10. These comments are indebted to Pentecost, *The Words and Works of Jesus Christ,* 423.

tice at Passover) had been supplied. Then the disciples were to prepare for the meal.

22:13   Peter and John went off and found everything to be as Jesus
said. They then made the preparations for the meal.

22:14   Verse 14 is a transitional statement, concluding the preparation for the Passover meal and leading into the meal itself. When the
set hour of the Passover arrived (sundown of Nisan 14, when the feast,
Nisan 15, was beginning), Jesus and the apostles arrived at the room.
But the term "hour" is more than chronological for Luke; it is also
theological—a critical moment in salvation history had come. They
dined at the table, a triclinium couch which was served by someone in
the inner section. On the outside of the table, Jesus and the apostles
reclined while they ate the meal, the customary practice at Passover.
Reclining at a meal was thought to symbolize freedom, an idea inherent in the Exodus of Israel.

THE LAST SUPPER, 22:15-20

G. B. Caird, in his commentary on Luke, calls the Lucan account
of the Last Supper "a scholar's paradise and a beginner's nightmare."[11]
He meant by this that Luke's account raises some taxing questions,
four of which we will attempt to answer as we move through the passage: (1) What is the textual solution to vv. 19b-20, verses not found in
some very reliable manuscripts? (2) What is the theological meaning
of the Last Supper? (3) What is the cultural background informing the
Last Supper? (4) Do vv. 15-20, together with vv. 21-38, form a particular literary genre?

22:15   Jesus began the evening by expressing His intense desire to
eat the Passover with His disciples. The grammatical construction consists of a cognate dative, "intensely (*epithymia*) I have desired (*epethy-
mēsa*)." The meaning of the statement is that Jesus had long desired to
eat the Passover, and now that wish had come true. Early Christian
readers would have heard a kind of play on words in Jesus' comment
—"to eat this *Passover* (*pascha*) with you before I *suffer* (*pathein*)"
—for, to their minds, since Jesus' death, Passover and suffering had
become synonymous. The pronoun "this" (*touto*) is in the emphatic
position, indicating that it is *this* particular Passover that Jesus wished
to eat with the disciples.

11. Caird, *Saint Luke,* 237.

22:16   The reason for Jesus' desire is provided in v. 16—this Passover that Jesus was eating with the disciples would be the last one He would partake of before He died (v. 15) and before the kingdom of God was fulfilled (cf. v. 18). The meaning of the last phrase is difficult, but it seems to anticipate the future consummation of the kingdom of God on earth, when the messianic banquet will be celebrated by the followers of Jesus (cf. 13:29; 14:15; Rev. 19:7-9). As such, it adds an eschatological perspective to the celebration of the Last Supper, akin to 1 Corinthians 11:26: "For as often as you eat this bread and drink this cup, you proclaim the Lord's death until he comes." The term "fulfill" (*plerōthe*) supports this eschatological interpretation (cf. 4:21; 9:31; 24:44).

22:17   Verse 17 describes Jesus' participation in the Passover seder. It would be helpful to set out in advance its order, as delineated in the oldest text on the subject, *m. Pesahim* 10:1-7 (cf. this account with Ex. 12:13-14; Num. 9:1-14: Deut. 16:1-8). Dwight Pentecost summarizes it well:

> (1) a benediction, (2) cup of wine, (3) the hands of the company washed, the master of the feast passing the basin while reciting a prayer, (4) bitter herbs dipped in sauce and eaten, (5) the lamb brought in with other portions of the meal, (6) a benediction and second eating of bitter herbs, (7) a second cup of wine with questions and answers as to the origin of the feast, (8) singing of the first part of the Hallel (Pss. 113, 114) followed by a benediction, (9) the master of the feast washes his hands and makes a sop by wrapping a bit of lamb with unleavened bread in bitter herbs and dipping it in the sauce, for each one present in turn, (10) each eats as much as he likes, finishing with a piece of lamb, (11) a third cup of wine after washing hands, (12) singing of second part of the Hallel (Pss. 115–118) in conclusion, (13) a fourth cup of wine.[12]

The Passover seder, then, is the key to understanding the cultural background of the Last Supper. Like the Passover seder, Jesus drank the cup of wine (quite possibly the first cup). Unlike the Passover seder, in which the participants drank from their own cups, Jesus distributed the one cup of wine among His disciples, signifying the communal aspect of the meal. The reference to Jesus giving thanks may confirm that the cup of wine being drunk was the first cup, because it

---

12. Pentecost, *The Words and Works of Jesus Christ,* 427.

was associated with an opening blessing (*qiddus*). In some Christian traditions, the Greek term for "thanks," *eucharist,* has become the title for the whole meal, usually accompanied by sacramental connotations.

22:18   Verse 18 is parallel to v. 16 in its assertion that Jesus will not drink of the fruit of the vine (wine) until the kingdom of God comes. Both verses state the matter in emphatic terms: v. 16, "never ever (*ou mē*) eat until the kingdom of God is fulfilled"; v. 18, "never ever (*ou mē*) drink until the kingdom of God comes." Both verses accentuate the future aspect of the kingdom of God: although it was present spiritually with the first coming of Christ, the kingdom will not be physically established on earth until the second coming of Christ.

22:19   With vv. 19-20, we encounter two significant changes that Jesus introduced into the Passover meal, forever modifying it and filling it with new meaning. We also meet in these two verses with a text critical problem. We begin with that first. There are two basic approaches in the manuscript evidence toward vv. 19b-20. Some manuscripts omit vv. 19b-20 (D [Bezae] and the Old Latin). Although the manuscript tradition favoring this reading is not strong, it apparently clears up the puzzling double reference to the cup of wine in vv. 17 and 20. Luke is the only gospel writer who mentions a second cup. This reading convinced so great text critics as B. F. Westcott and F. J. A. Hort (see their critical text of the Greek New Testament published in 1881) and was the preferred reading in the Nestle critical text of the New Testament in the first half of the twentieth century, up to the twenty-fifth edition.

The second reading is the longer one, which includes vv. 19b-20. There are three reasons it should be preferred as the most accurate text. First, the oldest manuscripts support it (p75, Sinaiticus, A, B, C). Second, it is the most difficult reading (*lectio difficilior*), because it creates two references to the cup of wine. The tendency of later New Testament scribes would have been to omit vv. 19b-20 in order to clear up that difficulty. Third, the two cups, in light of the cultural background, fit nicely into the four cups of wine around which the Passover seder was structured.

In proceeding to an analysis of vv. 19-20, we encounter two changes Jesus introduced into the Passover seder, which clue in the reader to the theological meaning of the Last Supper. In v. 19, we encounter the first change. Jesus took the unleavened bread (the *mat-*

zoh), which was equated in the Passover seder with the "bread of affliction" (see Deut. 16:34 and the association there of unleavened bread with Israel's affliction in Egyptian bondage), and identified it with His body. In other words, the bread of affliction was no longer to be equated with unleavened bread, but rather with Jesus' body and the affliction He was about to endure on the cross. The giving of thanks indicates the bread was eaten at the beginning of the main meal. With such bread, the participant would eat the Passover lamb and bitter herbs (cf. Ex. 12:8). Just as Jesus turned the cup of wine into a communal act (v. 17), so He did with the bread, breaking it from one loaf and distributing it to His disciples (cf. 1 Cor. 10:16; 11:24; see also Luke 24:30; Acts 2:46; 20:7, 11, 27:35). Jesus' words of institution, "This is my body, which is given for you; do this in remembrance of me," engender three comments: First, "this is my body" is metaphorical in expression. That is, Jesus compared the bread of affliction, the unleavened bread, with His body.[13] Jesus meant by the word "body" His flesh. Probably the reason Luke did not use the Greek word "flesh" (*sarx*) was because the Greek word for "body," *soma*, was assonant with "blood," *aima*; thus, body/blood, *soma/aima*. He undoubtedly inherited this pair from the traditions of the early church. Second, the words "given for (*hyper*) you" (cf. v. 20; 1 Cor. 11:24) are sacrificial in intent, referring to the offering up of Jesus' body on the cross. For a vicarious meaning attached to the word "for" (*hyper*, the "atoning" preposition), see Isaiah 53:5; Romans 5:6; 8:32; 1 Corinthians 15:3; 2 Corinthians 5:14; *2 Macc.* 7:9; 8:21; *4 Macc.* 1:9, 10. Compare also the sacrificial imagery used in v. 37 in terms of the suffering servant. Third, the phrase "do this in remembrance of me" is memorial in practice. The word Jesus used for "remembrance," *anamnēsis*, recalls Deuteronomy 16:3 and its challenge to Israel to remember the significance of the Passover, "that you may remember the day of your departure from the land of Egypt all the days of your life." Even so, whenever the followers of Jesus celebrate the Lord's Supper, they should remember His death on the cross for them.

22:20 In v. 20 we meet a second change Jesus introduced into the Passover meal; He identified the cup of redemption (the third cup) with His blood. In the same manner with which Jesus shared the bread, He then shared the cup after the meal saying, "This cup is the new covenant in my blood, which is poured out for you." Two of the

---

13. *Contra* Fitzmyer's literal equation of the two in *The Gospel According to Luke X–XXIV,* 1400.

points made with reference to v. 19 occur also in v. 20. First, the phrase, "This cup is the new covenant in my blood" is metaphorical in expression. The wine was being compared to Jesus' blood. Jesus further described the cup of His blood in terms of the new covenant, an allusion to Jerermiah 31:31 (cf. 2 Cor. 3:3, 6), which itself was based on the old covenant. The new covenant reflects the old covenant made by Yahweh and the people of Israel, "on the mountain, when Moses took the blood of twelve sacrificed oxen and sprinkled it, half on the people and half on the altar in token of the pact: 'See, the blood of the covenant which the Lord has made' (Exod 24:8). In this new form the covenant is established 'with my blood': Jesus' own blood is now involved in the . . . 'sacrifice of salvation' (Exod 24:5 . . .)."[14]

Second, the words "poured out for you" are sacrificial in intent. Jesus' death and shedding of His life's blood would be a sacrifice for the sins of others (cf. Isa. 59:7, 12; John 11:50; Rom. 3:15).

JESUS' DISCOURSE TO THE DISCIPLES, 22:21-38

Luke records Jesus delivering a discourse to His disciples after the Passover meal, a unique feature among the synoptic gospels (but cf. John 14–17). The Lucan discourse is composed of four parts: the prediction of the betrayal of Jesus (vv. 21-23); Jesus' correction of the disciples' misunderstanding of their role in the kingdom (vv. 24-30); the foretelling of Peter's denial of Jesus (vv. 31-34); the saying about the two swords (vv. 35-38).

THE PREDICTION OF THE
BETRAYAL OF JESUS, 22:21-23
22:21 Verses 21-23 consist of Jesus' prediction of His forthcoming betrayal at the hands of one of His own apostles. Having just depicted the divine perspective on the rationale for His death (vv. 15-20), in v. 21 Jesus alerts His disciples to the human involvement in that fate— it will come by the hand of one of those at the table with Jesus. Coming on the heels of the Passover meal itself, a testimony to Jesus' loyalty to His disciples, the very thought of one of them betraying Him intensifies the nature of the offense.
22:22 Verse 22 encapsulates the interfacing of the divine and human elements in Jesus' betrayal. From the divine perspective, the

14. The words are Fitzmyer's in *The Gospel According to Luke X–XXIV,* 1402.

death of Jesus, the Son of Man, has been planned all along by God. The term Luke uses for this plan is *hōrizmenon,* "horizoned off," or "determined," a word used by Luke elsewhere of the accomplishment of the divine will (Acts 2:23; 10:42; 11:29; 17:26, 31). With this word, then, Luke relates Judas's betrayal to the Father's plan of salvation history. But the phrase "Woe to that man by whom He is handed over" (*paradidotai*) emphasizes the human involvement pertaining to Jesus' death. The one who betrays Jesus, though acting unknowingly according to the divine plan, is nevertheless morally responsible for his actions and will be judged accordingly.

22:23   The disciples registered their shock and horror at such a dastardly deed, asking among themselves who would commit such an act.

JESUS' CORRECTION OF THE DISCIPLES' MISUNDERSTANDING
OF THEIR ROLE IN THE KINGDOM, 22:24-30
22:24   The next part of Jesus' discourse at the Passover table addressed the disciples' misconceptions as to their role in the kingdom of God, vv. 24-30. From this episode, the reader realizes that the eleven disciples who did not betray Jesus are not squeaky clean either. They, too, have their problems with Jesus' mission. In a sense, both Judas and the Eleven suffered from the same worldly desire for places of position and authority. The episode divides into two parts: the discussion of greatness (vv. 24-27) and the future role of the disciples in the kingdom (vv. 28-30). The latter part will come about only because the disciples will have learned the principle espoused in the former part—servanthood. Taken together, these two sections illustrate a theme dear to Jewish apocalypticism—suffering in this present age (vv. 24-28) leads to glory in the age to come (vv. 29-30); see also Luke 24:26; 2 Corinthians 3:16–5:10; Romans 8:17-25.

Verse 24 states the problem of perception under which the disciples labored—a dispute (*philoneikia,* "love of strife") arose among them as to who appeared to be the greatest. The word for "appear," *dokei,* pinpoints the apostles' problem—their understanding of greatness revolved around appearance's sake before others. The source of the argument is specified in Mark 10:35-37, where the sons of Zebedee asked Jesus for the highest positions of honor when He came into His kingdom, a request that made the other disciples indignant because they were jealous.

22:25   Jesus exposed the disciples' misunderstanding of their role in the kingdom by contrasting pagan rule over people with Christian service to people. Jesus gave two characteristics of the former. The kings (*basileis*) of the heathen lord their rule over them and then have the audacity to call themselves "benefactors." *Euergetēs,* "benefactor," was a title often given in the Hellenistic world to gods, princes, and Caesars. Caesar Augustus was implicitly so hailed in the Priene inscription, celebrating his birthday and giving thanks for his *euergē-mata,* "benefactions," as well as in the Decree of the Hellenes in Asia, recalling his *euergesia,* "benefaction." Nero was also given the title *euergetēs* (along with *sōtēr,* "savior") in an inscription from the Fayyum in Egypt.

22:26   But Jesus rejected that way of life for His followers. Rather, those who would be great among His followers must reverse the values of the world system. Kingdom ethics demand that those who would be the greatest should become like the youngest, i.e., less important (according to ancient standards). Those who want to lead must first learn to serve (*diakonōn*).

22:27   Jesus further illustrated the contrast between the kingdom of this world and the kingdom of God by raising a question, "By this world's standards, who is greater—the one who reclines at the table or the one serving that person at the table?" Obviously, the answer is the one reclining at the table. But that is not the way it is to be among Jesus' followers, for they must assume the role of a servant. Jesus used His own ministry as an illustration of that truth—"Yet I am here among you as the one who serves" (cf. Mark 10:45).

22:28   Despite the disciples' misunderstanding of the nature of greatness in the kingdom of God, Jesus encouraged them, praising their presence with Him during the trials of His ministry. Conzelmann's claim that the life of Christ (from Luke 4:13 to 22:3) was free of satanic temptation is surely disproved by Jesus' statement here.[15] The word used for Jesus' ministry, "trials," is *peirasmois,* the same term used of Jesus' temptation by Satan (4:2). This statement of praise may seem strange in light of the disciples' defection from Jesus during the events surrounding His trial and crucifixion, but, ultimately, they did prove faithful (cf. vv. 31-34).

22:29   Because of their faithfulness, Jesus promised the disciples a share in His kingdom, vv. 29-30. The promise is based on the spiritual

---

15. Conzelmann, *Theology of Luke,* 80-81.

and physical aspects of the kingdom. Verse 29 highlights the spiritual aspect—Jesus conferred on the disciples the kingship that was conferred on Him by the Father (cf. 1:32, 33; 19:11-27, 28-40). The word "confer" is based on the Greek word for covenant, *diathēke,* and accentuates the binding nature of Jesus' promise to His disciples.

22:30 The result of the promise to the disciples is that they will eat and drink in the kingdom of God and sit upon thrones as the judges of the twelve tribes of Israel. The reference to eating and drinking at the table in the kingdom recalls vv. 16 and 18 and the imagery there of the coming messianic banquet. The reference to the disciples sitting on the thrones as judges of the twelve tribes of Israel seems to draw on Psalm 122:4-5 and Daniel 7. Evans writes of this: "Since both OT passages in fact do appear together in Jewish exegesis and in the context of discussion concerned with the 'great ones of Israel' and the thrones that they will be given (see *Midrash Tanhuma* B, tractate *Qedoshim* 1.1), it seems that these are indeed the passages that ultimately lie behind Luke 22:30 and context. See also Rev. 21:12, 14."[16] Thus, v. 30 represents the physical aspect of the kingdom of God. It is an eschatological promise, the fulfillment of which awaits the second coming of Christ and the restoration of Israel.

In concluding this episode, we offer two further considerations. First, recalling our introduction to the Last Supper and the questions raised there, we have now answered three of those queries. (1) Text critically we argued that vv. 19b-20 are original to Luke's gospel. (2) The cultural backdrop of the Last Supper is the Passover seder. (3) From this we learned that the basic theological meaning of the Last Supper is twofold: historical and eschatological. Historically, the Last Supper is to be observed as a memorial of Christ's sacrificial death for our sins. Eschatologically, the Last Supper foreshadows the future messianic banquet and the arrival of the kingdom of God.

We now arrive at the fourth question relative to the Last Supper: What is the literary genre of the Last Supper, together with Jesus' discourse to the disciples after the meal? The answer is, a farewell speech. Raymond Brown has carefully shown that, in the Old Testament, famous people delivered farewell speeches before their deaths. In this regard note the farewell speeches of Jacob (Gen. 48:29–49:33), Moses (the whole book of Deuteronomy), Joshua (Josh. 22–24), and David (1 Chron. 28–29). These speeches attest to a well-established

16. Evans, *Luke,* 322.

pattern, comprised of some seven features.[17] We simply will list those features delineated by Brown and then point out what we suggest are the corresponding texts from Luke 22:15-46: (1) The speaker announces his imminent departure by way of death. Jesus' announcement of His death and betrayal fits this feature (vv. 15-22). (2) The announcement of impending death produces sorrow in the followers of the speaker/leader. The disciples' sorrowful, horrified reaction to Jesus' prediction of His betrayal corresponds here (v. 23), as does Peter's promise not to let Jesus die (v. 33). (3) The speaker provides instructions to his followers about how they should conduct their lives before the Lord subsequent to their leader's death. Jesus' admonition to the disciples to live as servants, not lords over, people fits this component (vv. 24-27). (4) The speaker appeals to his own past life in order to motivate his followers to serve the Lord. Jesus' words "But I am among you as the one who serves" (v. 27b) draw on the servant lifestyle of His ministry in order to properly motivate His disciples' behavior. (5) The leader forecasts the fate of his followers. Jesus' prediction about the disciples' future reign with Him (vv. 28-30), as well as His prophecy about Peter's denial and restoration (vv. 31-34), corresponds to this component. (6) The speaker/leader appoints a successor to carry on his work. Jesus' preformative statement conferring His kingship to the disciples (vv. 29-30) does this. (7) The speaker concludes his farewell address with a prayer. Jesus' prayer in the Garden of Gethsemane obviously reminds one of this aspect (vv. 39-46).

The second consideration we offer in concluding this episode is that the juxtaposition of the disciples' failure to properly perceive Jesus (vv. 24-27) with the prediction of their future reign over Israel (vv. 28-30) attests to our theory that certain persons or places in Luke's gospel foreshadow the coming restoration of Israel. There is an unmistakable, intimate connection between the twelve disciples (including Judas's future replacement, Acts 1:15-26) and the twelve tribes of Israel in v. 30. This prophecy that the disciples will one day judge Israel, alongside of Christ, surely bespeaks of Israel's future reconstitution. We can detect, therefore, a pattern existing between the disciples and Israel. The disciples' misunderstanding of Jesus (vv. 24-27) and subsequent forsaking of Him at the cross (v. 31) remind one of Israel's confusion over and rejection of Jesus the Messiah. Conversely, the disciples' restoration to Jesus and reign with Him in the kingdom

17. Brown, *The Gospel According to John xiii–xxi*, 597-601.

corresponds to Israel's future conversion and restoration to Jesus as their Messiah.

PETER'S DENIAL FORETOLD, 22:31-34

22:31   Having spoken of one of the Twelve who would betray Him and exposed an inappropriate attitude about greatness that arose among the apostles, Jesus went on to predict another form of infidelity that would surface among His followers—Peter's denial. Luke abruptly introduced another ominous note into the passion narrative, the forecasting of Peter's betrayal. The repetition of the vocative, "Simon, Simon," is for emphasis' sake. The reference to Satan's seeking after Simon reminds the reader of Judas's diabolical scheme (v. 3). The plural pronoun "you" (*hymas*) encompasses all twelve of the disciples. Satan's plot would involve sifting the disciples like a sieve separates chaff from wheat. In other words, the coming crucifixion of Jesus would sorely test the faith of the disciples. The thought in v. 31 approximates Job 1:7; 2:2. There Satan sought permission from God to test Job and thus to cause him to stumble in his faith.

22:32   But Jesus' prayer will prevail on behalf of Peter and the disciples. Peter now becomes the actor on center stage, with Satan accusing him on the one hand and Jesus defending him as his advocate on the other hand. Jesus' intercession for Peter would eventually reestablish the apostle's faith, that despite the momentary lapse in his walk with Christ. The intransitive participle *epistrepsas* means to turn and in Luke is a synonym for repentance from sin (17:4; Acts 3:19; 9:35; 11:21; 14:15; 15:19; 26:18, 20). By this word, then, Jesus indicated that Peter would repent of His denial and return to His Lord. Having done that, Peter would then be obligated to strengthen or establish the faith of his brothers in Christ. For Peter's role in strengthening the faith of the early church, see Acts 1–5; cf. also 1 Peter 5:10.

22:33   But Peter's impetuousness got the best of him. He told Jesus that, in effect, he would never deny Him. On the contrary, Peter intended to go with Jesus to prison and even death. Although these words of the apostle were not fulfilled before the crucifixion of Christ, they were afterward (see Acts 5:18; 12:3 and also the tradition of Peter's martyrdom upside down for Christ in Rome, *Acts of Peter* 30:41).

22:34   Jesus curtly responded that, before the rooster crowed that day, Peter would deny three times that he knew Jesus. Fitzmyer catches the sense of the prophecy—Peter's "triple denial will come so quickly that a cock will not even be able to crow twice."[18]

In concluding this episode, we mention the parallel existing between Peter and Israel, suggesting that the former is a proleptic picture of the latter. That there is an intimate connection between the two is hinted in v. 32, where Peter is told that, after having denied Christ and returning to Him, he should strengthen his brothers. As the commentators recognize, the scope of the challenge to Peter goes beyond the twelve disciples to encompass the early church, composed of Jewish Christians (see Acts 1–5). In other words, Peter is connected to the Jewish people. We may surmise, then, that Luke sees in Peter a pattern which Israel will one day follow. Just as Peter denied his Lord (cf. vv. 4, 54-62) but was later restored (vv. 31-33), so Israel, though presently rejecting her Messiah, will one day be "strengthened," i.e., restored to Him.

THE "TWO SWORDS," 22:35-38

22:35   Marshall's insightful introduction to vv. 35-38 and Jesus' saying about the two swords merits quoting:

> This is the final conversation-piece in the extended dialogue in the upper room. It brings to a climax the misunderstanding and earthly-mindedness of the disciples which has already figured three times in the dialogue, and which stands over against the promises and warnings of Jesus. . . . The section begins with an appeal by Jesus to the experiences of their earlier mission when they went out in faith and yet experienced no lack. But now conditions are different: the growth of opposition to Jesus and to his followers means that they must go out well prepared, even going to the length of regarding a sword as an indispensable accompaniment. The saying can be regarded only as grimly ironical, expressing the intensity of the opposition which Jesus and the disciples will experience, endangering their very lives. They are summoned to a faith and courage which is prepared to go to the limit. . . . This situation arises for there is an OT prophecy which must be fulfilled in Jesus, the saying that associates the Servant of Yahweh with evil-doers; Jesus sees it as a prophecy of his death, for his life is now drawing to an end. But the disciples fail to understand; taking Jesus literally, they produce two swords, and Jesus has to rebuke them for their lack of comprehension—a lack that will become even more evident when Jesus is arrested.[19]

18. Fitzmyer, *The Gospel According to Luke X–XXIV,* 1426.
19. Marshall, *Commentary on Luke,* 823-24.

Jesus concluded the Last Supper discourse by mentioning to the disciples the things He earlier forbade them to take on their missionary journey: purse, knapsack, and sandals (9:1-6; 10:1-12). He then asked His followers if they lacked anything on those journeys, to which they responded, "not a thing."

22:36 However, things would now be different. Whereas the followers of Jesus traveled lightly on those previous evangelistic forays, now the road ahead of them would be long and hard, requiring a different kind of preparation. The one having a purse should carry it, and likewise with the knapsack. The one not having those things (presumably the purse and knapsack) should sell his cloak and buy a sword. Jesus' command raises two questions. First, what is the understood object of "not having"? Two basic views have been offered. (1) The verb "not having" refers back to the purse and the knapsack (the sense of which is reflected in our translation). (2) The verb refers ahead to "sword." Thus, the one not having a sword should sell his cloak in order to buy one. But the problem with this view is that it is unlikely that the understood object of a verb would come as the last word in the sentence. The first view is therefore preferable. Its meaning then will be, the person who has a purse with money in it is to buy a sword, while the person who has no money is to sell his cloak and buy a sword.

Jesus' command raises a second question: What is the significance of the sword? Marshall identifies three suggestions which have been made.[20] (1) The sword is to be taken literally, with reference to an anticipated eschatological or messianic conflict between Jesus and the kingdoms of this world (cf. Rev. 19:11-21; see also the *War Scroll* of the Qumran community). But the problem with this view, as Marshall observes, is that such an idea does not play a role in either Luke's passion narrative or in the early church's thinking in the events surrounding the cross. (2) The sword is to be taken literally with reference to a political connotation, in the sense that Jesus was contemplating armed resistance against Rome in zealot fashion. But Luke's passion narrative itself rules out such an interpretation, for in vv. 38 and 51 Jesus categorically forbade the disciples from using their swords for defense. (3) The sword is to be taken figuratively in the sense that the disciples must prepare themselves for the spiritual conflict that was

20. Ibid., 825.

soon to accompany Jesus' crucifixion (cf. Eph. 6:11-17). This is the most accurate view of the three.

22:37 Jesus went on to apply Scripture to His impending fate: "All that has been written must find its end in me—'He was counted with transgressors'; for all that concerns me is coming to an end." The passage Jesus quoted was Isaiah 53:12, a text referring to the fate of the suffering servant. By applying the verb to Himself, Jesus was saying that He would share the destiny of criminals. This is seen most vividly in His crucifixion between two criminals (23:33). There may also be the idea of Jesus and His followers being classified by opponents of the faith as outlaws (as seen in Acts). The closing words of the verse, "for all that concerns me is coming to an end," refer to God's plan of salvation as adumbrated in the Old Testament coming to fulfillment in Jesus (cf. 24:27).

22:38 The disciples' response revealed their misunderstanding of Jesus' words about the sword. They pointed out to Him that they had two swords, supposedly with which to fight the entire Roman army (cf. vv. 49-50). Jesus' answer, "Enough of this" (*ikanon estin*), is to be preferred to that of, "it is enough." The latter might imply that Jesus affirmed the disciples' suggestion, acknowledging that two swords would be sufficient for the conflict. But the context clearly rules out that rendering. Rather, what Jesus meant was that, so complete was the disciples' misunderstanding of His saying about the need to buy a sword, that He refused to explain it any more. We might colloquially render Jesus' words thus, "I give up!"

JESUS' PRAYER ON
THE MOUNT OF OLIVES, 22:39-46

Commonly called the Garden of Gethsemene ("oil press") episode (see Matt. 26:36/Mark 14:32), Luke labels the place of Jesus' prayer on the night of His betrayal as the Mount of Olives, the mountain due east of the Kidron Valley. The plot thickens as Jesus courageously faces His upcoming ordeal, that in contrast to the sleeping, spiritually obtuse disciples.

22:39 After the celebration of the Passover meal, Jesus went up to the Mount of Olives, as was His custom (cf. 21:37). The place would have been familiar to Judas. The disciples of Jesus followed Him to the spot. Luke may intend that the word "follow" (*akolouthein*) evoke irony, for the word is used elsewhere of being a close follower of

Jesus (see 5:11), something not characteristic of the disciples in this particular episode (see v. 45).

22:40   When they reached the spot (Gethsemane, according to Mark 14:32), Jesus admonished His disciples to pray in order that they would not enter into temptation. Jesus understood that His forthcoming ordeal would be a test of the disciples' fidelity. The words "enter into temptation" (*perasmon*) mean to succumb to its evil power (cf. 46; 11:4).

22:41   Then Jesus withdrew from the disciples about a stone's throw away. The word for "withdraw" (*apestasthē*) means to pull away (cf. Acts 21:1) and bespeaks of the difficulty of Jesus' going to be alone. He knelt and prayed. The Lucan emphasis on prayer is clear in the episode as a whole (vv. 40-41, 45-46).

22:42   Jesus prayed, "Father, if you will, remove this cup from me. Yet not my will, but yours be done." Jesus' prayer generates at least four comments. First, it conveys the intimacy of Jesus and God. Jesus called God His father (*pater*; cf. 11:2). Mark uses an even dearer term of affection in Jesus' prayer in the Garden concerning God; He called Him *abba* (Aramaic for "daddy"). Second, the prayer acknowledges the destiny of Jesus. "Cup" (*potērion*) carries the Old Testament sense of destiny (Isa. 51:17, 22; Jer. 25:15; 49:12; Lam. 4:21), and not a pleasant one at that. Third, the prayer attests to the humanity of Jesus. Jesus, human being that He was, did not want to undergo the ordeal facing Him. He asked the Father to remove it from Him. The impending cross cast its shadow of horror upon Jesus. The physical, emotional, and spiritual agony of the crucifixion stirred up fear and dread, even in Jesus, the Son of Man. Fitzmyer puts it well, "Nowhere else in the gospel tradition is the humanity of Jesus so evident as here."[21] Fourth, the sentiments of Jesus forever immortalized in the words "not my will but yours be done" reveal His dependency on God the Father's desire.

22:43   The text critical difficulty of vv. 43-44 does not admit to a conclusive answer. The oldest manuscript evidence is divided. Those manuscripts retaining the verses include Sinaiticus, D, K. Those manuscripts omitting the verses are p75, A, B, and so on. Without being dogmatic about it, it seems to us that, on the one hand, because the manuscripts not containing the verses constitute the shortest reading, the verses

---

21. Fitzmyer, *The Gospel According to Luke X–XXIV,* 1442.

are probably not original to Luke.[22] On the other hand, with Ellis, we see no reason why the verses could not be part of a genuine extra-canonical tradition, but not Lucan[23] (cf. John 7:53–8:1, 7). For that reason, we believe it to be well advised to still analyze the two verses. According to v. 43, after Jesus' prayer an angel from heaven appeared to Him to strengthen Him.

22:44 Because of the angel's encouragement Jesus, in His agony (*agōnia*), prayed all the harder. His sweat became like drops of blood that fell to the ground. The words are figurative. Jesus did not literally sweat drops of blood. Rather His perspiration was so profuse that it was like blood spilling on the ground.

22:45 Rising up from praying, Jesus came to the disciples and found them sleeping, because of grief. In stark contrast to His struggle in prayer, Jesus found the disciples asleep. However, the Lucan comment "because of grief" somewhat excuses them, attributing their sleep to being worn out by grief, undoubtedly because of Jesus' imminent departure.

22:46 The episode concludes basically the way it began, with Jesus admonishing His disciples to get up, and not to sleep but rather to pray in order that they might not enter (succumb) into temptation. The "temptation" (*peirasmon*) immediately follows in the next episode.

THE ARREST OF JESUS, 22:47-53

Even as Jesus spoke about the temptation which would soon face Him and His disciples, Judas and the temple authorities arrived on the scene. The episode contains three elements: Judas's betrayal, vv. 47-48; the disciples' impulsive action, vv. 50-51; Jesus' explanation of His arrest, vv. 52-53.

22:47 Judas's notorious betrayal of Jesus occurs in vv. 47-48. Luke writes in v. 47 that just as Jesus told the disciples to awake, a crowd suddenly appeared. The crowd, as v. 52 will indicate, included the religious leaders. According to John 18:3, 12, Roman soldiers also formed part of the crowd. Leading the mob was Judas, one of the Twelve. Judas drew near to Jesus in order to kiss Him. From Mark 14:44-45 we learn that Judas's treachery consisted of identifying Jesus

22. See ibid., 1443-44.
23. Ellis, *The Gospel of Luke,* 258.

in the dark by approaching Him and kissing *philēin* Him. Although *philēin* could mean "to love," it was also used as a concrete expression of love, i.e., a kiss.

22:48   Jesus' reply was as quick as it was powerful. He asked Judas if it was with a kiss that he delivered up the Son of Man. The query exposed Judas's sordid plot—betraying Jesus with the kiss of death. The word for "deliver" became a technical term in the gospels for Jesus' arrest and death (*paradidōs*; see Luke 9:44; 18:31, 32; 22:22; 24:7).

22:49   Verses 49-51 recount the disciples' impulsive action at the arrest of Jesus. It is both humorous and tragic. In v. 49 we are told that some of the disciples around Jesus realized what was happening, and they asked Jesus if they should strike the captors with a sword. Apparently two of the disciples had carried with them the two swords referred to earlier in v. 38.

22:50   Then one of them (Peter according to John 18:10) cut off the ear of the high priest's servant! Only in Luke 22:50 and John 18:10 are we told it was the right ear. This has suggested to some that Luke was dependent in part on the gospel of John for his passion narrative. But that is debatable. It is more likely that both writers record the historical incident from their own sources.

22:51   Verse 51 makes clear that Jesus wanted no part in an insurrection against His government. He told His disciples who had resorted to violence, "Let it be as far as this." Colloquially we might render these words, "Stop it! No more of this!" Then Jesus touched the servant's ear (Luke uses the diminutive form here, *ōtiou,* i.e., the outer ear) and healed it. Jesus was practicing what He earlier preached, "Love your enemies, do good to those who hate you" (Luke 6:27; cf. vv. 28-33).

22:52   In vv. 52-53 Jesus exemplifies calmness and courage as He explains why He is being arrested. In doing so, He demonstrates that He, not the captors, is in control of the situation. In v. 52 Jesus addresses the chief priests, the temple officers, and the elders, asking them if they came with swords and clubs to arrest a robber (cf. 10:30). The word for "robber," *lēstēs,* can also mean revolutionary.

22:53   Jesus continued, inquiring why they had not arrested Him while He taught in the temple on a daily basis. From the human perspective, the religious authorities had not done so at that time because they were afraid of the inevitable public outcry that their action would precipitate (see 19:47-48). But Jesus provided the spiritual rationale behind the situation, "But now this is your hour, and the power of darkness." Jesus meant that the Jewish leaders were playing out the scheme of Satan. It was the climactic hour of evil's rule. But actually, even Satan and the forces of darkness, Jewish leaders included, were accomplishing the divine plan for achieving the means for saving humanity.

PETER'S DENIALS OF JESUS, 22:54-62

Despite their various perspectives and portrayals of Peter's denials,[24] the four gospels agree on the basics: all four record three accusations of Peter and his three denials; all four agree that the denials of Peter occurred at the house of the high priest; and all agree that the first accusation made of Peter was voiced by a female servant. We turn now to Luke's record of Peter's threefold denial.

22:54 The authorities arrested Jesus and brought Him to the house of the high priest. This incident marked the beginning of a twofold trial of Jesus—a religious one (22:54-71) and a civil one (23:1-25). Luke 22:54-66 seems to speak of a night trial (see v. 55, a fire was kindled; v. 66, day broke after the events of vv. 54-65). According to Matthew 26:57, the high priest's name was Caiaphas (who held that office from A.D. 18 to 36). John 18:13, 17, 24 record a prior meeting of Jesus with Annas, a former high priest and father-in-law of Caiaphas. Annas continued to exert his influence over the high priestly office after his own term expired. If he indeed was the owner of the money-changing operation in the temple, he will have relished the opportunity to have the first crack at Jesus. Jesus' meeting at night before the high priest already set the tone for the trial; it was a kangaroo court marred by numerous illegalities. Comparing the four gospels' presentations of the two trials of Jesus with the Mishnaic Code for the conduct of the Sanhedrin, some twenty-seven illegalities have been detected, including the following, according to Pentecost:

> The regular place for the meeting of the Sanhedrin was in the Temple, but they led Jesus away to the house of the high-priest Caiaphas, situated in a place just outside the present wall of the city, where all the chief priests and elders and scribes had been summoned to meet. Nor was the legal hour of meeting for trials in the night. Other features in the

24. On that relationship, see Evans, *Luke,* 327-29.

illegality practised in the trials of Jesus were: undue haste, seeking or bribing witnesses, neglecting to warn the witnesses solemnly before they should give evidence, forcing the accused to testify against Himself, judicial use of the prisoner's confession, and failure to release the prisoner when there was failure of agreement between witnesses.[25]

But Luke's major concern at this point in the narrative is to focus on Peter, who followed Jesus at a distance. The word "follow" (*ēkoloutbei*) again evokes irony—Peter followed Jesus as His disciple, but only at a distance. The statement forms, in effect, a theological oxymoron—one cannot follow Jesus as a disciple at a distance.

22:55 When they had kindled a fire in the middle of the courtyard and were sitting together, Peter sat in the midst of them. We are not told who "they" were, but they probably included underlings of the Jewish authorities (v. 63). The mention of the courtyard suggests that the high priest's house was spacious and luxurious, not unlike the expensive houses excavated outside the west wall of Jerusalem today in the Jewish quarter. In Jesus' time, the high priest's house was located there, in the elegant Herodian section.

22:56 Verse 56 records the first accusation made against Peter. A servant girl, also sitting with the others at the fire, began to stare at Peter. She exclaimed, "This one was also with Him."

22:57 Then came Peter's first denial, "I do not know Him, woman!" The word for "deny," *arneumai,* was a word laden with theological meaning in the early church. It meant to abandon the faith (cf. Matt. 10:33 with Luke 9:26; see also 2 Tim. 2:12-13).

22:58 The second accusation of Peter was made a little later by someone else. The Greek masculine pronoun, *heteros,* indicates that it was a male. The man also recognized that Peter was one of the disciples of Jesus. Peter's second denial was emphatic, "Man, I am not!"

22:59 After an hour passed, someone else insisted that Peter was one of the disciples. His Galilean accent gave him away (cf. Matt. 26:7). The third accusation had now been made.

22:60 For a third time Peter denied the accusation, this time telling the person that he did not know what he was talking about. Matthew 26:74 records that Peter cursed at this point. But even as Peter spoke, the cock crowed.

---

25. Pentecost, *The Words and Works of Jesus Christ,* 462-63. But see the cautious assessment of that evidence by Brown in *The Gospel According to John xiii–xxi,* 796-97.

22:61   Only Luke mentions that, at that moment, the Lord (Jesus) turned and looked at Peter. Jesus may have been guarded in the courtyard, or perhaps He was being taken from the high priest's house to the next stage of His trial. Jesus' look brought back to Peter's mind Jesus' prophecy that before the cock crowed, Peter would have denied his Lord three times.

22:62   Upon this realization, Peter went outside (probably the courtyard) and wept bitterly. The first part of Jesus' prophecy had come true; Peter did deny his Lord. But so would the second part eventually come true—Peter would be restored (v. 32).

THE MOCKING AND BEATING OF JESUS, 22:63-65

The religious trial of Jesus continued as He was brought to the Sanhedrin (vv. 66-71). Before that, He was treated cruelly by the underlings of the Jewish leaders, vv. 63-65.

22:63   The men who were holding Jesus in custody began to mock Him and beat Him. These men were the same ones who comprised part of the crowd which apprehended Jesus on the Mount of Olives (v. 47).

22:64   The guards played blindman's bluff with Jesus, blindfolding Him, and then asking Him to prophesy who it was that was hitting Him. Their ridicule and taunting of Jesus was designed to add insult to the injuries they inflicted on His body. However, the very thing they mocked, Jesus' prophetic ability, had just been ironically vindicated in the previous scene: Peter denied his Lord three times, just as Jesus predicted.

22:65   The guards hurled many other insults at Jesus, blaspheming (*blasphēmountes*) Him (cf. Acts 13:45; 18:6).

JESUS BEFORE THE SANHEDRIN, 22:66-71

Verses 66-71 record Jesus' appearance before the Sanhedrin. The council (v. 66) was made up of approximately seventy members, some of whom were priests and Sadducees, whereas others were Pharisees (see Acts 23:1-9). Many, whether aligning themselves with the Sadducees or the Pharisees, were professional scribes and teachers of the Law. This body represented the highest Jewish political and religious authority of the time. One of the tractates of the Mishnah named *Sanhedrin* describes this council's function.

22:66   When day came, which would still have been Nisan 15, or Passover, the elders of the people, both chief priests and scribes, assembled. Here Luke places the two groups of elder priests and scribes in apposition to the elders. Elsewhere Luke refers to the Sanhedrin in terms of three groups: elders, chief priests, and scribes (9:22; 20:1; Acts 4:5, 23; 6:12). Jesus was brought before the council (*synedrion* [Greek]; *Sanhedrin* [Hebrew]). According to the Mishnaic tractate *Sanhedrin*, the council was not to hold court on the Sabbath or a festival day. Their interrogation of Jesus on Passover apparently broke that rule.

22:67   The Sanhedrin tried to secure a confession from Jesus in order to charge Him. They asked Him point blank to tell them if He was the Messiah. If they could get Jesus to admit to that title, they would have political grounds for convicting Him, for they would tell the Roman government that Jesus was a dangerous revolutionary and should be dealt with accordingly. But Jesus deftly skirted the issue by responding that even if He were to confess to being the Messiah, the Sanhedrin would never ever (*ou mē*) believe Him. To even answer their question was, therefore, pointless. Jesus' answer was sort of a rendition of pleading the Fifth Amendment: "I refuse to answer on the grounds that it may incriminate me."

22:68   Jesus added that if He were to ask the authorities a question, they would not answer Him. The meaning of Jesus' reply is unclear. Perhaps He was "fighting fire with fire" by saying "I will not answer your question (v. 67) because you will not answer my question (v. 68)." If so, v. 68 may be an allusion back to the discussion recorded in 20:1-8, where the chief priests and the teachers of the Law refused to answer Jesus' question regarding the source of John's authority to baptize.

22:69   Sidestepping the issue of His messiahship, Jesus pronounced to the Sanhedrin that from then on the Son of Man would be seated at the right hand of the power, or throne, of God. Jesus' statement combines two Old Testament verses: Daniel 7:13, "the son of man," and Psalm 110:1, "sitting at the right hand." Jesus was forecasting His future exaltation as the Son of Man over His enemies, beginning with His resurrection (see Acts 2:32-36). His reign will be consummated at the Second Coming (see Luke 21:27). There was probably also a juridical connotation to Jesus' words here—one day He will be the judge over the very ones who put Him on trial (cf. 11:30).

22:70   The Sanhedrin replied, "Then you are the Son of God." Their conclusion that Jesus was claiming to be the Son of God was based on the Jewish belief that the Son of Man of Daniel 7:13 was heavenly in origin and therefore divine. The Sanhedrin thought they now had caught Jesus in blasphemy. Jesus' response, "You say that I am," was designed to both give tacit admission to the title but at the same time avoid self-incrimination. It was as though He said to the Sanhedrin, "If *you* say so." The tragedy was that the council said it, but they did not believe it.

22:71   The Sanhedrin understood Jesus' words to be a confession of the "crime" of claiming to be God. That was all the evidence they needed. Jesus, in the council's opinion, had not extricated Himself from the claim of being Messiah, the political overtone of which was sufficient enough testimony to send Him to the Roman governor, Pilate (23:1).

HOMILETICAL SUGGESTIONS

The difficult question that the preacher who wishes to preach Luke 22–23 faces is not how to do it. That is a relatively easy question, we think, if one is prepared to move through the twenty-one episodes therein. We believe our commentary on those sections should prove helpful for that task—culturally, historically, grammatically, and theologically. Rather, the difficult question confronting the minister concerning Luke 22–23 is when to preach the material. It is probably too much to ask one's congregation to focus a month of Sundays on the events of the passion, because its interest may wane. We suggest, therefore, that the preacher consider holding a Passion Week series the week of Good Friday and Easter Sunday. On Monday through Thursday nights, Luke 22–23 could be treated (albeit in cursory fashion). That would mean each evening would cover approximately five episodes. The advantage of this approach is that a church's sentiments about the passion narrative obviously run high during that Holy Week, which would sustain interest. It should, therefore, be receptive to an extended series on the subject, but in a short space of time.

Also, perhaps the preacher would consider assigning a few of the nights to church members who have speaking abilities. That would lighten the load of an already very busy week for the minister, as well as add creativity to the series. We have done something like this before, and it was extremely effective.

While we are on the subject of the passion narrative, we suggest two other types of sermonic genres for covering the passion narrative during Holy Week, especially the Last Supper. The first suggestion is to hold a "Living Lord's Supper." In this silent animation of the Last Supper, thirteen men are chosen to represent Jesus and the twelve apostles. A script has been composed for each character to be read by a narrator, with a musical backdrop provided. The drama is effective, sure to bring tears to the eyes of many. The play can be secured by writing to the Suburban Bible Church of Highland, Indiana, for a minimal cost. The second suggestion concerning the celebration of Holy Week, especially Maundy Thursday or Good Friday, is to celebrate the Christian version of the Passover, a two-hour meal, with an explanation of the Jewish feast, into which the Lord's Supper is interwoven. There are many messianic Jewish ministers and organizations (for example, Jews for Jesus) who provide their services to churches in accomplishing that task, one of the finest of whom is Dr. Louis Goldberg, Senior Professor of the Moody Bible Institute, Chicago, Illinois.

LUKE

CHAPTER

TWENTY THREE

THE TRIAL AND CRUCIFIXION
OF JESUS CHRIST

Luke 23 is given over to the three main events of the passion narrative—Jesus' trial before the Roman authorities (vv. 1-25), His crucifixion (vv. 26-43), and His death and burial (vv. 44-56). Before proceeding to the commentary proper, we will summarize the traditional understanding of the interplay of the roles of the Jewish and Roman rulers in the trial and crucifixion of Jesus. According to this viewpoint, the major portion of the fault rested with the Jewish leadership. Raymond Brown summarizes this position:

> The classical Christian position is that the Jewish authorities were the prime movers in Jesus' arrest, trial, and sentencing. They plotted against him because they disbelieved his messianic claims; the Sanhedrin tried him on a charge of blasphemy and sentenced him. However, either because the Romans alone could execute criminals or because the Jewish authorities wished to pass on to the Romans the public responsibility for killing Jesus, the Sanhedrin handed him over to Pilate on a political charge and blackmailed Pilate into passing sentence. (Some would even say that Pilate only ratified the Jewish death sentence.) In this view the Romans were little more than executioners.[1]

---

1. Brown, *The Gospel According to John, xiii–xxi*, 792, though the author provides qualifications for this viewpoint.

JESUS' TRIAL BEFORE THE ROMAN GOVERNMENT, 23:1-25

This section consists of four episodes: Jesus and Pilate, vv. 1-5; Jesus and Herod, vv. 6-12; Pilate's judgment, vv. 13-17; Jesus being handed over to be crucified, vv. 18-25.

JESUS AND PILATE, 23:1-5

23:1 We have in vv. 1-5 the account of Jesus' appearance before Pilate. The whole assembly of the Sanhedrin arose and led Jesus to him. The incident of Jesus appearing before Pilate is one of the few events from the life of Jesus referenced by extrabiblical literature. Tacitus, a Roman historian (ca. A.D. 56–116), wrote of this particular situation, "Christ, the source of that name [Christian] was executed by the procurator, Pontius Pilate, while Tiberius was reigning" (*Annals* 15.44.3).

23:2 The Sanhedrin proceeded to accuse Jesus of three things. First, referring derogatorily to Jesus as "this one" (*touton*), the council accused Jesus of perverting the nation of Israel. Here we find another incident attested to in extrabiblical literature, for the charges that Jesus was a sorcerer and deceiver of the people are found in Jewish tradition (Strack-B 2:262). The gist of the accusation was that Jesus supposedly turned the Jews against their God and His Law. Second, the Sanhedrin accused Jesus of forbidding the payment of taxes to Caesar, an obvious distortion of what Jesus said earlier (20:25). Third, they said Jesus claimed to be a messianic king. The accusation probably reflected the joyful shouts of the pilgrims at Jesus' triumphant entry, "Blessed is the king who comes in the name of the Lord" (19:38). The obvious intention of the Sanhedrin was to convince Pilate that Jesus was a rival king.

23:3 The third accusation caught Pilate's attention. He asked Jesus if He was the king of the Jews. Jesus answered Pilate diplomatically, if not nonchalantly, "If you say." His response was un-incriminating.

23:4 Pilate responded to the chief priests and the gathering crowd that he found nothing in Jesus that called for Him to die, that is, worthy of capital punishment. Pilate recognized that Jesus posed no threat to Roman authority (see vv. 14, 22; see also John 18:38; 19:4, 6).

23:5 The Sanhedrin was not content with Pilate's conclusion. They insisted that Jesus had stirred up the Jews with His teaching throughout Judea (the generic name for Israel; cf. 1:5), beginning in Galilee and continuing to that very place, i.e., Jerusalem (cf. v. 2b). The retort was not simply religious in nature. The Jewish council undoubtedly

wanted to implicate Jesus as a political insurrectionist. Other messianic claimants had also stirred up the Jews against Rome (Acts 5:35-37
records two of them). Josephus relates a number of such incidents
during the first century A.D.[2]

JESUS AND HEROD, 23:6-12

23:6   Verses 6-12 record Jesus' appearance before Herod Antipas.
Before examining this section we need to make mention of a once
popular theory that Luke's episode of Jesus before Herod was a leg-
end that grew out of Psalm 2, in which Herod and Pilate represent the
basileis and *archontes* who in the psalm plot against the Lord's anointed. Furthermore, Luke 23:6-12 is compared with Acts 4:27-28. Fitzmyer
summarizes the rationale of the view and then critiques it, a view popularized by the classical liberal theologian A. Loisy.[3] The reasons proposed for this view are: (1) Acts 4:27-28 speaks of Herod and Pilate
gathered in Jerusalem against God's holy servant, alluding to Psalm
2:1-2; this is the tradition that Luke has supposedly spun into a yarn.
(2) If the scene were historical, how could Mark have failed to come
across it? (3) Is it likely that Pilate would have sent a political prisoner
to be tried before Herod within his own jurisdiction? (4) The chief
priests and scribes seem to accompany Jesus to Herod (23:10), but v.
15 implies that they have remained with Pilate ("back to us"). (5) Ridicule of Jesus by Herod and his soldiers (23:11) is introduced here to
compensate for Mark 15:16-17, which Luke omits.

Yet, as Fitzmyer argues, none of these reasons is without a countering consideration: (1) Why is Acts 4:27-28 not merely a reflection of
Luke 25:6-12, the normal expectation in the second volume of any
author's work? That there may be an allusion to Psalm 2:1-2 is acceptable, but does that allusion certainly explain the genesis of the story
and its details? The allusion is at best vague. (2) Apart from Herod's
involvement in the execution of John the Baptist (Mark 6:14-22), how
much interest does Mark display in Herod? He could have omitted the
scene, just as John did. (3) Pilate may have sent Jesus to Herod to get a
problem off his hands. (4) Verse 15 does not tell whether the chief
priests and scribes had accompanied Jesus when He returned to Pilate. Pilate's use of "us" could refer to himself and his own entourage,
apart from the priests and scribes. (5) The reason for the Lucan omis-

2. *Ant.* 18:4.23; 20:97-102.
3. Fitzmyer, *The Gospel According to Luke X–XXIV,* 1478-79.

sion is obvious in the course of his passion narrative, where Roman soldiers do not appear until 23:36. Fitzmyer concludes that the upshot is that the evidence does not all point toward Lucan fabrication. The appearance of Jesus before Herod could be just as historical as the Lucan depiction of the morning session of the Sanhedrin interrogation. We concur with the view that asserts the historicity of Luke 23:6-16.

When Pilate heard the Sanhedrin mention that Jesus originated in Galilee, he saw a way to get rid of his "problem." He asked Jesus if He was indeed a man from Galilee.

23:7   When Pilate confirmed that Jesus was from Galilee, and therefore under Herod Antipas's jurisdiction, he sent Him to the Jewish ruler, who happened to be visiting in Jerusalem during those days. Herod was probably in town for Passover. He lodged in the family's palace in Jerusalem. The word "sent off" (*anepempsen*) was a technical word for sending a prisoner from one authority to another (see Acts 25:21).

23:8   Herod was very pleased to see Jesus, having wanted to meet Him for a long time because of the report of His accomplishments (see 9:9). He even hoped to get Jesus to perform a miraculous sign (*sēmeion*) for him.

23:9   Herod kept questioning Jesus with many words, but to no avail. Jesus would not answer him (cf. Isa. 53:7). Jesus' silence showed His strength of character and command of the situation.

23:10   All the while, the chief priests and the scribes stood by, vehemently accusing Jesus, obviously trying to get Herod to declare Him guilty.

23:11   But Herod could find no fault with Jesus. So he treated Him with contempt and ridicule instead (cf. 18:32; 22:63; 23:36). He and his soldiers, probably his bodyguard, threw a shining garment on Jesus, perhaps as a mockery of His supposed kingship (cf. Mark 15:17-20). Then Herod sent (cf. v. 7) Jesus back to Pilate.

23:12   There is sadistic irony in the statement that, thanks to their mutual mistreatment of Jesus, Herod and Pilate, who until then were enemies, became friends. It would have been natural for a Jewish tetrarch such as Herod to dislike a Roman overlord like Pilate. Perhaps one of the reasons Pilate sent Jesus to Herod (besides ridding himself of a problem) was to curry the favor of an enemy with a political courtesy. In any event, in light of Deuteronomy 19:15, Luke most probably included the episode of Jesus before Herod because he constituted the second witness to Jesus' innocence. Pilate was the first.

PILATE'S JUDGMENT OF JESUS, 23:13-17

23:13 When Jesus was returned to Pilate, the Roman prefect summoned the chief priests, the leaders, and the people to hear his verdict. As Fitzmyer notes, Pilate may have called the people in the hope of finding support among the populace for Jesus in opposition to their religious leaders.[4]

23:14 Pilate began by acknowledging the charge of the Jewish leaders that Jesus was brought to him because He perverted the people. But Pilate told the leaders that he had examined Jesus in their presence and found no basis for the charges they leveled against Him. This was Pilate's second declaration of Jesus' innocence.

23:15 Pilate added that neither did Herod find that Jesus had committed anything worthy of death, or else he would not have sent Him back. Thus, two secular authorities, Pilate and Herod, acquitted Jesus of any capital offense.

23:16 Pilate determined, therefore, to discipline Jesus and then to let Him go. The type of discipline Pilate had in mind was probably scourging (cf. *paideuein,* with the word Mark 15:15 uses, *fragelloō* [flagellate]), hardly light punishment, designed as a deterrent for any future thought by Jesus to cause trouble. Pentecost wrote of this flogging technique:

> It took place, it would appear, on the platform where the trial had been held, and in the eyes of all. The victim was stripped and stretched against a pillar, or bent over a low post, his hands being tied, so that he had no means of defending himself. The instrument of torture was a sort of . . . cat-o'-nine-tails, with bits of iron or bone attached to the ends of the thongs. Not only did the blows cut the skin and draw blood, but not infrequently the victim died in the midst of the operation. Some have supposed that Pilate, out of consideration for Jesus, may have moderated either the number or the severity of the strokes; but, on the other hand, his plan of releasing Him depended on his being able to show the Jews that He had suffered severely. The inability of Jesus to bear His own cross to the place of execution was no doubt chiefly due to the exhaustion produced by this infliction; and this is a better indication of the degree of severity than mere conjecture.[5]

4. Ibid., 1484.
5. Pentecost, *The Words and Works of Jesus Christ,* 474.

23:17   Some manuscripts (Siniaticus, D, W) add to the narrative the following words, "now he was obliged to release to them at the feast one prisoner" (v. 17). Other manuscripts (p75, A, B) omit it. The latter manuscripts are probably correct. The text may be a later scribal addition to Luke on the basis of Mark 15:6 and Matthew 27:15. However, it should be noted that without v. 17 the logic behind the crowd's demand for Pilate to release Barabbas in v. 18 is less than clear. The verse itself refers to a custom called the "Passover privilege" whereby, at every Passover, a prisoner popular with the Jewish people was released, in order to placate them (cf. John 18:39).[6]

JESUS HANDED OVER TO BE CRUCIFIED, 23:18-25
23:18   Having heard Pilate's decision to release Jesus, both leaders and people cried out for Pilate to take Jesus away and release to them Barabbas instead. Luke omits Mark's note that the crowds were instigated to a fever pitch by the chief priests (15:11). The word for "do away with" (*airō*), according to Acts 21:36; 22:22, means to kill (see also Acts 3:13-15). The man the crowd demanded to be released was Barabbas, a Greek form of two Aramaic words, *bar* (son) and *abbas* (father). Fitzmyer has not missed the sad irony of releasing Barabbas and killing Jesus: "The irony of the scene is apparent. . . . They scream for the release of one called Barabbas, 'son of the father,' and reject him who is really the Father's Son (recall 2:49; 10:21, 21-22; 11:2; 22:29, 42)."[7]
23:19   Luke offers an editorial comment on Barabbas, noting that he was thrown into prison for murder and for causing a riot to break out in the city (cf. Matt. 27:16; Mark 15:7; John 18:40).
23:20   Pilate, however, wished to release Jesus and accordingly tried to address the crowd.
23:21   But the crowds refused to listen to Pilate. They cried out, "Crucify, crucify Him." The double reference indicates the intensity level of the crowd. The term for "crucify" is *stauroun*; it comes from the word "stake" (*stauros*). Crucifixion was a form of execution whereby the victim was hanged, usually by nailing, upon a large wooden stake, often with a crossbeam. It was used by the Romans in cases of treason and insurrection.

---

6. See the article by C. B. Chavel, "The Releasing of a Prisoner on the Eve of the Passover in Ancient Jerusalem," *JBL* 60 (1941), 273-78.
7. Fitzmyer, *The Gospel According to Luke X–XXIV*, 1489.

23:22 For a third time Pilate declared Jesus' innocence. The Roman prefect asked the crowd what wrong Jesus had done, seeing that he himself found nothing worthy of His death. Once again, Pilate asserted that he was going to discipline Jesus and then let Him go.

23:23 But the crowds with loud outcries insisted that Jesus be crucified, and their voices prevailed.

23:24 Alas, Pilate acquiesced to the crowd's demand. His name has lived in infamy ever since.

23:25 Pilate released Barabbas, the man who was imprisoned for rioting and murder. But he delivered Jesus, the innocent one, over to the will of the people (cf. John 19:1-42).

Jesus' Crucifixion, 23:26-43

Before proceeding to Luke's account of Jesus' crucifixion, vv. 26-43, some important historical considerations need to be addressed. First, is Jesus' crucifixion attested to in extrabiblical literature? Second, why did Pilate show such cowardice in the face of the Jews' demand to crucify Jesus? Third, did the Jews have the power to implement capital punishment? Fourth, what happened at a crucifixion?

First, outside of the New Testament there are only a few brief reports of Jesus' crucifixion. Evans collects the data,[8] beginning with a letter by one Mara bar Serapion to his son (ca. A.D. 73): "For what advantage did . . . the Jews [gain] by the death of their wise king, because from the same time their kingdom was taken away?" From Josephus (ca. A.D. 90) we have: "Pilate, upon hearing him accused by men of the highest standing among us, had condemned him to be crucified" (*Ant.* 18.63-64). The Roman historian Tacitus (ca. A.D. 110–120) reported: "This name [i.e., "Christian"] originates from 'Christus' who was sentenced to death by the procurator, Pontius Pilate, during the reign of Tiberius" (*Annals* 15.44). According to the Babylonian Talmud: "On the eve of Passover they hanged Jesus the Nazarene. And a herald went out, in front of him, for forty days saying: 'He is going to be stoned, because he practiced sorcery and enticed and led Israel astray. Anyone who knows anything in his favor, let him come and plead in his behalf.' But not having found anything in his favor, they hanged him on the eve of Passover" (*b. Sanh.* 43a).

---

8. Evans, *Luke.*

Second, Pilate capitulated to the crowd's request to crucify Jesus because of his previous failed relationships with the Jews. Pilate, the Roman prefect of Judea from A.D. 26 to 36, was not well thought of by the Jews, to say the least. Josephus writes of his blundering dealings with the nation of Israel (*Ant.* 18.55-62; 4:85-89). Three in particular call for comment: (1) When he first became governor of Judea, Pilate sent his troops into Jerusalem with the ensigns on their standards. For the Jews, an image to Caesar was tantamount to idolatry. When the people protested Pilate's actions, he threatened them with death, but they were not intimidated. Pilate backed off from his threat. (2) Pilate confiscated funds out of the temple treasury to fund an aqueduct to bring water to Jerusalem. The Jews of Jerusalem were furious, but this time the governor carried through with his threat to kill those who opposed him. He did so by having his soldiers dress as civilians and then, at Pilate's signal, they attacked the protesters. (3) Pilate hung votive shields, engraved with emperor Tiberius's name, in the palace of Herod in Jerusalem. A Jewish delegation responded by appealing to the emperor, who rebuked Pilate and ordered the removal of the shields. The final straw had now come with the Jews' demand for Jesus' crucifixion. Were Pilate to refuse their request, the emperor would surely depose the governor, especially if he tolerated a rival king (see John 19:12-15).

Third, according to John 18:31, the Jewish authorities did not have the legal power to implement capital punishment. R. Brown evaluates the evidence:

There is no doubt . . . that the Roman governor had the power of capital punishment . . . [*J. W.* 2.8], or that he may have given the Sanhedrin this power for specific offenses, especially of a religious nature (the automatic death penalty for Gentiles caught trespassing in the inner parts of the temple precincts is attested by an inscription). But did the Sanhedrin have general competence to execute prisoners found guilty in serious religious, civil, and criminal cases? Those who think so point to a number of executions carried out by the Jewish authorities, some precisely affecting Christians. Stephen was stoned in the 30s (Acts vii 58-60); James, the leader of the Jerusalem church, was stoned in the 60s (Josephus, . . . [*Ant.* 20.9.1]). Paul's reluctance to be tried by the Sanhedrin in Jerusalem (Acts xxv 9-11) is more intelligible if that court had the power to pass capital sentence (see also acts xxii 30, xxiii 20). The story of the adulteress in John viii 3-5 may be interpreted as an indication that Jewish authorities could execute culprits. . . . However, those who think that the Sanhedrin did not have the general competence to execute offer another explanation for each instance. For example, they suggest that Stephen's case was "lynch law," and that, as Josephus indicates, James was executed in the interim between the terms of two Roman governors, with the result that the high priest involved was subsequently punished. There is a Jewish tradition . . . that jurisdiction over life was taken from Israel forty years . . . before the Temple was destroyed . . . (*b. San.* 1.18a, 34; 7.24b, 41). [After all the evidence is analyzed, Brown concludes that] the Romans zealously kept control of capital punishment; for in local hands the power of a death sentence could be used to eliminate pro-Roman factions. Turbulent Judea was the last place where the Romans would have been likely to make an exception.[9]

Fourth, concerning the horrors of the act of crucifixion, the *Harper's Bible Dictionary* provides the following description:

With a placard proclaiming the crime hung around the neck, the condemned prisoner carried the crossbar, not the whole cross, to the place of execution where the upright stake was already in place. There the offender was stripped and flogged. The prisoner's arms were affixed to the crossbar with ropes or nails, and the crossbar was then raised and attached to the upright stake. A small wooden block attached to the stake beneath the buttocks supported the weight of the suspended body, which was bound to the stake with ropes. Often the feet were also affixed to the stake with ropes or nails. Because deterrence was a primary objective, the cross was always erected in a public place. Death came slowly, often only after several days, and resulted from the cumulative impact of thirst, hunger, exhaustion, exposure, and the traumatic effects of the scourging. After death the body was usually left hanging on the cross. Because of the protracted suffering and the extreme ignominy of this manner of execution, it was viewed by the Romans as the supreme penalty, the "most wretched of deaths" (Josephus), and generally reserved for the lowest classes and the most heinous crimes.[10]

23:26 Verses 26-32 describe the road to the cross. Jesus was handed over to the Roman soldiers (vv. 32-33), undoubtedly accompanied by the Jewish authorities. They took hold of a man named Simon, from Cyrene (modern-day Libya; cf. Mark 15:21; see also Acts 6:9;

---

9. Brown, *The Gospel According to John xiii–xxi*, 849-50.
10. Achtemeier, *Harper's Bible Dictionary*, 194-95.

11:20; 13:1). This man happened to be coming out of the field when he was pressed into the service of helping to carry Jesus' cross. It was normal for the criminal to carry his own cross. Apparently Jesus was breaking down under its weight, having been scourged earlier. Surely Luke employs this incident as a reminder that disciples of Jesus must be prepared to take up the cross and follow Him.

23:27 The streets of Jerusalem leading to the site of the crucifixion were lined with people who had gathered to see the event. How quickly their theme had changed in a week's time (see 19:38). Many women, in professional mourning style, lamented over Jesus' impending fate. There is no reason to doubt the sincerity of the women.

23:28 Jesus addressed the women as the daughters of Jerusalem, telling them not to weep for Him but, rather, to weep for themselves and their children, because of the horror awaiting Jerusalem.

23:29 The tragic irony of Jesus' words at the thought of the coming fall of Jerusalem pierced even the shrill voices of the wailing women. Jesus prophesied that the days were coming when it would be better said of women, "Blessed are the barren, the womb that has never given birth and the breasts that have not nursed." Normally, Jewish custom did just the opposite, praised motherhood and stigmatized the barren. But the days of the fall of Jerusalem would be so severe that women would far prefer not to have children, rather than have them go through the ordeal that awaited the city.

23:30 In fact, in those days people in general would prefer death to life. They would cry to the mountains to fall on them and to the hills to cover them. The words echo Hosea 10:8, though in inverted order. The words of Hosea describe Israel's cry for death as a relief from divine punishment because of its apostasy from Yahweh.

23:31 Verse 31 literally reads, "If this is what they do with damp wood, what will happen to the dry?" Fitzmyer provides a good analysis of the remark Jesus makes: "If God allows the innocent Jesus (damp wood) to suffer such a fate as Jerusalem prepares for him, what will be the fate of Jerusalem (dry wood)?"[11]

23:32 Jesus was not alone in His misery. Two others were led away with Him. They were criminals who also were to be put to death. It is interesting that the best attested reading (p75, Sinaiticus, B), *heteroi kakourgoi dyo* ("two other criminals"), could suggest that Jesus was also considered to be a criminal. To avoid this impression, other manuscripts (A,

11. Fitzmyer, *The Gospel According to Luke X–XXIV*, 1498.

C, D) invert the word order, *heteroi dyo kakourgoi* ("two others, criminals"). Verse 32 obviously prepares the reader for vv. 33, 39-43. It is a telling criticism that Fitzmyer, a Jesuit theologian, observes in an aside comment on v. 32 that the account of Jesus' road to the cross says nothing about the fourteen stations of the cross, such as the falls of Jesus, the meeting with His mother or with Veronica ("true image"). Such later traditions, though certainly sentimental in appeal, seem to have no historical basis.[12]

23:33   Verses 33-49 are devoted to the episode of the crucifixion itself. The passage contains a number of threesomes: Three acts were perpetrated on Jesus (His crucifixion, v. 33; His garment was taken, v. 34; His dignity was affronted by the mockery, vv. 35-39). Three primary groups of actors surrounded the cross (the Jewish leaders, v. 35; the Roman soldiers, vv. 36-37; the condemned criminals, vv. 39-43). Three insults were hurled at Jesus by the leaders, soldiers, and one of the criminals, respectively. Three titles were applied to Jesus (God's Messiah, vv. 35, 39; God's chosen one, v. 35; king of the Jews, vv. 37-38). Three people were crucified, and there are at least three allusions to lament psalms (Ps. 22:18 in v. 34; Ps. 22:7 in v. 35; Ps. 69:22 in v. 36).

The crucifixion of Jesus was truly a divine drama. It was, in effect, a parody on kingship. Jesus, the king of the Jews (vv. 37-38), was enthroned on the cross, with the two highest seats of honor, the one on the right and the one on the left, occupied by criminals (v. 33). The subjects of the king—the leaders, the soldiers, and the people—taunted their royal ruler (vv. 34-49). Jesus' regal regalia, a tattered garment, was taken from Him (v. 34). His kingly drink was sour wine (v. 36), and His ensign was a placard attached to the cross, an instrument of capital punishment (v. 38). His kingdom was invisible and without apparent clout (vv. 42-43).

In v. 33 we are told that the group reached the place called "the skull" (the Greek word is *kranion*; *Golgotha,* not mentioned in Luke, is a Greek form of the Aramaic word, *gulgulta*). It was called so probably because the hill was shaped like a human skull. Today, most archaeologists identify Calvary with the site at the Church of the Holy Sepulchre,[13] though a few equate it with Gordan's tomb.[14] Upon arriv-

---

12. Ibid., 1499.
13. See Fitzmyer's discussion in ibid., 1503.
14. McBirne represents this view in *The Search for the Tomb of Jesus.*

ing at Golgotha, Jesus and the two criminals were crucified, one on the right side and the other on the left side of the Lord.

23:34   The earliest manuscripts do not contain the first part of v. 34: "Jesus said, 'Father forgive them, for they do not know what they are doing.'" The saying may have been inserted as a parallel to Acts 7:60b where Stephen offers a similar prayer of forgiveness. If original, it presents Jesus as willing to forgive those who have committed an inexcusable crime against Him. Jesus asks that they be forgiven on the grounds that they did not know what they were doing. According to Leviticus 4:2 and Numbers 15:25-29, atonement is possible for one who has sinned unwittingly. Perhaps this underlies Jesus' prayer.

According to v. 34b, the executioners divided up Jesus' garments by casting lots for them, an allusion to Psalm 22:19. It was a typical practice of Roman soldiers.

23:35   Luke records simply that the people stood by watching. If, however, the third evangelist is alluding to Psalm 21:8a, "all who look upon me have sneered at me," then the crowds were not excluded from mocking Jesus (cf. Mark 15:29). However, Luke focuses more on the Jewish leader's ridicule of Jesus at the cross. They taunted His apparent inability to save Himself, saying, "He saved others; let Him save Himself, if He is the Christ of God and His chosen one." The two titles recall Luke 9:20 and 9:35, respectively.

23:36   The soldiers joined the chorus of those ridiculing Jesus. They came up the hill to the cross and offered Jesus sour wine, probably as the offering of a cheap drink to the king of the Jews. The action recalls Psalm 69:21.

23:37   The soldiers, too, taunted Jesus, challenging Him to save Himself if He really was the king of the Jews.

23:38   The soldiers got the title from the inscription above Jesus on the cross, "This is the king of the Jews." Many later manuscripts add a reference about the three languages in which the inscription was written, Greek, Latin, and Hebrew, but this is a scribal gloss based on John 19:20. Josephus, the Jewish historian, provides an interesting interpretation of the inscription over Jesus: "At one of the gates leading into the temple with inscriptions hung a . . . tablet with inscription in these (Greek, Roman, and Jewish) characters, to the effect: Jesus has not reigned as king; he has been crucified by the Jews because he proclaimed the destruction of the city and the laying waste of the temple" (from the Slavonic version of *J. W.* 5.190-200, as quoted in Evans, *Luke*, 341).

23:39   Only Luke records that one of the criminals who was crucified joined in the mocking of Jesus. The criminal blasphemed Jesus by calling into question His messiahship. He challenged Jesus, if He really was the king of the Jews, to save both of them. Some commentators believe the man was a zealot who, therefore, could not have accepted Jesus as the Messiah if He made no attempt to overthrow the Roman government, the enemy of God. However, this is speculative.

23:40   But the second crucified criminal rebuked his companion. He asked him if he did not fear God, for he was under the same sentence as Jesus and about to face the Judge over all the earth.

23:41   The repentant criminal correctly assessed the situation. He rightly calculated that the two of them were getting what they deserved, but that Jesus had done nothing to deserve condemnation.

23:42   The criminal requested Jesus to remember him when Jesus entered His kingdom. The confession-like prayer generates at least three observations: (1) The criminal knew he was a sinner and that Jesus, in some sense, was a Savior. (2) The thief knew he had no merit to appeal to in order to persuade Jesus to help him. There was nothing more the criminal could do but cast himself on the mercy of Jesus. (3) For Luke, the entrance of Jesus into His kingdom began with His ascension and exaltation (24:26, 50; Acts 1:9-11; 2:33-36).

23:43   Jesus graciously granted the thief's request by assuring the man that that very day he would be with Christ in Paradise. Jesus' words raise two questions: When did that event happen? What is meant by Paradise? In answer to the first question, the time frame "today" (*sēmeron*) has been taken in one of two ways. Traditionally, the word "today" has been understood to be a chronological reference to a twenty-four-hour period. The difficulty with this view is its apparent conflict with biblical teaching elsewhere which suggests that Jesus first "descended" to hades after His death (Matt. 12:40; Acts 2:31; Rom. 10:7) and then afterward ascended to heaven (Luke 24; Acts 1:9-11), a time span covering three days. Therefore, more contemporary scholars tend to take the time frame eschatologically, with reference to the spiritual kingdom that was present in the first coming of Christ (see Luke's use of *sēmeron* in this manner in 2:11; 4:21; 5:26). Ellis expresses this view relative to v. 43 succinctly: "Today is sometimes a technical expression for the time of messianic salvation. Here that time is Jesus' exaltation at the resurrection."[15] The latter view seems to be what Luke intended.

---

15. Ellis, *The Gospel of Luke,* 368.

In answer to the second question, paradise (*paradeisos*), a Persian word meaning "garden, park," was used in the Septuagint for the Garden of Eden (Gen. 2:8). It then became a type of the future bliss for God's people in Isaiah 51:3, and received a technical sense in *T. Levi* 18:10-18. The future paradise was identified with the Garden of Eden, thus leading to the view that it existed in between the creation and the final age in hidden form. It came to be regarded as the intermediate resting place for the souls of righteous dead. It is used as a symbol for heaven and its bliss in 2 Corinthians 12:4; Revelation 2:7. In the present passage it represents the state of bliss which Jesus promised to the criminal directly after death.

THE DEATH AND BURIAL OF JESUS, 23:44-56

This section can be divided into two parts: the death of Jesus (vv. 44-49) and the burial of Jesus (vv. 50-56). In his description of the death of Jesus, Luke includes the following: two portents which took place at the time of Jesus' death on the cross, Jesus' committal of His spirit into God's care, and two admissions of Jesus' innocence. The episode of the burial of Jesus covers two points: the request of Joseph of Arimathea to bury the body of Jesus and the preparation of the women to anoint the body of Jesus.

23:44 The death of Jesus is depicted in vv. 44-49. According to vv. 44-45, two portents, or cataclysmic events, took place while Jesus was on the cross. The first was that darkness covered the land (v. 44). Following Mark 15:33, Luke observes that it was about the sixth hour (noon, or halfway through the twelve-hour period of daylight) when darkness came over the land (probably the immediate area of Jerusalem). The point is that, at a time when the sun usually shone brightly, darkness blocked out the daylight. The darkness continued until the ninth hour (three o'clock in the afternoon), that is, until Jesus' death.

23:45 Luke explains that the natural reason for the darkness was that the sun (*hēliou*) ceased to shine. Whether this is to be explained scientifically as an eclipse of the sun or as the consequence of the hot eastern wind, sirocco, hiding the sun from view, is uncertain.[16] We suspect that Luke is more concerned to accentuate theological factors that contributed to the scene of darkness. (See below at the conclusion of this section.)

16. See Marshall's discussion in *Commentary on Luke,* 874-75.

The second portent connected with the death of Jesus was the tearing of the veil in the temple, "the curtain of the temple was torn (*eschisthē*) in the middle." This portent raises two questions: Which veil was torn? What did it mean? Concerning the first question, in the temple hung thirteen veils or curtains. The two main ones were the one at the entrance of the Holy Place (see Josephus, *J. W.* 5.212, "a veil . . . of Babylonian tapestry, with embroidery of blue and fine linen, of scarlet also and purple, wrought with marvelous skill. . . . It typified the universe" [cf. Septuagint Ex. 26:36]) and one at the entrance of the Holy of Holies ("screened in like manner from the outer portion by a veil," *J. W.* 5.219; cf. Heb. 6:19; 9:3; 10:20). Strack-B 1:1043-45 says that it is impossible to say which of the two is meant. Older commentators in general merely assumed that the veil before the Holy of Holies was intended (for example, Ellis, *Gospel of Luke*, 260). But others insist on the veil at the entrance to the Holy Place (see, for example, Fitzmyer, *The Gospel According to Luke X–XXIV*, 1518). We are inclined toward the veil before the Holy of Holies.

Various answers have been proposed for the second question, What did the tearing of the veil mean? The answers vary: it was a sign of the destruction of the temple; it was a sign of divine displeasure; it signified that evil ruled during Jesus' passion; and so on. (We will offer our own interpretation below at the end of this section.)

23:46   Luke begins Jesus' last words with a nominative absolute, "crying with a loud voice" (*phōnēsas phōnē*), "Father, into your hands I commit my spirit." The utterance befittingly makes three points. First, the loud voice indicates that Jesus secured *victory* over death. The fact that He could raise His voice, when normally a crucified person could barely gasp for breath, indicates that Jesus was still in control of His destiny. Second, the word "father" reveals Jesus' *intimacy* with God on the cross, despite having been forsaken by Him because the sin of the world now laid on Jesus' shoulders (cf. Mark 15:34). Third, Jesus' committal of His spirit to the Father encapsulates His *dependency* on God, a reliance that carried Him all the way through life and, now, death. These words of Jesus are a quotation of Psalm 31:6. Psalm 31 is a psalm attributed to David, itself a prayer of lamentation and thanksgiving. Like Jesus, David was the object of lies and traps (vv. 4, 18, 20), scorned by enemies and abandoned by friends (v. 11), and sought refuge in God in the face of death (vv. 5, 13).

Having said this, Jesus expired, "breathed out His life." We conclude this section by briefly examining Luke's theology of the cross. It seems to us that there are at least three theological factors informing the third evangelist's portrait of Jesus' death. First, a *typological* theme is at work in Jesus' death on the cross, especially the Exodus motif. We noted earlier that Jesus' destiny in Jerusalem was specified to Him by Moses on the Mount of Transfiguration; it was to die on the cross and thereby to experience a new Exodus (9:30-31). Surely that idea is present in v. 44, as is also the background of the tenth plague on Pharaoh. That plague, the reader will remember, involved the killing of the Egyptian firstborn sons by the death angel, under the cover of darkness. It is hard not to see the same notion involved here in v. 44. Jesus as God's only Son took upon Himself the plague of God's wrath for sin. No wonder the sun refused to shine.

Second, there is an *eschatological* factor involved in Luke's presentation of the cross, particularly the enshrouding of the cross with darkness. The darkness should be understood as one of the cosmic phenomena often associated with the Day of Yahweh in the Old Testament (Joel 2:10; 3:3-4; Zeph. 1:15) and, itself, adumbrates the cosmic signs of the end time and the return of Christ (see Luke 21:25-26).

Third, we believe there is also a *primeval* interest at work in Luke's theology of the cross, one which is surprisingly overlooked by the commentators. Four intriguing correspondences between Luke 23:43-46 and Genesis 1–3 can be identified which, taken together, suggest that Jesus died on the cross as the new Adam. More specifically, Jesus, the last Adam, willingly experienced the consequences of the first Adam's sin in order that He might begin to restore the primeval past (cf. Luke 3:23–4:13). (1) According to v. 43, Jesus' death opened and thereby regained the paradise Adam and Eve lost because of their sin (see Gen. 2:8, 10; 3:23). (2) The darkness that covered the land at the death of Jesus (v. 44) reminds one of Genesis 1:1 and the darkness that covered the chaotic waters on the earth and to which the earth returned during Noah's flood in the aftermath of Adam's sin. It is not surprising, therefore, that Jesus called the hour of His cross, "the power of darkness" (Luke 22:53), for it symbolized the apparent triumph of sin over righteousness. (3) The rending of the veil of the temple at the death of Jesus (v. 44) we rather think is to be taken more positively than many have understood it. We prefer to see in it the sign from God that, because of the death of Jesus for sin, the way has been cleared for humans to enter directly into the presence of God (cf. Heb. 9). If we are accurate on this point, it would serve as the corrective for that day when Adam and Eve were cast out of Paradise and removed from the presence of God because of their sin (Gen. 3:24; cf. *T. Lev.* 18:2-14). (4) If we are on the right track in suggesting that a primeval theme is at work in Luke's theology of the cross, then the words of v. 46, "Jesus expired" ("breathed out His life"), can be seen to echo Genesis 2:7. There it is said that God breathed into Adam the breath of life, and he became a living soul. The one God breathed into the breath of life—Adam; the other breathed out the breath of life—Jesus. The latter paid the consequences for the sin of the former in order to inaugurate a new creation (cf. also Gen. 2:7 and 1 Cor 15:45).

23:47   Luke provides in vv. 47-48 two testimonies of Jesus' innocence, one by the Roman soldier at the foot of the cross and the other by the Jewish people gathered at the cross. According to v. 47, the Roman centurion ("commander of a hundred") at the foot of the cross glorified God (cf. 2:20; 5:25-26; 13:13; 17:15; 18:43; Acts 4:21; 11:18; 21:20) because of what he had seen happen. The circumstances that brought about this confession probably included the conversation about paradise between Jesus and the thief, the darkness, and the last words of Jesus. It is doubtful the soldier knew about the torn temple veil. The centurion specifically glorified God by vindicating Jesus' innocence: "Truly this man was innocent." For the translation of *dikaios* as innocent, see the Septuagint usages (Prov. 6:17; Joel 3:19; Jonah 1:14). The centurion's declaration joins the chorus of voices like Pilate (vv. 4, 14-15, 22), Herod (v. 11), and the thief (v. 41).

23:48   Verse 48 adds to that list the crowd's testimony. The Jewish people that gathered at the cross of Jesus to view the spectacle expressed their feelings by beating their breasts as they began to depart. They had finally realized that an innocent man had been executed (cf. 18:13). D. L. Tiede notes that the people returned/repented (*hypostrephein*) much as Jesus predicted that Peter would return/repent after denying his Lord (22:32). Luke's description anticipates the remorse and repentance that will be expressed at the Pentecost Sermon (Acts 2:37-38).[17] Luke intends the crowd's reaction to allude to Zechariah 12:10-14.

23:49   Perhaps Luke intends to identify a third testimony of Jesus' innocence, only this one came from the eloquent silence of His friends who watched Him from afar. The words "all who were known to Him" certainly refer to the womenfolk and possibly some of the disciples (cf. John 19:25), including perhaps Joseph of Arimathea

---

17. Tiede, *Luke*, 425.

(v. 51). The women mentioned recall the names of Mary Magdalene, Joanna, wife of Chuza, Susanna (see 8:2-3), and also Mary, Jesus' mother (24:10; cf. again John 19:25). The reference to the friends standing off afar may allude to Psalms 38:12 and 88:9.

23:50 The burial of Jesus is described in vv. 50-56. Two points are treated: the request of Joseph of Arimathea for the body of Jesus and the preparation of the women to anoint the body of Jesus. In v. 50 we find Joseph's character highlighted. All four gospel writers speak highly of Joseph of Arimathea (Matt. 27:57-60; Mark 16:43-46; Luke 23:50-53; John 19:38-42). Joseph was a member of the council, i.e., the Sanhedrin. He was a good and righteous man (cf. v. 47).

23:51 The explanation behind Luke's description of the moral character is provided—Joseph did not consent to the Sanhedrin's decision to crucify Jesus (22:4-5, 71; 23:1). The word translated "consent," *sugkatatithēmi*, means to "put down the same vote." Joseph was from the town of Arimathea in Judea, a site not yet conclusively determined. Furthermore, he was a man who awaited the arrival of the kingdom of God. By describing him thus, the evangelist is implying that Joseph was like one of the pious Israelites described in the birth narratives, such as Simeon (2:25) and Anna (2:38). He was probably sympathetic to John the Baptist (3:3) as well as to Jesus' proclamation of the kingdom (4:43). According to Matthew 27:57 and John 19:38, Joseph was a follower of Jesus, a testimony commensurate with Luke's description of him.

23:52 This man Joseph went to Pilate (probably in the pretorium in the Antonia Fortress that overlooked the temple mound) and requested permission to take the body of Jesus. Undoubtedly Joseph did so because he wanted to prevent Jesus' body from being dishonored by being thrown into a common grave, the fate of crucified criminals. He wanted to give Jesus' body a proper burial. It took courage on Joseph's part to ask Pilate for the body, because it implicated him as a follower of Jesus. By doing so, he went public with his faith.

23:53 Joseph performed three actions. First, he took the body of Jesus down from the cross, thus indicating that Jesus really did die (cf. 1 Cor. 15:4). Second, Joseph wrapped the body in linen cloth, i.e., a burial shroud. This phrase in the four gospels (cf. Matt. 27:59; Mark 15:46; John 19:40) has been connected by many with the Shroud of Turin. However, Fitzmyer, a Jesuit scholar, provides an illuminating discussion of the question of its authenticity, and concludes that it is inauthentic.[18]

The third action of Joseph of Arimathea with respect to the body of Jesus was that he laid it in a rock-cut tomb, where no one had yet been placed. Tombs hewn out of rock, dating from the first century, are found in abundance in the area around Jerusalem.[19] The tombs or caves had ledges or shelves carved within them out of the rock in order to make room for the burial of a number of bodies. After the bodies decomposed, the bones were placed in ossuaries, stone boxes. One of the most spectacular finds in this regard occurred recently when an ossuary was excavated on the Mount of Olives. The owner's name was inscribed on the outside (which was the custom)—Caiaphas (was this the high priest of Jerusalem who presided at the Sanhedrin's trial of Jesus?). Like Calvary, the location of the tomb of Jesus is identified by most biblical archaeologists as the site of the Church of the Holy Sepulcher, only a few hundred feet away from Golgotha.[20] The tomb was Joseph's own property, according to Matthew 27:60.

23:54 In v. 54 Luke provides a historical frame of reference for the burial of Jesus, noting that the day Jesus died was on the day of preparation (about 3:00 P.M., Friday), i.e., the day of preparing for the Sabbath, which was to follow at sundown (about 6:00 P.M., Saturday).

23:55 The account concludes with a note about the women's preparation to anoint the body of Jesus. The women who came with Jesus from Galilee (v. 49) followed along with Joseph. They observed which tomb Jesus was laid in, thus ruling out any possibility of later visiting the wrong grave site. The remark by Luke that the women noted how Jesus' body was placed may mean that they saw that the body was not yet washed and anointed.

23:56 The ladies went home to prepare spices and perfume for the anointing of their master's body. Then the women rested on the Sabbath, according to the commandment. The Sabbath is from sundown (6:00 P.M.) Friday until sundown Saturday. The command to rest, or cease from work, occurs in Exodus 20:10; Deuteronomy 5:12-15.

---

18. Fitzmyer, *The Gospel According to Luke X–XXIV,* 1528-29.
19. See Finegan, *The Archeology of the New Testament,* 191-96.
20. *Contra* McBirne, *The Search for the Tomb of Jesus.*

HOMILETICAL SUGGESTIONS

A couple of approaches would work well for preaching Luke 23. The first would be to proceed through the outline of the three major events in the passion narrative as we have expounded them: the trial of Jesus before the Roman government (vv. 1-25); the crucifixion of Jesus (vv. 26-43); His death and burial (vv. 44-56). Another approach which we have found to be quite effective is to preach a sermon entitled "Ironies around the Cross." There are several ironies, when the opposite effect of what was intended takes place, around the cross, as recorded in Luke 23, which center on some aspect of Jesus.

I. Jesus the Prophet (here we reach back to 22:54-65)
   A. Jesus was mocked as a prophet (22:63-65).
   B. Peter's denial fulfilled Jesus' prophecy (22:54-62).

II. Jesus the Righteous
   A. Jesus was pronounced innocent, but He was treated as though guilty (23:1-23).
   B. Barabbas, the false son of the father, was released while Jesus, the true Son of the Father, was executed (vv. 18-25).

III. Jesus the Peacemaker
   Two enemies, Pilate and Herod, became friends at the expense of Jesus (v. 12). Jesus' work on the cross could even reconcile two evil enemies.

IV. Jesus the Lamented
   The women wept for Jesus when they should have wept for themselves (vv. 26-32).

V. Jesus the Crucified
   A. The thief accepted the Messiah whereas the Jewish nation did not (vv. 33-43).
   B. At the cross, evil seemed to prevail (darkness was over the land when Jesus died, v. 43) when actually righteousness won the day (the veil of the temple was torn, thus opening the way to a holy God because of the death of Jesus, v. 44).
   C. The Jewish leaders thought they delivered up Jesus to death (vv. 33-45) when, in reality, Jesus, in control of the situation, delivered His own spirit up to death and the Father (v. 46).

D. The three groups who began the crucifixion with mockery (the leaders, v. 35; the people, vv. 18-23; and the soldiers, vv. 36-37) ended the crucifixion with sorrow and even repentance (Joseph of Arimathea, vv. 50-53; the people, v. 48; the centurion, v. 47), respectively. Not all of the three groups repented, of course, but some members of each did.

VI. Jesus the Savior (here we compare the birth of Jesus, according to 2:11-12 with the burial of Jesus, according to 23:53).
   When Jesus was born, He was wrapped in strips of linen cloth and placed in a cave (manger, 2:11-12). When Jesus was buried, He was wrapped in strips of linen cloth and placed in a tomb (23:53). Jesus was born to die in order to be the Savior of the world.

LUKE

CHAPTER

TWENTY FOUR

THE RESURRECTION AND
ASCENSION OF JESUS CHRIST

Luke 24 concludes the third evangelist's gospel. Fitzmyer provides a précis of the chapter, noting it contains five episodes:

(a) The finding of the empty tomb by the women (Mary Magdalene;
Mary, the mother of James; Joanna, and others) at the crack of dawn on
the first day of the week (23:56b–24:12); the *praeconium paschale* is
announced to them by two men in gleaming robes suddenly standing
by them. These persons charge the women to recall the words that
Jesus had addressed to them while he was still in Galilee; the women
leave and report it all to the Eleven, who regard their stories as so
much nonsense. Peter alone goes off to see for himself (and to him
Christ appears first, as one learns in v. 34). (b) The risen Christ appears
to disciples walking to Emmaus; they return to make known what they
had experienced (vv. 13-35). (c) Christ appears to the Eleven and their
companions in Jerusalem (vv. 36-43). (d) These he commissions to be
"witnesses of this" and to preach in his name (vv. 44-49); and finally (e)
he leads them out to Bethany, where he is parted from them and carried off to heaven on Easter Sunday night (vv. 50-53).[1]

---

1. Fitzmyer, *The Gospel According to Luke X–XXIV,* 1536.

THE EMPTY TOMB, 24:1-12

It is important to note that no New Testament writer provides an account of someone actually witnessing the Resurrection, that is, visibly perceiving God's act of raising the dead Jesus. This lack of spectacular detail itself speaks for the historicity of the New Testament documents. There is no attempt on the part of the writers to embellish the event of the Resurrection. Like the account in Genesis 1 of the creation of the world (which no human witnessed), the result of the Resurrection, not the event itself, is stated matter-of-factly by the biblical authors. One can appreciate the simplicity and straightforwardness of the gospel narratives when reading the later apocryphal gospel traditions, with their pronounced tendencies to exaggerate the truth. Consider, for example, the story of the resurrection of Jesus according to the *Gospel of Peter*:

> Now in the night in which the Lord's day dawned, when the soldiers were keeping guard, two by two in every watch, there rang out a loud voice in heaven. They saw the heavens opened, and two men came down from there in great brightness and drew near to the sepulchre. That stone which had been laid against the entrance to the sepulchre started to roll of itself and gave way to the side, and the sepulchre was opened, and both the young men entered in. When then these soldiers saw this, they woke up the centurion and the elders—for they also were there to assist at the watch. And while they were relating what they had seen, they again saw three men come out of the sepulchre, and two of them sustaining the other, and a cross following them. They saw the heads of the two reaching to heaven, but that of him who was led by them by the hand surpassing the heavens. Then they heard a voice crying out of the heavens, "Hast thou preached to them that sleep?" And from the cross there was heard the answer, "Yes." (35–42)

24:1   On the first day of the week (i.e., Sunday; cf. John 20:19; Acts 20:7; 1 Cor. 16:2) at dawn, the women came to the tomb, bringing with them the spices they had prepared to anoint Jesus' body.

24:2   They found that the stone had been rolled away from the tomb. Finegan observes that tombs in the neighborhood of Jerusalem from the first century A.D. have been found fitted with huge circular stone discs that were set in a transverse channel hollowed out of stone, along which the discs would be rolled in front of a rectangular doorway opening on to the tomb proper. As one faced the doorway from the outside, the stone would be rolled from left to right (or vice versa) to open or close the tomb. One such disc is found before the so-called Herodian Family tomb.[2]

24:3   When the women entered into the tomb, they did not find the body of the Lord Jesus. It is most appropriate that Luke calls Jesus "Lord" (*kyrios*), for He was now Lord over death.

24:4   While they were perplexed about the missing body of Jesus, two men in clothes that gleamed like lightening stood beside them. The appearance of two personages probably served to confirm their witness. The twofold witness continues throughout Luke 24: two men on the road to Emmaus, two appearances of the risen Jesus, two times the Scriptures are appealed to. The two men were undoubtedly angels (cf. 24:23; Matt. 28:2, 5).

24:5   The women were startled and bowed down to the ground. The heavenly personages asked them why they sought for the living among the dead. The angels' question served as a mild rebuff to the ladies' momentary lapse in faith.

24:6   The angels then clarified the situation with their immortalized words, "He is not here but is risen." The word for "risen," *ēgerthē*, is a theological passive, i.e., He has been raised (by God). The angels reminded the women of the prediction Jesus made in Galilee.

24:7   The angels specified the nature of that prophecy, recalling Jesus' words that the Son of Man must be delivered into the hands of sinful men and be crucified; and then He would be raised on the third day (see 9:22). The reference to the mode of Jesus' death—crucifixion—though not spelled out in the passion predictions of 9:22, 43-45; 18:31-34, was formulated by the angels with hindsight.

24:8   The women then recalled Jesus' words. This suggests that the ladies accompanied the disciples as they followed Jesus on the road to Jerusalem.

24:9   The women then departed from the tomb and reported their experience to the eleven disciples (now minus Judas; see Acts 1:16-19), as well as to the rest of Jesus' companions (see 24:13-35).

24:10   For the difficulty of the syntax and the text tradition of the opening words, *ēsan de,* see Marshall.[3] It is best to take the words as introducing the identification of the women mentioned in the previous verse. The names of the ladies were Mary Magdalene (see 8:2),

2. Finegan, *The Archeology of the New Testament,* 198.
3. Marshall, *Commentary on Luke,* 887.

Joanna (see 8:3), and Mary the mother of James (cf. Mark 16:1). The literal rendering is, "Mary, the one of James," probably referring to the mother of James (cf. Mark 15:40). Although Luke has not mentioned this person before, she must have been one of the women from Galilee who stood at a distance from the cross (23:49). These ladies, and the other women with them (see 23:49, 55), kept relating their experience with the angels to the apostles.

24:11   But the apostles did not believe the testimony of the women because their words seemed like nonsense.

24:12   Curiosity, however, got the best of Peter. He got up and ran to the tomb. Peter looked into the tomb and saw the strips of linen grave clothes laying by themselves, but the significance of the event did not yet dawn on the apostle. He was puzzled and left wondering as he went home.

In concluding this episode, perhaps we should address two historical critical issues: (1) the apparent contradiction in the gospel records concerning the events surrounding the Resurrection, and (2) the skeptical theories regarding the empty tomb. First, the Gospels record a multiplicity of events involving many different people, all occurring in a relatively brief period of time. This has led to confusion, seeming contradiction, and resultant charges that the Gospels cannot be reconciled and that therefore the accounts are untrustworthy. It will be helpful to attempt to a harmonization of the events and to develop the chronological sequence of events. We follow Pentecost who offers the following sequence:[4] The order of the events of this memorable Sunday, the resurrection day, are probably as follows: the earthquake, followed by the descent of the angel, the opening of the tomb, and the Resurrection (Matt. 28:2-4). The group of women came together and started for the tomb at the "very early" hour of "deep dawn," while it was yet dark. Mary Magdalene, being a young woman, eagerly ran ahead and came first to the tomb, finding it open. Immediately she ran back by the nearest way to inform Peter and John of this fact (John 20:1). The other women completed their two-mile walk from Bethany to the sepulcher, arriving a little after the rising of the sun (Mark 16:2). An angel suddenly appeared to them and gave them an urgent message to the disciples (Matt. 28:5; Mark 16:5). Another party of women came a little later and saw "two young

4. Pentecost, *The Words and Works of Jesus Christ,* 495-96.

men" dressed in white at the tomb, and received words of comfort and instruction (Luke 24:4). About 6:30 A.M. Peter and John arrived, John running ahead (John 20:3-10). Mary Magdalene came a little later and saw two angels (John 20:11-13). The other women had returned to bear the message to the other apostles (Luke 24:10). About 7:00 A.M. Jesus first revealed Himself to Mary of Magdala (John 20:14-18; Mark 16:9). A little later, He appeared to the company of women returning to the sepulcher and sent them with the charge to the brethren to go to Galilee (Matt. 28:9). About 4:00 P.M. He appeared to Simon Peter (Luke 24:34; 1 Cor. 15:5), and from 4:00 to 6:00 P.M. to Cleophas and his companion on the way to Emmaus. Finally, in the evening, probably about 8:00 P.M., He appeared to the Eleven (ten), and others in the room with barred doors (Mark 16:14; Luke 24:36; John 29:29).

Second, we offer the following rebuttals to those theories proposed to explain the empty tomb, using basically the Lucan text. To those claiming that the women went to the wrong tomb, it should be observed that Luke 23:55 makes clear that they knew precisely which tomb it was in which Jesus was buried. Regarding the theory that the disciples wanted so badly for Jesus to rise from the dead that they therefore imagined His resurrection, it should be noted that both the ladies (24:4) and the disciples (24:11) were taken by surprise at the empty tomb. In other words, they were not expecting a resurrection.

To those who say that animals entered the tomb and ate the body of Jesus or who subscribe to the swoon theory (Jesus did not really die on the cross, He only appeared to be dead on the cross and then crept out of the tomb later), it should be mentioned that the large stone blocking the entrance to the tomb would have obviously prevented either scenario (24:2). To the theory that grave robbers, or even the disciples, stole the body of Jesus, it should be remembered that the Roman government seal was placed over the tomb, and enforced by soldiers, thus threatening death to all who tampered with the grave site (Matt. 27:62-66). That leaves one other possibility. Did the Jewish leaders take the body of Jesus? Obviously not, for when they wanted to stop the apostolic preaching of the resurrection of Jesus, all they needed to do was to produce the body as evidence, which they were not able to do (Acts 1–9). Therefore, the only satisfactory explanation for the empty tomb was that Jesus arose bodily and left it.

THE ROAD TO EMMAUS, 24:13-35

The episode of the road to Emmaus is unique to Luke's gospel. Evans provides a perceptive introduction to this account of the risen Christ appearing to the two persons on the road to Emmaus. He observes several features:

> (1) The appearance takes place while the two persons were going along a road (24:13-15). This detail recalls the Central Section (9:51–19:27) in which Jesus taught while traveling along the road to Jerusalem. The idea of teaching and traveling might anticipate the traveling ministries of the apostles in the Book of Acts. (2) The risen Christ explains to his followers how Scripture was fulfilled in what has happened to him during the past few days (24:25-27, 32). This has been a characteristic mark of Jesus' ministry as presented in Luke. Beginning with his Nazareth sermon (4:16-30) Jesus announced that Scripture was fulfilled (see 4:17-21 where Isa. 61:1-2 is quoted as fulfilled). Later, in answer to the question of the messengers of the imprisoned Baptist, Jesus refers to his ministry as fulfilling Scripture (7:18-23, esp. v. 22). Moreover, in his third prediction of his coming passion (18:31-33) Jesus says that "everything that is written by the prophets about the Son of Man will be fulfilled." Twice in Luke 24 this theme is repeated. In the passage presently under consideration Jesus tells his confused followers that "all that the prophets have spoken" has been fulfilled and that "all the Scriptures" pertain to him (vv. 25-27). Later, he will tell his disciples that "everything must be fulfilled that is written about me" (v. 44). (3) There is also a eucharistic theme present in the walk to Emmaus (see v. 30): Jesus "took bread," "gave thanks," "broke it," and "g[a]ve it" to his followers, enabling them finally to see him. These words recall the similar words used when Jesus fed the five thousand (9:19-17, esp. v 16) and the words of the Last Supper (22:14-23, esp. v. 19). They also anticipate the "breaking of the bread" by Christians in Acts (2:42, 46; 20:7, 11; 27:35).[5]

24:13   On the same day of Jesus' resurrection, two of His followers were making their way to a village called Emmaus, which was about sixty stadia from Jerusalem. The two were probably not members of the eleven apostles, but rather were two other disciples (see vv. 9, 18). They were probably returning from the celebration of the Passover in Jerusalem. There is considerable uncertainty about the original loca-

5. Evans, *Luke,* 349.

tion of the village of Emmaus. Luke mentions that it was about seven miles (literally, "sixty stadia") from Jerusalem. If he meant round-trip, the reference would fit rather nicely with a town Josephus identified as Emmaus, which he located thirty stadia from Jerusalem (*J. W.* 7.217). However, it is difficult to be conclusive on the matter.

24:14   These two disciples were conversing with each other about all the things that had happened.

24:15   While they discussed these things Jesus Himself drew near and began to walk with them. He probably overtook them from behind. They perhaps thought He was another pilgrim returning from the celebration of the Passover in Jerusalem.

24:16   But the disciples' eyes were restrained from recognizing Jesus. "Restrained from recognizing," *kratounto,* is a theological passive, i.e., their spiritual blindness was divinely authored.

24:17   Jesus asked the disciples what the subject was of their discussion; literally, "What are these words that you exchange with one another?" The question stopped the two in their tracks; they were filled with gloom.

24:18   One of the men was named Cleopas, not to be confused with the Clopas of John 19:25. The other companion is unnamed in the narrative. Cleopas found it incredible that their fellow traveler was not aware of what had happened the last few days in Jerusalem. Was He the only pilgrim at the Passover not in the know?

24:19   Jesus feigned ignorance. "What things?" He asked. The travelers responded to the question by giving an encapsulated statement of who Jesus was—a prophet mighty in deed and word in both the presence of God and all of the people. For Jesus' background in Nazareth and as a Nazarene, see 4:34; 18:37. For His prophetic ministry, recall 7:16, 39; 9:8, 19. For the combination, "mighty in deed and word," see Acts 7:22 and the description used there of Moses. It may be that the description identifies Jesus as the prophet like Moses (Deut. 18:18-19). See 3:22; 9:35 for the divine approval of Jesus and 18:43 for the human approval, especially the general populace's positive reaction to Jesus' ministry.

24:20   The disciples continued their explanation, stating that their chief priests and the leaders delivered Jesus up to the sentence of death and crucified Him. The delivering up (*paradidomi*) of Jesus to death and crucifixion recalls 9:44; 23:13; 24:7. Only the Jewish leaders are mentioned here in v. 20, but the words "delivered up to the sentence (*krima,* judgment) of death" seem to implicate the Roman authorities as well.

24:21 The disciples' response revealed both dejection and disbelief. They were dejected because their hope that Jesus would be the one to redeem Israel did not come to fruition. Their hope was primarily political in orientation, centering on the freeing of Israel from the hands of Rome and establishing the kingdom of God (cf. 1:68 and 2:38). But now, three days had elapsed and no kingdom had appeared. Their remark reveals the disbelief of the disciples in Jesus' prediction to rise again on the third day. We might add in passing that the two disciples on the road to Emmaus seem to qualify for being pictures of the coming restoration of Israel. Like Israel, they suffered from a spiritual obtuseness that was divinely induced (cf. v. 16 with Rom. 11:25). Moreover, like the nation of Israel, they longed for the reestablishment of the Jews, God's chosen people (cf. v. 21 with Rom. 11:26, 27). If these connections are accurate, the progression of the disciples from partial to full understanding (v. 31) can be seen to mirror Israel's future journey of faith toward Jesus as her Messiah.

24:22 The two disciples went on to relate that some of the women from their group further confused them, astounding them when they went back to the tomb early that morning.

24:23 The women reported that they discovered the tomb to be empty and that they witnessed a vision (*optasia*) of angels who declared that Jesus was alive.

24:24 Some of the group of men (Peter and his companion, see v. 12; cf. John 20:3-10) went to the tomb. In the first century the testimony of women was not deemed authoritative. Luke's inclusion of the incident serves to emphasize his high regard for women. In any event, when some of the men arrived at the tomb, they found it to be just as the women had said, except that they did not see Jesus. The pronoun "Him" (*auton*) is in the emphatic position—"but Him they did not see." That is, despite what the women and the disciples said, no one had yet seen the risen Jesus.

24:25 The still incognito Jesus rebuked the two disciples. He called them foolish and slow of heart because they did not believe the prophetic testimony of the Old Testament. No specific prophet was referred to. Rather, Jesus had in mind the general witness of the Old Testament.

24:26 Jesus asked a rhetorical question: "Was not the Messiah bound to suffer these things and then enter into His glory?" The question raises the issue of whether or not the concept of a suffering Messiah existed in pre-Christian Judaism. Fitzmyer assesses the evidence:

> The notion of a suffering Messiah is not found in the OT or in any texts of pre-Christian Judaism. Str-B (2. 273-299) says that the "old Synagogue" knew of "a suffering Messiah, for whom no death was determined, i.e. the Messiah ben David" and "a dying Messiah, of whom no suffering was mentioned," i.e. the Messiah ben Joseph (ibid. 273-274). Yet when it cites the passages from rabbinic literature (ibid. 282-291) that speak of the suffering Messiah ben David, they are all drawn from late texts, which scarcely show that the expectation of such a figure existed among *Palestinian* Jews in or prior to the time of Jesus. The same has to be said of the texts about the dying Messiah ben Joseph (ibid. 292-299). Str-B rightly rejects the implication found at times in Christian commentators that Mark 8:31; 9:31; Matt 16:21 refer to a "suffering Messiah," since, if any title is used in these passages, it is a suffering "Son of Man," and the latter is not a "messianic" title without further ado. Where in pre-Christian Judaism does one find a "Son of Man" as an agent of Yahweh anointed for the salvation, deliverance of his people? True, in *Tg. Jonathan* the "servant" of Isa 52:13 is identified as "the Messiah": "See, my servant, the Messiah, shall prosper; he will be exalted, great, very mighty"; and 53:10c is made to read, "They will look upon the kingdom of their Messiah, many sons and daughters will be theirs." Yet no use of "Messiah" is made in the crucial verse, 53:12. It is not surprising that the "Servant" of Isaiah 52–53 was eventually identified with a messiah in the Jewish tradition; but it still remains to be shown that this identification existed in pre-Christian Judaism or in Judaism contemporary with the NT.[6]

In our opinion, Fitzmyer has judged the evidence too harshly, for there does seem to be some room for equating the concept of a suffering Messiah with the Servant in Isaiah. 53. Our suspicion is that because Israel later applied the suffering motif of Isaiah 53 to itself, Jesus redirected the nation's focus to the ultimate fulfillment of Isaiah 53—Himself. Having suffered, Jesus entered eschatological glory. The idea of righteous suffering leading to future glory was a widespread Jewish apocalyptic motif at the time of Jesus. It heavily influenced the thinking of the apostle Paul (see Rom. 5:2-5; 8:17-25; 2 Cor. 4:7–5:21)[7] and apparently Luke as well.

6. Fitzmyer, *The Gospel According to Luke X–XXIV,* 1565-66.
7. See Pate, *The Glory of Adam and the Suffering of the Righteous.*

24:27   Jesus then gave the two disciples a quick survey of the Old Testament, beginning with Moses and continuing with all the prophets' writings about Himself, in every part of Scripture. These parts of the Bible (Moses, the Law, and the Prophets) comprise the first two major sections of the Hebrew Bible (cf. Luke 16:16, 31; Acts 26:22; 28:23). In v. 44, the Psalms (the first book in the Writings) are mentioned, which comprise the third and final part of the Old Testament. The evangelist envisions all the passages of the Old Testament wherein early Christianity recognized messianic prophecies. Thus, Jesus' rejection and death, though not in keeping with popular expectation, was in fulfillment of Scripture.

24:28   By that time, the two disciples had drawn near to the village of their destination (Emmaus). Jesus pretended to be going further, probably to pique the disciples' interest.

24:29   But the disciples prevailed on Jesus to stay with them, because the day was about over. Jesus consented and entered into the village to stay with them for the night.

24:30   While dining with the disciples that evening, Jesus took bread, blessed it, broke it, and gave it to the other two. The act surely recalled Jesus' actions at the Lord's Supper (22:14-23), as well as the feeding of the five thousand (7:10-17).

24:31   With that action, the disciples' eyes were opened, and they recognized their guest as none other than Jesus Himself. The granting to the disciples the recognition of Jesus was a divine act. But no sooner did the two recognize Jesus than He disappeared from their midst, a feat now made possible because of Jesus' resurrection body.

24:32   When the full realization of what had just happened to them set in, the disciples could not contain their excitement. Jesus' presence with them on the road to Emmaus and in their home, along with His interpretation of Scripture was like fire burning in the disciples' hearts. Like John Wesley, their hearts were "strangely warmed."

24:33   Even at that late hour the two disciples rose up and returned to Jerusalem to share with the others their experience with the risen Jesus. When they arrived in town, they found the eleven apostles and their companions gathered together.

24:34   The best manuscripts read "they were saying" (*legontas* [the accusative form]; Sinaiticus, A, B), with reference to the eleven disciples. If the two disciples were the ones Luke had in mind, he would have written *legontes* (the nominative form). Thus, what transpired was that the two disciples found the Eleven in conversation, musing to one another that the Lord was indeed divinely raised (*ēgerthē,* a theological passive) and that He had been seen by Peter (cf. 1 Cor. 15:4). Jesus' appearance to Peter would serve as the basis for the apostle to strengthen the brethren (cf. Luke 22:32).

24:35   The two disciples entered into the discussion, explaining what had happened to them on the road, especially how Jesus became known to them in the breaking of the bread (cf. Acts 2:42). Marshall well applies these words to us today, "In the reading of Scripture and at the breaking of the bread the risen Lord will continue to be present, though unseen."[8]

JESUS' APPEARANCE TO THE DISCIPLES IN JERUSALEM, 24:36-43

This episode calls attention to the fact that the appearance of Jesus to the disciples served an apologetic purpose. The purpose was to counter arguments that the disciples saw only a vision, not Jesus in bodily form. But Jesus' invitation to the disciples to see the marks on His hands and His feet ensured that He was no ghost, but rather one who had arisen with a glorified body.

24:36   The truth of the testimonies of the disciples was confirmed when, even as they spoke, Jesus Himself suddenly stood in their midst. He said, "Peace be with you" (cf. John 20:19-20). The word "peace" (*eirēnē*) is the Greek counterpart to the Jewish word for "peace" (*shalom*). Christ's presence surely brings peace.

24:37   But rather than promoting peace, Jesus' presence caused the disciples to become terrified and afraid because they seemed to see a spirit or ghost. Two words in this verse call for comment. First, the Greek word for "seem" or "appear" is *dokoun,* from *dokeō.* The word became associated in the middle to late first century with the Christological heresy known as *doceticism,* a movement that taught that Jesus was *only* God but not human. He merely appeared (*dokeō*) to be human. The apostle John refuted such a notion in his epistle (see, for example, 1 John 1:1-4; 4:2-3). It may well be that Luke intends to counter docetism as well. His choice of the word "appear" (*dokoun*), along with the defense of the corporeality of Jesus' resurrection body that follows in vv. 38-42, suggest that to be the case. Second, the word for "spirit" is *pneuma,* the immaterial essence of a person's

---

8. Marshall, *Commentary on Luke,* 900.

being. But the account is precisely concerned to refute the notion that Jesus only arose in spirit, or as a ghost. Rather, He arose in spirit and in body; that is, in a spiritual body.

24:38 Jesus confronted the disciples' confusion by asking them why they were alarmed and why their hearts were filled with doubt. His rhetorical question was designed to allay the group's fears.

24:39 To convince them that He was truly risen from the dead, Jesus challenged the disciples to look at His hands and feet. The invitation was designed to identify Jesus by His nailprint hands and feet. In looking upon them, the disciples would be able to establish that it really was Jesus who stood in their midst (cf. John 20:25-27). Jesus further invited the group to touch Him, for a spirit does not have flesh and bones. Jesus' body, however heavenly it was, was tangible. Evans pinpoints the apologetic concern of the episode, "The purpose is to counter arguments that the disciples perhaps saw nothing more than a vision, but had not actually seen a real, living Jesus. This Jesus is indeed real and recognizable. His hands and feet are recognizable because of the nail prints. His physical reality is evident because they can feel him."[9]

24:40 Jesus then showed the disciples His hands and feet. The wording is so close to John 20:20 that some have postulated Lucan dependency on the gospel of John. It is more likely, however, that the two accounts represent independent traditions. Their close similarity speaks highly of the historical reliability of the process of the transmission of the gospel.

24:41 The disciples were still not quite convinced, partly out of fear and partly out of joy. It seemed too good to be true. So Jesus offered further proof by asking them if they had anything to eat (left over from the evening meal).

24:42 The group offered Jesus a piece of fish that they had broiled. Compare John 21:9-13 where Jesus and the disciples ate broiled fish on the shore of Luke Gennesaret.

24:43 Jesus took the fish and ate it in front of them, proof that He was not a ghost but a glorified, corporeal person.

JESUS' FINAL COMMISSION, 24:44-49

In this, the next to the last, episode in Luke's gospel, we encounter the risen Jesus' final commissioning of the disciples. Two compo-

---

9. Evans, *Luke*, 354-55.

nents were involved in that commissioning: the gospel as the fulfillment of the Scriptures, vv. 44-47, and the gospel as proclaimed by the
empowerment of the Spirit, vv. 48-49. The episode itself serves a transitional function in the Lucan writings. It returns the reader to the
beginning of the third gospel, especially with its assertion that the
salvation offered to both Jew and Gentile through Jesus Christ is the
fulfillment of the promise of the Old Testament (see chapter 1). But
vv. 44-49 also prepare the reader for the upcoming proclamation of
that message initiated at Pentecost and as continued throughout the
book of Acts.

24:44   Still in the presence of the disciples, the risen Jesus went on
to tell them that now, finally, His followers were about to understand
the words He had spoken to them while on earth with them. Those
words concerned the announcements of His death and resurrection
(9:22, 44; 17:25; 18:31-33; 22:37). The prophecy of Jesus' death and
resurrection was not restricted to Himself; it was also foretold by the
Law of Moses, the Prophets, and the Psalms. This threefold reference
to the Scripture is an advancement beyond the twofold reference that
is found in v. 27. It most probably reflects the tripartite division of the
Old Testament: the Law (*Torah*), the Prophets (*Nebiim*), and the Writings (*ketubim*).[10] There are perhaps two reasons why Jesus refers to
the writings as the Psalms. First, the Psalms are the first book in the
writings. Second, the Psalms yielded the greatest relevance for a messianic interpretation of the Old Testament. This can be seen, for example, in the allusions to the lament psalms (Pss. 22, 31, 69) in the Lucan
passion account (23:26-43). Concerning the testimony of the Law regarding the coming Messiah, perhaps we are to think of Deuteronomy
18:15-19 (cf. Acts 3:22-23; 7:37). For the prophets' testimonies, see the
comments on v. 46.

24:45   With that, Jesus then opened the disciples' minds to understand the Old Testament Scriptures. Until this illuminating moment,
the disciples had been unable to perceive that the Old Testament
prophecies about the Messiah were fulfilled in Jesus (cf. 24:32; Acts
17:3; cf. John 12:16).

24:46   Then Jesus explained the meaning of the Old Testament
prophecies. There were basically two parts to them. The first part was
that the Messiah would suffer and then rise from the dead on the third

---

10. The earliest attestation to the threefold division of the Old Testament occurs in the prologue
to the intertestamental book of *Sirach* (ca. 130 B.C.).

day. But where in the Old Testament is the suffering and resurrection of the Messiah predicted? Evans provides a fine answer to this question, which merits full quotation:

> Judging by which texts of Scripture are actually cited in the Lucan writings, we may infer which passages are in mind in v. 46. With reference to the need of the Messiah to suffer, the Lucan Jesus probably has in mind Isaiah 53, a portion of which is cited by the Ethiopian Eunuch in Acts 8:26-39 and applied to Jesus by Philip the Evangelist. When approached by Philip, the Ethiopian was reading Isa. 53:7-8: "As a sheep led to the slaughter or a lamb before its shearer is dumb, so he opens not his mouth. In his humiliation justice was denied him. Who can describe his generation? For his life is taken up from the earth" (. . . Acts 8:32-33). Since this OT text is actually cited in one of the Lucan writings and explicitly applied to Jesus of Nazareth (see Acts 8:35), it is quite reasonable to suppose that this is at least one of the OT passages understood as indicating that **the Christ will suffer** and die.
>
> Also found in Acts is the quotation of an OT passage which was understood as a promise that **the Christ will . . . rise from the dead.** In his Pentecost sermon Peter cites Ps. 16:8-11, in which the Psalmist, understood as David, the father of the Messiah (or Christ), declares: "For thou wilt not abandon my soul to Hades, nor let thy Holy One see corruption" (Ps. 16:10, as cited in Acts 2:27). The Lucan Paul also would later quote this OT text (Acts 13:35). According to the Lucan Peter's interpretation, this text has come to fulfillment in Jesus' physical death and resurrection. Since David's body is yet in its grave, this passage could not refer to him. Because Jesus has left his grave, the passage must refer to him instead (see Acts 2:29-32).
>
> Finally, there are allusions to OT writings in Luke's Gospel that may explain the necessity of **the Christ** to **rise from the dead on the third day.** One text that immediately comes to mind is the Jonah typology in Luke 11:29-32, where Jesus promises the evil people of his day no "miracle" (or sign) except the "sign of Jonah" (11:29). In his parallel passage, Matthew (12:39-41) states: "For as Jonah was three days and three nights in the belly of a huge fish, so the Son of Man will be three days and three nights in the heart of the earth." It might be objected that it is only in the Matthean version that reference to "three days" is found. This is true, but the possibility does remain that Luke had seen the fuller version of the saying, since in all likelihood the saying was part of the sayings source common to the Gospels of Matthew an Luke. It is also quite possible, however, that Luke 24:46 is actually alluding to Hos. 6:2: "After two days he will revive us; on the third day he will raise us up, that we may live before him." This may be the very Scripture that

Paul has in mind when he states: "... he was raised on the third day in accordance with the scriptures" (1 Cor. 15:4). That this similar formulation occurs in Paul indicates that the "third day" tradition was known prior to the time of Luke's writing.[11]

24:47   The second part of the Old Testament prophecies regarding the coming Messiah was that in the name of the Messiah, repentance for the forgiveness of sins would be preached to all the nations, beginning with Jerusalem. Again we may ask where in the Old Testament Scripture is this prediction found? Evans also helps to answer this question. He suggests that the Lucan writings themselves point us to the intended Old Testament texts:

> At least two OT passages are quoted in Acts that may have made up part of the scriptural testimony presupposed in Luke 24:47. In Acts 2:21 Peter quotes Joel 2:32: "Everyone who calls on the name of the Lord will be saved." Although the verse seems to be making a universal appeal, in the context of the Pentecost sermon, however, only Jews are addressed (both those of Palestine and those of the Diaspora). However, when Paul cites this same text in Rom. 10:13 his context indicates a universal meaning: both Jew and Gentile can freely call upon the name of the Lord. Another OT passage quoted in Acts applies to Gentiles as well. In Acts 13:47 the Lucan Paul quotes Isa. 49:6: "I have made you a light for the Gentiles, that you may bring salvation to the ends of the earth." The Greek word "ends" is the same as that in Acts 1:8 and 13:47. The idea of this proclamation "beginning at Jerusalem" could come from an OT text such as Isa. 2:2-3, where it is prophesied that "It shall come to pass in the latter days that ... all the nations ... and many peoples shall come.... For out of Zion shall go forth the law, and the word of the Lord from Jerusalem" (cf. also Mic. 4:1-2). Other OT texts used in early Christian circles that suggest that the Gentiles will have a part among God's people include Hos. 1:10 and 2:23, both of which are cited by Paul in Rom. 9:24-26. See also Paul's use of Isa. 65:1 in Rom. 10:20 and his use of Ps. 18:49; Deut. 32:43; Ps. 117:1; and Isa. 11:10 in Rom. 15:9-12.[12]

24:48   In addition to the gospel as the fulfillment of the Scriptures, the second component of Jesus' final commissioning of the disciples involved the empowerment of the Spirit to preach that gospel, vv. 48-

11. Evans, *Luke*, 358-59.
12. Ibid., 359-60.

49. Although the Spirit is not explicitly referred to in these verses, that is the obvious implication of the words "power from on high" (cf. Acts 1:8). According to v. 48, the disciples were commissioned to become witnesses of Jesus, proclaiming His life, death, and resurrection.

24:49   In His final commissioning of the apostles, Jesus asserted that He was going to send (*apostellō*) the promise of the Father upon them which, as Acts 1:4-5 makes clear, was the Holy Spirit. According to Tiede, the Father's promise constitutes "the fulfillment of the hopes for the consolation of Israel" (2:25), the "redemption of Jerusalem" (2:38), "the kingdom of God" (23:51), and the "redeeming of Israel" (24:21). That promise began to be actualized with the exaltation of Jesus and the subsequent sending of His Spirit.[13] This idea reinforces our theory that Luke is concerned to demonstrate that Israel will be restored to the Messiah in the future. To receive the Spirit, the apostles were to remain in Jerusalem until they were clothed with "power from on high." Comparing this last phrase with Luke 1:35 and Acts 1:8 permits us to say that the apostles were about to engage in an "incarnational" ministry. According to Luke 1:35, the Spirit as God's power on high was about to come upon Mary, who would then give birth to Jesus. Now, according to Luke 24:48 and Acts 1:8, the Spirit as God's power on high, in one sense, was about to come upon the apostles, who would then give testimony to Jesus. The Spirit was the divine link between Jesus and His church.

THE ASCENSION OF JESUS, 24:50-53

Unique to Luke is the episode of the ascension of Jesus (cf. Acts 1:9-11). Fitzmyer captures Luke's sentiments well:

This episode not only forms the end of the Lucan Gospel, but it is the climax of the whole latter part of it—from the crucial chap. 9 on. In 9:31 the transfigured Jesus converses with Moses and Elijah about his "departure" (*exodos*), which he is to complete in Jerusalem. Again, in 9:51 the reader learns about the days that were drawing near "when he was to be taken up to heaven." That *exodos*, which has been explained as "his entire transit to the Father" through death and resurrection "ending in the ascension" . . . has now been achieved. The goal and destiny toward which the Lucan Jesus has been resolutely moving have now been reached. It is the status to which he referred in his answer to

13. Tiede, *Luke*, 443.

the Sanhedrin in 22:69, "From now on the Son of Man will be seated at the right hand of the power of God." Indeed, from that "glory" (v. 26) he has appeared to Simon (v. 34), to the two disciples at Emmaus (vv. 15-31), and finally to the Eleven and all the others in this literary unit (vv. 36-53).[14]

24:50   Jesus then led His disciples out of Jerusalem as far as the village of Bethany. The word Luke uses of Jesus leading the disciples out of Jerusalem is *exagein,* the Septuagint term for Yahweh leading His people out of Egyptian bondage in the Exodus (see Ex. 3:10; 6:6-8; Lev. 19:36). It reminds the reader of Luke 9:31. Bethany was the village about two miles away from Jerusalem, on the eastern slope of the Mount of Olives (cf. Acts 1:12). After giving His final instructions to the disciples, Jesus raised His hands and blessed them, in good priestly fashion (cf. Lev. 9:22).

24:51   While blessing the disciples, Jesus was removed from them and carried up into heaven. This verse reminds one of the Transfiguration (9:28-31), as well as the Old Testament background of the translation of Enoch (Gen. 5:24) and the ascension of Elijah (2 Kings 2:11).

24:52   Like the shepherds at the birth of Jesus (2:20), so the disciples at the ascension of Jesus worshiped Him and were filled with great joy as they returned to Jerusalem.

24:53   The gospel of Luke closes with a scene in the temple, even as it began there (see 1:5-25). The disciples constantly stayed in the temple, praising God.[15] Evans's comments on this verse are an appropriate conclusion to the gospel of Luke as a whole: "The way Luke's Gospel concludes makes it evident that a sequel volume is planned. The disciples are left waiting in Jerusalem and are not engaged in their apostolic ministry of evangelism. This ministry does not begin in earnest until the sending of the Spirit, at which time the activities of the risen, glorified Christ will resume in the lives of his followers."[16]

HOMILETICAL SUGGESTIONS

Our suggestion for preaching Luke 24 is to deal with it in apologetic fashion, using the title, "Proofs for the Resurrection." Three

---

14. Fitzmyer, *The Gospel According to Luke X–XXIV,* 1587.
15. Some manuscripts read here, "blessing and praising God" (A, C), but the simple reading, "praising God," is to be preferred (p75, Sinaiticus, B).
16. Evans, *Luke,* 361.

pieces of evidence demonstrating the resurrection of Jesus surface in the chapter. An excellent resource to use for this approach is the work by Josh McDowell, *Evidence That Demands a Verdict*. The first proof is the empty tomb, vv. 1-12. Although various answers have been offered as reasons for the empty tomb, only one really explains the data. As we mentioned in our comments on vv. 1-12, the swoon theory, the stolen body theory, and the wrong tomb theory do not make sense of the data. The only reasonable cause for the empty tomb is the bodily resurrection of Jesus.

The second proof in Luke 24 of the resurrection of Jesus was His post-resurrection appearances (vv. 13-43), two of which are recorded here: the appearances to the two disciples on the Road to Emmaus (vv. 13-32) and to the eleven apostles and their group (vv. 33-43). Two counterarguments have been leveled against the validity of Jesus' post-resurrection appearances. First, some have said that the disciples so wanted Jesus to rise from the grave that they imagined that they saw Him, when in reality they did not. But as we noted in the commentary on these verses, the women at the tomb, the two disciples on the Road to Emmaus, and even the apostles were all taken completely by surprise when they encountered the risen Jesus.

Second, others accuse the disciples of fabricating the story of the resurrection of Jesus. However, two factors militate against this hypothesis. First, the accounts of the resurrection of Jesus are too embedded in the layers of the gospel tradition (see Matt. 28:1-20; Mark 16:1-8; Luke 24:1-53; John 20:1-29; 1 Cor. 15:3-10). Second, would the disciples have died for a lie they concocted? Hardly.

The third proof of the resurrection of Jesus attested to in Luke 24 is changed lives, vv. 44-53. Because of Jesus' death and resurrection the apostles, and all others who heed the message of the gospel, experienced forgiveness of sins (vv. 44-47) and the filling of the Spirit (vv. 48-50). Such a joyous transformation is based on the completed work of the exalted Christ (vv. 50-53). The proof, so to speak, is in the pudding. When all the objective evidence has been investigated, the final proof comes when people entrust themselves into the hands of the risen Christ. Those who do, like Theophilus of old, will come to know the truth whereof we speak (1:4).

Appendix A

THE JEWISH TEMPLE

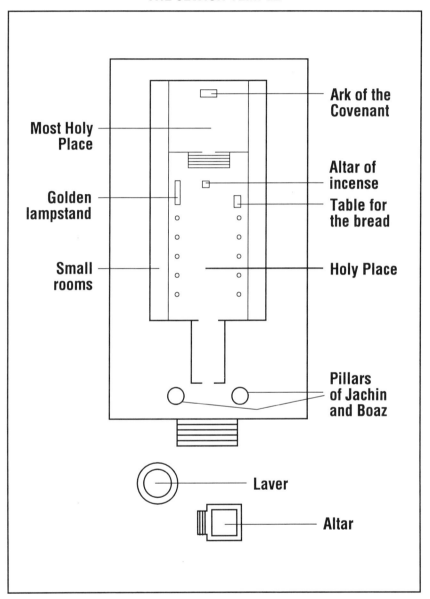

Most Holy Place

Golden lampstand

Small rooms

Ark of the Covenant

Altar of incense

Table for the bread

Holy Place

Pillars of Jachin and Boaz

Laver

Altar

Appendix B

NEW TESTAMENT PALESTINE

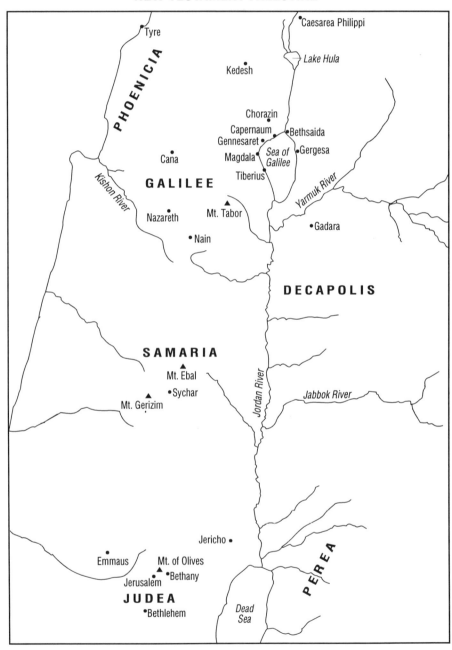

APPENDIX C

NEW TESTAMENT JERUSALEM

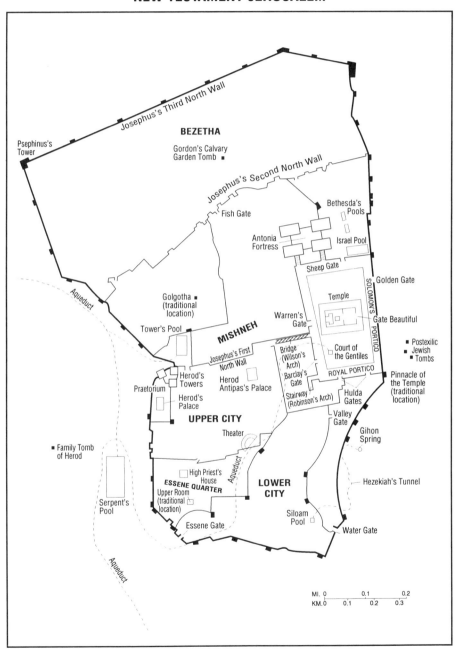

485

SELECTED BIBLIOGRAPHY:
FOR FURTHER STUDY

REFERENCE WORKS

Barrett, C. K. *The New Testament Background. Selected Documents*. San Francisco: Harper & Row, 1987.

Bauer-Gingrich-Danker. *Greek-English Lexicon of the New Testament*. Chicago: Univ. of Chicago, 1979.

Behm, J. *"Metamorphoō."* In vol. 4 of *TDNT*, edited by G. Kittel.

Beitzel, Barry J. *The Moody Atlas of Bible Lands*. Chicago: Moody, 1985.

Beyer, H. W. *"Blasphemia."* In vol. 1 of *TDNT*, edited by G. Kittel.

Bultmann, Rudolf. *"Agalliaomai."* In vol. 1 of *TDNT*, edited by G. Kittel.

Dittenberger, W. *Orientis Graeci Inscriptiones Selectae*. Leipzig: Hirzel, 1903–1905.

Gordon, C. H. *Ugaritic Textbook*. Analecta Orientalia 38. Rome: Biblical Institute, 1965.

Goppelt, Leonhard. *"Pēinaō."* In vol. 6 of *TDNT*, edited by G. Kittel.

Greeven, H. *"Plesion."* In vol. 6 of *TDNT*, edited by G. Kittel.

Hauck, Friedrich. "Mammon." In vol. 4 of *TDNT*, edited by G. Kittel.

Jeremias, Joachim. "Adam." In vol. 1 of *TDNT*, edited by G. Kittel.

———. *"Aren."* In vol. 1 of *TDNT*, edited by G. Kittel.

————. "Hades." In vol. 1 of *TDNT*, edited by G. Kittel.

————. "*Pollōi*." In vol. 6 of *TDNT*, edited by G. Kittel.

Kittel, Gerhard. *Theological Dictionary of the New Testament.* 10 vols. Grand Rapids: Eerdmans, 1964–1976.

Kuhn, Karl Georg. "Aaron." In vol. 1 of *TDNT*, edited by G. Kittel.

Michel, Otto. "*Telōnēs*." In vol. 8 of *TDNT*, edited by G. Kittel.

Rengstorf, Karl Heinrich. "*Apostolos*." In vol. 1 of *TDNT*, edited by G. Kittel.

Schneider, J. "*Elikīa*." In vol. 2 of *TDNT*, edited by G. Kittel.

Schrenk, G. "*Eklektos*." In vol. 4 of *TDNT*, edited by G. Kittel.

Schweizer, Eduard. "*Huios*." In vol. 8 of *TDNT*, edited by G. Kittel.

Sjöberg, Erik. "*Pneuma*." In vol. 6 of *TDNT*, edited by G. Kittel.

Strack, Hermann L., and Billerbeck, Paul. *Kommentar zum Neuen Testament aus Talmud und Midrash. 3 Die Briefe des Neuen Testaments und die Offenbarung Johannis.* Munich: C. H. Becksche Verlagsbuchhandlung, 1954.

SECONDARY MATERIALS

Achtemeier, Paul J., ed. *Harper's Bible Dictionary.* San Francisco: Harper & Row, 1985.

Audet, J. P. "L'Annonce à Marie." *RB* 63 (1956): 346-74.

Avi-Yonah, M. "The Caesarea Inscription of the Twenty-Four Priestly Courses." In *The Teacher's Yoke: Studies in Memory of Henry Trantham.* Edited by E. J. Vardaman and J. L. Garrett, 46-57. Waco, Tex.: Baylor, 1964.

Banks, R. J. *Jesus and the Law in the Synoptic Tradition.* Cambridge: Univ. Press, 1975.

Barrett, C. K. *The Holy Spirit and the Gospel Tradition.* London: SPCK, 1954.

Baur, F. C. *The Church History of the First Three Centuries.* 3d ed. London: Williams & Norgate, 1879.

————. *Paul, the Apostle of Jesus Christ: His Life and Work, His Epistles and His Doctrine.* London: Williams & Norgate, 1873.

Beasley-Murray, G. R. *Jesus and the Future.* London: SPCK, 1959.

Blomberg, Craig L. *Interpreting the Parables.* Downers Grove, Ill.: InterVarsity, 1990.

Braunert, H. "Die Römische Provinzialzensus und der Schätzungsbericht des Lukas-Evangeliums." *Historia* 6 (1957): 192-214.

Brawley, Robert L. *Luke-Acts and the Jews: Conflict, Apology, and Conciliation.* SBLMS. Atlanta: Scholars, 1987.

Brown, Raymond. *The Birth of the Messiah: A Commentary on the Infancy Narratives in Matthew and Luke.* Garden City, N.Y.: Doubleday, 1977.

————. *The Gospel According to John xiii–xxi.* Garden City, N.Y.: Doubleday, 1966.

————. "John the Baptist in the Gospel of John." In *New Testament Essays.* London, Dublin: Geoffrey Chapman, 1965.

Bultmann, Rudolf. *The History of the Synoptic Tradition.* New York: Harper & Row, 1963.

————. *Theology of the New Testament.* 2 vols. London: SCM, 1955–56.

Burkett, Larry. *The Coming Economic Earthquake.* Chicago: Moody, 1991.

Cadbury, H. J. *The Beginnings of Christianity, Part I: The Acts of the Apostles.* 5 vols. Edited by F. J. Foakes Jackson and Kirsopp Lake. London: Macmillan, 1920–27.

————. *The Style and Literary Method of Luke.* HTS 6. Cambridge, Mass.: Harvard Univ., 1920.

Caird, G. B. *St. Luke.* Pelican Gospel Commentary. Baltimore: Penguin, 1963.

Caragounis, C. C. "Opsōnion. A Reconsideration of Its Meaning." *Nov T* 16 (1974): 35-57.

Conzelmann, Hans. *The Theology of Luke.* New York: Harper & Row, 1966. Trans. of 2d ed. *Die Mitte der Zeit: Studien zur Theologie des Lukas.* BHT 17. Tübingen: J. C. Mohr, 1957.

Cranfield, C. E. B. *The Epistle to the Romans,* vol. I. ICC. Edinburgh: T. & T. Clark, 1975.

Creed, J. M. *The Gospel According to St. Luke.* London: Macmillan, 1930.

Cullman, Oscar. *Baptism in the New Testament.* Translated by J. K. S. Reid. London: SCM, 1951.

————. *The State in the New Testament.* New York: Scribner, 1956.

Danker, F. W. *Jesus and the New Age.* St. Louis: Clayton, 1972.

Deissmann, Adolf. *Light from the Ancient East: The New Testament Illustrated by Recently Discovered Texts of the Graeco-Roman World.* Translated by R. M. Strachan. New York: G. H. Doran, 1927.

Derret, J. D. *Law in the New Testament.* London: Darton, Longman, & Todd, 1970.

Dodd, C. H. "The Fall of Jerusalem and 'the Abomination of Desolation.'" *JRS* 37 (1947): 47-54.

_____. *The Parables of the Kingdom.* New York: Scribner, 1961.

Donahue, J. R. "Tax Collectors and Sinners: An Attempt at Identification." *CBQ* 33 (1971): 39-61.

Duff, Paul Brooks. "'The March of the Divine Warrior and the Advent of the Greco-Roman King: Mark's Account of Jesus' Entry into Jerusalem." *JBL* 111/1 (1992): 55-71.

Dunn, James D. G. *Baptism in the Holy Spirit.* SBT 15. Naperville, Ill.: Alec R. Allenson, 1970.

Ellis, E. Earle. *The Gospel of Luke.* NCB. London: Nelson, 1974.

_____. "Present and Future Eschatology in Luke." *NTS* 12 (1965, 1966): 27-41.

Eppstein, Victor. "The Historicity of the Gospel Account of the Cleansing of the Temple." *ZNW* 55 (1964): 42-58.

Eusebius. *Ecclesiastical History.* Grand Rapids: Guardian, 1976.

Evans, Craig C. *Luke.* Peabody, Mass.: Hendrickson, 1990.

Fee, Gordon. "'One Thing Is Needful?' Luke 10:42. Its Significance for Exegesis in New Testament Criticism." In *Essays in Honour of Bruce M. Metzger.* Edited by E. J. Epp and Gordon Fee, 61-76. Oxford: Clarendon, 1981.

Ferguson, Everett. *Backgrounds of Early Christianity.* Grand Rapids: Eerdmans, 1987.

Finegan, Jack. *The Archeology of the New Testament: The Life of Jesus and the Beginning of the Early Church.* Princeton, N.J.: University Press, 1969.

Fitzmyer, Joseph. *The Gospel According to Luke I–IX.* AB 28. Garden City, N.Y.: Doubleday, 1981.

_____. *The Gospel According to Luke X–XXIV.* AB 28a. New York: Doubleday, 1985.

Flender, Helmut. *St. Luke: Theologian of Redemptive History.* Translated by Reginald H. and Else Fuller. Philadelphia: Fortress, 1967.

France, R. T. *Jesus and the Old Testament. His Application of Old Testament Passages to Himself and His Mission.* Downers Grove, Ill.: InterVarsity, 1971.

Gartner, Bertil. *Iscariot.* FBBS 29. Philadelphia: Fortress, 1971.

Geisler, Norman, ed. *Inerrancy.* Grand Rapids: Zondervan, 1980.

Gerhardsson, Birger. *Memory and Manuscript.* Acta seminarii neutestamentici upsaliensis 22. Uppsala: C. W. K. Gleerup, 1961.

Gibson, M. D. "On the Parable of the Unjust Steward." *ExpTim* 14 (1902–1903): 334.

Glombitza, O. "Die Titel didaskalos und epistates für Jesus bei Lukas." *ZNW* 49 (1958): 275-78.

Gower, Ralph. *The New Manners and Customs of Bible Times.* Chicago: Moody, 1986.

Guelich, Robert A. *Mark 1:1–8:26.* WBC 34a. Waco, Tex.: Word, 1989.

————. *The Sermon on the Mount.* Waco, Tex.: Word, 1982.

Guthrie, Donald. *New Testament Introduction.* Downers Grove, Ill.: InterVarsity, 1978.

Haenchen, Ernst. *The Acts of the Apostles.* Philadelphia: Westminster, 1971.

Hay, David. *Glory at the Right Hand: Psalm 110 in Early Christianity.* SBLMS 18. Nashville: Abingdon, 1973.

Hill, David. *Greek Words and Hebrew Meanings.* Cambridge: University Press, 1967.

Hoehner, Harold. *Chronological Aspects of the Life of Christ.* Grand Rapids: Zondervan, 1977.

Jeremias, Joachim. *Abba: Studien zur Neutestamentlichen Theologie und Zeitgeschichte.* Göttingen: Vandenhoeck & Ruprecht, 1966.

————. *The Eucharistic Words of Jesus.* New York: Macmillan, 1955.

————. *Heiligengräben in der umwelt Jesu.* Göttingen: Vandenhoeck & Ruprecht, 1958.

————. *Jerusalem in the Time of Jesus.* Philadelphia: Fortress, 1969.

————. *New Testament Theology. The Proclamation of Jesus.* New York: Scribner, 1971.

————. *The Parables of Jesus.* Translated by S. H. Hooke. New York: Scribner, 1955.

————. *The Prayer of Jesus.* Naperville, Ill.: Alec R. Allenson, 1967.

Jervell, Jacob. *Luke and the People of God: A New Look at Luke-Acts.* Minneapolis: Augsburg, 1972.

Johnson, Luke T. *The Literary Function of Possessions in Luke-Acts.* SBLDS 39. Missoula: Scholars, 1977.

————. *The Writings of the New Testament: An Interpretation.* Philadelphia: Fortress, 1986.

Johnson, Marshall D. *The Purpose of the Biblical Genealogies with Special Reference to the Setting of the Genealogies of Jesus.* SNTSMS 8. Cambridge: University Press, 1969.

Jones, A. H. M. *Documents Illustrating the Reigns of Augustus and Tiberius.* Oxford: Clarendon, 1949.

Jülicher, Adolf. *Die Gleichnisreden Jesu I.* Freiburg: J. C. B. Mohr, 1899.

Keck, Leander E. "The Spirit and the Dove." *NTS* 17 (1970): 41-67.

Kee, Howard Clark. "The Terminology of Mark's Exorcism Stories." *NTS* 14 (1966–68): 232-46.

Klausner, J. *Jesus of Nazareth: His Life, Times, and Teaching.* New York: Macmillan, 1926.

Klausner, Joseph. *The Messianic Idea in Israel.* New York: Macmillan, 1955.

Knox, W. L. *The Acts of the Apostles.* Cambridge: University Press, 1948.

Kümmel, W. G. *Promise and Fulfillment: The Eschatological Message of Jesus.* SBT 23. Naperville, Ill.: Alec R. Allenson, 1957.

LaSor, William Sanford. *The Dead Sea Scrolls.* Chicago: Moody, 1962.

Ladd, George. *I Believe in the Resurrection of Jesus.* Grand Rapids: Eerdmans, 1975.

_____. *A Theology of the New Testament.* Grand Rapids: Eerdmans, 1974.

Leaney, A. R. C. *A Commentary on the Gospel According to St. Luke.* London: Black, 1958.

Liv, Peter. "Did the Lucan Jesus Desire Voluntary Poverty of His Followers?" *EQ* 64:4 (1922): 291-317.

Lyonnet, S. "*Chaire, kecharitōmene.*" *Bib* 20 (1939): 131-41.

Mains, Karen. *Open Heart, Open Home.* Elgin, Ill.: Cook, 1976.

Marshall, I. Howard. *I Believe in the Historical Jesus.* Grand Rapids: Eerdmans, 1977.

_____. *Commentary on Luke,* TNIGTC. Grand Rapids: Eerdmans, 1978.

_____. *Luke: Historian and Theologian.* Grand Rapids: Zondervan, 1970.

Martyn, J. Louis. *History and Theology in the Fourth Gospel.* Nashville: Abingdon, 1968.

McBirne, William Steuart. *The Search for the Tomb of Jesus.* Montrose: Acclaimed Books, 1975.

McCasland, S. V. "The Way." *JBL* 77 (1958): 222-30.

Metzger, Bruce M. *A Textual Commentary on the Greek New Testament: A Companion Volume to the United Bible Societies' Greek New Testament.* New York: United Bible Societies, 1971.

Morris, Leon. *The Gospel According to St. Luke.* TNTC. Grand Rapids: Eerdmans, 1974.

Munck, Johannes. *Paul and the Salvation of Mankind.* London: SCM, 1959.

Neyrey, Jerome. *The Passion According to Luke. A Redaction Study of Luke's Soteriology.* New York: Paulist, 1985.

Nolland, John. *Luke 1–9:20.* WBC 35a. Waco, Tex.: Word, 1989.

Pate, C. Marvin. *The Glory of Adam and the Afflictions of the Righteous: Pauline Suffering in Context.* Lewiston: Edwin Mellen, 1993.

Pentecost, J. Dwight. *The Words and Works of Jesus Christ.* Grand Rapids: Zondervan, 1981.

Perrin, Norman. *Rediscovering the Teaching of Jesus.* New York: Harper & Row, 1967.

Plummer, A. *A Critical and Exegetical Commentary on the Gospel According to St. Luke.* ICC. Edinburgh: T. & T. Clark, 1922.

Ramsay, William. *The Bearing of Recent Discoveries on the Trustworthiness of the New Testament.* London: Hodder & Stoughton, 1915.

————. "Luke's Authorities in the Acts, Chapters I–XII." *ExpTim* 7 (1909): 450-69.

Sahlin, Harold. *Studien zum dritten Kapitel des Lukasevangeliums.* Uppsala: Universitets Arsskrift, 1949.

Schmithals, Walter. *The Office of Apostle in the Early Church.* Translated by John E. Stelly. Nashville: Abingdon, 1969.

Schürer, Emil. *The History of the Jewish People in the Age of Jesus Christ.* Revised and edited by G. Vermes and F. Millar. Edinburgh: T. & T. Clark, 1973.

Selwyn, E. C. "The Carefulness of Luke the Prophet." *ExpTim* (1909): 547-58.

Stein, Robert. *The Synoptic Problem: An Introduction.* Grand Rapids: Baker, 1988.

Thielicke, Helmut. *The Waiting Father. Sermons on the Parables of Jesus.* Translated by John W. Doberstein. New York: Harper & Brothers, 1959.

Thompson, James A. *Handbook of Life in Bible Times.* Downers Grove, Ill.: InterVarsity, 1986.

Thrall, M. E. *Greek Participles in the New Testament*. NTTS 3. Leiden: E. J. Brill, 1962.

Tiede, David L. *Luke*. Augsburg Commentary on the New Testament. Minneapolis: Augsburg, 1988.

————. *Prophecy and History in Luke-Acts*. Philadelphia: Fortress, 1980.

Tyson, Joseph B., ed. *Luke-Acts and the Jewish People*. Minneapolis: Augsburg, 1988.

Vanhoye, Albert. "Structure du 'Benedictus.'" *NTS* 12 (1965–66): 382-89.

van Unnik, W. C. "Die rechte Bedeutung des Wortes treffen, Lukas II 19." In *Sparsa Collecta: The Collected Essays of W. C. van Unnik*. NovT Supp 29. Leiden: E. J. Brill, 1973.

Vielhauer, Paul. "On the 'Paulinism' of Acts." In *Studies in Luke-Acts*. SBT Edited by L. E. Keck and J. Louis Martyn, 33-50. Nashville: Abingdon, 1966.

Walvoord, John, Matthew. *Thy Kingdom Come*. Chicago: Moody, 1974.

Wilkinson, J. "The Case of the Bent Woman in Luke 13:10-17." *EQ* 49 (1977): 195-205.

Wrede, William. *The Messianic Secret*. Translated by J. C. G. Greig. Greenwood: Attic, 1971.

Wright, A. G. "The Widow's Mite: Praise or Lament? A Matter of Context." *CBQ* 44 (1982): 256-65.

Wright, N. T. "Adam in Pauline Christology." SBLSP 1983. Edited by Kent Harold Richards. Chico, Calif.: Scholars, 1983: 359-90.

Yoder, J. H. *The Politics of Jesus*. Grand Rapids: Eerdmans, 1972.

INDEX OF SUBJECTS

INDEX OF AUTHORS

INDEX OF SCRIPTURE
AND ANCIENT WRITINGS